MW01505098

Qur'ān The Dilemma

Former Muslims Analyze Islām's Holiest Book

Volume ONE

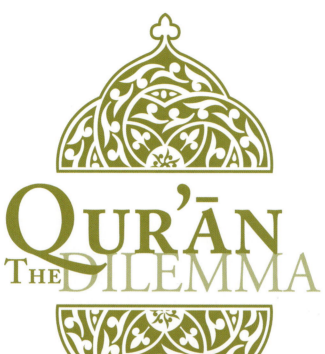

The Qur'ān Dilemma

by

TheQuran.com®

2011 © Copyright USA

ISBN 978-193557703-4
Print Code: 201101-01-10000
TheQuran.com®
www.thequran.com
Qdilemma@thequran.com

All rights reserved. No part of this book may be reproduced in any form without permission in writing from the publisher, except in the case of brief quotations embodied in critical articles or reviews.

Printed on 10% post consumer recycled paper.

Printed in Canada

Table of Contents

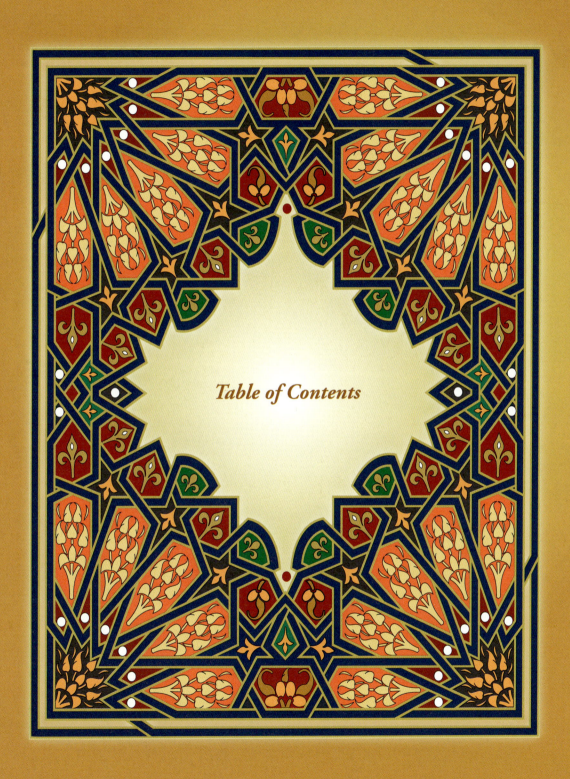

Table of Contents

Preface

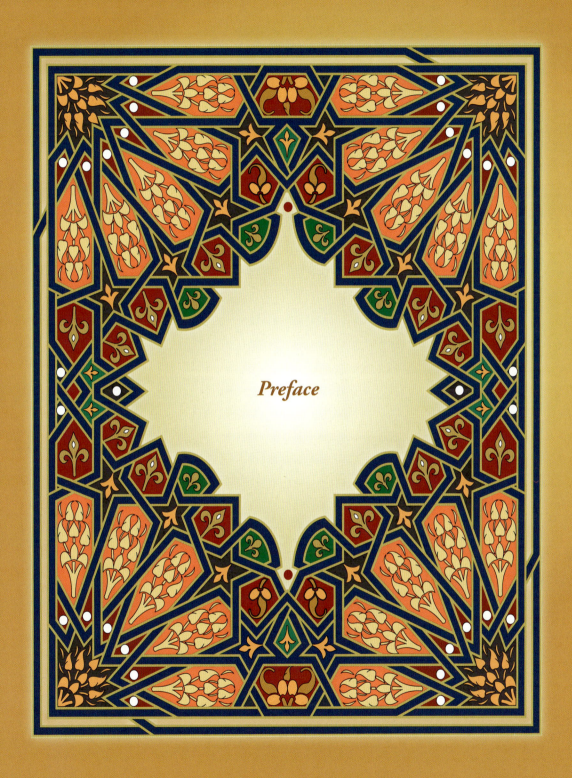

Preface

A book of terror or a book of peace? An inspired text or a political agenda? How is one to know the truth about the Qur'ān? Where does one even begin? How can an English-speaking reader ever hope to wade through the history, the translations, the sects, and the commentaries to begin making sense of the issues?

As the interest in Islām and the teachings of the Qur'ān has grown globally, the need to provide an objective tool to investigate the truth about Islām has become crucial. This in-depth scholarly work is that instrument. Translated from the Arabic, it allows English-speaking readers to see and study the Qur'ān through clear lenses not obscured by propaganda or missionary zeal. It also presents the text of the Qur'ān with parallel commentary, addressing important issues that Muslim scholars have wrestled with throughout the centuries, shedding light on their attempts to solve them and giving a rounded view of the various schools of thought.

This book is the fruition of ten years of planning and preparation. The idea of the book originated ten years ago, though the actual work on the manuscript—first written in Arabic—started seven years later and was published in 2010, followed by its English counterpart in 2011.

Both the Arabic book and its English translation represent the effort and production of many former Muslim writers, Islamic specialists, scholars, editors, researchers, and translators. Some members of this writing team have revealed their association with this project while others may publicize their participation after the publication of the book's second volume or other similar projects in the near future.

The critical methodology used in this book is inspired by the courageous tradition of those who dared to analyze the Qur'ān throughout history, while also incorporating the contemporary intellectual productions available in Arabic and foreign sources. The discoveries made through these scholarly critical methods are directed equally to non-Muslims and Muslims.

To non-Muslims who want to unravel the mysteries of Islām, this book presents information that Islāmic resources rarely disclose—to allow those seeking the truth to comprehend the full picture with all its outlines, colors, and dimensions.

To Muslims who seek genuine choices far from the culture of "indoctrination," this book opens a world of understanding to them, so that they can decide for themselves their intellectual and spiritual paths.

Approach of this Book

The commentary provided in this book examines the Qur'ān from three distinct perspectives. First, it systematically investigates and critically analyzes the historical, factual, and linguistic difficulties that the text of the Qur'ān presents to its reader.

The book then investigates the annulment of certain verses. Although the text of the Qur'ān is said to have been in a Preserved Tablet from the beginning of time, some of its verses abrogate, or nullify, other verses and render them ineffectual, as evidenced in the following example:

> Though it is popular in the West to highlight Allah's words in this verse, *"O ye folk! verily, we have created you of male and female, and made you races and tribes that ye may know each other. Verily, the most honourable of you in the sight of God is the most pious of you..."* (Q 49.13), the Qur'ān also instructs Muslims to persecute non-Muslims: *"But when the sacred months are passed away, kill the idolaters wherever ye may find them; and take them, and besiege them, and lie in wait for them in every place...."* (Q 9.5)

What is the Muslim to do? Have great relationships with the neighbors or kill them?

The answer to this dilemma is in the understanding of abrogation. For instance, the "peace" verses, such as Q 49.13 above, were given when early Muslims were still weak in their own tribal lands. After Muslims pacified the neighboring peoples, gaining followers and strength, they adopted Q 9.5, the Sword verse[D], as their modus operandi for forcibly spreading Islām and increasing their conquest of surrounding territories. To some exegetes, the Sword verse is viewed as an abrogator (nullifier) of all instructions for peace toward others in the rest of the verses in the Qur'ān.

The third issue that this book addresses is the problem of variant readings of the verses. There were many versions of the Qur'ān prior to the act by 'Uthmān Ibn 'Affān[N], the third caliph or successor after Muḥammad, to force a codified version—the 'Uthmānic codex—on Muslims and burn all the rest. In addition, this official Qur'ān (c. AH 34/ AD 654) did not have dots and diacritical marks in a language that relies heavily on them. The lack of such markings led to a variety of ways to read and understand the Qur'ān in Arabic. Certain propagators of particular readings became authorities on the proper way to read the Qur'ān. These variations spread throughout the Islāmic territories, leading to further disputes among Muslims as to the correct words and phrases for many verses of the Qur'ān.

This book provides, though not exhaustively, examples of some of the variant versions and variant readings. These variant versions and readings present compelling evidence refuting the claim that the current Arabic Qur'ān is the same from its past to its present form—contrary to what the Muslim historical and exegetical records attest.

This book also contains several articles to help the reader weigh and understand the issues surrounding the Qur'ān. These articles deal with such important topics as the treatment of women, the compilation process of the Qur'ān, the chronological sequence of its sūras, and the treatment of people of other faiths, to name a few.

Throughout the commentary and the articles the aim of this book is to supply the reader with many original sources from respected Muslim exegetes and scholars, in order to maintain the focus on the issues that are troublesome in the Qur'ān, even to committed Muslim scholars. The citations for these sources will be handled as endnotes rather than as embedded parenthetical references to improve the readability of the text.

Guide to Reading this Book

Before reading the articles in Part I, the reader is strongly advised to read "Key to Reading Part II" on page 147. This article provides critical information regarding translations, special text and styles used throughout the book.

The reader should also review the nine articles in Part I before reading the translated sūras with their corresponding commentary in Part II. These articles will provide the reader with the necessary background to understand the issues addressed in the commentary. The articles will also introduce the Islāmic scholars and authoritative readers who wrote down Muḥammad's "revelations," helped to compile the Qur'ān, issued rulings, presented their opinions, and offered variant readings so that the reader can become familiar with the names of the important Muslim leaders involved in these matters.

In addition, the following articles provide the reader with helpful information to better understand the ramifications of Islām and the teachings of the Qur'ān on specific groups. It is recommended to read these particular articles *before* reading the sūra listed next to them: "Women in the Qur'ān" (Sūra 4) and "The Qur'ān and People of Other Faiths" (Sūra 9).

The reader of this book is also supported with helpful resources at the back of the book (Part III):

- Suggested Readings, a list of references that offer more information on selected topics discussed in this book;
- Selected Proper Names, an annotated list of important people ([N]) mentioned in the articles and sūras;
- Selected Definitions, a glossary of unfamiliar or complex terms ([D]) used throughout the book;
- Timeline, a graphic illustration noting important dates, leaders, and events in the early history of Islam and the Qur'ān;
- Maps, a series of geographical and political representations of the Arabian Peninsula, including the expansion of Islam into the surrounding territories (c. seventh century AD).

A Subject Index is also provided to assist the reader in topic searches.

In conclusion, the reader is strongly encouraged to investigate different translations while reading this work, keeping in mind the following questions: Who is the author of the Qur'ān? And, is the Qur'ān in its current form without errors?

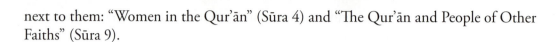

Part I
Background of the Qur'ān

Introduction

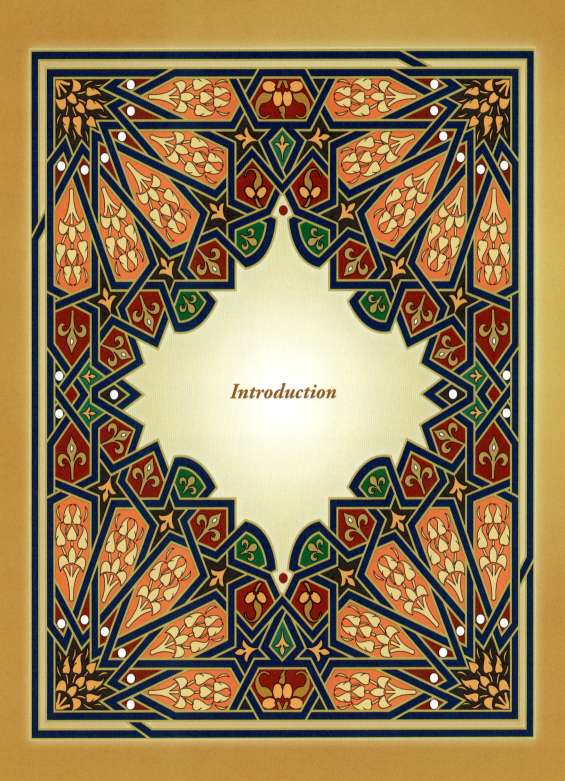

Introduction

Religion is man's systematic search for God and truth. It is a collection of beliefs and thoughts regarding the deity of God and his relationship to man. When one is considering the claims of a religion, one must consider the source of the authority upon which that religion bases its claims.

According to Islāmic doctrine, Muḥammad is the messenger[D] of Allah[D] (examples: Q 2.101, 279; Q 3.32) and the *"Seal of the Prophets"* (Q 33.40) on whom the Qur'ān was revealed through a heavenly intermediary. This intermediary is called *"the Faithful Spirit"* (Q 26.193) and other times *"Holy Spirit"* (Q 16.102). After Muḥammad's migration to Medina, this intermediary became known as "Gabriel" (Q 2.97-98). (See the article "Muḥammad's Jibrīl" on page 39.)

The Qur'ān was revealed to Muḥammad in the Arabic language (Q 12.2, Q 13.37, Q 20.113). Muḥammad gave this revelation to a people group that, previous to this time in history, had no heavenly revealed books, and had never had a prophet sent to them (Q 34.44). The Qur'ān makes the claim within its verses that it is part of the series of the holy books, e.g., the Torah[D], the Gospel (Q 2.41, 91, 97; Q 3.3, 50).

This period of revelation took place over the course of twenty-three years (AD 610-632), during which Muḥammad declared himself a prophet. After the death of Muḥammad, his Companions[D] gathered the Qur'ān into a book. (See the article "Compilation of the Qur'ān" on page 49.)

Names of the Qur'ān

Muslims have called their most holy book several different names, each with its own origin and meaning.

The Qur'ān

The common name for the holy book of Islām is *the Qur'ān* (Q 2.185). The name *Qur'ān* appears about seventy times in the Qur'ān. The opinions of scholars vary regarding the origin and meaning of the word *Qur'ān*:

1. *Qur'ān* comes from the word *qara'a,* meaning "to recite." Those who hold this view say that the expression *the Qur'ān* appears with this meaning in Q 75.17-18, where the Arabic reads with the word *Qur'ān* and its derivatives: *"It is for us to collect it and to read it; and when we read it then follow its reading."* [1]
2. *Qur'ān* is a description following the Arabic grammatical form *fu'lān. Qur'ān* then is considered a derivative of the word *qar'ī,* meaning "to gather." It is similar to the saying *"qara'ta al-mā'a fī al-ḥawḍ,"* which means "you gathered the water in the tub."[2]
3. *Qur'ān* is derived from *qarantu,* meaning "to pair one thing to another" or "to merge them together." The Qur'ān received this name because of the manner in which its sūras, verses, and letters were merged together to form the whole.[3]
4. *Qur'ān* "is derived from *qarā'in* because its verses confirm one another and, in many ways, look the same; hence, they are similar."[4]
5. *Qur'ān* is a unique proper noun, not borrowed from other known sources. It is applied to the words revealed to Muḥammad.[5]

It is interesting to note that many Muslim commentators and exegetes have disregarded the Semitic root of *qur'ān,* which is קרא (*qara'a*), meaning "to recite." This root word, *qara'a,* is likely to have come from the Aramaic-Canaanite region. The word *qur'ān* is present in Hebrew, Phoenician, Aramaic, and Syriac.[6]

One opinion maintains that the origin of the word *qur'ān* was influenced by the Hebrew expression מִקְרָא , which later came to mean "recitation, reading" according to the Old Testament (Neh. 8.8). This expression מִקְרָא is also repeated in rabbinical writings several times. However, most researchers lean toward the idea that *qur'ān* comes from the Syriac ܩܪܝܢܐ, which means "reading, recitation" and is used in connection to the study of the Bible.

The similarity between the Arabic and the Syriac words is clear. The Syriacs called the books, or chapters, of the Bible that are read in church ܩܪܝܢܐ, or lectionaries. Thus Muḥammad chose for his book the name that was familiar to him then. Without a doubt, the word *qur'ān* reached Muḥammad from Christian sources.[7]

In the Qur'ān the verb *qara'a* appears whenever Muḥammad shares a revelation—with the exception of four locations. Two of these exceptions refer to the other holy books (Q 10.94; Q 17.93). The other two refer to the *"Book"* (Record of Deeds) that are given to people on the Day of Judgment[D] (Q 17.71; Q 69.19). All of these references show that the inclusion of the verb *qara'a* in the Qur'ān is always associated with the heavenly books.[8]

Al-Muṣḥaf

A common name for the Qur'ān is *al-Muṣḥaf* ("the Codex"), the plural of which is *maṣāḥif.* The root of the word appears to be *ṣuḥuf.* According to an Islāmic narrative, the word has an Abyssinian root. When the first caliph Abū Bakr[N] had assembled the various parts of the Qur'ān, he gathered his advisors to discuss the issue of naming the book. Some of them wanted to name it *Injīl*[D] ("Gospel"), but that suggestion was rejected. Others proposed naming it *al-Sifr* ("the Book, the Record"), but this suggestion was rejected as well. One advisor, Ibn Mas'ūd[N], said that he had heard that the Abyssinians used the name *al-Muṣḥaf* and suggested it. His suggestion was accepted.[9]

Al-Furqān

The famous name *al-Furqān*[D] ("the Criterion") is used considerably but is less common than *al-Qur'ān* and *al-Muṣḥaf.* It is mentioned in Q 2.185, Q 3.4, and Q 25.1.

The expression *al-Furqān* is not limited to the Qur'ān but is mentioned when dealing with other holy books. For example, this phrase is used to describe the books of Moses (Q 2.53; Q 21.48). The Torah (the first five books of the Old Testament) and the New Testament are also collectively called by this name (Q 3.4).

The Qur'ān states that if a person believes in Allah, he would make that belief for the person a *furqān* (Q 8.29). In addition, the victory of Badr (Q 8.41) is called (in Arabic) "the day of *al-Furqān.*"[10]

All of the various uses of the name *al-Furqān* cause us to consider its Semitic root. This word is present in the rabbinical literature[D] as פֻּרְקָן, which means "to save or to redeem."[11]

In his book, *The Foreign Vocabulary of the Qur'ān*, Arthur Jeffery, Western Orientalist[D], traces the history of this word *furqān* and offers this summation:[12]

> No doubt Muḥammad himself borrowed the word 'Furqān' to use it as a technical term and gave it his own special meaning. The origin that was borrowed from was, without a doubt, the concordance of the Aramaic-speaking Christians.

Other Names

The Qur'ān is called by other common names:

- *al-Kitāb* ("the Book") in Q 2.2
- *al-Waḥī* ("the Inspiration") in Q 21.45
- *al-Dhikr* [D]("the Reminder") in Q 15.9

In the books of Qur'ānic science, there are fifty-five names given to the Qur'ān, including the following examples:[13]

- *Nūr* ("Light") in Q 4.174
- *Shifā'* ("Healing") in Q 17.82, Q 41.44
- *Maw'iẓa* ("Guidance") in Q 3.138, Q 10.57

Structure of the Qur'ān

There are four main structural elements to the Qur'ān:[14]

Al-Qur'ān is the book.

Al-Sūra is a chapter of the Qur'ān and is equivalent to a poem.

Al-Āya is similar to a line of poetry and will be called a "verse" in this book.

Al-Fāṣila is the end of the verse and acts as the rhyme.

The Sūra

The *sūra* is a chapter of the Qur'ān. Its plural is *suwar* (sūras). The word *sūra* appears in the Qur'ān in Q 2.23, Q 10.38, and Q 11.13.

Most of the verses that mention the word *sūra* belong to the later period of Muḥammad's activity, when he was mainly in Medina. The Islāmic sources do not contain information that indicates the origin of this word. Theodor Nöldeke and other Orientalists suggest that it came from the Hebrew שׁוּרָה, used in the Mishnah [D], and means "a lineup, or a chain." The problem with this view is that שׁוּרָה is not associated with the holy books, whereas the word *sūra* in the Qur'ān is exclusively associated with the holy books. This association compels Hartwig Hirschfeld to think that the word is equivalent to the Jewish word סדרה, which is a known term for section markers in the Hebrew books. Jeffery believes the word *sūra* comes from the Syriac word ܣܘܪܛܐ, which means "writing."[15]

According to the 'Uthmānic codex, which is the most widely used Qur'ān, there are 114 sūras. By some counts, Q 8 and Q 9 are considered to be one sūra, which makes the total number of sūras 113.[16] The number of sūras in the codex[D] of Ibn Mas'ūd is 112 sūras, since he does not include Q 113 and Q 114, known as *al-Mu'awwidhatayn*, the two refuge-seeking chapters. However, in the codex of Ubayy Ibn Ka'b the number of sūras is 116, because he adds the two sūras al-Ḥafd and al-Khal'.[17] (See Controversial Qur'ānic Texts, page 587.) Others say that the codex of Ibn Ka'b actually contains 115 sūras because he combines Q 105 and Q 106 into one sūra.[18] (See the article "Compilation of the Qur'ān" on page 49.)

A sūra may often have more than one name. For example, sūra Muḥammad (Q 47) is also called al-Qitāl ("The Fighting").[19] The formal name for Q 65 is sūra al-Ṭalāq, or "Divorce Chapter." Q 65 is nicknamed sūra al-Nisā' al-Qusrā ("The Smaller Chapter about Women") because it contains similar content (women's issues) as Q 4 but is shorter in length.

The Āya

The word *āya* is sometimes translated as "verse." The plural of *āya* is *āay* or *āyāt*. This word appears several times in the Qur'ān and its Arabic meaning is "the mark." It also "occurs in the old poetry…[of well-known Arab poet] Imrū' al-Qays…and so was in use before the time of Muḥammad."[20]

Later on, the expression *āya* came to mean a verse of the Qur'ān. Despite the fact that the word *āya* is repeated throughout the Qur'ān, it rarely appears in the Meccan verses[D].[21]

Even though there is no root for the word *āya (āyāt)* in Arabic, it likely reached the Arabs through the Syriac-speaking Christians. This Syriac word ܐܬܐ is used exactly like the Hebrew word אות. In Hebrew, the word *āya* is derived from the verb אוה , which means "to indicate or to mark." References of this word found in several Old Testament books indicate multiple meanings: the signs (marks) of the seasons (Gen. 1.14); standards, or military banners (Num. 2.2); signs for remembrance (Josh. 4.6); the miracles and wonders that reveal the divine presence (Deut. 4.34; Ps. 78.43); and signs or warnings that accompany and testify to the works of the prophets (Exod. 3.12; 1 Sam. 10.7, 9). What is readily noticeable is that the uses of אות are very close to the Qur'ānic meaning of the word.[22]

Disagreements about the totals of sūras (chapters) mentioned earlier similarly occur with the number of verses in the Qur'ān. Though based on the 'Uthmānic codex, even the most famous schools of reading[D] have tabulated the verses differently:[23]

- First Medinan (according to Kufa: 6217 verses; yet, according to Basra: 6214 verses)
- Latter Medinan: 6214 verses
- Meccan: 6210 verses
- Basran: 6204 verses
- Damascan: 6227 verses (and also 6226 verses)
- Hummusan: 6232 verses
- Kufan: 6232 verses

For another example, Q 112 has five verses according to the Meccan and the Syrian schools of reading but only four verses according to the rest of them.[24]

Al-Fāṣila

Al-fāṣila is the last word in a verse of the Qur'ān. These *fāṣilas* resemble the rhymes in the poetic lines of Arabic poem anthologies. The *fāṣila* often had to be taken into consideration during the composition of the current Arabic Qur'ān to preserve the poetic qualities of the sentence. This practice led to weak, irregular, or illogical construction of some of the syntax and sentence structures, as displayed in the following examples:[25]

- Q 54.41: The subject and object of the verb are out of place for the purpose of maintaining the rhyme. The Yusuf Ali English translation best represents this awkward syntax: "To the People of Pharaoh, too, aforetime, came Warners (from God)."
- Q 53.25: In the Arabic, the verse states that "it is to Allah that the End and the Beginning of all things belong." The "End" is placed before the "Beginning" to keep the rhyme; otherwise the "Beginning" would have been stated first as in Q 28.70.
- Q 40.5: The possessive *ya* ("my") is dropped in the Arabic and replaced with a *kasra*, "i" accent, to keep the *fāṣila* rhyme.
- Q 33.66: An unnecessary letter was added to the word *rasūl* ("messenger") in the Arabic Qur'ān, making it *rasūlā* (incorrect form of this word), in keeping with the rhyme.
- Q 21.33: Instead of using the normal irregular form of the plural, the regular plural is used to refer to the irregular object. Also, in Arabic grammar there are singular, dual form[D] (when referring to two subjects or entities), and plural nouns. In this verse the plural is used instead of the dual when the verse is talking about the sun and the moon. All these changes were done to keep the *fāṣila.*

There are many such examples in al-Raṣāfī's book, *Kitāb al-Shakhṣīya al-Muḥammadīya aw Ḥal al-Lughz al-Muqadas.*[26]

When the traditional grammar and clarity are apparently sacrificed to maintain rhyme (*fāṣila*) for these aberrant words and verses, one must ask how can this emphasis on rhyme benefit its readers?

Qur'ānic Challenge

Muslims view the Qur'ān as a miraculous text. Muslims believe that it is impossible to bring forth a Qur'ān that is equal to the one they currently have. They base this belief on the challenges of such a task as presented in the Qur'ān itself: *"Say, 'If mankind and ginns* [jinn] *united together to bring the like of this Qur'ān, they could not bring the like, though they should back each other up!'"* (Q 17.88). Similar examples include Q 11.13 (*"'Bring ten surahs like it devised...'"*) and Q 10.38 (*"'Bring a surah like it...'"*).

To the pagan tribesmen of the Quraysh[D] the challenge of replicating *"the like of this Qur'ān"* was not so much an impossible task but a ludicrous undertaking: "Revelations of the kind which Mohammed uttered, no unbeliever could produce without making himself a laughing-stock."[27] Furthermore, any attempt to exactly duplicate Muḥammad's compositions would be futile, since his compositions derived from his own unique educational reserve, psychological experiences, and personal language. If a pagan was to imitate the Qur'ān, his imitation would be no more than a weak approximation. The poet Ma'rūf al-Raṣāfī echoes these difficulties:[28]

> It is difficult for an objector to bring forth words similar to the ones to which he objected. Muḥammad knew that well, which is why he calmly and assuredly with all courage and valor challenged his people saying, *"And if ye are in doubt of what we have revealed unto our servant, then bring a chapter like it, and call your witnesses other than God if ye tell truth"* (Q 2.23).
>
> No one has been mentioned to have intended to oppose the Qur'ān… If one had intended to do so, he would have definitely failed. The one who opposes the Qur'ān must, first of all, have spirituality exactly like that of Muḥammad, and have intelligence like his and imagination like his….No one could oppose the Qur'ān and bring forth one like it except Muḥammad himself.

On the other hand, Muslims believe that the beauty of the Qur'ān's language is a given, ignoring the reality that the Qur'ān is different in composition from one period to another. The Meccan texts[D] are fiery and incitant, whereas the Medinan texts[D] are dry prose. (See the article "Chronological Sequence of the Qur'ān" on page 65.)

The objective reader may become bored when reading the Qur'ān. Orientalist Edward William Lane supports this likely reader reaction:[29]

> If not for the eloquence of the old Arabic language, which gave a sense of charm to some of the hard sentences and boring stories, the reading of the Qur'ān would be impossible. For one feels that one descended from the poetry to prose. The prose portion has nothing that deserves reading, which would compensate the loss of the poetic early texts, as the musical effect disappears.

Lane's view is commonly held by the great Arab author al-Raṣāfī:[30]

> What is unique to the Qur'ān and a characteristic that it does not share with the rest of the heavenly and earthly books is: redundancy. Take the Qur'ān and read one of its sūras (one of the longer ones), then continue on to another sūra after finishing the first, then move on to a third and a fourth sūra. Based on the subject matter, it does not feel like you moved from one sūra to another. That is because the redundant writings mainly contain mentioning prophets and what happened between them and their unbelieving people, and the mentioning of paradise, hell, the coming back to life, the resurrection, and the bashing of the unbelievers and their misleading others with idolatry….What is most amazing is that the Qur'ān is indebted to redundancy for its effect on the souls of those who read and hear it.

> **It is neither simple, nor customary among the learned to have a book use such redundancy, yet come out safe and blameless except the Qur'ān** [our emphasis]. Considering this, it is possible to call the Qur'ān "The Book of Influence Through Redundancy."

The Quraysh Opinion of the Qur'ān

Even though the first sūras of the Qur'ān were recited in the language of the tribe of Quraysh, the majority of Muḥammad's tribesmen were not impressed. In fact, the initial reaction to the Qur'ān by the people of the Quraysh was not particularly favorable:

- *"'These are but old folks' tales'"* (Q 6.25; Q 8.31; Q 23.83; Q 27.68)
- The Qur'ān was composed by *"a poet"* (Q 21.5; Q 37.36; Q 52.30; Q 69.41)

They also dismissed Muḥammad as

- *"an obvious sorcerer," "a magician, liar"* (Q 10.2; Q 38.4)
- *"a soothsayer"* (Q 52.29; Q 69.42)
- *"possessed," "mad"* (Q 15.6; Q 44.14; Q 52.29; Q 68.2, 51; Q 81.22)
- "bewitched" (Yusuf Ali trans. Q 17.47; Q 25.8)

This negative response is probably what prompted al-Raṣāfī to make these remarks:[31]

> They greatly magnify the inimitability of the Qur'ān, but they are unable to mention one clear effect of this miracle that lead to the success of the call to Islām (Islāmic *Da'wa*). For it is clear that the Islāmic Da'wa succeeded by the sword, not by the miracle of the Qur'ān.

Importance of Studying the Qur'ān

Reading and studying the Qur'ān is valuable for both its historical and religious significance.

A. Source for Studying the History of Muḥammad and Early Islām

The Qur'ān is the record of Muḥammad's call (*Da'wa*) of others to Islām. This ancient book helps us to understand the personality of Muḥammad. For example, one finds in it the depth of the various worries that Muḥammad experienced (Q 94); the fire of his anger against his uncle Abū Lahab (Q 111); or the rulings that he changed according to his human decisions, such as his position towards Zaynab Bint Jaḥsh (his adopted son's wife), where Muḥammad changed the rulings so he could marry her (Q 33.4, 36, 37, 53).

We also discover through the Qur'ān how Muḥammad viewed his context and how he dealt with it and produced his doctrines towards those who gave allegiance to him and those who opposed him. (See the article "The Qur'ān and People of Other Faiths" on page 133.)

B. Source for Understanding the Islāmic Context

According to Islāmic theory, the Qur'ān is Allah's address to the Muslims, the foundation of Islāmic teachings, and the source for legislations. It is the educational book that feeds the Islāmic mind and defines for the Muslim the philosophy of life and how to understand oneself as well as others. For Muslims, the Qur'ān is the tool that shapes their worldview.

Despite the centrality of the Qur'ān to the life of Muslims, most of them, even the Arab Muslims, have very limited knowledge of it. That knowledge is often filled with ambiguity and deficiencies and hedged with inherited prohibitions. For this reason, we have decided to shed light on the Qur'ān, mainly relying on the different Islāmic sources—the expositions, the narrations (*ḥadīth*), and the historical accounts. We have also made use of contemporary literary works in Arabic and other languages to help the reader gain a comprehensive knowledge of the Qur'ān.

This book also contains researched materials concerning historical matters ("Compilation of the Qur'ān," page 49), intellectual issues ("Women in the Qur'ān," page 117) and social issues ("The Qur'ān and People of Other Faiths," page 133).

This volume also examines the sūras of the Qur'ān according to their current arrangement, dealing with three areas concerning the verses: (1) critical analysis, (2) abrogation, and (3) variant readings. The aim behind this examination is to open serious and intellectual discussion concerning the Qur'ān.

Facts about the Qur'ān

Here are some interesting miscellaneous facts:[32]

- The longest word in the current Arabic Qur'ān is in Q 15.22: *fa'asqaynākumūh* (فَأَسْقَيْنَاكُمُوهُ), which means "so we give it to you to drink of."
- The longest verse is in Q 2.282 and is called "the Debt (Lending) Verse."
- The shortest verse is Q 93.1.
- The longest sūra is Q 2 and the shortest is Q 108.
- Q 12 is the only sūra that is over one hundred verses yet contains no mention of paradise or hell.

There are two copies of the current Arabic Qur'ān (based on the 'Uthmānic codex) that are in use today among the Muslims: (1) The (more prevalent) Qur'ān according to the reading of 'Āṣim as narrated by Ḥafṣ, which was issued in Cairo under the direction of al-Azhar in 1924 and (2) the Qur'ān according to the reading of Nāfi' as narrated by Warsh, which was issued in Algeria in 1905.

Critical Analysis

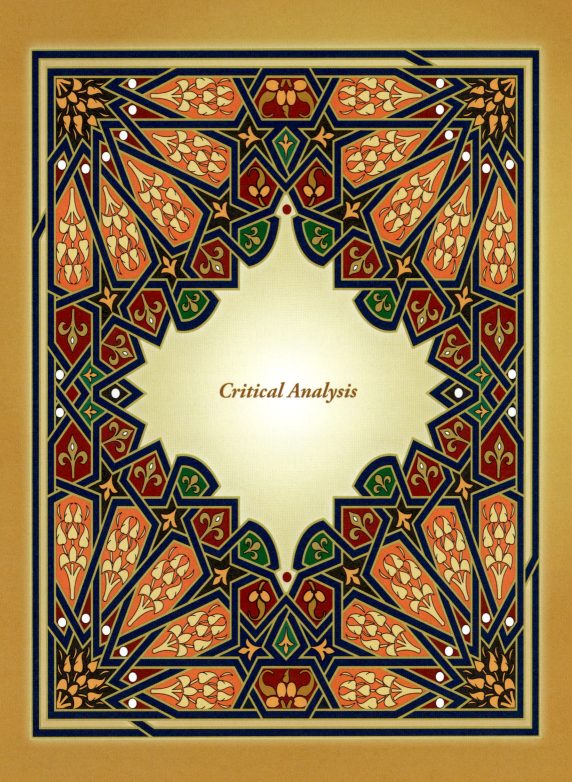

Critical Analysis

Perhaps the most sacrosanct belief of the Islāmic faith is that the Qur'ān is a miraculous book. It is believed to be the ultimate miracle of Islām: not only a book sent down from heaven but a perfect book in language and structure that could never be replicated by mankind.

As such, the Qur'ān is not to be challenged. When questions arise, most Islāmic scholars deal with them only from the perspective that the Qur'ān is a miraculous message from Allah. If, in fact, this assumption could be proven to be in error, Muslims would be empowered to subject the Qur'ān to true critical analysis, in the same fashion that all other religious texts in history have been analyzed.

Though Islām uniformly claims that the Qur'ān is a heavenly book, Muslim scholars hold three different views regarding its "revelation":[1]

- Jibrīl[D] (Gabriel) memorized the Qur'ān from the Preserved Tablet[D] and brought it down to Muḥammad in word and meaning.
- Jibrīl came down and shared with Muḥammad only the meanings, which Muḥammad learned and then expressed them to others in the Arabic language.
- Jibrīl *alqā* ("recited") the meanings to Muḥammad, who then expressed these meanings in the Arabic language.

To say that Jibrīl came with the content of the Qur'ān to Muḥammad and the latter expressed these meanings in his own language is a potentially dangerous theory. Such a theory would open the door wide to the critical analysis of the Qur'ān, because it would consider the Qur'ān to be Muḥammad's text and not a divine book. If the Qur'ān, in terms of structure, style, and formulation is a text authored by Muḥammad and not a text from Allah, it means it is a man-made book, subject to research and criticism.

This view could have helped scholars to understand the Qur'ān free from any previous restrictions. But few Muslims dared to tackle the consequences that would result from pursuing this view of Qur'ānic revelation.

In spite of the limitation of intellectual freedom for those seeking truth regarding the Qur'ān, this suppression did not prevent the emergence of fearless figures in Arabic and Islāmic studies who expressed opinions with deeper insight than the above theory. 'Abd Allah Ibn al-Muqaffa' (d. c. AH 139/AD 756), one of the geniuses in the Arabic language, wrote a book opposing the Qur'ān.[2] History also gives us the name of Abū al-Ḥussayn Aḥmad Ibn Yaḥyā Ibn Isḥāq al-Rāwandī, from the third century AH (ninth century AD), who wrote a book titled *al-Zumurrud*. In it, he addressed the biography of Muḥammad and dubbed him the false prophet. Ibn al-Rāwandī also criticized the Qur'ān in his book *al-Dāmigh*, a work that is, unfortunately, is no longer extant, though scattered excerpts of it are found in the books of his critics.[3]

In the third century AH, 'Abd al-Masīḥ Ibn Isḥāq al-Kindī wrote his famous apology known as *Risālat al-Kindī* in Arabic. It is a response to a letter by a Muslim scholar called Ismā'īl al-Hāshimī. In this apology, al-Kindī tackles many issues, such as defending the Christian doctrine, examining the biography of Muḥammad, and critiquing the Qur'ān. In the context of refuting the eloquence of the Qur'ān, he poses this provocative question:[4]

> When the poets compose their poetry, and weigh it to make sure that it is to the proper scale, which is harder and more precise in meaning, it stays cohesive. Their choosing the pure, crystal clear, and completely Arabic words with good consistent meaning is more perfect in adhering to the rules and better formed. For your book [the Qur'ān] is full of broken rhythm, incongruent words, and exaggerations in meanings that are meaningless. If you say its meanings are the most accurate, we ask you: what strange meaning did you come up with? Show it to us and inform us about it so we can learn it from you.

Later in the fourth century AH (tenth century AD), Muḥammad Ibn Zakarīyā Abū Bakr al-Rāzī (Abū Bakr al-Rāzī), the physician and chemist, critiques the Qur'ān in all its various aspects. He rejects the claim that states the Qur'ān is a miracle and responds to the demand to produce a religious book like it with the following comment:[5]

> If you want one like it in terms of better words we can get you a thousand like it from the words of the rhetoric, the eloquent, and the poets: words that are more fluent, more precise in meaning, more eloquent in function and expression, and more formed in rhythm. If that is not acceptable to you, then we demand of you to tell us what this "one like it" is that you are demanding of us to present.

He also remarks that "we find the words of Aktham Ibn Ṣayfī [an Arab known for his wise sayings and proverbs] better than some of the sūras of the Qur'ān."[6]

Abū Bakr al-Rāzī holds against the Qur'ān its lengthiness, repetition, and contradictions. He also objects that it contains myths from ancient sources. He describes them as matters that are of no benefit. Anyone who studies history is forced to agree with Abū Bakr al-Rāzī that the stories of the Qur'ān are merely myths and tales that are not true.

This painful criticism led a contemporary Islāmic researcher, Muḥammad Aḥmad Khalaf Allah, to try to find a way out of this trap. In his book *al-Fann al-Qaṣaṣī fi al-Qur'ān al-Karīm*, he presents the view that behind the stories of the Qur'ān are practical purposes, and the aim is not for historicity but for admonition. He concludes, therefore, that they are true stories from the perspective of the end result but not from the historical perspective. At any rate, the theory of Khalaf Allah refutes the depiction of the Qur'ān as a false, mythical book by quoting from it: *"...falsehood shall not come to it, from before it, nor from behind it—a revelation from the wise, the praiseworthy One"* (Q 41.42).

We also learn from Ibn al-Nadīm that other writers were critical of the Qur'ān's authenticity. They include Yaḥyā Ibn al-Ḥārith, Ibn Shabīb, Aḥmad Ibn Ibrahīm al-Warrāq, and Ya'qūb Ibn Abī Shayba.[7] Sadly, their works are lost, or more precisely, were intentionally disregarded and discarded by a culture of a singular authoritarian religion.

While scholars throughout history have attempted to critically analyze the Qur'ān, most have been silenced by a religion that violently rejects analysis. If the Qur'ān is indeed a holy and miraculous book, it should stand up to scrutiny. Throughout this text, we offer analysis by those historical scholars who have dared to speak out as well as from contemporary sources and our own Islāmic experts.

Muḥammad's Jibrīl

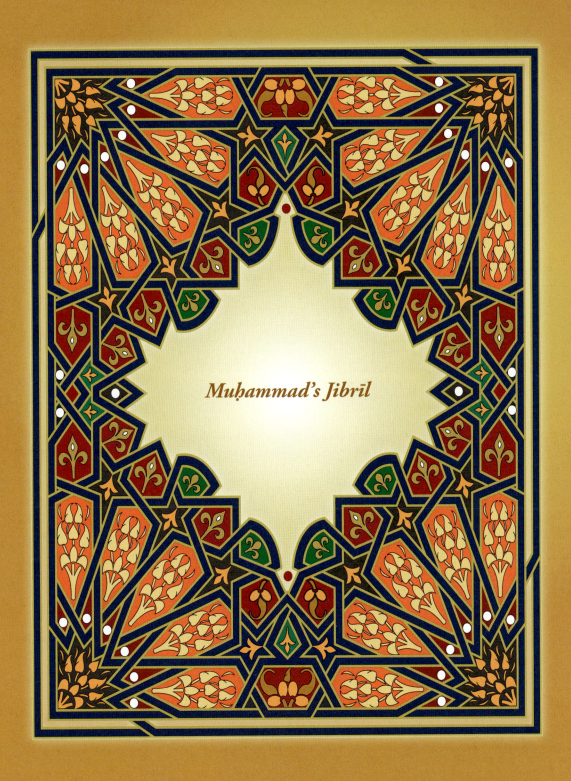

Muḥammad's Jibrīl

Jibrīl in the Islāmic narratives is the angelic messenger who carried (transported) the revelations to Muḥammad. Despite Jibrīl's vital role in establishing Islām as a religion, Muḥammad was silent about him for years. Jibrīl is not mentioned at all by Muḥammad in the Meccan portion of the Qur'ān. This spiritual messenger is not identified by Muḥammad until thirteen years later, after about eighty-six sūras of revelation had already been given. Jibrīl's name appears for the first time in sūra al-Baqara, where Muḥammad accused the Jews of being enemies of Jibrīl (Gabriel) (Q 2.97-98).

Afterwards, Muḥammad mentions Jibrīl's name only once in Q 66.4 to warn his insubordinate wives that Allah and Jibrīl are on his side against them.

There are, however, verses where hints of Jibrīl possibly appear, including *"One mighty in power"* (Q 53.5) and *"the Faithful Spirit"* (Q 26.193).

Muḥammad declared his revelations for many years before explicitly mentioning the name *Jibrīl.*

The Trance

The *sirat* literature (biography books) record that Muḥammad suffered from strange trancelike episodes. These unusual experiences were described by an eyewitness: "I looked at him, he had a snore...as the snore of a young camel."[1]

These trances actually led Muḥammad to question whether he had a touch of madness.[2] These symptoms stayed with him even after he declared himself a prophet. He continued to suffer from episodes of fainting, profuse sweating, and sounds of voices in his head. These symptoms then became explained as manifestations connected with the descending of inspiration, instead of possible symptoms of sickness.

Muḥammad described his condition during the process of his receiving a revelation:[3]

> Sometimes it comes like the ringing of a bell—which is the hardest on me—then it splits away from me. I then am aware of what he said. Other times the angel appears to me like a man and talks to me. Then I become aware of what he was saying. 'Ā'isha[N] [Bint Abī Bakr, Muḥammad's third wife]...said about it, "I saw him while the revelation was coming upon him on a bitterly cold day, then when it was split away from him, his [Muḥammad's] head would drip with sweat."

When we read history, we find that these symptoms are similar to the condition of the Arab diviners before Islām:[4]

> The priest during his divination enters a trancelike state, during which he would be in contact with a difficult arduous world no man can withstand. For the spirit to connect to it and be connected with the body of the diviner is a seriously dire matter during which the sweat is profuse, which especially happens when the speaker is the diviner himself.

Note that Muḥammad had openly declared that he used to hear a sound like the ringing of a bell. He also claimed, "The bell is the pipes of Satan."[5] Nonetheless, the question that seemingly has not been asked is if "the bell is the pipes of Satan," why does Muḥammad hear its ringing?

No matter the answer, Muḥammad treated these symptoms with *al-ruqya* ("spell-removing prayers or chants") and he would further advise Muslims to use *al-ruqya* for spells and chants.[6]

Muḥammad and the Pre-Islāmic (*Jāhilīya*) Divination

When the above-mentioned symptoms started to appear in Muḥammad, a great anxiety overtook and controlled him. When he compared what he was going through with the condition of the Arab diviners, he thought he too had become a diviner. He said to his first wife, Khadīja[N], "I am worried that I might be a diviner."[7]

In the Arabian Peninsula, divination was a common religious practice as well as a variety of other magical practices in use at the time, such as *al-ruqya* and astrology. The religious men would often belong to the priestly group, known as the *ruqya* performer *(al-rāqi)* or the astrologer.[8]

Such a diviner could make contact with hidden, spiritual forces. People with spiritually related questions would bring them to him at his home:[9]

> [Those] who sought him [the diviner] saw in him a super power and an ability to receive the revelation from that power which was seen in the form of an invisible person that would give the revelation to the diviner. Then the diviner would speak accordingly with what was appropriate to the situation and would answer their questions addressed to him.

Muḥammad admitted that he too experienced this process of divination: "Other times the angel appears to me like a man and talks to me. Then I become aware of what he is saying."[10]

Acts of similar divination by Muḥammad are presented in the Qur'ān, where he responds to questions with the expression, "They ask thee," as in these verses: *"They will ask thee of the spirit…"* (Q 17.85); *"They will ask thee about the mountains…"* (Q 20.105); and *"They shall ask thee about the Hour…"* (Q 79.42).

Furthermore, the "priests had a particular style in their talk while prophesying and divining known as *al-saj'* [rhymed prose]; that is why it was known as *al-saj'* of the diviners. Their *saj'* was characterized by the use of ambiguous words and general expressions that could be interpreted in a variety of opposing ways."[11]

The *saj'* and short expressions are characteristic of the Qur'ānic verses that belong to the first call (to Islām) period. An example of this can be seen in the Arabic rhymed prose of Q 102.1-8:

> *The contention about numbers deludes you*
> *till ye visit the tombs!*
> *Not so! In the end ye shall know!*
> *And again not so! In the end ye shall know!*
> *Not so! Did ye but know with certain knowledge!*
> *Ye shall surely see hell!*
> *And again ye shall surely see it with an eye of certainty.*
> *Then ye shall surely be asked about pleasure!*

For this reason, Muḥammad's contemporaries described him as one who had joined the diviners, an accusation that he vehemently denied. He announced to the Quraysh, that he was *"neither a soothsayer nor mad!"* (Q 52.29).

This reaction is significant, as the diviner was seen as one who would be inspired with the revelation by the "satan of the diviner." The Arabs believed that this satan would eavesdrop "on heaven and bring what he heard and recite it. Then the diviner would recite to the people what his satan had recited to him."[12]

Based on this imagery, Muḥammad believed that every man had his companion satan. He declared, "'Each one of you, without exception, has been assigned a companion of the jinn.' The Muslims asked him, 'Even you?' He said, 'Even I, except that Allah aided me against him. So, he became a Muslim and would command me with nothing but good.'"[13] He also said to 'Ā'isha, "'Yes! But my Lord aided me against him until he became a Muslim.'"[14]

Khadīja's Verdict

In the midst of these hallucinations and voices, when some suspected that madness could have befallen Muḥammad or that he might have become a diviner, Khadīja stepped forward to deliver Muḥammad out of his condition and suffering:[15]

> Khadīja...said to the messenger of Allah..."Cousin [husband], can you tell me about your companion that appears to you when he comes?" He said, "Yes!" She said, "Then when he comes to you, tell me about it." Jibrīl...came to him as he used to do. The messenger of Allah...said to Khadīja, "Khadīja! Jibrīl has come to me." She said, "Get up, cousin [husband], and sit on my left thigh...." The messenger of Allah...got up and sat on her. She said, "Do you see him?" He said, "Yes!" She said, "Move and sit on my right thigh." She reported that the messenger of Allah...moved and sat on her right thigh. She asked, "Do you see him?" He said, "Yes!" She said, "Move and sit in my lap." She reported that the messenger of Allah...moved and sat in her lap. She said, "Do you see him?" He said, "Yes!" She reported that she felt distressed and cast her veil while the messenger of Allah...was in her lap. Then she said to him, "Do you see him?" he said, "No!" She said, "O cousin [husband], be steadfast and of good cheer, for by Allah he is indeed an angel and not a satan."
>
> [Another slightly different story adds that Khadīja] tucked the messenger of Allah...between her and her undergarment [*dir'ihā*]. At that point Jibrīl left. She then said to the messenger of Allah..."This is an angel, not a satan."

We notice the following troubling issues in this story:

1. Khadīja said to Muḥammad, "This is an angel, not a satan," which indicates that Muḥammad believed that a satan was the one who was appearing to him (and not Jibrīl) as the text of the story mentions. For if Muḥammad had thought that Jibrīl was the one that was appearing to him, his wife would probably have said, "You are right! He is Jibrīl." Instead, she rejected the description of the being as a satan without mentioning Jibrīl, which means the name *Jibrīl* may have been inserted later into the original story.
2. Even though Khadīja was not able to see this being, she still decided its nature—despite the fact that Muḥammad, who could see the being, was not able to identify it. (Muḥammad only identified this being as Jibrīl in later revelations.)
3. This story presents another perplexing question: Why would the angel overlook the fact that Muḥammad was sitting on the thigh of Khadīja (a suggestive, provocative position) yet leave later when she unveiled her face (a less erotic action)?
4. Khadīja conducted her experiment to an explicit extreme. She made Muḥammad sit one time on her left thigh, then again on her right thigh, and then in her lap. Finally, according to the second story, she tucked Muḥammad under her undergarments, "tucked the messenger of Allah...between her and her garments [*dir'ihā*]," to judge if the being would remain to watch these explicit scenes. If this being continued to watch, then this being would be a satan. What is clear is that Khadīja was lavishing compassion and kindness on Muḥammad to calm his fears, so she would find it easy to convince him that what he saw was an angel and not a satan.

Conclusion

For many long years Muḥammad suffered different trancelike symptoms. On occasion he suspected that he had become mad, as he said to Khadīja, "I hear a voice and see a light. I fear that I have madness in me."[16]

At other times, Muḥammad believed that he had become a diviner like those soothsayers who "see their companion, who could appear to them in a human form."[17] But Khadīja delivered him from this condition because she had a sharp insight into Muḥammad's psyche. Then she experimented to find out the identity of what appeared to her husband and to testify afterwards that it was an angel and not a satan. Her pronouncement means Muḥammad discovered the nature of what he saw through a woman, "who lacks in reason and religion," according to the view of women in Islām. Based on her witness, Muḥammad established his evidence that what came to him was an angel. Muslims, then, rely in turn on the single testimony of a woman. (See the article "Women in the Qur'ān" on page 117.)

The testimony of Khadīja did not cure Muḥammad of this phenomenon, which plagued him throughout his adult life. He continued hearing the voices and seeing the shadows.

These symptoms resemble those of a condition known as auditory aura. They are auditory hallucinations that may be accompanied with other sensory hallucinations, and they can take place during an epileptic seizure. If Muḥammad did not suffer from auditory aura, it seems certain that he had a lesser problem known as akoasm, which is an auditory hallucination where symptoms include hearing ringing sounds, knocking sounds, shuffling sounds, and the like. Because of these sounds, Muḥammad continued to believe that he had a companion satan, as he told 'Ā'isha.

After Khadīja convinced Muḥammad that what appears to him is the deliverer of revelation, Muḥammad refers to this being as the *"Holy Spirit"* (Q 16.102), and calls him *"a noble apostle"* (Q 81.19). He did not mention Jibrīl's name as the one delivering the revelation until he moved to Medina.

This eventual declaration concerning Jibrīl must have resulted from Muḥammad's contact with the Jews. The name גַּבְרִיאֵל (Jibrīl/Gabriel) is a Hebrew name mentioned in an Old Testament book (Dan. 8.16, 9.21). Did Muḥammad learn the name *Jibrīl* from the Jews, or did he learn it just before this contact?

We do not have any available written text that would help specify the time period when Muḥammad directly introduced the name *Jibrīl.* If Muḥammad acquired that name from the Jews, it explains why the name did not appear except in Medina. However, if we are to accept the probability offered by Arthur Jeffery, noted scholar and historian of Semitic languages, its source originated from the Syriac form of the name ܓܒܪܝܠ.[18]

It is possible that Muḥammad could have heard the name in Mecca, but in Medina he saw the necessity of updating all the Qur'ānic texts to show that Jibrīl delivered all the revelations Muḥammad had received.

Therefore, Jibrīl, in his true nature, was those voices and images that would come to Muḥammad. These manifestations were transformed by the suggestive power of Khadīja into an angel who later could have become Gabriel through the influence of Jewish or Christian acquaintances.

Note: Because of an apparent misinterpretation of the Annunciation story in the New Testament (Luke 1.19-31), Muḥammad created a mix-up between the spirit and Jibrīl and merged the two into one being. He said about Mary, *"...we sent unto her our spirit"* (Q 19.17) as well as *"a messenger of"* the Lord (Q 19.19).[19] Therefore, Muḥammad made the spirit of Allah and the messenger of Allah one and the same.

This issue of Jibrīl as both spirit and messenger appear to run counter to other verses of the Qur'ān that mention *"angels and the Spirit"* (Q 70.4; Q 97.4), distinguishing between the angels and the spirit without paying attention that Jibrīl is an angel. Who is the spirit in these verses? In response, the exegetes say that Jibrīl is the spirit.[20] But if Jibrīl is one of the angels, then why make this distinction? (See comment on Q 2.97, page 195.)

Compilation of the Qur'ān

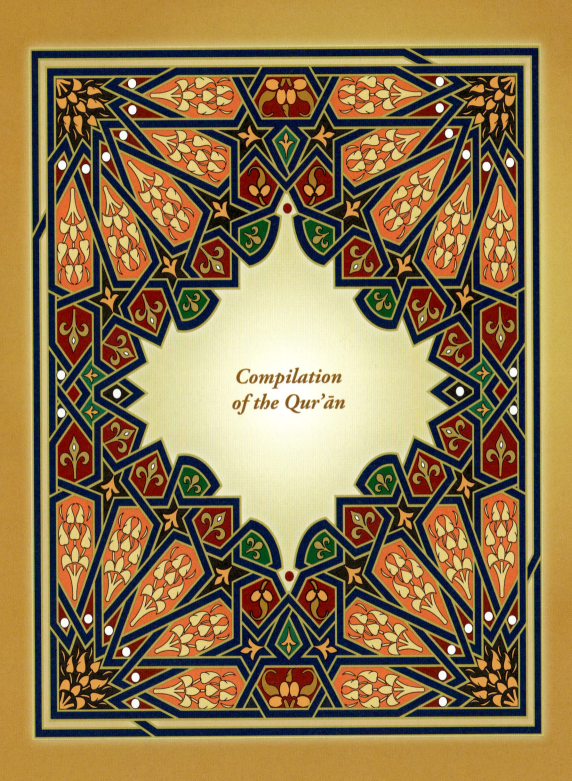

Compilation of the Qur'ān

According to Islāmic beliefs, the Qur'ān was revealed when Muḥammad began proclaiming his faith and reciting portions of it for his followers to memorize. When the Meccans persisted in rejecting Muḥammad and his followers, they emigrated to Medina around AD 621. This migration is known in Islāmic sources as the *Hijra*[D], or Hegira. Then, in Medina, another portion of the Qur'ān was given.

Muḥammad was in the habit of asking his scribes to add new verses to different texts.[1] However, this procedure did not apply to all the Qur'ānic passages. What he had left before his death (AH 11/AD 632) were merely scattered fragments written on primitive materials, like leather, clay, and palm leaves. These pieces were not kept with Muḥammad or anyone in particular. When the compiling of the Qur'ān was initiated, the compilation committee did not designate any specific person to collect these pieces but asked everyone who held any portion of the Qur'ān to bring it forth. It seems clear that Muḥammad had never sought to collect the Qur'ān. One Muslim scholar explained that "Muḥammad did not compile the Qur'ān in a book because he anticipated abrogations[D] of some of its rulings or recitations."[2]

A partial writing of the Qur'ān took place in Medina, which means the Meccan portion of the Qur'ān (two-thirds of the Qur'ānic material) was never written. If there was a possibility that Muḥammad wrote some of the texts in Mecca, they must have been lost, because the historical annals do not mention the Muslims taking Qur'ānic texts with them during the *Hijra*.

In addition, we don't find in the historical sources any mention of scribes in Mecca. The only possible reference suggesting the existence of a scribe at that time mentions 'Abd Allah Ibn Abī Sarḥ, who recounted that he wrote the Qur'ān for Muḥammad in Mecca.[3] Later, he broke off his association with Muḥammad and joined the Quraysh after the falsehood of Muḥammad's claims to prophethood became apparent to him.[4]

Ibn Sa'd quoted a list of "those who compiled the Qur'ān" during Muḥammad's time: Ubayy Ibn Ka'b, Mu'ādh Ibn Jabal, Abū al-Dardā', Zayd Ibn Thābit, Sa'd Ibn 'Ubayd, Abū Zayd Ibn 'Ubayd, and Mujma' Ibn Jārīya. It is further said that Ibn Mas'ūd learned part of the Qur'ān from Mujma' Ibn Jārīya. Another report mentioned by Ibn Sa'd adds more names: 'Uthmān Ibn 'Affān, Tamīm al-Dārī, Mu'ādh Ibn Jabal, 'Ubāda Ibn al-Ṣāmit, and Abū Ayūb.[5]

It seems that the meaning of "compilation" here is actually memorization. The Islāmic historiographers unanimously agree that the first compilation of the Qur'ān, in terms of writing it down, happened later under the supervision of Zayd Ibn Thābit. There is no doubt, however, that those who "compiled" the first Qur'ān, whether in writing or by memorizing, gathered it in part, not in whole; there was no written text yet and Muḥammad was still amending it by adding to parts of the Qur'ān, abrogating some, and removing others.

We notice that the figures who are said to have collected the Qur'ān during Muḥammad's lifetime, except for 'Uthmān Ibn 'Affān[N], had no social status because they were distant from the decision-making arena. It seems that they were merely loyal to the call of Islām. Considering that 'Uthmān Ibn 'Affān was under the criticism of numerous Muslims during his reign, perhaps his name might have been added to this list to confer a kind of holiness upon him.

Therefore, throughout the Meccan period and during some of the Medina periods, memory was the main tool to record the Qur'ānic passages. However, memory is not a reliable tool, for it failed Muḥammad himself. "Hence, we see him comforting the believers in Q 2.106, saying that Allah will grant them a better one in place of each verse that fell victim to forgetfulness."[6]

Abu Bakr and 'Umar's Compilation

Two major compilations, assembled during two different caliphs but under the direction of the same committee leader, eventually produced the first rudimentary codex. The primary purpose of the first compilation was to collect and preserve manuscripts to ensure the survival of the Qur'ān.

Zayd's First Compilation

The first compilation of the Qur'ān was done by Abū Bakr, who succeeded Muḥammad in leading the Muslims (AH 11-13/AD 632-634).[7] He fought a series of wars against the tribes that refused to submit to the authority of Muslims. These wars (known in the Islāmic sources as *Ḥurūb al-Ridda,* or Wars of Apostasy) ended with a bloody war against Musaylima[N], a rival of Muḥammad who also claimed prophethood, in al-Yamāma (AH 12/AD 633). There, the Muslims achieved a great victory but at a high human toll.

According to the narrations, some of those who were killed in this decisive war were those who had memorized the Qur'ān. Consequently, 'Umar Ibn al-Khaṭṭāb[N] suggested to Abū Bakr that he compile the Qur'ān. In response, Abū Bakr asked him how he could do something that Muḥammad wouldn't do. But 'Umar defended the rightness of his opinion, saying that more wars would follow the al-Yamāma war, and if more preservers of the Qur'ān are killed a large portion of the Qur'ān would be lost.[8] Therefore, "Abū Bakr, concerned that the Qur'ān might be lost," charged 'Umar Ibn al-Khaṭṭāb and Zayd Ibn Thābit with the duty of compiling the Qur'ān.[9]

Some accounts alluded to the fears of Abū Bakr concerning the loss of the Qur'ān (without mentioning 'Umar's advice) and states in short that "when the Muslims were killed in the al-Yamāma war, Abū Bakr was terrified. He feared that a group of preservers of the Qur'ān might perish. So, people came forth with what they had till it was collected on paper during the time of Abū Bakr, the first to compile the Qur'ān into manuscripts."[10]

The mentioning of "paper" in the narration reveals the manipulation of the stories in the Islāmic sources, because the Arabs used papyrus after the occupation of Egypt during the reign of 'Umar, and paper was made a century and a half later in Samarqand. Its production in Baghdad did not start until the end of the eighth century AD with the help of the Chinese.[11]

Abū Bakr assigned the duty of compiling the Qur'ān to Zayd[N] because Zayd used to write the Qur'ān for Muḥammad: "You are a sensible youth; we have nothing against you. You wrote the revelation to the prophet. Follow the trace of the Qur'ān in order to collect it."[12]

This assignment was not easy, as explained by Zayd: "If they had assigned me the burden of moving mountains, it would have been easier than what they assigned me. I followed the trace of the Qur'ān from the chests of men [meaning: what the men had committed to memory], the palm leaves, leather pieces, ribs, and pieces of stone and pottery."[13]

The collection process took place in the following manner:

> Abū Bakr sent after those people who were known for their high quality of memorization and asked them to work under the leadership of Zayd. A meeting was held in the house of 'Umar to discuss the manner of how to compile the Qur'ān and to divide the tasks.[14] They asked Bilāl to announce in Medina to those who had in their possession written Qur'ānic pieces to submit them to the writing committee.[15] The testimony of two people was required to confirm a piece was Qur'ānic.[16]

One interesting story is told that 'Umar brought to the committee the verse on stoning (*al-rajm*), but Zayd did not notate it because 'Umar had no one to bear witness except himself.[17]

The process of compiling lasted about a year.[18] After completing the task, Zayd handed it over to Abū Bakr. Then 'Umar received it when he became the second successor (caliph) following Muḥammad's death. The manuscripts ended up with his daughter, Ḥafṣa, after his death.[19]

'Uthmān's Compilation

Multiple *maṣāḥif* (codices) and variant readings escalated conflicts among Muslims. To help reduce these tensions and unify the different Muslim groups, 'Uthmān Ibn 'Affān (third caliph) established a compilation committee to create one standard Qur'ān for all.

Zayd's Second Compilation

A singular story narrates that 'Uthmān Ibn 'Affān collected the Qur'ān during the reign of 'Umar Ibn al-Khaṭṭāb.[20] It is not understood from this story if 'Uthmān compiled the Qur'ān by himself or if he participated in the committee work under Zayd. However, if what is meant is that he participated in the committee, the story is acceptable.

Approximately the year AH 25, (or, it is also said, AH 30), 'Uthmān Ibn 'Affān made the decision to compile the Qur'ān.[21] That decision was made after conflicts arose between Muslims about the Qur'ānic variant readings. The conflict concerning the difference in wording was widespread:

- **Iraq:** The Islāmic armies included competing tribes and clans. Based on this clan division, conflicts arose among the Muslims on various issues, including the Qur'ān. A schism occurred between the people of Basra who recited their Qur'ān according to how Abū Mūsā read it and the people of Kufa who recited their Qur'ān according to how Ibn Mas'ūd read it.[22]

- **Iraq/Syria (al-Shām):** The dissension over which *muṣḥāf* was the correct Qur'ān spread outside Iraq. When the Muslim combatants from Iraq and those from the Syria (al-Shām) were together fighting at the borders of Armenia and Azerbaijan, they started quarrelling about the question of who had the right Qur'ān.[23] The people of Hums considered the codex of al-Miqdād Ibn al-Aswad the most credible one, while the rest of the people of the Syria held to the codex of Ibn Ka'b. The people of Kufa considered Ibn Mas'ūd's recitation to be the standard one, while the people of Basra considered Abū Mūsā's text to be the most reliable one.[24] The reports about the quarrels reached 'Uthmān.[25]

- **Medina:** The dissension over the reading had also spread in Medina, which was the heart of Islām at that time. Even the teachers of the youngsters were in dispute: "Some of them even counted the others' reading to be blasphemous. That news reached 'Uthmān as well, so he rose up and said, 'You are in my presence, yet you disagree about it and say it incorrectly. Those who are in faraway regions are even in more disagreement and grammatical incorrectness. Gather ye, O Companions of Muḥammad, and write for the people an *Imām* [a standard to follow].'"[26] He also said, "Your prophet was just taken fifteen years ago, and you already disagree about the Qur'ān's text itself!?"[27]

Moreover, the expansion of Muslims and their mixing with other people groups led to the blending of languages. So it appeared that the evolutionary linguistic process would put the Qur'ān "in jeopardy of corruption, distortion, addition and deletion."[28]

Reliance on Ḥafṣa's Manuscript

There is no doubt that the presence of hundreds of Qur'ānic manuscripts among the Muslims nurtured the schism in the different cities (Kufa, Basra, Medina) and regions (Iraq, Syria) over which Qur'ān was the standard one. A historian estimated the number of codices at the end of 'Umar Ibn al-Khaṭṭāb's reign (AH 13-23/AD 634-644) to be 100,000 codices distributed in Iraq, Syria, and Egypt.[29]

We do not agree with this estimate, because it is not based on historical data but only on assumptions. Even if there was a large number of manuscripts at that time in each city, there should have remained at least a few.

Certainly all the copies of the Qur'ān were partial ones and not the complete manuscript. Some might have had a few sūras, while others could have had larger portions. However, it is highly unlikely that 100,000 complete copies of the Qur'ān existed then. If this large total was true, we would have at least dozens of these manuscripts today. The first compilation attempt revealed that the written Qur'ānic manuscripts were spread among many Muslims, not taking into account the parts of the Qur'ān that were committed to memory only. The only copy that was completed by Zayd's first committee took more than a year to compile. It was the only copy that was considered somewhat complete and was ultimately given to Ḥafṣa for safekeeping. No extra copies of it were made for circulation.

Since the only unique compiled copy was the one entrusted to Ḥafṣa, 'Uthmān asked her to submit it so that it would become the basis for the work he was about to start. He appointed an editing committee consisting of Zayd Ibn Thābit, Sa'īd Ibn al-'Āṣ, 'Abd al-Raḥmān Ibn al-Ḥārith Ibn Hishām, and 'Abd Allah Ibn al-Zubayr. In another account the list included Zayd Ibn Thābit, 'Abd Allah Ibn 'Amr Ibn al-'Āṣ, 'Abd Allah Ibn al-Zubayr, Ibn 'Abbās, and 'Abd al-Raḥmān Ibn al-Ḥārith Ibn Hishām.[30] From another source we see that 'Uthmān appointed a committee of twelve men from the two groups, the Emigrants (*al-Muhājirūn*)[D] and the Helpers (*al-Anṣār*)[D].[31]

'Uthmān asked the compiliation committee to write the Qur'ān in the language of the Quraysh. This condition is attributed to 'Umar Ibn al-Khaṭṭāb, who had required the members of Zayd's initial committee to write the Qur'ān in "the language of Muḍar."[32]

After the committee completed the task entrusted to it, several copies were made and distributed to those present. 'Uthmān also sent copies to the Islāmic governing centers, ordering the governors to destroy the codices in their possession.[33] He sent a copy each to Kufa, Basra, and Syria, and he kept one for himself. It is said that seven copies were made and that 'Uthmān sent them to Mecca, Syria, Yemen, Bahrain, Basra, and Kufa. He also left one in Medina. The Islāmic view tends to prefer the story that he sent four copies.[34]

After that, 'Uthmān returned Ḥafṣa's copy to her, and she kept it until the days of the rule of Marwān Ibn al-Ḥakam.[35] After her death, Marwān asked 'Abd Allah Ibn 'Umar (Ḥafṣa's brother) to send him the copy.[36] 'Abd Allah Ibn 'Umar sent it to Marwān, who burned it, "fearing something might be different from what 'Uthmān copied."[37]

No opposition was reported to 'Uthmān's action, except the objection of Ibn Mas'ūd.[38] The prominent figures in Medina supported the decision of unifying the Qur'ān. Historical sources agree that 'Alī Ibn Abī Ṭālib recognized 'Uthmān for his work in compiling the Qur'ān and said, "O ye people, do not malign 'Uthmān and say nothing but good to him regarding the burning of the *maṣāḥif* [codices], for by Allah he did what he did to the *maṣāḥif* in the presence of us all."[39] 'Alī Ibn Abī Ṭālib[N] announced that if he was in power, he would have done what 'Uthmān did about this matter.[40]

Ibn Mas'ūd's Rejection

Ibn Mas'ūd refused to acknowledge the 'Uthmānic codex for personal reasons. His heart was filled with bitterness because he was excluded from the compilation committee. He said, "O Muslims! I get removed from writing down the Qur'ān's copies, and the charge is given to a man [Zayd], that by Allah, when I became a Muslim, he was still in the custody within the inner being of his father [before conception], a *kāfir*[D] [an infidel, or unbeliever]."[41]

Ibn Mas'ūd believed that he had the right to supervise the writing of the Qur'ān. He said bitingly, "I learned from the mouth of (Muḥammad) seventy sūras, while Zayd Ibn Thābit barely had two locks of hair and was playing with the boys."[42]

Ibn Mas'ūd pushed the people of Kufa to reject the official Qur'ān imposed by 'Uthmān's decision.[43] As a result, the people of Kufa stayed firm to the codex of Ibn Mas'ūd until al-Ḥajjāj Ibn Yūsuf al-Thaqafī[N] came to power.[44]

Difference Between the Two Compilations

Even though the two major compilation committees had different purposes for developing a written Qur'ān, the outcomes were similar—a flawed codex.

Abū Bakr's Compilation vs. 'Uthmān's Compilation

The story that claims that the decision of Abū Bakr to compile the Qur'ān was the result of the outcome following the Battle of Yamāma cannot be accepted, for very few men who were killed in the battle had knowledge of the Qur'ān. "Actually, we find…only two of those who fell dead in the battle were clearly recognized for their knowledge of the Qur'ān. They are 'Abd Allah Ibn Ḥafaṣ Ibn Ghānim and Sālim, both followers of Abū Ḥudhayfa."[45] It is obvious that the decision of Abū Bakr and 'Umar to compile the Qur'ān aimed to secure a comprehensive copy of the Qur'ānic passages in one place. In other words, the compiling and archiving of the Qur'ān was motivated by the fear that it could get lost.

The compilation of 'Uthmān, on the other hand, was motivated by a desire to unify and standardize the differences between the versions. After the spread of Islām across the Arabian Peninsula, the Arabs started reading the Qur'ān according to their various languages. 'Uthmān saw that this led "to some of them calling others deviant in their reading. He feared the escalation of this matter and therefore copied those Qur'ānic copies into one Qur'ān organized in sūras. Of all the languages he could have chosen, he selected the Quraysh language, arguing that the revelation came down in that tongue. If the Qur'ān was spread in different languages for ease and comfort at the beginning, now that need was no longer there. Hence he limited it to one language."[46]

Al-Ḥārith al-Muḥāsibī explains, "What is known among the people is that the compiler of the Qur'ān is 'Uthmān. It is not so. 'Uthmān made the people read one version, a choice made between him and his contemporaries, the Emigrants and the Helpers."[47]

'Uthmān's endeavor for unification was based on political motivations. The Muslims were in need of a bond to hold them together and Islām was the common agent. Since the Qur'ān is the holy book of Islām, differences over the book would weaken the bond among Muslims. Imposition of one single reading (one book) was needed to promote political unity. The fear of weakening the unity was more important than maintaining variety in the Qur'ān. When Muḥammad allowed individuals to read the Qur'ān according to their tribal language and allowed the multiplicity of readings, he was then a leader of political and religious formation confined to Medina and its surrounding areas. Later, during 'Uthmān's time, the political and religious situation became more complicated. 'Uthmān had to tackle the Qur'ānic text in accordance with the needs of a society undergoing developmental growth and military expansion.

The completion of the Qur'ān was not free from flaws:

> **First**, when the Qur'ān was presented to 'Uthmān, he said, "It [the Qur'ān] has grammatical flaws (*laḥn*) and the Arabs will fix them according to their tongues."[48] He further said, "If the writer was from Thaqīf such issues would not be found in it."[49] Some requested that he endeavor to complete the necessary revisions. When the verse Q 20.63 was recited in his presence, it was suggested to him that it should be corrected. But he refused, saying, "Let it be. It does not forbid what is permitted nor permit what is forbidden."[50]
>
> **Second**, there was another imperfection in the Qur'ān, in that it did not have the dots on the letters or the accents. Still, this omission was no different from other versions of the Qur'ān:[51]
>
>> It was up to the reader himself to place the dots on the letters of the words and to set the accents according to the meaning of the verses. For example, one would read the word بعلمه as يُعَلِّمُهُ [*Yu'allimuhu* ("He teaches him")], another نُعَلِّمُهُ [*Nu'allimuhu* ("We teach him")], yet another تُعْلِمُهُ [*Tu'limhu* ("You inform him")], and بِعِلْمِهِ [*bi'ilmihi* ("by his knowledge")], etc., by placing the dots and the accents according to the reader's interpretation of the verse. Moreover, many readers chose [preferred] readings of the Qur'ān that were forbidden by 'Uthmān, as can be seen in the books of the variant readings of the Qur'ān.

The absence of dotting and other diacritical markings[D] kept the issue of the multiple readings present, which required a new intervention by the political authority. This intervention took place when al-Ḥajjāj Ibn Yūsuf al-Thaqafī revised some of the Qur'ānic passages.[52]

Multiple *Maṣāḥif*

When 'Uthmān initiated the unification of the Qur'ānic readings, he relied on Ḥafṣa's *muṣḥāf* but did not strictly copy it. His committee started the process of reviewing and revising Ḥafṣa's *muṣḥāf*, or codex, as well as organizing the sūras. Even though 'Uthmān ordered the unified reading, he did not destroy Ḥafṣa's copy, allowing certain individuals to keep their own different *maṣāḥif*. He also did not pursue the owners of other copies, or *maṣāḥif*:[53]

Other *Maṣāḥif* Concurrent with 'Uthman's Codex	
Sālim Ibn Ma'qal	'Abd Allah Ibn Mas'ūd[N]
'Abd Allah Ibn 'Abbās[N]	'Ā'isha[N]
'Uqba Ibn 'Āmir*	'Alī Ibn Abī Ṭālib[N]
Al-Miqdād Ibn al-Aswad	'Abd Allah Ibn al-Zubayr[N]
Abū Mūsā al-Ash'arī**	'Abd Allah Ibn 'Umar
Ubayy Ibn Ka'b[N]	Um Salma***

* He later ruled Egypt. His codex was discovered in the year AH 313/AD 925, but it is now lost.

** His codex spread in Basra. It greatly resembles the codices of Ibn Mas'ūd and Ibn Ka'b but disagrees with the 'Uthmānic codex.

*** She was one of Muḥammad's wives.

Historical sources also list names of people belonging to the second generation of Muslims (the successors), who had their own codices (*maṣāḥif*): 'Ubayd Ibn 'Umayr al-Laythī, 'Aṭa' Ibn Abī Rabāḥ, 'Akrama, Mujāhid, Sa'īd Ibn Jubayr[N], al-Aswad Ibn Yazīd, 'Alqama Ibn Qays, Muḥammad Ibn Abī Mūsā, Ḥaṭṭān Ibn 'Abd Allah al-Raqāshī, Ṣāliḥ Ibn Kīsān, and Ṭalḥa Ibn Muṣarrif.[54]

We will address below two other codices, for they hold more material than the one in circulation.

Ubayy Ibn Ka'b's Codex

Accounts tell us that Ubayy[N] participated in the first compilation committee.[55] It seems that it helped him in preparing his own special codex. It differs from 'Uthmān's approved codex in the order of sūras. However, what most distinguishes Ubayy's version is that it contains two additional sūras: al-Khal' and al-Ḥafd. (See Controversial Qur'ānic Texts, page 587.) These were published in an edited form by Hammer. Nöldeke later reedited and published them.[56]

'Alī's Codex

'Alī Ibn Abī Ṭālib supposedly had his own Qur'ān. According to some Islāmic sources, 'Alī collected the Qur'ān after Muḥammad's death, when he swore he would not to leave his house "until the Qur'ān is compiled in one book." However, this claim has no solid ground. If 'Alī had actually collected a codex of his own, he would have had to stay home and work on it during the entire ruling period of Caliphs Abū Bakr and, perhaps, 'Umar. (See an examination of this issue in the article "Chronological Sequence of the Qur'ān" on page 70.) In defense of 'Alī's claim, al-Sijistānī explains that the expression "compile the Qur'ān" means to memorize it.[57]

Over the next several decades the different Muslim groups increasingly clashed over religious leadership, proper religious practices, and a correct Qur'ān. According to Shiite opinion, 'Alī should have been the first successor to Muḥammad so they believe his copy of the Qur'ān is the correct version and any other copy is corrupted:[58]

> [Some Shiites said,] "We found the nation (*umma*) differing in its [the Qur'ān's] transfer greatly and horrendously. Due to the greatness of their difference, we became unable to distinguish its correct from its corrupt, or its shortage from excess [what was taken out or added to it], nor do we know the order of everything in what was revealed, neither what comes before nor after." Some of their people said, "No one knows about what is missing of it except the imām[D], who was given the knowledge thereof, and to his followers [as well]." Those who denied any addition to it (the Qur'ān) but affirmed that it was missing [portions] said, "Abū Bakr and his followers were the ones who took charge of setting and organizing it, and putting it, or most of it, in sūras (chapters), bringing up the rear and pushing back the front; hence, many verses were misplaced and verses were removed from their deserving places."

The Shiites accused Abū Bakr and 'Uthmān of tampering with the Qur'ān. The Shiites said that Abū Bakr and 'Uthmān deleted all the paragraphs referring to 'Alī and his family and omitted from the current version verses directing criticism to the "Helpers and Emigrants for committing improper behavior."[59] In the fourth century AH, the writings of the Shiites referred to corruption in about five hundred verses in the Qur'ān.[60]

In spite of this contention, the Shiites today consider the circulated Qur'ān a holy book and they will continue to use it until the coming of al-Mahdī[D], who they believe will bring the true uncorrupted Qur'ān.[61]

Since the fourth century AH, the Shiite school has doubted the truthfulness of the current Arabic Qur'ān being Muḥammad's Qur'ān. It has adhered to its view that the Qur'ān has been subjected to different corruptions, including a change of sequence of the sūras and verses, omissions and additions. At one time, a version of the Qur'ān with two additional sūras, al-Nūrayn and al-Wilāya, was circulated in Shiite clerical groups. (See Controversial Qur'ānic Texts, page 587.) In 1842, Joseph Garcin de Tassy published sūra al-Nūrayn, but Mirza Kazem Beg doubted its originality, while William St. Clair-Tisdall accepted the possibility of its authenticity. In 1913, he published sūra al-Wilāya after he found it in a Shiite manuscript, where the name of 'Alī is explicitly mentioned.[62] The Shiite fabrication in sūra al-Wilāya is unquestionable. However, sūra al-Nūrayn suggests certain authenticity, and it is worth mentioning since it is the subject of debate among researchers.[63]

Conclusion

The political issues of the time motivated the compilation of the Qur'ān, and that initiation came from 'Umar Ibn al-Khaṭṭāb. The work started during the caliphate of Abū Bakr, but it appears that the compiling was not completed in the time of Abū Bakr. Therefore, 'Umar continued with the task of compiling and that is why some sources claim that 'Umar was the first to compile the Qur'ān.[64] One source says that 'Umar ordered the collection of the Qur'ānic passages, but he was killed while work was underway, so 'Uthmān worked to complete the task.[65]

In all these accounts, Zayd Ibn Thābit was always the head of the compilation committee, although he had not reached ten years of age when Muḥammad arrived at Medina. However, Abū Bakr chose him for many reasons, which he reveals in a comment to Zayd: "You are a righteous youth; [we have nothing against you,] we don't accuse you. You used to write the revelation." Apparently, Zayd's young age and lack of personal ambition removed any possible animosity with Abu Bakr and 'Umar. Also, Zayd was writing the Qur'ān for Muḥammad, and they say he learned the Jewish language.

After years of 'Uthmān's reign, Muslims started fighting over the readings of the Qur'ān: the Kūfis and the Basran, the Iraqis and the Syrians. There were conflicts within Medina as well. Therefore, 'Uthmān decided to release an official copy. He chose Zayd for the same reasons that led Abū Bakr to choose him. Moreover, Zayd had developed significant experience in the compiling and writing of the manuscript. 'Uthmān also had to work to keep certain persons, such as 'Abd Allah Ibn Mas'ūd, away from the committee.

'Uthmān intended that his manuscript unify the Qur'ānic readings and eliminate the cause of discord among the Muslims. He collected the readings into one version so that he could provide a basis for consensus. It is said that what 'Uthmān did was merely "put the sūras in order."[66] There is no doubt that this compilation served a political agenda, but it was at a historical cost. The readings of that period were missed, and by that omission we lost part of the Qur'ānic heritage, even though some of the readings are scattered and preserved in the commentaries and in rare works. Most notable among these works are *Kitāb al-Maṣāḥif* by Ibn Abī Dāwūd al-Sijistānī (third century AH) and *al-Muḥtasib* by Abū al-Fatḥ 'Uthmān Ibn Jinnī (fourth century AH).

However, 'Uthmān's attempt to make one unified text was not successful, for 'Uthmān himself kept Ḥafṣa's codex, as well as the personal codices belonging to the first generation of Muslims. Furthermore, the followers owned their own special codices. Within a few years conflict again arose over the reading because the new 'Uthmānic version was not dotted and required a reader with prior knowledge of the reading material. (See the chart "Illustration of Variant Readings," concerning the effect of dots on one transcription, page 102.)

As a result, the verses were merely interpreted according to the understanding of the reader most of the time. Three centuries would pass after the compilation of the 'Uthmānic codex before the final copy of a dotted Qur'ān would appear in the fourth century AH (tenth century AD).[67]

In the modern era, Muslims still have two separate readings:[68]

- **Reading of Ḥafṣ** (d. AH 190/AD 805) according to 'Āṣim (d. AH 127/AD 744), which was approved by al-Azhar in its print of the Qur'ān in 1925 and circulated in the largest part of the Islāmic world.

- **Reading of Warsh** (d. AH 197/AD 812) according to Nāfi' (d. AH 169/AD 785) used in north Africa.

Today, the Qur'ān that is circulated among Muslims with both readings is nothing but two versions that have been revised repeatedly over three centuries.

Fortunately, the Ṣan'ā' (Sana) manuscript was discovered in 1972, during the restoration of an ancient mosque on the brink of falling. This manuscript contains unknown readings.[69] It is the oldest Qur'ānic manuscript currently available. The German Orientalist, G. Puin, conducted research on the manuscript and found that significant changes were made to the Qur'ān. What this discovery tells us is that the present Qur'ān is not Muḥammad's Qur'ān. As a result of these serious discoveries, Yemeni authorities consequently banned Puin from further access to these manuscripts.[70]

The issue of the history of the Qur'ānic text is still subject to research. The most controversial hypothesis was raised by researcher John Wansbrough, who announced that the Qur'ān continued to be compiled for two to three centuries after the death of Muḥammad.[71] He added that the final wording of the Qur'ān emerged outside the Arabian Peninsula in monotheistic societies, particularly in Iraq and Palestine. However, another researcher of this issue observed that the internal structure of the Qur'ān does not support Wansbrough's assumption but reveals instead that it was compiled before (AH 41/AD 661).[72]

The discovery of more manuscripts and newer, more advanced research methods will allow us to identify the layers added to the Qur'ān during the process of the compilation, writing, and repeated revision. One day science may be able to access the first edition of the Qur'ān—the original version that was declared by Muḥammad to the Muslims.

Summary

- Muḥammad leaves some parts of the Qur'ān on primitive writing materials while others commit his words to memory.
- Abū Bakr and 'Umar take action to archive the Qur'ānic material, fearing its potential loss.
- 'Uthmān works on revising the Qur'ān that was organized by the first compilation committee, and, in the meantime, tries to destroy the other versions.
- The issue of variant readings remains persistent because of the absence of dotting and supplementary diacritical marks.
- The political and religious authorities revise the Qur'ān repeatedly until the dotted Qur'ān is published.

Chronological Sequence of the Qur'ān

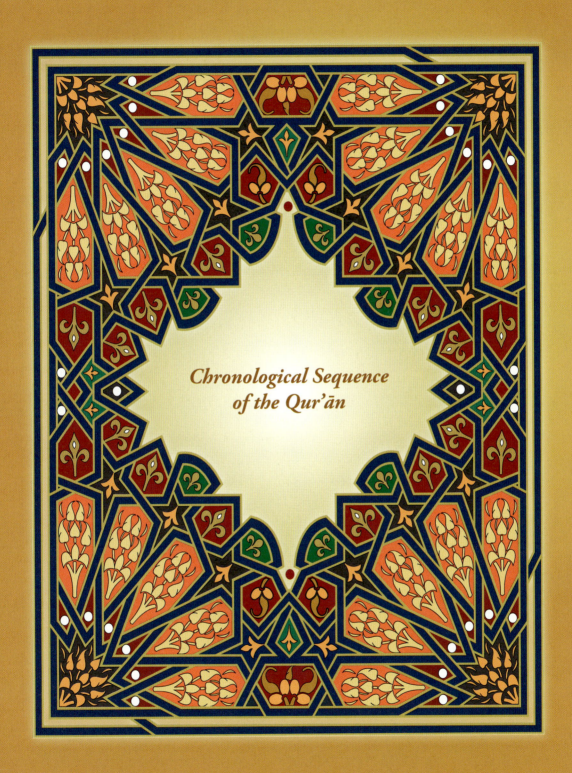

Chronological Sequence of the Qur'ān

One difficulty that faces the student of the Qur'ān is that its order is not based on the principle of chronological sequence. Because of its relation to theological issues, Muslim scholars gave careful attention to the issue of arrangement of the Qur'ānic text. For example, in the field of abrogation, the verse that abrogates another cannot be ascertained without specifying the chronological sequence of the verses.

The earliest attempt of chronological sequencing is attributed to Ibn 'Abbās[N] (d. AH 68/AD 688), the traditional father of exegesis. Al-Bayḍāwi (d. AH 716/ AD 1316) highlighted this point in his commentary. Islāmic research on the Qur'ān reached the pinnacle of its development in the hands of al-Suyūtī (d. AH 911/AD 1505) in his book *al-Itqān fī 'Ulūm al-Qur'ān,* which became the starting point of Western study in regard to the arrangement of the Qur'ān.[1]

In the modern era, a Muslim scholar named Muḥammad al-Ṭāhir Ibn 'Āshūr, in his commentary *al-Taḥrīr wa al-Tanwīr,* resumed the issue of arranging the texts by attempting to address the problem of chronological sequence at the beginning of each sūra.

The study of the arrangement of the Qur'ānic texts falls within a field of research in the study of the Qur'ān known as *M'arifat al-Makkī wa al-Madanī* ("Knowing the Meccan and the Medinan"). Muslim Qur'ānic scholars coined the terms *Meccan* and *Medinan* and gave them three distinct definitions:[2]

1. Meccan: The portion of the Qur'ān revealed in Mecca before and after the Hegira. Medinan: The portion of the Qur'ān revealed in Medina.
2. Meccan: Each speech addressed to the people of Mecca. Medinan: Each speech addressed to the people of Medina.
3. Meccan: The portion of the Qur'ān revealed in Mecca before the migration. Medinan: The portion of the Qur'ān revealed after the migration, whether in Medina, or Mecca, or in any other place during the raids of Muḥammad.

This last definition (number three) is the most popular one and is adopted by the majority of Muslim scholars of the Qur'ān, as well as by the Orientalists, the Western scholars of Middle Eastern Studies. Hence, we will use this last definition because it helps in defining the chronological succession—as opposed to the first two definitions that lack the chronological sequence. We have also chosen this third definition because the first definition is connected to the revelation only in terms of geography, and the second is concerned only with the identity of Muḥammad's audience.

When examining the arrangement of the Qur'ān, there are three major issues that should be considered: the arrangement of the sūras, the arrangement of the verses within the sūras, and the dating of the Qur'ānic text. A grasp of all three issues is crucial to understanding the discontinuity of the Qur'ān. It is also important to examine the lack of arrangement of verses within the same sūra, the intermingling of verses that belong to different periods, and the incoherence of verse succession within the 'Uthmānic text as noted by Shiite scholars.

Arrangement of the Sūras

According to a narrative attributed to Ibn 'Abbās, the Meccan portion of the Qur'ān consists of eighty-five sūras, while the Medinan portion is twenty-eight sūras.[3] It is noteworthy that the Ibn 'Abbās total is only 113, not 114 sūras. Perhaps the source of this view may have dropped al-Fātiḥa (Q 1) from his count, or it may be that his count relied on a certain copy that combined two sūras. In some codices, sūras al-Ḍuḥā (Q 93) and al-Sharḥ (Q 94) are combined into one sūra.[4] In fact, there is still debate today on the Meccan or Medinan origins of seventeen sūras:[5]

Seventeen Sūras with Disputable Origins		
al-Ra'd (Q 13)	al-Muṭaffifīn (Q 83)	al-Takāthur (Q 102)
Muḥammad (Q 47)	al-Tīn (Q 95)	al-Mā'ūn (Q 107)
al-Raḥmān (Q 55)	al-Qadr (Q 97)	al-Ikhlāṣ (Q 112)
al-Ḥadīd (Q 57)	al-Bayyina (Q 98)	al-Falaq (Q 113)
al-Ṣaff (Q 61)	al-Zalzala (Q 99)	al-Nās (Q 114)
al-Taghābun (Q 64)	al-'Ādiyāt (Q 100)	

Regarding the arrangement of the Qur'ān, Islāmic scholars have presented two opinions:

- The arrangement of the Qur'ān is "instituted," meaning by the order and guidance of Muḥammad.
- The arrangement of the Qur'ān is "adaptable," based on the labors of the compilation committees.

A group of Islāmic scholars also state that the arrangement of most of the sūras is instituted.[6]

However, academic examination of the Qur'ān reveals that the Qur'ān underwent simple systemic arrangement. After gathering the verses in an independent sūra, the collectors decided to set a simple arrangement based on a quantitative basis—from longer to shorter. The current breakdown of the Qur'ān is based on four categories:[7]

1. The "lengthy" (*al-ṭuwāl*)—long sūras (more than 100 verses)
2. The "one-hundreds" (*al-ma'ūn*)—which follow the seven longest sūras, each containing approximately 100 verses
3. The "double digits" (*al-mathānī*)—following the one-hundreds and containing less than one hundred verses each
4. The "sectioned" (*al-mufaṣṣal*)—following the double digits. These are the shortest of the sūras. Scholars said this portion is named *al-mufaṣṣal* for the many divisions among the sūras. Others said it was so named because these sūras contain fewer abrogations.

Alternative Qur'ānic Arrangements

It is important to note that the current arrangement of the Qur'ān is not the only arrangement and that the overall arrangement of the Qur'ān—its sūras, verses and sometimes even the arrangement of words within the verses—seemed of little importance to Muḥammad.

In addition to the adopted text arranged by 'Uthmān's committee, some references give us a list of other arrangements. The following table will present the sequence of the first fifteen and last sūras of the Qur'ān as arranged by Ibn Mas'ūd and Ibn Ka'b:

Alternate Sūra Arrangements		
Current Qur'ān	Codex (*Muṣḥaf*) of Ibn Mas'ūd*	Codex (*Muṣḥaf*) of Ubayy Ibn Ka'b*
al-Fātiḥa **(Q 1)**	al-Baqara (Q 2)	al-Fātiḥa (Q 1)
al-Baqara **(Q 2)**	al-Nisā' (Q 4)	al-Baqara (Q 2)
Āl-i 'Imrān **(Q 3)**	Āl-i 'Imrān (Q 3)	al-Nisā' (Q 4)
al-Nisā' **(Q 4)**	al-A'rāf (Q 7)	Āl-i 'Imrān (Q 3)
al-Mā'ida **(Q 5)**	al-An'ām (Q 6)	al-An'ām (Q 6)
al-An'ām **(Q 6)**	al-Mā'ida (Q 5)	al-A'rāf (Q 7)
al-A'rāf **(Q 7)**	Yūnus (Q 10)	al-Mā'ida (Q 5)
al-Anfāl **(Q 8)**	al-Tawba (Q 9)	Yūnus (Q 10)
al-Tawba **(Q 9)**	al-Naḥl (Q 16)	al-Anfāl (Q 8)
Yūnus **(Q 10)**	Hūd (Q 11)	al-Tawba (Q 9)
Hūd **(Q 11)**	Yūsuf (Q 12)	Hūd (Q 11)
Yūsuf **(Q 12)**	al-Isrā' (Q 17)	Maryam (Q 19)
al-Ra'd **(Q 13)**	al-Anbiyā' (Q 21)	al-Shu'arā' (Q 26)
Ibrāhīm **(Q 14)**	al-Mu'minūn (Q 23)	al-Ḥajj (Q 22)
al-Ḥijr **(Q 15)**	al-Shu'arā' (Q 26)	Yūsuf (Q 12)
...	...	...
Last sūra: al-Nās **(Q 114)** Total number of sūras: **114**	Last sūra: al-Ikhlāṣ (Q 112) Total number of sūras: 111**	Last sūra: al-Nās (Q 114) Total number of sūras: 116***

* The arrangement of the suras for the codex of Ibn Mas'ūd and Ubayy Ibn Ka'b is recorded in the book *al-Fihrist* by Ibn al-Nadīm.[8]

** Ibn Mas'ūd dropped Q 113 and Q 114 from his codex, which is why al-Suyūtī says of him that he has 112 sūras in his codex. However, the total number of sūras in his codex must have been 111 because he does not add sūra al-Fātiḥa (Q 1) either.[9]

*** Ibn Ka'b added sūras al-Ḥafd and al-Khal' for a total of 116 sūras. Al-Suyūtī says that the codex of Ibn Ka'b contains only 115 sūras, because he combined sūras al-Fīl (Q 105) and Quraysh (Q 106).[10] (See Controversial Qur'ānic Texts, page 587.)

Arrangement and Compilation of 'Alī Ibn Abī Ṭālib's Codex

According to al-Ya'qūbī, 'Alī divided his codex *(muṣḥaf)* into seven parts, using the following arrangement:[11]

Arrangement of 'Alī Ibn Abī Ṭālib's Codex						
Part one	Part two	Part three	Part four	Part five	Part six	Part seven
al-Baqara (Q 2)	Āl-i 'Imrān (Q 3)	al-Nisā' (Q 4)	al-Mā'ida (Q 5)	al-An'ām (Q 6)	al-A'rāf (Q 7)	al-Anfāl (Q 8)
Yūsuf (Q 12)	Hūd (Q 11)	al-Naḥl (Q 16)	Yūnus (Q 10)	al-Isrā' (Q 17)	Ibrāhīm (Q 14)	al-Tawba (Q 9)
al-'Ankabūt (Q 29)	al-Ḥajj (Q 22)	al-Mu'minūn (Q 23)	Maryam (Q 19)	al-Anbiyā' (Q 21)	al-Kahf (Q 18)	Ṭa Ha (Q 20)
al-Rūm (Q 30)	al-Ḥijr (Q 15)	Ya Sīn (Q 36)	al-Shu'arā' (Q 26)	al-Furqān (Q 25)	al-Nūr (Q 24)	al-Ṣāffāt (Q 37)
Luqmān (Q 31)	al-Aḥzāb (Q 33)	al-Shūrā (Q 42)	al-Zukhruf (Q 43)	al-Qaṣaṣ (Q 28)	Ṣād (Q 38)	al-Aḥqāf (Q 46)
Fuṣṣilat (Q 41)	al-Dukhān (Q 44)	al-Wāqi'a (Q 56)	al-Ḥujurāt (Q 49)	al-Ghāfir (Q 40)	al-Zumar (Q 39)	al-Fatḥ (Q 48)
al-Dhāriyāt (Q 51)	al-Raḥmān (Q 55)	al-Mulk (Q 67)	Qāf (Q 50)	al-Mujādila (Q 58)	al-Jāthiya (Q 45)	al-Ṭūr (Q 52)
al-Insān (Q 76)	al-Ḥāqqa (Q 69)	al-Muddathir (Q 74)	al-Qamar (Q 54)	al-Ḥashr (Q 59)	al-Bayyina (Q 98)	al-Najm (Q 53)
al -Sajda (Q 32)	al-Ma'ārij (Q 70)	al-Mā'ūn (Q 107)	al-Mumtaḥana (Q 60)	al-Jumu'a (Q 62)	al-Ḥadīd (Q 57)	al-Ṣaff (Q 61)
al-Nāzi'āt (Q 79)	'Abasa (Q 80)	al-Masad (Q 111)	al-Ṭāriq (Q 86)	al-Munāfiqūn (Q 63)	al-Muzzammil (Q 73)	al-Taghābun (Q 64)
al-Takwīr (Q 81)	al-Shams (Q 91)	al-Ikhlāṣ (Q 112)	al-Balad (Q 90)	al-Qalam (Q 68)	al-Qiyāma (Q 75)	al-Ṭalāq (Q 65)
al-Infiṭār (Q 82)	al-Qadr (Q 97)	al-'Aṣr (Q 103)	al-'Ādiyāt (Q 100)	Nūḥ (Q 71)	al-Naba' (Q 78)	al-Muṭaffifīn (Q 83)
al-Inshiqāq (Q 84)	al-Zalzala (Q 99)	al-Qāri'a (Q 101)	al-Kawthar (Q 108)	al-Jinn (Q 72)	al-Ghāshiya (Q 88)	al-Falaq (Q 113)
al-A'lā (Q 87)	al-Humaza (Q 104)	al-Burūj (Q 85)	al-Kāfirūn (Q 109)	al-Mursalāt (Q 77)	al-Fajr (Q 89)	al-Nās (Q 114)
al-Bayyina (Q 98)	al-Fīl (Q 105)	al-Tīn (Q 95)		al-Ḍuḥa (Q 93)	al-Layl (Q 92)	
	Quraysh (Q 106)	al-Naml (Q 27)		al-Takāthur (Q 102)	al-Naṣr (Q 110)	

It is noteworthy, that al-Ya'qūbī's sequence (shown in the table above), does not contain these sūras: al-Fātiḥa (Q 1), al-Ra'd (Q 13), al-Saba' (Q 34), and Muḥammad (Q 47).

Question: Did 'Alī Ibn Abī Ṭālib pen a codex?

During the course of narrating the story of 'Alī's compilation of the Qur'ān, the Shiite sources state that 'Alī compiled the Qur'ān in accordance with the chronology of the revelation. Immediately after the death of Muḥammad, 'Alī went into isolation in his home "for three days until he compiled the Qur'ān. It was the first Qur'ān he collected in one book from memory. That Qur'ān belonged to the people of Ja'far."[12]

When subjecting the story to scrutiny, it appears to hold no credibility for the following separate or collective reasons:

1. The need for penning the Qur'ān emerged only after Muslim armies had expanded beyond the borders of the Arabian Peninsula, when the soldiers began to quarrel over the accuracy of their codices. This situation forced 'Uthmān to intervene and unify the Qur'ānic text. Many believe this unification was an act that the Islāmic society of Medina did not need, neither during Muḥammad's life nor immediately following his death.
2. 'Alī was busily engaged in political conflicts with regard to governance since the death of Muḥammad. Hence, he had no time for the task of compiling the Qur'ān.
3. The documented compiling of the Qur'ān required a committee of several individuals who worked diligently to examine the available texts and hear the testimony of the memorizers of the Qur'ān. How, then, would 'Alī be able to accomplish what it took an entire committee to do? And further, how was he able to write down the Qur'ān in just a few days?
4. 'Alī Ibn Abī Ṭālib received the reins of power after the murder of 'Uthmān. Why didn't he impose his Qur'ān on all the regions during his caliphate? Assuming that political conditions did not allow him to disseminate his Qur'ān, because of the prevailing unrest and chaos during his reign, why wasn't his Qur'ān circulated and used by his Shiite followers?

Moreover, if we take the list transmitted by al-Ya'qūbī (see table "Arrangement of 'Alī Ibn Abī Ṭalib's Codex," page 69), we will find that 'Alī's codex is not based on the chronological sequence. Rather, it leans toward the quantitative arrangement but according to different rules. For example, the seven long sūras are distributed among the seven parts. The shorter sūras are also distributed among the seven parts, and so on. It is clear that this categorization relied on "'Uthmān's revision."[13] Therefore, it is a post-'Uthmānic text, meaning the allegation that 'Alī compiled the Qur'ān, let alone that he arranged it, is propaganda generated by those who opposed the Umayyads to belittle the status of the 'Uthmānic codex.

Arrangement and Compilation of the Qur'ān Based on the Probable

The Qur'ān is organized by the length and not the chronology of its sūras. To understand this unusual arrangement, one must understand the context regarding the beginnings of the Qur'ān and how it eventually reached the Muslims. It appears Muḥammad showed no interest in writing down the Qur'ān but would sporadically write parts of it at different times. He would add verses to this sūra or that sūra with no clear methodology. Sometimes, Muḥammad appeared as if he did not care about the precision of the Qur'ānic text, which is an issue exposed by 'Abd Allah Ibn Abī Sarḥ, who was a scribe for Muḥammad.

'Abd Allah Ibn Abī Sarḥ started having doubts when Muḥammad recited, *"We have created man from an extract of clay..."* (Q 23.12-14). Ibn Abī Sarḥ said to Muḥammad, "And blessed be God, the best of creators!" To which Muḥammad replied, "Write it down! For it was revealed like that." The phrase was added to the body of the verse's text.

Consequently, Ibn Abī Sarḥ became suspicious of the call of Muḥammad.[14] He decided to test the veracity of Muḥammad's heavenly connection. One day, Muḥammad dictated, "Exalted in Power, Wise." In response, Ibn Abī Sarḥ wrote, "Oft-forgiving, Most Merciful." Then, when he read the changes, Muḥammad said to him, "Yes, it is the same."

In another story we read that Ibn Abī Sarḥ manipulated the revelation. When Muḥammad dictated, "Heareth and knoweth all things," Ibn Abī Sarḥ wrote, "Knoweth all things, Most wise." And when Muḥammad dictated, "Knoweth all things, Most wise," Ibn Abī Sarḥ wrote, "Heareth and knoweth all things"[15] This experience led Ibn Abī Sarḥ to reject Islām and return to the Quraysh, where he declared to them the falsehood of Muḥammad's prophetic claims.[16]

Muḥammad taunted him with this response:

> *Who is more unjust than he who devises against God a lie, or says, 'I am inspired,' when he was not inspired at all? and who says, 'I will bring down the like of what God has sent down;' but didst thou see when the unjust are in the floods of death, and the angels stretch forth their hands, 'Give ye forth your souls; today shall ye be recompensed with the torment of disgrace, for that ye did say against God what was not true, and were too proud to hear His signs.* (Q 6.93)

In addition, Muḥammad did not stick to the Qur'ānic text literally but was lenient with the readings. There are many reports of Muḥammad's negligence concerning the accuracy of the Qur'ān. We read in a narrative that 'Umar Ibn al-Khaṭṭāb noticed when he heard Hishām Ibn Ḥakīm reciting sūra al-Furqān (Q 25), that he was reading it "with many letters [i.e., words]" he had never heard before from Muḥammad. When Hishām finished praying, 'Umar grabbed him by his garment and asked him who taught him the sūra. He replied to him that it was Muḥammad. 'Umar called him a liar. Then they went together to Muḥammad who, after he heard the recitation of Hishām, said, "It was revealed like this," and added, "This Qur'ān was sent down on seven letters [dialects]. Read ye, therefore, of the Qur'ān what is easy for you."[17]

Another story tells of a man who came to Muḥammad and said to him, "'Abd Allah Ibn Mas'ūd taught me a sūra," then said, "Ubayy Ibn Ka'b taught it to me, but their readings differed. Which of the readings should I take?" Muḥammad kept silent. 'Alī, who was sitting next to him, replied, "Let each man read as he was taught. All are good and beautiful!"[18]

Muḥammad did not see the need to write down the Qur'ān precisely, which is why he did not put into effect any methodology to compile it. The task of accomplishing this mission and the laying down of its essential rules was left to his followers.

After 'Uthmān's committee compiled the Qur'ān, it used the quantitative arrangement (from longer to shorter). This arrangement relied, however, on what the eye estimated the size of the pages to be and not on the number of verses. For example, sūra al-Nisā' (Q 4) consists of 176 verses, while sūra al-A'rāf (Q 6) consists of 201 verses. Thus, this categorization based on verse totals is not entirely accurate. Perhaps the editorial committee was dealing with manuscripts of different lengths and script sizes that concealed the true length of the sūras.

Nonetheless, this categorization does not explain the strongest and most prominent violations against the quantitative principle mentioned here. For instance, al-Ra'd (Q 13), Ibrāhīm (Q 14), and al-Ḥijr (Q 15), which do not exceed more than 3 or 3½ pages in length, were placed among sūras whose lengths are about 7 pages each.

Also, it is not clear why al-Anfāl (Q 8), consisting of 5 pages, was put before al-Tawba (Q 9), consisting of 10 pages, or, for that matter, why al-Sajda (Q 32), consisting of 1½ pages, was put before al-Aḥzāb (Q 33), consisting of 5⅓ pages.[19]

Nöldeke presented one reason for this arbitrary ordering: "The motive behind this noteworthy method might be the fear of fully completing the task, which might incite the hidden evil forces. This myth is still widespread among the primitive people groups."[20]

Arrangement of the Verses

The arrangement or sequence of the verses in the Qur'ān is very unusual. Not only are the verses not in chronological order but verses from different eras (Meccan and Medinan) have been intermingled together in the same context or sūra.

A. **The lack of arrangement of verses within the same sūra**

In many cases, the arrangement of the verses lacks a chronological sequence. We find the first verses of a particular sūra placed far from the beginning of that sūra. For example, verses 15 and 16 are the first two verses to be revealed of sūra al-Mā'ida (Q 5).[21] According to chronological order, they should have been placed at the beginning of the sūra and numbered verses 1 and 2.

B. **The intermingling of verses that belong to different eras**
There is another issue concerning the order of the verses. We find Medinan verses within Meccan sūras and vice versa. Islāmic sources reference the sūras that are made up of different parts—mixed Meccan and Medinan verses:[22]

Meccan Sūras Containing Medinan Verses	Medinan Sūras Containing Meccan Verses
al-An'ām (Q 6)	al-Anfāl (Q 8)
al-A'rāf (Q 7)	al-Tawba (Q 9)
Ibrāhīm (Q 14)	al-Ra'd (Q 13)
al-Naḥl (Q 16)	al-Ḥajj (Q 22)
al-Isrā' (Q 17)	al-Mā'ūn (Q 107)
al-Kahf (Q 18)	
al-Qaṣaṣ (Q 28)	
al-Zumar (Q 39)	
al-Aḥqāf (Q 46)	

In fact, the above chart does not include all the sūras with intermingled verses. A methodological study reveals a kind of intermingling that requires the patience and careful detailed examination of the researcher. One observes that the inner structure of the intermingled sūras lacks unison and the method of organizing the verses shows that they were arranged, even within the same sūra, without following any particular method. For example, the verse of usury (Q 2.278), *"O ye who believe! fear God, and remit the balance of usury, if ye be believers"* is placed at the end of al-Baqara (Q 2), even though it is a verse that belongs to the first two years of migration (*Hijra*).[23]

In another example, some narratives say that the following text is the last verse of the Qur'ān: *"They will ask thee for a decision; say, 'God will give you a decision concerning remote kinship…'"* (Q 4.176).[24] This verse is placed in sūra al-Nisā' (Q 4), a sūra that belongs to the period between the third and fifth years of migration, AH 3-5.

Shiite Observations
In addition to what is stated above, the Shiite scholars agreed that the verses are not properly arranged. They considered it evidence of the neglect in the arrangement of the verses in the 'Uthmānic codex.

They also considered it as evidence for the existence of intermittence and distortion in the text. For instance, the natural succession of one verse is not found in the verse that follows, for it shows up in a much farther place. This discontinuity affects the cohesion of the verse's context. The natural sequence can only occur if the verse's complements are found and rejoined together from the various separate places.[25]

Here are some of the Shiites' additional remarks:

1. The verse, *"Said he* [Moses], *'Do ye ask what is meaner instead of what is best? Go down to Egypt,—there is what ye ask…'"* (Q 2.61) must be followed by the verse, *"They said, 'O Moses! Verily, therein is a people, giants; and we will surely not enter therein until they go out from thence…'"* (Q 5.22).[26]
2. The verse, *"But if ye fear that ye cannot do justice between orphans, then marry what seems good to you of women…"* (Q 4.3) was sent down together with, *"They will ask thee a decision about women; say, 'God…'"* (Q 4.127). Therefore, the verses must be read in this way: "They will ask thee a decision about women; say, 'God decides for you about them, and that which is rehearsed to you in the Book; about orphan women to whom ye do not give what is prescribed for them, and whom ye are averse from marrying. Then marry what seems good to you of women, by twos, or threes, or fours."[27]
3. Verses 104 of Q 4 and 140 of Q 3 must be placed in Q 3, as both contexts are describing the Battle of Uḥud.[28]
4. Verse 46 of Q 26 completes what is said in Q 20 from verse 10 and on.[29]
5. Verse 28 of Q 32 belongs after verse 21 of the same sūra.[30]
6. Verse 24 of Q 29 should have come immediately after verse 18 of the same sūra and the section that comes between these two verses has a place somewhere else. It has been placed where it is now [only] as a result of negligence during the compilation.[31]
7. Verse 16 of sūra Luqmān (Q 31) must come immediately after verse 13 of the same sūra and what is between them is an abnormal interruption to Luqmān's bequest for his son.[32]
8. What came out of the mouth of Muḥammad's enemies about the Qur'ān, *"'Old folks' tales, which he has got written down while they are dictated to him morning and evening,'"* (Q 25.5) must be followed with (Q 29.48): *"Thou couldst not recite before this any book, nor write it with thy right hand, for in that case those who deem it vain would have doubted."*[33]
9. Regarding Q 75.16, al-Rāzī mentions in his commentary that some of the Shiites made this statement: "A group of the earliest rejecters claimed that this Qur'ān had been changed and altered, added to and taken from. They objected to it, saying that there is no correlation between this verse and the one before it; and if this arrangement was from Allah the matter will not be as such."[34]

Dating Qur'ānic Text

If the Qur'ān was not subject to a methodology in its arrangement, how then is it possible to conclude that a certain text (sūra or verse) is Meccan or Medinan?

Muslims scholars found what they believed to be an honorable answer to this question in the scientific study of the revelation of the Qur'ān:[35]

> Of the most honorable sciences of the Qur'ān is the science of its revelation and its interpretation. The arrangement of: what was revealed in Mecca and Medina; what was sent down in Mecca while its authority is Medinan, and what was revealed in Medina while its authority is Meccan; what was sent down in Mecca concerning the people of Medina, and what was sent down in Medina concerning the people of Mecca; what is similar to the Meccan revelation in the Medinan, and what is similar to the Medinan revelation in the Meccan;...what was revealed in Ta'if, and what was revealed in Ḥudaybīya; what was revealed at night, and what was revealed in the day; what was revealed with other revelation, and what was revealed singularly; the Medinan verses in Meccan sūras, and the Meccan verses in Medinan sūras;...and what they differed about where some of them said: it is Medinan, while others said: it is Meccan.

Hence, they sought to know the arrangement of the text. They set out ideas for how to know what is Meccan and what is Medinan. Later, rules were developed by Western researchers. The Western school, started by Gustav Weil in his book, *Historisch-Kritishce Einleitung in den Koran* (1844), was improved upon by Theodor Nöldeke with his encyclopedic work, *History of The Qur'ān* (*Geschichte des Qorāns*) (1860). This work was revised and published as a second edition by Schwally. Later, other Orientalists released a second and a third part of the *History of The Qur'ān*. Following that publication, Régis Blachère worked on refining and arranging Nöldeke's book in his work, *Introduction au Coran*, which was published in three volumes in Paris (1947-1950).

Furthermore, the Orientalists presented their opinions regarding the arrangement of sūras, among the most prominent being Hartwig Hirschfeld in his book, *New Researches into the Composition and Exegesis of the Qoran* (1902). Hirschfeld establishes and describes five critical criteria for understanding the Qur'ān (Confirmatory, Declamatory, Narrative, Descriptive, and Legislative). William Muir, in his book, *The Corân: Its Composition and Teaching* (1875), also presents an arrangement free of Nöldeke's influence and introduces a theory stating that some of the Qur'ānic texts belong to the period that preceded Muḥammad's declaration of prophethood.[36]

We will summarize for the reader the general rules (based on the work by al-Ḥaddād) of the Muslim scholars and the Orientalists for distinguishing the Meccan from the Medinan Qur'ānic Text:[37]

1. The Meccan message focused on the call to Allah and rejection of polytheism. In Medina, when Muḥammad established a society submissive to his (Muḥammad's) authority, he presented a message that had liturgical, regulative, and legislative aspects.
2. Every argument with the idolaters is in Mecca and every debate with the People of the Book[D] is in Medina.

3. Each verse that calls for forgiveness belongs to Mecca and each verse that encourages fighting belongs to Medina. All sūras that contain a call to a defensive military stance belong to the early years of Muḥammad's stay in Medina. All sūras that contain a call to an offensive military stance belong to the second period in Medina after the Treaty of Ḥudaybīya[D] (AH 6/AD 628).
4. The stories of prophets and ancient nations go back to the Meccan period. Also, all sūras that talk about the story of Adam and Satan, with the exception of al-Baqara (Q 2), are Meccan.
5. The messages that warn about eternal consequences belong to the first Meccan period, while the messages that contain a campaign against idols are from the second Meccan period.
6. Sūras that contain swearing (oaths) are Meccan. This style is absent in the Medinan sūras.
7. Each passage that has the name "al-Raḥmān: the Beneficent" is from the second period in Mecca.
8. All passages that show courtesy toward the Jews or cite them are Meccan. On the other hand, all passages that level accusations against the Jews are Medinan.
9. Citing the People of the Book is Meccan, while verses campaigning against them and their doctrines are Medinan.
10. In the Medinan period, terms such as "Emigrants" (Muhājirūn), "Helpers" (Anṣār), and "hypocrites" (opponents of Islām) are mentioned.
11. Short sūras, in general, are from the first Meccan period (especially the ones with a fiery style), while the lengthy sūras that appear comparatively calm are from the second period in Mecca. Long sūras are Medinan.
12. In Mecca, Muḥammad declared himself using descriptions that were acceptable to the Meccan polytheistic and scriptural environment, descriptions such as *"bringer of good news"* and *"warner."* In Medina, when he became the obeyed master, he portrayed himself as a *"Prophet and Messenger."*
13. In Mecca, when the Qur'ān refers to the past sacred books in general, it calls them *"the Book"* without details. In Medina the names of the books are specified—Torah, Injīl, Zabūr (Psalms), and al-Ḥikma (Wisdom). Therefore, the verses that contain the distinctive names of the books are Medinan, even if they were inserted into Meccan sūras.
14. In Mecca and Medina the Qur'ān names those who have the Scriptures *"the People of the Book," "those who possess the Message [al-Dhikr],"* and *"those endowed with knowledge."* But when it calls them *"the Jews"* or *"people of the Gospel,"* this specification is Medinan, even though it was inserted in Meccan sūras.

15. The style differs between the Meccan and Medinan texts:
    - Meccan sūras tend to be in the rhymed prose, especially the sūras of the first period, a style that is rare in the Medinan Qur'ānic text, whose verses are longer.
    - The Meccan Qur'ānic text is narrative, similar to a novel, in nature. It tells of the hereafter, the angels, and the jinn[D]. On the other hand, this narrative style is rare in the Medinan Qur'ānic text.
    - The Meccan language is a fervidly poetic language, especially in the early stages of Mecca, while the Medinan language is determinative. It tackles referendums, legal questions, social questions, moral questions, family questions, and their legislative answers.

These are the general rules, though there may be deviations here and there. One example is particularly apparent in the first Medinan sūra al-Baqara (Q 2), where Muḥammad initiated the formulation of his new language.

Conclusion

When reviewing the arrangement of sūras in the codex of Ibn Mas'ūd and Ibn Ka'b, we find the sūras follow a quantitative arrangement, longer to shorter. We also find the quantitative rule applied in the alleged codex of 'Alī Ibn Abī Ṭālib. Since these versions of the Qur'ān, including the official 'Uthmānic codex, relied on the quantitative rule, they indicate that this quantitative principle, from longer to shorter, was the best resolution, and maybe the only one, to the problem of Qur'ānic arrangement. This method allowed the compilers to bypass the dilemma of dating.

Arranging the Qur'ān according to a chronology was almost impossible. First of all, Muḥammad left the written Qur'ānic texts scattered in pieces in the hands of Muslims. Most of the texts were merely committed to memory. Secondly, the Muslims did not have the knowledge or tools to perform the task of chronological sequencing.

However, the simplicity of the arrangement created a difficulty in investigating the chronological sequence of the sūras. This difficulty was increased by the lack of context for the verses, because of the insertion of Medinan verses into Meccan sūras and vice versa. Therefore, the Qur'ānic researcher must study carefully and thoroughly to understand the text.

In spite of this, the Sunnī scholars sought to use this chaos as a sign of inimitability. They wrote books about the creative side in the arrangement of sūras, the most prominent of which are *al-Burhān fī Munāsabat Tartīb Suwar al-Qur'ān* by Ja'far Ibn al-Zubayr, *Naẓm al-Durar fī Tanāsub al-Āyāt wa al-Suwar* by Burhān al-Dīn al-Buqā'ī, and *Asrār Tartīb al-Qur'ān* by al-Suyūtī. While the authors of these books sought to defend the "correlation, cohesion, and unison in the arrangement of verses and sūras," it is likely these scholars were responding implicitly to the non-Muslim critics of the Qur'ān in general, and, specifically, to the Shiites who had proven the arbitrary nature of the arrangement of the Qur'ān.

Abrogation and the Abrogated

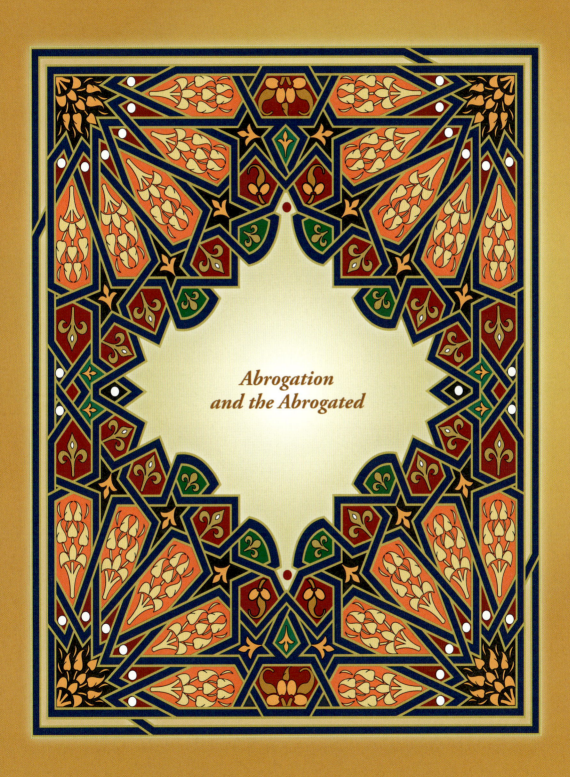

Abrogation and the Abrogated

In the fifth year of Muḥammad's call in Mecca, where the people of the Quraysh, pagans and Muslims were gathered, Muḥammad came and joined their gathering. Shortly thereafter, he recited to them the first verses of sūra al-Najm, *"Have ye considered Allat and Al'Huzza, and Manat the other third?"* (Q 53.19-20), adding, "These are the idols of superior status; their intercession is expected."[1]

In this phrase, Muḥammad admitted that the Quraysh idols had the power to intercede. He did this, no doubt, to receive the approval of his audience. Immediately, everyone in the council, Muslim and idolater, including Muḥammad, rushed to prostrate themselves before heaven. It seemed to the Quraysh that a new era had begun, during which the factions of Mecca would grow closer.[2]

But just days later, Muḥammad retracted what he had proclaimed, stating that what he had said was a slip of the tongue, an intrusion by Satan, and that Allah had abrogated the words of Satan. Then he recited, *"We have not sent before thee any apostle or prophet, but that when he wished, Satan threw not something into his wish; but God annuls what Satan throws; then does God confirm his signs, and God is knowing, wise..."* (Q 22.52).

This verse (Q 22.52) contains one of the earliest allusions to abrogation[D] in the Qur'ān. Later, abrogation would occupy a crucial role in the science of interpretation.

Abrogation in the Qur'ān

The Arabic word for *abrogation* is *naskh*, which means "to copy." To *naskh* a book means "to copy the book and write it, word for word." The word *abrogation* also means "to annul." For example, when one says the legislator *naskh* a law, it means he annulled it.

Abrogation in the Qur'ān means the annulment of the authority or ruling of a verse. It also means substituting one verse for another. The term *abrogation* in the Qur'ān includes the following cases:[3]

- **Removing** the verse from the Qur'ān. This removal is readily visible in the verse pertaining to the incident of the omitted "Satanic verses" mentioned above: *"but God annuls what Satan throws; then does God confirm his signs..."* (Q 22.52).
- **Substituting** one verse with another. This case is alluded to in the following verse: *"And whenever we change one verse for another..."* (Q 16.101).
- **Altering** the ruling of a verse, where one position is transferred to another (e.g., the right to inherit was transferred from one group to another regarding inheritances).

Abrogation is one of the scientific branches of the Qur'ān. Islamic scholars require knowledge of the principles and incidents of abrogation as a precondition before practicing the interpretation of the Qur'ān. It has been said, "[N]o one is allowed to interpret the [Qur'ān], until he knows the abrogating [verses] and the abrogated [verses] of it."[4] Books of Qur'ānic science abound with recommendations stressing the necessity of comprehending abrogation.[5]

The domain of abrogation is the jurisprudential system wherein abrogation makes "the permitted forbidden, and the forbidden permitted. It made the permissible unlawful and unlawful permissible."[6]

Abrogation also includes sociopolitical issues. For instance, every tendency towards peace in the Qur'ān is abrogated. The most famous abrogating verse is the Sword (*al-Sayf*) verse: *"But when the sacred months[D] are passed away, kill the idolaters wherever ye may find them..."* (Q 9.5). This particular verse abrogates 114 other verses that call for peace with and tolerance for non-Muslims.[7]

Modes of Abrogation

Abrogation divides verses into the following modes:

1. **The verses whose recitations are abrogated but whose rulings remain in effect.** An example is the stoning verse[D] (*al-rajm*): "If an elderly man and an elderly woman committed adultery, stone them. Certainly it's a punishment from Allah."[8] It is told that the verse of *al-rajm* was part of the sūra al-Aḥzāb (Q 33).[9] Muslim scholars assert that the reason here for cancelling the reading of such verses (by removing them from the Qur'ān—when the ruling is still in effect) to test the obedience of Muslims.

The truth is that the existence of this sort of abrogation stems from the dubious nature of the compilation of the Qur'ān. (See the article "Compilation of the Qur'ān" on page 49.) Dr. Naṣr Ḥāmid Abū Zayd[N] believes that the reason for not including the verse of *al-rajm* in the Qur'ān is due to the prevalence of adultery "in society, as if not writing down the text [according to one account] was so as to not cause people to be repelled from coming to Islām."[10]

2. **The verses whose ruling was abrogated but whose recitation remains in effect.** This mode is the sort found in the writings on "the abrogating and the abrogated."[11] Al-Zarkashī says that this kind of abrogation is found in sixty-three sūras.[12] One example is this verse: "*...but pardon and shun them till God brings His command...*" (Q 2.109). This verse commands Muslims to be kind to the People of the Book, but its ruling is abrogated by the texts that command them to fight (Q 9.5, 29).[13]

3. **The verses whose readings and rulings are abrogated.** An example of this mode has been described by 'Ā'isha. She said that there are in the Qur'ān "ten known suckles [breast feedings]. Then they are abrogated by five known ones. Then he [Muḥammad] died and they are among what is read in the Qur'ān."[14] Muslim scholars explained, saying, "and they [verses] are what is read" does not mean their recitation was still taking place when Muḥammad died, but that their recitation was abrogated just before his death. It can also mean that their recitation was abrogated before his death, but the news did not reach all Muslims. Therefore, some of these unaware Muslims continued to use it. About these verses, Abū Mūsā al-Ash'arī said, "They were sent down[,] then taken back up."[15]

Another case, "the forgotten verses," can also be perceived as a mode of abrogation. These "forgotten verses" are referred to in Q 2.106: "*...or cause thee to forget....*" In this situation, Muḥammad's forgetfulness is considered a sort of abrogation.[16] In some of the readings of the Qur'ān, the word *forgetfulness* is mentioned. The phrase, "*Whatever verse we may annul or cause thee to forget,*" is read in the codex of Ibn Mas'ūd as "We do not make you forget a verse nor abrogate it." On the other hand, Sa'd Ibn Abī Waqqāṣ[N] has a variant reading of the verse that reads, "None of our revelations do we abrogate or you forget it," where Sa'd's reading means "or you forget it, O Muḥammad."[17]

Tools of Abrogation

Muslim scholars, who have sought the abrogation of a verse, primarily rely on the Qur'ān for guidance. However, some believe Muḥammad's sayings and actions can also be used as a tool:

1. Based on the verse, *"Whatever verse we may annul or cause thee to forget, we will bring a better one than it, or one like it…"* (Q 2.106), Islāmic scholars say that the Qur'ān can only be abrogated by the Qur'ān. There is no disagreement about this principle among Muslim scholars.
2. Others say that it is possible for Muḥammad's *sunna*, a prescribed Islāmic way of life based on narrative records of Muḥammad's sayings[D] (*ḥadīths*) or actions, to abrogate the Qur'ān. However, Muslim scholars disagree about this. Though some reject the principle of the *ḥadīth* abrogating the Qur'ān, the majority say if the *ḥadīth* is reliable, then abrogation is permissible. This view is based on the depiction of Muḥammad in this verse: *"…nor speaks he out of lust!"* (Q 53.3).[18] As a basis for their decision, scholars adopt yet another verse that commands obedience to Muḥammad: *"And what the Apostle gives you, take; and what he forbids you, desist from…"* (Q 59.7).[19] An example of such an application is that *"the legacy…to…parents"* (Q 2.180) is abrogated with Muḥammad's saying, "[D]o not bequest for an heir."[20]

Abrogation Unique to the Qur'ān

The scholars of Islām say the phenomenon of abrogation is a distinctive feature of Islām and does not apply to any other religion.[21] To understand why this phenomenon is unique to the Qur'ān, we have to study the history of the Qur'ānic text. The composition of the Qur'ān is tied to the circumstances of Muḥammad's call in Mecca and Medina. There, through the Qur'ān, Muḥammad tried to deal with various political and social issues. Since the local realities were constantly changing, Muḥammad continued to abrogate, substitute, and remove parts of the Qur'ān.

Therefore, we find the phenomenon of abrogation to be a clearly explainable phenomenon. But, since Muḥammad had said that the verses of the Qur'ān were revealed to him from above, he changed this understandable phenomenon to a phenomenon that causes confusion, wherein the abrogation process makes Allah look like one who cannot make up his mind, a perception which goes against the nature of deity as understood by Christians and Muslims alike.

Importance of Studying Abrogation

Muḥammad worked for twenty-three years to spread his message. Throughout these years, he experienced political and social changes, which are echoed in the Qur'ān, including abrogation. Therefore, to approach the abrogation phenomenon, the daily record of the Islāmic proselytizing must be studied.

When Muḥammad was in Mecca he was merely a giver of good news and a *"warner."* Hence, his oratories were given in an instructive or enlightening manner. However, in Medina, when he became a leader with no rival, the Qur'ān started dealing with legislative and political issues.

Therefore, the study of abrogation is one of the tools of discovering the theoretical and doctrinal development of Islām. Knowing the abrogated ruling, why a verse was abrogated, and by whose authority it was abrogated helps in understanding the history of Muḥammad in particular, and the early history of Islām in general.

Also, since the abrogated verses belong to the earlier period of Muḥammad's ministry, the study of abrogation helps in studying the arrangement of the Qur'ānic texts. When the Qur'ān was compiled, the issue of arranging the abrogating and the abrogated was not taken into consideration. As a result, there are cases in the Qur'ān in which the abrogating verse precedes the abrogated verse, instead of following it, as it should. Such inconsistencies resulted from the arbitrary procedure of the Qur'ān's compilation. The book *al-Burhān fi 'Ulūm al-Qur'ān* by al-Zarkashī discusses this issue and includes these examples:[22]

1. The verse *"...let these wait by themselves for four months and ten days..."* (Q 2.234) abrogated *"Those of you who die and leave wives, should bequeath to their wives maintenance for a year, without expulsion (from their home)..."* (Q 2.240).
2. The verse *"O thou prophet! verily, we make lawful for thee thy wives..."* (Q 33.50) abrogated *"It is not lawful to thee to take women after (this), nor to change them for (other) wives..."* (Q 33.52).

Conclusion

Why didn't Muḥammad abrogate according to the first mode, omitting both the words and the ruling? The answer is not available to us. But we do suggest that Muḥammad did not consider the compilation of the Qur'ān a priority in his lifetime. Since he did not compile it, he was apparently not concerned about dealing with the phenomenon of abrogation. Therefore, he left this "gap" as an opportunity for us to discover the inconsistencies between the Qur'ānic text and the historical reality, which revealed the earthly historical nature of the text. This characteristic allows us the opportunity to understand the Qur'ānic text and to scrutinize it scientifically.

Even during the lifetime of Muḥammad, the Qur'ān faced criticism because of the phenomenon of abrogation. The Quraysh saw "the rules of Allah...fixed and unchangeable. If what the Qur'ān was saying came from Allah, then abrogation would not be permissible."[23] The Jews of Medina also doubted the sacredness of the Qur'ān and saw abrogation as a personal act by Muḥammad. They said to those around them, "[D]o you see not that Muḥammad orders his Companions to do something, then he forbids them to do it and instructs them otherwise? Doesn't he say something today and goes back on it tomorrow?"[24]

The phenomenon of abrogation in the Qur'ān caused confusion to some significant Muslim thinkers. They observed that the abrogation suggests that the will of Allah is changing and his knowledge is evolving, which subjects the affirmations of faith to doubt.[25]

Therefore, some Mu'tazilites[D], such as Abū Muslim al-Aṣfahānī, said that the occurrence of abrogation in the Qur'ān is not acceptable, based on how the Qur'ān depicts itself: *"...falsehood shall not come to it, from before it, nor from behind it—a revelation from the wise, the praiseworthy One"* (Q 41.42). Regarding this issue, Shu'la writes, "[I]f abrogation happened to some of the Qur'ān's verses[,] then it would [mean] falsehood would approach it, which is impossible, because Allah reported that falsehood cannot approach it."[26]

The Mu'tazilite opinion attempted to reconcile the phenomenon of abrogation with the claim of the Qur'ān's divine inspiration. Otherwise, the acceptance of abrogation would impose on the scholars this question: "Does not abrogation make the theory of the presence of [the] Qur'ān in the Preserved Tablet (*al-Lawḥ al-Maḥfūẓ*)[D] questionable?"[27]

In fact, Muslim scholars do not discuss if "the phenomenon of abrogation of recitation, nor that of omitting texts, whether its ruling remained or was abrogated as well, would lead to complete elimination of their perception...of the eternal presence of the written text in the Preserved Tablet."[28]

Muslims agree that any abrogation of the Qur'ān after Muḥammad's death is not acceptable, even if scholars unanimously want to carry it out. Nonetheless, two caliphs practiced it.

Abū Bakr, the first caliph, cancelled the portion, *"those whose hearts are reconciled"* (Q 9.60), which speaks of the leaders of Mecca, whom Muḥammad had granted a share in the spoils after the Battle of Ḥunayn (AH 8/AD 630), in order to draw them to Islām. It is likely that this cancellation was proposed by 'Umar Ibn al-Khaṭṭāb.[29]

'Umar Ibn al-Khaṭṭāb, during his caliphate, also annulled the "temporary marriage for pleasure" (*mut'a*[D] marriage), which is permissible in the Qur'ān in the sūra al-Nisā' (Q 4.24).

In addition, the Shiites ceased practicing an Islāmic observance when they "abrogated the fixed Friday prayer with a Qur'ānic text (Q 62.9)."[30]

Aside from these exceptional cases, no one has since dared to abrogate any more Qur'ānic verses, regardless of the need for it. Without abrograting many problematic verses of the Qur'ān, such as the Sword verse (Q 9.5), the Qur'ān cannot evolve to adapt to the changing world of its followers in their everyday lives and their dealings with non-Muslims.

The study of abrogation in the Qur'ān reveals the correlation of the Qur'ān with the daily realities of Muḥammad's life. In the composition of the Qur'ān, Muḥammad took into consideration the circumstances of that changing reality. Today, the advance of Islām is conditionally dependent, no doubt, on the awareness of the need to again activate the phenomenon of abrogation in the Qur'ān, thus completing the journey of abrogation.

Variant Readings of the Qur'ān

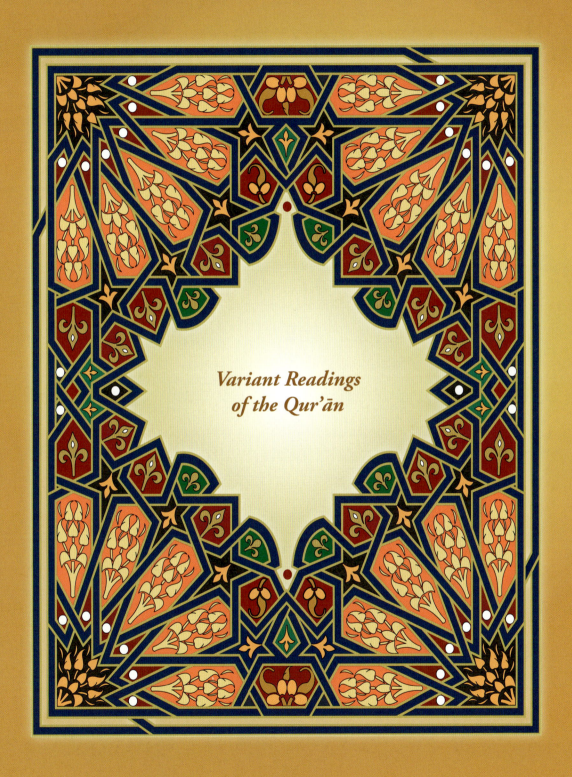

Variant Readings of the Qur'ān

The roots of the variant readings of the Qur'ān go back to the time of Muḥammad. The historical record shows an event that sheds light on the presence of differences in the various readings of the Qur'ān among the Muslims. We are told that 'Umar Ibn al-Khaṭṭāb happened to hear Hishām Ibn Ḥakīm reading sūra al-Furqān (Q 25). He noticed that Hishām was saying it in a different form than he ('Umar) had heard from Muḥammad. When 'Umar asked Hishām for the source of his recitation of the Qur'ān, Hishām responded that he had heard it from Muḥammad. 'Umar did not believe him, so they both went to Muḥammad to have him judge between them as to who was quoting the portion of the Qur'ān correctly.

When Muḥammad heard their request, he asked Hishām to recite the passage, which he did. Muḥammad responded, "Thus it was revealed." Then Muḥammad asked 'Umar to recite his version, which he did. Muḥammad responded, "Thus it was revealed." He added, "This Qur'ān was revealed in seven different *aḥruf* letters (readings or dialects). Read of it what you find to be easier."[1]

What this story shows is that not only did the variant readings appear in the time of Muḥammad, but that he himself approved them.

Among the first generation of Muslims, each reader of the Qur'ān rendered it in a different form than the other readers. Eventually, the differences became so important that they led to quarrels among Muslims of the different regions, especially in Iraq and Syria (al-Shām). These quarrels moved 'Uthmān Ibn 'Affān to unify the text of the

Qur'ān during his reign (c. AH 25-30/AD 645-650). (See the article "Compilation of the Qur'ān" on page 49.)

Once 'Uthmān's committee adopted an official text of the Qur'ān ('Uthmānic codex), 'Uthmān sent copies of it to the various regions where the Muslim armies were present. Since this "official" Qur'ān was without dots on the letters or other diacritical marks, those who read these copies read them based on their own linguistic knowledge.

An examination of this issue is vital to understand the impact of the diacritical marks. For example, the transcription "ـ", when connected to the following letters can be read as the letter "N: نـ", if one adds a dot on top. If the reader puts the dot underneath, he gets a "B: بـ ". If two dots are put on top, one will have a "T: تـ". Add another and get a "Th: ثـ". Move the dots below and get a "Y: يـ". Imagine having to determine the letters in order to adopt certain interpretations and then propagate them in one's province as the way the Qur'ān should be read.

Again, a reader may say that a word without the dots is "ٮٮٮ". Some may read it as "BYT", whereas someone else looks at those same dot-less letters and deduces that they are "NBT" and then propagates that way of reading through recitation. At the end, we would have two variant readings of that word: one reading with readers memorizing and reciting the Qur'ān using the word BYT and another reading where the word NBT would be used instead. There could be a myriad of combinations and potential variances based on the dot issue without even taking into account the diacritical markings. (See the "Illustration of Variant Readings," page 102.)

As a result, the intended unified reading of the Qur'ān that the committee of 'Uthmān was trying to accomplish did not materialize. Instead, based on this "official" Qur'ān, several new ways of reading it appeared.

In addition to the variant readings of the official text transmitted through the recitation channels, there remained other readings that 'Uthmān was trying to abolish. Most prominent among these were the readings of Ibn Mas'ūd and Ubayy Ibn Ka'b. Indeed, by the second century of Islām, the variant readings of the Qur'ān were more in number than before 'Uthmān's attempt to unify the text.[2]

Ibn Mujāhid and the Seven Readings versus the Fifty Readings

The first one to write about the various readings was Abū 'Ubayd al-Qāsim Ibn Salām (d. AH 224/AD 839). He gathered twenty-five variant readings in a book.[3]

The Shiites consider Ibbān Ibn Taghlub al-Kūfī (d. AH 141/AD 759) to be the first to categorize the readings.[4] Ibbān Ibn Taghlub al-Kūfī followed Yaḥyā Ibn Ya'mur (d. AH 90/AD 708), who was the first to write in the field of the readings.[5]

Around the year AH 300/AD 912, the readings multiplied in an astonishing manner and the number of readers reached "thousands of thousands," studying the Qur'ān in approximately fifty variant readings.[6] Among these readings appeared certain currents that evoked fear among those who held to the official copy of 'Uthmān:

- The first current took its reading from those outside of the official reading of ʻUthmān. One of its representatives was Ibn Shannabūdh.
- The second current used the official text of ʻUthmān, deriving different readings from it according to the linguistic tastes of the reader. This current was established by Ibn Miqsam al-ʻAṭṭār, in addition to those who were not proficient in the grammar of the Arabic language.

During this time period, Ibn Mujāhid took on the duty of eradicating these variant readings. His response to Ibn Shannabūdh and Ibn Miqsam was to bring them to trial.[7]

Ibn Shannabūdh (d. AH 328/AD 939)

Muḥammad Ibn Aḥmad Ibn Shannabūdh was the reader of Baghdad in his time. He did not commit himself only to the official text of the Qur'ān (ʻUthmānic codex) but studied the Qur'ān according to the readings of many scholars. He also taught many future readers the variant readings of the Qur'ān. He was considered a key reference in this field.

During prayer, he used to read the Qur'ān according to the readings of Ubayy Ibn Kaʻb and Ibn Masʻūd. This practice was used by Ibn Mujāhid as a reason to turn the authorities against Ibn Shannabūdh. Ibn Mujāhid incited the minister, Ibn Muqla, against Ibn Shannabūdh, and persuaded the minister to send Ibn Shannabūdh to trial.

During the trial, Ibn Shannabūdh argued that he had roamed the different Islāmic countries and had gained an encyclopedic knowledge of the variant readings of the Qur'ān. He further accused Ibn Muqla and Ibn Mujāhid of having insufficient knowledge in the variant readings of the Qur'ān. Their response to this defense was to strip Ibn Shannabūdh of his clothes and severely whip him. He then retracted his position and declared his repentance. He died during his confinement.[8]

Ibn Miqsam al-ʻAṭṭār (d. AH 354/AD 965)

Muḥammad Ibn al-Ḥassan Ibn Miqsam al-ʻAṭṭār was a grammarian and a reader from the Kufan school in Baghdad. He was known for his precision and his extensive knowledge of the sciences of the Arabic language and the Qur'ān. It was said about him that "[h]e was one of the greatest keepers of the grammar of the Kufans and most knowledgeable in recitations in all its forms; the famous ones, the strange ones, and the deviant ones."[9]

He thought it permissible to read the Qur'ān in ways that are not mentioned in the sources as long as these readings were appropriate to the context of the text, and if they were linguistically correct. He allowed even the versions that were not read by the early readers, "and the saying is attributed to him that every reading that agrees with the script of the Qur'ān is a permissible way to recite [read] even if it had no material [support], meaning from transmission."[10] This opinion was seen to be against the inerrancy of the Qur'ān because it allowed the reading of the Qur'ān based on *ijtihād*, one's individual judgment. He was summoned to trial in AH 222/AD 836 because of the agitation stirred up by Ibn Mujāhid.

The trial was attended by both jurisprudents and readers. When he was made to stand for a beating, he made a plea to Ibn Mujāhid, despite the fact that it was Ibn Mujāhid who was the real instrument behind this ordeal. Ibn Mujāhid heard his pleas and made it a condition that Ibn Miqsam sign an affidavit disowning the readings that he had promoted and accepting only the transmitted readings. Ibn Miqsam remained true to his affidavit until the death of Ibn Mujāhid.[11]

Ibn Mujāhid

Abū Bakr Aḥmad Ibn Mūsā Ibn Mujāhid (Baghdad AH 245-324/AD 859-935) was the imām of the readers in Baghdad.[12] Increasingly hostile toward those who represented readings other than that of 'Uthmān, like Ibn Shannabūdh and Ibn Miqsam, Ibn Mujāhid even spoke against al-Ḥallāj and became one of the most prominent figures against him.[13]

Ibn Mujāhid specified three conditions for considering a reading to be sound:[14]

1. Reading is transmitted through trustworthy scholars from Muḥammad himself (the chain of transmission is sound).
2. Reading is permissible (palatable) in Arabic (agrees with the Arabic language).
3. Reading is in accordance with the text of the Qur'ān (agrees with the way a word is drawn in the text of 'Uthmān).

When Ibn Mujāhid applied these conditions on the commonly used readings of his time, he found there were far too many in existence. Consequently, he decided to adopt seven readings from among the most common found among the people.[15] As to the reason for his specifying seven only, it is said it was in remembrance of the fact that 'Uthmān had sent out seven copies.[16]

Regarding Ibn Mujāhid's choice to adopt only seven readings, many scholars believe that it was "based on coincidence and agreement. The number of readers was much larger than that. **And among those whom he had left out of his seven were those who were more excellent** [our emphasis]."[17] Several linguists and scholars have remained firm in their rejection of the seven he chose.[18]

Widening the Seven Readings

Over a period of centuries, the number of accepted readings doubled.

The Ten Readings

Around the year AH 800/AD 1397), after five centuries had passed since the institution of the seven readings of Ibn Mujāhid, a discussion among the scholars of the Qur'ān took place on whether it was necessary to add the condition of *tawātur* ("frequency") to accept the validity of a reading.[19] During the discussion, Ibn al-Jizrī (AH 751-833/AD 1350-1429) endorsed the condition of *tawātur* for accepting a reading.[20] He added three more readings, making a total of ten readings.

The Fourteen Readings

After three more centuries, Aḥmad Ibn Muḥammad al-Bannā al-Dumyāṭī (d. AH 1117/AD 1705) added four other readings to the body of the approved readings. In AH 1082/AD 1671), he composed his book, *Itḥāf Fuḍalā' al-Bashar bi-l-Qira'āt al-Arba'at 'Ashar*.[21] Its first edition was issued in AH 1285/AD 1868) and contained 561 pages. It has been reprinted several times since.

Deviant Readings

Readings excluded from these lists were considered to be deviant readings. However, this specification was not without its issues, as a new disagreement ensued among the scholars of the Qur'ān concerning which readings should be considered deviant: the ones outside the Seven, the Ten, or the Fourteen readings.[22]

However, any decision to set some of the readings outside the list of the approved readings did not lessen their authority. Instead, in several instances the deviant readings were considered stronger than the approved ones. Ibn Jinnī states that the people (of his time period) considered certain readings to be deviant, but in actuality those readings were characterized by the same reliability, possessing the same conditions for acceptance, as the rest. And, "**many of which were equal in eloquence to those that were agreed upon** [our emphasis]."[23]

He adds that, even though he remains committed to the approved readings, he still sees the "strength of those called deviant." He notes the presence of weak readings among the approved readings, like that of Ibn Kathīr, such as the archaic word *di'ā'* ("ضئاء") instead of *dīā'* ("ضياء") both of which mean "lights" in Q 10.5, Q 21.48, and Q 2.71. In the reading of Ibn 'Āmir in Q 6.137, the word *shurakā'ihim* ("their associates") grammatically comes in place of the word "*children*", making the children both the associates and the ones killed in the verse: "made seemly to many of the idolaters the killing of their children, their associates."[24] (See the comment on Q 6.137.)

In other instances, the scholars deem the deviant reading to be the correct one. For example, in Q 5.38 the word *"thief"* and in Q 24.2 the word "*adulteress*" were both read with a *ḍamma* (long "oo") ending. Some read it with a *fātiḥa* ("ah" sound) ending, which was a deviant reading. However, Sibawayh considers it "stronger Arabic than the common way of reading."[25] It is the opinion of the linguistic scholars that some of the deviant readings are better quality linguistically than the common ones. Al-Akhfash (Sa'īd Ibn Mas'ada al-Baṣrī) comments that some of the deviant readings were of "a better quality than that of the majority readings."[26] Such words are also heard from al-Mubarrid (Abū 'Abbās Muḥammad Ibn Yazīd).[27]

Discussions Among Muslims

The use of seven (and later, more) variant readings produced ongoing and often divisive discussion by Muslim scholars regarding the meanings and differences among all these readings.

Meaning of the Seven

A discussion took place between the scholars of the Qur'ān regarding what is meant by the seven letters (readings) in a narrative (*ḥadīth*) of Muḥammad: "This Qur'ān came down according to seven letters." These scholars were divided in their opinions:

- One group of scholars said that the seven letters referred to the dialects of seven tribes: Quraysh, Kināna, Assad, Hadhīl, Banū Tamīm, Ḍabba, and Qays.[28]
- A second group said that having seven letters permits freedom in applying grammar, allowing those who had different dialects to overcome the difficulties that are particular to them, such as the *hamza* (guttural "a") for those of the Quraysh and the *fatḥa* (short "a") for those of the Assad tribe.[29]
- Yet another group believed that the seven letters were a symbolic representation of a wider number—that the number is not limited to seven readings, but each group could read according to its dialect.[30] The aim was to make it easier for the people, so that each group could read by its own language.[31]

Differences in the Readings

According to Ibn Qutayba, there are seven differences in the readings:

1. **The difference in grammar without changing the transcription of the word.** In this difference only the diacritical marks are different, such as the word *al-bukhli* in Q 4.37 being read by some as *al-bakhali* and *al-bikhli* all meaning "stinginess."[32]

2. **The difference in grammar that changes the meaning without changing the transcription of the word**. In Q 34.19 the supplication using the word *bā'id* ("make the distance more remote") had its grammar changed in some readings, changing its diacritical marks and meaning to *bā'ada* ("he made the distance more remote"). Thus the verb was changed from the imperative to the past tense. Instead of asking Allah to create the distance, he already had done so.

3. **The difference in the letters of the words, which in turn changes their meanings, without changing the grammar.** An example is found in Q 2.259, where the word *nunshizuhā* ("to reanimate, to set together") was changed in some readings to *nunshiruhā* ("to resurrect from the dead").

4. **The difference in the entire word, without changing the meaning.** An example is found in Q 36.29 where the word *ṣayḥatan* was replaced by the word *zaqya,* both meaning "a scream."

5. **The difference in the word and its meaning.** An example is found in Q 56.29 where the word *ṭalḥin* ("a massive thorny tree found in Ḥijāz")[33] was substituted with the word *ṭal'in* ("bananas").[34] Another example is found in Q 2.36 where the word *fa'azallahumā* ("he made them slip") was substituted by the word *fawaswasa* ("he whispered").[35] (See the comment on Q 2.36, page 179.)

6. **The difference in the order of the words.** An example is found in Q 50.19 where the words of the verse *"and came the stupor of death with truth"* was read by Abū Bakr in this order: "and came the stupor of truth with death." Ibn Mas'ūd, on the other hand, read it "and came the stupors of truth with death."[36]

7. **The difference by addition and omission.** An example is found in Q 31.26: *"...verily, God, He is the independent, worthy of praise..."* was read by some as "Indeed, the Rich one the Worthy of praise."[37]

Ibn Qutayba omitted two more kinds:

8. **The difference by deletion.** One example is the deletion of two sūras (chapters) Q 113 and Q 114 from the codex of Ibn Mas'ūd.[38]

9. **The difference by addition.** The codex of Ubayy Ibn Ka'b includes two additional sūras: al-Khal' and al-Ḥafd.[39] (See Controversial Qur'ānic Texts, page 587.)

(See the article "Compilation of the Qur'ān" on page 49.)

Current Variant Readings of the Qur'ān

There are ten readings of the Qur'ān present today in the hands of the Muslims. Each reading has two narrators. Therefore, there are twenty narrations of the Qur'ān proceeding out of ten readings. We want to point out that Islāmic scholars explain "the readings" as merely differences in pronunciations, not in meanings.

It is understandable that very minute changes, like the dropping of a *hamza* without changing the meaning, might take place in a text that is said to be inspired. (A *hamza* is the sign "ء" that is placed over a letter, or by itself, to signify a glottal stop in Arabic and usually expressed in English as an apostrophe.) Such minute changes do not present any significant problems since there might be a difference in the pronunciation, while retaining the meaning from one environment to another.

However, the more significant problem discovered in our research comes from the fact that there are many words that have a different meaning when one reads from one variant reading to another. Furthermore, the important issue is that these differences cannot be labeled simply as variations in pronunciations between different tribes and different localities, because the words themselves are used among all the Arabs. Evidence of this research will be documented in this book.

Because these variant readings do not corroborate each other, one finds that they are no longer just different readings of the same Qur'ān. Instead, the intellectually honest seeker discovers there are, in fact, several codices that differ in meanings and exegetical interpretations. As a result, one will find different religious rulings based on those different meanings.

Most Common Variant Readings of the Qur'ān

Of the present ten readings, there are four major variant readings by different readers still in recent circulation:

- **Reading of Ḥafṣ:** Originally the reading of Kufa in Iraq, this reading now represents the reading of the majority of Muslims in the world. It is read in the Persian Gulf, as well as in Egypt, Turkey, Afghanistan, Pakistan, and some of the South and East Asian countries, such as Malaysia, Uzbekistan, China and Indonesia.
- **Reading of Warsh:** This reading continues to be used mainly in the northwest African Arab-dominated countries of Tunis, Algeria and Morocco. Originally, it was the reading of Medina (Yathrib), where Warsh studied under Nāfi', the most prominent reader of Medina. For that reason, the reading of Warsh carries his name, *The Qur'ān According to the Reading of Warsh.*
- **Reading of Qālūn:** Qālūn was one of the narrators who related the Qur'ān from Nāfi' as well. It is a variant reading by the people of Libya, whose Qur'ān is still printed according to Qālūn's reading.
- **Reading of al-Dūrī according to Abū 'Amr:** This reading spread in Sudan, where recently several editions of this version were printed by the publisher Dār Muṣḥaf Afriqia at the International University of Africa in Khartoum.

If all these readings are taken from one codex—that of 'Uthmān—why are there numerous differences among them despite the one origin? This question must be considered, especially since we are not talking only about different pronunciations and utterances but also about differences in meaning from the original.

Note that if these differences are still present, even after 'Uthmān Ibn 'Affān burned all the variant codices, one wonders what differences were present before he destroyed the other variant versions.

The research provided in this book contains some examples (out of hundreds) of core differences present in the different readings of the Qur'ān. The common saying that "there is only one Qur'ān from China to Morocco" needs to be reexamined and revised.

Conclusion

The Qur'ān was recited according to different readings during the life of Muḥammad. After his death, the gap widened between the readers. The most prominent readers of that time were Ibn Mas'ūd and Ubayy Ibn Ka'b, both whose texts had additions and differences in comparison to the codex of 'Uthmān's committee. Both of these men enjoyed the trust and confidence of Muḥammad. Ibn Mas'ūd had personally heard more than seventy chapters as recited by Muḥammad himself.[40] Ubayy Ibn Ka'b used to write down the Qur'ān for Muḥammad and is considered one of the most important among the group of readers who were the Companions of Muḥammad.[41]

When the Muslim armies marched outside of the Arabian Peninsula, the problem of variant readings grew, which led 'Uthmān to impose a standard copy of the Qur'ān. Indeed, an "official codex" was penned down and copies of it were sent out to the different regions. However, the solution by 'Uthmān's committee to the problem of the variant readings created other variant readings as the 'Uthmān codex employed no diacritical markings or dots (in a language where a dot would change a given letter into a completely different one).

Many variant readings arose based on the 'Uthmānic codex. In addition, there were already variant codices in circulation that differed from the 'Uthmānic codex. For three consecutive centuries the text of the Qur'ān remained a source of quarrel and dispute among the Muslims, until the number of acknowledged readings reached fifty. Ibn Mujāhid tried to solve the problem by settling on seven readings based on two factors:

- Superstition—namely, the sacredness of the number seven.
- Familiarity—based on the widespread acceptance of the reading.

Afterwards, more readings were approved, increasing the total to ten various readings, then fourteen. The Islāmic books continued to contain the unorthodox readings, which were later called "deviant readings," despite the fact that some of these versions were of better linguistic quality and had better composition than the "authoritative" ones. These "deviant readings" are found in a variety of sources, the most famous of which are the books *al-Muḥtasib* by Ibn Jinnī and *I'rāb al-Qira'āt al-Shādha* by Abū al-Baqa' al-'Akbarī (d. AH 616/AD 1219).

A manuscript of the Qur'ān was discovered in 1972 in Ṣan'ā'(Yemen). It is one of the oldest extant manuscripts of the Qur'ān today and could give much insight into the problem of the variant readings. However, scholars have not been granted permission to examine it, except for Dr. Gerd Puin, who had limited access for a short period of time. (See the article "Compilation of the Qur'ān" on page 49.)

Of the four readings mentioned earlier (Ḥafṣ, Warsh, Qālūn, and al-Dūrī), most Muslims recite the Qur'ān according to two main different readings:[42]

- **First Reading:** In the east, Muslims employ the reading of 'Aṣim as told by Ḥafṣ. It was issued in 1925 under the supervision of al-Azhar in Cairo.
- **Second Reading:** Used in North Africa, this is the reading of Nāfi' as told by Warsh. The Qur'ān printed in Algeria in 1905 by al-Tha'labīya Press is based on this reading.

What do these readings reveal?

Islāmic doctrine states that the Qur'ān has one source, Allah. It declares that the Qur'ān has one copy in *al-Lawḥ al-Maḥfuẓ* (the Preserved Tablet). But this belief generates many questions concerning these variant readings:

- Does not the presence of many different readings of the Qur'ān debunk the claim of its being from a single source?
- Does not the presence of fifty readings rescind the claim that the Qur'ān is in a Preserved Tablet?
- Do not the numerous readings and their variances reveal the human element in the composition of the Qur'ānic text?
- Does not the development of the readings reveal that the Qur'ān was subject to changes, as it remained in the stages of writing and correcting for centuries? It is for this reason that we find Shiite and Mu'tazilite readings, in addition to the various non-'Uthmān text-based readings.

There are two benefits from studying the Qur'ānic variant readings:

- Familiarity with old linguistic grammatical, morphological, and verbal forms that are no longer in use.
- Evidence refuting the Qur'ān's claim of *i'jāz* ("inimitability"). A famous common example concerns Muḥammad's prophesy that the Romans (translated by Palmer as "The Greeks") would have victory over the Persians in Q 30.2-4:

> *The Greeks are overcome in the highest parts of the land; but after being overcome they shall overcome in a few years; to God belongs the order before and after; and on that day the believers shall rejoice....*

Sources state that when the Persians had victory over the Romans in AD 616, the news reached Mecca. The tribe of Muḥammad, the Quraysh, rejoiced at the defeat of the Romans because they were Christians, whereas the Persians were Magi. Muḥammad was not happy with that, so he declared, *"The Greeks are overcome...but...they shall overcome...."* The scholars of Islām have declared that the verse is evidence to the prophethood of Muḥammad as it foretold the victory of the Romans over the Persians that took place in AH 4/AD 625.[43]

However, this claim has no support in the text. What is clear is that Muḥammad was responding to the rejoicing people of the Quraysh by reminding them that history will turn and the Persians would face defeat one day.[44] The Quraysh might have interpreted the victory of the Magi as evidence to the supremacy of that faith over Christianity, as al-Rāzī deduced. He wrote in his commentary that these verses came "to show that victory does not indicate rightness."[45]

There is another variant reading that says, "The Romans overcome…and they shall be overcome…."[46] The commentaries on this reading state that after the Battle of Badr (AH 2/AD 624), when the news of the Romans' victory over the Persians reached the Muslims, this verse came to promise the Muslims' victory over the Romans in the future.[47] Those who end up victorious in the first reading, end up defeated in the second.[48] According to the first reading, where the Romans would defeat the Persians at the end, the "prophecy" would have been revealed in Mecca three to five years before the *Hijra*.[49] According to the second reading, this "prophecy" was revealed in Medina.

Therefore, we have a disagreement in the historical background and the nature of the promise. (Will the Romans overcome or be overcomed?) Despite this discrepancy, the Islāmic scholars did not hesitate to draw the curtains over these details to justify the saying that the text is a prophetic miracle. The gratitude for unveiling this "inimitability" goes to the variant readings of the Qur'ān.

List of Readers

The following fourteen readers are grouped in the order of their acceptance. The fourteen readers were accepted in three successive groups.

A. **Seven Readers:**[50]

1. Abū 'Amr Ibn al-'Alā' from Basra (d. c. AH 154/AD 770). Yaḥyā Ibn al-Mubārak (d. AH 202/AD 817) read according to al-'Alā'. According to al-Mubārak there are the two readings of Abū 'Amr al-Dūrī (d. AH 246/AD 860) and Abū Shu'ayb al-Sūsī (d. AH 261/AD 874).
2. 'Āṣim Ibn Abī al-Nujūd Bahdala from Kufa (d. AH 128/AD 745). Abū Bakr Shu'ba (d. AH 193/AD 808) and Ḥafṣ (d. AH 180/AD 796) read according to the reading of al-Nujūd Bahdala.
3. Ḥamza Ibn Ḥabīb al-Zaīyāt from Kufa (d. AH 156/AD 772). Sulaym Abū 'Īsā read according to al-Zaīyāt. Khalaf (d. AH 229/AD 843), and Khallād (Abū 'Īsā al-Shībānī) (d. AH 220/AD 835) read according to Sulaym Abū 'Īsā.
4. 'Abd Allah Ibn 'Āmir al-Yaḥṣubī from Damascus (d. AH 118/AD 736). Ibn Dhakwān (d. AH 242/AD 856) and Hishām al-Silmī (d. AH 245/AD 859) read according to al-Yaḥṣubī.
5. 'Abd Allah Ibn Kathīr from Mecca (d. AH 120/AD 738). Qunbul (d. AH 291/AD 903) and al-Bazzī (d. AH 250/AD 864) read according to Ibn Kathīr.

6. 'Alī Ibn Ḥamza al-Kissā'ī from Kufa (d. AH 189/AD 805). Abū al-Ḥārith al-Layth Ibn Khālid al-Baghdādī (d. AH 240/AD 854) and al-Dūrī (who is mentioned in (1) above) read according to Ḥamza.
7. Nāfi' Ibn Abī Nu'aym (a.k.a. Abū 'Abd al-Raḥmān) from Medina (d. AH 169/AD 785). Qālūn (d. AH 220/AD 835) and Warsh (d. AH 197/AD 812) read according to 'Abd al-Raḥmān.

B. **Next Three after the Seven:**[51]

8. Abū Ja'far (d. AH 130/AD 747). Abū al-Ḥārith 'Īsā Ibn Wardān (d. AH 160/AD 776) and Ibn Jammāz (Abū al-Rabī' Sulaymān Ibn Muslim) (d. AH 170/AD 786) read according to Abū Ja'far.
9. Ya'qūb al-Ḥaḍramī from Basra (d. AH 205/AD 820). Rūways Muḥammad Ibn al-Mutawakil (d. AH 238/AD 852) and Rawḥ Ibn 'Abd al-Mu'īn (d. AH 234-235/AD 848-849) read according to al-Ḥaḍramī.
10. Khalaf Ibn Hishām al-Bazzār from Kufa (d. AH 229/AD 843). Isḥāq al-Warrāq (d. AH 286/AD 899) and Idrīs al-Ḥaddād (d. AH 292/AD 904) read according to al-Bazzār.

C. **Next Four after the Ten:**[52]

11. Muḥammad Ibn 'Abd al-Raḥmān Ibn Muḥayṣin from Mecca (d. AH 123/AD 740).
12. Yaḥyā Ibn al-Mubārak Ibn al-Maghīr al-Yazīdī from Basra (d. AH 202/AD 817).
13. Al-Ḥassan al-Baṣrī[N] from Basra (AH 21-110/AD 641-728)
14. Sulaymān Ibn Mahrān al-A'mash from Kufa (AH 60-148/AD 679-765).

Illustration of Variant Readings

The chart on the following page illustrates the problematic word choices a reader might face in the Qur'ān compiled by 'Uthmān's committee. If the reader was to see the script ٮٮ, he could add the dots and accents as he thinks a word should be read, based on his knowledge and linguistic taste. These variant ways of reading this one word demonstrate how the myriads of variant readings developed from the official codex of 'Uthmān. Over time and by force, as explained in this book's articles, certain readings were imposed, despite the fact that not everyone agreed that they are the best way to read the text.

ٮٮ			
English Meaning	**Transliteration**	**Modern Arabic**	**Classical Arabic**
she pounces	*tathibu*	تَثِبُ	تَثِبُ
we pounce	*nathibu*	نَثِبُ	نَثِبُ
he broadcasts	*yabuthu*	يَبُثُّ	يَبُثُّ
she broadcasts	*tabuthu*	تَبُثُّ	تَبُثُّ
(it) she broadcasted	*bathat*	بَثَّتْ	بَثَّتْ
we broadcast	*nabuthu*	نَبُثُّ	نَبُثُّ
it was ascertained	*thabata*	ثَبَتَ	ثَبَتَ
perseverance, stability, etc.	*thabātu*	ثَبَاتُ	ثَبٰتُ
steadfast, stable, etc.	*thābit*	ثَابِت	ثٰبِت
woman who is not a virgin	*thayīb*	ثَيِّب	ثَيِّب
clothes, garments	*thiyāb*	ثِيَاب	ثِيٰب
camel's udder	*tay'ab*	تَيْأَب	تَيٰب
to lose, to go astray	*tabbat*	تَبَّتْ	تَبَّتْ
she repented	*tābat*	تَابَتْ	تٰبَتْ
I built	*bayyattu*	بَيَّتُ	بَيَّتُ
builders	*bunāt*	بُنَاة	بُنٰت
she built	*banat*	بَنَتْ	بَنَتْ
she spent the night OR it became	*bātat*	بَاتَت	بٰتَت
must, necessitated	*battat*	بَتَّتْ	بَتَّتْ
plants	*nabāt*	نَبَات	نَبٰت
I repented	*tubtu*	تُبْتُ	تُبْتُ
you repented	*tubta*	تُبْتَ	تُبْتَ
to make final	*tabuttu*	تَبُتُّ	تَبُتُّ
house	*bayt*	بَيْت	بَيْت
to stay overnight	*bayāt*	بَيَات	بَيٰت
girl	*bint*	بِنْت	بِنْت
girls	*banāt*	بَنَات	بَنٰت
sprout	*nabata*	نَبَتَ	نَبَتَ
to do something (at night)	*bayyata*	بَيَّتَ	بَيَّتَ

Muqaṭṭaʿāt
(The Stand-alone Letters)

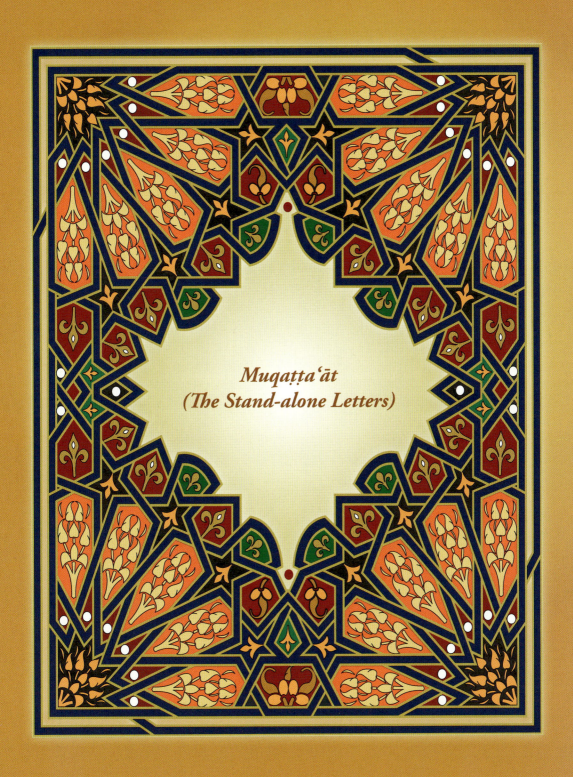

Muqaṭṭaʿāt
(The Stand-alone Letters)

Some Qurʾānic sūras begin with one or more individual letters of the alphabet, most commonly referred to as *muqaṭṭaʿāt*, which translated, means "disjointed letters." They are also called *fawātiḥ*, or "openers," because they form the opening of multiple sūras. One of these is *"A.L.M.,"* or *"Alif Lām Mīm."* These letters appear at the beginning of Q 2, as well as at the beginning of five other sūras.

In total, *muqaṭṭaʿāt* appear in twenty-nine sūras of the Qurʾān. In Arabic, they are written in the image of the letter but not in the name or pronunciation of the letter. For example, in the Arabic Q 38.1, the letter appears as *"**Ṣ.** By the Qurʾān with its reminder"* rather than *"**Ṣād.** By the Qurʾān with its reminder."* Most English translators of the Qurʾān translate the *Ṣ* as *Ṣād*, because an Arabic speaker would pronounce it this way. (See table "Sūras Containing *Muqaṭṭaʿāt*," page 112.)

Some of these opening letters are counted as a verse; for example, *"A.L.M."* or *"Alif Lām Mīm"* is counted as the first verse of Q 2. However, others are considered part of a verse. For example, the *N* that appears at the beginning of Q 68 is counted as part of the verse: *"N. By the pen, and what they write"* (Q 68.1). (See table "List of Opening Letters," page 113.)

There are many unanswered questions surrounding the *muqaṭṭa'āt*:

- Why were some *muqaṭṭa'āt* counted as verses while others were considered part of a verse? What was the basis for these classifications?
- Why do *muqaṭṭa'āt* appear in only twenty-nine sūras, and why were the remaining eighty-five sūras left without these opening letters?

But the primary question that continues to puzzle many readers of the Qur'ān is the meaning of these opening letters. Scholars have different perspectives on this issue. The following is a summary of their opinions from Islāmic sources.

Muqaṭṭa'āt are Attention Grabbers

It was said that the idol worshippers would stay away from Muḥammad when he started reciting the Qur'ān, so these *muqaṭṭa'āt* were revealed to draw the attention of those who refused to hear the Qur'ān. Al-Rāzī states, "It was revealed so that they might feel puzzled and, as a result, open their ears to hear more, which would, in turn, enable them to hear the verses of the Qur'ān that follow."[1] He also comments that as "they were hearing it, they would say in amazement: 'Listen to what Muḥammad is revealing!' But as they focus on hearing, the Qur'ān would take them by surprise. This [use of the *muqaṭṭa'āt*] was a reason for them to hear the Qur'ān and a way to benefit them."[2]

Another similar opinion supports the same purpose (drawing the attention of the listener) but not in terms of those who might turn away to resist hearing the Qur'ān. This opinion states that these letters are a form of "call letters" to command the attention of even the devout listener, such as saying, "Hey!" when calling to someone.[3]

Al-Zarkashī agrees with this opinion: [4]

> They [the letters] are as enticers to any who hear it [the Qur'ān] out of those who are wise, and an awakening to any who are lazy out of those who are eloquent in speech, who seek debate and higher status. They [the letters] are considered at the same level as the sound of thunder, which helps the onlooker watch for rain, appreciate the clouds, and save what is poured out unto him of blessings.

Critique of the First Opinion

Let us hypothetically assume that Muḥammad did intend to grab the attention of those who refused to hear the Qur'ān. Why then are the same *muqaṭṭa'āt* not found in all of the sūras revealed in Mecca?

When we analyze the sūras that are adorned with *muqaṭṭa'āt*, we find several contradictions and inconsistencies:

1. The letter *N* appears in Q 68.1, which is one of the earliest sūras. In fact, some early writings indicate that this verse (and its opening letter) was the first verse to be revealed to Muḥammad. Because Muḥammad began his message of Islām in secret, the argument that these letters were intended to alert the hearers of the Qur'ān to its recitation or to draw their attention contradicts the intention to keep the message secret during the beginning phases of Islām.
2. We find *muqaṭṭa'āt* in the following sūras that date between three years before the *Hijra* and the year of the *Hijra*: Q 46, Q 45, Q 44, Q 43, Q 42, Q 40, and Q 41. During this period, the enmity between Muḥammad and the Quraysh tribe had reached its climax. It would have been impossible for these letters to command the attention of Muḥammad's idol-worshipping tribesmen.
3. The phrase *"A.L.M."* or *"Alif Lām Mīm"* appears in Q 2 and Q 3, which were both revealed in Medina. However, Muḥammad never suffered rejection in Medina, indicating that the purpose behind the letters was not to grab his listeners' attention.
4. If we accept the opinion that these letters were intended as "call letters" to summon the attention of the devout listener, then why did Muḥammad use something unrecognizable to his hearers? Was it necessary for Muḥammad to use such meaningless phrases in order for Muslims to hear him? And if these letters were indeed "call letters" written by Muḥammad for this purpose during recitation, why did his scribes include them in the Qur'ān as if they were divine revelations?
5. Finally, if the purpose of the *muqaṭṭa'āt* was a tool for Muḥammad himself to command attention, then there is no longer any use for them in modern times. However, if there is indeed no use for them today, then these letters contradict the Islāmic claim that the entire Qur'ān is valid and applicable for every time period, season and location.

Muqaṭṭa'āt are a Divine Secret

Another group of scholars stated that these letters are "Allah's secret in the Qur'ān, and it is not befitting for anyone to discuss them." All of the four caliphs after Muḥammad, as well as Ibn Mas'ūd, were proponents of this opinion. They said, *"Muqaṭṭa'āt* are of that which is kept hidden and cannot be explained."[5]

Critique of the Second Opinion

The Qur'ān is believed to be a practical book that deals with daily issues and legal matters. This belief is the primary source of pride for many Muslims. Therefore, the introduction of phrases and words like *muqaṭṭa'āt* is in conflict with the practical nature of the Qur'ān. However, if the proponents of this opinion are correct, and the opening letters of these sūras are indeed divine secrets, then Muḥammad himself added this mystic element to the Qur'ān.

At any rate, the opinion that these letters "are Allah's secret in the Qur'ān" indicates that the scholars supporting this theory believed implicitly in the existence of meaninglessness in these letters.

Muqaṭṭa'āt are Symbolic

The third opinion, which occupies a large section in the exegetical sources, states that these letters are merely symbols and signs. The letters *"K.H.Y.A.S. (kāf-hā'-yā'-'ayn-ṣād)"* (Q 19) appear to be such an example. The *K* or *Kāf* is the first letter of the Arabic word for "sufficient" (*kāfī*) and signifies Allah being sufficient. The *H* or *Ha* is the first letter of the Arabic word for "guide" (*hādī*) and is symbolic of Allah being "the Guidance." The *A* or *'Ayn* is the first letter of the Arabic word for "all-knowing" (*'alīm*) and is symbolic of Allah being omniscient. Finally, the *S* or *Ṣad* is the first letter in the Arabic word for "truthful" (*sādiq*) and is symbolic of Allah being the truthful one.[6]

Overall, the symbolism claim includes the following points:

1. **Some of these letters symbolize Allah's names and others signify one of his attributes.** Al-Rāzī records that Ibn 'Abbās believes *"A.L.M."* stands for "I am Allah who knows [is more knowledgeable]." Regarding Q 10, Ibn 'Abbās believes that *"A.L.R."* stands for "I am Allah who sees" and that *"A.L.M.S."* in Q 13 stands for "I am Allah the best."[7]

   Other interpretations indicate that the *A* in *A.L.M.* symbolizes Allah being one, everlasting, or eternal; the *L* symbolizes his gentleness; and the *M* symbolizes Allah being the king, the glorified, or the giver. Still others believe that these letters are symbolic of Allah's names. Sa'īd Ibn Jubayr believes that the combination of *A.L.R.*, *H.M.*, and *N* is the name *al-Raḥmān*, which means "the gracious or beneficent one." However, he acknowledges that he was unable to combine the rest of the opening letters to make names of Allah or even attributes out of them.[8]

   Both Ibn 'Abbās and 'Alī Ibn Abī Ṭālib reportedly have said, "[T]he *muqaṭṭa'āt* in the Qur'ān are Allah's greatest names; however, we do not know how to derive it from them [the letters]."[9]

2. **Some of these letters symbolize Allah's names, while others symbolize other names.** Some scholars believe that in *A.L.M.*, the *A* stands for Allah, the *L* for Gabriel, and the *M* for Muḥammad. They believe that the group of letters stands for the phrase, "Allah revealed the Book [the Qur'ān] through the tongue of Gabriel to Muḥammad."[10]

3. **These letters symbolize names for the Qur'ān.** "There are other names that refer to the Qur'ān, such as *al-Furqān* ("the Criterion") and *al-Dhikr* ("the Remembrance")."[11] These other Qur'ānic names are similar to such common references as "God's Word" or "Holy Book" for the Bible. Using these comparisons, some interpret these letters to mean the "names for the sūras."[12]

4. **These letters contain prophetic knowledge of time periods concerned with major historical events.** This claim is based upon the principles of numerology. The proponents of this belief assert that numerology is the only way to determine the meaning of these letters. They claim that if numerology is not considered, the meaning of these letters cannot be attained.[13] It is important to note that many Qur'ānic commentators do not support this claim.[14]

Critique of the Third Opinion

This opinion attempts to avoid dealing with the problems associated with the Second Opinion, which states that the *muqaṭṭa'āt* are a divine secret that cannot be discussed or understood. However, this third theory, which focuses on symbolism, contradicts the Qur'ān itself, because the Qur'ān claims to be written *"in plain* [clear] *Arabic language"* (Shakir trans. Q 26.195).

Furthermore, these letters, with all their possible meanings, contradict the Qur'ān: *"O ye folk! proof has come to you from your Lord, and we have sent down to you manifest light"* (Q 4.174). If its meanings are difficult to understand, argue Muslim scholars, (*Mutakalimūn*[D]), how can the Qur'ān be a *"proof"* and a *"light"*?

Muslim scholars deny that the Qur'ān contains anything that people cannot understand: "Anyone who directs meaningless speech is similar to someone who speaks to an Arab in an Abyssinian language." In other words, whoever utters words that are not understandable is similar to someone who speaks to an Arab in a language he does not understand. The scholars add "that what is intended by words is to make one understand it; however, if it cannot be understood, then using it to communicate will be vain and foolish."[15]

Question: Does this sentiment apply to *muqaṭṭa'āt* and all of the opinions mentioned in the symbolism theory?

Note: Other phrases that can be generated from these letters can be found in books dealing with the systematic study and exegesis of the Qur'ān.

Sūras Containing *Muqaṭṭa'āt*						
Number of Letters	Opening Letter		Arabic Letter	Frequency	Sūra(s) in which the Letter(s) Appear	Is it considered a verse?
	The Letter	Letter Name				
1	S	Ṣād	ص	1	Ṣād (38)	No
	Q	Qāf	ق	1	Qāf (50)	No
	N	Nūn	ن	1	Al-Qalam (68)	No
2	T. H.	Ṭā' Hā'	طه	1	Ṭa Ha (20)	Yes
	T. S.	Ṭā' Sīn	طس	1	al-Naml (27)	No
	Y. S.	Yā' Sīn	يس	1	Ya Sīn (36)	Yes
	H. M.	Ḥā' Mīm	حم	6	al-Mu'min [Ghāfir] (40), Fuṣṣilat (41), al-Zukhruf (43), al-Dukhān (44), al-Jāthiya (45), al-Aḥqāf (46)	Yes
3	A. L. M.	Alif Lām Mīm	الم	6	al-Baqara (2), Āl-i 'Imrān (3), al-'Ankabūt (29), al-Rūm (30), Luqmān (31), al-Sajda (32)	Yes
	A. L. R.	Alif Lām Rā'	الر	5	Yūnus (10), Hūd (11), Yūsuf (12), Ibrāhīm (14), al-Ḥijr (15)	No
	T. S. M.	Ṭā' Sīn Mīm	طسم	2	al-Shu'arā' (26), al-Qaṣaṣ (28)	Yes
4	A. L. M. S.	Alif Lām Mīm Ṣād	المص	1	al-A'rāf (7)	Yes
	A. L. M. R.	Alif Lām Mīm Rā'	المر	1	al-Ra'd (13)	No
5	K. H. Y. 'H. Z.	Kāf Hā' Yā' 'Ayn Ṣād	كهيعص	1	Maryam (19)	Yes
	H. M. 'H. S. Q.	Ha Mīm 'Ayn Sīn Qāf	حم عسق	1	al-Shūrā (42)	2 verses

Note: The Basran school never considered the *muqaṭṭa'āt* to be independent verses but rather a part of the following verse. The division of these letters into independent verses, or a part of a verse, dates back to the Kufan school.[16]

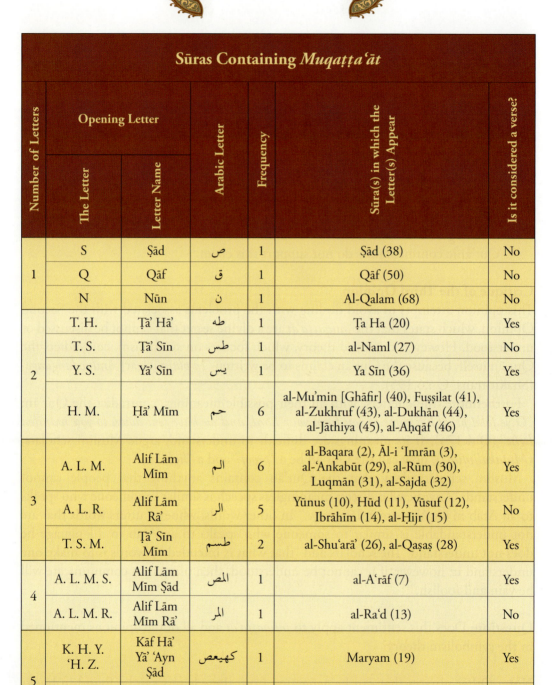

List of Opening Letters		
English Letter	**English Transliteration**	**Arabic Letter**
A	Alif	أ
Ḥ	Ḥā’	ح
R	Rā’	ر
S	Sīn	س
Ṣ	Ṣād	ص
Ṭ	Ṭā’	ط
‘	‘Ayn	ع
Q	Qāf	ق
K	Kāf	ك
L	Lām	ل
M	Mīm	م
N	Nūn	ن
H	Hā’	هـ
Y	Yā’	ي

Note: These letters can be collected together to formulate this phrase in Arabic as نصٌّ حكيمٌ قاطعٌ لهُ سرٌّ or in English as "NS-HKYM-QAT‘-LH-SR." After adding the diacritical marks, this phrase means "an absolutely wise text that has [contains] a secret."[17]

Women in the Qur’ān

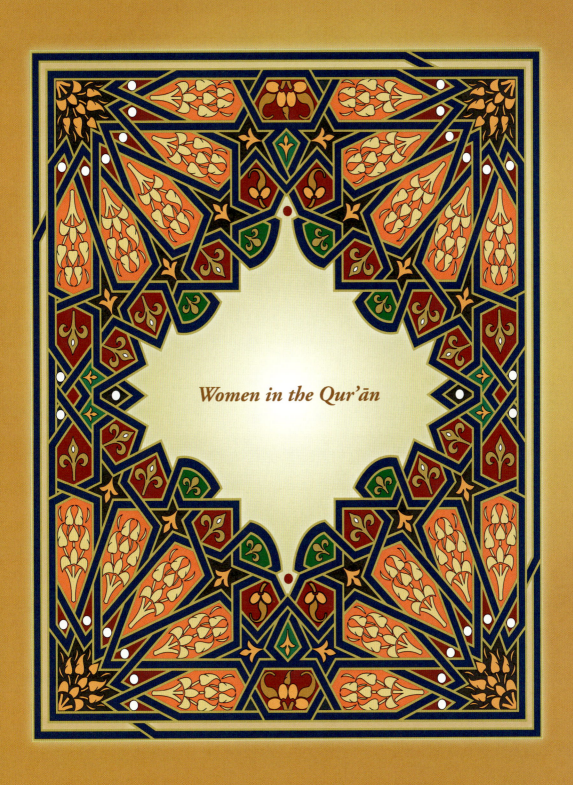

Women in the Qur'ān

The Qur'ān is the source of all personal status laws in Islāmic countries. Therefore, the rules of religious jurisprudence concerning the position and treatment of women are also based on the Qur'ān. In order to fully understand the position of women in Islām, one must first examine the Qur'ānic rules concerning them.

The Qur'ānic Image of Women

The Qur'ān provides many provocative descriptions regarding the nature of women and their intrinsic value in comparison to men:

A. Evil Beings

The Qur'ān treats women with an attitude of suspicion. It presents them as a source of danger to men. In the story of Joseph, the Qur'ān describes women as possessing great maliciousness or *kayd* ("tricks"): *"...verily, your tricks are mighty!"* (Q 12.28). On the other hand, the Qu'ran uses similar language to describe Satan: *"...verily, Satan's tricks are weak"* (Q 4.76).

It is important to note that the word *kayd* is not always used as an insult. However, the description of women in Q 12, portraying them as possessing *kayd,* is clearly used in the context of an insult. This word appears three times (verses 33, 34, and 50). Based on these three verses, one may conclude that the innate, malicious *kayd* of women comes out of their "nature and temperament." Thus their innocence is a façade that hides the evil or cunning that is within them. Furthermore, this *kayd* keeps them busy contriving plots.[1]

B. Incomplete Beings

According to the Qur'ān, a woman is an incomplete being. This depiction is illustrated by the following laws:

> **First,** the Qur'ān dictates that a woman's portion of an inheritance should be only half of what a male receives: *"God instructs you concerning your children; for a male the like of the portion of two females...."* (Q 4.11, 176)
>
> **Second,** the testimony in a court of law by a woman does not carry as much weight as it does by a man. Instead, her testimony is valued at half a man's testimony. In fact, her legal statements cannot even be accepted as true unless there are two women testifying. Furthermore, the Qur'ān dictates that when a business transaction takes place between two people, two men must witness it, or one man and two women. That way, if one woman forgets what transpired, *"the second of the two may remind the other..."* (Q 2.282).

Not only is a woman's mental capacities considered weak, but the Qur'ān compares her to a man with weak reasoning and an inability to argue his case: *"What! one brought up amongst ornaments, and who is always in contention without obvious cause?"* (Q 43.18).

The commentators on the Qur'ān see these verses as proof of "the mental weakness of women and of their deficiencies, as compared to the instincts of men. It is said that when a woman spoke to present her cause, she presented the cause against herself."[2] They feel that women are incapable of engaging in reasonable discussion. If a woman "needed to argue and fight, she would be unable [to do so], and would not prevail. This is due to her weakness of tongue, mental deficiency, and dullness of temperament."[3]

Moreover, the Muslim commentators state that a woman understands she is an incomplete being. Hence, she tries to build her self-confidence "by adorning herself with trinkets and such, to compensate for what is deficient in her."[4]

In addition, the commentators state that men outperform women even in duties that "are exclusively carried out by women, [even though] her share of them has been greater and began much earlier than a man." Therefore, even though women have been busy since the beginning of history learning how to prepare food properly, a woman can never hope to reach the skill of a man "who dedicates only a few years to it."[5] Men are even better than women in designing and embroidering fabrics. In the field of dancing, men are considered to be professional in it, whereas women's dancing tends to be based on performance rather than originality.[6] Women who are geniuses in any given field and those who were queens throughout history are exceptional cases that do not change this rule.[7]

The Qur'ān's Ruling on the Veil

The wearing of a veil has been widely practiced by women in the Arabian Peninsula since before Islām. Women wore scarves and left the upper part of their chests, as well as their necks and ears, uncovered.[8] Such was the appearance of a woman when she was out in public before men, including the Muslim women who initially kept their traditional clothing.[9]

However, social changes in Medina convinced Muḥammad that he should mandate the wearing of a veil. When women, including Muḥammad's wives, went out at night to relieve themselves between the palm trees and the fields, "the youth and those who were opportunistic" used to harass female slaves who were going out to answer the call of nature. Sometimes they would even approach and harass a free woman, claiming that they could not differentiate between her and a slave. So the women went to Muḥammad to complain about the matter.[10] And thus, he ordered the free women to wear a veil, which would distinguish them from slaves: *"O thou prophet! tell thy wives and thy daughters, and the women of the believers, to let down over them their outer wrappers; that is nearer for them to be known and that they should not be annoyed..."* (Q 33.59).[11]

Based on the commentary of Ibn Kathīr, this effort was very successful. He states that some of "the fornicators of the people of Medina" who used to roam at night to accost women were no longer bothering the free ones. In fact, "if they saw a woman wearing a full *ḥijāb* [head covering], they would say, 'This is a free one,' and would not harass her. But if they saw a woman not wearing one, they would say, 'This is a female slave,' and they would pounce on her."[12]

Therefore, Muḥammad declared in Q 33.59 that a distinction could be made between a free woman and a female slave. This distinction would stop those who might accidentally harass free women.[13] Because being unveiled became one of the characteristics of a female slave, 'Umar Ibn al-Khaṭṭāb forbade them from wearing a veil: "[I]f he saw a female slave veiled, he would beat her with a whip to preserve the apparel of the free ones."[14]

The Qur'ān's Rules on Marriage

The Qur'ān uses the term *al-nikāḥ* for marriage (Q 33.49). While the Qur'ān does not put a minimum limit on the marriageable age for women, it clearly states that it is permissible for a young girl to be given in marriage before she reaches adulthood. This ruling is evidenced by the verse discussing the prescribed waiting period, or *'idda*[D], of a young female divorcee who has not yet begun menstruation. Her waiting period is set at three months (Q 65.4). The following text provides further understanding of the marital relationship in Islām and the tenets upon which it is based.

A. Man's Supreme Authority

The Qur'ān gives a man complete authority in marriage: *"Men stand superior to women..."* (Q 4.34). The Qur'ān justifies giving this authority to the man for the following reasons:

> **First,** preference is given to him by nature: *"God hath preferred some of them over others..."* (Q 4.34).
>
> **Second,** preference is given to him by reason of his financial ability: *"and in that they expend of their wealth..."* (Q 4.34).

This higher position of man does not change even if "a woman has enough money to support herself without needing him to spend money on her, or even if she has so much money that she can spend it on him."[15] This preference is because a man has authority over a woman according to the Qur'ān, regardless of his economic situation. The leading authorities of Islām state that this ruling of the Qur'ān is an everlasting one: "[I]t precedes the development of civilizations and general legislations and [remains] past them."[16]

Furthermore, "among the instinctual and natural evidences of a man's role as leader are a woman's feelings of deprivation, lack, worry, and loss of happiness when she lives with a man who does not carry out his responsibilities as the leader and lacks the necessary leadership characteristics."[17]

B. Wife's Relationship to Husband

In Islām, the wife is a slave to her husband. Muḥammad ascribed this characterization to women during a speech made during his final pilgrimage. When he addressed the subject of women, he told men that women are *'awān*, meaning that they are equivalent to captives.[18]

The *sunna*[D] (prescribed actions and customs) of Muḥammad stress that a woman should obey her husband's commands. The story is told of a man who ordered his wife not to leave the house while he was traveling. During his absence, her father became ill, so she sent to Muḥammad asking for permission to go to her father. Muḥammad answered her by saying, "Obey your husband." Her father died, so she then requested permission from Muḥammad to go see her father's body before burial. He said to her again, "Obey your husband." When her father was buried, Muḥammad sent her a message saying, "Allah has forgiven her father because of her obedience to her husband."[19]

In addition to absolute obedience, a woman should revere her husband because Muḥammad stated, "If a woman knew the right of a husband, she would not sit at his lunch and supper time until he finishes."[20]

One time, a woman came to Muḥammad to ask about her obligations to her husband. He said, "If he had pus from his hair part to his foot [from head to toe] and you licked him, you would not have shown him enough gratitude."[21] Furthermore, in another source, Muḥammad said, "If he had an ulcer and she licked it, or if pus and blood started coming out of his nose and she licked it, she would not fulfill her obligation towards him."[22]

This *ḥadīth* (or narrative) is repeated in several sources and in several variations.

Another *ḥadīth* records Muḥammad's following statement: "It is a husband's right that his wife, if his nose was to be running with blood and pus and his wife licked it with her tongue, she would not fulfill her obligation to him. If it was required for a human to bow down to another human, I would have decreed that a wife should prostrate herself before her husband when he comes to her. That is because of how gracious Allah has been to her."[23]

Obedience and reverence towards her husband are two of the wife's duties. These duties form an element of worship for her. As Muḥammad said, "If a woman prays her five prayers, fasts the month of fasting, keeps her chastity, and obeys her husband, she will enter the paradise of her Lord."[24] In addition, Allah will not accept the prayer of a woman if her husband is angry with her.[25]

C. Husband's Right to Punish His Wife

The Qur'ān gives the husband the right to punish his wife if she goes outside the parameters that he draws for her. It provides men with instructions: *"But those whose perverseness ye fear, admonish them and remove them into bed-chambers and beat them; but if they submit to you, then do not seek a way against them..."* (Q 4.34).

If a wife expresses her dislike about a matter, refuses to have sexual intercourse with her husband, or leaves the house without her husband's permission, she is considered disloyal.[26] The man should deal with sexual and behavioral "disobedience" with the "surgical tools" given to him by the Qur'ān's rulings: instructing, sexual punishing, and beating.

1. **Instructing**

   At the beginning of marriage, a husband reminds his wife about the rights that are given to him by *sharī'a* (Islāmic laws). He can say to her, "Fear Allah! I have rights due to me from you. Repent from what you are doing. Know that obedience to me is one of your obligations."[27] If the wife refuses to fulfill the sexual desires of her husband, then he should remind her of his rights over her body.[28]

2. **Sexual Punishing (*al-Hajr*)**
   This word has two interpretations:
   - **Desertion**
     If a wife remains "disobedient," her husband should ignore her. This means he should cease talking to her as well as sharing a bed with her.[29] Some sources have included abstaining from sexual intercourse with her as part of this phase of punishment.[30] However, the common view among Muslim scholars is that ignoring or deserting means he should not talk to her, but he can still have sexual relations with her. So according to *sharī'a* a husband can verbally mistreat his wife without letting go of his "legally given right" to her body. "He [verbally] deserts her with his tongue and mistreats her but does not refrain from intercourse with her."[31]
   - **Forced Sexual Intercourse ("tightening the bindings")**
     Another form of discipline is given in Q 4.34. This verse prescribes *hajr* as an appropriate way to deal with an insubordinate wife. While *hajr* is interpreted to mean "to refuse to share their beds," the word *hajr* has several meanings. One of these meanings indicates the *hajr* of the camel when the owner binds the animal with a *hijār,* or rope. A *hijār* is tied to the front and back legs on one side of the animal to impede its movement.[32] This interpretation means that the term *wa'hjurūhunna* in Q 4.34 ("refuse to share their beds") actually means to tighten the bindings of the wife and force her to have sexual intercourse. This meaning is the adopted view of al-Ṭabarī, as he bases the meaning of *hijār* as being the binding of a camel with a *hijār*.[33] Other scholars, who also support this interpretation, state "it means to tie them up and force them to have [sexual] intercourse."[34]

     The Qur'ānic principle of a man's right to a woman's body is not open for discussion. Regardless of her psychological or physical state, she has to obey the man's command to lie in bed and have sexual relations with him. Muḥammad repeatedly made statements advocating this view:

> One of the rights of a husband upon his wife is that if she was riding on a camel's back and he approached her with sexual desires, she should not deny him.[35]
>
> If a man calls his woman to his bed, and she does not come, and then he goes to bed angry at her, the angels will curse her until the morning.[36]

These same statements are repeated in the *ḥadīth*, such as *Ṣaḥīḥ al-Bukhārī* and *Ṣaḥīḥ Muslim*, but with variations in the wording.[37]

3. **Beating**

If the previous methods, including instruction and verbal abuse, fail to correct a wife's behavior, then a husband is given the right to beat his wife. Verse Q 4.34 does not specify the mode or limit of the beating. However, it is believed that Muḥammad put a condition on the beating, classifying it as "not excessive."[38]

When interpreting the phrase "not excessive beating," scholars offer the following guidelines:

- Avoid hitting the wife's face.[39]
- Do not break any of the wife's bones.[40]
- Use nonfatal implements or physical force:[41]
  - *al-siwāk* (a twig of the *Salvadora persica* tree), or shoe laces, etc.
  - hand, etc. [hitting, slapping, punching the neck and chest, etc.]

The wife may receive a beating for every behavior that incites the anger of her husband or for every act that her husband does not like.[42] Current Islāmic literature supports the legitimacy of beating and its benefit for "upbringing." For example, the Egyptian scholar Muḥammad Mitwallī al-Shaʿrāwī (AD 1911-1998), who was considered among the top Muslim thinkers in the twentieth century, records his position:[43]

> Beating is not a sign of hatred. It could be a sign of love. As long as it is not excessive, it would only cause a small amount of pain. A person might resort to lightly beating the loved one due to desiring what is in the person's [best] interests and due to caring about the person. A woman, by her very nature, understands that, coming from her husband. She knows that his anger at her and his punishing her...will soon pass away and with its passing, its causes will pass. Therefore, they remain in their relationship as if nothing happened.

D. Husband's Rights over Wife's Body

The Qur'ān regards sexual intercourse as an act of the man that a woman receives. She is merely an object used for his enjoyment: *"Your women are your tilth, so come into your tillage how you choose..."* (Q 2.223).

Because a husband has the right to control his wife's body, like a farmer with his plow, Muslim scholars started a discussion over the meaning of the term *annā*, translated in the verse above as "how." This word can also mean "where," "when," and "however." Therefore, they have determined that this verse indicates the following sexual rights of a husband over his wife:

1. He has the right to choose any sexual position he desires.[44]
2. He has the right to have sexual relations whenever he feels like it, except during menstruation.[45]
3. He has the right to have sexual relations wherever he wishes. Therefore, some claim that this verse permits anal intercourse, a view that was supported by the Companions and some Medinan religious scholars.[46] (See comment on Q 2.223, page 238.)

According to the Qur'ān, a wife has no right over her own body. She is merely like farmland that her husband plows, according to an exegete's description.[47]

E. Polygamy

The Qur'ān permits polygamy. Q 4.3 states *"then marry what seems good to you of women, by twos, or threes, or fours,"* as long as they are dealt with justly. The commentators explain that to "be equitable" means that the husband should have equal desire towards all his wives.[48] Also, with all of his wives, he is to be just in "intercourse, fellowship, and distribution."[49] In other words, he is not to spend an undue amount of time with one wife, thereby neglecting the others.

Polygamy was known in the period before Islām, at which time the number of wives was unlimited. However, Islām limits the number of wives to four at a time.[50] Some interpret the phrase *"by twos, or threes, or fours,"* to permit up to nine wives by using Muḥammad as an example (since he, at certain times, had nine wives at the same time). However, this interpretation is rejected by the majority of commentators who considered Muḥammad to be a special case.[51] (Compare with comment on Q 4.2-3, page 320.)

Even though Muḥammad allowed polygamy, he was against it when it came to his son-in-law marrying another woman. When 'Alī Ibn Abī Ṭālib (husband of Muḥammad's daughter Fāṭima) wanted to take a second wife, both Fāṭima and her father were angry with him.[52] Muḥammad was "hurt that his most beloved daughter would be intimidated by a rival wife. He had pity on her and did not want her to go through such a harsh experience."[53] Thus, Muḥammad warned 'Alī publicly that if he wanted to marry again, he would have to divorce his wife, Muḥammad's daughter.[54]

Overall, polygamy strengthened the ability of the Muslims to invade. It became somewhat of a production machine to reinforce Muslim armies with hoards of men able to go forth into battle. Even today, Muslim writers look at polygamy from the angle of invasion. One modern writer proposes the following about polygamy and its importance to the spread of Islām by the power of increased might:[55]

> Polygamy is the best way to increase the birth rate in the environments that need a lot of hands for war or for work, such as in agricultural lands. The Muslims are charged with *jihād* for the sake of spreading the good news about Islām and inviting others to accept Islām. Hence, polygamy is able to replace what was lost in the *jihād* and recompenses many women for the loss of their husbands in the war.

F. Divorce and Remarriage

The Qur'ān endorses a method of divorce whereby a husband has the right to divorce his wife twice. However, it states that after the third time, a divorced woman is not allowed to return to her first husband *"until she marr*[ies] *another husband"* (Q 2.230).

The Islāmic sources mention that the Qur'ān instituted this ruling to overturn a societal practice that gave the husband the right to return to the wife he divorced, as long as she was in the prescribed waiting period (*'idda*). Thus, some men were using this practice to torture their wives by returning to them before the prescribed waiting period was over, then immediately divorcing them again.[56]

Therefore, the Qur'ān's legislation put an end to this activity by requiring that a divorced woman remarry and have sexual intercourse with her new husband before she can return to her first husband. In the event a wife is divorced for the third time by her husband, she must then marry another man before she can return to her first husband. The following stages must be completed before she can even return to her first husband, provided she is divorced by her new husband:

1. Waiting during the prescribed period (*'idda*) before the next marriage;
2. Marrying a second husband (contract marriage);
3. Having intercourse with her new husband;
4. Receiving a divorce from her second husband;
5. Returning to her first husband.

(See the comment on Q 2.229-231, page 242.)

G. Prescribed Waiting Period

In the event that her husband dies, a woman is instructed to remain as a prisoner in her own home for four months and ten days. She is not allowed to adorn herself. After this period has ended, she then has the right to leave her house and get married (Q 2.234).

In the case of divorce, a woman has to abide by the prescribed waiting period. For an older woman who is postmenopausal and for a young woman who has not yet started her menstrual period, the duration of this period is three months. The waiting period for a pregnant woman is the remainder of her pregnancy (Q 65.4).

Islām took these provisions from the pre-Islāmic Arabs and modified them. The prescribed waiting period for a widow had previously been one full year.[57] However, under Islām, it became four months and ten days. As to the divorced woman, she had no prescribed waiting period before Islām and had the right to marry whenever she chose. The Qur'ān, however, imposed a prescribed waiting period on her.[58]

The Qur'ān's Rules on Temporary Marriage (*al-Mut'a*)

The enjoyment marriage (*al-mut'a*) is a temporary marriage similar to a normal marriage in that it is based on a contract, but it differs in that divorce occurs automatically at the end of the period agreed upon in the contract.

This type of marriage was practiced before Islām.[59] Quite often the children of *al-mut'a* are attributed genealogically to their mother because the father was often just a passerby in the mother's town. Contact between the father and the mother would often cease at the end of the contract, and the children would take the name of the mother and her tribe.[60] Muḥammad incorporated this practice into Islām, as shown in this verse: "*...but such of them as ye have enjoyed, give them their hire as a lawful due...*" (Q 4.24).

There is no mention of an abrogation of this verse that refers to *al-mut'a*. However, Sunnī Muslims believe that Muḥammad abrogated *al-mut'a*.[61]

History points to 'Umar Ibn al-Khaṭṭāb as being the first one to ban this type of marriage.[62] Ibn Ḥabīb mentions the names of other Companions of Muḥammad who supported the continued practice of *al-mut'a*:[63]

- Khālid Ibn 'Abd Allah al-Anṣārī
- Zayd Ibn Thābit al-Anṣārī
- Salma Ibn al-Akwa' al-Aslamī
- 'Umrān Ibn al-Ḥuṣn al-Khuzā'ī
- 'Abd Allah Ibn al-'Abbās Ibn 'Abd al-Muṭṭalib

Today, Shiite Muslims continue to hold to the legality of *al-mut'a*.

The number of wives in *al-mut'a* is not limited to four, as in a permanent marriage. When Ja'far al-Ṣādiq was asked about the number of wives allowed in *al-mut'a*, and if it was limited to four, he answered, "No, not even seventy." In fact, he said that it was limitless. He advised another, "Marry a thousand of them." And when al-Hādī was asked if there was a specific limit to the number of wives a man could have in *al-mut'a*, he too answered that there was "no limit."[64]

Female Slaves *"that your right hand possesses"*

The Qur'ān deals with another category of women: female slaves. The Qur'ān gives a man the right to sexually enjoy his female slaves without regard for their familial status before being taken captive—that is, whether they were married or not (Q 4.3, 24). Because the Qur'ān views a female slave as property, she has to obey all of her owner's commands.

Since the Qur'ān views a male slave as property as well, the Muslim owner has the right to deal with his male slave's marital tie. One of the Shiite sources of law states that if an owner marries his male slave to his female slave, but then the owner desires her, he can command the male slave to renounce her. If she has completed her menstrual period, then the owner can sleep with her.

Shiite jurisprudence further allows a practice called "lending the pudendum." This practice allows the owner to lend his female slave to a relative or friend for sexual enjoyment. When he is finished with her, the relative or friend returns her to her owner. Again, because a female slave is considered property, her owner had the legal right to lend her to whomever he chooses.[65]

Moreover, the Shiite rulings allow the practice of *al-fahr*, which permits a man to have sexual intercourse with two female slaves simultaneously. He could also have sexual intercourse with one while the other watches.[66] In addition to other variations of "threesome" sexual intercourse, it appears that *al-fahr* was practiced among the Arabs. In Arabic it is said that "the man, *afhar,* if he steps aside with his female slave to do what he needs, while having another one of his female slaves with him at home, and after he is finished with the first, that is, he entered her but did not ejaculate, he enters the other one and ejaculates within her."[67]

Modern Muslim scholars refuse to criticize this treatment of female slaves; not only that, but they even accept it in theory. Although modern political and international conditions do not allow Muslim armies to freely invade or allow the taking of female captives as concubines, we find one of the leading Egyptian scholars defending this practice, considering it a form of marriage.[68]

Al-Shaʿrāwī holds that even though it is no longer possible to purchase slaves, this "does not indicate a weakening of the text. The legal text is still valid. If a case occurs that it can be applied to, then it would be valid. If there is not a case, then the concept is still permissible and can be applied once a case is found."[69] As for today's society, modern Muslim scholars consider the international treaties concerning the treatment of captives the result of earthly legislations to which Muslims should not have to abide.

Conclusion

This article has examined the Qur'ān's rules pertaining to the status of women, along with the sayings of Muḥammad used by scholars to interpret the Qur'ānic texts. Two factors dictate the position of women in Islām. The first is the written record found in the Qur'ān and the sayings of Muḥammad as recorded in the *ḥadīth*. These sources are fixed and remain unchanged by time and place. The second is the social environment. This latter factor can change according to historical context and culture.

Islāmic literature claims that Islām improved the position of women in the Arabian Peninsula and is the only religious doctrine that honors women. History shows that Islām did accomplish some advancement in the position of women during the seventh century in certain aspects. For example, limiting the number of wives to four was a positive change in comparison to the practices during that era in the Arabian Peninsula.

Another positive legislation concerned the rules governing inheritance. During the *jāhilīya,* the pre-Islāmic era, the laws of inheritance were very unfavorable to women. Inheritance belonged only to older males but not to females, as long as the male heir was able to fight. Therefore, women and young males were not eligible to claim their rightful inheritance.[70] Although this practice was not prevalent throughout the Arabian Peninsula and women were allowed to inherit in some areas of the Peninsula, Islām gave the right of inheritance to all children, without the condition of being able to fight. Islām also gave women half the inheritance of men. Therefore, compared to the practice of the time, this was positive legislation. However, the expanded rights of inheritance did not originate with Islām. There are known pre-Islāmic instances where some Arab tribes decreed that a male would inherit "the same as two females."[71]

Conversely, many of the changes implemented by Islām were not positive. The Qur'ān permits men to beat their wives, making domestic abuse a divinely permissible act rather than just an individual behavior. Furthermore, Islām permits a man to have sexual intercourse, even if it is nonconsensual, with his female slaves, thereby condoning and even making sacred the act of rape.

In various ancient societies and throughout human history, women have lived under the oppression of social injustice. But the difference between the position of women in Islām as compared to other societies and cultures is that Islām is seen as the final religion and source of law by its followers. Hence, the position of women is fixed, and rulings, such as the lot of women in inheritance, must remain in place as specified by the Qur'ān. Though in modern society a woman may work and share in the financial burdens of life, she will still be deprived of equality in inheritance because the Qur'ān commands it so. While many modern Muslim men do not practice polygamy, the fact remains that a man still has the legal right to marry a second, third, or even fourth wife.

Overall, the Qur'ānic rules regarding the treatment of women can still be used today as tools of oppression in the hand of the Muslim man. In all likelihood Muslim women will never achieve the full and equal rights with men because Muslim thinkers still claim, even today, that "the sole occupation of a woman is to marry and have a family. Any effort she exerts other than that is of no value."[72]

The Qur'ān and People of Other Faiths

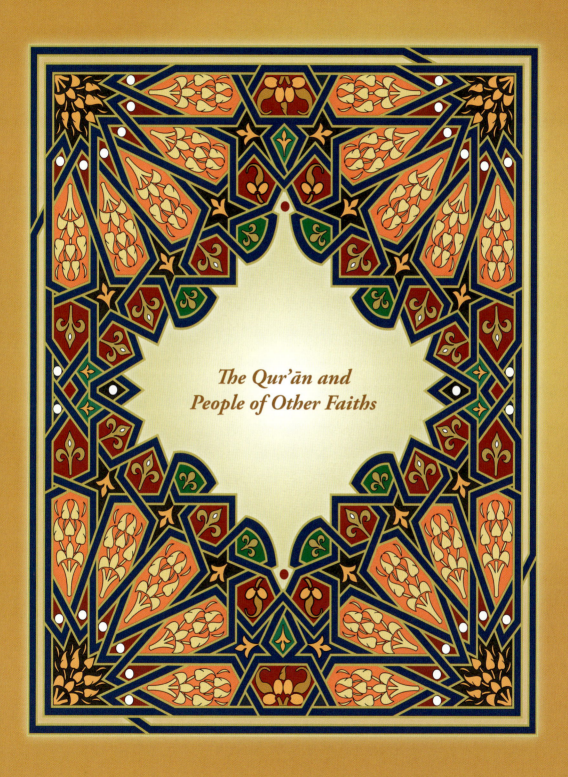

The Qur'ān and People of Other Faiths

Islām's relationship with people of other faiths can be traced to sūra al-Tawba (Q 9), one of the most definitive chapters of the Qur'ān regarding interpersonal relations between Muslims and non-Muslims. As one of the last "revealed" chapters, sūra al-Tawba (Q 9) is the foundation for Islām's perception and treatment of non-Muslims. It provides value judgments regarding all other religions and organizes a set of principles for dealing with their adherents. Finally, this sūra settles the understanding of *jihād*[D] by describing it as a duty-bound tool for dealing with the unbelievers, *"the misbelievers,"* of Islām.

Warlike Tone of al-Tawba

In general, this sūra conveys a warlike quality, as evidenced in two areas.

A. Names of the Sūra

Exegetical sources mention different names for the sūra. The most common are *al-Barā'a* ("Disavowal by God") and *al-Tawba* ("Repentance"). But other names and descriptions embody a more combatant spirit of the sūra: *al-Mukhzīya* ("the Shaming One"), *al-Munakkila* ("the Torturer"), and *al-Musharrida* ("the Displacer").[1] It is told that Ḥudhayfa said, "You call it sūra al-Tawba [Repentance], but it is indeed sūra al-'Adhāb [Torment]."[2]

B. Omission of *al-Basmala*

Q 9 is the only sūra in the Qur'ān that does not begin with the Basmala[D] (*"In the name of the merciful and compassionate God..."*). Listed below are two of the most common reasons that have been offered to explain its absence:[3]

1. Basmala refers to mercy and security, yet this sūra contains verses that encourage fighting. For this reason, many believe the Basmala was dropped from this sūra.
2. During the time of this sūra's revelation, the Arabs would typically remove the Basmala when writing a document that contained a breach to a covenant. Thus, this sūra was read without the Basmala, according to that tradition.

The imprinting of this sūra with the "war brand" goes back to the fact that it was composed during several stages of time that were full of military battles. This historical theater of operations included several important military campaigns:

- **Making preparations to occupy Mecca** (verses 13-15), a conquest that took place in the eighth year of the Hegira (AH 8/AD 630). Plans were also underway for the Battle of Ḥunayn, which took place immediately after the conquest of Mecca (Q 9.25).
- **Carrying out the Raid of Tabūk along the Syrian borders** (AH 9/AD 631), the first battle for Muslims with opponents from outside the Arabian Peninsula.
- **Annulling the peace treaties.** In the ninth year of the Hegira (AH 9/AD 631), Muḥammad sent Abū Bakr to Mecca to lead the pilgrims. As soon as Abū Bakr arrived at Mecca, 'Alī Ibn Abī Ṭālib caught up with him with a command from Muḥammad to read the first part of Q 9 to the pilgrims.[4] This part included the annulment of every peace agreement Muḥammad had contracted with the idolatrous Arab tribes, as well as the banning of other religions in the heart of the Arabian Peninsula so that Islām would become the only religion.

The sūra divides the people of other religions into two groups:
- *al-mushrikūn* ("the idolaters"): People who believe in nonbiblical faiths
- People of the Book: Jews and Christians

Based on this division, Q 9 specifies the rules for the treatment of these groups.

Treatment of *al-Mushrikūn* ("the idolaters") (verses 1-28)

As prescribed in Q 9, Muslims must force, if necessary, idolators to accept Islām or risk captivity or death by Muslim forces, because *al-mushrikūn* are dishonest, evil, and unclean.

A. Extermination Campaign (verses 1-6)
Verse 1 of the sūra annuls every covenant that was made between Muḥammad and the Muslims on one side and the *al-mushrikūn* on the other side. It also gives a grace period, in verse 2, of *"four months,"* during which the idolaters could move freely. Afterward, they would become targets of the sword of Islām. Muḥammad wanted to give the four-month period a chance to frighten the idolaters so that they would have "in it plenty of time to consider their matter and to think about their end: to choose between Islām or the preparation for resistance and clashing."[5] In verse 3 it threatens that although the idolaters had been given a chance, Allah will bring upon them killing and captivity in this world and torment in the next. Then it advises the idolaters to adopt Islām, trying to persuade them that it would be better for them. So verse 3 gives the idolaters two choices: accept Islām or face war.

Verse 5 then says that after the four-month grace period has expired, it becomes permissible to spill the blood of the idolaters wherever they may be found in the Arabian Peninsula, even if they are on the premises of *al-Ka'ba*[D]. Everyone who has adopted the religion of Islām would be spared. This verse also commands the Muslims to lie in wait for the idolaters in all their paths and to kill them wherever and whenever possible. Thus, this verse imposes on the Muslims the requirement to treat the believers of other nonbiblical religions as enemies.

This verse states the following rules of combat:

- Kill idolaters immediately if they fall into the hands of the Muslims.
- Besiege the idolaters in their homes and forbid them to move.
- Lie in wait for idolaters everywhere so that they would find it impossible to move without Islāmic supervision. (The scholars say that lying in wait for the idolaters is a "general" ruling.[6] It is not limited to the Arabian Peninsula during that time only but applies to every time and place.)
- Offer freedom and peace if the idolaters adopt Islām and abandon their own religion, committing themselves to prayer and almsgiving:

The two conditions of prayer and almsgiving are strictly emphasized because prayer is the symbolic expression of the individual's submission to the god of Islām, and almsgiving is the tangible expression of submission to the Islāmic government and recognition of the legitimacy of that government. The following verse also stresses that adopting Islām as a religion must be accompanied by prayer and almsgiving: *"But if they repent and are steadfast in prayer and give alms, then they are your brethren in religion..."* (Q 9.11).

At the end of verse 5, Muḥammad announces that the idolater's adoption of Islām (or his surrender) prevents him from being killed because *"God is forgiving and merciful."*

Forgiveness and mercy are only offered on the condition of surrendering to the will of the Muslims.

Verse 6 indicates a situation where a idolater may be given temporary security if he expresses a desire to become acquainted with Islām. If the idolater refuses to accept Islām, he is permitted to leave safely. However, war would then be declared on him anew. Therefore, the aim of the temporary easement was only to deliver and spread the message of Islām.

B. Discredit of the Idolaters (verses 7, 8, and 10)

Q 9 questions the honesty of the idolaters. Verse 7 asks the negative question, "How do the idolaters have the right to attain a covenant with the Muslims?" when, according to the accusation of this verse, the idolaters would not honor such a relationship or a covenant if they overcame the Muslims. The same accusation is repeated in verse 10.

The following verse (Q 9.8) claims that the idolaters will practice a policy of dissimulation when they are weak (and cannot prevail) even as their hearts are full of resentment and hatred. All these verses aim to make the idolaters look dishonest and evil so that the Muslim would see it to be his duty to implement the tasks appointed by the previous verses: killing, besieging, and lying in wait.

C. Idolaters' Uncleanliness (verse 28)

The incitement against the idolaters continues with the text in verse 28: *"It is only the idolaters [idolaters] who are unclean...."* The word *najasun* ("unclean") is a root word, the use of which makes "masculine and feminine; singular, dual, and plural equal. [This word's] **intent is to exaggerate in the description by making the described to be the definition of that description** [our emphasis]."[7] This word does not appear anywhere else in the Qur'ān.

The Muslim scholars give two opinions regarding the meaning of *najasun*:

- The word *najasun* used as a description is a metaphor meant to show contempt. Others also say that the idolaters are described as unclean because they do not hold to the Muslim cleansing rituals.[8]
- Idolaters are unclean by nature. It is told that Ibn 'Abbās said, "Their notables are unclean like the dogs and the pigs."[9] In another source he states "that their notables are as dirty as dogs."[10] The Twelvers (the largest branch of Shiite Islām) also declare that non-Muslims are literally *"najasun."*[11]

The term *najasun* generates several repulsive descriptions in the mind of the Muslim:

- Unclean: meaning unhygienic and dirty; a thought that aims to create a pathological aversion towards the other.
- Moral impurity: meaning corrupt morals, which plays a role in feeding into the hatred towards the other by portraying him as impure; thus, the world must be purified of him.

The sūra also uses a similar term, *al-rijsu* ("abomination"), which means "dirty," a thing that is nasty or an ugly act. This word was used as a description of a party that refused to participate in the Raid of Tabūk; so it was said about them, *"Verily, they are a plague..."* (Q 9.95).

Treatment of People of the Book (verses 29-35)

These verses address the People of the Book (Jews and Christians) and contain several accusations to justify Islāmic law against them. The verses state that the People of the Book should be fought for the following reasons:

1. They do not believe in Allah.
2. They do not believe in the Day of Judgment.[D]
3. They do not keep the prohibitions of Islām: *"...and who forbid not what God and His Apostle have forbidden..."* (Q 9.29).
4. They do not adopt Islām as their religion: *"...and who do not practice the religion of truth..."* (Q 9.29).

The first and second items show a lack of understanding regarding the doctrines of Judaism and Christianity. Instead, the content resembles a political statement, the goal of which is to incite fighting and not introduce the Muslims to these two religions or start a dialogue with them.

A. *Al-Jizya* (verse 29)

If the People of the Book would not adopt Islām as their religion, then verse 29 gives the condition that fighting them would only stop if they gave *al-jizya*[D], a fine (tribute) for living in Islāmic lands: *"...until they pay the tribute by their hands and be as little ones..."* (Q 9.29). So what does this mean?

1. ***"by their hands"* (*'an yadin*)**
   - The Christian or the Jew would pay the fine personally; no one else can do it in his place.[12]
   - The Christian or the Jew, helpless and powerless, would feel compelled (forced) to pay the fine.[13]
   - The Christian or the Jew would pay the fine in appreciation of the graciousness of Islām [for sparing his life and letting him live in a Muslim land].[14]

2. ***"and be as little ones"* (*wa hum ṣāghirūn*)**
   - It means that while a Jew or Christian is cowering and submissive, "The lowly despicable person is called *ṣaghir* ["subdued"]. "[15]
   - Scholars provide even more detailed meanings for *subdued*:

> The Christian or the Jew should pay it standing straight, while the one receiving it would be seated.[16] When the payee of the *jizya* reaches the person receiving it, the Muslim man receiving it would take him by the throat and say to him, "pay the *jizya*. "[17] Others say, once he pays, he gets slapped on his behind. It is also said that he is to be taken by his beard and beaten on his jaw. It is said as well that he is to be taken violently by the collar of his clothes and dragged to the place of payment.[18]
>
> *Subdued* means that the Christian or the Jew would present the *jizya* in spite of his hatred of it.[19]

The commentaries on this verse say that the People of the Book who reside within the borders of the Islāmic country should not be respected, nor should they be held in a higher regard than the Muslims. Such a policy was implemented after Muḥammad gave this order to the Muslims: "Do not greet the Jews and Christians first, and, if you meet one of them along the way, force him to take the narrowest of it."[20]

B. False Accusations

Just like the previous verses aimed at discrediting the idolaters, other verses in Q 9 seem designed to plant hatred in Muslims by presenting allegations to create a negative image of the People of the Book:

1. Verse 29 considers their doctrines to be null and void, that they *"do not practice the religion of truth…."*
2. Verse 30 attributes to the Jews the false saying: *"Ezra is the son of God…."*
3. Verse 30 disputes and belittles the claim that "Christians say that the Messiah [Christ] is the son of God…."
4. Verse 31 claims that the Jews "take their doctors [rabbis and religious leaders]… as lords" and the Christians "take…their monks…and the Messiah the son of Mary" to be their lords.
5. Verse 32 adds that these doctors and monks *"desire to put out the light of God with their mouths…."*
6. Verse 34 claims a large percentage of *"the doctors and monks devour the wealth of men openly"* and hinders them from adopting Islām.

To many Muslims, these accusations justify fighting against the People of the Book. In his commentary on verses 30-31, Ibn Kathīr makes this blunt declaration: "**This is an enticement from Allah almighty for the believers to fight the blaspheming idolatrous Jews and Christians** [our emphasis], for their saying this heinous fabrication against Allah."[21] In verses 34-35 the inclusion of Jewish and Christian leaders expands the incrimination against the Jews and Christians and serves to introduce yet more inflammatory text to the rest of the sūra that incites fighting against the People of the Book.

The description by Ibn Kathīr of the Jews and the Christians as idolaters echoes the previous passage in verse 28, which describes idolaters as unclean. Now the description of *najasun* ("unclean") is no longer limited to the believers in nonbiblical religions only but also includes the People of the Book, because—according to Ibn Kathīr—they are idolaters as well. In one verse, the Qur'ān describes the Jews as "the idolaters." The Qur'ān also accuses Christians of denying the oneness of God and believing there are three gods (Q 5.73; compare with Q 4.171). In Q 3.64, Jews and the Christians are accused of associating others with Allah [worshipping others along with Allah].

Based on these Qur'ānic descriptions, the Arabic concordance offers this definition of the word *shirk*: "To have *shirk* in Allah: to have a partner in his reign...the noun *is al-shirku*...to associate with Allah a partner in his Lordship...."[22]

Hence, the term *al-shirk* in the Qur'ān includes the idolatrous religions found in the Arabian Peninsula at that time, as well as the biblical religions, Judaism and Christianity. Based on this denotation, the Muslim legislators state that the People of the Book "are of the same status as the unclean notables in the imperative to avoid them."[23] Al-Ḥassan says, "He who shakes hands with a *mushrik* [idolater] must perform *wuḍū'* [ablutions] again."[24] The *Ẓāhiriya*[D], the Shiite Twelvers[D], and the Sunnīs concur with this opinion.[25] These three groups constitute the largest currents in Islām.

A modern scholar states that the People of the Book are "evil ones [and] wicked, due to the *shirk*, oppression, and ugliness of morals."[26] This suspicion with regard to the non-Muslim's ethics and morals established the principle of "Loyalty and Repudiation."

C. Loyalty and Repudiation (verses 23, 24, 71, 113, 114)

Sūra Q 9 commands the Muslims to establish their ties on the basis of religious sectarianism and not of kinship. It says that there is no such thing as loyalty between a Muslim and his fathers or brothers. Furthermore, the Muslim who befriends one who is not Muslim is considered one of the oppressors. The Qur'ān points out the necessity of being at enmity with all who are at enmity with Islām, *"even if they were their fathers, or their sons, or their brethren, or their clansmen..."* (Q 58.22).

In Q 60.16, the Qur'ān stresses that it is not permissible to establish a relationship between a Muslim and a non-Muslim. In Q 35.5, it completely forbids being loyal to (befriending) the People of the Book. In Q 9.71, a Muslim is to be loyal only to another Muslim. On the psychological level, it is not permissible, according to verse

113, to even think about seeking forgiveness *"for the idolaters, even though they be their kindred."*

The commentaries say that verse 113 was revealed in Mecca to stop Muḥammad from praying for forgiveness for his uncle who had just died.[27] It is told that Muḥammad came to Abū Ṭalib at the time of his dying and asked him to say the expression, "There is no god but Allah," but Abū Ṭalib refused. So the verse came following his death: "Then it was added to this Medinan sūra because it was suitable to its rulings….It is also narrated by a group that it was revealed when he [Muḥammad] visited his mother's tomb and asked forgiveness for her."[28]

Thus, it is not permissible for a Muslim to ask for forgiveness for a non-Muslim, even if it is his dead mother. The sūra underscores this point in the following verse (114) by offering Ibrahīm (Abraham) as an example to be followed. When Abraham realized that his father did not believe in his religion, *"he dissociated himself from him."*

Treatment of Both Groups by Means of *Jihād* ("holy war")

Despite the differences between the People of the Book and *al-mushrikūn*, Q 9 makes both groups the focused target of *jihād*.

A. Imperative to fight non-Muslims (verses 14-16)

The Muslim has to fight anyone who is a non-Muslim. In verses 14-16, the Qur'ān incited the Muslims to storm Mecca (AH 8/AD 630). Q 9 states Allah would make the Quraysh taste suffering at the hands of the Muslims. In verses 14-15, it states that killing the Quraysh would *"remove* [the] *rage"* from the hearts of Muslims. Al-Zuḥailī notes that killing the enemy had a psychological benefit for Muslims: "It is a removal of the anguish or the sorrow of the hearts of the Muslims who were hurt by the idolaters breaking their covenant."[29]

Killing gives the Muslims the joy of revenge—it "heals the chests of [the Muslims] by the killing of the idolaters." Subduing the idolaters at the hands of the Muslims heals the anger and hatred that are in the hearts of the Muslims because of what had come to them "of harm and abomination."[30] Based on these verses, killing for the cause of Islām has become an enjoyable act for the Muslim fighter in every time and place.

Jihād is a duty of every Muslim because as verse 16 states (compare with Q 29.2-3), it reveals the true Muslim from the one whose faith is impure. The goal behind the fighting, according to Q 9.33, is that Islām will prevail over all religions *"averse although idolaters may be."*

The necessity to fight to raise the banner of Islām over all other religions is mentioned in several places in the Qur'ān. The most well-known of these verses are located in Q 9:

- Q 9.5: *"...kill the idolaters wherever ye may find them; and take them, and besiege them, and lie in wait for them in every place of observation...."* This verse concerned the idolatrous Arabs of the Arabian Peninsula, but it became a jurisprudence base for all nonbiblical persons.
- Q 9.29: *"Fight those who believe not in God...and who do not practice the religion of truth from amongst those to whom the Book has been brought, until they pay the tribute by their hands and be as little ones."* This verse demands the fighting of the People of the Book (Jews and Christians) to either subdue them and impose the *jizya* or force them to adopt Islām as their religion.
- Q 9.36: *"...but fight the idolaters, one and all, as they fight you one and all."* This passage demands the fighting of all who are non-Muslim and considers the non-Muslims as one anti-Islāmic camp.

B. Foreign Invasion

In the ninth year of the Hegira, Muḥammad carried out a raid on the Syrian borders that became known later as the Raid of Tabūk (AH 9/AD 631). This was the first Islāmic military skirmish outside the Arabian Peninsula. Verses 38-39 of Q 9 helped to incite the invasion and threaten those who refused to take up arms with the punishment of hellfire. As a continuation to this call to battle (verses 88-89), the sūra commends the fighters and promises them *"gardens beneath which rivers flow."* Even today, this agitation to invade remains active in the Islāmic doctrine and the Islāmic mind.

In verse 73 commands Muḥammad to fight *"the unbelievers and the hypocrites."* He is also exhorted to be severe and rough as he makes war on his enemies. This directive has become the duty of Muslims in every time and place. Ibn Mas'ūd comments that verse 73 states that a Muslim must carry out *jihād* "by his hand, but if he cannot, then with his tongue, but if he could not, then with his heart, yet if he could not, then let him scowl with his face."[31]

Verse 111 states that Allah has made a deal with Muslims, in which he has purchased of Muslims *"their persons and their wealth, for the paradise they are to have...."* That is, Muslims have to put forth their lives and possessions in the cause of lifting the banner of Islām over the world. In return for this sacrifice, Allah will give them paradise. In the text of the contract, we read that the Muslims are obligated to fight, *"and they shall slay and be slain...."*

C. Elimination of Critics

In the second part of Q 9.12 is a command to fight anyone who criticizes Islām. Thus, criticizing Islām, or critiquing the life of Muḥammad, is considered a crime punishable by death. [32]

A modern exegete states that any critical discussion about the Qur'ān, Islām, or the life of Muḥammad is a form of war on Islām.[33] If a Christian or a Jew who resides within the borders of an Islāmic country dares to discuss subjects that are related to Islām, "his killing becomes permissible, because the covenant has already been contracted with him that he would not discredit. If he discredits Islām, he will have broken his covenant and left *al-dhimma*[D]."[34] In his commentary on verse 13, this same exegete considers that any evangelism by non-Muslims is a product of political colonialism.[35] So he gives the prohibition for non-Muslims to evangelize in the Islāmic world a false nationalistic justification.

Conclusion

Sura Q 9 divides the believers of other religions into two groups:

- **Those who belong to nonbiblical religions.** The Muslims must fight them until they adopt Islām or are killed. This ruling used to apply to the idolaters of the Arabian Peninsula. However, now it covers all the nonbiblical religions, including the other major religions: Hinduism, Buddhism, Confucianism, and so on. This ruling also applies to nonreligious groups. The sura specifies a fixed principle to deal with this group, which means that this first group has only two choices: to become Muslims or to be killed.
- **People of the Book.** According to the Qur'ān, Muḥammad is the Seal (the Last) of the Prophets, and Islām abrogates all previous religions. Hence, this sura formulates a rule that states that the People of the Book have to either accept Islām or pay the *jizya*. Furthermore, Islām divides Muslim society into two classes: Muslims (first class) and People of the Book (second class).

Regarding relations between countries, the Muslim doctrine divides the world into two groups: Dār al-Islām (House of Islām) where Islām rules, and Dār al-Ḥarb (House of War), which is every country that has not submitted to the Islāmic ruling, regardless of whether or not it is in a real state of war with Muslims and regardless of the prominent religion in it.

The Qur'ān imposes on Muslims the obligation to fight in order to raise the banner of Islām over all the earth. The imposition of *jihād* in Q 9 is an absolute command—not for defense but for this one consideration: forcing the world to accept Islām, even by the power of the sword (Q 9.5, 29, 33, 36, 73, 111, and 123). Verse 123 commands Muslims to start their holy war on their neighboring countries: *"O ye who believe! fight those who are near to you of the misbelievers…"*—the height of good neighborly conduct among the nations.

Part II

The Qur'ānic Text

Key to Reading Part II

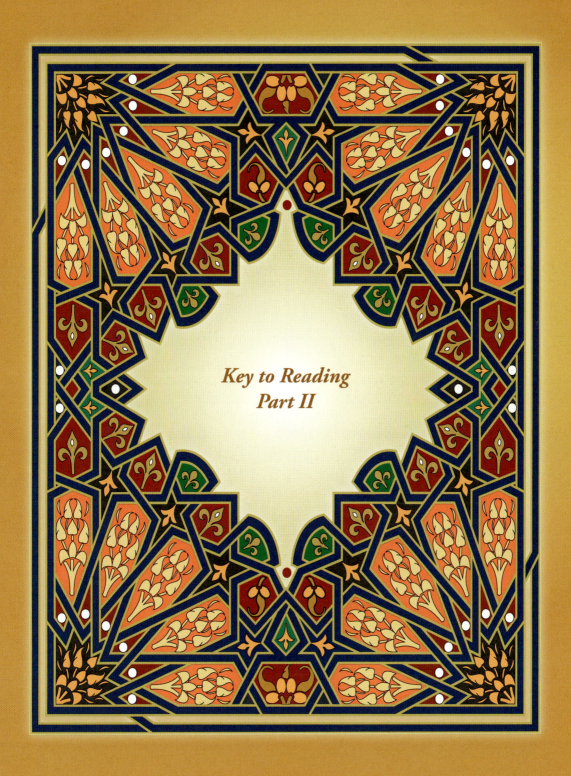

Key to Reading Part II

Each chapter (sūra) will be preceded by a short introduction that will summarize the main topics addressed in that sūra and alert the reader to related historical, linguistical, exegetical and other important issues.

Each sūra (as translated by Palmer) will be presented in its original form, ornately boxed, as is customary to see the Qur'ān in an Arabic text. Generally, these decorative text boxes will be placed at the top of the pages (though some will span several full pages) with the related commentary placed below these boxes.

Qur'ānic Text and Citations

When the word "Qur'ān" is used in this book without further explanation, it refers to the 'Uthmānic codex because this reading is the official version of the Qur'ān in circulation today. Throughout this book, the readings of the official Qur'ān ('Uthmānic codex) and the Palmer English translation will be italicized; the other readings, or codices, will use normal text.

For all Qur'ānic citations, the letter "Q" refers to the Qur'ān. In the example Q 4.3, the number 4 refers to sūra 4 and the number 3 refers to the verse.

Note: 'Uthmānic Codex

Sometimes this book will mention that a reading of a particular verse is attributed to the "codex of 'Uthmān." How can there be a reading from the codex of 'Uthmān when the official Qur'ān is the 'Uthmānic codex? The answer is that several readings of the Companions of Muḥammad have been transmitted to us, including one from 'Uthmān Ibn 'Affān, the third successor or caliph after Muḥammad's death. These readings were not included in the official Qur'ān because the official version was a development of an earlier copy.

This earlier copy was prepared on the orders of Abū Bakr, the first caliph, and 'Umar Ibn al-Khaṭṭāb, the second caliph, and kept with Ḥafṣa, 'Umar's daughter and one of Muḥammad's wives. When 'Uthmān formed his committee to transcribe the official Qur'ān, the committee took the copy from Ḥafṣa and created a text based on it that was acceptable to all. Therefore, many individual readings of the Qur'ān were left out of the official copy. Some of these ignored readings belonged to Abū Bakr, 'Umar Ibn al-Khaṭṭāb—and 'Uthmān—themselves. (See the article "Compilation of the Qur'ān" on page 49.)

Reliability of non-Arabic Qur'āns

The Qur'ān states in verses such as Q 16.103 and Q 26.195 that it is an Arabic book that was revealed to Arabs in their own language. However, in order for Islām to grow beyond the limitations of time and space, the Muslims had to translate the Qur'ān and propagate it in a way that would attract the target cultures.

A reader might approach any translation of the Qur'ān with the assumption that it is an honest rendering of the original and, thus, might not be aware of the many differences that might exist between the original and the translation.

The Arabic and English languages are very different, which opens the door for several reasons behind inaccurate translations:

1. The translator's pursuit of an equivalent word in another language might prove difficult. Therefore, the translator may choose, out of preference, one word over another based on the translator's knowledge or linguistic taste. For example, the Arabic word *fitna* (found in Q 2.191) has several English translations:
   - "persecution" by Pickthall
   - "tumult and oppression" by Yusuf Ali
   - "sedition" by Palmer

   Another example, with possible serious theological ramifications upon translation, is found in Q 33.56. The verse, presented here in three English translations, literally states that Allah and his angels pray upon (*yuṣallūna 'ala*) Muḥammad:

   PICKTHALL: "Lo! Allah and His angels **shower blessings** on the Prophet. O ye who believe! **Ask blessings** on him and salute him with a worthy salutation."

Yusuf Ali: "God and His angels send blessings on the Prophet: O ye that believe! **Send ye blessings** on him, and salute him with all respect."

Palmer: "Verily, God and His angels **pray for** the prophet. O ye who believe! **pray for** him and salute him with a salutation!"

2. The translator might belong to a particular school of thought within Islām, which would motivate the translator to choose the foreign words that would be interpreted closest to the religious views of the translator. For example, the Arabic phrase *mutawaffika* (found in Q 3.55) means "causing you to die." However, Muslims who believe that Jesus did not die just yet (but was gathered up and will come back and die), translate this phrase as "gathering you," "taking you," or "terminating your period of stay on earth." Again, there are several English translations for this verse:

   Pickthall: "when Allah said: O Jesus! Lo! I am gathering thee and causing thee to ascend unto Me...."

   Sher Ali: "when ALLAH said, 'O Jesus, I will cause thee to die a natural death and will raise thee to Myself...."

   Yusuf Ali: "God said: "O Jesus! I will take thee and raise thee to Myself...."

   Palmer: "When God said, 'O Jesus! I will make Thee die and take Thee up again to me...."

   Note: Some of the authoritative exegetes hold that Jesus died for a short period of time. They disagree about the length of his death, which some hold to be only a few hours, while others suggest that it lasted up to three days.[1] (See the comment on Q 3.55, page 285.)

3. The translator may intentionally attempt to adorn the language to present a better image of the Qur'ān and its rulings. This questionable partiality is a serious issue as it shows that the translator is not necessarily in agreement with what the Qur'ān actually states. Conversely, others might present a worse image than one might get from reading the Qur'ān in Arabic. An example of this possible negative bias is seen in Q 4.34:

PICKTHALL: "Men are **in charge** of women, because Allah hath made the one of them to excel the other, and because they spend of their property (for the support of women). So good women are the obedient, guarding in secret that which Allah hath guarded. As for those from whom ye fear rebellion, admonish them and banish them to beds apart, and **scourge them**...."

YUSUF ALI: "Men are **the protectors and maintainers** of women, because God has given the one more (strength) than the other, and because they support them from their means. Therefore the righteous women are devoutly obedient, and guard in (the husband's) absence what Allah would have them guard. As to those women on whose part ye fear disloyalty and ill-conduct, admonish them (first), (next), refuse to share their beds, (and last) **beat them (lightly)**...."

PALMER: "Men **stand superior** to women in that God hath preferred some of them over others, and in that they expend of their wealth: and the virtuous women, devoted, careful (in their husbands') absence, as God has cared for them. But those whose perverseness ye fear, admonish them and remove them into bed-chambers and **beat them**...."

The Palmer translation most closely resembles the Arabic text. Notice how Yusuf Ali translates "beat them," by adding the word "lightly." Notice in contrast how Pickthall translates the Arabic word *wa ḍribūhunna* as "scourge." Yusuf Ali tries to downplay what the Qur'ān states or maybe inject his own belief, by modifying its words to present a more palatable Qur'ān to the Western audience. Nonetheless, is beating women lightly an acceptable practice when women are not obedient to their men? Both Pickthall and Yusuf Ali show their partiality in their translation, whereas Palmer more closely mirrors the Arabic.

In addition, the Palmer translation more closely aligns with the opinion of the Muslim exegetes on this issue. They hold that men are in charge of disciplining women, and that they are to take their women by the hand and discipline them.[2] They further state that men's words and commands to women are final.[3] This perspective best supports the Palmer translation, "stand superior." (For more details, see the article "Women in the Qur'ān" on page 117.)

Verses Q 3.54 and Q 8.30 also serve to illustrate this point of possible translator partiality in several English-translated descriptions of Allah as the **best of *al-mākirīna***, a term, which in Arabic, is considered insulting to the receiver:

Pickthall

- Q 3.54: "And they (the disbelievers) schemed, and Allah schemed (against them): and **Allah is the best of schemers**."
- Q 8.30: "And when those who disbelieve plot against thee (O Muḥammad) to wound thee fatally, or to kill thee or to drive thee forth; they plot, but Allah (also) plotteth; and **Allah is the best of plotters**."

Yusuf Ali

- Q 3.54: "And (the unbelievers) plotted and planned, and God too planned, and the **best of planners is God**."
- Q 8.30: Remember how the Unbelievers plotted against thee, to keep thee in bonds, or slay thee, or get thee out (of thy home). They plot and plan, and God too plans; but the **best of planners is God**.

Notice that Ali uses "plotted" for the unbelievers but uses "planned" for Allah. This translation is inconsistent with the Arabic, which uses the same root word for both verbs.

Palmer

- Q 3.54: "But they (the Jews) were crafty, and God was crafty, for **God is the best of crafty ones**!"
- Q 8.30: "And when those who misbelieve were crafty with thee to detain thee a prisoner, or kill thee, or drive thee forth; they were crafty, but God was crafty too, for **God is best of crafty ones**!"

These variances in the translations are due in part because Arab exegetes tried to resolve the issue themselves by offering a different definition for the word *al-mākirīna* when it applies to Allah. Al-Baghawī offers two definitions for the word *mākir* (singular of *mākirīna*). When applying this adjective to people, he provides the meaning "malign [be evil-minded], deceive, cheat." However, when applying it to Allah, he suggests that Allah "lures the person and takes that person by surprise."[4]

However, the word *al-mākirīna* literally means to "con," "swindle," "be sly," "double-deal," "be crafty," or "deceive." Hence, the phrase should be translated as Allah is the best at cunning, or Allah is the best deceiver.

The reader needs to be mindful of these translation issues, especially in such areas as the rulings toward the treatment of women, the treatment of people of other faiths, and the like.

Palmer Translation

Among most of the compared verses, Palmer is closest, from a literal standpoint, to what the current Arabic Qur'ān states. His command of both languages, Arabic and English, is clear. Another advantage to using Palmer's translation is its language style. Unlike today's vernacular, the Palmer translation is written in an earlier form of English, which gives not only unusual spellings and words (e.g., befel, vicegerents) but also the feel that the Arabic reader would have when approaching the Qur'ān with its nearly 1500-year-old Arabic. These qualifications make Palmer the choice translation for this book.

Finally, the reader must be aware that different translations may have different numbering sequences. Older translations might follow a numbering system based on a copy of the Qur'ān (issued in Leipzig in AD 1834) by German Orientalist, Gustav Leberecht Flügel. On the other hand, newer translations might use the numbering system based on a copy of the Qur'ān issued in AD 1925 by al-Azhar Islāmic University. For the Palmer translation used in this book, the current Arabic Qur'ān's numbering system was used to divide and enumerate the verses to make reading and searching easier for readers.

Because of these different numbering sequences, the reader may sometimes need to look at the verses that precede or follow the verse number mentioned in this book if a particular verse in the book is not the same as another edition found online or in print.

The reader should also note that there is one verse (Q 7.179) and parts of two other verses (Q 6.57, 58) where the Palmer translation is missing for unknown reasons. For these rare occurrences, the English translation by Orientalist George Sale has been inserted and will be identified with square brackets.

Any other translated verses other than Palmer (e.g., Yusuf Ali, Sher Ali, Pickthall) will be identified in the text. In all cases, the aim is to present the reader with the English translation that best explains the research and commentary of this book, which is based on the original Arabic text of the Qur'ān.

Biblical References

The primary source for cited passages or verses from the Bible will be the *NIV Study Bible* (*NIV*). If another version is used, it, too, will be identified in-text and listed in the Works Cited on page 645.

Arabic Pronunciations

Throughout the book, the reader will often encounter transliterated Arabic text with dots and diacritical markings. These markings are designed to aid the reader in pronouncing these words. Examples of these markings as well as English approximations of the major vowel sounds are provided in the following chart:

Arabic Pronunciation Guide			
Symbol	**Sound**	**Example**	**Arabic letter**
ʿ	deep **a** sound	Baal	ع
ʾ	gutteral stop as **a** in **a**pple	apple	ء
z	**z** as in **z**oom	zoom	ز
ẓ	**z** as in **zu**m	zum	ظ
dh	**th**e	the	ذ
t	**t** as in **t**in	tin	ت
ṭ	**t** as in **tu**ff	tuff	ط
d	**d** as in **d**ad	dad	د
ḍ	**d** as in **du**d	dum	ض
h	**h** as in **h**at	hat	ه
ḥ	stressed **h** with the sound **hu**t	haughty	ح
kh	gutteral **h** as in lo**ch**	Bach, bochwurst	خ
s	**s** as in **s**ee	see	س
ṣ	**s** as in **s**od	sod, some	ص
ā	short vowel **a** as in dad	dad	ا
ū	long vowel **u** as in d**u**de	dude, doom	و
ī	long vowel **e** as in d**ee**d	deed, please	ي

ⓖ [104] O ye who believe! say not 'ra'hina,' but say 'un*th*urna,' and hearken; for unto misbelievers shall be grievous woe.

[105] They who misbelieve, whether of those who have the Book or of the idolaters, would fain that no good were sent down to you from your Lord; but God specially favours with His mercy whom He will, for God is Lord of mighty grace.

ⓑ

ⓡ [106] Whatever verse we may annul or cause thee to forget, we will bring a better one than it, or one like it; dost thou not know that God is mighty over all?

Ⓖ *Q 2.104*

It is recorded that the Anṣār said to Muḥammad, "*ra'inā,*" which meant they wanted him to explain more to them. However, in this verse, Muḥammad commanded them to use the word *unẓ urnā* in its place, because he considered *ra'inā* to be Jewish slang for an expletive....

Ⓑ *Q 2.106*

The text of this verse is mentioned in different forms:

- In the codex of Ibn Mas'ūd it is read as "we do not hold back a verse or abrogate it, but we come with one better than it or similar to it."
- It is also told that Ibn Mas'ūd read it as "we do not make you forget a verse or abrogate it"....

Ⓡ *Q 2.106*

In the midst of the doctrinal controversy between Muḥammad and the Jews in Medina, the Jews noticed that Muḥammad was annulling, time and again, rulings that he had enacted....

Color-coded Sections

As exemplified in the above illustration, three colors are used to help the reader identify and understand the three main sections:

- Sections with a green motif introduce commentary regarding the abrogation of the verse. (See Ⓖ.) The text of the corresponding Qur'ānic verse (in the decorated box) will be underlined in green. (See ⓖ.)
- Sections with a blue motif introduce commentary that discuss the variant readings of the verse. (See Ⓑ.) The text of the corresponding Qur'ānic verse will be colored blue. (See ⓑ.)
- Sections with a red motif introduce the critical analysis of the verse. (See Ⓡ.) The text of the corresponding Qur'ānic verse will also be colored red. (See ⓡ.)

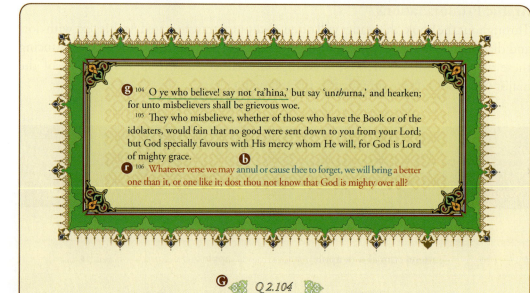

[102] And they follow that which the devils recited against Solomon's kingdom;—it was not Solomon who misbelieved, but the devils who misbelieved, teaching men sorcery,—and what has been revealed to the two angels at Babylon, Harut and Marut; yet these taught no one until they said, 'We are but a temptation, so do not misbelieve.' Men learn from them only that by which they may part man and wife; but they can harm no one therewith, unless with the permission of God, and they learn what hurts them and profits them not. And yet they knew that he who

Q 2.102

Most readers read it as rendered above, where the word ***al-shayāṭīnu*** (Q) ("**the devils**" (P)) is in the Arabic irregular (broken) plural form. However, there is a reading that says *al-shayāṭūn*. (V) They read it as *wa lakin al-shayāṭūn*—using the weaker *lakin* ("but") instead of the stronger ***lakinna*** ("**but**"), which is what the current Arabic Qur'ān reads—and keeping *al-shayāṭūn* according to the previous reading. This substitution of words presents a great grammatical difference in parsing words.

Special Text

In the above illustration, the blue, italicized, and bold-faced text represents the reading in the current Arabic Qur'ān (see (Q)); its Palmer English translation is blue, bold faced, but not italicized (see (P)). Variant readings (with their English translations) will also be blue and italicized but not bold-faced (see (V)).

Superscripts

The insertion of the superscripts [D] and [N] after words or phrases will be used as references for entries in the Selected Definitions (page 567) and Selected Proper Names (page 555), respectively.

Conclusion

While reading, the reader is strongly encouraged to investigate different translations, keeping in mind the following questions: Who is the author of the Qur'ān? And, is the Qur'ān in its current form without errors?

Introduction

The first sūra in the Qur'ān, al-Fātiḥa (Q 1), is known by a number of different names. Islāmic scholars list more than twenty, including these most familiar and prominent names:[1]

- *Fātiḥat al-Kitāb* ("The Opener of the Book")
- *Al-Sab' al-Mathānī*[D]
- *Um al-Qur'ān* ("The Mother of the Qur'ān")
- *Um al-Kitāb* ("The Mother of the Book")

Scholars disagree about the date of its revelation, an issue which will be examined further as we analyze this sūra.

The Kufan and Meccan schools[D] counted the Basmala (*"In the name of the merciful and compassionate God"*) as the first verse of Q 1. However, the Medinan school counted this opening phrase, the Basmala, as part of the first verse. On the other hand, al-Ḥassan al-Baṣrī (a well-known Muslim theologian and scholar) divided Q 1 into eight verses.[2]

Al-Fātiḥa is the only sūra which Muslims end its recitation with the word Āmīn (*Amen*).

1 In the name of the merciful and compassionate God.
2 Praise belongs to God, the Lord of the worlds,
3 the merciful, the compassionate,
4 the ruler of the day of judgment!
5 Thee we serve and Thee we ask for aid.
6 Guide us in the right path,
7 the path of those Thou art gracious to; not of those Thou art wroth with; nor of those who err.

Q 1.4

Different readings give varying meanings to the key word in this verse.

In addition to the meaning ***māliki*** (“**the ruler**”) found in the Qur'ān, there are other meanings given from different readings:

- *malik* (“king”): Al-Ṭabarī considers this meaning to be the most accurate among all the readings.[3]
- *malaka* (“owned”): The word is read as a verb in the past tense.[4]
- *malīk* (“master/owner”): This word carries a similar meaning to *māliki* (“the ruler”). However, al-ʿAkbarī says that *malīk* is more eloquent than *māliki*.[5]

Q 1.6

The most common reading is ***ihdinā*** (“**guide us**”). However, in the codex[D] of Ibn Masʿūd, the word *arshidnā* (“instruct us, show us”) is used.[6] In another reading, the word *baṣṣirnā* (“give us insight”) is used.[7]

The reading of the Qur'ān (*ihdinā* or “guide us”) asks Allah[D] to point out the right path. Whereas in the codex of Ibn Masʿūd, the use of *arshidnā* (“instruct us, show us”) indicates that the ones who are asking see themselves as being lost and wish to be delivered from their situation. The reading of *baṣṣirnā* (“give us insight”) is a request from the ones reciting it to Allah—to give them insight into all things.

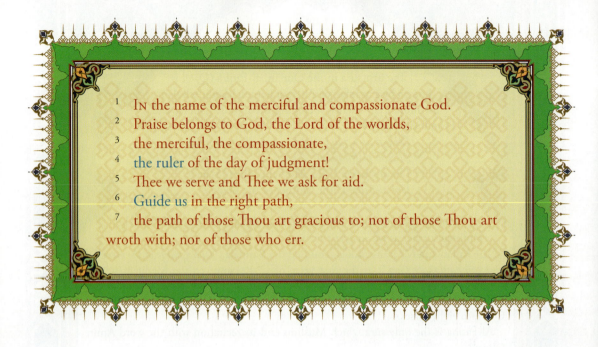

Q 1.1-7

In the Islāmic books that recount the history of the codices, records show that Ibn Mas'ūd refused to include Q 1, Q 113, and Q 114 in his codex of the Qur'ān, because he believed that these sūras were never intended to be a part of Islām's holiest text (the Qur'ān).

Ibn Mas'ūd[N], a profoundly influential person in the history of Islām who enjoyed the highest respect from both Sunnī and Shiite Muslims, resisted the efforts of 'Uthmān[N], the third caliph, to impose a uniform, written copy of the Qur'ān upon Muslims. Mas'ūd was also opposed to 'Uthmān's committee[D] and its leader, Zayd Ibn Thābit[N]. About him, Mas'ūd said, "I recited seventy sūras from the mouth of the messenger[D] of Allah when Zayd barely had two locks of hair and was playing with other boys." He also said, "I recited seventy sūras of the Qur'ān from the mouth of the messenger of Allah, while Zayd was still a boy. Do I then abandon what I received from the mouth of the messenger of Allah?"[8]

Ibn Mas'ūd did not include sūra al-Fātiḥa (Q 1) in his codex of the Qur'ān, as he did not consider it to be part of the Qur'ān.

Perhaps his primary reason was that Muḥammad described this passage as an incantation, or *al-ruqya* ("spell-removing prayers or chants"), not a sūra.[9] It is possible that Ibn Mas'ūd believed that describing a text as a *ruqya* no longer made it worthy of being included in the Qur'ān.

In addition, Ibn Mas'ūd could have further built his objection based upon other facts connected with this sūra. Q 1 is comprised of seven verses, including the opening Basmala[D]. Yet, despite its brevity, scholars are divided concerning the revelation date of this sūra. It was said that it was a Meccan sūra[D], while others believed it to be a Medinan sūra[D]. However, there is also a third opinion stating that this sūra was revealed to Muḥammad twice: once in Mecca[D] and once in Medina[D]. Parallel to this belief is yet another opinion that half of it was revealed in Mecca and the other half in Medina.[10]

The brevity of this sūra and the fact that it may have been revealed twice, or in two stages, undoubtedly had a profound influence upon Ibn Mas'ūd's opinion of sūra al-Fātiḥa (Q 1).

The general rule in the textual science of the Qur'ān states that short sūras were revealed in Mecca during the early stage of Islām. While it is held that this sūra was composed by Muḥammad for the first time in Mecca, it does not contain the Meccan language of this early stage. Instead, it has a unique structure. The sūra is actually used as a religious hymn, and when examined closely, can be seen to contain biblical phrases, such as the following examples:

- Q 1.2: *"Praise belongs to God...."* *Al-Ḥamdulillāh* in the Arabic text is similar to a Syriac phrase found in the New Testament of the Bible (Luke 1.68; 2 Cor. 1.3) and is often used in the Old Testament (example: Exod. 18.10). The phrase is also used with little variation in Hebrew liturgy.[11]
- Q 1.3: The name "the merciful" or *al-Raḥmān* in Arabic comes from a shared Semitic root רחם. In addition, it is used as one of the names of God in the Talmud רחמנא, the Targum, and the Palmyrian inscription[D]. This exact phrase exists in the Syriac language and was also mentioned in southern Arabic writing 𐩢𐩣𐩬𐩬 multiple times.[12] Moreover, the Islāmic historical sources report that Musaylima Ibn Ḥabīb[N], who also claimed to be a prophet during the time of Muḥammad, was preaching about *al-Raḥmān*.

After his migration to Medina, Muḥammad improved upon this hymn.[13] For this reason, some scholars formulated the opinion that this sūra was revealed twice, or in two stages.

It is possible to conclude that Muḥammad and his Companions[D] used to recite al-Fātiḥa during ceremonial rituals; Muḥammad did not regard it as part of the Qur'ān, and his Companions, such as Ibn Mas'ūd, were aware of this view. However, for reasons unknown to us, 'Uthmān's collection committee decided to include it in its official copy of the written Qur'ān. Ibn Mas'ūd, on the other hand, refused to comply and did not add this sura to his codex of the Qur'ān, because of his knowledge of the sūra's liturgical status. It is also possible that he intended to use his objection to weaken the credibility of the 'Uthmānic codex of the Qur'ān.

Question: Why did 'Uthmān's committee refuse to accept the opinion of a person with the religious stature of Ibn Mas'ūd by including a passage that he believed had no place in the written Qur'ān?

Q 1.6-7

During prayer, Muslims ask Allah to guide them to *"the right path."* In Arabic, this phrase implies that the petitioner is lost and cannot find the right path. Therefore, Allah is asked to guide the way to the correct path. According to Islāmic scholars, *"the right path"* could mean the Qur'ān, Islām, or paradise. Furthermore, Muslims believe that Islām is the true religion. They follow its teachings, glorify the Qur'ān, and believe that they are already guided to *"the right path"* and that heaven will be their future abode. Therefore, all the various definitions given by the Islāmic commentators cause the verse to be contradictory to Islāmic belief. If a Muslim already believes that he or she has found *"the right path,"* then why would Allah be repeatedly petitioned to help the believer find it?

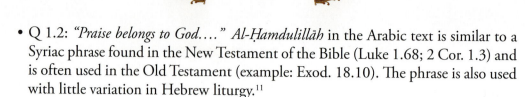

Guide Us to the Right Path

Without a doubt, al-Fātiḥa (Q 1) constitutes Muḥammad's prayer all his life, which is evidenced by the fact that his followers continued using it as well. The request of Muḥammad and his followers for guidance to the right path until the end of time is an astonishing mystery. On the other hand, the Book of Psalms includes thanks to *al-Raḥmān, al-Raḥīm* ("The Merciful, the Compassionate") for guiding Moses to His way (Psa. 102)....

The Merciful (*al-Raḥmān*): This biblical majestic name was used in the northern region of the Arabian Peninsula, especially in the southern part of it. Then the Qur'ān introduced it to the Ḥijāz region [...].[The two linguistic scholars] al-Mubarrid and Tha'lab say that the origin of this name is Hebrew and originally had the foreign sound of the guttural letter *kha.* The name was also referenced in the Hebrew and Syriac Torah and in the Talmud. Then it spread among the Arabs during the biblical call [to faith when the message of the Bible was brought to the Arab lands]....

Therefore, al-Fātiḥa, which is a supplication to Allah to guide his followers to the right path, is a biblical prayer both in letter and meaning. It is found in Psalms 47 and 148, which were repeatedly used in the prayers of the Jewish and Christian Arabs in Ḥijāz and Mecca.

The sixth and seventh verses were added to al-Fātiḥa in Medina after Muḥammad had become independent (established a separate religion) from the People of the Book. Al-Jalālayn said, "[*T*]*hose Thou art wroth with'* are the Jews, and *'those who err'* are the Christians [....]" Yet, al-Jalālayn and others have missed the point that the Qur'ān commands Muḥammad to follow in the footsteps of the Bible and its people (Q 6.90). How then would it describe them with such phrases?

Apart from the sixth and seventh verses, al-Fātiḥa is essentially a Meccan sūra. During the Meccan phase there was unity between Muslims and the People of the Book. At that time, Muḥammad also believed in what was revealed by God to the People of the Book (Q 42.15). This is why al-Bayḍāwī, in his commentary, declines to accept that "those Thou art wroth with" are the Jews, and "those who err" are the Christians. Rather, [he said], "'[T]hose Thou art wroth with' are the rebellious (stiff-necked) ones and 'those who err' are those who are ignorant about Allah.'"

(Excerpt from al-Ḥaddād, *Aṭwār al-Da'wa al-Qur'ānīya* 380)

Question: What is the purpose of praying this prayer if a Muslim already has been guided to the straight path (Islām)? To Muslims, is not the answer to this prayer already an established fact?

In the face of this dilemma, Muḥammad Ibn Abī Bakr Ibn 'Abd al-Qādir al-Rāzī (M. al-Rāzī) offers this comment about this verse: "[I]t means hold us steadfast on it [the right path] and keep us in this behavior, out of fear of a bad ending."[14] This statement does not resolve the contradiction mentioned above about this verse. The early Islāmic scholars also said that the phrase *"those Thou art gracious to"* is about Muslims; in other words, it is about Muḥammad and his Companions.[15] However, it is improbable and contradictory for Muḥammad to ask Allah to help him find the right path; he already believes himself to be walking on it.

It is illogical for Muḥammad and his Companions to ask Allah for the guidance of those upon whom Allah has bestowed his grace if they think they were the ones upon whom Allah has already bestowed his grace.

If we accept these Islāmic explanations, then the contradictions between these two verses become even stronger. Therefore, in order to understand these two verses (Q 1.6-7), we must understand their historical context.

When Muḥammad and his followers recited Q 1, the "Praise Hymn," in their minds they were thinking of a generation that preceded them, a generation whom they wanted to imitate. Al-Rāzī refers to this way of thinking in his commentary on the phrase, *"those Thou art gracious to,"* when he states, "It means, 'show us the right path of those upon whom you bestowed your grace before us [or before our time].' And those who preceded the Muslims of other nations did not have the Qur'ān or Islām." Then he adds, "The intent is, 'show us the right path of those truthful ones who deserved paradise.'"[16]

When we view these two verses according to this interpretation, the contradiction is clear. Muḥammad is asking Allah to put him on the path of those "who preceded Muslims of other nations"—that is, the People of the Book[D] (Jews and Christians). It appears that these two verses were from the Meccan part of Q 1. However, resolving the contradictions in these verses will create other contradictions in the Qur'ān. While Q 1 hails "those nations who preceded the Muslims," we find severe attacks against Jews and Christians within the Medinan portions of the Qur'ān, especially in Q 9.

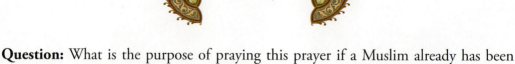

Introduction

Al-Baqara is the longest sūra in the Qur'ān. Named al-Baqara, ("The Cow"), it contains an account of Moses instructing the Israelites to offer a cow as a sacrifice to Allah (Q 2.67-71). This sūra addresses a wide variety of practical topics, including significant portions of Islāmic law. It retells stories of famous biblical characters such as Adam, Abraham, and Moses.

The sūra is classified as Medinan because it was revealed over the course of the first two years of the *Hijra*[D], Muḥammad's migration period (AH 1-2/AD 622-623). However, certain verses in this sūra belong to earlier and later periods. For example, Q 2.21-39 and the phrase *"O ye folk"* (verses 21 and 168) are believed to have been revealed while Muḥammad was in Mecca. After Muḥammad migrated to Medina, he began using a different phrase: *"O ye who believe!"* (Q 2.104).

On the other hand, there are other verses believed to have been revealed after the second year of Muḥammad's migration to Medina, such as these examples:

- Verse 114 was revealed c. AH 6/AD 627-628 (refers to the Treaty of Ḥudaybīya[D]).
- Verses 190-194 discuss the doctrine of *jihād*[D] after the Treaty of Ḥudaybīya.
- Verses 111-113 were revealed c. AH 9/AD 630-631 (deals with the year of delegations).

Moreover, verses 278-281 are believed to have been revealed during the last year of Muḥammad's life because they are connected to the "Farewell Pilgrimage[D]," performed by Muḥammad before his death. At the end of the sūra there is a condemnation of *riba* (usury).[1] The verses pertaining to usury are believed to be among the last verses revealed in the entire Qur'ān.

The composing of sūra al-Baqara, including the modifications and corrections, took more than eight years, from AH 1-8/AD 622-629.

Sūra al-Baqara addresses the following topics:

- **Legislation**—the major pilgrimage (Ḥajj), minor pilgrimage ('Umra), fasting, and *jihād*. The laws found in Q 2 were revealed early in Muḥammad's period in Medina. However, while gathering the written Qur'ān, many changes were inserted into Q 2 from different time periods. As a result, al-Baqara became the largest legislative sūra in the Qur'ān.[2]
- **Controversies**—criticism of, debates with, and incitements against the Jews (Q 2.83-105, 174-177) as well as other volatile issues occupy a large part of this sūra.
- **Politics**—criticism of Muḥammad's opponents in Medina (Q 2.206), who are labeled "the hypocrites."

In this sūra, Muḥammad introduces rituals, e.g., *qibla*, the pilgrimages, that some of his contemporaries questioned because they believed these rituals contained paganistic elements.

This sūra also contains stories originally found in biblical and rabbinical literature.[3]

In the name of the merciful and compassionate God.
1 A.L.M.
2 That is the book! there is no doubt therein; a guide to the pious,
3 who believe in the unseen, and are steadfast in prayer, and of what we have given them expend in alms;
4 who believe in what is revealed to thee, and what was revealed before thee, and of the hereafter they are sure.
5 These are in guidance from their Lord, and these are the prosperous.
6 Verily, those who misbelieve, it is the same to them if ye warn them or if ye warn them not, they will not believe.
7 God has set a seal upon their hearts and on their hearing; and

Q 2.1

The first verse of this sūra begins with individual letters of the alphabet called *muqaṭṭaʿāt*. They are also called *fawātiḥ*, or "openers," because they form the opening of multiple sūras. For a discussion about their possible origin and meaning, see the article *"Muqaṭṭaʿāt* (The Stand-alone Letters)" on page 107.

Q 2.3

In the Arabic text, the verb for *"expend in alms"* is related to the word *nafaqa*. However, Ibn al-Jawzī recorded four scholarly opinions on the meaning of the word *nafaqa* as used in the context of this verse:[4]

1. Spending on the family;
2. Giving the required alms or *zakāt*[D];
3. Giving a voluntary offering; and
4. Giving a required offering, called *nafaqa* (prior to the *zakāt* being mandated in Islām).

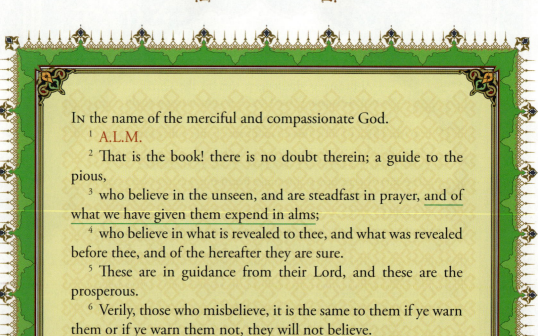

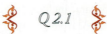

on their eyes is dimness, and for them is grievous woe.
8 And there are those among men who say, 'We believe in God
and in the last day;' but they do not believe.
9 They would deceive God and those who do believe; but they
deceive only themselves and they do not perceive.
10 In their hearts is a sickness, and God has made them still
more sick, and for them is grievous woe because they lied.
11 And when it is said to them, 'Do not evil in the earth,' they
say, 'We do but what is right.'
12 Are not they the evildoers? and yet they do not perceive.
13 And when it is said to them, 'Believe as other men believe,'
they say, 'Shall we believe as fools believe?' Are not they themselves
the fools? and yet they do not know.

One group of scholars ruled that a Muslim is required to keep enough finances on hand to cover his daily needs and then give the remainder away to the poor. Later, this requirement was abrogated, or annulled, with the verse that mandated the *zakāt*: *"Take from their wealth alms to cleanse and purify them thereby..."* (Q 9.103).

They explained that Q 9.103 abrogated all commandments regarding the giving of alms, just as the verses implementing the fast at Ramadan[D] abrogated all prior verses that governed fasting.[5]

Ibn al-Jawzī disagrees with this opinion because he believes that this verse encouraged spending. Therefore, he believes that this verse is not abrogated.[6]

Al-Naḥās, al-Makkī, and Ibn Ḥazm do not address the abrogation of this verse.

Q 2.7

Dimness is written in the current Arabic Qur'ān as ***ghishāwatun*** (literally "covering or veil"); however, the readers accent it differently: *ghushāwatun*, *ghishāwatan*, *ghashāwatan*, and *ghashāwatun*.[7] There is also a group of readers that read it with the

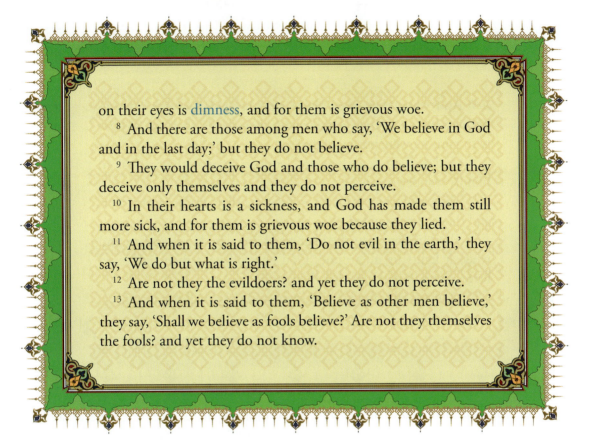

[14] And when they meet those who believe, they say, 'We do believe;' but when they go aside with their devils, they say, 'We are with you; we were but mocking!'
[15] God shall mock at them and let them go on in their rebellion, blindly wandering on.
[16] Those who buy error for guidance, their traffic profits not, and they are not guided.
[17] Their likeness is as the likeness of one who kindles a fire; and when it lights up all around, God goes off with their light, and leaves them in darkness that they cannot see.
[18] Deafness, dumbness, blindness, and they shall not return!

letter *'ain* instead of *ghain*: *'ashāwatun*. They disagree in its accenting here as well: *'ushāwatun*, *'ishāwatan*, *'ashāwatan*, and *'ashāwatun*.[8] Furthermore, some read it as *ghashwatun* and *ghashyatun*.[9]

Whether or not there is a difference in meaning (such as "covering" or "dimness in sight"), the interesting part about this word is that it has two readings: *ghishāwatun* and *'ashāwatun*, each having four forms of accenting. That means we have eight forms, in addition to the two readings, *ghashwatun* and *ghashyatun*. Hence, in the different codices' readings of the same verse, we have a total of ten forms of recitation for the one word.

Question: Which word did Jibril[N] give to Muḥammad?

Q 2.19

Some read the word ***ṣawā'iq*** ("**thunder-clap**") as *ṣawāqi'* ("thunder-clap"), according to the dialect of Tamīm and some of the branches of Rabi'a.[10] This difference shows that some of the readers altered the Qur'ānic words to agree with their local dialects. Such dialect alteration was similarly applied to *"but do not draw near this tree"* (Q 2.35), where the word ***shajara*** ("**tree**") is read by a group as *shiyara*. This latter version was

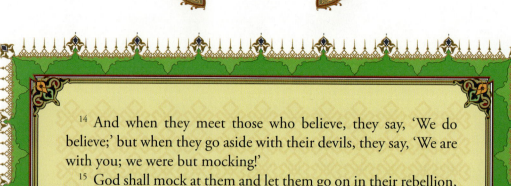

[19] Or like a storm-cloud from the sky, wherein is darkness and thunder and lightning; they put their fingers in their ears at the thunder-clap, for fear of death, for God encompasses the misbelievers.
[20] The lightning well-nigh snatches off their sight, whenever it shines for them they walk therein; but when it is dark for them they halt; and if God willed He would go off with their hearing and their sight; verily, God is mighty over all.
[21] O ye folk! serve your Lord who created you and those before you; haply ye may fear!

hated by some of the readers because it was an utterance "that is read with by the uncivilized of Mecca as well as its blacks."[11]

Question: Should a reading of the Qur'ān be hated and rejected because it is the reading of the blacks of Mecca?

Q 2.20

The word ***mashaw*** ("**walk**") in the current Arabic Qur'ān is written as *marrū* ("passed") in the codex of Ubayy Ibn Ka'b[N]. Further, in the codex of Ibn Mas'ūd, it is written *maḍaw* ("went").[12]

The three words that appear here do not have the same meaning. The verb *masha* indicates moving from one place to another on foot. The verb *marra* means "to go by, to pass." Further, the verb *maḍa* means "went," as in the Qur'ānic verse Q 15.65 *"but go on to where ye are bidden."*

These movement-indicating verbs mentioned in the readings—*masha*, *marra*, and *maḍa*—are not the same.

Question: Which verb is most precise?

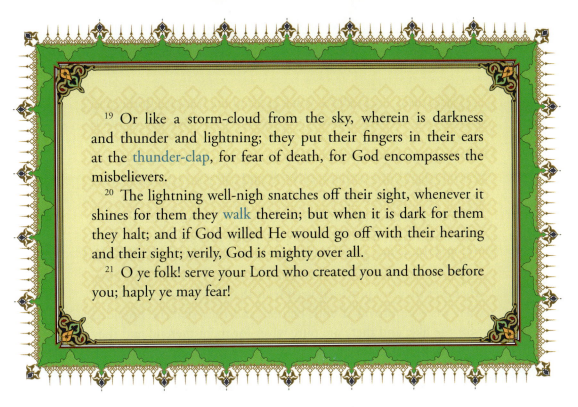

[22] who made the earth for you a bed and the heaven a dome; and
sent down from heaven water, and brought forth therewith fruits as
a sustenance for you; so make no peers for God, the while ye know!
[23] And if ye are in doubt of what we have revealed unto our
servant, then bring a chapter like it, and call your witnesses other
than God if ye tell truth.
[24] But if ye do it not, and ye shall surely do it not, then fear the
fire whose fuel is men and stones, prepared for misbelievers.
[25] But bear the glad tidings to those who believe and work
righteousness, that for them are gardens beneath which rivers flow;
whenever they are provided with fruit therefrom they say, 'This is
what we were provided with before,' and they shall be provided
with the like; and there are pure wives for them therein, and they
shall dwell therein for aye.

Q 2.22

In addition to the Qur'ānic reading of ***firāshan*** ("**bed**"), there are three other readings: *bisāṭan* ("rug"), *mihādan* ("resting place"), and *mahdan* ("cradle").[13]

The word *al-firāsh* means "a bedspread." The word *al-bisāṭ* means "all that is stretched out [on the floor]." The word *al-mihād* is a synonym of *al-firāsh*, whose plural is *muhūd*. However, the word *al-mahd* is an infant's bed, whose plural is *muhūd*.

All three words (*al-firāsh*, *al-bisāṭ*, *al-mihād*) have similar meanings. However, the word *al-mahd* is the farthest from the correct meaning because it has to do with the world of infancy. This variation in words is based on the readers' educational background.

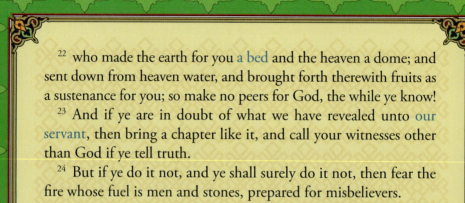

[26] Why, God is not ashamed to set forth a parable of a gnat, or anything beyond; and as for those who believe, they know that it is truth from the Lord; but as for those who disbelieve, they say, 'What is it that God means by this as a parable? He leads astray many and He guides many;'—but He leads astray only the evildoers;
[27] who break God's covenant after the fixing thereof, and cut asunder what God has ordered to be joined, and do evil in the earth;—these it is who lose.
[28] How can ye disbelieve in God, when ye were dead and He made you alive, and then He will kill you and then make you alive again, and then to Him will ye return?
[29] It is He who created for you all that is in the earth, then he made for the heavens and fashioned them seven heavens; and He knows all things.

Q 2.23

This verse was read in the plural as *'ibādina* ("our servants") and in the singular as ***'abdinā*** ("**our servant**"). Those who read it in the plural say that those addressed in the verse are Muḥammad and the Muslims. Those who read it in the singular said that it is only Muḥammad.[14]

Question: To whom is this revelation addressed? Is it meant for Muḥammad alone, or Muḥammad and the Muslims?

Q 2.25

The address is to Muḥammad, but some read it as *wa bushira* ("But they were given the glad tidings") in the passive past tense.[15] Therefore, the identity of the one giving glad tidings is not indicated. It could be Muḥammad or it could be another person.

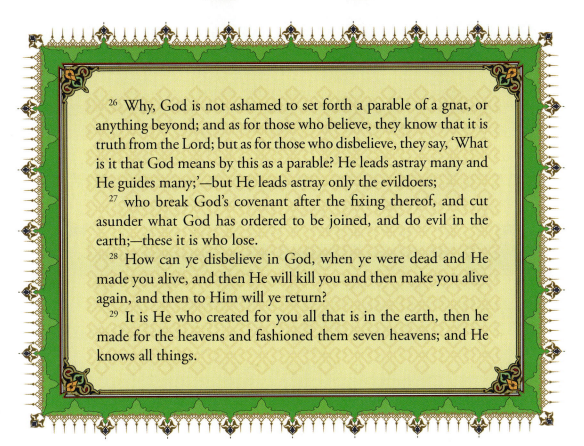

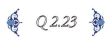

[30] And when thy Lord said unto the angels, 'I am about to place a vicegerent in the earth,' they said, 'Wilt Thou place therein one who will do evil therein and shed blood? we celebrate Thy praise and hallow Thee.' Said (the Lord), 'I know what ye know not.'

[31] And He taught Adam the names, all of them; then He propounded them to the angels and said, 'Declare to me the names of these, if ye are truthful.'

Q 2.30

This verse recounts Allah telling the angels that he was planning to create a human being, yet they replied with an implied objection, saying, "'*Wilt Thou place therein one who will do evil therein and shed blood?...*'" (Q 2.30).

The Qur'ānic commentaries confirm the implied objection of the angels. Al-Ṭabarī states, "[T]his report was from Allah, may His name be exalted, telling us that His angels, who said, '*Wilt Thou place therein one who will do evil therein and shed blood?*' were shocked to know that Allah, great is His praise, would make creatures that will disobey him, and were surprised to be told that this matter would take place."[16]

It is important to note that al-Ṭabarī also adds, "He [Allah] consulted with the angels regarding the creation of Adam."[17] This statement also appears in Ibn Kathīr's commentary, where he reports al-Suddī as saying, "He [Allah] consulted the angels concerning the creation of Adam."[18]

Therefore, this verse provides us with an image of Allah consulting with the angels, yet they are objecting. Al-Zamakhsharī, though a Mu'tazilite[D], declares that "'*Wilt Thou place therein...?*'" is a statement of surprise that the creation of obedience is going to be replaced by the creation of disobedience, "but He [Allah] is the all-wise, who does righteousness and wants nothing but righteousness."[19]

Question: How can Allah, the omniscient and the omnipotent, be glorified by consulting with angels? Is it reasonable that angels should advise or even rebuke what Allah does?

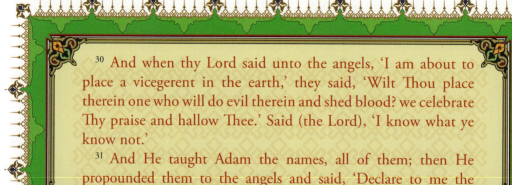

[32] They said, 'Glory be to Thee! no knowledge is ours but what
Thou thyself hast taught us, verily, Thou art the knowing, the wise.'
[33] Said the Lord, 'O Adam declare to them their names;' and
when he had declared to them their names He said, Did I not say
to you, I know the secrets of the heavens and of the earth, and I
know what ye show and what ye were hiding?'

Note: Most commentators explain that the angels' objection to Allah was due to their knowledge regarding what the humans were going to do—namely, disobey Allah—even though the angels are not omniscient. Hence, the commentators invented many interpretations of this verse to avoid any criticism.

Q 2.31 – 33

Verses 31–33 are a continuation of the conversation between Allah and the angels concerning the creation of man. These verses state that Allah taught Adam the names of *"all of them."* Then Allah asks the angels to repeat these names, *"'if ye are truthful.'"*

The commentary of al-Jalālayn explains the meaning of Allah's question to the angels, *"'if ye are truthful'"*:[20]

> Allah meant that He did not create someone who is more knowledgeable than the angels, nor that they [the angels] are eligible to become vicegerents. In saying this, Allah was making it clear to the angels that they were mistaken in their assumption, and that their knowledge is not superior: *"'Glory be to Thee! no knowledge is ours but what Thou thyself hast taught us, verily, Thou art the knowing, the wise'"* [Q 2.32], to which Allah would reply: *"'O Adam declare to them their names'"* [Q 2.33].

Regarding the statement in Q 2.31 that Allah *"taught Adam the names of all,"* some Islāmic scholars say that the names that Allah taught Adam were the names of the

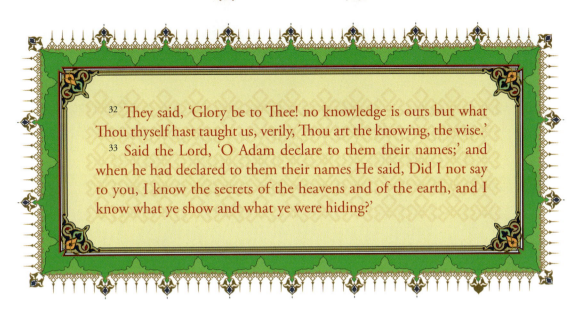

34 And when we said to the angels, 'Adore Adam,' they adored him save only Iblis, who refused and was too proud and became one of the misbelievers.

creatures. Others believe that they were the names of everything in the world. However, another group of scholars believe that they were the names of the angels. Still others reason that they were the names of Adam's descendents.

Another example of improper handling of the divine nature of Allah is found in the commentary of al-Ṭabarī:[21]

> 'Alī Ibn al-Ḥassan told us: narrated by [a man named] Muslim, who narrated from Muḥammad Ibn Muṣ'ab, who narrated from 'Āṣim Ibn Kulayib, who narrated from Sa'īd Ibn Ma'bad, who narrated from Ibn 'Abbās[N] concerning Allah's saying, "And He taught Adam the names of all things." He said: "Allah taught him the names of all things, including trifles, the corrupted and bad things, and the breaking of wind [flatulence]."

Q 2.34

In the Qur'ānic story of Creation, after man is brought into being, Allah tells the angels to lie prostrate before Adam. The angels obey except for Iblīs (the Devil), who refuses because he is too proud. In context, these verses do not provide an explanation regarding the nature of this command to bow down to Adam. Therefore, it is very surprising that this command comes from Allah.

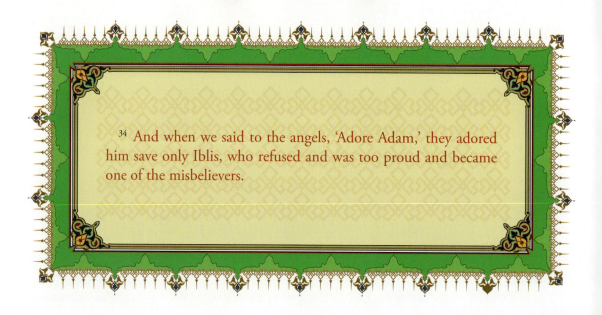

Two Contradictions

First, the act of bowing down to Adam is an act of worship, and worship of any being, except Allah, is a complete contradiction of the other teachings of the Qur'ān. Hence, this command portrays Allah as a god who condones idolatry, which contradicts the Qur'ānic description of Allah's divine nature.

Second, the verse says, *"And when we said to the angels, 'Adore Adam,' they adored him save only Iblis...."* It is clear that this command is directed to the angels. By the context of this verse it is also clear that Iblīs (the Devil) is considered to be of the same nature as the angels. Why then does he refuse to bow down, since the angels are described in the Qur'ān as those who *"disobey not God in what He bids them"* (Q 66.6)? Hence, this verse contradicts the Qur'ānic description of angels as obedient servants, which would have included Iblīs.

Muḥammad's Dilemma

How did Muḥammad fall into such contradictions as these?

Ample evidence confirms that Muḥammad heard many stories from the Bible via the oral traditions. However, it appears that he might not have learned them in an accurate manner. This faulty learning was either because he heard incomplete versions, or because he was introduced to them through erroneous versions of the Gospel. Therefore, Muḥammad included some of these accounts in the Qur'ān without confirming their accuracy.

It is possible that this account of the angel's prostration before Adam originated from Muḥammad's misunderstanding of a verse recorded in the New Testament of the Bible: "[W]hen God brings his firstborn into the world, he says, 'Let all God's angels worship him'" (Heb. 1.6). Conceivably, this verse may have made its way to Muḥammad, who then assumed it applied to Adam rather than Christ.

In conclusion, this misunderstanding could have logically resulted in this passage concerning the angels' prostration before Adam. Furthermore, similar misunderstandings might have also caused other contradictions in the Qur'ān regarding the nature of Iblīs (the Devil), which will be examined in other entries.

Note: The story of Iblīs is also mentioned in Q 7.11-19, Q 15.31-33, Q 17. 61-63, Q 18.50, Q 20.116-117, Q 38.71-86.

[35] And we said, 'O Adam dwell, thou and thy wife, in Paradise, and eat therefrom amply as you wish; but do not draw near this tree or ye will be of the transgressors.

Q 2.35

Allah said to Adam and his wife that they may eat whatever they desire in Eden but adds, *"...but do not draw near this tree, or ye will be of the transgressors"* (Q 2.35).

The use of the definite article *this* indicates that the hearers knew which tree the command is referencing. However, the identity of the tree is not known to any except the ones to whom the command was directed, Adam and his wife. Thus, despite the use of the definite article in the phrase *"this tree,"* the actual type of tree remains a mystery. Therefore, where is the clarity of the Qur'ān?

Since Islāmic commentaries recount stories of missing Qur'ānic verses, is it possible that this tree is mentioned in another verse but was omitted during the collection of the written Qur'ān? For instance, 'Ā'isha Bint Abī Bakr[N] (Muḥammad's third wife) states that Q 33 was two hundred verses long, "but when 'Uthmān assembled the Qur'ān in writing we only received of it the portion we have now."[22] Today, Q 33 comprises only seventy-three verses, which means that after 'Uthmān assembled the written Qur'ān, 127 verses were lost or removed.

The Tree According to Islāmic Scholars

In their efforts to resolve this mystery, the Islāmic scholars offer different interpretations concerning the tree mentioned in this verse. The commentary of Ibn Kathīr suggests these interpretations:[23]

- **Corn Shoot:** "Each bean of it was the size of a cow's kidney, sweeter than honey, and softer than butter."
- **Wheat Plant**
- **Vine:** This interpretation is another reason given for the prohibition of wine in Islām.
- **Fig Tree**
- **Supernatural Tree:** A tree with special fruit that the angels ate to remain immortal. The scholar who offered this interpretation then added that "it is the fruit which Allah forbade Adam and his wife from eating."

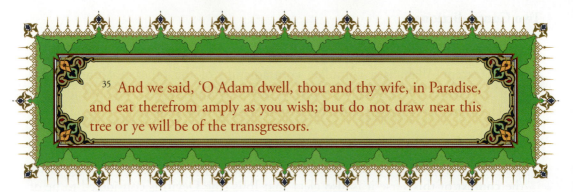

[36] And Satan made them backslide therefrom and drove them out from what they were in, and we said, 'Go down, one of you the enemy of the other, and in the earth there is an abode and a provision for a time.'

[37] And Adam caught certain words from his Lord, and He turned towards him, for He is the compassionate one easily turned.

[38] We said, 'Go down therefrom altogether and haply there may come from me a guidance, and whoso follows my guidance, no fear is theirs, nor shall they grieve.

[39] But those who misbelieve, and call our signs lies, they are the fellows of the Fire, they shall dwell therein for aye.'

[40] O ye children of Israel! remember my favours which I have favoured you with; fulfil my covenant and I will fulfil your covenant; me therefore dread.

Q 2.36

Most readers read this phrase as ***fa-azallahumā*** ("[Satan] **made them backslide**"). However, there are those who read it as *fa-azallahum* in the plural, instead of the dual form[D] above. Others read it as *fa-azālahumā* ("he removed them [dual]") from the verb *zāla*.[24] Ibn Mas'ūd, on the other side, adds a completely different word: *fa-waswasa lahumā* ("he [Satan] whispered to them").[25]

We observe here a significant difference in meaning regarding Satan's participation depending on the reading: *fa-azallahumā* ("[Satan] made them backslide") and *fa-azallahum,* meaning "he made them fall into sin." But, *fa-azālahumā* ("he removed them") comes from "removing," meaning "he removed them."

On the other hand, Ibn Mas'ūd writes a completely different word, which is *waswasa* ("he [Satan] whispered"). These variances prove that the writing of the Qur'ān was subject to the understanding of the different readers.

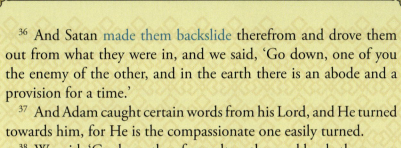

[41] Believe in what I have revealed, verifying what ye have got,
and be not the first to disbelieve in it, and do not barter my signs
for a little price, and me do ye fear.
[42] Clothe not truth with vanity, nor hide the truth the while ye know.
[43] Be steadfast in prayer, give the alms, and bow down with
those who bow.
[44] Will ye order men to do piety and forget yourselves? ye read
the Book, do ye not then understand?
[45] Seek aid with patience and prayer, though it is a hard thing
save for the humble,
[46] who think that they will meet their Lord, and that to Him
will they return.
[47] O ye children of Israel! remember my favours which I have
favoured you with, and that I have preferred you above the
worlds.
[48] Fear the day wherein no soul shall pay any recompense for
another soul, nor shall intercession be accepted for it, nor shall
compensation be taken from it, nor shall they be helped.
[49] When we saved you from Pharoah's people who sought to

Q 2.46

Most readers declare this phrase as ***yaẓunnūna*** ("[they] **think**"). However, Ibn Mas'ūd reads it as *ya'lamūna* ("[they] know").[26] There is an obvious difference between thinking or guessing and knowing. To think or guess expresses doubt, whereas to know something is certain.

Q 2.48

Instead of the current Arabic Qur'ān's ***nafsun*...*nafsin*** ("**soul...soul**"), Abū al-Sirrar al-Ghanawi read this verse as *nasamatun*...*nasamatin* ("a person [or soul]...a person [or soul]").[27] It is true that substituting *nafsin* with *nasmatin* does not change the meaning,

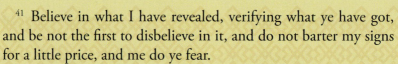

wreak you evil and woe, slaughtering your sons and letting your
women live; in that was a great trial for you from your Lord.
50 When we divided for you the sea and saved you and drowned
Pharoah's people while ye looked on.
51 When we treated with Moses forty nights, then ye took the
calf after he had gone and ye did wrong.
52 Yet then we forgave you after that; perhaps ye may be grateful.
53 And when we gave Moses the Scriptures and the
Discrimination; perhaps ye will be guided.
54 When Moses said to his people, 'O my people! Ye have
wronged yourselves in taking this calf; repent unto your Creator
and kill each other; that will be better for you in your Creator's
eyes; and He turned unto you, for He is the compassionate one
easily turned.'
55 And when ye said to Moses, 'O Moses! we will not believe in
thee until we see God manifestly,' and the thunderbolt caught you
while ye yet looked on.
56 Then we raised you up after your death; perhaps ye may be
grateful.

but it seems that Abū al-Sirrār read according to a formulation that he considered clearer in meaning.[28]

Q 2.55

This verse describes a scene from Moses' journey with the Israelites in the wilderness after leaving Egypt. According to al-Ṭabarī's commentary, prior to this response from Moses (verse 55), he was with a group of Jewish people who had said to him: "O Moses, we will not believe you or endorse what you have revealed to us until we see Allah, eye to eye, by removing the barrier between us and him, and by removing the cover that separates us so that we can see him with our eyes."[29] Then, Allah responds to their request with a deadly thunder.

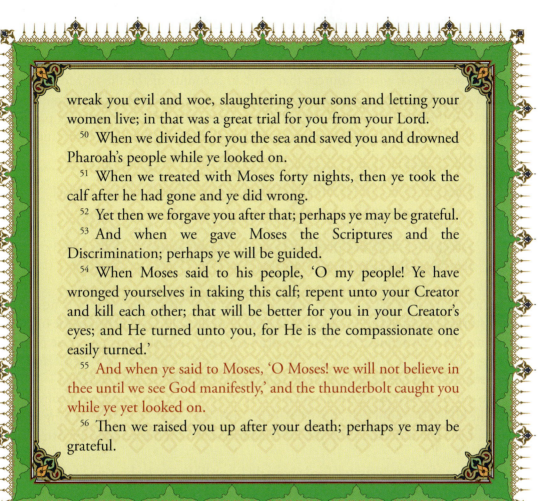

Who are the people mentioned in this verse (Q 2.55)?

The commentators offer different interpretations concerning the identity of this group. However, al-Rāzī states decisively that this group is "the chosen seventy."[30]

When we go back to the sources that contain accounts of the life of Moses, none confirms the version of the account found in this verse (Q 2.55). In addition, we do not find in the Old Testament of the Bible any mention of this event. It is possible that the Qur'ānic account is a corrupted version of a story in the Bible concerning the coming of the Spirit of the Lord upon the seventy elders:

> Moses and Aaron, Nadab and Abihu, and the seventy elders of Israel went up and saw the God of Israel. Under his feet was something like a pavement made of sapphire, clear as the sky itself. But God did not raise his hand against these leaders of the Israelites; they saw God, and they ate and drank. (Exod. 24.9-11)

The account found in Q 2.55 of the Jews requesting to *"see God manifestly"* contradicts the historical record of the Torah[D] (first five books of the Old Testament). In the biblical account, the Jews request that Moses speak to them, and they express their fear of having God speak to them directly. They say to Moses, "Speak to us yourself and we will listen. But do not have God speak to us or we will die" (Exod. 20.19).

As to the thunder, it seems Muḥammad was not aware that this version was inconsistent with the biblical account, which separates these two occasions—God's appearing to the elders of Israel and the fire from the Lord coming down on the people—by two years:

> Now the people complained about their hardships in the hearing of the Lord, and when he heard them, his anger was aroused. Then fire from the Lord burned among them and consumed some of the outskirts of the camp. (Num. 11.1)

It seems that this Qur'ānic account might have confused and combined the coming of the Spirit of the Lord "upon the seventy elders" as a deadly thunder, as mentioned in Exodus 20.19. The likely reason for this confusion is that Muḥammad had been exposed to incomplete information and accounts from the surrounding Jewish and Christian tribes.

Furthermore, the Qur'ān's detailing of the Jews' request to *"see God manifestly"* most likely did not stem from Muḥammad's ignorance of the actual biblical account but from a deliberate change. The primary intent of this change was to lessen the influence of the Jews among the Muslims. Q 2 is one of the Medinan sūras. When Muḥammad was in Medina, it became obvious to him that it would be impossible to convince the Jews that he was a prophet[D].

[57] And we overshadowed you with the cloud, and sent down the manna and the quails; 'Eat of the good things we have given you.' They did not wrong us, but it was themselves they were wronging.
[58] And when we said, 'Enter this city and eat therefrom as plentifully as ye wish; and enter the gate worshipping and say 'hi*tt*atun. So will we pardon you your sins and give increase unto those who do well.'
[59] But those who did wrong changed it for another word than that which was said to them: and we sent down upon those who did wrong, wrath from heaven for that they had so sinned.

In a similar scenario recorded in Q 4, Muḥammad responds to the Jews' request for evidence regarding his claim of prophethood by saying that their arguments with him would expose them to Allah's judgment. Then Muḥammad recites a verse to them that is almost identical to Q 2.55: *"but they asked Moses a greater thing than that, for they said, 'Show us God openly;' but the thunderbolt caught them in their injustice"* (Q 4.153).

Al-Rāzī raises another question in his commentary concerning Q 2.55:[31]

> Why did they [the Jews] deserve to die, since they have repented from their apostasy and the one who repents from his apostasy should not be killed? The answer to this question has to do with the differences in the Laws. It is possible that the Law of Moses...commanded the death of the one who has repented, whether in general, concerning the rights of all people, or in particular, concerning that group.

Question: Does al-Rāzī's attempted solution effectively answer the question?

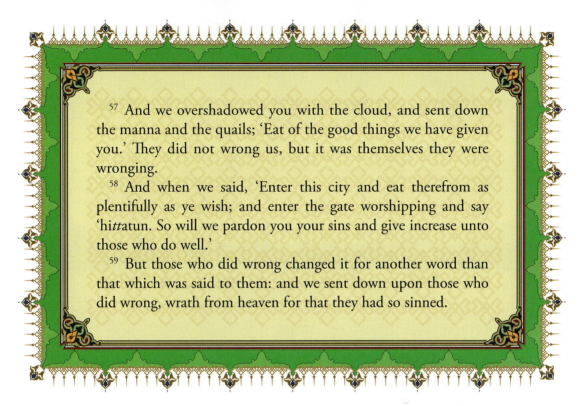

[60] When Moses, too, asked drink for his people and we said, 'Strike with thy staff the rock,' and from it burst forth twelve springs; each man among them knew his drinking place. 'Eat and drink of what God has provided, and transgress not on the earth as evildoers.'

[61] And when they said, 'O Moses, we cannot always bear one kind of food; pray then thy Lord to bring forth for us of what the

Q 2.60

The verse informs us that Moses sought to find a water source for his people. The Lord commanded him to strike *"the rock"* with his staff. The rock split and *"and from it burst forth twelve springs"* (Q 2.60; Q 7.160).

The verse mixes together two biblical incidents. In the first incident, Moses went with the sons of Israel to "Elim, where there were twelve springs" (Exod. 15.27). In the second incident, Moses struck a rock (while he was in Horeb) and water—though not twelve springs—gushed out of it (Exod. 15.27). (See the Old Testament book of Exodus, chapters 15 and 17.)

Q 2.61

The Old Testament mentions that as the people of Israel were running away from Pharaoh and his soldiers, they arrived at the edge of the sea, where they could go no further. There, in the depth of their despair, they said to Moses, "It would have been better for us to serve the Egyptians than to die in the desert!" (Exod. 14.12). However, when the Qur'ān retells this account, it contradicts the story by saying that the children of Israel beg Moses to ask Allah to bring forth *"of what the earth grows, its green herbs, its cucumbers, its garlic, its lentils, and its onions…"* (Q 2.61).

The verse levels another accusation against the Jews by saying they were being punished because they *"…kill the prophets"* without specifying the names of the prophets. What is unusual is that the great exegetical scholars do not make any concerted efforts to find the identity of these prophets. However, the commentary of al-Jalālayn mentions Yaḥyā (John the Baptist), son of Zakarīyā (Zechariah), as one of those slain prophets.[32]

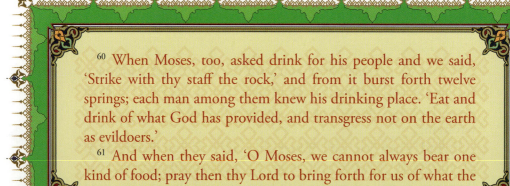

earth grows, its green herbs, its cucumbers, its garlic, its lentils, and its onions.' Said he, 'Do ye ask what is meaner instead of what is best? Go down to Egypt,—there is what ye ask.' Then were they smitten with abasement and poverty, and met with wrath from God. That was because they had misbelieved in God's signs and killed the prophets undeservedly; that was for that they were rebellious and had transgressed.

Thus, the commentary unintentionally supports a corrupted history, initiated by the Qur'ān, because John the Baptist was not even a contemporary of Moses. In fact, he was born centuries later.

Two Linguistic Comments

First, we read in the verse *"...killed the prophets undeservedly."* The phrase *"undeservedly"* confuses the alert reader of the Qur'ān. How is a prophet deservedly slain? That conundrum is why many exegetes neglect to mention this phrase. However, some of them address it briefly, such as the following example:[33]

> ..."without just cause": to magnify the awfulness of the crime that they committed. It is common knowledge that a prophet is not slain with just cause; however, in case one was to imagine that possibility, [the Qur'ān] says: "without just cause," concerning the obvious awfulness of the crime.

Question: Is this comment considered a sufficient or conclusive response?

Second, the verse states *"of what the earth grows, its green herbs,... its onions...."* The Arabic word that the translators of the Qur'ān render as "onions" in English is *fūm*. The exegetes offer two meanings for this word:

- **The first opinion:** is that *fūm* means "wheat" and is a reference to bread. The exegetes further explained the word means all kinds of grains. The readers say, "[I]t is an old language whose speakers say: *'Fūmū*, meaning to make bread.'"[34]

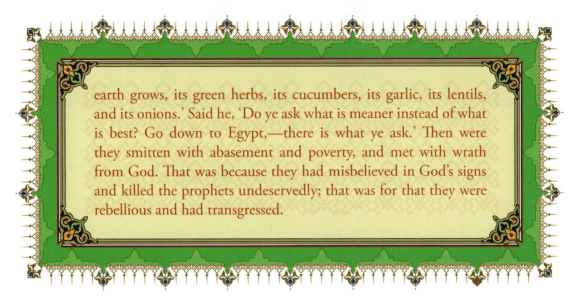

[62] Verily, whether it be of those who believe, or those who are Jews or Christians or Sabaeans, whosoever believe in God and the last day and act aright, they have their reward at their Lord's hand, and there is no fear for them, nor shall they grieve.

- **The second opinion:** holds that *fūm* is *thūm*, the Arabic word for garlic. There is a Qur'ānic reading of Ibn Mas'ūd that says the verse using *thūmhā* instead of the current word now in the Qur'ān, *fūmhā*.[35]

Question: If the Qur'ān offers clear guidance, why do the exegetes not know the exact meaning of these words?

Q 2.62

This verse puts the Jews, Christians, Sabaeans[D], and Muslims into one group (the believers in Allah) and promises them their reward at the end of time (Q 2.62). Another verse, Q 5.69, repeats this promise word for word. However, if we continue to read Q 5, we find that the Qur'ān accuses the Christians of blasphemy and threatens them with hellfire (Q 5.72-73). In another verse, the circle of those who are bound for hellfire becomes even larger, including all who do not embrace Islām: *"Whosoever craves other than Islām for a religion, it shall surely not be accepted from him, and he shall, in the next world, be of those who lose"* (Q 3.85).

Question: What then is the destiny of the Jews, Christians, and Sabaeans, according to the Qur'ān: paradise or hellfire?

Q 2.62

Islāmic scholars issued a variety of opinions regarding the identity of those listed in this verse. Ibn al-Jawzī records the following opinions:[36]

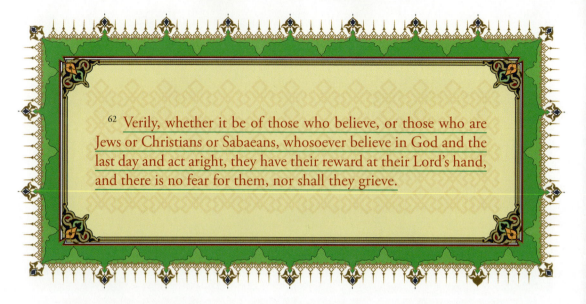

[63] And when we took a covenant with you and held the mountain over you; 'Accept what we have brought you with strong will, and bear in mind what is therein, haply ye yet may fear.'
[64] Then did ye turn aside after this, and were it not for God's grace towards you and His mercy, ye would have been of those who lose.

A. First Opinion
   1. *"Those who believe"* refers to the Muslims;
   2. *"those who are Jews"* ("those who follow the Jewish") refers to the Jews;
   3. *"Christians"* (*al-Nassara* [*Nazarene*]) refers to the Christians;
   4. *"the Sabaeans"* refers to those who embrace Islām; and
   5. *"any who believe"* refers to those who remain in the faith (Islām).

B. Second Opinion
   1. *"Those who believe"* refers to people who only declare Islām outwardly (hypocrites);
   2. *"those who are Jews"* ("those who follow the Jewish") refers to the Jews;
   3. *"Christians"* (*al-Nassara* [*Nazarene*]) refers to the Christians;
   4. *"the Sabaeans"* refers to a category of unbelievers called the *kuffār*[D]*;* and
   5. *"any who believe"* refers to those who embrace Islām.

C. Third Opinion
   This verse refers to Muslims and any of those who embrace Islām from the aforementioned categories.

Scholars also disagree on the abrogation of this verse.

One group believes that this verse is abrogated by Q 3.85: *"Whosoever craves other than Islām for a religion, it shall surely not be accepted from him…."*[37]

Another group of scholars believes that the meaning of this verse is conserved. "For it is a *khabar* [report] from Allah, about what he does with his servants, those who were following their own religion before Islām."[38] A *khabar* "does not get abrogated."[39]

Al-Naḥās does not comment on the abrogation of this verse.

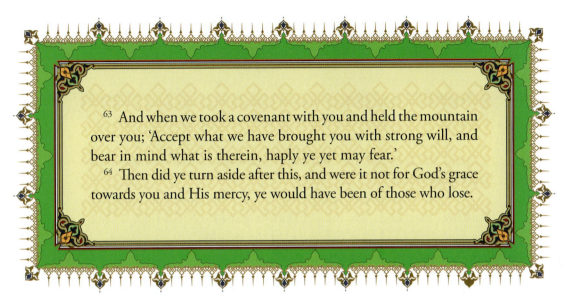

[65] Ye know too of those among you who transgressed upon the Sabbath, and we said, 'Become ye apes, despised and spurned.'
[66] Thus we made them an example unto those who stood before them, and those who should come after them, and a warning unto those who fear.
[67] And when Moses said to his people, 'God bids you slaughter a cow,' they said, 'Art thou making a jest of us?' Said he, 'I seek refuge with God from being one of the unwise.'

Q 2.65

This verse tells about the residents of a Jewish village who break the sanctity of the Sabbath. The exegetes explain that these Jews defiled the Sabbath by fishing on that day, *"so Allah metamorphosed them into monkeys because of their disobedience."*[40]

The scholars of Islām discussed the destiny of those who were metamorphosed, as to whether they lived or perished. They arrived at two different opinions:

- **The first opinion:** states that the Jews lived and multiplied. It further states that the current monkeys may have descended from them.
- **The second opinion:** which is supported by the bulk of Muslim scholars, states that a metamorphosed being does not beget. The group that metamorphosed perished after three days. It is told that Ibn 'Abbās was a supporter of this opinion. He states, "No metamorphosed being ever lived beyond three days, for it does not eat, drink, or beget."[41]

Al-Rāzī considers both opinions "reasonably possible," but he leans towards Ibn 'Abbās' view that they perished after three days.[42]

This tale is not found in any other reference except for the Qur'ān. No other historical books mention it.

Question: Why then does the Qur'ān weave this myth?

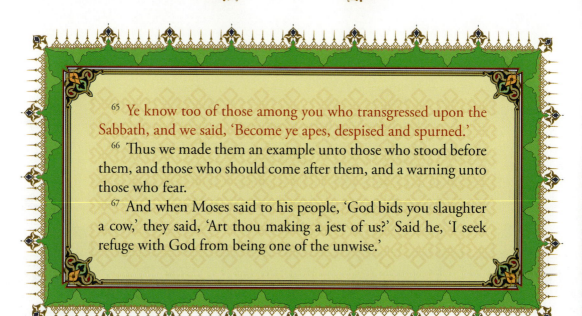

[68] They said, 'Then pray thy Lord for us to show us what she is to be.' He answered, 'He saith it is a cow, nor old, nor young, of middle age between the two; so do as ye are bid.'
[69] They said, 'Pray now thy Lord to show us what her colour is to be.' He answered, 'He saith it is a dun cow, intensely dun, her colour delighting those who look upon her.'
[70] Again they said, 'Pray thy Lord to show us what she is to be; for cows appear the same to us; then we, if God will, shall be guided.'

To answer this question, we must look at the intent of the verse. Its objective was to plant fear in the heart of the Jews of Medina so that they would follow Muḥammad. The verse even declares that Allah does not only turn that village population into monkeys but into the lowest kind of monkeys: "*'Become ye apes, despised and spurned.'*"

A classical exegete understands the objective of the tale:[43]

> That it would be as if the Almighty, when he told them about how he dealt with the Sabbath-breakers, was telling them, "Don't you fear that the suffering that befell them would befall you because of your rebelliousness? Do not be deceived by the respite extended to you!"

In conclusion, the verse's purpose is to terrorize the Jews of Medina. This purpose was an earthly goal of Muḥammad, which prompted him to weave this story.

Q 2.70

The reading of most readers is ***baqar*** ("**cows**"). However, there are those who read this as *bāqir* ("the group of cows with their shepherds").[44]

Question: Does the verse mean that the cows only looked alike to the Jews, or was it both the cows and their shepherds?

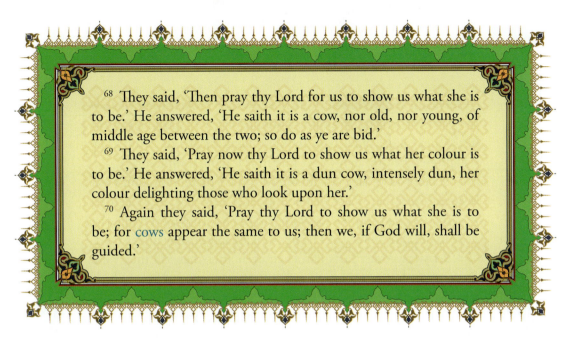

[71] He answered, 'He saith, it is a cow, not broken in to plough
the earth or irrigate the tilth, a sound one with no blemish on
her.' They said, 'Now hast thou brought the truth.' And they
slaughtered her, though they came near leaving it undone.
[72] When too ye slew a soul and disputed thereupon, and God
brought forth that which ye had hidden,
[73] then we said, 'Strike him with part of her.' Thus God brings the
dead to life and shows you His signs, that haply ye may understand.
[74] Yet were your hearts hardened even after that, till they were
as stones or harder still, for verily of stones are some from which
streams burst forth, and of them there are some that burst asunder
and the water issues out, and of them there are some that fall
down for fear of God; but God is never careless of what ye do.
[75] Do ye crave that they should believe you when already a sect

Q 2.71

The phrase ***fa-dhabaḥūhā*** (“**they slaughtered her**”) in the current Arabic Qur'ān is rendered in the codex of Ibn Mas'ūd as *fa-naḥarūhā* (“they cut her jugular vein”).[45] Though there might not be a real difference between the meanings of *fa-dhabaḥūhā* and *fa-naḥarūhā*, the difference presented proves that linguistic taste plays a part in the writing of the codices.

Another example of these linguistic differences is shown in the verse, *“Or every time they make a covenant, will a part of them repudiate it?”* (Q 2.100). There, the word ***nabadhahu*** (“**repudiate it**”) is used, whereas the codex of Ibn Mas'ūd reads *naqaḍahu* (“abolished or broke it”).[46]

of them have heard the word of God and then perverted it after
they had understood it, though they knew?
76 And when they meet those who believe they say, 'We believe,'
but when one goes aside with another they say, 'Will ye talk to
them of what God has opened up to you, that they may argue with
you upon it before your Lord? Do ye not therefore understand?'
77 Do they not then know that God knoweth what they keep
secret and what they make known abroad?
78 And some of them there are, illiterate folk, that know not the
Book, but only idle tales; for they do but fancy.
79 But woe to those who write out the Book with their hands
and say 'this is from God;' to buy therewith a little price! and woe
to them for what their hands have written, and woe to them for
what they gain!

Q 2.75

Most readers read this phrase according to the current Arabic Qur'ān as ***afataṭmā'ūna*** ("**Do ye crave**"). However, some of them read it as *afayaṭmā'ūna* ("do they crave") in the third person.[47]

In the Qur'ān, the reading is in the second person, but the variant reading is in the third person. This variance means the readers differed in their determination of who is being addressed. Are the addressed "you" or "they"? Such an issue appears in the Qur'ān quite often. Several similar examples can be found in Q 2:

- *"Do they not then know that God knoweth"* (Q 2.77); some read this pronoun in the second person, "Know you not...."[48]
- *"Do ye say that Abraham..."* (Q 2.140); some read it as "Do they say that Abraham...."[49]
- "And Allah is not unaware of what they do" (Pickthall trans. Q 2.144); some readers read it as "And Allah is not unaware of what ye do...."[50]
- *"God is not careless of that which ye do"* (Q 2.149); others read it as "God is not careless of that which they do."[51]

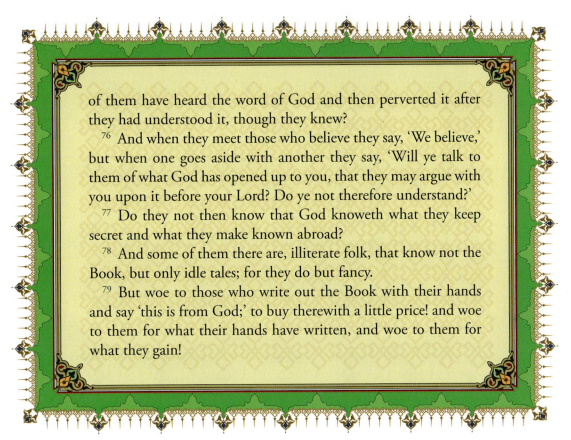

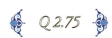

[80] And then they say, 'Hell fire shall not touch us save for a
number of days.' Say, 'Have ye taken a covenant with God?' but
God breaks not His covenant. Or do ye say of God that which ye
do not know?
[81] Yea! whoso gains an evil gain, and is encompassed by his sins,
those are the fellows of the Fire, and they shall dwell therein for aye!
[82] But such as act aright, those are the fellows of Paradise, and
they shall dwell therein for aye!
[83] And when we took from the children of Israel a covenant,
saying, 'Serve ye none but God, and to your two parents show
kindness, and to your kindred and the orphans and the poor, and
speak to men kindly, and be steadfast in prayer, and give alms;'

Q 2.81

There are two opinions concerning the abrogation of this verse. Some scholars believe that its meaning is abrogated, while another group believes its meaning is conserved.

Scholars who interpret the word *evil* as "the sins that one gets punished for," consider this verse abrogated by Q 4.48: *"Verily, God pardons not associating aught with Him, but He pardons anything short of that to whomsoever He pleases...."*[52] This verse clarifies that Allah can forgive any sin except the sin of idolatry.

However, the scholars who define the phrase *"an evil"* (as found in Q 2.81) as meaning idolatry, believe that this verse is not abrogated.[53] According to their ruling, Q 4.48 is merely a restatement of Q 2.81.

Q 2.83

Because of this phrase, *"and speak to men kindly,"* Islāmic scholars disagree on the abrogation of this verse. Some believe its meaning is abrogated, while others believe that its meaning is conserved.

and then ye turned back, save a few of you, and swerved aside.
84 And when we took a covenant from you, 'shed ye not your kinsman's blood, nor turn your kinsmen out of their homes:' then did ye confirm it and were witnesses thereto.
85 Yet ye were those who slay your kinsmen and turn a party out of their homes, and back each other up against them with sin and enmity. But if they come to you as captives ye ransom them!— and yet it is as unlawful for you to turn them out. Do ye then believe in part of the Book and disbelieve in part? But the reward of such among you as do that shall be nought else but disgrace in this worldly life, and on the day of the resurrection shall they be driven to the most grievous torment, for God is not unmindful of what ye do.

One group of scholars believe this phrase represents a call for peace, as it urges Muslims to speak kindly or politely to non-Muslims.

These scholars ruled that this verse is abrogated because they hold that every call for peace found in the Qur'ān is abrogated by Q 9.5: *"...kill the idolaters wherever ye may find them...."*[54]

A second group ruled that it is conserved and based its decision on the phrase *"to men."* This group believes that this phrase obligates a person to speak to others in an appropriate manner.[55] A member of this group, al-Naḥās, ruled that the meaning of this verse is conserved "because the verse means invite them to Allah as in Q 16.125, *"Call unto the way of thy Lord with wisdom and goodly warning...."*[56]

This opinion of al-Naḥās did not find favor with another Muslim scholar, al-Makkī, who said that even though the meaning of the verse is conserved, it includes "the promotion of virtue and the prevention of vice."[57]

"[S]peak to men kindly" means that you must speak to people in a way that is appropriate to the occasion; if what is being promoted is good, condone it, but if what is being promoted is evil, then condemn it.

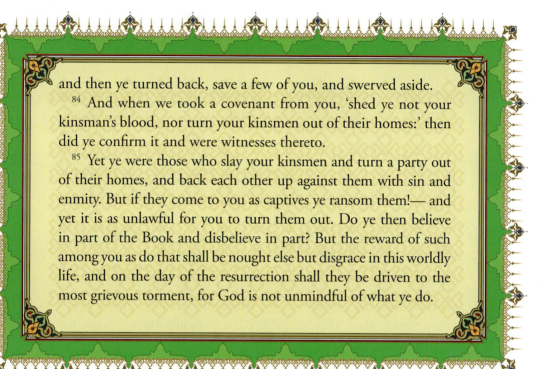

86 Those who have bought this worldly life with the Future, the
torment shall not be lightened from them nor shall they be helped.
87 We gave Moses the Book and we followed him up with other
apostles, and we gave Jesus the son of Mary manifest signs and
aided him with the Holy Spirit. Do ye then, every time an apostle
comes to you with what your souls love not, proudly scorn him,
and charge a part with lying and slay a part?
88 They say, 'Our hearts are uncircumcised;' nay, God has cursed
them in their unbelief, and few it is who do believe.
89 And when a book came down from God confirming what
they had with them, though they had before prayed for victory
over those who misbelieve, yet when that came to them which
they knew, then they disbelieved it,—God's curse be on the
misbelievers.
90 For a bad bargain have they sold their souls, not to believe
in what God has revealed, grudging because God sends down of
His grace on whomsoever of His servants He will; and they have
brought on themselves wrath after wrath and for the misbelievers
is there shameful woe.
91 And when they are told to believe in what God has revealed,
they say, 'We believe in what has been revealed to us;' but they
disbelieve in all beside, although it is the truth confirming what
they have. Say, 'Wherefore did ye kill God's prophets of yore if ye
were true believers?'
92 Moses came to you with manifest signs, then ye took up with
the calf when he had gone and did so wrong.
93 And when we took a covenant with you and raised the
mountain over you, 'Take what we have given you with resolution
and hear;' they said, 'We hear but disobey;' and they were made to
drink the calf down into their hearts for their unbelief. Say, 'An evil
thing is it which your belief bids you do, if ye be true believers.'
94 Say, 'If the abode of the future with God is yours alone and

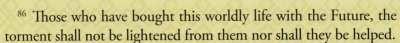

not mankind's: long for death then if ye speak the truth.'
95 But they will never long for it because of what their hands
have sent on before; but God is knowing as to the wrong doers.
96 Why, thou wilt find them the greediest of men for life; and
of those who associate others with God one would fain live for a
thousand years,—but he will not be reprieved from punishment
by being let live, for God seeth what they do.
97 Say, 'Who is an enemy to Gabriel?' for he hath revealed to
thy heart, with God's permission, confirmation of what had been
before, and a guidance and glad tidings to believers.
98 Who is an enemy to God and His angels and His apostles and
Gabriel and Michael?—Verily, God is an enemy to the unbelievers.

Q 2.97

This verse states that the angel Gabriel (Jibrīl[D]) is the one who transmitted the Qur'ān to Muḥammad. However, another Qur'ānic text states that the Holy Spirit is the one who carried out this task: *"Say, 'The Holy Spirit brought it down from thy Lord…'"* (Q 16.102). Yet a third verse, in Q 26, identifies *"the Faithful Spirit came down with it"* as the one responsible for transmitting the Qur'ān (Q 26.193).

Because Islāmic literature seeks to spread the viewpoint that the Holy Spirit is Gabriel, this might not seem like a contradiction. However, the reality is that the name "Holy Spirit" appears in the Qur'ān only four times. Three of these times, the Holy Spirit is associated with Christ, as in this verse: *"we gave Jesus the son of Mary manifest signs and aided him with the Holy Spirit"* (Q 2.87). This verse is repeated word for word in verse Q 2.253 and is stated in a similar way in Q 5.110.

Concerning the meaning of the Holy Spirit, scholarly sources say that he, or it, could be Gabriel, Injīl[D] (Gospel), "the name through which he (Christ) would raise the dead," or "it is the Spirit that was breathed into Mary, and the Holy is Allah."[58]

To understand the origin of this contradiction, we must look at the historical context of these terms. The expression *"the Faithful Spirit"* (Q 26.193) was introduced during

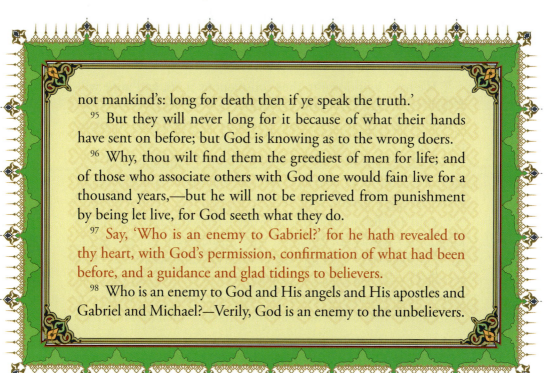

[99] We have sent down to thee conspicuous signs, and none will
disbelieve therein except the evildoers.
[100] Or every time they make a covenant, will a part of them
repudiate it? Nay, most of them do not believe.
[101] And when there comes to them an apostle confirming what they
have, a part of those who have received the Book repudiate God's
book, casting it behind their backs as though they did not know.
[102] And they follow that which the devils recited against Solomon's
kingdom;—it was not Solomon who misbelieved, but the devils
who misbelieved, teaching men sorcery,—and what has been
revealed to the two angels at Babylon, Harut and Marut; yet these
taught no one until they said, 'We are but a temptation, so do not
misbelieve.' Men learn from them only that by which they may part

Muḥammad's call in Mecca. Later (probably as he came to know more about Christian ideologies albeit in a questionable manner), Muḥammad added the name "Holy Spirit" to his concordance and attributed the transmitting of the Qur'ān to the Holy Spirit in Q 26 (one of the late Meccan sūras). Further, in Medina, Muḥammad mentioned the name "Gabriel" (Q 2.97-98 and Q 66.4).

What is obvious is that these names—the spirit of Faith and Truth, the Holy Spirit, and Gabriel—were not one and the same in the mind of Muḥammad. Rather, he was using a variety of religious terms that reflected the environmental changes in his life, such that, as he moved from place to place, he would use the words that were common to that locale and appropriate to the conditions of the day.

The Angel Israfil

We have a confirmed narrative (*ḥadīth*[D] *ṣaḥīḥ)* that says that the angel Israfil had the responsibility of delivering the Qur'ān to Muḥammad: "...he would bring him word by word. Then Gabriel came down upon him with the Qur'ān." This narrative speaks of not one, but two angels (Israfil and Gabriel) charged with the same task: to deliver the Qur'ān to Muḥammad. And, in yet another text, we read about a third angel, the one who transmitted the al-Fātiḥa (Q 1) to Muḥammad: "an angel who had never come down to earth at all."[59]

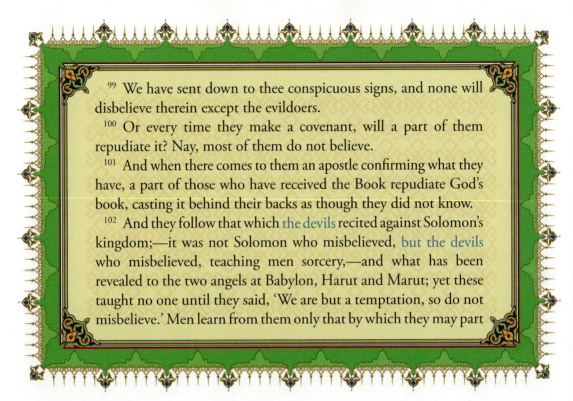

man and wife; but they can harm no one therewith, unless with the permission of God, and they learn what hurts them and profits them not. And yet they knew that he who purchased it would have no portion in the future; but sad is the price at which they have sold their souls, had they but known.

103 But had they believed and feared, a reward from God were better, had they but known.

104 O ye who believe! say not 'ra'hina,' but say 'un*th*urna,' and hearken; for unto misbelievers shall be grievous woe.

105 They who misbelieve, whether of those who have the Book or of the idolaters, would fain that no good were sent down to you from your Lord; but God specially favours with His mercy whom He will, for God is Lord of mighty grace.

Q 2.102

Most readers read it as rendered above, where the word ***al-shayāṭīnu*** ("**the devils**") is in the Arabic irregular (broken) plural form. However, there is a reading that says *al-shayāṭūn*. They read it as *wa lakin al-shayāṭūn*—using the weaker *lakin* ("but") instead of the stronger ***lakinna*** ("**but**"), which is what the current Arabic Qur'ān reads—and keeping *al-shayāṭūn* according to the previous reading.[60] This substitution of words presents a great grammatical difference in parsing words.

Q 2.104

It is recorded that the Anṣār[D] said to Muḥammad, *"ra'inā,"* which meant they wanted him to explain more to them. However, in this verse, Muḥammad commanded them to use the word *unẓurnā* in its place, because he considered *ra'inā* to be Jewish slang for an expletive.[61]

Because this command from Muḥammad does not abrogate the meaning of a Qur'ānic verse but rather changes a particular behavior, this verse is not considered abrogated.[62] However, this verse is mentioned in different sources on abrogation, the

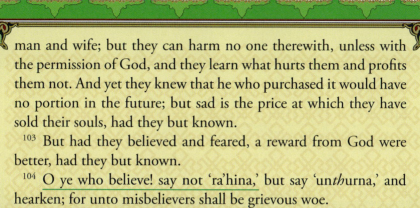

106 Whatever verse we may annul or cause thee to forget, we will bring a better one than it, or one like it; dost thou not know that God is mighty over all?

first of which is Ibn al-Jawzī: "And they [other scholars] mentioned this verse among the abrogated, and it is not [abrogated] in any way. If this had not been brought up in [the study of] abrogation, I would not have mentioned it."[63]

Q 2.106

The text of this verse is mentioned in different forms:

- In the codex of Ibn Mas'ūd it is read as "we do not hold back a verse or abrogate it, but we come with one better than it or similar to it."[64]
- It is also told that Ibn Mas'ūd read it as "we do not make you forget a verse or abrogate it."[65]
- Further, Sa'd Ibn Abī Waqqāṣ[N] used to read it as "we do not abrogate a verse or forget it," meaning, "or you forget it, O Muḥammad."[66]

Q 2.106

In the midst of the doctrinal controversy between Muḥammad and the Jews in Medina, the Jews noticed that Muḥammad was annulling, time and again, rulings that he had enacted. This issue became a subject of their criticism. They said, "Don't you see that Muḥammad commands his Companions to do something, then forbids them from it and commands them with its contrary. Doesn't he say something today, then takes it back the next?"[67]

Muḥammad answered their criticism with this verse, telling them that annulling, abrogating, cancelling, or forgetting the verses, is evidence of the power of Allah. With this verse, Muḥammad pointed to two phenomena of the Qur'ān, which are explained below.

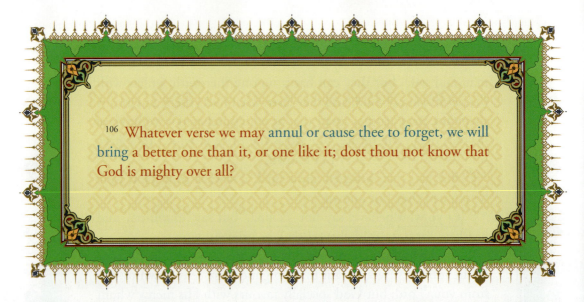

First Phenomenon: Abrogation

Abrogation means to annul a ruling and enact another in its place.

Al-Ṭabarī identifies the scope of abrogation[D]: "That is, it makes the lawful (*ḥalāl*) unlawful (*ḥarām*), and the unlawful, lawful. It changes the permissible to impermissible, and the impermissible to permissible. That only applies to commands and prohibitions, to restrictions and releases, and to forbidding and allowing. However, reports (*akhbār,* the plural for *khabar,* or report) do not come under abrogation."[68]

Muslim scholars support the abrogation of the Qur'ān. However, some scholars believe the word *naskh* ("copy, replace, or abrogate") here means to copy or transcribe a script. This viewpoint is based on an arbitrary interpretation of the word *naskh* and does not agree with the context of the verse, which very clearly means the annulling of legislation. Hence, al-Qurṭubī rejects this view, saying, "[I]t has nothing to do with this verse."[69]

In another verse, the Qur'ān affirms abrogation and calls it "substitution," saying, *"And whenever we change one verse for another,—God knows best what He sends down. They say, 'Thou art but a forger!'—Nay, most of them do not know"* (Q 16.101) (See the article "Abrogation and the Abrogated" on page 81.)

Muḥammad's Forgetfulness

The books of *ḥadīth*[D] and *sunna*[D] admit to the phenomena of Muḥammad's forgetfulness in a manner that leaves us no room for doubt.

Al-Ṭabarī reported from Qatāda that, "the prophet of Allah reads a verse or more, then it is forgotten and lifted up." Further, "Allah made his prophet forget whatever he [Allah] willed." And from Mujāhid, "'Ubayd Allah Ibn 'Umayr[N] used to say, 'we cause it to be forgotten, then we lift it up from you.'" And from al-Ḥassan, "[Y]our prophet was made to read a Qur'ān that he forgot." And from al-Rabi', "[W]e cause it to be forgotten, we lift it up. Allah had brought down Qur'ānic matters that he lifted up."

In reality, what has been said by the scholars about the meanings of the verb *nonsiha* "to cause to forget," are similar. Lifting the rulings of a verse of the Qur'ān, delaying it, forgetting it, or erasing it from the heart of the prophet…are all a stab to the heart of its inerrancy. Allah, who made his prophet infallible, in order to make by his infallibility, the infallible Qur'ān, then 'lifts' its infallibility due to changes in the conditions of Muḥammad, his circumstances, and historical events.

(al-Harīrī, *'Ālam al-Mu'jizāt* 112)

Second Phenomenon: Forgetting

Qur'ānic verses could be subject to forgetting with this text: *"Whatever verse we may annul or cause thee to forget…"* (Q 2.106). The person addressed here is Muḥammad, meaning, "we make you [Muḥammad] forget it: that is, we erase it from your heart."[70]

The scholars considered a verse subject to being forgotten as part of the process of abrogation. They said, "The prophet reads a verse or more, then he is made to forget it, then it is recalled [to heaven]." In another *ḥadīth* (saying or naration of Muḥammad) it says, "Allah, Almighty, was making his prophet forget whatever he [Allah] wanted and abrogated whatever he [Allah] wanted."[71]

In the codex of Ibn Mas'ūd, the verse states, "We make you not forget a verse or abrogate it." On the other hand, Sa'd Ibn Abī Waqqāṣ read it as "we abrogate not a verse or you forget it," a reading that considers that Muḥammad is being addressed, "as if he meant: You forget it, O Muḥammad."[72]

The scholars have said that one of the meanings of *"we…cause to be forgotten"* is "we erase it." Erasure is stipulated by the Qur'ān in another verse, where it states, *"God blots out what He will, or He confirms; and with Him is the Mother of the Book"* (Q 13.39).

Just as some commentators tried to avoid the embarrassment of abrogation by explaining that it means "copying the book by hand" [instead of saying that Allah annulled the verses], other commentators have read the verse using the expression *nansa'aha* as "we delay it, we do not transmit down its ruling and we lift up its recitation" or "we delay it in the Preserved Tablet," instead of *nonsiha* ("to cause to forget").[73] However, the meaning of *nansa'aha* is inconsistent with the internal idea of the verse and proves that the text of the Qur'ān was subject to the demands of Muḥammad's environment.

Another Problem

In addition to the two phenomena of abrogation and forgetting, the verse points to the variations in the equivalence of verses. It says, *"we will bring a better one than it, or one like it"* (Q 2.106). This statement means the substituted verse is better than the one that was abrogated or forgotten, or at least just like the one annulled or forgotten. This begs the question, "Why wasn't the *"better"* transmitted in the first place, since the Qur'ān is there in heaven, in the Preserved Tablet[D] (*al-Lawḥ al-Maḥfūẓ*)? Also, if a "similar" is brought forth, what is new in this case?"

These problems found in Q 2.106 refute several understandings held by Muslims regarding the inerrancy of the Qur'ān and its preservation in the Preserved Tablet.

Another Contradiction

Abrogation in itself presents a contradiction within the Qur'ān. The verse, *"And whenever we change one verse for another,"* (Q 16.101) contradicts the verse, *"there is no changing the words of God!"* (Q 10.64). (See the comment on Q 10.64 in the second volume of this book.)

107 Dost thou not know that God's is the kingdom of the heavens and the earth? nor have ye besides God a patron or a help.
108 Do ye wish to question your apostle as Moses was questioned aforetime? but whoso takes misbelief in exchange for faith has erred from the level road.

Muʿtazilite View on the Creation of the Qur'ān

By this verse [Q 2.106], the Muʿtazilite concluded that the Qur'ān is created for several reasons. One reason is that if the words of Allah were ancient, then the abrogated verse and the abrogating verse would both be ancient. But that is impossible because the abrogating verse should come after the abrogated one. Accordingly, the verse coming after cannot be called ancient. As to the verse being abrogated, it has to be removed and "lifted up." By agreement then, neither can that which has been removed be considered ancient.

The second reason is that the verse indicates that some parts of the Qur'ān are better than others. If this is so, then these better parts cannot be considered ancient.

The third reason is, when the Qur'ān states *"dost thou not know that God is mighty over all?"* it intends to show that Allah Almighty is the one able to abrogate a verse and bring another in its place. That which comes under the scope of ability and is an action, is considered causal.... (al-Rāzī, *al-Tafsīr al-Kabīr* 3: 252)

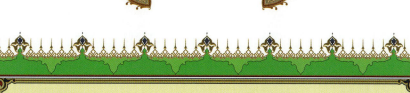

[109] Many of those who have the Book would fain turn you back
into misbelievers after ye have once believed, through envy from
themselves, after the truth has been made manifest to them; but
pardon and shun them till God brings His command; verily, God
is mighty over all.
[110] Be ye steadfast in prayer, and give alms; and whatsoever good
ye send before for your own souls, ye shall find it with God, for
God in all ye do doth see.
[111] They say, 'None shall enter Paradise save such as be Jews or
Christians;' that is their faith. Say thou, 'Bring your proofs, if ye
be speaking truth.'
[112] Aye, he who resigns his face to God, and who is kind, he shall

Q 2.109

This phrase describes a lenient stance toward the People of the Book, for it urges Muslims to offer amnesty and pardon. However, after Islām settled its position toward the Jews and Christians, some scholars say the meaning of this verse is abrogated by either of the following verses:

A. Q 9.29: *"Fight those who believe not in God ...."*[74]
B. Q 9.5: *"...kill the idolaters wherever ye may find them...."*[75]

Another group of scholars did not believe this verse is abrogated and justified their position by ruling that the pardon mentioned here is not absolute. Instead, the pardon is limited by the time period indicated by the phrase, *"till God brings His command...."* Ibn al-Jawzī provides this explanation:[76]

> That it would be as if the Almighty, when he told them about how he dealt with the Sabbath-breakers, was telling them, "Don't you fear that the suffering that befell them would befall you because of your rebelliousness? Do not be deceived by the respite extended to you!"

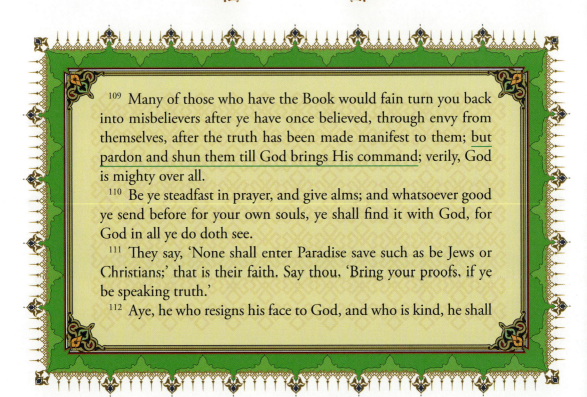

have his reward from his Lord, and no fear shall be on them, and they shall not grieve.

113 The Jews say, 'The Christians rest on nought;' and the Christians say, 'The Jews rest on nought;' and yet they read the Book. So, too, say those who know not, like to what these say; but God shall judge between them on the resurrection day concerning that whereon they do dispute.

114 But who is more unjust than he who prohibits God's mosques, that His name should not be mentioned there, and who strives to ruin them? 'Tis not for such to enter into them except in fear, for them is disgrace in this world, and in the future mighty woe.

Q 2.114

Some read ***khā'ifīna*** ("**in fear**") as *khuīyafān* ("afraid"), which is the plural of *khā'if* ("afraid").[77] This reading is not different in meaning from the text in the Qur'ān. However, the codex of Ibn Mas'ūd reads this phrase as *ḥunafā'* ("believers in the Hanif faith").[78] Fear is a psychological feeling, whereas a Hanif is one who believes in the Ḥanīfiya[D] religion.

Question: Given the extreme difference between these two meanings, which meaning is correct?

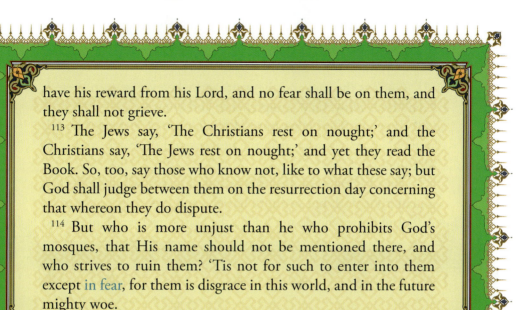

[115] God's is the east and the west, and wherever ye turn there is
God's face; verily, God comprehends and knows.
[116] They say, 'God takes unto Himself a son.' Celebrated be His
praise! Nay, His is what is in the heavens and the earth, and Him
all things obey.
[117] The Originator of the heavens and the earth, when He decrees
a matter He doth but say unto it, 'BE,' and it is.
[118] And those who do not know (the Scriptures) say, 'Unless God

Q 2.115

Muslims are taught to face the Ka'ba[D] in Mecca when they pray. However, this verse's phrase grants permission for a Muslim to pray in any direction. One historical account records the story of a Muslim military company on assignment. When the members of the company wanted to pray, they were doubtful as to whether the *qibla* (the direction of prayer) they followed was correct. Upon return, they told Muḥammad about their confusion, and he responded with Q 2.115.

Based upon this account, one group of Muslim scholars believe that the instruction given in this verse remains valid whenever a Muslim is in a similar situation and has no means by which to discern the correct direction of prayer.[79]

Other scholars believe that the intended meaning of this verse is "wherever you are, face the direction of the Ka'ba as your *qibla*."[80]

However, other Islāmic scholars believe this verse should be abrogated and cited various reasons:

A. Q 2.115 contains permission to pray facing in any direction. Therefore, its meaning has been abrogated by Q 2.144: *"Turn then thy face towards the Sacred Mosque...."*[81]

B. Early in his mission, Muḥammad prayed toward the Ka'ba in Mecca. After he migrated to Medina, he began to pray toward Jerusalem. Later, he returned to praying toward the Ka'ba, and reconfirmed the direction of the *qibla* with Q 2.144: *"Turn then thy face towards the Sacred Mosque; wherever ye be, turn your faces towards it."* Therefore, Q 2.115 is abrogated by Q 2.144.[82]

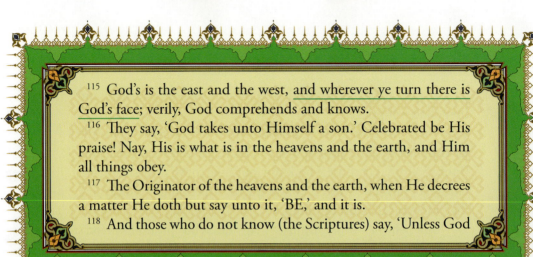

speak to us, or there comes a sign.' So spake those before them like unto their speech. Their hearts are all alike. We have made manifest the signs unto a people that are sure.
119 We have sent thee with the truth, a bearer of good tidings and of warning, and thou shalt not be questioned as to the fellows of hell.
120 The Jews will not be satisfied with thee, nor yet the Christians, until thou followest their creed. Say, 'God's guidance is the guidance;' and if thou followest their lusts after the knowledge that

C. Authoritative sources indicate the true reason for the final change in the direction of prayer: "Some of the Jews were saying, 'He [Muḥammad] was not guided to a direction until we directed him.' Muḥammad loathed their saying that, and lifted up his face toward the sky." Thus, Q 2.144 was sent down to him from Allah: *"We see thee often turn about thy face in the heavens, but we will surely turn thee to a qiblah thou shalt like."* [83]

These scholars believed that this is the first instance of abrogation in the Qur'ān.[84]

Other scholars deny any occurrence of abrogation in Q 2.115. They clearly state that there is absolutely no abrogation in this verse, either in part or in whole.[85]

Q 2.119

The majority read ***wa lā tus'alū*** ("**thou shalt not be questioned**").[86] Ubayy Ibn Ka'b read *wa mā tus'alu* ("thou shalt not be questioned"), whereas Ibn Mas'ūd read *wa lan tus'ala* ("thou shalt not be questioned").[87] All these readings have the same meaning: You are not responsible, O Muḥammad.

Others read *wa lā tas'al* ("do not question") in the prohibitive form.[88] This reading has this meaning: Do not seek information, O Muḥammad, about the condition of the dwellers of hellfire. It is not in your area of concern.

Question: Does the verse then mean that Muḥammad is not responsible, or does it command Muḥammad not to ask?

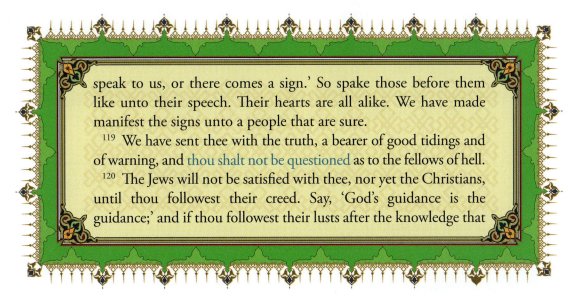

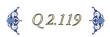

has come to thee, thou hast not then from God a patron or a help.
121 They to whom we have brought the Book and who read it as
it should be read, believe therein; and whoso disbelieve therein,
'tis they who lose thereby.
122 O children of Israel! remember my favours with which I
favoured you, and that I have preferred you over the worlds.
123 And fear the day when no soul shall pay a recompense for
a soul, nor shall an equivalent be received therefrom, nor any
intercession avail; and they shall not be helped.

Q 2.124

Within this verse we notice that the reading that would make the word *"evildoers"* more proper in Arabic would be in the nominative instead of the accusative case of the noun, i.e., "The evildoers are not within the reach of My Promise." *"Evildoers"* should read in Arabic *al-ẓālimūn* instead of *al-ẓālimīn.* But *"evildoers"* is written in the current Arabic Qur'ān in the accusative (objective case), the case that some Muslim exegetes try to defend. For example, al-Ṭabarī gives the following explanation:[89]

> [I]t is possible to use the nominative or the accusative of *'al-ẓālimīn'*;... that is, because everything a man achieves, has been achieved by him.... [It could be stated]: The good of so-and-so has reached me, or I have received of his good. One time the action of the verb is directed to the good [that the person has received], and another time it is directed to the person himself.

However, we find the nominative case was present in other codices. In the codex of Ibn Mas'ūd, the word is found in the nominative: "But My Promise is not within the reach of evildoers (*al-ẓālimūn*)," meaning that the evildoers are the ones who do not reach the Promise of Allah.[90]

Reading the word in the nominative case has been affirmed by others. "Some of them read: "'But My Promise is not within the reach of evildoers,' *al-ẓālimūn*, meaning that the one who is an evildoer among your descendents will not reach my Promise."[91]

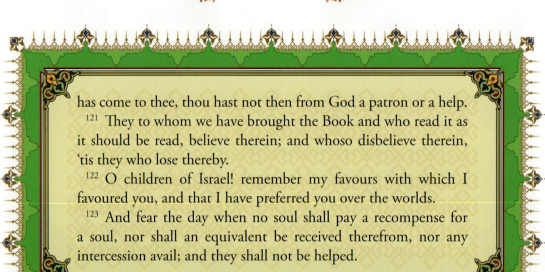

[124] And when his Lord tried Abraham with words, and he fulfilled them, He said, 'Verily, I will set thee as a high priest for men.' Said he, ' And of my seed?' God said, 'My covenant touches not the evildoers.'
[125] And when we made the House a place of resort unto men, and a sanctuary, and (said) take the station of Abraham for a place of prayer; and covenanted with Abraham and Ishmael, saying, 'Do ye two cleanse my house for those who make the circuit, for those who pay devotions there, for those who bow down, and for those too who adore.'

There are also those who admit to the erroneous use of *al-ẓālimīn* found in the common Qur'ān. Abū Raja', Qatāda, al-A'mash, Ibn Mas'ūd, and Ṭalḥa Ibn Muṣarrif read it as *"al-ẓālimūn"* in the nominative, because a promise is not achieved. Thus, the meaning is ["]My Promise does not extend to the evildoers["] or ["]the evildoers will not reach it["].

Al-Zajjāj[N] commented, "It is a very good and eloquent reading. However, I do not read by it; neither should it be read as such because it contradicts the Qur'ān."[92]

Q 2.125

A large number of readers read ***itakhidhū*** ("[you] **take**") in the imperative form. Others read *itakhadhū* ("they took") in the past tense.[93]

The imperative form *itakhidhū* ("[you] take") is found in the reading of the current Arabic Qur'ān, which means the station of Abraham is not taken as a place of prayer yet. However, the second reading uses the verb in the past tense, *itakhadhū* ("they took"), meaning the station of Abraham has actually been taken as a place of prayer and renders the command null.

Q 2.125-129

The Qur'ānic narrative found in these verses informs us that Abraham and Ishmael raised the structure of the Ka'ba and asked Allah to send a messenger among the people of Mecca: *"and send them an apostle from amongst themselves,"* beseeching him to provide

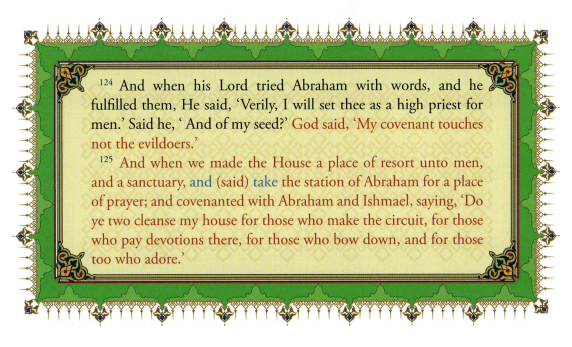

[126] When Abraham said, 'Lord, make this a town of safety, and provide the dwellers there with fruits, such as believe in God and the last day!' (God) said, ' And he who misbelieves, I will give him but little to enjoy, then will drive him to the torment of the fire, an evil journey will it be.'

[127] And when Abraham raised up the foundations of the House with Ishmael, 'Lord! receive it from us, verily, thou art hearing and dost know.

[128] Lord! and make us too resigned unto Thee, and of our seed also a nation resigned unto Thee, and show us our rites, and turn towards us, verily, Thou art easy to be turned and merciful.

[129] Lord! and send them an apostle from amongst themselves, to read to them Thy signs and teach them the Book and wisdom, and to purify them; verily, Thou art the mighty and the wise.'

this town with various sources of income. But when we compare this story in the Qur'ān with the original sources, it becomes evident that it differs substantially from the biblical accounts. The life of Abraham is mapped differently in the Old Testament:

- God told Abraham, who was living in a pagan environment near the Euphrates, to leave his home and go to a land that God would show him (Josh. 24.2).
- Abraham's family departed from "Ur of the Chaldeans to go to the land of Canaan," where he lived in Shechem (modern day Nablus) around 1850 BC.
- Because of the famine that came upon Canaan (Gen. 12.1-10), Abraham departed from Canaan and went to Egypt. From Egypt, he moved to Bethel, where he built a temple for the Lord (Gen. 13.1-4).

Three regions are mentioned in the biblical narrative of Abraham's journey: the Euphrates, Canaan, and Egypt. At the same time, no mention of the Arabian Peninsula (regarding Mecca) or a connection between Abraham and the Ka'ba is given. If Abraham had been the builder of the Ka'ba, it would have been a holy site for the Jews, or at least the historical tales would have mentioned their regard for it.

According to classical Islāmic sources, the name for this sacred house found in Mecca derives from its cubical shape. In the Arabic, the word *ka'ba* means "cube." The worship

130 Who is averse from the faith of Abraham save one who is
foolish of soul? for we have chosen him in this world, and in the
future he is surely of the righteous.
131 When his Lord said to him, 'Be resigned,' he said, 'I am
resigned unto the Lord of the worlds.'
132 And Abraham instructed his sons therein, and Jacob (saying),
'O my sons! verily, God has chosen for you a religion, do not
therefore die unless ye be resigned.'
133 Were ye then witnesses when Jacob was facing death, when
he said to his sons, 'What will ye serve when I am gone?' They
said, 'We will serve thy God, the God of thy fathers Abraham, and
Ishmael, and Isaac, one God; and we are unto Him resigned.'
134 That is a nation that has passed away, theirs is what they
gained; and yours shall be what ye have gained; ye shall not be
questioned as to that which they have done.

of Ka'ba is connected to Arab paganism because the Arabs of the Peninsula considered the Ka'ba holy before Islām.[94]

The historic sources also inform that the pagan Arabs regarded other houses named *ka'bat* (*ka'bas*) to be sacred as well:[95]

- Ka'ba of Yemen
- Ka'ba of Najran
- Ka'ba of Shaddād
- Ka'ba of Ghaṭafān

According to the historical sources, the number of *ka'bat* (*ka'bas*) may have been as many as twenty-three. Regardless of the accuracy of this number, the consensus is that there are other *ka'bat* (*ka'bas*) besides the one in Mecca.

Question: Since Abraham had not visited the southern Arabian Peninsula, and since the Ka'ba was at the heart of Arabian paganism, how could Abraham be tied to the Ka'ba?

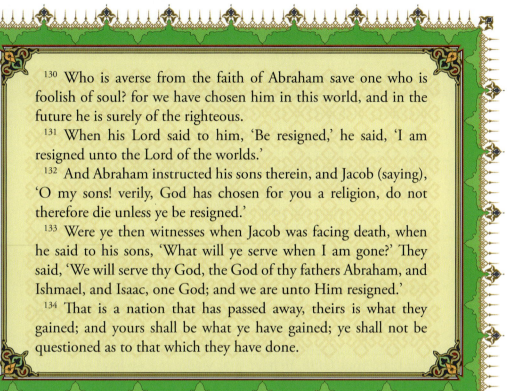

[135] They say, 'Be ye Jews or Christians so shall ye of Abraham be guided.' Say, 'Not so! but the faith of Abraham the 'Hanif, he was not of the idolaters.'

[136] Say ye, 'We believe in God, and what has been revealed to us, and what has been revealed to Abraham, and Ishmael, and Isaac, and Jacob, and the Tribes, and what was brought to Moses and Jesus, and what was brought unto the Prophets from their Lord; we will not distinguish between any one of them, and unto Him are we resigned.

[137] If they believe in that in which ye believe, then are they guided; but if they turn back, then are they only in a schism, and God will suffice thee against them, for He both hears and knows.

[138] The dye of God! and who is better than God at dyeing? and we are worshippers of Him.

[139] Say, 'Do ye dispute with us concerning God, and He is our Lord and your Lord? Ye have your works and we have ours, and unto Him are we sincere.'

[140] Do ye say that Abraham, and Ishmael, and Isaac, and Jacob, and the Tribes were Jews or Christians? Say, 'Are ye more knowing than God? Who is more unjust than one who conceals a testimony

Q 2.137

The verse says about the Jews and Christians: *"If they believe in that in which ye believe, then are they guided,"* a reading that is criticized by Ibn 'Abbās. According to his interpretation, this stipulation means that if the People of the Book believe in one like Allah, *"then are they guided."* He says, "[D]o not say '*in that in which ye believe*' for Allah has no one like him." He said to the Muslims that they have to read "if they believe in what you believe."[96]

Moreover, Ubayy Ibn Ka'b follows in the footsteps of Ibn 'Abbās by reading the verse "if they believe in what you believe."[97]

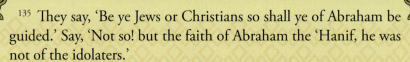

that he has from God?' But God is not careless of what ye do.
141 That is a nation that has passed away; theirs is what they
gained, and yours shall be what ye have gained; ye shall not be
questioned as to that which they have done.
142 The fools among men will say, 'What has turned them from
their qiblah, on which they were agreed?' Say, 'God's is the east
and the west, He guides whom He will unto the right path.'
143 Thus have we made you a middle nation, to be witnesses
against men, and that the Apostle may be a witness against you.
We have not appointed the qiblah on which thou wert agreed,
save that we might know who follows the Apostle from him who
turns upon his heels; although it is a great thing save to those
whom God doth guide. But God will not waste your faith, for
verily, God with men is kind and merciful.
144 We see thee often turn about thy face in the heavens, but
we will surely turn thee to a qiblah thou shalt like. Turn then thy
face towards the Sacred Mosque; wherever ye be, turn your faces
towards it; for verily, those who have the Book know that it is the
truth from their Lord;—God is not careless of that which ye do.
145 And if thou shouldst bring to those who have been given the

Q 2.139

Scholars have issued various opinions on this verse, resulting in two views about its abrogation and conservation.

One group ruled that it is abrogated because it extends leniency towards non-Muslims. Therefore, its meaning is replaced with Q 9.5: *"...kill the idolaters wherever ye may find them..."* [98]

Another group ruled that it is conserved for the following reasons:[99]

A. This verse is simply states that each man bears the consequences of his own actions.
B. This verse is citing a report.
C. If a verse is abrogated, it loses its authority. But in this case, the authority of the verse remains because the ruling is that each man receives a reward for his own actions.

Book every sign, they would not follow your qiblah; and thou art
not to follow their qiblah; nor do some of them follow the qiblah
of the others: and if thou followest their lusts after the knowledge
that has come to thee then art thou of the evildoers.
146 Those whom we have given the Book know him as they know
their sons, although a sect of them do surely hide the truth, the
while they know.
147 The truth (is) from thy Lord; be not therefore one of those
who doubt thereof.
148 Every sect has some one side to which they turn (in prayer);
but do ye hasten onwards to good works; wherever ye are God will
bring you all together; verily, God is mighty over all.
149 From whencesoever thou comest forth, there turn thy face
towards the Sacred Mosque, for it is surely truth from thy Lord;
God is not careless about what ye do.
150 And from whencesoever thou comest forth, there turn thy
face towards the Sacred Mosque, and wheresoever ye are, turn your
faces towards it, that men may have no argument against you, save
only those of them who are unjust; and fear them not, but fear me
and I will fulfil my favours to you, perchance ye may be guided yet.
151 Thus have we sent amongst you an apostle of yourselves, to
recite to you our signs, to purify you and teach you the Book and
wisdom, and to teach you what ye did not know;
152 remember me, then, and I will remember you; thank me, and
do not misbelieve.
153 O ye who do believe! seek aid from patience and from prayer,
verily, God is with the patient.
154 And say not of those who are slain in God's way (that they
are) dead, but rather living; but ye do not perceive.
155 We will try you with something of fear, and hunger and loss
of wealth, and souls and fruit; but give good tidings to the patient,
156 who when there falls on them a calamity say, 'Verily, we are

God's and, verily, to Him do we return.'
[157] These, on them are blessings from their Lord and mercy, and they it is who are guided.
[158] Verily, Zafa and Merwah are of the beacons of God, and he who makes the pilgrimage unto the House, or visits it, it is no crime for him to compass them both about; and he who obeys his own impulse to a good work,—God is grateful and doth know.

Q 2.158

In the codex of Ibn Mas'ūd the verse reads *an lā yaṭṭawafa* ("to not compass") by adding *lā* ("not").[100] Instead of the Qur'ān's ***an yaṭṭawafa*** (**"to compass"**), Ibn 'Abbās and Anas Ibn Mālik read *an lā yataṭawafa* ("that he should not compass").[101]

The reading of the Qur'ān means that if a Muslim is to compass the two hills near the east side of the Ka'ba, Ṣafā and Marwa, there is no sin on him. Whereas, according to the reading of Ibn Mas'ūd, if the Muslim does not compass them, there is no sin on him. (See the critical analysis of Q 2.158, page 213.)

Q 2.158

The Anṣār were embarrassed to retrace the route of Hajar between Ṣafā and Marwa. Therefore, the verse came to Muḥammad to calm the concerns of their hearts. Later, the meaning of this verse was abrogated by Q 2.130: *"Who is averse from the faith of Abraham save one who is foolish of soul?"* Hence, retracing this route became a duty.[102] (See the critical analysis of Q 2.158, page 213.)

Q 2.158

This verse continues to address what Muḥammad initiated in Q 2.144 when he changed the *qibla* for Muslims from the Sacred House (Jerusalem) to Mecca. Muḥammad reached the conviction that there was no future hope with the Jews of Medina, no chance of winning them to his cause. Furthermore, Muḥammad grew ambitious about broadening the base of his followers. So he started wooing the pagan

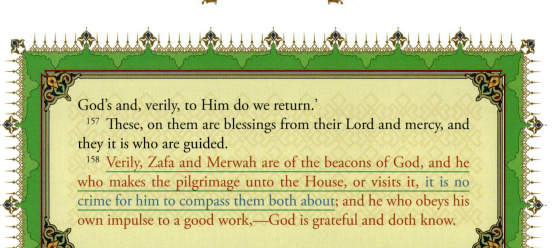

Arabs instead. Muḥammad began to draw nearer to the pagans of the Arab regions by changing the direction of the *qibla* and incorporating pagan pilgrimage rituals within Islām. For instance, the procession between the Ṣafā and Marwa was already a pagan pilgrimage ritual, and the circumambulation ritual was a uniquely Quraysh[D] ritual apart from the rest of the Arabians.[103]

The Ṣafā and Marwa used to contain two idols, Isāf (in Ṣafā) and Nā'ila (in Marwa), during the time of Muḥammad.[104] Several years after he made the decision to change the direction of *qibla*, Muḥammad performed 'Umra (the minor pilgrimage), which took place before the conquest of Mecca. While Muḥammad was performing the rituals, he proceeded to perform the ritual of the procession between the Ṣafā and Marwa, following the ceremonial practice of the pagan Quraysh. Since this ritual was not practiced by all Arabs, the Muslims who were not of the Quraysh backgrounds said to him, "How do we proceed, knowing that the glorification of idols and all such things that constitute their worship rather than Allah is a *shirk* ("blasphemy")?"[105]

This objection was also shared by a group of Muslims who detested "the circumambulation in Islām of the Ṣafā and the Marwa."[106] Anas Ibn Mālik said, "[W]e hated the procession between them [the hills], because it was one of the rituals of [the] *jāhilīya* (pre-Islāmic era) period." This practice remained detestable until the revelation of this verse: *"Verily, Zafa [Ṣafā]and Merwah [Marwa] are of the beacons of God."*[107]

We have a narrative that says some Muslims advised Muḥammad not to perform the ritual of procession and said, "O messenger of Allah! Do not walk in procession between Ṣafā and Marwa; it is a blasphemous act we used to do in *jāhilīya*." Hence, the Qur'ān eventually responds with this verse: *"and he who makes the pilgrimage unto the House, or visits it, it is no crime for him to compass them both about."*[108]

The narrative also tells us that the Anṣār were the ones who expressed their concern. They used to worship the goddess Manat before Islām. Because of their recent pagan past and the presence of the other gods (idols) Isāf and Nā'ila, "they found it embarrassing to walk in procession between the Ṣafā and Marwa."[109] Historical sources state that those who criticized the request to walk in the procession said to Muḥammad, "Walking in procession between these two stones is a *jāhilīya* practice."[110]

At the same time, other narratives say that the verse concerns the Muslims who descended from the people of Tehama, a province of Arabia. These people did not practice this ritual of the Quraysh before Islām, and thus were afraid to perform it when Muḥammad gave the command to do so.[111]

The sources do not reveal whether or not the embarrassment of these Muslims was because the processional originated from pagan rituals of the Quraysh, which would indicate their rejection was an anti-Quraysh expression. But there is no disagreement that those who rejected the ritual did so because of its pagan origin.

It seems that some people of influence remained embarrassed about the ritual of walking between the Ṣafā and Marwa because they believed that the context of the verse does not make compassing (the walking ritual) a necessary requirement. They

159 Verily, those who hide what we have revealed of manifest signs
and of guidance after we have manifested it to men in the Book,
them God shall curse, and those who curse shall curse them too.
160 Save those who turn and do right and make (the signs) manifest;
these will I turn to again, for I am easy to be turned and merciful.
161 Verily, those who misbelieve and die while still in misbelief, on
them is the curse of God, and of the angels, and of mankind altogether;

based their convictions on a reading written in the codex of Ibn Masʿūd: "There is no sin in him if he does not compass them." It is said that Ibn ʿAbbās also embraced this reading.[112] Another source states "that Ibn ʿAbbās, Anas Ibn Mālik, Shahr Ibn Ḥawshab read 'that he compasses not.'"[113]

Question: How did Allah make a pagan practice religiously permissible? Not only that, but how did he sanction, in particular, a pagan ritual belonging to the Quraysh?

Verse Contradiction

Verse 158 also contains an internal contradiction. The first part says, *"Verily, Zafa and Merwah are of the beacons of God,"* which would make the compassing ritual a requirement. On the other hand, the second part of it says that the one who compasses the Ṣafā and Marwa is not considered a sinner, *"and he who makes the pilgrimage unto the House, or visits it, it is no crime for him to compass them both about."*

Q 2.159

Some scholars believe that the meaning of this verse is abrogated by the exception cited in the verse that follows it, which is Q 2.160: *"Save those who turn and do right and make (the signs) manifest...."*[114]

However, Ibn al-Jawzī disagrees with this assertion in its entirety, stating, "[T]he exception is not an abrogation, but it is revealing some of what is included in the term."[115]

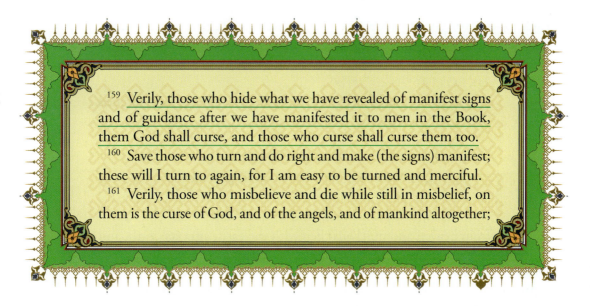

162 to dwell therein for aye; the torment shall not be lightened
for them, nor shall they be looked upon.
163 Your God is one God; there is no God but He, the merciful,
the compassionate.
164 Verily, in the creation of the heavens and the earth, and the
alternation of night and day, and in the ship that runneth in the sea
with that which profits man, and in what water God sends down
from heaven and quickens therewith the earth after its death, and
spreads abroad therein all kinds of cattle, and in the shifting of
the winds, and in the clouds that are pressed into service betwixt
heaven and earth, are signs to people who can understand.
165 Yet are there some amongst mankind who take to themselves
peers other than God; they love them as they should love God
while those who believe love God more. O that those who are
unjust could only see, when they see the torment, that power is
altogether God's! Verily, God is keen to torment.
166 When those who are followed clear themselves of those who
followed them, and see the torment, and the cords are cut asunder,
167 those who followed shall say, 'Had we but another turn, then

Q 2.173

Scholars have issued differing opinions on the abrogation of this verse. Some believe that its meaning is abrogated by the exception found in the second part of the same verse: *"but he who is forced...."*[116]

However, others believe that its meaning is abrogated by a saying of Muḥammad recorded in the *ḥadīth*: "He [Allah] had allowed us two [types of] dead meat and two [types of] blood: fish and locusts, liver and spleen."[117] Therefore, these scholars believed that although dead animals and blood are generally forbidden to the Muslim, in a case of dire necessity, based on Muḥammad's statement from the *ḥadīth*, they could consume two types of dead meat, fish and locusts, and two types of blood from the liver and spleen.

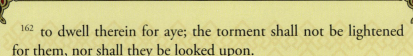

would we clear ourselves of them as they have cleared themselves
of us.' So will God show them their works; for them are sighs, and
they shall not come forth from out the fire.
168 O ye folk! eat of what is in the earth, things lawful and things
good, and follow not the footsteps of Satan, verily, to you he is an
open foe.
169 He does but bid you evil and sin, and that ye should speak
against God what ye do not know.
170 When it is said to them, 'Follow what God has revealed,' they
say, 'Nay, we will follow what we found our fathers agreed upon.'
What! and though their fathers had no sense at all or guidance—?
171 The likeness of those who misbelieve is as the likeness of him
who shouts to that which hears him not, save only a call and a cry;
deafness, dumbness, blindness, and they shall not understand.
172 O ye who do believe! eat of the good things wherewith we
have provided you, and give thanks unto God if it be Him ye serve.
173 He has only forbidden for you what is dead, and blood, and
flesh of swine, and whatsoever has been consecrated to other than
God; but he who is forced, neither revolting nor transgressing, it
is in no sin for him; verily, God is forgiving and merciful.
174 Verily, those who hide what God has revealed of the Book, and
sell it for a little price, they shall eat nothing in their bellies save
fire; and God will not speak to them on the day of resurrection,
nor will He purify them, but for them is grievous woe.
175 They who sell guidance for error, and pardon for torment,
how patient must they be of fire!
176 That (is), because God has revealed the Book with truth, and
verily those who disagree about the Book are in a wide schism.
177 Righteousness is not that ye turn your faces towards the east
or the west, but righteousness is, one who believes in God, and the
last day, and the angels, and the Book, and the prophets, and who
gives wealth for His love to kindred, and orphans, and the poor,

and the son of the road, and beggars, and those in captivity; and who is steadfast in prayer, and gives alms; and those who are sure of their covenant when they make a covenant; and the patient in poverty, and distress, and in time of violence; these are they who are true, and these are those who fear.

178 O ye who believe! Retaliation is prescribed for you for the slain: the free for the free, the slave for the slave, the female for the female; yet he who is pardoned at all by his brother, must be prosecuted in reason, and made to pay with kindness. That is an alleviation from your Lord, and a mercy; and he who transgresses

Q 2.178

The verse stipulates reciprocal treatment for the punishment of the crime of murder. According to this verse, "If a free man murders a slave, the murderer is not executed. Also, a man is not executed for murdering a woman, or a woman for [murdering] a man, [nor is a] slave [executed] for a free, or a free for a slave."[118]

The exegetes' opinion is divided on whether or not this verse is abrogated. Some scholars ruled that it is abrogated by Q 5.45: *"We have prescribed for thee therein 'a life for a life….'"*[119] When these scholars were questioned as to how this rule applied to Muslims, (since Q 5.45 seems to be directly discussing Jewish laws and practices), they replied that these rules of punishment are applicable to Muslims because of the second part of Q 5.45, which states *"but he whoso will not judge by what God has revealed, these be the unjust."*[120] Thus, it became incumbent to kill a man if he murdered a woman and vice versa, as well as to kill a slave if he killed a free person.

Another group believes that Q 2.178 is abrogated by Q 17.33: *"for he who is slain unjustly we have given his next of kin authority; yet let him not exceed in slaying; verily, he is ever helped."*[121]

However, there is also a group of scholars who hold the view that what is mentioned in the verse concerns the Jews only.[122] Accordingly, they feel that the meaning and relevance of both verses Q 2.178 and Q 5.45 are conserved, since each one is concerned with a different subject.[123]

Al-Makkī believes the reason for the conservation of Q 2.178 is due to one of two possibilities:[124]

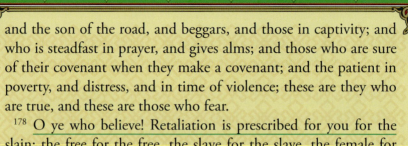

after that for him is grievous woe.
179 For you in retaliation is there life, O ye possessors of minds!
it may be ye will fear.
180 It is prescribed for you that when one of you is face to face
with death, if he leave (any) goods, the legacy is to his parents, and
to his kinsmen, in reason. A duty this upon all those that fear.
181 But he who alters it after that he has heard it,—the sin thereof
is only upon those who alter it; verily, God doth hear and know.
182 And he who fears from the testator a wrong intention, or a
crime, and doth make up the matter between the parties, it is no

A. This verse may refer to a specific incident. Later, it is possible that it became the rule and was made into law. Therefore, it is conserved.
B. The verse came to abolish a social custom. Thus, it is conserved.

Eventually, Islāmic legal experts formulated the following law, based on Q 2.178 and Q 5.45: The free [person] is killed for murdering a free person, regardless of gender, according to these verses in Q 2 and Q 5. A man is killed for murdering a woman and a woman for murdering a man, according to the verse in Q 5.[125]

Q 2.180

The scholars have offered differing opinions on whether or not bequeathing possessions to parents or next of kin is mandatory for Muslims. Some believe that this verse merely indicates a suggested course of action. They ruled that the phrase *"in reason"* is proof that this action is not mandatory. They also believe that a *"duty this upon all those that fear,"* but "duty is not unique to Allah-fearers."[126]

However, the majority of Muslim scholars ruled that this bequest is mandatory for Muslims because they believe that the word *"prescribed"* indicates that this is a required duty, as is the case with Q 2.183: *"There is prescribed for you the fast."* However, they also believe that the details set forth in this verse have been abrogated by other verses, and thus they issued a variety of opinions:

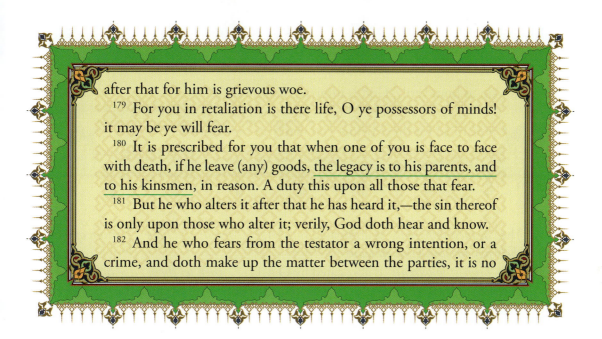

sin to him; verily, God is forgiving and merciful.
183 O ye who believe! There is prescribed for you the fast as it was prescribed for those before you; haply ye may fear.

A. The *"bequest to parents"* is abrogated by Q 4.7: *"Men should have a portion of what their parents and kindred leave...."* [127]
B. The *"bequest to parents"* is abrogated by Q 4.11: *"...then let them have two-thirds of what (the deceased) leaves...."* [128] The bequest henceforth became due [belonged] to the relatives.[129]
C. What is abrogated is the bequest to parents and all relatives who are heirs. In other words, there is no need to leave a will for those who have already been given specific portions of the inheritance legally, according to this *ḥadīth* of Muḥammad: "No bequest to an heir."[130] Instead, the will would be used to specify what should be given to those who do not have legal inheritances.

Q 2.183

Some scholars believe it is permissible to eat, drink, and engage in sexual relations during the period of *ifṭār*[D]. Each day during Ramadan, a Muslim must fast until the sunset (*al-maghrib*) prayer. After the nightfall (*al-'ishā'*) prayer, a Muslim will again abstain from food, drink, and sexual relations until the following night (changed later to be from sunset to sunrise). However, if a Muslim oversleeps and misses this original short *ifṭār* period between the two prayers, then he will not be permitted, when he awakes, to do any of these activities. Rather, he must continue fasting until the *ifṭār* of the next day. But many scholars believe that this strict rule is abrogated by Q 2.187: *"Lawful for you on the night of the fast is commerce with your wives...."* [131]

Others believe that Q 2.183 abrogates the Fast of 'Āshūra[D] that was prescribed in the pre-Islāmic era. Later, fasting during Ramadan was imposed upon the Muslims, so Muḥammad then said to them: "Whoever wants to, can fast ['Āshūra], and whoever does not want to, can leave it."[132] A second opinion suggests that Q 2.183 abrogates another fast of three days each month that Muḥammad had imposed.[133]

Finally, another group of scholars ruled that this verse is neither abrogated, nor does it abrogate any other verse.[134] Al-Ṭabarī, in turn, leans also toward the view that this verse does not deal with abrogation.[135]

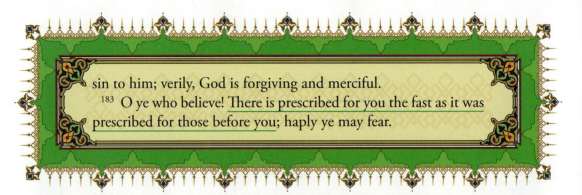

[184] A certain number of days, but he amongst you who is ill or on a journey, then (let him fast) another number of days. And those who are fit to fast may redeem it by feeding a poor man; but he

Q 2.184

The scholars have issued different opinions on the abrogation of this verse.

Some scholars ruled that the verse was revealed to offer Muslims an option to choose between fasting and breaking the fast (*ifṭār*) in exchange for feeding *"a poor man."* As a result, the rich began to break their fasts by feeding the poor, while those with less ample funds had no option but to fast. This practice resulted in a differentiation in fasting among Muslim social classes. Therefore, the choice given in this verse is abrogated by Q 2.185: *"And he amongst you who beholds this month then let him fast it...."*[136]

Other scholars believe that the entire meaning of this verse is conserved. They ruled that the verse is not abrogated because it refers to those who cannot fast for health reasons (like the elderly, pregnant, nursing, and infirm). Therefore, such persons have to feed one poor person for each day of missed fasting, since they are unable to fast themselves.[137]

Q 2.184

This verse has two issues regarding the variant readings:

1. Ubayy Ibn Ka'b read "then (let him fast) another successive number of days," adding the word *mutatābi'āt* ("successive").[138] According to the reading of Ubayy, the substituted fast should be done in a successive manner, contrary to the reading of the current Arabic Qur'ān that allows for breaks. Further, the condition is repeated by Ubayy Ibn Ka'b later when he read the verse, *"...and he who cannot find (anything to bring), then let him fast three days..."* (Q 2.196) as "And he who cannot find (anything to bring), then let him fast three days successively (*mutatābi'āt*)," adding the word *mutatābi'āt* as well.[139]
2. The word ***miskīn*** ("**a poor man**") appears in the singular in the Qur'ān; whereas, another group read *masākīn* ("poor") in the plural.[140] This difference in reading the word leads to a religious legal difference.

Question: Should one feed a single poor, indigent person or several?

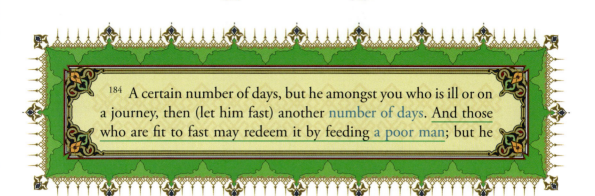

who follows an impulse to a good work it is better for him; and if ye fast it is better for you, if ye did but know.

185 The month of Rama*dh*an, wherein was revealed the Qur'an, for a guidance to men, and for manifestations of guidance, and for a Discrimination. And he amongst you who beholds this month then let him fast it; but he who is sick or on a journey, then another number of days;—God desires for you what is easy, and desires not for you what is difficult,—that ye may complete the number, and say, 'Great is God,' for that He has guided you; haply ye may give thanks.

186 When my servants ask thee concerning me, then, verily, I am near; I answer the prayer's prayer whene'er he prays to me. So let them ask me for an answer, and let them believe in me; haply they may be directed aright.

187 Lawful for you on the night of the fast is commerce with your wives; they are a garment unto you, and ye a garment unto them. God knows that ye did defraud yourselves, wherefore He has turned towards you and forgiven you; so now go in unto them

Q 2.190

Both parts of this verse are abrogated. The beginning phrase, *"Fight in God's way with those who fight with you,"* gives the precondition that a non-Muslim must initiate any conflict that occurs; a Muslim should not fight unless he is attacked by a non-Muslim. Therefore, Ibn al-Jawzī records that the first phrase is believed to be abrogated by the following verses:[141]

A. Q 9.36: *"...but fight the idolaters, one and all, as they fight you one and all."*
B. Q 2.191 and Q 4.36: *"...kill them wherever ye find them...."*
C. Q 9.29: *"Fight those who believe not in God and in the last day[D]...."*
D. Q 9.5: *"...kill the idolaters wherever ye may find them...."*

and crave what God has prescribed for you, and eat and drink
until a white thread can be distinguished by you from a black one
at the dawn. Then fulfil the fast until the night, and go not in unto
them, and ye at your devotions in the mosques the while. These
are the bounds that God has set, so draw not near thereto. Thus
does God make manifest His signs to men, that haply they may
fear.
188 Devour not your wealth among yourselves vainly, nor present
it to the judges that ye may devour a part of the wealth of men
sinfully, the while ye know.
189 They will ask thee about the phases of the moon; say, 'They
are indications of time for men and for the pilgrimage.' And it
is not righteousness that ye should enter into your houses from
behind them, but righteousness is he who fears; so enter into
your houses by the doors thereof and fear God; haply ye may
prosper yet.
190 Fight in God's way with those who fight with you, but
transgress not; verily, God loves not those who do transgress.

The second view holds that the phrase *"but transgress not,"* is what is abrogated in the verse. The scholars define *"transgress not"* as the killing of any women and children. These transgressions also include Muslims instigating the killing of those who do not want to fight and initiating fights during the sacred month.[142]

These scholars state that *"but transgress not"* is abrogated by Q 9.36: *"...but fight the idolaters, one and all, as they fight you one and all"* and by Q 9.5: *"...kill the idolaters wherever ye may find them...."*[143]

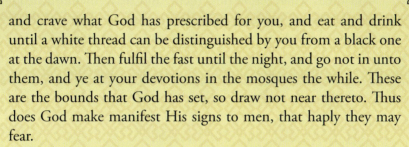

[191] Kill them wherever ye find them, and drive them out from whence they drive you out; for sedition is worse than slaughter; but fight them not by the Sacred Mosque until they fight you

Q 2.191

This verse, described as "one of the most complex in the study of abrogation," states that Muslims are not to fight others in the sacred area unless they are attacked first. One group of scholars claim that the verse is not abrogated and use some *sunans* to support their view. However, another group alleges that it is abrogated and uses other verses and *ḥadīths* from the *sunan.*"[144] They offer these verses to support their argument:

A. Q 9.5: *"...kill the idolaters wherever ye may find them...."* This verse orders fighting at any time and place.[145]
B. Q 2.193, Q 8.39: *"But fight them that there be no sedition...."*[146]
C. Q 2.191: *"Kill them wherever ye find them...."*[147]
D. Q 2.191: *"...until they fight you there; then kill them."*[148]
E. Q 9.36: *"...but fight the idolaters, one and all, as they fight you one and all...."*[149]

However, another group of scholars holds that the verse is conserved—meaning that it is not permissible for Muslims to fight in the sacred area unless they are being attacked. Those who hold this view rely on a *ḥadīth* of Muḥammad spoken at the conquest of Mecca, in which he said, "It is not permissible [to fight in the sacred area] to anyone after me; it was only made permissible for me for one hour of a day."[150]

Q 2.191

The reading in the current Arabic Qur'ān is "...**but fight them not** at the Sacred Mosque, unless **they** (first) **fight you** there; but if **they fight you**, slay them." (Yusuf Ali trans.; Palmer translation does not include the third phrase *fight you.*)

A group of readers read the above rendered words with an *alif* (long "a" sound) *wa lā tuqātilūhum...yuqātilūkum...qātalūkum* ("**but fight them not...they fight you...they fight you**"). Others read it as *wa lā tuqatilūhum...yuqatilūkum...qatalūkum* ("but kill them not...they kill you...they kill you").[151]

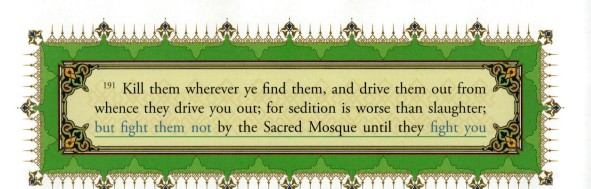

there; then kill them, for such is the recompense of those that misbelieve.
192 But if they desist, then, verily, God is forgiving and merciful.

Reading it the first way forbids initiating the fighting. The second reading forbids killing, or it could be understood to permit fighting on the condition that bloodshed is avoided.

Q 2.192

The scholars divided on the meaning of *"if they cease"* fall into two groups:

Some ruled that the meaning of this verse is conserved because they believe *"if they desist"* indicates the end of all nonbelief [in Allah and Muḥammad as his messenger].[152]

But other scholars believe *"if they desist"* means that [the idolaters] have stopped fighting the Muslims.[153]

This belief, in turn, has led to these two opposing views:

A. Q 2.192 states *"verily, God is forgiving and merciful."* Allah is declared such because he does not order that the idolaters be fought while in the sacred area but only to be fought after they leave it (Q 2.191). Therefore, the meaning of this verse is conserved.[154]

B. Others believe that the command in Q 9.5, *"...kill the idolaters wherever ye may find them...,"* replaces the forgiveness and mercy found in Q 2.192.[155] Therefore, abrogation is probable here.

Al-Naḥās and al-Makkī do not address the abrogation of this verse.

[193] But fight them that there be no sedition and that the religion
may be God's; but, if they desist, then let there be no hostility save
against the unjust.
[194] The sacred month for the sacred month; for all sacred things
demand retaliation; and whoso transgresses against you, transgress
against him like as he transgressed against you; but fear ye God,
and know that God is with those who fear.
[195] Expend in alms in God's way and be not cast by your own hands
into perdition; but do good, for God loves those who do good.

Q 2.194

This verse refers to the prohibited months or sacred months[D] during which Muslims are traditionally forbidden to fight or wage war. However, some scholars believe this phrase of Q 2.194 is abrogated by the second part of the same verse: *"and whoso transgresses against you, transgress against him like as he transgressed against you. . . ."*[156]

Those who believe in abrogation reason that Q 2.192 was revealed in Mecca where Muḥammad and his followers experienced persecution. Therefore, this verse came to give the Muslims the permission to either respond (fight) or be patient. After Muḥammad migrated to Medina, the verse was abrogated with verses about fighting.[157]

On the other hand, those who did not believe in the abrogation of this verse stated that in the event that a Muslim is attacked during the sacred months, he should respond likewise. They ruled that this portion of Q 2.194 is not abrogated because "repelling an attack is permitted at all times by all scholars." Al-Naḥās also leans toward this ruling.[158]

Q 2.194

Humans create laws to achieve justice, and there is no concept of forgiveness written into the law. However, the absence of "forgiveness" from legal transcriptions does not mean that the law is a means of revenge. So if human law, as imperfect as it is, rejects the idea of vengeance, how is it normal that a book, considered to be "brought down from heaven," would state that the normal response to an assault is an assault? Could

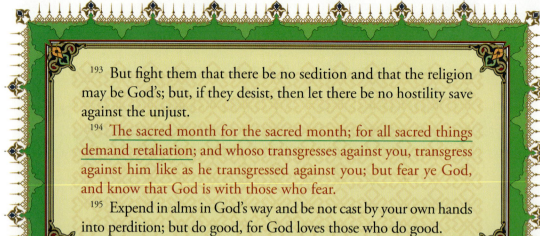

196 And fulfil the pilgrimage and the visitation to God; but if ye be besieged, then what is easiest for you by way of gift. But shave not your heads until your gift shall reach its destination; and he amongst you who is sick or has a hurt upon his head, then the redemption is by fasting or by alms or by an offering. But when ye are safe again, then let him who would enjoy the visitation until the pilgrimage (bring) what is easiest as a gift. And he who cannot find (anything to bring), then let him fast three days on the pilgrimage

the principle of *"and whoso transgresses against you, transgress against him like as he transgressed against you"* be a divine legislation?

Q 2.196

Scholars define the completion of the Ḥajj (major pilgrimage) and ʿUmra (minor pilgrimage), as mentioned in Q 2.196, as merely the fulfillment of religious rituals with no reference to conducting commercial activities during these events.[159] Based on this interpretation, the scholars ruled that this verse is abrogated by Q 2.198: *"It is no crime to you that ye seek good from your Lord...."*[160]

Q 2.196

The verse commands Muslims to perform both the major and minor pilgrimages, specifying some of the rituals that must be performed. The principle requirements of the Islāmic pilgrimage rituals consist of wearing the Ḥajj clothes (*al-Iḥrām*), shaving the head, going between the Ṣafā and Marwa, compassing the Kaʿba, kissing the black stone, casting stones, and offering a sacrifice.

What captures the attention is how astonishingly similar the Islāmic pilgrimage rituals are to the pagan pilgrimage rituals. To demonstrate this strong similarity, consider the elements of the pagan pilgrimage.

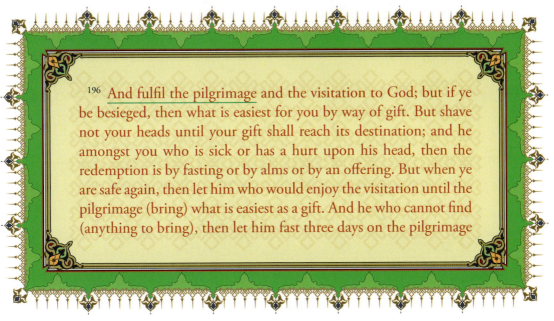

and seven when ye return; these make ten days complete. That is, for him whose family are not present in the Sacred Mosque; and fear God and know that God is keen to punish.

197 The pilgrimage is (in) well-known months: whosoever then makes it incumbent on himself (let him have neither) commerce with women, nor fornication, nor a quarrel on the pilgrimage; and whatsoever of good ye do, God knoweth it; then provide yourself for your journey; but the best provision is piety. Fear ye me ye who possess minds.

The Ḥajj [Major Pilgrimage] and the 'Umra [Minor Pilgrimage]

Before Islām, the Arabs used to perform their pilgrimage in the month of Dhū-l-Ḥijja every year. They performed the very same ceremonies that Muslims continue to perform today.

The Talbiyya [answering the call], the Ihram [consecration], the wearing of the garments of Ihram, the leading of Hudī [leading of the sacrificial animal] and its rituals—standing at 'Arafāt, dashing forward at Muzdalifa, heading to Mina to cast stones, *naḥr* [sacrificing by cutting the jugular vein] the Hudī and compassing the Ka'ba [as well] seven times [neither increased or decreased in Islām], kissing the black stone [to glorify it], and the Sa'ī [retracing Hajar's route] between the Ṣafā and Marwa]—all remain the same. They [pre-Islāmic Arabs] also used to call the eighth day of Dhū-l-Ḥijja [*Yawm al-Tarwīya*] stand at 'Arafāt on the ninth day, and start on the tenth, the days of Mina and the casting of stones. They [also] called these days [*al-Tashrīq* days]. They further performed the minor pilgrimage on months other than that of the Ḥajj.

('Abd al-Karīm, *al-Judhūr al-Tārīkhīya li-l-Sharī'a al-Islāmīya* 16-17)

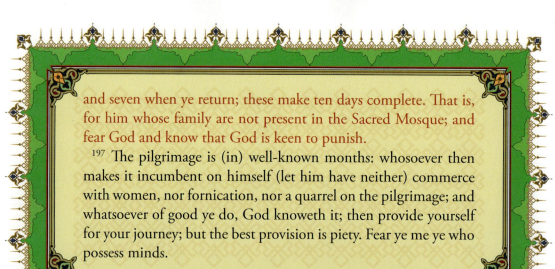

The time of the pilgrimage is in the month of Dhū-l-Ḥijja, which is why it is called the month of Ḥajj. This is the last month in the Islāmic calendar, and it was also known by this name before the advent of Islām. The ancient texts mention the month by the name *Dhū-Ḥijjatin*, which means Dhū-l-Ḥijja, and indicates that the Arabs regarded this month as their month of pilgrimage before the founding of Islām as a religion.[161]

Historical sources say that because of the presence of numerous holy sites (*ka'bas*) in the Arabian Peninsula, the pilgrimage did not take place in only one location. So the pilgrimage was not only to Mecca but to different holy sites as well. In addition, the ceremonial practices of both the major and minor pilgrimages were not the same in all locations. These ceremonial practices differed from one tribe to another. When Muḥammad considered adopting Ḥajj as a pillar of Islām, he adopted the Quraysh form of *ḥajj* (pagan pilgrimage). One of the most distinctive rituals of the Quraysh was to go hastily between the Ṣafā and Marwa.

When we compare the pagan rituals with the Islāmic, we find complete commonality between them.

For example, the scholars relate several different forms of *talbīya* ("answering the call by a religious chant"). Every tribe answered its special idol's call in its own form. The people of Mecca had their unique form as well. Ibn Ḥabīb mentions the Quraysh form of *talbiyya* to the idol Isāf: *"Labayk Allahuma labayk, labayk lā sharīka laka illā sharīk howa laka. Tamlikuhu wa mā malak"* ("We answer you, Allah, we answer you. We answer you. There is no partner with you except the one that you own. You own that one and all that one owns").[162] We find that the Muslim form of *talbiyya* is very similar to it: *"Labayk Allahuma labayk, lā sharīka laka labayk, inna al-ḥamda wa al-ni'mata laka wa almulk, la sharīka lak"* ("We answer you, Allah, we answer you. We answer you. There is no partner with you, we answer you. Praise and grace belong to you as well as reign, there is no partner with you").[163]

The commonality between the pagan pilgrimage rituals and the Islāmic rituals reveals a disquieting side to Islām—that is, one of Islām's pillars is completely derived from Arabian paganism.

Despite the spiritual danger, the act of including the pagan pilgrimage rituals in Islām was a brilliant strategic move by Muḥammad, because it helped him gain the affection of the pagan Arab tribes. However, it also exposes the earthly, human nature of Islām and strips Muḥammad of his claim to the divine origin of the Qur'ān.

The Islāmization of the pagan *ḥajj* demonstrates Muḥammad's political genius, yet it topples his claim as a prophet sent from God.

Question: How could Allah accept the sanctioning of pagan pilgrimage rituals? If we overlook the politically beneficial dimension of sanctioning the *ḥajj*, this question remains unanswered.

198 It is no crime to you that ye seek good from your Lord; but
when ye pour forth from 'Arafat, remember God by the sacred
beacon. Remember Him how He guided you, although ye were
surely before of those who err.
199 Then pour ye forth from whence men do pour forth and ask
pardon of God; verily, God is forgiving and merciful.
200 And when ye have performed your rites, remember God as
ye remember your fathers, or with a keener memory still. There is
among men such as says, 'Our Lord! give us in this world;' but of
the future life no portion shall he have.
201 And some there be who say, 'Our Lord! give us in this world good
and in the future good; and keep us from the torment of the fire!'
202 These,—they have their portion from what they have earned;
for God is swift at reckoning up.
203 Remember God for a certain number of days; but whoso

Q 2.198

Ibn Mas'ūd and others read "good from your Lord during the pilgrimage…," adding the phrase "during the pilgrimage."[164] This addition clearly authorizes engaging in commerce, which is contrary to what is found in the Qur'ān. This verse does not speak clearly about the permissibility of engaging in commerce during the pilgrimage. Ibn 'Abbās read the verse with the addition as well.[165]

Q 2.213

In the codex of Ubayy Ibn Ka'b the word *al-basharu* ("mankind") is used instead of ***al-nāsu*** ("**Men**"; literally "the people") found in the current Arabic Qur'ān.[166]

Ibn Mas'ūd read "The people were one single nation, but they disagreed," adding *fa-ikhtalafū* ("but they disagreed").[167] This addition clarifies the verse because it explains the reason behind Allah's sending of the prophets. Therefore, the context becomes "Mankind was one single nation, but they disagreed, so Allah sent Messengers."

hastens off in two days, it is no sin to him, and he who lingers on it is no sin to him,—for him who fears. So fear ye God and know that unto Him shall ye be gathered.

204 There is among men one whose speech about the life of this world pleases thee, and he calls on God to witness what is in his heart; yet is he most fierce in opposition unto thee.

205 And when he turns away, he strives upon the earth to do evil therein, and to destroy the tilth and the stock; verily, God loves not evil doing.

206 And when it is said to him, 'Fear God,' then pride takes hold upon him in sin; but hell is enough for him! surely an evil couch is that.

207 And there is among men one who selleth his soul, craving those things that are pleasing unto God; and God is kind unto His servants.

208 O ye who believe! enter ye into the peace, one and all, and follow not the footsteps of Satan; verily, to you he is an open foe.

209 And if ye slip after that the manifest signs have come to you, then know that God is the mighty, the wise.

210 What can they expect but that God should come unto them in the shadow of a cloud, and the angels too? But the thing is decreed, and unto God do things return.

211 Ask the children of Israel how many a manifest sign we gave to them; and whoso alters God's favours after that they have come to him, then God is keen at following up.

212 Made fair to those who misbelieve is this world's life; they jest at those who do believe. But those who fear shall be above them on the resurrection day. God gives provision unto whom He will without account.

213 Men were one nation once, and God sent prophets with good tidings and with warnings, and sent down with them the Book in truth, to judge between men in that wherein they disagreed; but none did disagree therein save those who had been given it after

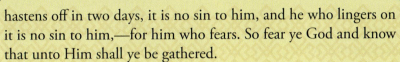

that manifest signs had come to them, through greed amongst
themselves; and God guided those who did believe to that truth
concerning which they disagreed by His permission, for God
guides whom He will unto the right path.
214 Did ye count to enter Paradise, while there had nothing come
to you like those who passed away before you; there touched them
violence and harm, and they were made to quake, until the Apostle
and those who believed with him said, 'When (comes) God's help?
Is not God's help then surely nigh?'
215 They will ask thee what they are to expend in alms: say,

Q 2.214

The codex of Ibn Mas'ūd presents the verse in a variant form: "and they were so shaken and shaken again until…", by adding *thumma zulzilū* ("then they were shaken").[168]

Q 2.215

One group of scholars define *"what they are to expend in alms"* as charity given to the various groups mentioned (parents, family, orphans, etc.). Therefore, they ruled that this verse is abrogated by Q 9.60, which mandates charitable giving (*Ṣadaqa*): *"Alms are only for the poor and needy…."*[169]

Another group of scholars ruled that the meaning of Q 2.215 is conserved because they believe that this verse discusses the spending of bounties (surplus) and voluntary acts of charity. Therefore, it is not proper to speak of its abrogation.[170]

Q 2.216

In the Arabic text the word translated here as *"prescribed"* literally means *imposed or ordained*. Therefore, this verse indicates that fighting is imposed upon, or required, of all Muslims.[171] However, the meaning of this verse is considered abrogated by the following verses:

A. Q 2.286: *"God will not require of the soul save its capacity…."* Therefore, if a Muslim is physically unable to fight, fighting is not required.[172]

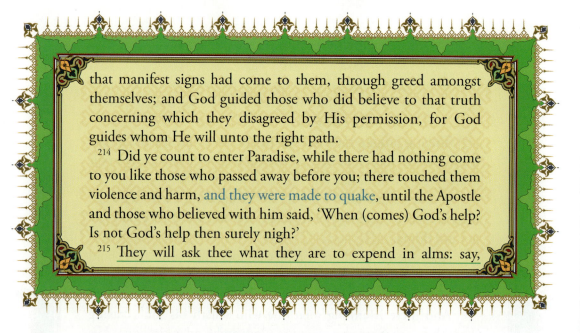

'Whatsoever good ye expend it should be for parents and kinsmen, and the orphan and the poor, and the son of the road; and whatsoever good ye do, verily, of it God knows.'
216 Prescribed for you is fighting, but it is hateful to you. Yet peradventure that ye hate a thing while it is good for you, and peradventure that ye love a thing while it is bad for you; God knows, and ye,—ye do not know!
217 They will ask thee of the sacred month,—of fighting therein. Say, 'Fighting therein is a great sin; but turning folks off God's way, and misbelief in Him and in the Sacred Mosque, and turning His

B. Q 9.122: *"...if a troop of every division of them march not forth, it is only that they may study their religion...."* If some Muslims are able to fight, then they are representative of all in their community; the rest of the community is thereby not required to physically engage in fighting.[173]
C. Q 9.41: *"March ye then, light and heavy...."*[174]

Q 2.217

Once Muḥammad sent a company of men, led by 'Abd Allah Ibn Jaḥsh[N], to survey an area. While surveying, the Jaḥsh's company raided a commercial camel train of the Quraysh during the Arab holy lunar month Jumada al-Akhira.

This raid led to several deaths among the ranks of the Quraysh and disturbed the Anṣār. Furthermore, the non-Muslims viewed this act as a violation of the sanctity of this month. In describing the sanctity of such months, Ibn al-Jawzī declared, "[I]f one of us were to pass by the murderer of his father, he would not [even] wake him up [i.e., disturb him]."[175] Therefore, Q 2.217 was abrogated to defend the act of Ibn Jaḥsh's company.[176]

This verse acknowledges the sanctity of the month and that violence is a violation. However, it justifies Ibn Jaḥsh's act by laying the responsibility on the Quraysh because they persecuted the Muslims and forced them to leave Mecca: *"turning His people out therefrom, is...greater in God's sight..."* (Q 2.217).

Later, the Muslims felt that fighting under such circumstances, even in sacred places, is not forbidden. Therefore, with the consensus of several Islāmic scholars, this verse is considered abrogated by the following verses:

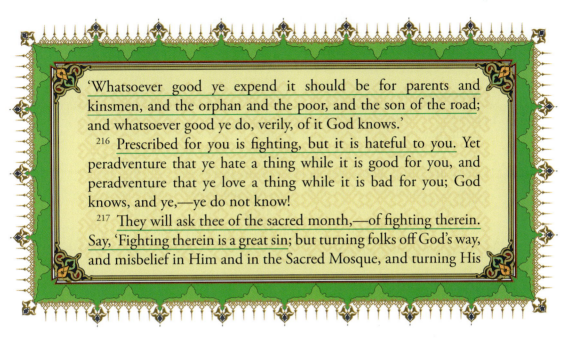

people out therefrom, is a greater in God's sight; and sedition is a greater sin than slaughter.' They will not cease from fighting you until they turn you from your religion if they can; but whosoever of you is turned from his religion and dies while still a misbeliever; these are those whose works are vain in this world and the next; they are the fellows of the Fire, and they shall dwell therein for aye.
218 Verily, those who believe, and those who flee, and those who wage war in God's way; these may hope for God's mercy, for God is forgiving and merciful.

A. Q 9.5: *"...kill the idolaters wherever ye may find them...."*[177]
B. Q 9.29: *"Fight those who believe not in God and in the last day...."*[178]
C. Q 9.36: *"...but fight the idolaters, one and all, as they fight you one and all...."*[179]

Q 2.219

This verse has two issues regarding abrogation:

1. The context of the verse considers the consumption of alcohol an undesirable act. According to many scholars, it abrogates the condition of absolute permissibility that was prevalent in early Islām.[180] However, there is ambiguity in the verse. Does it completely prohibit the consumption of alcoholic drinks? For this reason, 'Umar Ibn al-Khaṭṭāb[N] asked Muḥammad to explain more about the verse. Hence, verse Q 5.90 came to finally and completely eradicate the practice of drinking alcohol: *"...avoid them then...."*[181]
2. In the second part of Q 2.219, *'The surplus,'* is defined as a surplus of money. Scholars explained that this verse urges Muslims to spend money left over after satisfying their needs. But Muslims disliked this request. Therefore, Q 9.103 regarding the *zakāt* (mandatory almsgiving) was revealed by Muḥammad: *"Take from their wealth alms to cleanse and purify them thereby."* This verse (Q 9.103) then abrogates Q 2.219.[182]

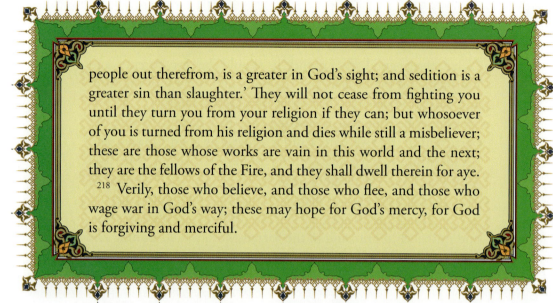

219 They will ask thee about wine and el maisar, say, 'In them both is sin and profit to men; but the sin of both is greater than the profit of the same.' They will ask thee what they shall expend in alms: say, 'The surplus.' Thus does God manifest to you His signs; haply ye may reflect on this world and the next!

220 They will ask thee about orphans: say, 'To do good to them is best.' But if ye interfere with them—they are your brethren, and God knows the evildoer from the well doer; and if God will He will surely trouble you. Verily, God is mighty, wise.

Other scholars ruled that '*The surplus*' means the *zakāt*. Therefore, Q 2.219 is conserved.[183]

Q 2.219

In the Palmer translation, the word "great," found in the current Arabic Qur'ān, is omitted from the verse. However, this word is included in the Yusuf Ali translation: "They ask thee concerning wine and gambling. Say: "In them is great sin, and some profit, for men…"

This verse has two issues regarding the variant readings for this adjective:

1. The readers collectively read ***ithmun kabīrun*** ("**great** sin"), whereas Ibn Mas'ūd as well as others read it *ithmun kathīrun* ("numerous sins").[184]
2. In the codex of Ibn Mas'ūd *ithmahumā aktharu* ("the sin of both is more numerous") is used instead of ***akbaru*** ("**greater**") found in the Qur'ān. The codex of Ubayy Ibn Ka'b' reads *ithmahumā aqrabū* ("the sin of both is nearer") instead.

The word *kabīrun* ("great") is an adjective that describes size rather than number, whereas, the word *kathīrun* ("numerous") is an adjective that describes number rather than size. Finally, *aqrabū* ("nearer") gives an entirely different meaning.

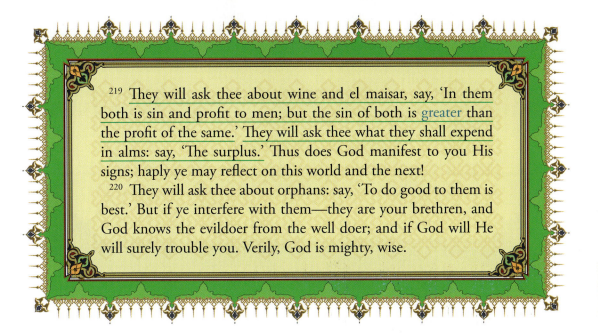

[221] Wed not with idolatrous women until they believe, for surely a believing handmaid is better than an idolatrous woman, even though she please you. And wed not to idolatrous men until they believe, for a believing slave is better than an idolater, even though he please you. Those invite you to the fire, but God invites you to paradise and pardon by His permission, and makes clear His signs to men; haply they may remember.

Q 2.221

In this verse, the Qur'ān forbids Muslim men and women from marrying "unbelievers": *"Wed not with idolatrous women…And wed not to idolatrous men…."* Because the Qur'ān accuses the Christians of being unbelievers (idolaters), marriage is prohibited between Muslims and Christians (Q 5.72-73, Q 9.31). Nonetheless, the Qur'ān allows Muslim men—**only**—to marry Jewish and Christian women (Q 5.5). Muslim women are not mentioned in Q 5.5, so they must abide by the prohibition of Q 2.221 to not marry a Jew or a Christian.

Since Q 5.5 does not abrogate Q 2.221, the contradiction still stands between these two opinions in the Qur'ān.

Question: Are Christians really *mushrikūn*[D] (unbelieving idolaters) or not? Is it permissible to have them as in-laws?

Q 2.221

There are differing opinions about the definition of *"unbelieving women."*

Some scholars believe this phrase refers to pagan, idolatrous women. Therefore, for these scholars the passage does not apply to Jewish or Christian women. Hence, the verse is conserved.[185]

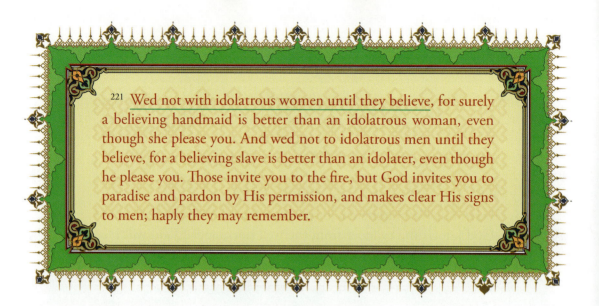

222 They will ask thee about menstruation: say, 'It is a hurt.' So keep apart from women in their menstruation, and go not near them till they be cleansed; but when they are cleansed come in to them by where God has ordered you; verily, God loves those who turn to Him, and those who keep themselves clean.

Other scholars believe that the word *"unbelieving"* is a description of all non-Muslim women. They feel that this group includes women who are part of the group referred to as "the People of the Book" (Jews and Christians), women from other religious backgrounds, and women from people groups who have no holy scriptures. However, those who hold this general opinion are divided on this verse's abrogation, terms, and application:

A. The purpose of Q 2.221 is to forbid the marriage of Muslims to "women of the Book" (Jews and Christians). However, this prohibition is abrogated by Q 5.5: *"Lawful for you…chaste women of those who believe, and chaste women of those to whom the Book has been given before you…."* [186]

B. The phrase *"Do not marry unbelieving women"* is a general expression and Q 5.5 explains, not abrogates, the command in this verse. Therefore, Q 5.5 does not abrogate Q 2.221; it merely specifies the type of women who are acceptable to marry.[187] "Therefore, Q 5.5 is conserved and not abrogated; it specifies and explains Q 2.221."[188]

C. Some have said that the prohibition found in Q 2.221 concerns "women of the Book" who reside outside of Islāmic countries and territories. Therefore, such women are not under Islāmic control. Based on this interpretation of Q 2.221, the verse is conserved. It is neither abrogated, nor is it specific.[189]

Question: Why do Muslim men marry European and American women when such women are in non-Muslim countries?

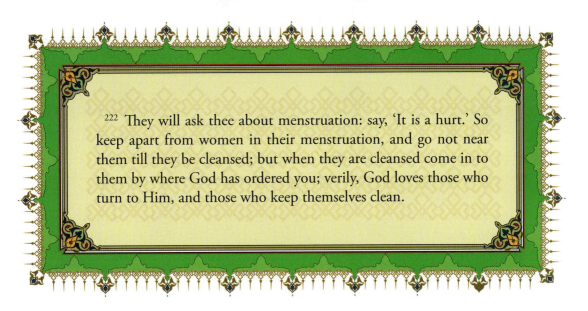

[223] Your women are your tilth, so come into your tillage how you choose; but do a previous good act for yourselves, and fear God, and know that ye are going to meet Him; and give good tidings unto those who do believe.
[224] Make not God the butt of your oaths, that ye will keep clear and fear and make peace amongst men, for God both hears and knows.
[225] He will not catch you up for a casual word in your oaths, but He will catch you up for what your hearts have earned; but God is forgiving and clement.

Q 2.223

This verse views women as farms (or *tilth*, meaning "tilled earth or soil") that men plow. In the commentary by al-Ṭabarī, al-Suddiy describes a woman as "a farm that can be plowed" by a man.[190] It also allows Muslim men to have sexual relations with no limits (*annā shi'tum*), which can be interpreted to mean when, where, or however he desires. The verse also gives the Muslim man the right to do whatever he pleases with the body of a woman.

But the question regarding this verse is not concerned with whether the Qur'ān gives men the right to treat a woman's body as they please, because this issue is not disputed among Muslim scholars. Rather, the question is, what does the expression, *"so come into your tillage how you choose,"* mean?

To understand this expression, we have to determine what is meant by *annā shi'tum*, translated in the English above as *"how."* Does *annā shi'tum* mean "however, whenever, or wherever?" The scholars offered divergent views:

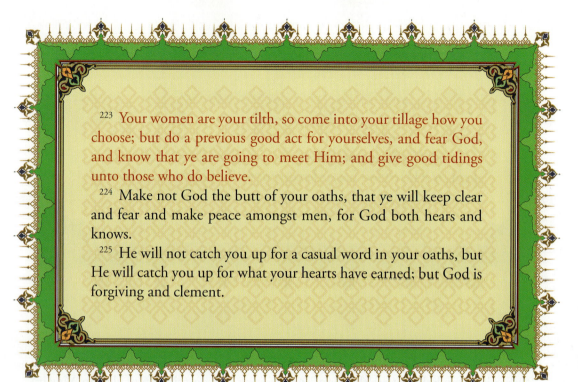

A. Some scholars believed this expression means a Muslim man may have intercourse in any position he prefers. Some Jews criticized the Muslims for having different sexual positions during intercourse. A Jew also said, "You are like the animals, for we only approach her in one position," so this verse came in response to him.[191]
B. A Muslim man may have intercourse whenever he desires, except during her menstrual period.[192]
C. A Muslim man may have intercourse whenever and wherever he desires. And some believe that the verse permits anal intercourse. Ibn 'Umar commented on this verse: "[I]t came down regarding approaching women in their anuses."[193]

Concerning the above viewpoint, several stories are told about why this verse was handed down (revealed). One story relates "that a man approached a woman in her anus and was not settled in his soul about it." Therefore, this verse was revealed.[194]

Another story tells of "a man who had anal intercourse with his wife...but the people considered it *munkar* (meaning "abhorable, abominable")...so Allah sent down" this verse.[195]

The legal scholars of Medina felt that anal intercourse should be allowed.[196] Purportedly, in one of Mālik's books, *Kitāb al-Sirr* [*The Book of the Secret*], he is said to have agreed as well. There are other reports that indicate several of Muḥammad's Companions also supported this view.[197]

In addition, Ibn al-'Arabī, in his book *Aḥkām al-Qur'ān* [*The Rulings of the Qur'ān*], states that a group of scholars supported anal intercourse. He adds that a scholar named Ibn Sha'ban collected opinions supporting this viewpoint in a book titled *Jimā' al-Niswān wa Aḥkām al-Qur'ān* [*Intercourse with Women and the Rulings of the Qur'ān*]. Ibn al-'Arabī "found support to its permissibility among a noble group of the Companions and the followers of Mālik in several stories."[198]

Regardless of the sources that gave credence to the various viewpoints, it is undeniable that an argument emerged among the followers of each opinion. It is said that Ibn al-Jawzī authored a book titled, *Taḥrim al-Maḥal al-Makrūh* [*Forbidding the Detestable Spot*], in which he objects to the opinion allowing anal intercourse.[199]

Despite all these scholarly arguments, this verse gives the man the right to take any sexual position he desires and allows him to satisfy his sexual yearning at any time, regardless of the woman's physical and psychological state. The reality remains that, even with a more moderate interpretation, this verse does away with the personhood of a woman.

Question: If the "divine" permission in the verse means "allowing a variety of sexual positions but not anal intercourse," why does the Qur'ānic revelation come in such an ambiguous way that it would allow those leaning towards deviant sexual practices to fulfill their desires?

[226] Those who swear off from their women, they must wait four
months; but if they break their vow God is forgiving and merciful.
[227] And if they intend to divorce them, verily, God hears and
knows.

Q 2.226

Before Islām, a custom among the Arab tribes permitted a man angry with his wife to take an oath to forego any sexual relations with her for one year or more without divorcing her. Some scholars reported that it was "not an oath but was said in anger," while others said that oath taking is swearing "in anger or without."[200] Therefore, Q 2.226 came to change this custom, reducing potential abstention to a period of four months. Q 2.226 also states that if the husband's abstention exceeds this time period, then the wife is entitled to divorce her husband.[201]

This verse does not abrogate any other known verse in the current written Qur'ān. However, it was included in the scholars' list of Qur'ānic abrogations. It is possible that some unrecorded text, which would have been abrogated by Q 2.226, was inadvertently omitted during the writing down of the Qur'ān. (See the article "Compilation of the Qur'ān" on page 49.)

Q 2.228

Scholars state that the *"three courses"* mentioned here refer to three menstrual periods.[202] Therefore, the divorcée has to wait for three menstrual periods to conclude before remarrying. This waiting period is known as the *'idda*[D]. Scholars disagree on whether the rule found in this verse is abrogated or conserved.

Some scholars believe that the length of the waiting period is abrogated by verses which delineate the following situations:

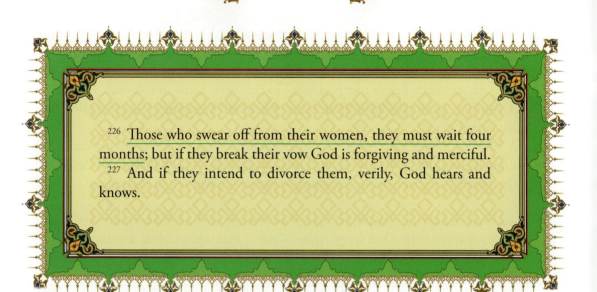

228 Divorced women must wait for themselves three courses; and it is not lawful to them that they hide what God has created in their wombs, if they believe in God and in the last day. Their husbands will do better to take them back in that (case) if they wish for reconciliation; for, the same is due to them as from them; but the men should have precedence over them. God is mighty and wise.

A. If the divorcée is pregnant, then Q 2.228 is abrogated by Q 65.4: *"And those who are heavy with child their appointed time is when they have laid down their burden...."* [203]
B. If the divorcée no longer menstruates or has not yet begun menstruation, then Q 2.228 is abrogated by another portion of Q 65.4: *"And such of your women as despair of menstruation,—if ye doubt, then their term is three months; and such as have not menstruated too...."* [204]
C. If the divorcée's marriage was never consummated, then Q 2.228 is abrogated by Q 33.49: *"O ye who believe! when ye wed believing women, and then divorce them before ye have touched them, ye have no term that ye need observe...."* [205]

Other scholars believe that the beginning of Q 2.228 is conserved, but the phrase, *"Their husbands will do better to take them back in that (case)"* is abrogated. According to this phrase, a husband has the right to reclaim his wife within three menstrual periods or less after divorcing her. However, these scholars ruled that this portion of Q 2.228 is abrogated by Q 2.230: *"But if he divorce*[s] *her (a third time) she shall not be lawful to him after that, until she marry another husband...."* [206]

However, Ibn al-Jawzī believes the entire verse should be conserved: "For its beginning is general, about the divorcee [Q 2.228]; [and] what is included about the pregnant, elderly [Q 65.4]...is distinct from the overall, and is not a matter of abrogation." [207] Hence, Ibn al-Jawzī believes that verses, such as Q 65.4, merely provide additional details but do not alter the meaning of Q 2.228.

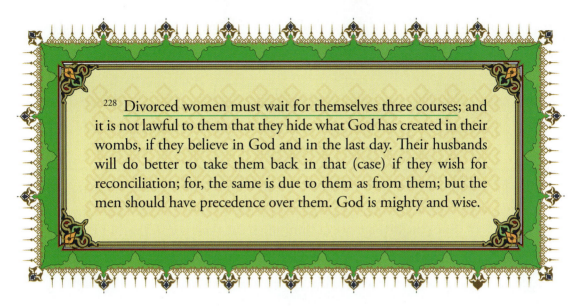

[229] Divorce (may happen) twice; then keep them in reason, or let
them go with kindness. It is not lawful for you to take from them
anything of what you have given them, unless both fear that they
cannot keep within God's bounds. So if ye fear that ye cannot keep
within God's bounds there is no crime in you both about what she
ransoms herself with. These are God's bounds, do not transgress
them; and whoso transgresses God's bounds, they it is who are unjust.
[230] But if he divorce her (a third time) she shall not be lawful to
him after that, until she marry another husband; but, if he divorce

Q 2.229

Ubayy Ibn Ka'b uses a variant reading using two substitutions in this verse:[208]

- He substitutes the first verb ***yakhāfā*** ("[they] **both fear**") in the Qur'ān with *yaẓunnā* ("[they] both think").
- He also substitutes the dual form *ẓannā* ("[they] both thought") for the plural ***khiftum*** ("**ye** [plural] **fear**").

The difference between the current and Ibn Ka'b's reading is that the intended two people (main subject) in his reading are the ones who are thinking, whereas in the current Arabic Qur'ān's reading the intended people are the ones who might fear. Note that Palmer erroneously translates "ye cannot keep," but the Arabic states that "they both cannot keep."

Q 2.229-231

The Qur'ān justifies, or approves, repeated divorces. According to verse 229, the man is given the right to divorce his wife twice and to remarry her after the first and second divorces. But, if he divorces her a third time, she is not allowed to return to her ex-husband, *"until she marry another husband"* (Q 2.230). (See the article "Women in the Qur'ān" on page 117.)

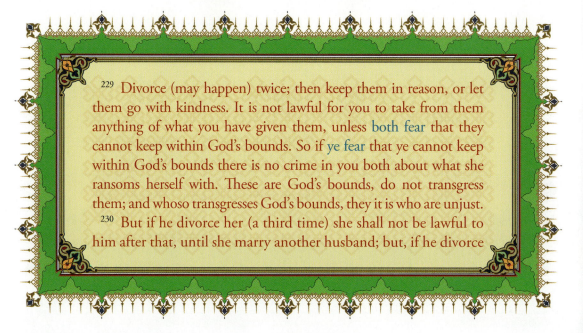

A story is told that a Muslim called Thābit Ibn Yasar from the Anṣār divorced his wife. When her period of waiting (*'idda*) was near its end, he would take her again and

her too, it is no crime in them both to come together again, if they think that they can keep within God's bounds. These are God's bounds which He explains to a people who know.

231 When ye divorce women, and they have reached the prescribed time, then keep them kindly, or let them go in reason, but do not keep them by force to transgress; for whoso does that, he is unjust to his own soul: and do not take God's signs in jest; and remember God's favours to you, and what He has sent down to you of the Book and wisdom, to admonish you thereby; and fear God, and know that God doth all things know.

then divorce her again. He would do that just to hurt her. To end this type of abuse, the verse Q 2.231 came down, saying, *"but do not keep them by force to transgress...."*[209]

Did the above-mentioned man find support for his practice in a *jāhilīya* (pre-Islāmic) custom or in an Islāmic principle that was later annulled? Because there is no information about the basis for this practice, we cannot come to a final verdict. However, this principle used to allow the man, if he divorced his wife, to take her back before the end of her *ʿidda*, no matter how many times he divorced her.

This pre-Islāmic principle allowed men to toy with the destiny of their wives, taking them back and then rejecting them. The Muslim scholars explain that the reason for enacting *"until she marry another husband"* is to prevent the husband from playing with his wife's emotions and to liberate her from being a pawn of his moods.

Muslim scholars further studied the meaning of *"until she marry another husband"* and gave two viewpoints on the application of this statement:

In the first viewpoint, scholars believe that what is meant by the word *nikāh* ("marry") in the verse is "having a marriage contract." Once the other person (wife) is "contracted," even if the couple (wife with second husband) does not have sexual intercourse, she could go back to the first husband.

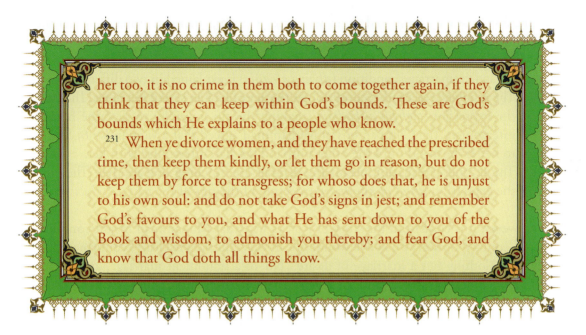

In the second viewpoint (the view held by most scholars) *nikāh* means sexual contact. They supported this opinion with a story about the wife of Rifāʿa al-Quradhiy, whose name was Tamīma bint Waheb. She was divorced by her husband but she married another man simply to enable her to return to her ex-husband under Islāmic laws. But Muḥammad said to her, "Do you want to go back to Rifāʿa? Not until you experience *dhawq al-ʿasīla* with him [her second husband], and he with you."[210] While this expression is usually translated as "experiencing orgasm," there are other views on the meaning of these words.

Muḥammad's remarriage condition (*dhawq al-'asīla*) is explained in two different ways:

1. The scholars explain this condition as the act of having sexual relations. They use the expression *taghyīb al-ḥashafa* (making the tip invisible) to describe having intercourse. The Companions of Muḥammad agreed that a woman is not lawful to her ex-husband until the other husband has had intercourse with her.
2. The second explanation means the genitals are touching one another. They use the expression *iltiqā' al-khitānayn* (meeting of the tips of the parts).

However, it is clear from the story of Rifā'a's wife that Muḥammad meant complete sexual contact; option two above would not fit this criteria. He clearly confirmed this, saying, "Nothing but a marriage of desire. 'No' to a fraudulent marriage, and 'no' to making a mockery of the book of Allah. Then, he must experience *dhawq al-'asīla* with her." Thus, he warned against *taḥlīl*, an intervening marriage contracted for the sole purpose of legalizing a remarriage between a divorced couple. Muḥammad said, "Allah['s] curses be upon the *muḥalil,* the one making it permissible, and the *muḥalal lahu*, the one that it would become lawful to." Muḥammad further described the person who would play the role of the *muḥalil*, saying he is "a borrowed billy goat."[211]

Hence, the process of going back to the first husband necessitates going through the following stages:[212]

- Waiting the mandated period of time (*'idda);*
- Making a marriage contract with the second husband;
- Having sexual intercourse with the second husband (*dhawq al 'asīla*);
- Divorcing the second husband;
- Waiting the mandated period of time (*'idda*).

Without any doubt, removing the custom allowing a man to overly manipulate a woman was necessary. However, does the enactment by Muḥammad that is based on *"until she marry another husband"* and "experiencing *dhawq al-'asīla* with him" show that it is a heavenly ruling? This method of dealing with divorce requires the education of legislators and their own personal understanding of the relationship between a man and a woman rather than a divine or theological view.

Note: The rule of divorcing three times does not apply to all Muslims. Islāmic scholars ruled that a slave can marry only two women and only divorce twice. The waiting period for a slave woman before remarrying is two menstrual cycles; however, if she is not experiencing menses, then it is two months. This waiting period is shorter than for a free woman, who must wait through three menstrual cycles.[213]

[232] When ye divorce women, and they have reached their
prescribed term, do not prevent them from marrying their (fresh)
husbands, when they have agreed with each other reasonably. That
is what he is admonished with who amongst you believes in God
and in the last day. That is more pure for you and cleaner. But God
knows, and ye know not.
[233] Mothers must suckle their children two whole years for one
who wishes to complete the time of suckling; and on him to
whom it is born its sustenance and clothing are incumbent; but in
reason, for no soul shall be obliged beyond its capacity. A mother
shall not be forced for her child; nor he to whom it is born for his
child. And the same (is incumbent) on the heir (of the father). But
if both parties wish to wean, by mutual consent and counsel, then
it is no crime in them. And if ye wish to provide a wet-nurse for
your children, it is no crime in you when you pay what you have
promised her, in reason. Fear God, and know that God on what
ye do doth look.
[234] Those of you who die and leave wives behind, let these wait
by themselves for four months and ten days; and when they have

Q 2.233

This verse describes the recommended period for breastfeeding a child. Scholars disagree on whether the meaning of this verse is abrogated or conserved.

Some scholars ruled that the term of *"two whole years"* is abrogated by the second part of Q 2.233: *"But if both* [the father and mother] *parties wish to wean, by mutual consent and counsel, then it is no crime in them."*[214]

However, another group of scholars believe this entire verse is conserved, because the primary purpose is to demonstrate the recommended period of breastfeeding.[215] They ruled that there is no abrogation since this verse grants the opportunity to choose and the two-year period is not mandatory.[216]

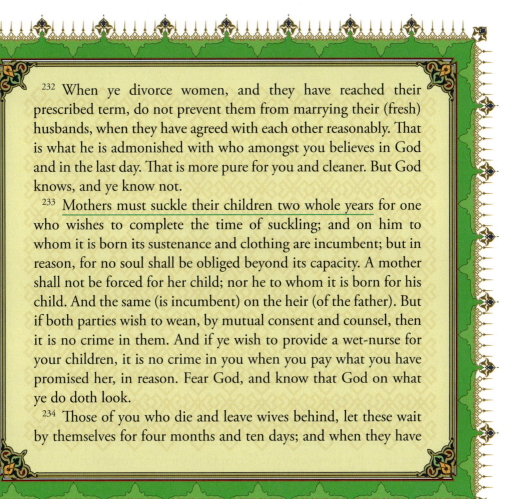

reached their prescribed time, there is no crime in them for what they do with themselves in reason; for God of what ye do is well aware.

235 Nor is there any crime in you for that ye make them an offer of marriage, or that ye keep it secret, in your minds. God knows that ye will remember them; but do not propose to them in secret, unless ye speak a reasonable speech; and resolve not on marriage tie until the Book shall reach its time; but know that God knows what is in your souls; so beware! and know that God is forgiving and clement.

236 It is no crime in you if ye divorce your women ere you have yet touched them, or settled for them a settlement. But provide maintenance for them; the wealthy according to his power, and the straitened in circumstances according to his power, must provide, in reason;—a duty this upon the kind.

237 And if ye divorce them before ye have touched them, but have already settled for them a settlement; the half of what ye have settled, unless they remit it, or he in whose hand is the marriage tie remits it; and that ye should remit is nearer to piety, and forget not liberality between you. Verily, God on what ye do doth look.

238 Observe the prayers, and the middle prayer, and stand ye attent before God.

239 And if ye fear, then afoot or on horseback; but when ye are in safety remember God, how He taught you while yet ye did not know.

240 Those of you who die and leave wives, should bequeath to their wives maintenance for a year, without expulsion (from their home); but if they go out, there is no crime in you for what they do of themselves, in reason; but God is mighty and wise.

241 And divorced women should have a maintenance in reason,—a duty this on those that fear.

242 Thus does God explain to you His signs; haply ye may

understand.
[243] Dost thou not look at those who left their homes by thousands, for fear of death; and God said to them 'Die,' and then He quickened them again? Verily, God is Lord of grace to men, but most men give no thanks.
[244] Fight then in God's way, and know that God both hears and knows.

Q 2.238

The exegetes disagreed concerning the meaning of "**the middle prayer**":

- It is the dawn (*al-fajr*) prayer.[217]
- It is the noon (*al-ẓuhr*) prayer.[218]
- It is the afternoon (*al-'aṣr*) prayer.[219]
- It is the sunset (*al-maghrib*) prayer.[220]

'Ā'isha, the third wife of Muḥammad, wrote in her Qur'ān: "Observe the prayers, and the middle prayer and the afternoon prayer; and stand ye attent before God," by adding *wa ṣalāt al-'aṣr* ("and the afternoon prayer"). She said that she heard it from Muḥammad.[221] There were others who read this verse according to 'Ā'isha's reading.[222] Among them is Ḥafṣa, the daughter of 'Umar and 'Ubayd Ibn 'Umayr.[223]

Q 2.240

It was customary before Islām that a widow was entitled to stay in the marital home for one year from the time of her husband's death and use the money she inherited for living expenses. Other heirs were not entitled to request the division of the estate until the end of that year. However, if the widow willingly moved out of the house before the end of the year, then the heir was free to manage the inheritance without guilt in regards to the widow's situation.[224] Islām incorporated this social custom with Q 2.240.

However, this rule was soon changed as Q 2.240 was abrogated by Q 2.234: *"Those of you who die and leave wives behind, let these wait by themselves for four months and ten days."* Thus, the yearlong period was changed to four months and ten days.[225]

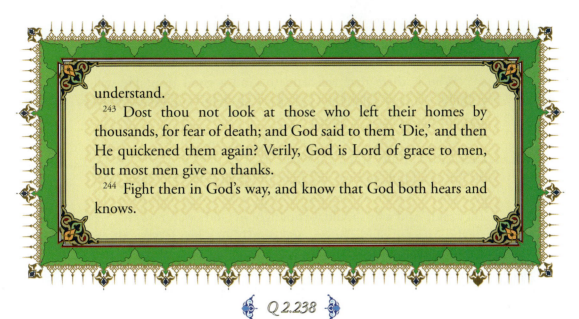

245 Who is there that will lend to God a good loan? He will redouble it many a double; God closes His hand and holds it out, and unto Him shall ye return.

246 Dost thou not look at the crowd of the children of Israel after Moses' time, when they said to a prophet of theirs, 'Raise up for us a king, and we will fight in God's way?' He said, 'Will ye perhaps, if it be written down for you to fight, refuse to fight?' They said, 'And why should we not fight in God's way, now that we are dispossessed of our homes and sons?' But when it was written down for them to fight they turned back, save a few of them, and God knows who are evildoers.

247 Then their prophet said to them, 'Verily, God has raised up for you *T*alut as a king;' they said, 'How can the kingdom be his over us; we have more right to the kingdom than he, for he has not an amplitude of wealth?' He said, 'Verily, God has chosen him over you, and has provided him with an extent of knowledge and of form. God gives the kingdom unto whom He will; God comprehends and knows.'

248 Then said to them their prophet, 'The sign of his kingdom is that there shall come to you the ark with the shechina in it from your Lord, and the relics of what the family of Moses and the family of Aaron left; the angels shall bear it.' In that is surely a sign to you if ye believe.

249 And when *T*alut set out with his soldiery, he said, 'God will try you with a river, and he who drinks therefrom, he is not of mine; but whoso tastes it not, he is of mine, save he who laps it lapping with his hand.' And they drank from it save a few of them, and when he crossed it, he and those who believed with him, they said, 'We have no power this day against *G*alut and his soldiery,' those who thought that they should meet their Lord said, 'How many a small division of men have conquered a numerous division, by the permission of God, for God is with the patient.'

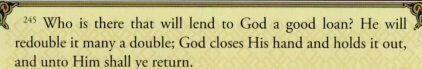

Q 2.247-251

These verses tell the story of a prophet who told the Israelites, "Allah, in answer to your request, has appointed Ṭālūt (Saul) as your king." The leaders objected to this choice because, in addition to lacking enough money to give him the right to be a leader, the candidate did not come from the tribe of the kings nor from the house of prophecy. But the prophet answered them, saying, "The matter is Allah's will and Ṭālūt will bring the Ark as a sign of his reign."

After Ṭālūt became king, he went out with his army to fight his enemies. He told his soldiers that they would cross a river and that Allah would test them by requiring that they not drink from the river. Anyone who drinks from it, *"save he who laps it lapping with his hand,"* would fail the test (Q 2.249). Most of the soldiers failed the test, so those who eventually crossed with Ṭālūt were few. (Most of the tales told in the commentaries speculate the number to be a little over three hundred men.)

When these few soldiers saw the enemy's leader, Jālūt (Goliath), they were terrified. But a few who were pure in faith said to the scared among them, "History teaches us that a small group with faith and perseverance is able to conquer, by the might of Allah, an oppressive group of a large number." Then they called to Allah to give them victory against the enemy. Indeed, the believers vanquished their enemies with a great victory, and David, who later became King David, killed Jālūt.

This narrative in the Qur'ān tells the story of Saul (Ṭālūt) but introduces into it an event from the life of David and a chapter from the life of Gideon. The biblical story tells us that the prophet Samuel anointed Saul to be king over the Israelites (1 Sam. 15.1). During the reign of Saul, a war takes place against the Philistines where David fights Goliath (Jālūt) and kills him (1 Sam. 17.33-58). However, the Qur'ān diverges from the biblical text:

A. When mentioning the subject of the Ark, the Qur'ān associates the Ark with Saul, not David. The Qur'ān says, *"The sign of his kingdom is that there shall come to you the ark..."* (Q 2.248). But it is David, not Saul, who takes control of Jerusalem and brings the Ark of the Covenant to that city (2 Sam. 6.6-19).

B. As to the story of the river, it is Gideon who says, after routing the Midianites, "Come down against the Midianites and seize the waters of the Jordan ahead of them as far as Beth Barah" (Judg. 7.24). The three hundred fighters who cross the river are with Gideon: "Gideon and his three hundred men, exhausted yet keeping up the pursuit, came to the Jordan and crossed it" (Judg. 8.4). But the Qur'ān adds to the story the description of the drinking water test, which is either a result of an oral tale that had spread in the Arabian Peninsula, or Muḥammad added it.

The Qur'ān clearly mixes several incidents. Saul is credited with bringing the Ark into Jerusalem, when it is David who brought it there. The Qur'ān considers Saul [Ṭālūt] and Gideon to be the same person, a misunderstanding that leads the author

[250] And when they went out against *G*alut and his soldiery, they
said, 'Lord, pour out patience over us, and make firm our steps,
and help us against the misbelieving people!'
[251] And they put them to flight by the permission of God, and
David killed *G*alut, and God gave him the kingdom and wisdom,
and taught him of what He willed. And were it not for God's
repelling men one with another the earth would become spoiled;
but God is Lord of grace over the worlds.
[252] These are the signs of God, we recite them to thee in truth,
for, verily, thou art of those who are sent.
[253] These apostles have we preferred one of them above another.
Of them is one to whom God spake; and we have raised some of
them degrees; and we have given Jesus the son of Mary manifest
signs, and strengthened him by the Holy Spirit. And, did God
please, those who came after them would not have fought after
there came to them manifest signs. But they did disagree, and of
them are some who believe, and of them some who misbelieve,
but, did God please, they would not have fought, for God does
what He will.

of the Qur'ān to equate the war with the Philistines with the war with the Midianites, even though there is a substantial time difference between the two. Goliath was killed in 1062 BC, but the battles of Gideon took place in 1245 BC, which means the time difference between the two incidents is 180 years.

Q 2.252

The majority of the readers read ***natlūhā*** ("**we recite them**") with a *nūn* (sound of "n,") where the subject in the verse is Allah and the person addressed is Muḥammad. However, it is also read with a *ya'* (sound of "y") in the singular *yatlūhā* ("he recites them"). This reading apparently means that Gabriel would recite it to Muḥammad.[226]

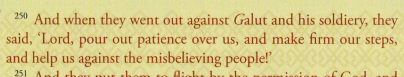

[254] O ye who believe! expend in alms of what we have bestowed
upon you, before the day comes in which is no barter, and no
friendship, and no intercession; and the misbelievers, they are the
unjust.
[255] God, there is no god but He, the living, the self-subsistent.
Slumber takes Him not, nor sleep. His is what is in the heavens
and what is in the earth. Who is it that intercedes with Him save
by His permission? He knows what is before them and what
behind them, and they comprehend not aught of His knowledge
but of what He pleases. His throne extends over the heavens and
the earth, and it tires Him not to guard them both, for He is high
and grand.
[256] There is no compulsion in religion; the right way has been
distinguished from the wrong, and whoso disbelieves in Ta*gh*ut
and believes in God, he has got hold of the firm handle in which
is no breaking off; but God both hears and knows.
[257] God is the patron of those who believe, He brings them forth
from darkness into light. But those who misbelieve, their patrons
are Ta*gh*ut, these bring them forth from light to darkness,—fellows

Q 2.256

Some scholars ruled that this verse is abrogated by the following verses:

A. Q 9.5: *"...kill the idolaters wherever ye may find them...."* [227]

B. Q 9.73: *"...strive strenuously against the misbelievers and the hypocrites."* [228]

Other scholars ruled that Q 2.256 is conserved:

A. Some scholars presumed that the People of the Book must not be coerced to convert to Islām but should be able to freely decide between converting to Islām or paying the *jizya*[D] tax, according to the command found in Q 9.29: *"until they pay the tribute by their hands and be as little ones."* [229]

B. Other scholars ruled this verse simply describes "believing in heart," not outward statements of faith; therefore, it is not abrogated. [230]

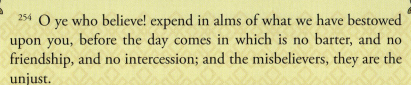

of the Fire, they dwell therein for aye.

258 Do you not look at him who disputed with Abraham about his Lord, that God had given him the kingdom? When Abraham said, 'My Lord is He who giveth life and death,' he said, 'I give life and death.' Abraham said, 'But verily, God brings the sun from the east, do thou then bring it from the west?' And he who misbelieved was dumbfounded, for God does not guide unjust folk.

Q 2.258

In various Qur'ānic verses, we read about the debate between Abraham and Nimrod. We will consider one of these verses here. We start our commentary with a summary of the story of Abraham and Nimrod. This story did not originate with the author of the Qur'ān, but Muḥammad quoted it from the oral literature of the Jews of the Arabian Peninsula:[231]

> Azar [the father of Abraham] was a professional idol maker. He would give his idols to [his son] Abraham to sell, who would then take them and call out, "Who would like to buy something that would bring him harm and not benefit him?"
>
> Then Allah commanded Abraham to call his people to monotheism. Abraham called them, including his father, but his father did not respond to the calling. When news about Abraham spread and reached King Nimrod, he asked Abraham to come and talk with him. The talk ended with Nimrod taking Abraham and throwing him into a great fire. But the fire did not burn him. Instead, the fire upon Abraham was *"cool and a safety"* (Q 21.69). After a number of days, when Abraham came out of the fire, a group of men from his people believed in him.

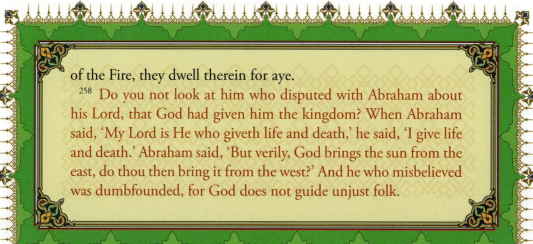

This Qur'ānic narrative has no historical basis because the two men, Abraham and Nimrod, did not live at the same time. Abraham left Ur of the Chaldeans in 1921 BC, while Nimrod lived approximately three hundred years before that. In the Old Testament, Nimrod is described as "a mighty hunter" (Gen. 10.8-12) and "a mighty warrior on earth" (1 Chron. 1.10). His kingdom is known by the name "the land of Nimrod" (Mic. 5.6).

Furthermore, when the story is analyzed as it appears in the Qur'ān and Islāmic sources, it is clear that the author of the Qur'ān took the complete Qur'ānic story of Abraham and Nimrod from a story found in a Jewish book called *Midrash Rabbah*[D]:[232]

> Terah [Abraham's Father] was a manufacturer of idols. He once went away somewhere and left Abraham to sell them in his place.
>
> A man came and wished to buy. 'How old are you?' Abraham asked him. 'Fifty years,' came the reply. 'Woe to such a man!' he exclaimed, 'you are fifty years old and would worship a day-old object!' At this he [the man] became ashamed and departed.
>
> On another occasion a woman came with a plateful of flour and requested him, 'Take this and offer it to them. So he took a stick, broke them, and put the stick in the hand of the largest.
>
> When his father returned he demanded, 'What have you done to them?'
>
> 'I cannot conceal it from you,' he [Abraham] rejoined. 'A woman came with a plateful of fine meal and requested me to offer it to them. One claimed, "I must east first," while another claimed, "I must eat first." Thereupon the largest arose, took the stick, and broke them.'
>
> 'Why do you make sport of me,' he [Terah] cried out; 'have they then any knowledge!'
>
> 'Should not your ears listen to what your mouth is saying,' he retorted.
>
> Thereupon he [Terah] seized him and delivered him to Nimrod.
>
> 'Let us worship the fire!' he [Nimrod] proposed.
>
> 'Let us rather worship water, which extinguishes the fire,' he [Abraham] replied.
>
> 'Then let us worship water!'
>
> 'Let us rather worship the clouds which bear the water.'

> 'Then let us worship the clouds!' [Nimrod]
>
> 'Let us rather worship the winds which disperse the clouds.' [Abraham]
>
> 'Then let us worship the wind!'
>
> 'Let us rather worship human beings, who withstand the wind.'
>
> 'You are just bandying words,' he exclaimed; 'we will worship nought but the fire. Behold I will cast you into it, and let your God whom you adore come and save you from it.'
>
> ...[Abraham] descended into the fiery furnace and was saved....

Muḥammad literally repeated this story in the *Midrash Rabbah*, though he made a slight change when he called the father of Abraham, "Azar" (Q 6.74). The name of Abraham's father is Terah in the Torah, a name that even appears in *Midrash Rabbah*, the source of the story of Abraham and Nimrod found in the Qur'ān.

The name Azar (given to Terah by Muḥammad) goes back to Eusebius, the Greek historian whose book was translated into Syriac. Eusebius mistakenly said that the name of Abraham's father is "Athar" (ἀθάρ). Since Muḥammad had traveled to the Levant (the eastern Mediterranean region), it is probable that he heard the name, Athar, there.

Origin of the Fire Story

The basis for this story most likely originated from the book of Genesis in the Old Testament, where God says to Abraham, "I am the Lord who brought you out of Ur of the Chaldeans..." (Gen. 15.7). The meaning of *ur*, in the old language of Babylon, is "city." This word is incorporated in the first part of the word *Jerusalem*, which means "City of Peace." On the other hand, there is another word found in Hebrew, Aramaic, and Chaldean that looks like *ur*, both in speaking and writing. However, the word in Hebrew means "light."

Many years after the writing of the Torah, a Jewish scholar by the name of Jonathan Ibn Uzz'iel, who did not have knowledge of old Babylonia, translated this verse into Chaldean: "I am the Lord who brought you out of the furnace of the fire of the Chaldeans." In his explanation of Genesis 11.28 this scholar said, "When Nimrod threw Abraham into the furnace of fire because of his refusal to bow down to his [Nimrod's] idols, the fire was prohibited from hurting him."[233]

The story in the Qur'ān literally repeats the *Midrash* myth that Muḥammad heard.

[259] Or like him who passed by a village, when it was desolate
and turned over on its roofs, and said, 'How will God revive this after its death?' And God made him die for a hundred years, then He raised him, and said, 'How long hast thou tarried?' Said he, 'I have tarried a day, or some part of a day.' He said, 'Nay, thou hast tarried a hundred years; look at thy food and drink, they are not spoiled, and look at thine ass; for we will make thee a sign to men. And look at the bones how we scatter them and then clothe them with flesh.' And when it was made manifest to him, he said, 'I know that God is mighty over all.'
[260] And when Abraham said, 'Lord, show me how thou wilt
revive the dead,' He said, 'What, dost thou not yet believe?' Said he, 'Yea, but that my heart may be quieted.' He said, 'Then take four birds, and take them close to thyself; then put a part of them on every mountain; then call them, and they will come to thee in haste; and know that God is mighty, wise.'
[261] The likeness of those who expend their wealth in God's way
is as the likeness of a grain that grows to seven ears, in every ear a hundred grains, for God will double unto whom He pleases; for God both embraces and knows.
[262] Those who expend their wealth in God's way, then do not
follow up what they expend by taunting with it and by annoyance, these have their hire with their Lord, and no fear is on them, neither shall they grieve.
[263] Kind speech and pardon are better than almsgiving followed
by annoyance, and God is rich and clement.
[264] O ye who believe! make not your almsgiving vain by taunts
and annoyance, like him who expends what he has for the sake of appearances before men, and believes not in God and the last day; for his likeness is as the likeness of a flint with soil upon it, and a heavy shower falls on it and leaves it bare rock; they can do nought with what they earn, for God guides not the misbelieving folk.

[265] But the likeness of those who expend their wealth craving the goodwill of God, and as an insurance for their souls, is as the likeness of a garden on a hill. A heavy shower falls on it, and it brings forth its eatables twofold; and if no heavy shower falls on it, the dew does; and God on what ye do doth look.

[266] Would one of you fain have a garden of palms and vines, with rivers flowing beneath it, in which is every fruit; and when old age shall reach him, have weak seed, and there fall on it a storm wind with fire therein, and it gets burnt? Thus does God manifest to you His signs, mayhap ye will reflect.

[267] O ye who believe! expend in alms of the good things that ye have earned, and of what we have brought forth for you out of the earth, and do not take the vile thereof to spend in alms,—what you would not take yourselves save by connivance at it; but know that God is rich and to be praised.

[268] The devil promises you poverty and bids you sin, but God promises you pardon from Him and grace, for God both embraces and knows.

[269] He bringeth wisdom unto whom He will, and he who is brought wisdom is brought much good; but none will remember save those endowed with minds.

[270] Whatever expense ye expend, or vow ye vow, God knows it; but the unjust have no helpers.

[271] If ye display your almsgiving, then well is it; but if ye hide it and bring it to the poor, then is it better for you, and will expiate for you your evil deeds; for God of what ye do is well aware.

[272] Thou art not bound to guide them; but God guides whom He will; and whatever good ye expend it is for yourselves, and do not expend save craving for God's face. And what ye expend of good, it shall be repaid you, and ye shall not be wronged,—

[273] unto the poor who are straitened in God's way, and cannot knock about in the earth. The ignorant think them to be rich because

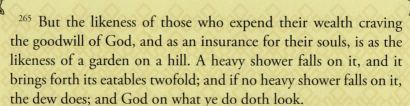

of their modesty; you will know them by their mark, they do not beg
from men importunately; but what ye spend of good God knows.
274 Those who expend their wealth by night and day, secretly and
openly, they shall have their hire with their Lord. No fear shall
come on them, nor shall they grieve.
275 Those who devour usury shall not rise again, save as he riseth
whom Satan hath paralysed with a touch; and that is because they
say 'selling is only like usury,' but God has made selling lawful and
usury unlawful; and he to whom the admonition from his Lord
has come, if he desists, what has gone before is his: his matter is
in God's hands. But whosoever returns (to usury) these are the
fellows of the Fire, and they shall dwell therein for aye.
276 God shall blot out usury, but shall make almsgiving profitable,
for God loves not any sinful misbeliever.
277 Verily, those who believe, and act righteously, and are steadfast
in prayer, and give alms, theirs is their hire with their Lord; there
is no fear on them, nor shall they grieve.
278 O ye who believe! fear God, and remit the balance of usury, if
ye be believers;
279 and if ye will not do it, then hearken to the proclamation of
war from God and His Apostle; but if ye repent, your capital is
yours. Ye shall not wrong, nor shall ye be wronged.

Q 2.275

The sources mention two readings of Ibn Masʿūd that are different in form and expressions:

1. Adding *yawm al-sāʿa* ("the day of the hour [of judgment]") thus reading "will not stand the day of the hour except...."
2. Adding *yawm al-qiyāma* ("judgment day") and *al-majnūn* ("the mad one") thus reading "will not stand the day of judgment except as stand one who is mad...."[234]

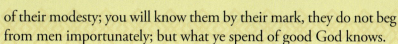

280 And if it be one in difficulties, then wait for easy circumstances;
but that ye remit it as alms is better for you, if ye did but know.
281 Fear the day wherein ye shall return to God; then shall each
soul be paid what it has earned, and they shall not be wronged.
282 O ye who believe! if ye engage to one another in a debt for
a stated time, then write it down, and let a scribe write it down
between you faithfully; nor let a scribe refuse to write as God
taught him, but let him write, and let him who owes dictate; but
let him fear God his Lord, and not diminish therefrom aught;
but if he who owes be a fool, or weak, or cannot dictate himself,
then let his agent dictate faithfully, and let them call two witnesses
out from amongst their men; or if there be not two men, then a
man and two women, from those whom he chooses for witnesses,
so that if one of the two should err, the second of the two may
remind the other; and let not the witnesses refuse when they
are summoned; and let them not tire of writing it, be it small
or great, with its time of payment. That is more just in the sight
of God, and more upright for testimony, and brings you nearer
to not doubting. Unless, indeed, it be a ready-money transaction
between you, which ye arrange between yourselves, then it is no
crime against you that ye do not write it down; but bring witnesses
to what ye sell one to another, and let not either scribe or witness
come to harm, for if ye do it will be abomination in you; but fear
God, for God teaches you, and God knows all things.
283 But if ye be upon a journey, and ye cannot find a scribe, then
let a pledge be taken. But if one of you trust another, then let him
who is trusted surrender his trust, and let him fear God his Lord,
and conceal not testimony, for he who conceals it, verily, sinful is
his heart: God knows what ye do.
284 God's is what is in heaven and in the earth, and if ye show
what is in your souls, or hide it, God will call you to account; and
He forgives whom He will, and punishes whom He will, for God

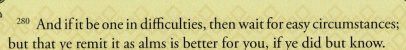

Q 2.282

This verse instructs Muslims to provide a witness for the activities of buying or borrowing. However, scholars have been divided on whether this instruction is a mandatory act or merely a desirable preference.

Those who maintain that this verse indicates a required duty ruled that it is mandatory to provide a witness for each sale, even if the commodity being sold is something as insignificant as beans. However, to lighten the burden of this duty, Q 2.282 is abrogated by Q 2.283: *"But if one of you trust another, then let him who is trusted surrender his trust…."*[235] According to this analysis, the verse is abrogated. But the observance of the instruction therein is optional. A Muslim is free to abide by the principles of either Q 2.282 or Q 2.283.[236]

Other scholars who maintain that the principle described in Q 2.282 is simply a desirable option, ruled that this verse is merely indicating a preference and giving guidance. Hence, they consider its meaning conserved with no abrogation, as there is no abrogation where a choice is given.[237]

Q 2.284

This verse states that a man will give account for what he conceals within himself. The scholars have been divided in their opinions on this issue.

Some ruled that this verse is abrogated. When Q 2.284 was revealed, the Muslims confessed to Muḥammad that the terms and consequences of this verse were too strict, and it was beyond their ability to avoid transgression at this level. Therefore, Muḥammad abrogated it by revealing Q 2.286: *"God will not require of the soul save its capacity."*[238]

Other scholars believe that Q 2.284 is not abrogated for the following stated reasons:

A. Allah punishes the thoughts of whomever he pleases and forgives whomever he pleases. Thus, its meaning and authority is still valid.[239]

B. "Culpability in it is a fact," meaning that transgressing this command is indeed inescapable. But Allah, on the Day of Judgment[D], will tell the people what was in their souls. Then he will forgive the Muslims and judge the others.[240]

C. The judgment insinuated by the phrase, *"God will call you to account,"* means Allah will afflict the person with sadness and sorrow during his or her lifetime; therefore, this verse does not affect the afterlife.[241]

Yet another opinion claims that the meaning of Q 2.284 is not about hiding personal thoughts but instead refers to hiding any truth. Hence, this verse rules that concealing truth is a sin.[242]

is mighty over all.
285 The Apostle believes in what is sent down to him from his Lord, and the believers all believe on God, and His angels, and His Books, and His apostles,—we make no difference between any of His apostles,—they say, 'We hear and obey, Thy pardon, O Lord! for to Thee our journey tends.
286 God will not require of the soul save its capacity. It shall have what it has earned, and it shall owe what has been earned from it. Lord, catch us not up, if we forget or make mistake; Lord, load us not with a burden, as Thou hast loaded those who were before us. Lord, make us not to carry what we have not strength for, but forgive us, and pardon us, and have mercy on us. Thou art our Sovereign, then help us against the people who do not believe!'

Q 2.285

Most readers read ***Kutubihi*** ("**His books**") in the plural.[243] But some readers read it in the singular, or *Kitābihi* ("His book").[244] Between these two readings is a grave doctrinal difference: *Kutubihi* ("His books") means the books of the Law (*Tawrāt* or Pentateuch), the Psalms (Zabūr) and the Injīl[D] and the Qur'ān; whereas *Kitābihi* ("His book") means only the Qur'ān.

Ibn Mas'ūd read, "The Messenger believeth in what hath been revealed to him from his Lord, and he believeth as do the men of faith. Each one (of them) believeth in His book, His meeting, and His messengers," hence, repeating the verb "believeth," adding "His meeting," using the singular for "His book."[245]

Q 2.286

Though some scholars believe that this verse abrogates Q 2.284 (see prior discussion for Q 2.284), others disagree on whether the meaning of Q 2.286 is abrogated or conserved.

One group believes that the word *"require"* mentioned in the verse refers to how much a man can withstand or bear. They ruled that this verse is abrogated by Q 2.185: *"God desires for you what is easy,"* where *"what is easy"* means whatever can be accomplished easily. This specification relieves the amount a soul can bear (*"save its capacity"*).[246] However, the majority ruled that the meaning of Q 2.286 is conserved. They believe that it is to be taken literally. Allah places on a man only as much of a burden as he can bear.[247]

Al-Naḥās and al-Makkī do not address the potential abrogation of this verse.

Introduction

The name of this sūra, Āl-i ʿImrān, means "the house (or family) of ʿImrān." In Islām, ʿImrān is considered the father of Mary and this family (house) includes ʿImrān, Anne, Mary, and Jesus.

This sūra consists of two distinct sections:

- Teachings and prohibitions from AH 2/AD 624 to AH 3/AD 625, from the victory at Badr to the defeat at Uḥud (Q 3.1-139)
- Verbal castigations against those who doubted or opposed the power of the Muslims (Q 3.140-200)

This second section also addresses the aftermath following the defeat at Uḥud and tackles its negative consequences for Muslims. Later verses mention the second Battle of Badr[D] and promise "great reward" to those "who answered the call of Allah" and went forth to fight (Q 3.172-200). Also included in this section are certain hostile verses against the Jews (Q 3.121-170).

From the context of this sūra, it is clear that its composition took about three years, from the second to the fourth *Hijra* years (AD 624-626). Yet, some parts of the sūra obviously belong to times before this period. Other parts, however, indicate inclusion later than AD 626:

- The language of verses 26 and 27 is absolutely Meccan, with key phrases and wording an apparent residual of the late Meccan period.[1]
- The sūra refers unfavorably to the visit of the Christian delegation from Najran in the year of delegations, AH 9/AD 631. However, it is known that during the time of the initial writing of this sūra, Christians were viewed somewhat favorably, so scholars feel that "this insertion is incompatible with both the timeline and the topic of the sūra…."[2]
- The two verses, Q 3.96-97, refer to pilgrimage rituals. Hence, their dating belongs to the later years of Muḥammad (c. AH 10/AD 631).
- Verses 130-136 discuss the interest on loans (*riba*); however, the presence of this topic here seems incompatible within its context because verses 121-170 are a unit with an independent topic.[3] Instead, this portion (Q 3.130-136) appears to be a repetition of the condemnation of *riba* quoted in sūra al-Baqara (Q 2).

In the name of the merciful and compassionate God.
1 A.L.M.
2 God, there is no god but He, the living, the self-subsistent.
3 He has sent down to thee the Book in truth, confirming what
was before it, and has revealed the law, and the gospel
4 before for the guidance of men, and has revealed the
Discrimination. Verily, those who disbelieve in the signs of God,
for them is severe torment, for God is mighty and avenging.
5 Verily, God, there is nothing hidden from Him in the earth,
nor in the heaven;

Q 3.3-4

These verses address Muḥammad, stating that the book that came down to him "is confirming to what was sent down before of Allah's books, which he had sent down upon his prophets and messengers."[4] It is "confirming…what they have told about Allah."[5]

It adds that Allah sent down the Torah and the Injīl of Jesus, which contain *"guidance"* to mankind.

To prove the reliability of the Qur'ān, the verse presents the Qur'ān as equal to the other divine books and describes it as a witness to these books, not as a book that has contradicted, abrogated or exceeded all others. Then verse 4 warns the people of the danger of disbelieving in these books, which it calls *"signs of God,"* and threatens that the result of rejecting these books is *"severe torment."*

Though the English translation uses the phrase *"what was before it,"* the Arabic original is *"that which is between his hands,"* thereby implying that Muḥammad had access to (i.e., had in his hands) the other divine books at the time this verse was first recited. Therefore, this verse does not acknowledge any distortions in these other books or offer evidence that these books were not considered "distorted" during Muḥammad's lifetime.

Hence, there is obvious contradiction here. Although the Qur'ān uses the basis of its similarity to these books as a standard for its own authenticity and credibility, Muslims claim that the other books became distorted. Even if we assume that these books were distorted later on, then where are the undistorted versions? Why did

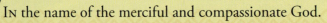

Muslims neglect to keep copies of these undistorted books when their armies invaded vast areas of the Old World and their military and governmental authority included the confiscation of non-Muslim temples, churches, and their libraries?

The verse says that the Qur'ān is *"confirming what was before it"* (in the Arabic, *"that which is between his hands"*), meaning that Muḥammad thought that his book was a continuation of prior books. Meanwhile, Islāmic reference books and the Qur'ān itself state that Islām has abrogated (cancelled) all preceding religions.

Question: How can the abrogator use the abrogated as its proof and reference?

The *Furqān*: An Obscure Phrase

Another issue avoided in some English translations but apparent in the Arabic text is the fact that this verse points to another book, called the *Furqān*[D], as shown in this translation: "revealed to you the Book with truth…and He sent the Furqān…" (Shakir trans. Q 3.3-4). The scholars state that the *Furqān* might mean all the heavenly books or another, a fourth book, which is *al-Zabūr* (Psalms). *Furqān* is also seen to mean the Qur'ān itself. "The text repeated the mention of the Qur'ān with the term *Furqān* to magnify its position and demonstrate its virtues."[6] Other scholars believe that the *Furqān* means the Torah.[7]

If one is to accept that the *Furqān* is the Zabūr, then why does the verse use an adjective to describe it instead of mentioning it by name as it does with the Torah and the Injīl?

If we accept that the *Furqān* means the Zabūr, then what exactly is the Zabūr? There is no consensus regarding the meaning of the Zabūr, since the scholars have said that it was all the books of the prophets: the Torah, the Injīl, the Qur'ān, and the books of the Bible that were sent down after Moses and the Psalms of David.[8]

If one considers the *Furqān* to be a description of all the books mentioned in this verse, or only the Torah, or only the Qur'ān, all of these scenarios make the text very weak and redundant, because the word *and* in this sentence, *"**and** He sent the Furqān,"* was added to what preceded it. In the Arabic language, the word preceding *and* must be different from the word after it. This means that *Furqān* cannot mean the Qur'ān, or any of the books already listed, because this is "weak and far away from the eloquence of speech that should be appropriate for Allah's words," according to al-Rāzī's point of view.[9]

Thus, al-Rāzī tries to explain this obscurity by stating the following in his commentary: "What was meant by this *Furqān* are the miracles that Allah associated with sending down these books…so the miracle is the *Furqān*." Since this meaning is never mentioned in any verse, this suggestion by al-Rāzī seems far from the truth. Most likely he was not satisfied with it himself and noticed some twisting of the meaning, so he adds, "This is what I have as an interpretation to this verse." His excuse might have been that he was trying to rid the Qur'ān of the "weakness and redundancy that went against its eloquence."[10]

The Qur'ān Testifies to the Truth of the Bible

The Qur'ān testifies in several different verses that it had come "confirming" and "verifying" the Scriptures. The following statements confess the divine origin of the Scriptures:

1. *"Believe in what I have revealed, verifying what ye have got, and be not the first to disbelieve in it, and do not barter my signs for a little price, and me do ye fear"* (Q 2.41).

   This verse addresses the Jews, asking them to accept the Qur'ān because it agrees with the Torah that is with them. The verse does not say that the Qur'ān is confirming the true Torah or the undistorted Torah, but it declares "*what ye have got*"—meaning, that is with the Jews at the time the Jews are being addressed, not confirming that which "*was*" once with them as the exegetes would desire.

2. *"And when they are told to believe in what God has revealed, they say, 'We believe in what has been revealed to us;' but they disbelieve in all beside, although it is the truth confirming what they have..."* (Q 2.91).

   When Muḥammad invited the Jews to believe in all the scriptures that were sent down, they replied that they believed only in their scripture and did not believe in any other scriptures (i.e., the Injīl and the Qur'ān). Muḥammad answered them that the scripture they rejected, the Qur'ān, is the truth, and it validates the Jewish scripture.

   Once more the term *"what they have"* is used to indicate that the Qur'ān confirms the truth of the Jewish scripture that was in the hands of the Jews at that time. The Qur'ān uses the present tense, "*what they have*" and not the past tense, "what they had."

3. *"Say, 'Who is an enemy to Gabriel? For he hath revealed to thy heart, with God's permission, confirmation of what had been before, and a guidance and glad tidings to believers"* (Q 2.97).

   The Qur'ān confirms that it is identical to the Holy Scriptures, which was present with the Jews and the Christians at that time.

4. *"And when there comes to them an apostle confirming what they have, a part of those who have received the Book repudiate God's book, casting it behind their backs..."* (Q 2.101).

   This verse states that even though Muḥammad came to the Jews confirming their scriptures, they still rejected him. The verse further testifies to the divine origin of the Torah, which was in the form present with the Jews at that time and describes the Jewish scripture as "*God's book.*"

5. *"O ye who have been given the Book! believe in what we have revealed, confirming what ye had..."* (Q 4.47).

   This verse addresses the People of the Book in general, telling them that the Qur'ān verifies their books.

6. *"This is the Book which we have revealed, a blessing and a confirmation to those which were before it* [between his hands]*: and that the mother of cities may be warned, with those who are round about her..."* (Q 6.92).

   This verse considers the Qur'ān as verification for other Holy Scriptures and includes the idea that the Qur'ān is an Arabic version of these books. Compare this idea with the explanation of the verse Q 46.12 below (number 8).

7. *"What we have inspired thee with of the Book is true, verifying what* [is between his hands] *was before it..."* (Q 35.31).

   The Qur'ān is described in this verse as a book of truth verifying other books.

8. *"But before it was the Book of Moses, a model and a mercy; and this is a book confirming it in Arabic language, to warn those who do wrong and as glad tidings to those who do well"* (Q 46.12).

   This verse states that the Torah is a guide and that the Qur'ān is considered a verifying Arabic copy of the Torah.

9. *"Said they, 'O our people! verily, we have heard a book sent down after Moses, verifying what came before it...'"* (Q 46.30).

   Here, the jinn discuss among themselves the news of the Qur'ān describing it as a confirmation to the Torah.

6 He it is who fashions you in the womb as He pleases. There is no God but He, the mighty, the wise.

7 He it is who has revealed to thee the Book, of which there are some verses that are decisive, they are the mother of the Book; and others ambiguous; but as for those in whose hearts is perversity, they follow what is ambiguous, and do crave for sedition, craving for (their own) interpretation of it; but none know the

Dilemma of *Nazzala* Versus *Anzala*

In Q 3.3-4, two verbs are used to describe the revelation process. These two verbs are *nazzala*, translated by Palmer as *"sent down"* and *anzala*, translated by Palmer as *"has revealed."* Muslim scholars say that *nazzala* means to send down a little at a time, time after time, and is used in reference to the Qur'ān because it was revealed to Muḥammad in increments. However, they say *anzala* means to send down altogether at one time, which applies to the other books.[11]

But since the Qur'ān came down in stages and it was appropriate to use the term *nazzala*, why then was the term *anzala* used in reference to the Qur'ān in another verse: *"Praise belongs to God, who sent down* [*"sent down"* is *anzala* in the Arabic Qur'ān] *to His servant the Book and put no crookedness therein"* (Q 18.1).

If one argues it meant that the Qur'ān came down at one time to the lower heaven, we would answer that the verse makes this statement: *"Who hath sent to* [*anzala*] *His Servant (Muḥammad) the Book...."*

This verse also contains a historical error because the Bible, in fact, consists of sixty-six books. The process of inspiration and its documentation extended over fifteen hundred years. Therefore, the term *anzala* (sent down at one time in its totality) is not correct concerning any portion of the Bible.

Q 3.6

The current Arabic Qur'ān reads ***yūṣawirukum*** ("**fashions you**"). This verse was read by one of the readers as *taṣawarakum* ("he imagined you to be") in the past tense.[12]

The difference in this reading, thus, has led to a difference in the intended meaning. One reading means that Allah creates man and the other means that he knows the man's image.

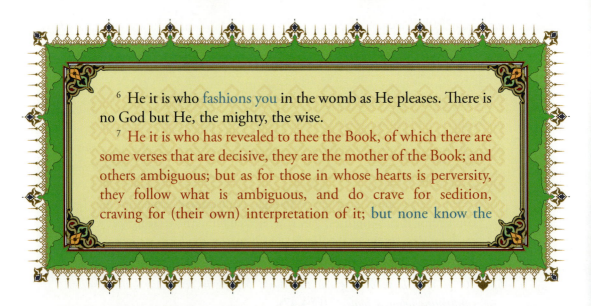

interpretation of it except God. But those who are well grounded in knowledge say, 'We believe in it; it is all from our Lord; but none will remember save those who possess minds.

8 'O Lord! pervert not our hearts again when Thou hast guided them, and grant us mercy from Thee, for Thou art He who grants.

9 O Lord! Thou shalt gather together men unto the day wherein is no doubt. Verily, God will not depart from His promise.'

Q 3.7

This verse states that some of the verses of the Qur'ān are *muḥkamāt*[D] ("decisive") and others are *mutashābihāt*[D] ("similar, allegorical, or ambiguous"). The *muḥkamāt* verses are of established meaning, without a need for interpretation, while the *mutashābihāt* verses can have more than one interpretation.

However, this statement contradicts another one that states that all the verses of the Qur'ān are *muḥkamāt*, "a Book, whose verses are made decisive…" (Shakir trans. Q 11.1).

Q 3.7

The readers render this verse in different ways:[13]

- Ibn Masʿūd: "Indeed its hidden meanings are with Allah [alone]. And those who are firmly grounded in knowledge say: 'We believe in it [the Book].'' It is also told that he read, "Indeed its true hidden meanings are with Allah [alone]. And those who are firmly grounded in knowledge say: 'We believe in it [the Book].'"
- Ubayy Ibn Kaʿb, Ibn ʿAbbās, and ʿĀ'isha: "but no one knows its hidden meanings except Allah. And *says* those who are firmly grounded in knowledge: 'We believe in it [the Book].'"

Notice that in Arabic, *wa yaqūlu* ("[and he or they] say") is used in the codex of Kaʿb instead of ***wa yaqūlūna*** ("[and they] **say**") of the current official Qur'ān. Notice also that the word order is not the same.

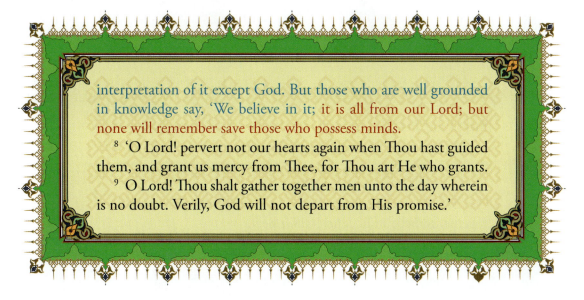

10 Verily, those who misbelieve, their wealth shall not help them,
nor their children, against God at all; and they it is who are the
fuel of the fire.
11 As was the wont of Pharaoh's people, and those before them,
they said our signs were lies, and God caught them up in their
sins, for God is severe to punish.
12 Say to those who misbelieve, 'Ye shall be overcome and driven
together to hell, an ill couch will it be.'
13 'Ye have had a sign in the two parties who met; one party

- It is told that in the codex of Ibn 'Abbās the verse is read, "Its hidden meanings are not knowable, but those who are firmly grounded in knowledge say: 'We believe in it [the Book].'"

Notice the effect of the diacritical marks on the meaning here. The verse in the codex of Ibn 'Abbās has *wa mā yu'lamu* ("it is not knowable") instead of ***ya'lamu*** ("[he] **knows**") that is found in the Qur'ān today.

The differences in these texts show that the readers took the meaning and worked the verse according to their linguistic tastes.

Q 3.13

Some read the word ***yarawnahum*** ("**[they] saw [them]**") with the third person *ya*, meaning that the crowd of Muslims saw the enemy crowd as twice their number. Others read it *tarawnahum* ("you saw them") with the second person *ta*, meaning the address is to all Muslims and the *hum* ("them") refers to all the idolaters."[14] The difference leads to a difference in meaning.

Question: Is the subject of the verb "the Muslims" or is the subject "their enemies"?

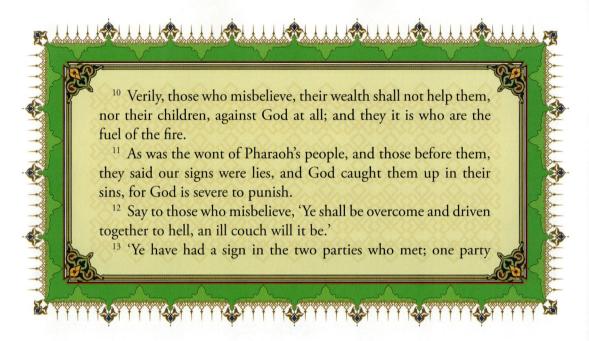

fighting in the way of God, the other misbelieving; these saw twice
the same number as themselves to the eye-sight, for God aids with
His help those whom He pleases.' Verily, in that is a lesson for
those who have perception.
14 Seemly unto men is a life of lusts, of women, and children,
and hoarded talents of gold and silver, and of horses well-bred, and
cattle, and tilth;—that is the provision for the life of this world;
but God, with Him is the best resort.
15 Say, 'But shall we tell you of a better thing than this?' For

Q 3.14

The majority of the readers read the verb ***zuyyina*** ("**[it was made] Seemly**") in the passive with the subject missing. Hence, a disagreement ensued as to the identity of the subject. Some said that the one adorning is Allah, and others said that it is Satan.[15]

Some of the readers, however, read *zayyana…ḥubba* ("he adorned...the love") where the pronoun refers to Allah as the subject.[16]

The difference in the two readings results in two understandings with regard to the identity of the one making the adornment. In the reading of the Qur'ān, *zuyyina* ("it was made fair or seemly; it was adorned or beautified") the stylist could be Allah or Satan, whereas in the second reading, *zayyana* ("he adorned") the stylist is definitely Allah.

Q 3.14

Regarding this verse, most of the scholars said, "Allah has beautified to people the love of desires and things they covet."[17]

Al-Zamakhsharī explains that Allah beautified for people the love of desires and things they covet to test them, as mentioned in Q 18.7: *"Verily, we have made what is on the earth an ornament thereof, to try them, which of them is best in works."*[18]

This verse astonished the early Muslims. It might have even pleased some of them. So another verse, Q 3.15, came immediately following it, saying that better than the listed earthly desires are *"gardens with their Lord, beneath which rivers flow…and pure wives…."*[19]

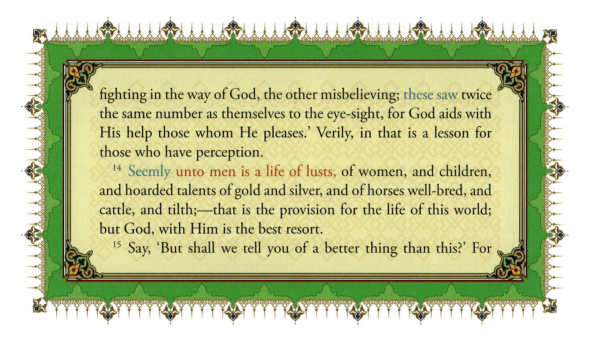

Some of the scholars thought that it was not appropriate for Allah to beautify the *"life of lusts"* and coveting, so they said that the one who made it seemly was the devil.

The Mu'tazila[D] disagreed among themselves about the identity of the beautifier. Some of them thought it to be Allah, while others thought that it was the devil that beautified the love of desires.

However, Abū 'Alī al-Jubā'ī presented a compromise, saying that "the beautification of good things is from Allah, but that of forbidden things is from the devil."[20]

The opinion that the devil was the one who *"beautified the life of lusts"* faced opposition from other Muslim scholars. They argued, "If the beautifier was the devil, then who beautified disbelief and heresy for the devil? If it was another devil, then that necessitates a sequence."[21] Thus, the majority of the scholars have collectively agreed that Allah is the beautifier.

Question: How could Allah beautify for people *"the life of lusts,"* then punish them for their lusts?

Women

This verse states, *"Seemly unto men is a life of lusts, of women, and children, and hoarded talents of gold and silver, and of horses well-bred, and cattle, and tilth,"* thereby placing women and sons on the same level as gold, silver, horses, cattle (camels, cows, and sheep) and land.

This verse addresses men and considers them "mankind," but it excludes women from mankind. The verse encourages the man to look at women and sons in the same way as he looks at possessions. It equates the relationships within the family (women and children) with the relationship an owner has with his possessions (wealth and animals).

Therefore, in this verse the value of women is expressed as follows:

Women = children = wealth = animals = land (= means "equals")

As to the reason why the verse starts the list with women, al-Qurṭubī makes this statement:[22]

> As the souls [of men] [lust after] them [women], as they are the snares of the devil and the desire of men....The temptation of women is the greatest one of all because it is said that in women there are two temptations...the first one is to break the closest [of family ties], as women instruct husbands to disconnect from their mothers and sisters. The second comes when, for the sake of women, men are tempted to gather money [by all possible means] legally and illegally.

those who fear are gardens with their Lord, beneath which rivers
flow; they shall dwell therein for aye, and pure wives and grace
from God; the Lord looks on His servants,
16 who say, 'Lord, we believe, pardon Thou our sins and keep us
from the torment of the fire,'—
17 upon the patient, the truthful, the devout, and those who ask
for pardon at the dawn.
18 God bears witness that there is no god but He, and the angels,
and those possessed of knowledge standing up for justice. There is
no God but He, the mighty, the wise.

This is how the Qur'ān views a woman: an instrument in the devil's hand, a temptation, a destroyer of family relationships, and a motivator for collecting ill-gained money.

Q 3.18

The Qur'ān reads ***shahida Allahu*** ("**God bears witness**"). It contains a verb and a subject, where Allah testifies to himself. There is more than one reading of this verse. The most prominent include these two variant readings:

- *shuhida Allahu* ("it is testified that Allah") where the verb is in the passive.[23] Here it is testified that Allah is one without identifying the subject.
- *shuhadā'a Allahi* ("Allah's testifiers") where the phrase describes (as an adjective) the *wa al-mustaghfirīn* ("and who ask for pardon")[24] Hence, the text is read "the patient, the truthful, the devout, and those who ask for pardon at the dawn[:] *Allah's testifiers...*" (Q 3.17-18). Therefore, the ones who pray for forgiveness are the testifiers.

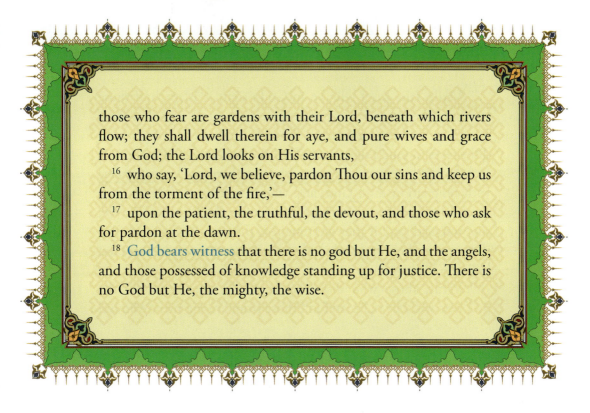

[19] Verily, (the true) religion in God's sight is Islam, and those
to whom the Book was given disagreed not until after that there
was given to them knowledge, through mutual envy. But whoso
disbelieves in God's signs, truly God is quick at reckoning up.
[20] And if they would dispute with thee, then say, 'I turn my face
with resignation unto God, and whoso follows me.' And say to
those who have been given the Book, unto the Gentiles, 'Are ye,
too, resigned' and if they are resigned, then are they guided. But
if they turn their backs, then thou hast only to preach, and God
looks on his servants.
[21] Verily, those who disbelieve in God's signs, and kill the
prophets without right, and kill those from among men, who bid

Q 3.19

Ibn Mas'ūd read, "The religion before Allah is Ḥanfiya."[25] He replaces the current Arabic Qur'ān's "**Islām**" with Ḥanfiya. (See the comment on Q 3.67, page 290.)

Ubayy Ibn Ka'b said that the transmitted reading from Muḥammad is "the religion before Allah is *al-Ḥanfiya*, not Judaism, not Christianity and not Magian,"[26] adding "not Judaism, not Christianity and not Magian[D]."

Question: Why was the rest of the verse omitted in the Qur'ān? And who made the decision to omit it?

Q 3.20

This verse has two issues regarding abrogation:

1. The first part is seen as abrogated by Q 16.125: *"and wrangle with them in the kindest way…."*[27] However, some scholars believe that this portion of Q 3.20 is not abrogated by Q 16.125 because each of the phrases refers to a different style of argument.[28]

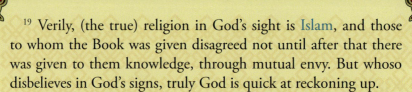

what is just,—to them give the glad tidings of grievous woe!
22 These are they whose works are void in this world and the
next, and helpers have they none.
23 Did ye not see those who have been given a portion of the
Book? they were called unto the Book of God to decide between
them; and then a sect of them turned their backs and turned
away;—
24 that is because they say the fire shall not touch us save for a
certain number of days. But that deceived them in their religion
which they had invented.
25 How will it be when we have gathered them together for a
day whereof there is no doubt, when each soul shall be paid what

2. The second part states that the duty of Muḥammad is to deliver the message. However, Muslim scholars are divided on the abrogation of this verse.
   - One group believes that this phrase is abrogated by *al-Sayf*[D] (the Sword) verse Q 9.5, *"...kill the idolaters wherever ye may find them...."*[29]
   - Another group believes that this phrase is not abrogated but instead simply gives a description of Muḥammad. They base their decision on the fact that Muḥammad is described elsewhere in the Qur'ān as the "one who warns." For example, Q 11.12 makes this statement regarding Muḥammad: *"thou art only a warner...."*[30]

Q 3.21

Ubayy Ibn Ka'b read "and kill the prophets and those from among men, who bid what is just...."[31]

The expression ***bi-ghayri haq*** ("**without right**") is perplexing; the killing of prophets is never justified. Hence, Ubayy's removal of the phrase saved the verse from unnecessary wording.

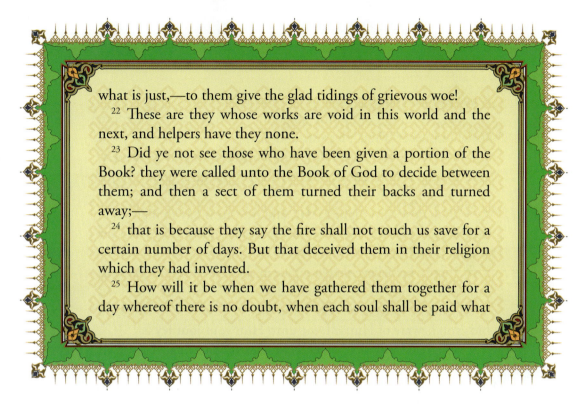

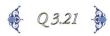

it has earned, and they shall not be wronged?
26 Say, 'O God, Lord of the kingdom! Thou givest the kingdom
to whomsoever Thou pleasest, and strippest the kingdom from
whomsoever Thou pleasest; Thou honourest whom Thou pleasest,
and abasest whom Thou pleasest; in Thy hand is good. Verily,
Thou art mighty over all.
27 Thou dost turn night to day, and dost turn day to night, and
dost bring forth the living from the dead, and dost provide for
whom Thou pleasest without taking count.'
28 Those who believe shall not take misbelievers for their patrons,
rather than believers, and he who does this has no part with God
at all, unless, indeed, ye fear some danger from them. But God
bids you beware of Himself, for unto Him your journey is.
29 Say, 'If ye hide that which is in your breasts, or if ye show it,

Q 3.28

The scholars disagree regarding whether to abrogate or conserve this verse.

One group of scholars believes this verse to be abrogated. This group has said the purpose of this verse is to warn Muslims not to make friends with unbelievers in order to protect themselves from the dangerous consequences of such friendships. But they believe this verse is abrogated with *al-Sayf* (the Sword) verse, Q 9.5: *"...kill the idolaters wherever ye may find them...."* [32]

Another scholar explains that this permission to guard the Muslim believer from unbelievers was established because of the weakness of Islām in its early stages. Later, when Islām grew stronger, this precept was abrogated.[33]

Another group of scholars states that this verse is conserved because if a Muslim is compelled by idolaters to blaspheme his religion, then he is permitted to submit to the idolaters in order to keep himself from harm. This verse substantiates and explains that position: *"unless it be one who is forced and whose heart is quiet in the faith..."* (Q 16.106).[34]

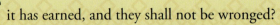

God knows it: He knows what is in the heavens and what is in the
earth, for God is mighty over all.'
30 The day that every soul shall find what it has done of good
present before it; and what it has done of evil, it would fain that
there were between itself and that a wide interval. 'God bids you
beware of Himself, but God is gentle with His servants.'
31 Say, 'If ye would love God then follow me, and God will love
you and forgive you your sins, for God is forgiving and merciful.'
32 Say, 'Obey God and the Apostle; but if ye turn your backs
God loves not misbelievers.'
33 Verily, God has chosen Adam, and Noah, and Abraham's
people, and Imran's people above the world,—
34 a seed, of which one succeeds the other, but God both hears
and knows.

Note: The Sunnīs hold against the Shiites their belief in *al-taqīya*[D] ("avoidance of danger, dissimulation") even though some of the Sunnī scholars also believe this verse to be conserved. The verse then is a legal support for the avoidance of danger. It is told that Ibn 'Abbās commented on this verse by saying, "Avoidance is by the tongue. Whoever is forced to speak of that which is disobedience to Allah, and he says it for fear of the people, *'heart is quiet in the faith,'* this harms him not."[35]

Q 3.33

Unlike the current Arabic Qur'ān's reading "**and Imran's people**," Ibn Mas'ūd reads "and the family of Muḥammad," which was also read by some of the Shiite readers.[36] The historical and doctrinal difference between "the family of 'Imrān" and the "family of Muḥammad" is clear without needing to explain.

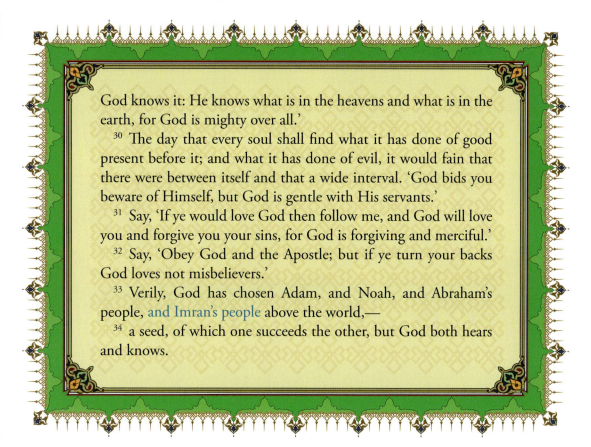

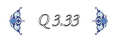

[35] When Imran's wife said, 'Lord! I have vowed to Thee what is within my womb, to be dedicated unto Thee, receive it then from me. Verily, Thou dost hear and know.'
[36] And when she brought it forth she said, 'Verily, I have brought it forth a female'—but God knew best what she brought forth; and a male is not like a female—'I have called her Mary, and I seek a refuge in Thee for her and for her seed from Satan the pelted.'

Q 3.35-37

This text tells us of 'Imrān's wife, who is Hannah, according to the scholars. When she felt that she was pregnant, she offered what was in her womb as a servant to Allah. However, after she delivered, she discovered that the baby was female and pleaded with Allah that her newborn was not fit to serve him because she was a female. So she named the baby Maryam (Mary) and prayed, asking Allah to protect her and her offspring from *"Satan the pelted* [outcast]."

Allah answered her prayer and protected Maryam. Later the verse declares, *"[A]nd Zachariah took care of her."* Whenever Zachariah visited her in her prayer chamber, *"he found beside her a provision."* When he asked her about the source of the food, Maryam told him that it was *"from God."*

The scholars agree that the man named 'Imrān mentioned in this text is the father of the Virgin Mary (the mother of Jesus) and not the father of Miriam, the sister of Moses and Aaron.

They base their argument on two points:

- The context of these verses inform us that Zachariah took care of Maryam.
- Sūra Āl-i 'Imrān (Q 3) is concerned with Christ's biography and does not recount the story of Moses or Aaron.[37]

This story, as mentioned in the Qur'ān, contains several inconsistencies from the biblical account:

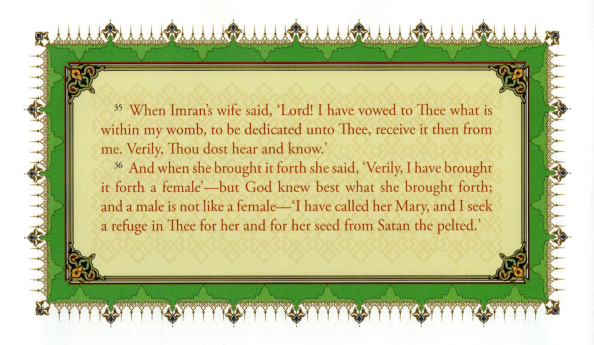

[37] And her Lord received her with a good reception, and made her grow up with a good growth, and Zachariah took care of her. Whenever Zachariah entered the chamber to her he found beside her a provision, and said, 'O Mary, how hast thou this?' She said, 'It is from God, for God provides for whom He pleases without count.'
[38] Therefore prayed Zachariah to his Lord, and said, 'Lord, grant me from Thee a good seed. Verily, Thou hearest prayer.'

Maryam, daughter of 'Imrān

- First the name of 'Imrān appears with an *n* at the end instead of *m* ending found in the Torah. According to the Bible, Maryam's mother was Jochebed, the daughter of Levi (not Hannah): "To Amram she bore Aaron, Moses and their sister Miriam" (Num. 26.59).
- Maryam had no children because she was not married. (See the comment on sūra Maryam, Q 19.27-28, in the second volume of this book.)

Hannah

The Islāmic commentaries state that Hannah is Maryam's mother and that she vowed to give the fruit of her womb to serve in the temple. However, the biblical account does not mention the names of Mary's parents, while the Islāmic sources state that her mother's name was Hannah. After comparing biblical references to Hannah and the story of making a vow in the temple, the Qur'ānic version of the story clearly seems to be a fabrication based upon the Old Testament story of Hannah, the mother of Samuel, who is mentioned in the Old Testament book of 1 Samuel 1.11, 24, 28 and 2.11, 18-19.

The analysis of the Qur'ānic version of the story leads us to the apocryphal[D] books from which Muḥammad most likely derived this account. Since the analysis of all elements of this story would require a detailed and lengthy study, we will only highlight

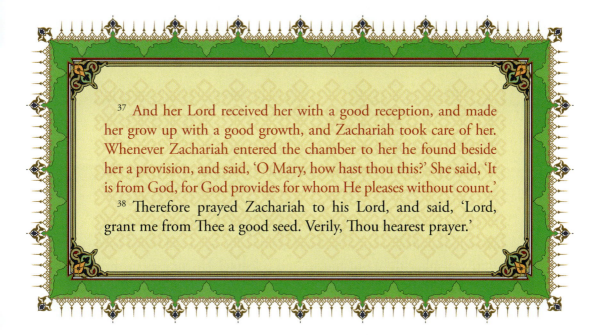

[39] And an angel cried out to him as he was standing praying in the chamber (and said) that 'God gives thee the glad tidings of John, to confirm the Word from God,—of a chief and a chaste one, and a prophet from amongst the righteous.'

[40] He said, 'My Lord, how can there be to me a boy when old age has reached me, and my wife is barren?' Said he, 'Thus God does what He pleaseth.'

[41] He said, 'My Lord, make for me a sign.' He said, 'Thy sign is that thou shalt not speak to men for three days, save by gesture; but remember thy Lord much, and celebrate His praises in the evening and the morning.'

[42] And when the angels said, 'O Mary! verily, God has chosen

one detail. The issue of the food that was given to Maryam on a daily basis seems to originate in a Coptic book called *The Biography of the Virgin*. This book states that when Hannah put her daughter Maryam in the temple, "She was provided for like a dove, and the angels used to bring her food from heaven…and frequently brought her fruit to eat from the tree of life."[38]

Q 3.39

Ibn Mas'ūd recorded in his Qur'ān, "Gabriel called unto him, while he was standing in prayer in the chamber."[39] According to the reading of the Qur'ān in Arabic, there are a group of angels (Yusuf Ali trans.): "While he was standing in prayer in the chamber, the angels called unto him." In the codex of Ibn Mas'ūd it is one particular angel: Gabriel.

Q 3.42, 45

This verse states that angels brought glad tidings to Mary about the birth of Jesus. But another verse states that only one angel came to her (Q 19.17-21).

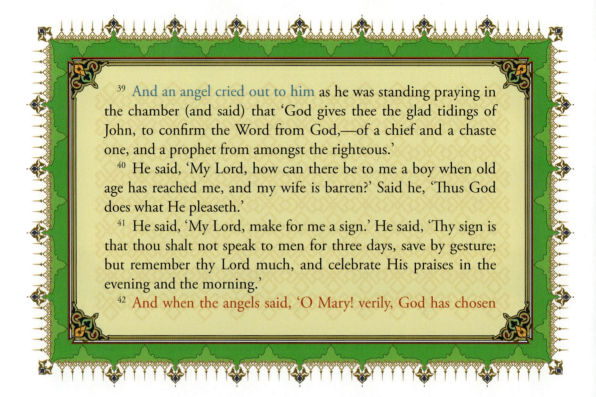

The scholars ignored this contradiction. However, the commentary *Tafsīr al-Jalālayn* indicates that Gabriel was the angel indicated by the phrase *"the angels said"* in

thee, and has purified thee, and has chosen thee above the women of the world.

[43] O Mary! be devout unto thy Lord, and adore and bow down with those who bow.

[44] That is (one) of the declarations of the unseen world which we reveal to thee, though thou wert not by them when they threw their lots which of them should take care of Mary, nor were ye by them when they did dispute.'

[45] When the angel said, 'O Mary! verily, God gives thee the glad tidings of a Word from Him; his name shall be the Messiah Jesus the son of Mary, regarded in this world and the next and of those whose place is nigh to God.

Q 3.42, 45 and in *"He said: Nay, I am only a messenger"* found in Q 19.19.[40] (Unlike Palmer, the current Arabic Qur'ān uses the plural *angels* in verse 45.)

Al-Rāzī explained the phrase *"the angels said"* in his commentary, stating, "It was said: the word 'angels' in that context referred to Gabriel alone, and although it might seem a deviation from the obvious, nonetheless it could not be understood otherwise, because sūra Maryam (Q 19) indicates that the one speaking with Mary is Gabriel: *"and we sent unto her our spirit; and he took for her the semblance of a well-made man* [Q 19.17].'"[41]

In order to rid the Qur'ān of this contradiction, al-Rāzī was obliged to accept the statement that the plural word *angels* actually meant Gabriel alone.

Q 3.43

The Arabic of the current official Qur'ān literally reads, ***wa irkaʿi maʿa al-Rākiʿīn*** ("and kneel down with those who kneel"). The codex of Ibn Masʿūd reads, "O Mary! Worship your Lord devoutly, *wa isjudi fī al-sājidīn* ("and bow down among those who bow down").[42]

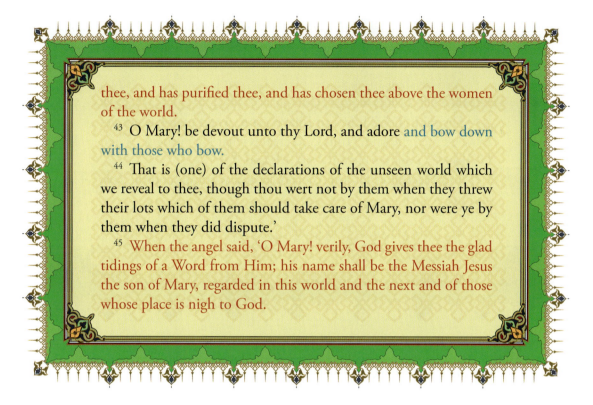

[46] And he shall speak to people in his cradle, and when grown up, and shall be among the righteous.'

[47] She said, 'Lord! how can I have a son, when man has not yet touched me?' He said, 'Thus God creates what He pleaseth. When He decrees a matter He only says BE and it is;

[48] and He will teach him the Book, and wisdom, and the law, and the gospel,

[49] and he shall be a prophet to the people of Israel (saying), that I have come to you, with a sign from God, namely, that I will create for you out of clay as though it were the form of a

Question: According to these readings, there is a difference in the form of worship that is required of Mary. Should she kneel or bow?

Q 3.49

The verse talks about Christ as he enumerates the miracles that he would perform. He declares, *"I have come to you, **with a sign** from God."* However, the codex of Ibn Mas'ūd reads, "I have come to you, with Signs from your Lord" instead of "with a sign."[43]

It appears that Ibn Mas'ūd found that the singular does not fit with the Qur'ānic context that says, *"I have come to you, with a sign from God,* [1] *namely, that I will create for you out of clay as though it were the form of a bird,...* [2] and I will heal the blind from birth, and lepers; [3] *and I will bring the dead to life....* [4] *and I will tell you what you eat and what ye store up in your houses."* Hence, he wrote, "I have come to you, with Signs" instead of "I have come to you, with a Sign."

Q 3.46, 49

These passages indicate that Jesus used to *"speak to people in his cradle,"* and that he later created *"out of clay as though it were the form of a bird"* and breathed *"thereon and it shall become a bird"* (Q 3.46, 49).

These two detailed accounts seem to have been taken from an apocryphal writing.

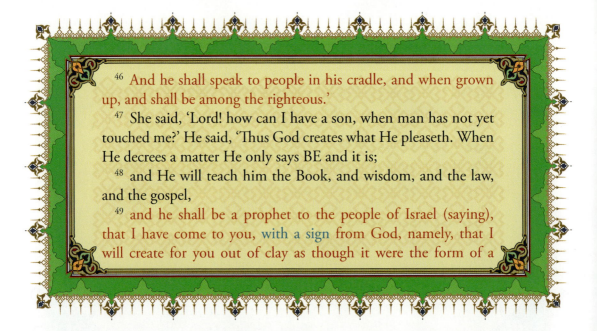

bird, and I will blow thereon and it shall become a bird by God's
permission; and I will heal the blind from birth, and lepers; and I
will bring the dead to life by God's permission; and I will tell you
what you eat and what ye store up in your houses. Verily, in that is
a sign for you if ye be believers.
50 And I will confirm what is before you of the law, and will
surely make lawful for you some of that which was prohibited
from you. I have come to you with a sign from your Lord, so fear
God and follow me,
51 for God is my Lord, and your Lord, so worship Him:—this

Speaking in his cradle (verse 46)

The story of Jesus speaking while still a babe in the cradle is found in *The Infancy Gospel*[D]. This account details that Caiaphas, the high priest during Jesus' lifetime, said, "Jesus spoke when he was in the cradle. He said to his mother Mary, 'I am the Christ the Son of God, whom Gabriel had informed you about, and my Father (God) has sent me for the salvation of the world.'"[44]

It is possible that Muḥammad heard this story and added it to the Qur'ān after tailoring its details to match the teachings of Islām.

The canonical Gospels do not mention this incident at all. In addition, a passage found in the Gospel of John suggests that Jesus did not perform any miracles during his childhood and that his first miracle was at a wedding in Cana of Galilee when he was approximately thirty years old. "This, the first of his miraculous signs, Jesus performed in Cana of Galilee. He thus revealed his glory, and his disciples put their faith in him" (John 2.11).

Additional Comment on Verse 46

The Qur'ān repeats the story of Jesus speaking from the cradle in Q 19. When people saw Maryam (Mary) carrying an infant, they reproached her. When she pointed to Jesus to defend her, they said to her, *"How are we to speak with one who is in the cradle a child?"* Jesus answered, *"Verily, I am a servant of God; He has brought me the Book, and He has made me a prophet…"* (Q 19.29-30).

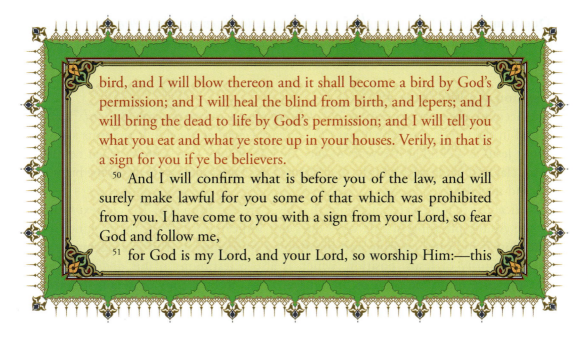

Question: Q 3.46 says, *"...he shall speak to people in his cradle, and when grown up...."* Without a doubt, it is a miracle for an infant to speak, but what is so miraculous about the ability of an older man to speak?

Creation of a Bird (verse 49)

This account, the story of creating *"out of clay as though it were the form of a bird,"* is also found in the Greek apocryphal text, *The Infancy Gospel of Thomas*. It recounts a story about Jesus as a child at five years of age. He was playing near a brook when he took some clay and made twelve birds, then clapped his hands and commanded the birds to fly, and they flew.[45]

Notice first that the verse mentions that Jesus created from clay. The context found in the Arabic phrasing of this verse does not indicate just the actual making of a bird, but it indicates creating and breathing a spirit into it. This is a testimony of the superiority of Jesus' position, which is also a testimony of his divine nature. The presence of this account in the Qur'ān seems to be a copy of details found in apocryphal texts.

Secondly, the ability to create is a measure of divinity. According to the Qur'ān, *"Is He who creates like him who creates not?—are they then unmindful?"* (Q 16.17). Compare Q 16.20, Q 25.3, Q 3.49, and Q 5.110 and notice that in the Qur'ān this standard is also applied to Christ: *"I will create for you out of clay as though it were the form of a bird, and I will blow thereon and it shall become a bird by God's permission…"* (Q 3.49).

Is the One Who Creates like the One Who Does Not?

The attribute of creation, as indicated in the Qur'ān, was ascribed by Allah to Jesus alone. Even Muḥammad himself did not have this attribute. Although Muḥammad is viewed by Muslims as the best of Allah's creatures and the seal [last] of all prophets and messengers, in fact, Allah denied Muḥammad even the ability to heal the deaf, as mentioned in the Qur'ān: *"Verily, thou canst not make the dead to hear, and thou canst not make the deaf to hear the call..."* (Q 27.80).

This [the power to heal] is, of course, a lot easier than creating from nothing; nevertheless, Muḥammad was not able [to heal or create].

In the Qur'ān, Allah challenged all mankind and all the gods of the idols to create even a fly: *"Verily, those on whom ye call beside God could never create a fly if they all united together to do it"* (Q 22.73). Meanwhile, Jesus is given the power to create a bird. (Qazzī, *Masīḥ al-Qur'ān* 75-76)

is the right path.'
52 And when Jesus perceived their unbelief, He said, 'Who are
my helpers for God?' Said the apostles, 'We are God's helpers. We
believe in God, so bear witness that we are resigned.
53 Lord, we have believed in what Thou hast revealed, and we
have followed the Apostle, so write us down with those which bear
witness.'
54 But they (the Jews) were crafty, and God was crafty, for God
is the best of crafty ones!
55 When God said, 'O Jesus! I will make Thee die and take Thee
up again to me and will clear thee of those who misbelieve, and
will make those who follow thee above those who misbelieve,
at the day of judgment, then to me is your return. I will decide

Q 3.54

The closest translation to the Arabic is found in the Pickthall translation: "Allah is the best of schemers" (Q 3.54). The Arabic text is clear in discussing Allah's fight against evil by stating that Allah answers deception with deception, and that he is the best of all *mākirīn* ("deceivers, schemers"). (For more information about this term *mākirīn*, see the article "Key to Reading Part II" on page 150.)

Question: Is it appropriate for a book that is believed to be heavenly to attribute deception to Allah?

Q 3.55

Allah is addressing Jesus, telling him that Allah will deliver him from those who rejected him (Jews). Allah also promises Jesus that Allah will make Jesus' followers (Christians) above the disbelievers and that Allah will judge between the Christians and their enemies on the Day of Judgment.

At the beginning of this verse, Allah states, *"I will make Thee die and take Thee up again to me."* The scholars have offered a variety of different suggestions regarding the meaning of this phrase.

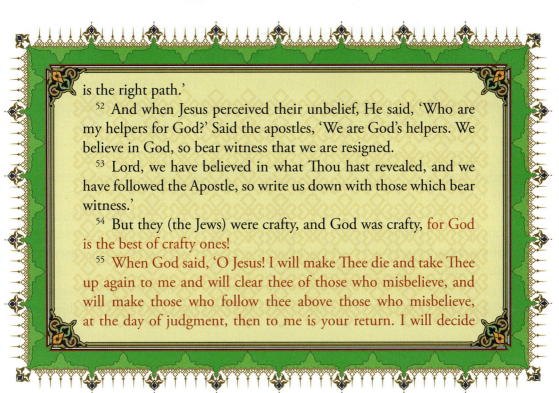

Some state, *"I will make Thee die"* means "I will put you to death"[46] and is explained as "I will complete your lifetime and then make you die, so as not to leave you until they kill you."[47]

It was also said, "It was the sleep of death; as if to say: I will cause you to sleep, then I will raise you from your sleep."[48]

They also give the phrase an allegorical meaning, saying, "I will make you like a dead person, because when Jesus was raised to heaven and ceased to be on earth, he would be like a dead person."[49]

Another suggestion explains the statement in its correct context: "make you die" literally means "cause you to die." Supporters of this suggestion explain this statement by saying that Jesus died for three hours and then was raised, or that he died for seven hours and then Allah made him come back to life when Allah raised him up to heaven.[50]

Another commentary states, "Allah made him die for three days, then raised him from the dead and then ascended him up to heaven."[51]

The conjunction *and* in this phrase, *"I will make Thee die* ***and*** *take Thee up again to me..."* indicates a sequence of events, which seems to agree with al-Rāzī's suggested meaning.

According to Islāmic doctrine, Christ was raised to heaven without being crucified. However, this verse records the occurrence of death first and then ascension. This sequence of death, then ascension, was a source of embarrassment among Islāmic scholars.

A Mu'tazilite scholar tried to defend the Islāmic doctrine by ignoring all opinions of the other scholars on the topic of Jesus' death and ascension. He stated, "The word [*and*] does not necessitate a sequence; Allah could have raised him, then caused him to die. Another possibility could have been that he made him dead without him feeling it, then ascended him and returned him to life."[52]

The first part of this explanation states that Jesus died after his ascension into heaven. Even more humorous is the further suggestion that, "[Allah] made him dead without him feeling it."

The opinion concerning (first) the death and (second) the resurrection of Jesus, which is supported by a group of Islāmic scholars, coincides with the Christian belief on this topic. Therefore, this verse supports Jesus' death, resurrection, and ascension.

There is a gap in the verse concerning the death of Jesus. The scholars who suggested his death (for three hours, seven hours, or three days) do not address when or how death occurred. Their reluctance to explain the details is probably due to their realization that this verse implies supporting testimony for the crucifixion of Jesus, which Islāmic doctrine clearly denies.

It is noteworthy that the Qur'ān testifies to the death and the resurrection of Jesus in other verses as well: *"and peace upon me the day I was born, and the day I die, and the day I shall be raised up alive," and "when Thou didst take me away to thyself..."* (Q 19.33; Q 5.117).

between you concerning that wherein ye disagree.
56 And as for those who misbelieve, I will punish them with grievous punishment in this world and the next, and they shall have none to help them.'
57 But as for those who believe and do what is right, He will pay them their reward, for God loves not the unjust.
58 That is what we recite to thee of the signs and of the wise reminder.
59 Verily the likeness of Jesus with God is as the likeness of Adam. He created him from earth, then He said to him BE, and he was;—
60 the truth from thy Lord, so be thou not of those who are in doubt.
61 And whoso disputeth with thee after what has come to thee

Despite the clarity of this implicit testimony to the death (crucifixion) and resurrection of Jesus as mentioned in the Qur'ān (Q 3.55; Q 5.117; Q 19.33), what is demonstrated by these Qur'ānic verses is in direct contradiction with Q 4.157: *"...but they did not kill him, and they did not crucify him, but a similitude* [resemblance] *was made for them...."*

Q 3.59

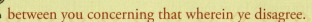

This verse demonstrates the similarity of the origin of Jesus and Adam as they were both created without a father. However, the difference is that Adam was created from dust or clay, while Jesus was created by the word of Allah, according to the Qur'ānic narrative. Some of the earlier critics have noticed this descrepancy in the alleged similarity, again because Adam was created from dust, while Jesus from the spirit of Allah. Adam was without a father or a mother, but Jesus was without a father only. However, the Muslim scholars replied that the similarity was still true because Jesus was created without a father like Adam, not because he was created from dust; therefore, Jesus and Adam do share the absence of a father.[53] They said that the purpose of the similarity was to point to the absence of a father only, not necessarily their similarity in all aspects.[54]

However, another conflict results from the phrase, "Be! and he become" [or *yakūn,* as found in the Arabic] (Pickthall trans. Q 3.59). It should read, *"BE and he was* [*kāna*]*,"* as corrected by other English translators. The difference between these two Arabic terms is significant because the first one indicates the present tense (*yakūn*) and the second one is in a past tense (*kāna*).

Al-Qurṭubī, in an attempt to rid the verse of this incorrect verb tense, stated, "The future could be in the place of the past if the meaning was understood."[55]

Even if we accept al-Qurṭubī's explanation, there still exists a contradiction in the verse because it states that Allah created Adam from dust, then Allah said to him, *"BE! and he is* [*yakūn*]." How could Allah say *"BE"* to Adam after he created him from the dust?

This conflict was ignored by all scholars except al-Rāzī, who attempted to resolve this issue by presenting three suggestions:

> **First,** creation is the process of estimation and settlement (making), meaning that Allah knew his will and how it would take place before the existence of Adam. The term *"BE"* indicates "bringing into existence," meaning that creation is an occurrence in the mind of the Creator, while *"BE"* is the action of it.[56]
> Our Comment: Is it proper to say that Allah creates in his mind, then takes the action of creation?
>
> **Second,** creation is the formation from clay, and *"BE"* is the action of tranferring life into it.
> Our Comment: If the process of making Adam from clay was in the phase of becoming, then Adam was not yet created. The process of creation would be at the point of transmitting life into Adam. Therefore, the word *"BE"* should be said in synchronization with the action of creation.
>
> **Third,** the verse should be read as "I created him by saying to him '*BE,*' then I made him a wholesome creation."[57]
> Our Comment: When Allah said to Adam *"BE,"* he was instantly created because the term *"BE"* indicates a direct command.

The Qur'ān Confesses the Uniqueness of Christ among all People

The Qur'ān declares the unique and miraculous birth of Christ among all people. The Qur'ān also describes Christ using four adjectives and gives him four titles that were not given to any other messenger. This [attention] demonstrates the greatness of his message, because he, unlike any other, received all his inspiration directly from Allah....It was as if all inspiration was within him.

The Qur'ān mentions five types of signs, or miracles, that supported his [Christ's] message, some of which he shared with other messengers, like healing and prophesying. Other signs were exclusively his own, unlike any other messenger, as in the ability to create and to raise the dead—abilities that only the Creator possesses.

Al-Rāzī states, "They confessed and admitted that Allah Most High had honored Jesus with certain distinctions:

First: The miracle of death.

Second: The miracle of ascension to Allah's kingdom, the place of the Most High's honor. The phrase "lifting up" indicates glorification and honor. The miracle of raising him up alive to heaven was exclusive to Christ above all messengers and creations.

Third: Purifying him of disbelivers. Just as he was glorified by being lifted up as the means for purifying him of the disbelievers.

Fourth: The superiority of believers in Jesus, over those who do not believe in him, in power, authority, and a higher position until the Day of Resurrection [the Day of Judgment]; and also by reason, proof and evidence as well as by a more highly exalted position. Allah Most High had declared he would give to Jesus these honorable qualities and this superior, prestigous and high position on earth. While on the Day of Judgment, Jesus will judge between those who believed in him and those who did not believe in his message," as if this means that the final verdict on the Day of Judgment will be based on whether one believes in Christ or not!

(al-Ḥaddād, *Aṭwār al-Da'wa al-Qur'ānīya* 999-1000)

of knowledge, say, 'Come, let us call our sons and your sons, and our women and your women, and ourselves and yourselves: then we will imprecate and put God's curse on those who lie.'
62 Verily, those are the true stories, and there is no god but God, and, verily, God He is the mighty, the wise;
63 but if they turn back, God knows the evildoers.
64 Say, 'O ye people of the Book, come to a word laid down plainly between us and you, that we will not serve other than God, nor associate aught with him, nor take each other for lords rather than God.' But if they turn back then say, 'Bear witness that we are resigned.'

Q 3.67

This verse says that Ibrāhīm (Abraham) was neither a Jew nor a Christian, but that he was an upright man (Hanif), a Muslim.

The Hanifs, according to the Qur'ān, were those who abandoned idol worship but were neither Jews nor Christians.

This verse is correct in its first conclusion that Abraham was neither a Jew nor a Christian. In fact, he lived three and a half centuries before Moses, who died circa 1451 BC, and nineteen centuries before the birth of Jesus. It is also correct in stating that he was not a polytheist because he was a man of God.

However, describing Abraham as a Hanif does not coincide with historical fact because the Ḥanīfiya formed several centuries after Abraham's lifetime.

Who are the Hanifs?

The name Hanifs is derived from the root word *ḥanafa*. In the Arabic language dictionaries we find the following definition:

> ***ḥanafa,*** to deviate. This verb means to turn from the straight path to the unguided path or to go astray. Therefore, since *ḥanafa* could mean turning away from the straight path to unguided path, the Arabic root does not always yield a positive connotation.

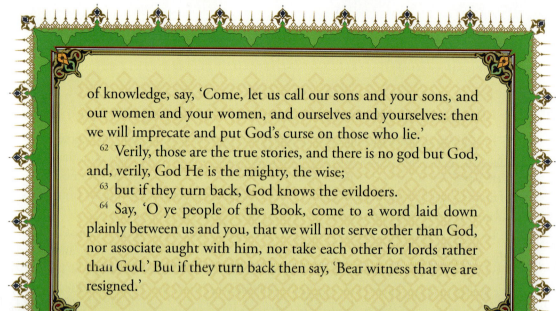

[65] O people of the Book, why do ye dispute about Abraham, when the law and the gospel were not revealed until after him? What! do ye not understand?

[66] Here ye are, disputing about what ye have some knowledge of; why then do ye dispute about what ye have no knowledge of? God knows and ye know not.

[67] Abraham was not a Jew, nor yet a Christian, but he was a 'Hanif resigned, and not of the idolaters.

[68] Verily, the people most worthy of Abraham are those who follow him and his prophets, and those who believe;— God is the patron of the believers.

Comparative linguistics reveals that the singular form of this word has a Syriac root. In the Syrian language, this word has a decidely negative connotation, as shown in the following definitions:[58]

- *ḥinfā*: pagan, infidel, idol worshipper
- *ḥinfūtū*: paganism, infidelity and idolatry
- *aḥnuf*: to become an infidel

Therefore, the Christians in Syria would have considered the Hanifs to mean idol worshippers or misguided people.

Historical annals record that the Ḥanifiya movement existed with a small number of followers and originated before Islām. They were known to worship the one God and to reject idol worship. Researchers have suggested varying theories concerning them:

1. They were a group of Arabs who were neither Jews nor Christians but followed an ancient local religion.[59]
2. The beliefs of the Hanifs are a mixture of paganism, Judaism, and Christianity. Therefore, this Ḥanifiya movement could not be considered pagan or Jewish or Christian but a new movement in the earliest phase of formation.[60]

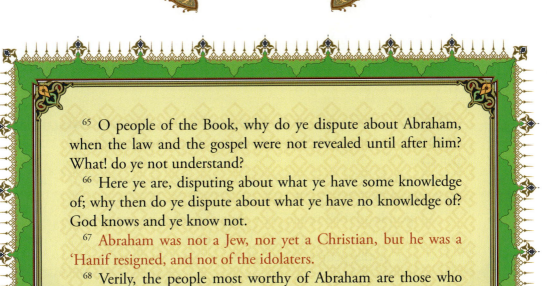

[69] A sect of the people of the Book would fain they could lead you astray, but they only lead themselves astray, and they do not perceive.
[70] O people of the Book! why do ye disbelieve in the signs of God, the while ye witness them?
[71] O people of the Book! why do ye clothe the truth with falsehood and hide the truth the while ye know?
[72] A sect of the people of the Book say, 'Believe in what was

3. Some of the Orientalists considered the Hanifs a sect of Christianity (Nazarenes), who settled in the Arabian Peninsula and were influenced by various beliefs from the different religions that existed there at that time. Louise Shikho adopts this theory. [61]
4. Another theory suggests they were a Judeo-Christian movement that originated in Palestine whose followers then moved to Ḥijāz[D]. The Christians of Syria had used the label *Hanifs* concerning a Christian sect "from the Israelites…meaning "the deviated ones from the nation" or "perverts" [as translated from] the Syriac language. So the members of the sect adopted this title and called themselves Hanifs in Ḥijāz."[62]

All of these opinions agree that the term *Ḥanīf* used to describe Abraham in this verse refers to the Ḥanīfiya movement that was active in the Arabian Peninsula. It was monotheistic and its roots can be traced back to a sect from Syria that deviated from traditional Christianity. This information means that it started after the time of Jesus. Therefore, how could Abraham have been a Ḥanīf when he preceded the Ḥanifiya movement by at least two thousand years?

Notes: Hanīf in the Qur'ān

The Qur'ān mentions the Ḥanīf in conjunction with Abraham. (The biblical account of the life of Abraham can be found in the Old Testament, Genesis 11.27-24.10; 25.)

The word *Ḥanīf* is mentioned ten times in the Qur'ān: Q 2.135; Q 3.67, Q 3.95; Q 4.125; Q 6.79, Q 6.161; Q 10.105; Q 16.120, Q 16.123; Q 30.30.

The word Hanifs is mentioned twice: Q 22.31 and Q 98.5.

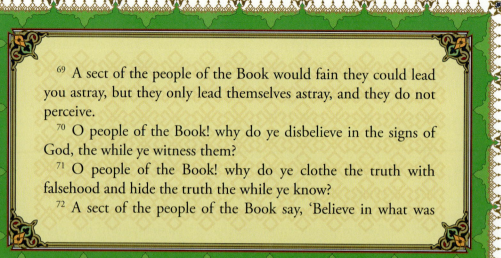

revealed to those who believed at the first appearance of the day,
and disbelieve it at the end thereof,'—that (others) may perchance
go back (from their faith)—
73 'do not believe save one who followeth your religion.' Say,
'Verily, the (true) guidance is the guidance of God, that one should
be given like what ye are given.' Or would they dispute with you
before your Lord, say, 'Grace is in the hand of God, He gives it to
whom he pleases, for God both comprehends and knows.
74 He specially favours with his mercy whom he pleases, for
God is Lord of mighty grace.
75 And of the people of the Book, there are some of them who,
if thou entrust them with a talent give it back to you; and some
of them, if thou entrust them with a dinar, he will not give it
back to thee except so long as thou dost stand over him. That is
because they say, 'We owe no duty to the Gentiles;' but they tell a
lie against God, the while they know.
76 Yea, whoso fulfils his covenant and fears,—verily, God loves
those who fear.
77 Those who sell God's covenant and their oaths for a little
price, these have no portion in the future life. God will not speak
to them, and will not look upon them on the resurrection day, and
will not purify them; but for them is grievous woe.
78 And, verily, amongst them is a sect who twist their tongues
concerning the Book, that ye may reckon it to be from the Book,
but it is not from the Book. They say, 'It is from God,' but it is not
from God, and they tell a lie against God, the while they know.
79 It is not right for a man that God should give him a Book, and
judgment, and prophecy, and that then he should say to men, 'Be
ye servants of mine rather than of God;' but be ye rather masters
of teaching the Book and of what ye learn.
80 He does not bid you take the angels and the prophets for your

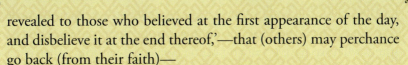

lords; shall He bid you misbelieve again when you are once resigned?
81 And when God took the compact from the prophets '(this is)
surely what we have given you of the Book and wisdom. Then shall
come to you the Apostle confirming what is with you. Ye must
believe in him and help him.' He said, moreover, 'Are ye resolved
and have ye taken my compact on that (condition)?' They say, 'We
are resolved.' He said, 'Then bear witness, for I am witness with you;
82 but he who turns back after that, these are sinners.'
83 What is it other than God's religion that they crave? when to
Him is resigned whosoever is in the heavens and the earth, will he
or nill he, and to him shall they return!
84 Say, 'We believe in God, and what has been revealed to thee,
and what was revealed to Abraham, and Ishmael, and Isaac, and
Jacob, and the tribes, and what was given to Moses, and Jesus,

Q 3.81

Ibn Mas'ūd, Ubayy Ibn Ka'b, and others read, "And when God took the covenant of those who were brought the Book [i.e., People of the Book]…."[63]

Mujāhid said, "The Qur'ān is as such, and affixing ***"the prophets"*** is a mistake made by the scribes…."[64]

The disagreement is about whether the phrase was concerning *"the prophets"* or "those who were brought the book [i.e., People of the Book]."

At the same time, Ibn Mas'ūd interchanges "the prophets" and "those who were brought the Book" in different verses, so instead of *"When God took the compact from those who have had the Book"* ("those who were brought the book") in Q 3.187, he and Ibn 'Abbās read, "When God took the compact of the prophets…."[65]

It appears that Ibn Mas'ūd and others hold that verse 81 belongs at 187, and verse 187 belongs at 81.

and the prophets from their Lord,—we will make no distinction
between any of them,—and we are unto Him resigned.
85 Whosoever craves other than Islam for a religion, it shall
surely not be accepted from him, and he shall, in the next world,
be of those who lose.'
86 How shall God guide people who have disbelieved after
believing and bearing witness that the Apostle is true, and after
there come to them manifest signs? God guides the unjust folk.
87 These, their reward is, that on them is the curse of God, and
of the angels, and of men together;
88 they shall dwell therein for aye—the torment shall not be
alleviated from them, nor shall they be respited;
89 save those who repent after that, and act aright, for verily,
God is forgiving and merciful.

Q 3.86-88

Scholars have varying opinions concerning the individuals intended by *"who have disbelieved"*:

1. It is said that this verse relates to al-Ḥārith Ibn Suwayd[N] who abandoned Islām and followed his people. It is said that when these verses reached him through one of his people, he returned to Islām and proclaimed his faith.[66]
2. This verse relates to six men who abandoned Islām. Later, one of the six, Suwayd Ibn al-Ṣāmit, was excluded.[67]
3. This verse relates to ten people who proclaimed, then later reneged, on their faith in Islām. Al-Ḥārith Ibn Suwayd was one of them, but he later repented and returned to Islām.[68]
4. The verse is about the People of the Book. According to Islāmic myths, the People of the Book are awaiting the coming of a prophet named Muḥammad. However, when Muḥammad announced his message, they refused to believe in him.[69]

90 Verily, those who misbelieve after believing, and then increase in misbelief, their repentance shall not be accepted; these are those who err.

91 Verily, those who misbelieve and die in misbelief, there shall not be accepted from any one of them the earth-full of gold, though he should give it as a ransom. For them is grievous woe, and helpers have they none.

92 Ye cannot attain to righteousness until ye expend in alms of what ye love. But what ye expend in alms, that God knows.

93 All food was lawful to the children of Israel save what Israel made unlawful to himself before that the law was revealed. Say, 'Bring the law and recite it, if ye speak the truth.'

94 But whoso forges against God a lie, after that, they are the unjust.

95 Say, 'God speaks the truth, then follow the faith of Abraham, a 'hanif, who was not of the idolaters.'

96 Verily, the first House founded for men was surely that at Bekkah, for a blessing and a guidance to the worlds.

97 Therein are manifest signs,—Abraham's station, and whosoever enters in is safe. There is due to God from man a pilgrimage unto the House, for whosoever can find his way there. But whoso misbelieves—God is independent of the worlds.

98 Say, 'O people of the Book! why do ye misbelieve in God's signs, while God is witness of what ye do?'

99 Say, 'O people of the Book! why do ye turn from the way of God him who believes, craving to make it crooked, while ye are witnesses? But God is not careless of what ye do.'

100 O ye who believe! if ye obey the sect of those to whom the Book was brought, they will turn you, after your faith, to unbelievers again.

101 How can ye misbelieve while unto you are recited the signs of God, and among you is His Apostle? But whoso takes tight hold

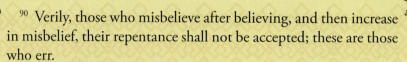

on God, he is guided into the right way.
102 O ye who believe! fear God with the fear that He deserves,
and die not save ye be resigned.
103 Take tight hold of God's rope altogether, and do not part in
sects; but remember the favours of God towards you, when ye
were enemies and He made friendship between your hearts, and
on the morrow ye were, by His favour, brothers. Ye were on the
edge of a pit of fire, but he rescued you therefrom. Thus does God
show to you His signs, perchance ye may be guided;

Some say that these verses are abrogated with this one: *"...save those who repent after that..."* (Q 3.89). This opinion is rejected by Ibn al-Jawzī, saying that this is an exception, not an abrogation, because the aforementioned verses are a report (*khabar*).[70]

Al-Naḥās and al-Makkī do not speak of the abrogation of this verse.

Q 3.97

This clause contains the mandate of pilgrimage (Ḥajj) on all Muslims: the rich and the poor, the able and the infirm. But the second part of the verse abrogates that obligation for those unable to perform the Ḥajj: *"for whosoever can find his way there."*

The Arabic uses "able" for *"can find,"* meaning having the physical ability or strength to perform the journey, as well as having sufficient financial resources for the trip.[71]

Ibn al-Jawzī expresses a conservative opinion about the verse's abrogation. He says that the word *mann* ("who") [grammatically] is the substitutable *mann*, which means, "Allah requires that those among the people **who** can perform the pilgrimage to do so."[72]

Q 3.102

Scholars differ on whether this verse is abrogated or conserved.

Some scholars believe it is abrogated. When Muslims first heard the verse, they found the demand burdensome because they understood that the verse required that their labor be genuine, stemming from the heart.

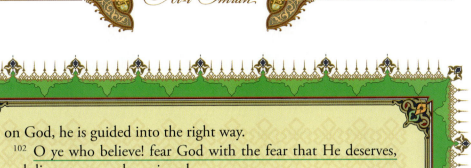

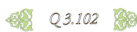

[104] and that there may be of you a nation who shall invite to good, and bid what is reasonable, and forbid what is wrong; these are the prosperous.
[105] Be not like those who parted in sects and disagreed after there came to them manifest signs; for them is mighty woe,
[106] on the day when faces shall be whitened and faces shall be blackened. As for those whose faces are blackened,—'Did ye misbelieve after your faith, then taste the torment for your misbelief!'
[107] But as for those whose faces are whitened, they are in God's mercy, and they shall dwell therein for aye.
[108] These are the signs of God. We recite them to you in truth,

Accordingly, their situation is portrayed as "they were annoyed by its revelation a great deal." As a result, another verse was revealed to confirm this verse: *"...and fight strenuously for God, as is His due..."* (Q 22.78). However, the impact of the second verse on Muslims was even greater: "Their minds almost were in a stupor."[73] Later, an abrogating verse came down to relieve the Muslims: *"Then fear God as much as ye can..."* (Q 64.16).[74]

Another group of scholars believes the verse is conserved. They attributed to Ibn 'Abbās an opinion in which he says the *"fear"* mentioned in the verse means *jihād* (to struggle, strive, or fight). They added that what is contained in the verse falls within the area of what is doable.[75]

Another group of scholars states that the intention here is to fear (revere), in general. Therefore, there is no abrogation.[76]

Q 3.104

'Uthmān Ibn 'Affān and Ibn Mas'ūd and others read "and forbidding what is wrong, and seeking Allah's help with what had befallen them..." adding *"wa yasta'īnūna Allaha 'ala mā aṣābahum* ("and seeking Allah's help with what had befallen them").

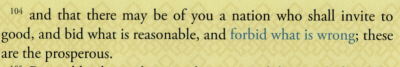

for God desires not wrong unto the worlds.
109 God's is what is in the heavens and what is in the earth, and
unto God affairs return.
110 Ye were the best of nations brought forth unto man. Ye bid
what is reasonable, and forbid what is wrong, believing in God.
Had the people of the Book believed, it would have been better
for them. There are believers among them, though most of them
are sinners.
111 They shall surely not harm you save a hurt; and if they fight
you, they shall show you their backs, then they shall not be helped.
112 They are smitten with abasement wherever they be found,
save for the rope of God and the rope of man; and they draw on

Others read with a reading similar to Ibn Mas'ūd's, substituting the word *nāhūna* ("forbidders") for *yanhawna* ("forbidding").[77]

Q 3.111

A group of exegetes has given the following meaning for this sentence: "They will do you no lasting harm in body or money (wealth), but whatever harm may occur will be easily dealt with and quickly pass. Furthermore, you will be rewarded for it." Some scholars consider what is in the verse to be a *khabar* (report); hence, it contains no abrogation. But a minority has said, since the reference to the *"people of the Book"* (Q 3.110) preceded the order to fight, then the verse is abrogated with Q 9.29: *"Fight those who believe not in God and in the last day…."* (Q 9.29).[78]

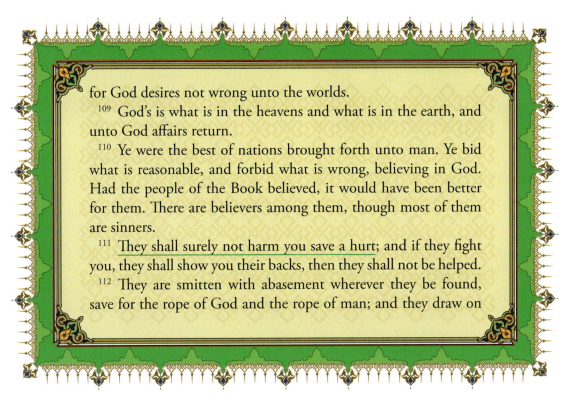

themselves wrath from God. They are smitten, too, with poverty; that is because they did disbelieve in God's signs, and kill the prophets undeservedly. That is because they did rebel and did transgress.

113 They are not all alike. Of the people of the Book there is a nation upright, reciting God's signs throughout the night, as they adore the while.

114 They believe in God, and in the last day, and bid what is reasonable, and forbid what is wrong, and vie in charity; these are among the righteous.

115 What ye do of good surely God will not deny, for God knows those who fear.

116 Verily, those who misbelieve, their wealth is of no service to them, nor their children either, against God; they are the fellows of the Fire, and they shall dwell therein for aye.

117 The likeness of what they expend in this life of the world, is as the likeness of wind wherein is a cold blast that falls upon a people's tilth who have wronged themselves and destroys it. It is not God who wrongs them, but it is themselves they wrong.

118 O ye who believe! take not to intimacy with others than yourselves; they will not fail to spoil you; they would fain ye came to trouble,—hatred is shown by their mouths; but what their breasts conceal is greater still. We have made manifest to you our signs, did ye but understand.

119 Ye it is who love them, but they love not you; and ye believe in the Book, all of it. But when they meet you they say, 'We believe;' and when they go aside they bite their finger tips at you through rage. Say, 'Die in your rage, for God doth know the nature of men's breasts.'

[120] If good luck touch you it is bad for them, but if bad luck befal
you they rejoice therein; yet if ye are patient and fear, their tricks
shall not harm you, for what they do God comprehends.
[121] When thou didst set forth early from thy people to settle for
the believers a camp to fight;— but God both hears and knows;—
[122] when two companies of you were on the point of showing
cowardice; but God was their guardian, for on God surely the
believers do rely.
[123] Why! God gave you victory at Bedr when ye were in a poor
way; fear God, then, haply ye may give thanks.
[124] When thou didst say unto the believers, 'Is it not enough for
you that your Lord assists you with three thousand of the angels
sent down from on high?
[125] Yea, if ye are patient and fear God, and they come upon you
on a sudden, now, your Lord will assist you with five thousand of
His angels, (angels) of mark.
[126] God only made this as glad tidings for you to comfort your
hearts withal,—for victory is but from God, the mighty, the
wise;—
[127] to cut off the flank of those who misbelieve, or make them
downcast, that they may retire disappointed.'
[128] Thou hast nothing to do with the affair at all, whether He
turn towards them again or punish them; for, verily, they are
unjust.
[129] God's is what is in the heavens and in the earth. He forgives
whom He pleases, and punishes whom He pleases; for God is
forgiving and merciful.
[130] O ye who believe! devour not usury doubly doubled, but fear
God, perchance ye may be prosperous;

[131] fear the fire which is prepared for the unbelievers,
[132] and obey God and His Apostle, perchance ye may get mercy.
[133] And vie with one another for pardon from your Lord, and for Paradise, the breadth of which is as the heaven and the earth, prepared for those who fear;—
[134] for those who expend in alms, in prosperity and adversity, for those who repress their rage, and those who pardon men; God loves the kind.
[135] Those who when they do a crime, or wrong themselves, remember God, and ask forgiveness for their sins,—and who forgives sins save God?—and do not persevere in what they did, the while they know;—
[136] these have their reward:—pardon from their Lord, and gardens beneath which rivers flow, dwelling therein for aye; for pleasant is the hire of those who act like this.

Q 3.133

This verse identifies the width of paradise, "a Garden whose width is that (of the whole) of the heavens and of the earth…." (Yusuf Ali trans. Q 3.133) Yet another verse mentions that the width of paradise is the width of one heaven: "...and a Garden (of Bliss), the width whereof is as the width of heaven and earth" (Yusuf Ali trans. Q 57.21).

The scholars were questioned on the subject of the length of paradise. Some of the scholars ignored this question, while others considered the distance mentioned in the Qur'ān to be metaphorical in nature, reflecting the vastness of paradise and not its exact measurements.[79] However, a third group of scholars saw a divine mystery in this verse, as narrated by Ibn 'Abbās: "The heavens and earth are attached to each other as pieces of cloth are laid down and attached to each other. This is the width of paradise and only Allah knows its length."[80]

It was said that Muḥammad's opponents ridiculed this verse by asking him, "Then where is hell?"[81]

Which opinion is the correct one? Is the width of paradise equal to that of all the heavens and earth, or equal to the width of one heaven only?

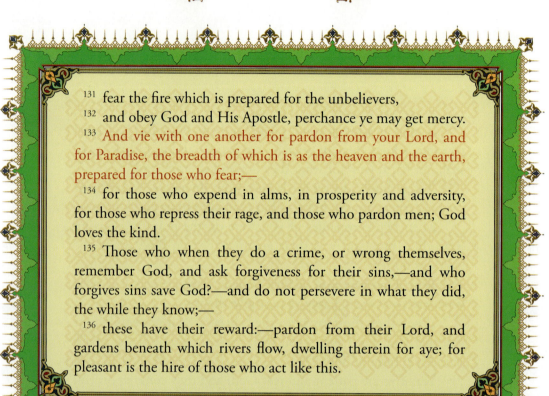

[137] Incidents have passed before your time, go on then in the earth,
and see what was the end of those who called (the prophets) liars.
[138] This is an explanation unto men, and a guidance and a
warning unto those who fear.
[139] Do not give way nor grieve, for ye shall have the upper hand
if ye but be believers.
[140] If a sore touch you, a sore like it has touched people: these are
days which we make to alternate amongst mankind that God may
know who it is that believe, and may take from you witnesses, for
God loves not the unjust;
[141] and that God may assay those who believe, and blot out the
misbelievers.
[142] Do ye think that ye can enter Paradise and God not know
those of you who have fought well, or know the patient?
[143] Why, ye longed for death before ye met it! Now ye have

The above opinions can be expressed as equations:

- Paradise = The heavens + the earth
- Paradise = One heaven + the earth
- Paradise = One heaven

Question: Which of these equations is correct?

Note: A Muʿtazilite group said that paradise and hell are not created yet. They believe that Allah will start creating paradise and hell after the end of the universe.[82]

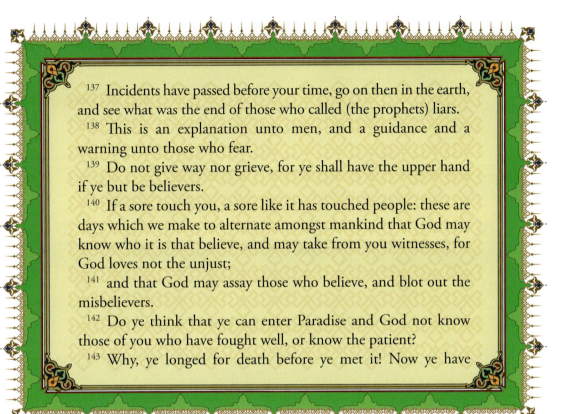

looked upon it and ye halt!
144 Mohammed is but an apostle; apostles have passed away before his time; what if he die or is killed, will ye retreat upon your heels? He who retreats upon his heels does no harm to God at all; but God will recompense the thankful.
145 It is not for any soul to die, save by God's permission written down for an appointed time; but he who wishes for the reward of

Q 3.144

This verse was unknown to the Muslims of Muḥammad's day, even to Muḥammad's friends. The account of its revelation was recorded by the scholar al-Qurṭubī:[83]

> When Muḥammad died and the news spread, 'Umar Ibn al-Khaṭṭāb went to Muḥammad's house and declared that the death was not real, but that Muḥammad was in a coma. He warned that he would cut the neck of (slaughter) anyone who said Muḥammad was dead. In the meantime, Abū Bakr[N] arrived at Muḥammad's house, inspected the body, then came out to the people that were gathered. Among this group was 'Umar Ibn al-Khaṭṭāb, who was threatening and warning. Abū Bakr quieted the chaos and announced to the people the news of Muḥammad's death. In order to emphasize that Muḥammad's death was real and to refute 'Umar's statement, he quoted two Qur'ānic passages on announcing the death:
>
> *Mohammed is but an apostle; apostles have passed away before his time; what if he die or is killed, will ye retreat upon your heels?* (Q 3.144)
>
> *We never made for any mortal before thee immortality; what, if thou shouldst die, will they live on for aye? Every soul shall taste of death!* (Q 21.34-35)

These verses convinced 'Umar of Muḥammad's death, and he fell to the ground in astonishment. However, since Muslims never knew of these verses but heard them for

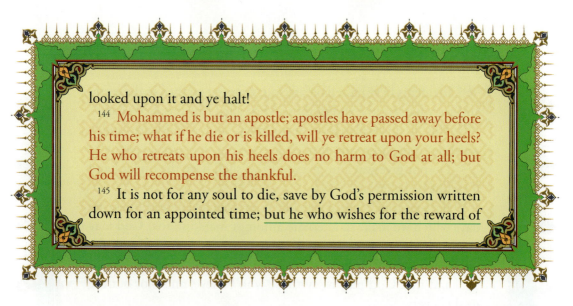

this world we will give him of it, and he who wishes for the reward of the future we will give him of it, and we will recompense the grateful.
146 How many prophets have myriads fought against! yet they did not give way at what befel them in God's way! Nor were they weak, nor did they demean themselves:—God loves the patient.
147 And their word was only to say, 'Lord, forgive us our sins and

the first time from Abū Bakr, 'Umar was not the only one who was surprised by the existence of these verses. According to the sources, people started reciting Q 3.144 "as if it was never sent down before that day."[84]

Question: How could it be proper that prominent Companions of Muḥammad had no knowledge of these verses? Does this not suggest that when Abū Bakr saw the dangerous political situation, he decided to fabricate a Qur'ānic portion to calm the fear and anxiety of Muḥammad's followers?

Q 3.145

The scholars differ on whether the verse is abrogated or conserved.

One group of scholars believes it is abrogated.

The verse says that each man has a predetermined lot. To him who wants the rewards of this life, Allah will give him what was predestined for him according to what Allah wills. Some of the scholars have said that the ruling of the verse is abrogated with *"Whoso is desirous of this life that hastens away, we will hasten on for him therein what we please,—for whom we please"* (Q 17.18).[85]

Another group of scholars believe it is conserved.

Ibn al-Jawzī rejects the abrogation of Q 3.145 by verse Q 17.18, saying both verses confirm that the giving of a reward is related to the will of Allah. He adds, "This is not a proper saying for whoever understands abrogation. So, it should not be relied on." He continues, that Q 3.145 is conserved, and those that speak of it being conserved reached that verdict because it is a report (*khabar*). A report (*khabar*) cannot be abrogated.[86]

Al-Naḥās and al-Makkī do not mention any abrogation of this verse.

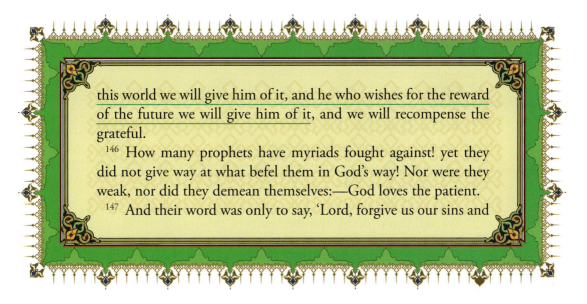

our extravagance in our affairs; and make firm our footing, and help us against the misbelieving folk!'

148 and God gave them the reward of this world, and good reward for the future too, for God doth love the kind.

149 O ye who believe! if ye obey those who misbelieve, they will turn you back upon your heels, and ye will retreat the losers.

150 Nay, God is your Lord, He is the best of helpers.

151 We will throw dread into the hearts of those who misbelieve, for that they associate that with God which He has sent down no power for; but their resort is fire, and evil is the resort of the unjust.

152 God has truly kept His promise, when ye knocked them senseless by His permission, until ye showed cowardice, and wrangled, and rebelled, after he had shown you what ye loved. Amongst you are those who love this world, and amongst you are those who love the next. Then He turned you away from them to try you; but He has pardoned you, for God is Lord of grace unto believers,—

153 when ye went up and looked not round upon any one, although the Apostle was calling you from your rear. Therefore did God reward you with trouble on trouble that ye should not grieve after what ye had missed, nor for what befel you, for God is well aware of what ye do.

154 Then He sent down upon you after trouble safety,—drowsiness creeping over one company of you, and one company of you getting anxious about themselves, suspecting about God other than the truth, with the suspicion of the ignorant, and saying, 'Have we any chance in the affair?' Say, 'Verily, the affair is God's.' They conceal in

Q 3.156

Ibn Mas'ūd read the verse in a different order: *"wa Allahu baṣīrun bimā ta'malūna*: and God sees what you do."[87] In Ibn Mas'ūd's codex the word *baṣīrun* ("sees") comes after Allah and not at the end of the verse as it appears in the current official Qur'ān.

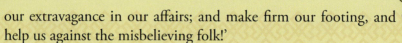

themselves what they will not show to thee, and say, 'If we had any chance in the affair we should not be killed here.' Say, 'If ye were in your houses, surely those against whom slaughter was written down, would have gone forth to fight even to where they are lying now; that God may try what is in your breasts and assay what is in your hearts, for God doth know the nature of men's breasts.'

155 Verily, those of you who turned your backs on that day when the two armies met, it was but Satan who made them slip for something they had earned. But God has now pardoned them; verily, God is forgiving and clement.

156 O ye who believe! be not like those who misbelieve, and say unto their brethren when they knock about in the earth, or are upon a raid, 'Had they but been at home, they had not died and had not been killed.' It was that God might make a sighing in their hearts, for God gives life and death; and God on what ye do doth look.

157 And if, indeed, ye be killed in God's way or die, surely forgiveness from God and mercy is better than what ye gather;

158 and if ye die or be killed it is to God ye shall be assembled.

159 It was by a sort of mercy from God thou didst deal gently with them, for hadst thou been rough and rude of heart they had dispersed from around thee. But pardon them, and ask forgiveness for them, and take counsel with them in the affair. As for what thou hast resolved, rely upon God; verily, God loves those who do rely.

160 If God help you, there is none can overcome you; but if He leave you in the lurch, who is there can help you after Him? Upon God then let believers rely.

Q 3.159

Ibn ʿAbbās and Ibn Masʿūd read "and consult them in some of the affairs" by adding *baʿḍ* ("some.")[88] The difference is that the verse in the Qurʾān asks Muḥammad to consult his Companions about his different matters; whereas, it commands him, according to the reading of Ibn ʿAbbās and Ibn Masʿūd, to consult them in some of his matters.

161 It is not for the prophet to cheat; and he who cheats shall
bring what he has cheated on the resurrection day. Then shall each
soul be paid what it has earned, and they shall not be wronged.
162 Is he who follows the pleasure of God, like him who has
drawn on himself anger from God, whose resort is hell? An evil
journey shall it be!
163 These are degrees with God, and God sees what ye do.
164 God was surely very gracious to the believers, when He sent
amongst them an apostle from themselves, to recite to them His
signs, and purify them, and teach them the Book and wisdom,
although they surely were before his time in manifest error.
165 Or when an accident befals you, and ye have fallen on twice
as much, ye say, 'How is this?' Say, 'It is from yourselves. Verily,
God is mighty over all.'
166 And what befel you the day when the two armies met, it was
by God's permission; that He might know the believers,
167 and might know those who behaved hypocritically; for it was
said to them, 'Come, fight in God's way,' or 'repel (the foe);' they
said, 'If we knew how to fight we would surely follow you.' They
were that day far nigher unto misbelief than they were to faith.
They say with their mouths what is not in their hearts, but God
doth know best what they hid.
168 Those who said of their brethren, whilst they themselves stayed
at home, 'Had they obeyed us they would not have been killed.'
Say, 'Ward off from yourselves death, if ye do speak the truth.'
169 Count not those who are killed in the way of God as dead,
but living with their Lord;— provided for,
170 rejoicing in what God has brought them of His grace, and being
glad for those who have not reached them yet,—those left behind
them; there is no fear for them, and they shall not be grieved;
171 glad at favour from God and grace, and that God wasteth not
the hire of the believers.
172 Whoso answered to the call of God and of His prophet after

Q 3.161

We have two readings here that belong to two separate historical occasions:

- The first, the reading of the Qur'ān: ***yaghulla*** ("**to cheat**").
  This is a reading of a group of readers from the Ḥijāz and Iraq schools. The word *yaghulla* means "to betray." Those readers said that a plush (blanket trimmed with fringes) went missing from among the loot after the Battle of Badr. Some of them said that maybe Muḥammad took it. A lot of clamor arose concerning the issue.[89] Therefore, the verse came to deny that Muḥammad would have covertly taken anything.
- The second reading: *"yughalla."*
  This reading has several different meanings. The first meaning is "to be betrayed." Hence, the phrase in the verse would mean that no prophet would be betrayed by his Companions. The second meaning of *yughalla* is "to be accused of betrayal."[90] A third meaning, offered by al-Ṭabarī in his commentary, interprets *yughalla* as "to withhold from giving." According to al-Ṭabarī, Muḥammad sent a vanguard before one of the battles. While they were absent, the Muslims were able to loot. Muḥammad did not give any share to the vanguards, so the verse came to show that what he did was wrong.[91]

The first reading acquits Muḥammad of the stealing charge, whereas the second reading has three meanings. It could deny that Muḥammad faced betrayal by his Companions, that he should not be accused of betrayal, or that he should not be accused of withholding from giving. Thus, there are a total of four meanings to this word.

These readings are attributed to two different events with different conclusions.

Question: Does the verse deny that Muḥammad stole, or does it only call what he did wrong?

Q 3.169-170

It is mentioned in Islāmic sources that after Muslims were killed in a battle, their souls were taken to heaven where they said to each other, "[W]e wish that our people could know what reward our Lord has granted us." Allah answered them that he would inform the Muslims. Indeed, he revealed to Muḥammad the verse, "[I]nform our people we met our Lord, well-pleased he is with us as we are with him." This verse is a Qur'ānic passage that has been omitted from the circulated Qur'ān. The verse was in the Qur'ān for some time but was later abrogated with Q 3.169-170.[92]

Note: The field of abrogation shows here that a Qur'ānic text was removed from the current Arabic Qur'ān in circulation.

sorrow had befallen them, for those, if they do good and fear God, is a mighty hire.

173 To whom when men said, 'Verily, men have gathered round you, fear then them,' it only increased their faith, and they said, 'God is enough for us, a good guardian is He.'

174 Then they retired in favour from God and grace; no evil touched them; they followed the pleasure of God, and God is Lord of mighty grace.

175 It is only that Satan who frightens his friends. Do not ye fear them, but fear me, if ye be believers.

176 Let them not grieve thee who vie with each other in misbelief. Verily, they cannot hurt God at all. God wills not to make for them a portion in the future life; but for them is mighty woe.

177 Verily, those who purchase misbelief for faith, they do not hurt God at all, and for them is grievous woe.

178 Let not those who misbelieve reckon that our letting them range is good for themselves. We only let them have their range that they may increase in sin. And for them is shameful woe.

179 God would not leave believers in the state which ye are in,

Q 3.175

Ibn Mas'ūd, Ibn 'Abbās, and others read *yukhawifikum awliyā'ah*, meaning "his votaries frighten you."[93] Whereas, the verse in the current Arabic Qur'ān reads ***yukhawifu awliyā'ahu*** ("**frightens his friends** [or votaries]"). Ubayy Ibn Ka'b, as well as others, read *yukhawifikum bi-awliyā'ihi* ("he frightens by his votaries").[94]

The reading of the Qur'ān means that Satan scares his votaries (devotees). Whereas, the reading of the others means that Satan scares the Muslims by the power of his votaries.

Further, we have another reading: *"yukhawifikum awliyā'uhu,"* which makes the subject of the verb, the "votaries of Satan."[95] The meaning thus becomes that the votaries of Satan cause Muslims to fear.

until He discerns the vile from the good. And God would not
inform you of the unseen, but God chooses of His apostles whom
He pleases. Wherefore believe ye in God and His Apostle; and if
ye believe and fear, for you is mighty hire.
180 And let not those who are niggard of what God has given
them of His grace, count that it is best for them;—nay, it is worse
for them. What they have been niggard of shall be a collar round
their necks upon the resurrection day. And God's is the heritage of
the heavens and the earth, and God of what ye do is well aware.
181 God heard the speech of those who said, 'Verily, God is poor
and we are rich.' We will write down what they said, and how they
killed the prophets undeservedly, and say, 'Taste ye the torment of
burning;'
182 this shall they suffer for what their hands have sent on
before;—for, verily, God is no unjust one to His servants,—
183 who say, 'Verily, God has covenanted with us that we should
not believe in an apostle until he gives us a sacrifice which fire
devours.' Say, 'There have come to you apostles before me with
manifest signs, and with what ye talk about; why then did ye kill
them, if ye speak the truth?

So, who scares who? Is it Satan who scares his votaries? Or, does Satan scare the Muslims by his votaries? Or do the votaries of Satan themselves scare the Muslims? The difference is quite grave among the three meanings.

Q 3.183

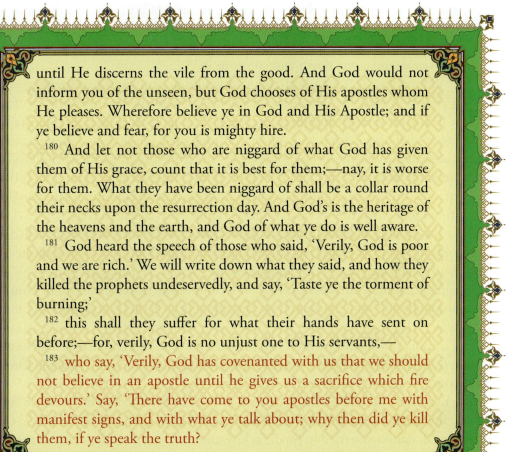

The reports tell that a group of Jews (including Kaʿb Ibn al-Ashraf, Mālik Ibn al-Ṣiyīf, Wahb Ibn Yahūdhā, Finḥāṣ Ibn ʿĀzūr, and others) entered into a discussion with Muḥammad. To prove that Muḥammad's prophecy was true, they required him to bring an "offering that would be consumed by fire."[96] They explained the reason behind their request, saying, "God, in the Torah, had commanded us not to believe in any prophet until he performed that miracle…just like the prophets of Israel used to bring an offering and when the prophet prayed, fire would come down from heaven to consume it."[97] It seemed that this occurrence during an offering was a widespread belief in the Arabian Peninsula. It also might have been believed by some pagans, as we can see from this account: "[W]hen someone brought an offering and it was accepted, fire from heaven would come down and consume it."[98]

Why did the Jews request an offering that would be "consumed by fire?"

This argument made by the Jews seems to originate in the recorded history of Israel. When in the presence of prophets, fire would come down to the people. The Torah informs us that after Moses and Aaron had presented the offering, "the glory of the LORD appeared to all the people. Fire came out from the presence of the LORD and consumed the burnt offering and the fat portions on the altar…" (Lev. 9.23-24).

Therefore, this was an established belief among the Jewish community that originated from times past when fire was a sign that a sacrifice was accepted (Lev. 6.13).

After the prophet Elijah had offered the sacrifice on Mount Carmel and called upon the Lord, "...the fire of the LORD fell and burned up the sacrifice, the wood, the stones and the soil, and also licked up the water in the trench" (1 Kings 18.38).

"[W]hen Solomon finished praying, fire came down from heaven and consumed the burnt offering and the sacrifices, and the glory of the LORD filled the temple" (2 Chron. 7.1).

Fire coming down from heaven was evidence of God's acceptance of man's sacrifice (Judg. 6.21; 1 Kings 18.38). It was also sent to establish a religious covenant. On other occasions, fire accompanied divine manifestations (Gen. 15.17; Exod. 3.2).

The rabbinical literature[D] states that when the Lord wanted to intervene in human issues, fire would come down from heaven.

When Muḥammad settled in Medina, he wanted the Jews to follow him as a prophet. Most likely the Jews of Medina were expecting him to perform the sign of the offering as evidence to the truth of his message. But when Muḥammad did not perform this sign, while still insisting on his message, the Jews of Medina went to Muḥammad to request that he perform the sign. So a group was delegated to go and ask him to show them *"a sacrifice which fire devours."*

This request tested Muḥammad's honesty according to the standards of the Torah. However, Muḥammad did not seem to be acquainted with that detail. Therefore, when asked by the Jews to bring an offering, knowing that their request was based on a scriptural standard, he became certain that unless he performed this miracle, it would be impossible to win them to his side. Since he was unable to bring an offering that would be *"a sacrifice which fire devours,"* he answered them, "There have come to you apostles before me with manifest signs, and with what ye talk about; why then did ye kill them, if ye speak the truth?"

By this answer, Muḥammad both confessed the authenticity of the standard of proof requested by the Jews and made an accusation against them that has no basis.

Muḥammad's insistence that there were prophets who brought *"a sacrifice which fire devours"* but were still rejected by the Jews does not agree with the recorded history of the Jewish people; prophets who brought *"a sacrifice which fire devours"* were offering the sacrifice with fire, not performing miracles to prove the truth of their prophecy.

Muḥammad did not mention the names of the prophets who brought *"a sacrifice which fire devours"* and were killed by the Jews. Later, commentators pulled information from Jewish history in an attempt to offer an explanation. One of them believed that the murdered prophets to whom Muḥammad referred were Isaiah, John the Baptist, and Zechariah.[99]

However, upon biblical review, we find the following disparities:

- **Isaiah:** The son of Amoz, Isaiah was the most prominent of the Hebrew prophets. He was active in the eighth century BC. He was killed as a martyr during the reign of Manasseh, son of Hezekiah (c. 643 BC). The exact date of his death is not known. He was buried in northern Palestine and later his remains were moved to Constantinople in AD 442.

- **John the Baptist:** Herod killed him because of Herodias' plot.

- **Zechariah:** More than one Zechariah can be found in the Bible. Three of the most prominent were Zechariah, son of the high priest Jehoiada, who was killed in the temple by the order of Joash (ninth century BC); Zechariah, son of Berechiah (fifth century BC); and Zechariah, the father of John the Baptist.

The assumption made by the commentators that these men were the ones referenced by Muḥammad in this verse seems to be based upon either hearsay or a superficial reading of the biblical accounts. The deaths of all of these men were in no way related to sacrifices and burnt offerings.

Even though Muḥammad was unable to refute the biblical standard, he still needed to rid himself of the Jews' request. Therefore, he responded with an accusation that they had killed whoever performed this miracle in the past.

However, this is not a convincing response. Even if his accusation was accurate, he still bore the burden of proof: to prove his prophecy true by bringing *"a sacrifice which fire devours."*

Performing this miracle would have confirmed Muḥammad's prophecy and, in turn, would have obliged the Jews to believe in him according to their own conditions of proof, which he himself testified as to its authenticity.

Muḥammad performing the miracle → Jews follow Muḥammad's religion

Had Muḥammad been honest in his message, he certainly would have tried to bring *"a sacrifice which fire devours,"* or any other sign immediately.

[184] And if they did call thee a liar, apostles before thee have been
called liars too, who came with manifest signs, and with scriptures,
and with the illuminating Book.
[185] Every soul must taste of death; and ye shall only be paid your
hire upon the resurrection day. But he who is forced away from
the fire and brought into Paradise is indeed happy; but the life of
this world is but a possession of deceit.
[186] Ye shall surely be tried in your wealth, and in your persons,
and ye shall surely hear from those who have had the Book brought
them before you, and from those who associate others with God,
much harm. But if ye be patient and fear,—verily, that is one of
the determined affairs.
[187] When God took the compact from those who have had the
Book brought them that 'Ye shall of a surety manifest it unto
men, and not hide it,' they cast it behind their backs, and bought
therewith a little price,—but evil is what they buy.
[188] Count not that those who rejoice in what they have produced,
and love to be praised for what they have not done,—think not
that they are in safety from woe,—for them is grievous woe!

Q 3.186

Regarding the patience mentioned here, a group of scholars has said the verse is abrogated with the following two verses:

A. Q 9.5 (Sword verse[D]): *"...kill the idolaters wherever ye may find them...."*[100]
B. Q 9.29: *"Fight those who believe not in God and in the last day, and who forbid not what God and His Apostle have forbidden, and who do not practice the religion of truth from amongst those to whom the Book has been brought, until they pay the tribute by their hands and be as little ones...."*[101]

The majority of scholars believe that the verse is conserved, for it contains a reference to patience and piety, both of which are obligations for the Muslim.[102]

Al-Naḥās and al-Makkī do not discuss the abrogation of this verse.

[189] God's is the kingdom of the heavens and the earth, and God is mighty over all!
[190] Verily, in the creation of the heavens and the earth, and in the succession of night and day, are signs to those possessed of minds;
[191] who remember God standing and sitting or lying on their sides, and reflect on the creation of the heavens and the earth. 'O Lord! thou hast not created this in vain. We celebrate Thy praise; then keep us from the torment of the fire!
[192] Lord! verily, whomsoever Thou hast made to enter the fire, Thou hast disgraced him; and the unjust shall have none to help them.
[193] 'Lord! verily, we heard a crier calling to the faith, "Believe in your Lord," and we did believe. Lord! forgive us our sins and cover our offences, and let us die with the righteous.
[194] Lord! and bring us what Thou hast promised us by Thy apostles, and disgrace us not upon the resurrection day; for, verily, Thou dost not break Thy promises!'
[195] And the Lord shall answer them, 'I waste not the works of a

Q 3.188

Ibn Masʿūd read, "Count not that those who rejoice in what they have produced, and love to be praised for what they have not done, are in safety from woe…" by omitting the second *fa-lā taḥsabannahum* ("[count or] think not that they.")[103]

Q 3.192

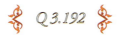

This verse declares that whoever Allah sends to hell will be humiliated: *"Lord! verily, whomsoever Thou hast made to enter the fire, Thou hast disgraced him."* It is well known that the Qur'ān states that everyone will go to hell: *"There is not one of you who will not go down to it…"* (Q 19.71). This means Muslims will be humiliated (dishonored), even though the Qur'ān promises them that Allah will not dishonor them on the Day of

worker amongst you, be it male or female,—one of you is from the other. 'Those who fled, and were turned out of their houses, and were harmed in my way, and who fought and were killed, I will cover their offences, and I will make them enter into gardens beneath which rivers flow.' A reward from God; for God, with Him are the best of rewards.

196 Let it not deceive you that those who misbelieve go to and fro in the earth.

197 It is a slight possession, and then their resort is Hell; an evil couch shall it be.

198 But those who fear their Lord, for them are gardens beneath which rivers flow, and they shall dwell therein for aye,—an entertainment from God; and that which is with God is best for the righteous.

199 Verily, of the people of the Book are some who do believe in God, and in what has been revealed to you, and what was revealed to them, humbling themselves before God, and selling not the signs of God for a little price. These shall have their reward with their Lord; verily, God is quick at reckoning up.

200 O ye who believe! be patient and vie in being patient, and be on the alert, and fear God, that haply ye may prosper.

Judgment: *"...the day God will not disgrace the Prophet nor those who believe with him..."* (Q 66.8).

Question: Which of these beliefs is the right one?

Introduction

This sūra's name, al-Nisā', means "The Women." The name comes from its many rulings about women, particularly in the initial verses (up to Q 4.34). Muslim scholars disagree about the date of this sūra. The majority believes that it was revealed after Q 3 and so dated it after the third year of the *Hijra* (AH 3/AD 622). Others suggest it was revealed in the fourth or the beginning of the fifth year of the *Hijra*, AH 4-5.[1] The scholar Wherry leans towards adopting this date because he considers that its revelation occurred the beginning of AH 4 to the middle or end of AH 5.[2] Still others date it between the end of the third and fifth year of the *Hijra*, AH 3-5, between the Battle of Uḥud[D] and the Battle of the Trench[D].[3]

Some parts of this sūra clearly do not belong to the aforementioned time period, AH 3-5. For instance, we find the phrase, *"O ye folk!"* (Q 4.1, 133), which is considered a Meccan expression. It is probable, however, that this was indeed an early Medinan expression used by Muḥammad before he coined his new terms. The use here of *"O ye folk!"* leads some Muslims to say that this is a Meccan sūra (revealed in Mecca).[4] However, most Muslim scholars reject this position, as the sūra deals with events that occurred in Medina. Therefore, verses 1 and 133 are thought to have been added to the sūra at a later date.

We also find that some verses in this sūra belong to a period beyond the fifth year of the *Hijra*, AH 5. For example, Q 4.43—the verse mandating *al-tayamum* (performing the ritual washing with sand when no water is available)—came during the Raid of al-Muraysī', which occurred in AH 5 or 6. Verse 176, also known as the *kalāla* verse (governing the rules of inheritance), comes at the end of this sūra and is considered by some as the last verse of the Qur'ān to be revealed.[5] This chronology indicates that the sūra was not revealed at one time as a complete sūra but was instead patched together with verses from different time periods.

Overall, this sūra is concerned with three main issues:

- Rules concerning women
- Aftereffects of the defeat at the Battle of Uḥud
- Laws regarding inheritance and the care of orphans

The sūra also provides various admonitions to Muslims.

In dealing with the political situation after the Battle of Uḥud, verses 44-55 and 155-158 introduce anti-Jewish rhetoric. Then verses 60-68, 81-83, 138, and 141-143 severely criticize Muḥammad's opponents (*al-munāfiqūn*, or "the hypocrites"). We also find that verses 74-78 and 84 encourage fighting. Moreover, verses 171-172 insult Christians. However, since the Qur'ān had not yet begun its campaign of accusations against Christians, these verses must have been added to the sūra at a later time.

In the name of the merciful and compassionate God.
1 O ye folk! fear your Lord, who created you from one soul, and created therefrom its mate, and diffused from them twain many men and women. And fear God, in whose name ye beg of one another, and the wombs; verily, God over you doth watch.
2 And give unto the orphans their property, and give them not the vile in exchange for the good, and devour not their property to your own property; verily, that were a great sin.
3 But if ye fear that ye cannot do justice between orphans, then marry what seems good to you of women, by twos, or threes, or fours; and if ye fear that ye cannot be equitable, then only one, or what your right hands possess. That keeps you nearer to not being partial.
4 And give women their dowries freely; and if they are good enough to remit any of it of themselves, then devour it with good digestion and appetite.
5 But do not give up to fools their property which God has made you to stand by; but maintain them from it, and clothe them, and speak to them with a reasonable speech.

Q 4.2-3

In the first verse, the Qur'ān warns Muslims against seizing the money of orphans, considering it a great sin (Q 4.2). In the next verse, it tells Muslim men *"if ye fear"* that they shall not be able to deal justly with orphans, then *"marry what seems good to you of women, by twos, or threes, or fours..."* (Q 4.3).

So, what is the connection between being afraid of dealing unjustly with orphans and choosing to marry any number of women?

According to the Arabic grammar, *"if ye fear that ye cannot do justice* [act equitably]*"* is a condition and *"marry"* is the result or reply. Therefore, how can this reply be connected to that condition?

Muslim scholars have expressed their opinions on this verse:

- **The first opinion:** According to 'Ā'isha, this verse refers to the orphans' custodians. They were infatuated with the beauty of the orphan girls in their care and married them at a reduced dowry. The verse directs these men to pay the girls a fair dowry. However, if they feared that they would not be able to act equitably in this regard, then they should marry foreign women.[6]
- **The second opinion:** After the Qur'ān demanded the just dealing of orphans (Q 4.2), men felt intense pressure lest they failed to be equitable. Therefore, the following verse tells them, "[I]f you were afraid to neglect justice to orphans' rights and are in distress over it, then also be afraid to neglect justice to women, and so reduce the number of women you marry."[7] It was mentioned by Sa'īd Ibn Jubayr[N], al-Sadī, Qatāda, and Ibn 'Abbās that as far as the orphans' money was concerned, Arab men felt pressured to act responsibly, but they did not feel that same responsibility when it came to women, even if they married ten or more women. Therefore, the verse directs men, "[A]s you fear being unjust with orphans, likewise feel an obligation towards women and marry only up to the limit that would avoid injustice."[8]

"If You Fear…Marry"!

This verse [Q 4.3]…is a wonder of wonders. It gathered two matters that could not be joined together unless it was possible to mix oil with water. In spite of all my readings in the commentaries of things that are acceptable, or rejectable; of nonsensical chatter, or forced meanings; I am still unable to understand the relationship between injustice with orphans' money and marriage.

Between the condition "*if ye fear*" and the response "*then marry*" in the verse… there most likely had to be a third verse that was either missing, abrogated, or intentionally or unintentionally dismissed; unless there was "infinite wisdom" or a "rhetorical joke" that the talkative scholars have gotten us used to! Otherwise, all their trials to rescue this verse remain futile.

This verse, in its current written form, is meaningless. The rigid stance [in this matter] has led to a refusal to contemplate the exclusion of this verse. A refusal to accept anything other than keeping it—in the same way it came down—for fear of distortion and attribution to Allah's word of something he did not say.

('Abd al-Nūr, *Miḥnatī ma'a al-Qur'ān wa ma'a Allah fi al-Qur'ān 130*)

- **The third opinion:** Muslim men felt hard-pressed to take care of orphans, so they were told, if they feared for the rights of orphans, so be afraid of adultery, and, thus, marry only the number of women allowed and try not to circumvent what is prohibited.
- **The fourth opinion:** It was said that married men with several wives were taking care of orphan girls and when they spent money on their wives, the money came from the orphans' allotment. As a result, the verse came to warn against this shameful conduct and request that men be satisfied with a maximum of four wives as a way to eliminate the cause of this misbehavior. If they were worried that they would be unjust to even four wives, then they were instructed to marry just one.[9] Explains the commentary found in *al-Muḥarir al-Wajīz*: "If you feared the lack of money as to do injustice to orphans, then be limited."[10]

Notice the contradiction. One suggestion declares that Arabs were accustomed to seizing the money of orphans for personal gain, either through reducing the dowry (the first opinion) or through direct misappropriation of orphans' money for personal reasons, such as spending it on their wives (the fourth opinion).

Meanwhile, the second opinion states that men were trying to be fair to orphans and that was why the Qur'ān asks the man to deal justly with his wife (or wives) in a way similar to his conduct with orphans. However, this opinion does not agree with the context of the verse, because the preceding verse warns men against robbing the orphans of their money, a statement that insinuates they are guilty of robbing orphans. Notice the verse does not tell Muslims, *"as you fear being unjust with orphans, so fear similarly with women,"* but uses the phrasing, "if…then." In other words, it shows a relationship between the two.

As for the third opinion stating that the verse pertains to adultery, it is a weak opinion because the verse is speaking of marriage. Even if we accept the third opinion, the conditional connection "if…then" remains incomprehensible. Nevertheless, none of these four opinions gives the reader a clear reason to link the fear of being unjust with orphans' money and the solution, marrying multiple women of their choice.

Notes:

- **Allowing marriage to more than four women**
  According to the fourth opinion, if a man does not confiscate the orphans' money to cover his own expenses, then he has the right to marry as many women as he pleases. Muslim scholars support lawful marriage to more than four women, basing this judgment on Q 4.3.[11]
- **Allowing marriage to female orphans before puberty**
  Basing his opinion upon Q 4.3, Abū Ḥanīfa[N] said it was permissible to marry an orphan girl before she reached the age of puberty.[12]

[6] Prove orphans until they reach a marriageable age, and if ye perceive in them right management, then hand over to them their property, and do not devour it extravagantly in anticipation of their growing up. And he who is rich, let him abstain; but he who is poor, let him devour in reason, and when ye hand over to them their property, then take witnesses against them; but God sufficeth for taking account.

Q 4.6

This verse prohibits the rich (well-off) guardian of an orphan's money from benefiting from it in any way. However, if the guardian is poor, then he is allowed to benefit by it: *"let him devour in reason,"* meaning let him have what is just and reasonable. Moreover, the scholars say *"devour in reason"* means one of the following intentions:

A. It is permissible to borrow from the orphan's money.[13]

B. "It is permissible to consume (*"devour"*) but one should avoid being wasteful."[14] Another scholar says, "[Use] just enough to stave off hunger and hide private parts." Yet another says, "Eating using the fingertips [i.e., a small portion], without excessiveness in food consumption. He should not be buying clothes from the money."[15]

C. It is permissible for the poor guardian to take only what is necessary from the orphan's funds. Then, if he can, he ought to pay back what he took. If he cannot afford to pay it back, then he is released from having to return it.[16]

D. The poor guardian is permitted to take as much as is needed for his necessary expenditures.[17]

Therefore, according to these views, the verse is considered to be conserved. However, other scholars say the verse is abrogated by the following two verses:

A. Q 4.29: *"...devour not your property amongst yourselves vainly...."*[18]

B. Q 4.10: *"Verily, those who devour the property of orphans unjustly, only devour into their bellies fire, and they shall broil in flames...."*[19]

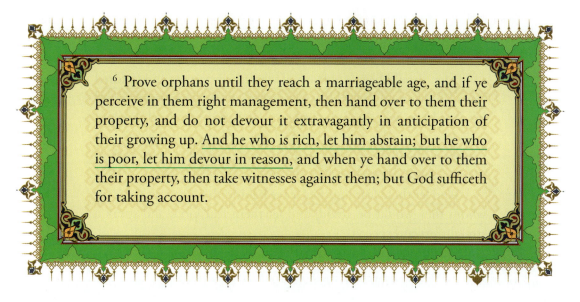

[7] Men should have a portion of what their parents and kindred
leave, and women should have a portion of what their parents and
kindred leave, whether it be little or much, a determined portion.
[8] And when the next of kin and the orphans and the poor are
present at the division, then maintain them out of it, and speak to
them a reasonable speech.
[9] And let these fear lest they leave behind them a weak seed, for
whom they would be afraid; and let them fear God, and speak a
straightforward speech.
[10] Verily, those who devour the property of orphans unjustly,

Q 4.7

Some scholars believe that verse 7 refers to the requirement of giving an inheritance to women without specifying the amount but is abrogated with the inheritance verse, Q 4.11: *"God instructs you concerning your children; for a male the like of the portion of two females. . . ."*[20]

However, Ibn al-Jawzī does not agree. He considers that verse 7 establishes the principle of women's inheritance, while the inheritance verse came to specify the portion.[21]

Q 4.8

It is told that during the distribution of an inheritance, various people (such as the neighbor, the poor, and the orphan) attended the proceedings to receive charity from the heirs.[22] There are two differing beliefs concerning this practice:

A. Some scholars believe the verse is abrogated with the inheritance verse, Q 4.11: *"God instructs you concerning your children; for a male the like of the portion of two females. . . ."*[23]

B. Others believe the verse is conserved. One story recounts that Ibn 'Abbās said the verse is not abrogated, "but it is what people took lightly." Another scholar has said, "[I]t is not abrogated. It is the one that stands. However, the people were stingy and miserly."[24] Yet others say the verse urges and entices but contains no specific command.[25]

Q 4.9

There are several differing scholarly opinions about whom this verse addresses.

The first opinion states that the verse addresses the attendants present with the testator (the one making the will):

A. The verse warns those who are in attendance while the testator is allocating his money not to order him to designate it to anyone other than the legal heirs. According to this explanation, the attendants ought to persuade him to reserve his money for the legitimate heirs.[26]

B. In contrast to the above, the verse prohibits those present from forbidding the testator from bequeathing his money to his relatives.[27]

The second opinion holds that the verse is an address to the guardians of orphans to do their duty with sincerity and honesty.[28]

The third opinion states that this verse is an address to the guardians to execute the bequest according to the testator's orders. It is abrogated with verse Q 2.182: *"And he who fears from the testator a wrong intention, or a crime, and doth make up the matter between the parties, it is no sin to him."* Here, Q 2.182 allows the guardian to amend the bequest if he sees in it a deviation from what is right. According to this viewpoint, the verse is considered abrogated, whereas in the first two opinions, the verse is conserved.[29]

Q 4.10

It is said that because the verse warns of consuming the money of orphans some guardians set the orphan's food and drink apart from food given to others. But some believed that dividing up the food and drink made the guardianship too complicated. Therefore, verse Q 2.220 came to abrogate this part of Q 4.10, disposing of the necessity to set apart the orphan's food and drink: *"But if ye interfere with them* [mix their affairs with yours]*—they are your brethren...."*[30]

Yet there are those who say the verse is abrogated with verse Q 4.6: *"...but he who is poor, let him devour in reason."* However, this view is rejected by Ibn al-Jawzī, who believes that the two verses do not cancel each other out.[31] Thus, he declared that the verse is conserved.

Q 4.10

The verse appears in a different form in the codex of Ibn Mas'ūd. He substitutes the singular for the plural throughout the verse: "Whoever unjustly eats up the property of orphans, eats up a fire into his own belly, and he will be broiling in flames."[32]

only devour into their bellies fire, and they shall broil in flames.
11 God instructs you concerning your children; for a male the like
of the portion of two females, and if there be women above two,
then let them have two-thirds of what (the deceased) leaves; and if
there be but one, then let her have a half; and as to the parents, to
each of them a sixth of what he leaves, if he has a son; but if he have
no son, and his parents inherit, then let his mother have a third, and
if he have brethren, let his mother have a sixth after payment of the
bequest he bequeaths and of his debt. Your parents or your children,
ye know not which of them is nearest to you in usefulness;—an
ordinance this from God; verily, God is knowing and wise!
12 And ye shall have half of what your wives leave, if they have
no son; but if they have a son, then ye shall have a fourth of what
they leave, after payment of the bequests they bequeath or of their
debts. And they shall have a fourth of what ye leave, if ye have no
son; but if ye have a son, then let them have an eighth of what
ye leave, after payment of the bequest ye bequeath and of your
debts. And if the man's or the woman's (property) be inherited by
a kinsman who is neither parent nor child, and he have a brother
or sister, then let each of these two have a sixth; but if they are
more than that, let them share in a third after payment of the
bequest he bequeaths and of his debts, without prejudice,—an
ordinance this from God, and God is knowing and clement!
13 These be God's bounds, and whoso obeys God and the Apostle
He will make him enter into gardens beneath which rivers flow,
and they shall dwell therein for aye;—that is the mighty happiness.
14 But whoso rebels against God and His Apostle, and
transgresses His bounds, He will make him enter into fire, and
dwell therein for aye; and for him is shameful woe.
15 Against those of your women who commit adultery, call
witnesses four in number from among yourselves; and if these bear
witness, then keep the women in houses until death release them,
or God shall make for them a way.

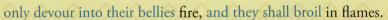

Q 4.12

Ubayy Ibn Ka'b read this as "and he has a brother or a sister from the mother…"[33] by adding "from the mother."

Ibn Mas'ūd and Sa'd Ibn Abī Waqqāṣ remove the definite article "the" and read this phrase as "and he has a brother or a sister from a mother." Others read it as "and he has a brother or a sister from his mother."[34]

The disagreement here is that the verse in the Qur'ān discusses who would get a portion of the inheritance and mentions *"have a brother or a sister"* without specifying from which parental side of the family. The other readings, however, specify that the siblings are from the mother's side.

Q 4.15

The verse determines the penalty for women who *"commit adultery"* by confining them to their houses *"until death release them."* In Arabic, this phrase is more literally translated "until they pass away by death." Since there is no difference between "passing away" and "death," it is as if the verse says "until death kills them." Therefore, to the Arabic reader, the content of the verse is redundant. While some scholars ignored this redundancy, others made this comment: "It is possible to mean 'until the angels of death kill them…or until they are taken by death and their spirits pass away.'"[35]

The commentators were not confident about the correctness of their view, which can be seen by the phrase "it is possible." However, if their view is correct, it means that the Qur'ān has a weakness when it comes to forming expressions.

Q 4.15, 16

In these passages, the first (verse 15) indicates that the penalty of either adultery or fornication for a woman (married or single) is confinement until she dies. The second (verse 16) says the penalty for a man is injury only (beating with sandals, shaming, and cursing). The conclusion of both verses is that only the woman would be confined in addition to being injured, whereas the man is punished with injury only.[36] But some scholars say the penalty of injury is inflicted only on the unmarried (man and woman).[37]

However, both of these rulings (confinement and injury) are abrogated. Therefore, the penalty for married men and women became one hundred lashes, then stoning. For single men and women, it became one hundred lashes and a year in exile.[38] The abrogation of this verse is qualified with the following authoritative text:

A. Q 24.2: *"The whore and the whoremonger. Scourge each of them with a hundred stripes…."* If they are married, then stoning is their punishment, according to a narration (*ḥadīth*) attributed to Muḥammad.[39]

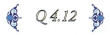

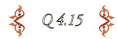

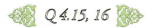

[16] And if two of you commit it, then hurt them both; but if they turn again and amend, leave them alone, verily, God is easily turned, compassionate.

[17] God is only bound to turn again towards those who do evil through ignorance and then turn again. Surely, these will God turn again to, for God is knowing, wise.

[18] His turning again is not for those who do evil, until, when death comes before one of them, he says, 'Now I turn again;' nor yet forth those who die in misbelief. For such as these have we prepared a grievous woe.

[19] O ye who believe! it is not lawful for you to inherit women's estates against their will; nor to hinder them, that ye may go off with part of what ye brought them, unless they commit fornication manifestly; but associate with them in reason, for if ye are averse from them, it may be that ye are averse from something wherein God has put much good for you.

[20] But if ye wish to exchange one wife for another, and have given one of them a talent, then take not from it anything. What! would you take it for a calumny and a manifest crime?

B. The penalty is abrogated by the *ḥadīth* attributed to Muḥammad. It states that the punishment of an adulterous woman is one hundred lashes, followed by stoning. As to the punishment of unmarried woman, the punishment is one hundred lashes only.[40]

Additionally, please note that the verse on stoning[D] (*al-rajm*) is not recorded in the Qur'ān. Hence, scholars say that while its words are abrogated, its ruling remains.[41]

Q 4.17, 18

Both verses specify the conditions of repentance. In regard to non-Muslims, some scholars consider both verses abrogated with this phrase from Q 4.18: *"...nor yet forth those who die in misbelief."*[42]

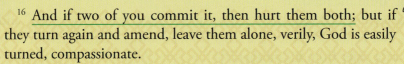

Other scholars say the first part of verse Q 4.18, *"His turning again is not for those who do evil...,"* is abrogated with Q 4.48: *"Verily, God pardons not associating aught with Him, but He pardons anything short of that to whomsoever He pleases...."*[43] This last verse means that God pardons all sins except that of idolatry, which is the worship of anything other than him.

Q 4.19

In the case of a wife committing adultery, the husband is entitled to take back everything he has given her. Most scholars consider the verse conserved, holding that in the case of adultery, a husband is permitted to divorce his wife without giving her compensation. In their opinion, committing *"fornication manifestly"*—that is, disobedience, rebelliousness, or a foul tongue—means adultery.[44] Therefore, "if a woman became disobedient to her husband [became rebellious to him and refused to obey him], it is lawful to divorce her without giving her compensation and leave her."[45] Thus, the first part of the verse is abrogated by the second part.

Q 4.19

Ubayy Ibn Ka'b read this as "unless they commit an abominable act against you," by removing "**manifestly**."[46] This reading gives the abominable act a specific meaning, which is mistreating the husband.

On the other hand, Ibn Mas'ūd, Ibn 'Abbās and others read this as "unless they *yafḥashna* ("commit abomination,") by removing "manifestly."[47] This reading gives abomination a wider meaning, which would be anything outside the moral boundaries.

Q 4.20

Ibn Mas'ūd read this as "even if ye had given the latter a whole treasure of gold for dower," by adding "of gold."[48]

Q 4.20

This verse commands men not to take a woman's dowry *"for a calumny."* The term *"calumny"* was used in this verse outside of its proper linguistic meaning. *Calumny* means slander. However, the act of not giving the woman her dowry is an act of oppression, not of slander.

The scholars were confused about the use of this term. Some said, "The term *calumny* indicated injustice." Al-Zajjāj said, "It meant 'in vain,'" and others said it referred to the act of "a man denying that he owes the woman her dowry." However, since none of these suggested meanings coincided with the actual definition of the term, some scholars said the verse was addressing the men who accused their wives of adultery in order to force the women to abandon their right to a dowry. [49]

Among the scholars, al-Rāzī preempted other attempts to provide suggestions for the meaning of the term *calumny* by presenting the following suggestions:[50]

- **The first opinion:** Allah has imposed a dowry for the wife. If the husband takes the dowry back, it would appear as if he is denying his duty to allow her to keep it. As a result, the act becomes slander.
- **The second opinion:** At the signing of the marriage contract, the husband gives the wife a dowry and is not supposed to take it back. If he does, this action makes his initial promise a slander.
- **The third opinion:** Men used to accuse their wives of adultery in order to secure a divorce and to frighten women into giving up their right to a dowry rather than face a scandal.
- **The fourth opinion:** Q 4.19 reads, *"Nor to hinder them, that ye may go off with part of what ye brought them, unless they commit fornication manifestly...."* While a Muslim should not disobey Allah's command to give his wife a dowry, if he takes part of his wife's dowry back, that would indicate that she had committed adultery (illegal sexual intercourse), which—if it were not true—would then be considered slander.
- **The fifth opinion:** The punishment of slander and evident sin was well known to Muslims, so the phrase, *"would you take it for a calumny and a manifest crime?"* actually means, "would you take the punishment of slander?" Q 4.10 reads, *"Verily, those who devour the property of orphans unjustly, only devour into their bellies fire, and they shall broil in flames...."*

All these opinions are merely arbitrary interpretations, futile attempts to make the term *"calumny"* match the meaning of the verse. Moreover, the multiple and various possibilities created by the use of this word are only further proof of the contradictions found in the verse.

[21] How can ye take it when one of you has gone in unto the other, and they have taken from you a rigid compact?
[22] And do not marry women your fathers married,—except bygones,—for it is abominable and hateful, and an evil way;
[23] unlawful for you are your mothers, and your daughters, and your sisters, and your paternal aunts and maternal aunts, and your brother's daughters, and your sister's daughters, and your foster mothers, and your foster sisters, and your wives' mothers, and your step daughters who are your wards, born of your wives to whom ye have gone in; but if ye have not gone in unto them, then it is no crime in you; and the lawful spouses of your sons from your own loins, and that ye form a connexion between two sisters,—except bygones,—verily, God is forgiving, merciful;

Q 4.22

Before Islām, some sons used to marry their stepmothers. The practice continued until this verse came to prohibit the custom.[51] This verse is conserved. However, since the phrase *"except bygones"* means "after what had already occurred during *jāhilīya*, then that is forgiven." Some scholars say this ruling does not apply to prior cases.[52] Ibn al-Jawzī believes this statement was an exception, and not an abrogation.[53]

Q 4.23

Before Islām, it was also permitted for a man to marry two sisters at the same time. This verse abolishes that behavior. However, the phrase *"except bygones"* caused a debate similar in content to that of the previous verse (22).[54]

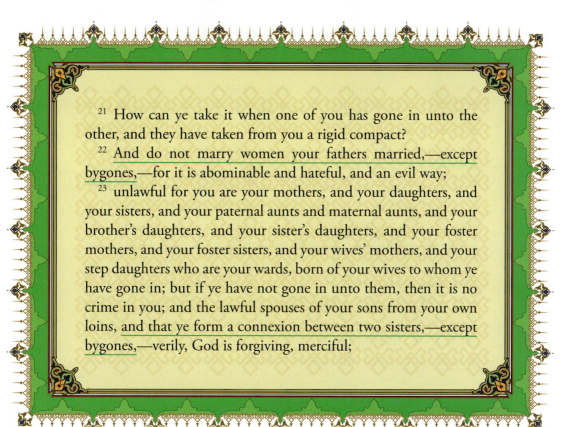

[24] and married women, save such as your right hands possess,—
God's Book against you!—but lawful for you is all besides this,
for you to seek them with your wealth, marrying them and not
fornicating; but such of them as ye have enjoyed, give them their
hire as a lawful due; for there is no crime in you about what ye agree
between you after such lawful due, verily, God is knowing and wise.
[25] But whosoever of you cannot go the length of marrying
marriageable women who believe, then take of what your right
hands possess, of your maidens who believe;—though God knows
best about your faith. Ye come one from the other; then marry
them with the permission of their people, and give them their
hire in reason, they being chaste and not fornicating, and not
receivers of paramours. But when they are married, if they commit
fornication, then inflict upon them half the penalty for married
women; that is for whomsoever of you fears wrong; but that ye

Q 4.24

Ibn Mas'ūd, Ibn 'Abbās and others read this as "but such of them as ye have enjoyed until a mentioned time, give them their hire as a lawful due." Ibn 'Abbās ascertains that this is the correct reading.[55]

The difference between the two readings is that the Qur'ān's reading refers to marriage in general, which is why the Sunnīs explain that the wages are the marriage dowry. However, the reading that adds "until a mentioned time" connects the verse with the temporary marriage, *al-mut'a*[D]. This variance means that either the Sunnīs removed the phrase to confirm their saying that the *mut'a* marriage has been abrogated, or that the Shiites added the phrase to bolster their saying that the *mut'a* marriage is religiously legal. Either way, one sect of the Muslims altered the wording in the Qur'ān to shape opinion regarding the *mut'a* marriage. (See the article "Women in the Qur'ān" on page 117.)

Q 4.24

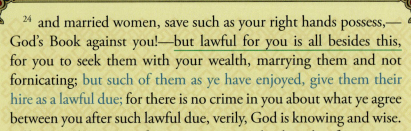

Verses 22-24 identify the categories of women whose marriages are not permissible. Therefore, it became understood that marriage to anyone not mentioned in these verses is permissible. In other words, a man could marry both a woman and her paternal aunt or a woman and her maternal aunt. But this practice was abrogated with Muḥammad's narration (*ḥadīth*): "Do not combine (in marriage) a woman and her paternal aunt, or a woman and her maternal aunt."[56]

Scholars differ about the meaning of "enjoyed" (*istimtā'* or "enjoyment') in this verse, dividing their opinions into the following two positions:

- *istimtā'* ("enjoyment") = marriage and *"lawful due"* (*ujūr* or "their pay") = dowry. This is the position of the majority of scholars.[57]
- *istimtā'* ("enjoyment") = marriage for pleasure (*mut'a*), which is a temporary marriage that was practiced during the early years of Islām. A disagreement arose concerning the abolition of *mut'a*.[58]

In the first view, *mut'a* marriage is abrogated with these verses and other sources:

A. The Qur'ānic imposition of a prescribed period (*'idda*), which is mentioned in the following verses:[59]
   1. Q 65.1: *"O thou prophet! when ye divorce women, then divorce them at their term...."*
   2. Q 2.228: *"Divorced women must wait for themselves three courses,"* meaning three menstrual periods.
   3. Q 65.4: *"And such of your women as despair of menstruation,—if ye doubt, then their term is three months...."*

B. A saying that is attributed to a wife of Muhammed, 'Ā'isha, is that the pleasure marriage (*mut'a*) is abrogated with verses Q 23.5-6 and Q 70.29-30 (entirely identical in the current Arabic Qur'ān): *"And who guard their private parts—except for their wives or...their right hands possess...verily, they are not to be blamed."* Since the woman in the *mut'a* is neither a permanent wife nor a maid, this verse (Q 4.24) is abrogated.[60] And this ruling is affirmed by some of the Sunnī legal scholars.[61]

C. A prohibition concerning the *mut'a* marriage is attributed to Muḥammad.[62]

In the second scholarly opinion, the temporary marriage (*mut'a)* is conserved. According to this view, the group of scholars say *mut'a* is not abrogated.[63] This is the position of the Shiites.

Q 4.25

This phrase refers to slave women, married to Muslims, who later *"commit fornication"* (i.e., adultery). However, there is no penalty for unmarried slave women who commit adultery. (See the article "Women in the Qur'ān" on page 117.)

This verse came to specify that the punishment for married slave women committing adultery is half of what falls on the married free women. Other scholars were of the

should have patience is better for you, and God is forgiving and
merciful.
26 God wishes to explain to you and to guide you into the
ordinances of those who were before you, and to turn towards
you, for God is knowing, wise.
27 God wishes to turn towards you, but those who follow their
lusts wish that ye should swerve with a mighty swerving!
28 God wishes to make it light for you, for man was created weak.
29 O ye who believe! devour not your property amongst
yourselves vainly, unless it be a merchandise by mutual consent.
And do not kill yourselves; verily, God is compassionate unto you.
30 But whoso does that maliciously and unjustly, we will broil
him with fire; for that is easy with God.
31 If ye avoid great sins from which ye are forbidden, we will
cover your offences and make you enter with a noble entrance.
32 And do not covet that by which God has preferred one of you
over another. The men shall have a portion of what they earn, and
the women a portion of what they earn; ask God for His grace,
verily, God knows all.
33 To every one have we appointed kinsfolk as heirs of what parents
and relatives and those with whom ye have joined right hands leave;
so give them their portion, for, verily, God is over all a witness.
34 Men stand superior to women in that God hath preferred

opinion that this verse abrogates Q 24.2: *"Scourge each of them with a hundred stripes...."* Whereas, before this verse the punishment used to be the same for both groups, now the female slave takes half the punishment of a free woman.[64]

Q 4.29

There are two views regarding the abrogation of this verse. Some scholars believe that the verse forbids a man from eating the food of another unless he purchases the food.[65] In other words, a man could not accept the free gift of food or hospitality from another. It was said, after the verse came, that it became an embarrassment for a man to eat at another's home, or at anyone else's expense. Therefore, it was abrogated with verse Q 24.61: *"There is no crime on you, that ye eat all together or separately. And when ye enter houses then greet each other with a salutation from God, blessed and good."*[66]

Others said that some understood the verse to prohibit eating with "special needs" people so that they are treated justly with regard to their share of the food. Therefore, they quit eating with the blind, the lame, and the ill. So, verse Q 24.61 came to abrogate this supposed prohibition: *"There is no hindrance to the blind, and no hindrance to the lame, and no hindrance to the sick...."*[67]

While one group of scholars believes that the verse prohibits ill gain through unlawful means like usury, gambling and other means, it is considered conserved.[68]

Q 4.31

Ibn 'Abbās read this as *"We will cover from your offences..."* by adding "from."[69]

In the Qur'ān's verse, the promise is to expel or remit all the evil, whereas the promise, according to the reading of Ibn 'Abbās, is to expel or remit part of the evil.

Q 4.33

Regarding this verse, scholars said that *"give them"* could mean a variety of different things:

1. **Bequeathing property to another.** Two men could make an agreement to inherit one another's wealth. One might say to the other, "You are my heir and I am your heir." So this rather unusual manner of bequeathing an inheritance is abrogated with verse Q 8.75: *"But blood relations are nearer in kin by the Book of God...."*[70] In other words, blood relations have prior rights to inheritance than to those who are not related.
2. **Supporting each other.** Two or more people could make an agreement to support the other(s).[71]
3. **Agreeing on these two matters: support and inheritance.** But this is abrogated with the inheritance verse, Q 8.75: *"But blood relations are nearer in kin by the Book of God...."*[72]
4. **Granting adopted children an inheritance with their natural children.** However, that is abrogated with verse Q 8.75: *"But blood relations are nearer in kin by the Book of God...."*[73]

some of them over others, and in that they expend of their wealth: and the virtuous women, devoted, careful (in their husbands') absence, as God has cared for them. But those whose perverseness ye fear, admonish them and remove them into bed-chambers and beat them; but if they submit to you, then do not seek a way against them; verily, God is high and great.

35 And if ye fear a breach between the two, then send a judge from his people and a judge from her people. If they wish for reconciliation, God will arrange between them; verily, God is knowing and aware.

36 And serve God, and do not associate aught with Him; and to your parents show kindness, and to kindred, and orphans, and the poor, and the neighbour who is akin, and the neighbour who is a stranger, and the companion who is strange, and the son of the road, and what your right hands possess, verily, God loves not him who is proud and boastful;

37 who are miserly and bid men be miserly too, and who hide what God has given them of His grace;—but we have prepared for the misbelievers shameful woe.

38 And those who expend their wealth in alms for appearance sake before men, and who believe not in God nor in the last day;—but whosoever has Satan for his mate, an evil mate has he.

39 What harm would it do them if they believed in God and in the last day, and expended in alms of what God has provided them with? but God knows about them.

40 Verily, God would not wrong by the weight of an atom; and if it's a good work, He will double it and bring from Himself a mighty hire.

41 How then when we bring from every nation a witness, and bring thee as a witness against these

42 on the day when those who misbelieve and rebel against the Apostle would fain that the earth were levelled with them? but they cannot hide the news from God.

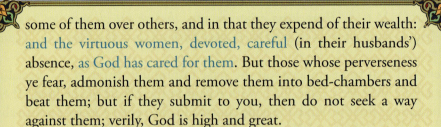

43 O ye who believe! approach not prayer while ye are drunk, until ye well know what ye say; nor yet while polluted,—unless ye be passing by the way,—until ye have washed yourselves. But

Q 4.34

Ibn Masʿūd read the verse as "and the virtuous women, devoted, careful (in their husbands') absence, as God has cared for them. Therefore, be good unto them."[74] Though it is not visible in English, this reading uses the broken plural *fāl-ṣawāliḥ qawānit ḥawāfiẓ* instead of the sound feminine plural found in the Qur'ān ***fāl-ṣāliḥāt qānitāt ḥāfiẓāt***.

It is noteworthy that the reading of Ibn Masʿūd differs in two ways:

- He followed different grammatical rules, which makes one wonder which form of plural is the appropriate one here?
- He added, "Therefore, be good unto them."

Question: Did Ibn Masʿūd add to the Qur'ān, or did others remove from it?

Q 4.40

Ibn Masʿūd read it as "Allah is not unjust, not even the weight of *namla* ["an ant"].[75]

The Arabic word used in the Qur'ān is ***dharratin***, which was understood to mean the "**smallest ant**." Today, this word *dharra*(*tin*) is used as an equivalent to the English word "atom." There is no disagreement between the two readings with regard to the meaning. However, the difference is actually in the technical form of the expression. What is also interesting is that the readers chose the words according to their artistic taste, which shows how individual differences in reading styles can affect the recording of the Qur'ān.

Q 4.43

This verse allows the drinking of alcohol outside of prayer times. Later, it was abrogated with verse Q 5.90: "*...wine and* [other evils]*...are an abomination of Satan's work! Avoid them....*"[76] Others say the verse is abrogated with Q 5.91: "*...will ye not, therefore, abstain from them?*"[77]

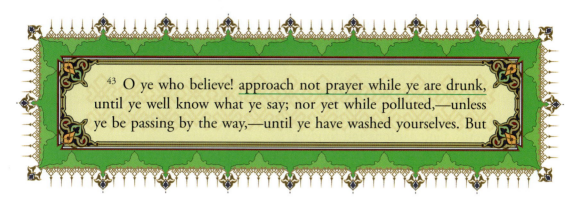

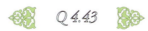

if ye are sick, or on a journey, or one of you come from the privy,
or if ye have touched a woman, and ye cannot find water, then use
good surface sand and wipe your faces and your hands therewith;
verily, God pardons and forgives.
44 Do ye not see those who have been given a portion of the
Book? they buy error, and they wish that ye may err from the way!
45 But God knows best who your enemies are, and God suffices
as a patron, and sufficient is God as a help.
46 And those who are Jews, and those who pervert the words
from their places, and say, 'We hear but we rebel, and do thou
listen without hearing,' and (who say) 'rahina,' distorting it with
their tongues and taunting about religion. But had they said,
'We hear and we obey, so listen and look upon us,' it would have
been better for them and more upright;—but may God curse
them in their misbelief, for they will not believe except a few.
47 O ye who have been given the Book! believe in what we have
revealed, confirming what ye had before; ere we deface your faces
and turn them into hinder parts, or curse you as we cursed the
fellows of the Sabbath when God's command was done.
48 Verily, God pardons not associating aught with Him, but He
pardons anything short of that to whomsoever He pleases; but he
who associates aught with God, he hath devised a mighty sin.
49 Do ye not see those who purify themselves? nay, God purifies
whom He will, and they shall not be wronged a straw.
50 Behold, how they devise against God a lie, and that is manifest
sin enough.
51 Do ye not see those to whom a portion of the Book has been
given? They believe in *G*ibt and Ta*gh*ut, and they say of those who
misbelieve, 'These are better guided in the way than those who
believe.'
52 These are those whom God has cursed, and whom God has
cursed no helper shall he find.
53 Shall they have a portion of the kingdom? Why even then

Q 4.44

The majority of the readers read this as *"**they wish**,"* meaning non-Muslims,[78] while some read this as "You wish," where the Muslims are the addressee.[79]

Question: Who is being addressed, the Muslims or the non-Muslims?

Q 4.49

The reports state that the Jews and Christians used to boast, saying, *"We are the sons of God and His beloved…"* (Q 5.18).

So Muḥammad answered them by saying that it was not permitted for people to praise themselves, and that praise is strictly limited to Allah (Q 4.49).

Muḥammad repeatedly warned against praising oneself. Thus, he said in the Qur'ān, *"Make not yourselves out, then, to be pure; He knows best who it is that fears"* (Q 53.32). On another occasion he told Muslims, "Do not justify yourselves; Allah knows better those who are rightous among you."[80] But Muḥammad did not abide by this teaching. When accused by some Muslims of being biased toward his own Quraysh tribe, he answered, "By Allah I am indeed faithful in heaven and faithful on earth." This contradictory behavior was noted by al-Rāzī, who commented on Muḥammad's self-praise by saying, "Since Allah justified him first by a sign [the miracle], he was permitted to act unlike any other."[81]

Question: How could Muḥammad forbid something, then do it himself? Is he not "the best example"? Is it not written in the Qur'ān, *"Will ye order men to do piety and forget yourselves? ye read the Book, do ye not then understand?"* (Q 2.44). And is it not also written, *"O ye who believe! say not what ye do not"* (Q 61.2)? Or was it, as stated by al-Rāzī, that according to Islāmic doctrine, a prophet is permitted to do what is considered forbidden to everyone else?

Q 4.51

This verse accuses *"those to whom a portion of the Book has been given"* that they *"believe in Gibt and Taghut."* According to the Arabic concordance *al-Qāmūs al-Muḥīṭ*, *Gibt* means idols or other false deities and *Ṭāghūt*[D] means the devil.

However, some of the commentaries interpret *Gibt* as a sorcerer, sorcery, or the devil, and *Ṭāghūt* as a diviner [priest] or the devil himself.[82]

How could it be said that a biblical group believes in *Gibt* and *Ṭāghūt*?

In their interpretation of this verse, the scholars said that Ḥuyaiy Ibn Akhṭab and Ka'b Ibn al-Ashraf[N] went to Mecca with a group of Jews to form an alliance to go into battle against Muḥammad. When the people of the Quraysh feared there was a trick

they would not give to men a jot.
54 Do they envy man for what God has given of His grace? We have given to Abraham's people the Book and wisdom, and we have given them a mighty kingdom.
55 And of them are some who believe therein, and of them are some who turn from it, but Hell is flaming enough for them.
56 Verily, those who disbelieve in our signs, we will broil them with fire; whenever their skins are well done, then we will change them for other skins, that they may taste the torment. Verily, God is glorious and wise.
57 But those who believe and do aright, we will make them enter gardens beneath which rivers flow, and they shall dwell therein for ever and aye, for them therein are pure wives, and we will make

or secret agreement between Muḥammad and the Jews, they asked the Jews to prove their loyality by worshipping the Quraysh idols.[83] In another narrative, the Quraysh had asked the Jews to believe in their idols.[84] After the Jews granted their request, the Quraysh agreed to enter into an alliance with them against Muḥammad.

The people of the Quraysh were not so naïve as to ask a Jewish group to worship idols just to confirm their honest intentions. The Quraysh would have known that if the Jews were plotting against them, the Jews would bow down to idols to win their trust. Therefore, this story appears to be a fabrication. Besides, the verse uses the present tense of the verb *"believe,"* which indicates an ongoing action from the past until now. Hence, this verse does not say that they (the People of the Book) believed in *Gibt* and *Ṭāghūt* only once. Even if a person is Jewish at one time, anyone who actively believes in sorcery, idols, or the devil is a pagan.

Therefore, another clear contradiction arises with the verse declaring that Jews *"believe in sorcery* (*Gibt* or idols) *and evil* (*Ṭāghūt* or the devil)*."* Furthermore, it seems that the purpose of this verse was to defame the Jews and undermine their prestige in Medina after their refusal to follow Muḥammad or accept that he was a true prophet of God.

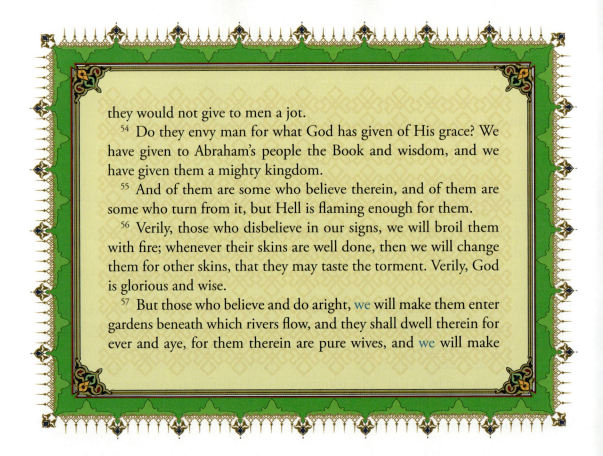

them enter into a shady shade.
[58] Verily, God bids you pay your trusts to their owners, and when ye judge between men to judge with justice. Verily, God, excellent is what He admonishes you with; verily, God both hears and sees.
[59] O ye who believe! obey God, and obey the Apostle and those in authority amongst you; and if ye quarrel about anything, refer to God and the Apostle, if ye believe in God and the last day; that is better and fairer as a settlement.
[60] Do ye not see those who pretend that they believe in what has been revealed to them, and what was revealed before thee; they wish to refer their judgment to Ta*gh*ut, but they are bidden to disbelieve therein, and Satan wishes to lead them into a remote error.

Q 4.57

Ibn Mas'ūd and others read this as "[b]ut those who believe and do deeds of righteousness, he shall soon admit to Gardens…he shall admit them to shades, cool and ever deepening."[85]

There is a difference with regard to the person. In the Qur'ānic text, Allah is the speaker, whereas, according to Ibn Mas'ūd's reading, another person is talking about Allah.

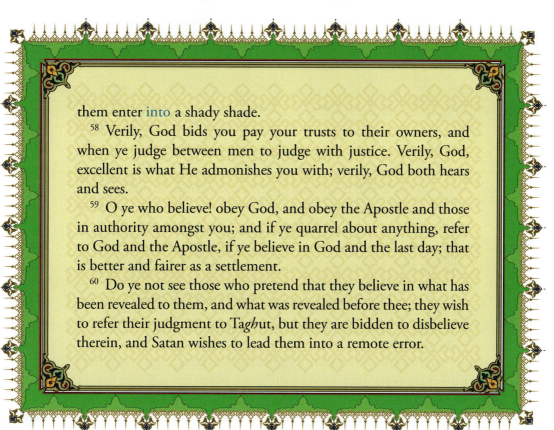

61 And when it is said to them, 'Come round to what God has
sent down and unto the Apostle,' thou seest the hypocrites turning
from thee, turning away.
62 How then when there befalls them a mischance through what
their hands have sent on before? then will they come to you, and
swear by God, 'We meant naught but good and concord.'
63 These, God knows what is in their hearts. Turn thou away
from them and admonish them, and speak to them into their
souls with a searching word.
64 We have never sent an apostle save that he should be obeyed
by the permission of God; and if they, when they have wronged
themselves, come to thee and ask pardon of God, and the Apostle
asks pardon for them, then they will find God easy to be turned,
compassionate.
65 But no! by thy Lord! they will not believe, until they have
made thee judge of what they differ on; then they will not find in
themselves aught to hinder what thou hast decreed, and they will
submit with submission.
66 But had we prescribed for them, 'Kill yourselves, or go ye
forth out of your houses,' they would not have done it, save only
a few of them; but had they done what they are admonished, then
it would have been better for them, and a more firm assurance.
67 And then we would surely have brought them from ourselves
a mighty hire,
68 and would have guided them into a right path.
69 Whoso obeys God and the Apostle, these are with those God
has been pleased with, of prophets and confessors and martyrs and
the righteous;—a fair company are they.
70 That is grace from God, and God knows well enough.
71 O ye who believe! take your precautions and sally in detachments
or altogether.
72 Verily, there is of you who tarries behind, and, if a mischance

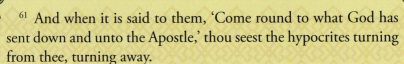

befalls you, says, 'God has been gracious to me, since I am not with them a martyr.'

[73] But if there befalls you grace from God, he would say—as though there were no friendship between you and him—'O would that I had been with thee to attain this mighty happiness!'

[74] Let those then fight in God's way who sell this life of the world for the next; and whoso fights in God's way, then, be he killed or be he victorious, we will give him a mighty hire.

Q 4.63

This is a principle at the beginning of the call to Islām. But after the Muslims became stronger in numbers and influence, the verse was abrogated with verse Q 9.5: *"...kill the idolaters wherever ye may find them...."*[86]

Q 4.64

This verse is abrogated with verse Q 9.80: *"Ask forgiveness for them or ask not forgiveness, for them! if they shouldst ask forgiveness for them seventy times, yet would not God forgive them."*[87]

Q 4.71

The verse contains an order for Muslims to take caution and be prepared with weapons for battle, organizing each squad and each company. But it is abrogated with Q 9.122: *"Nor should the Believers all go forth together...."*[88]

But some scholars say that no abrogation applies here. In the words of Ibn al-Jawzī, "the fighters' situations differ, and it is up to the imām[D] how he evaluates the matter, and there is no abrogation in this verse, but the whole of it is conserved."[89]

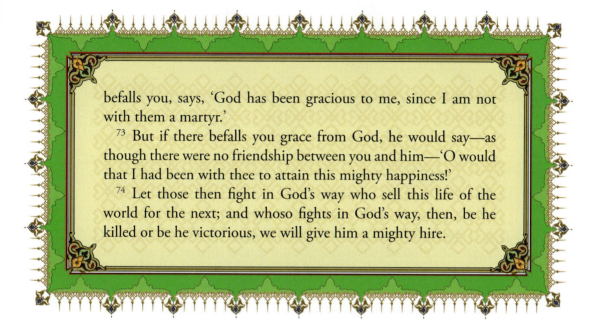

75 What ails you that ye do not fight in God's way, and for the weak men and women and children, who say, 'Lord, bring us out of this town of oppressive folk, and make for us from Thee a patron, and make for us from Thee a help?'
76 Those who believe fight in the way of God; and those who disbelieve fight in the way of Ta*gh*ut; fight ye then against the friends of Satan, verily, Satan's tricks are weak.
77 Do ye not see those to whom it is said, 'Restrain your hands, and be steadfast in prayer and give alms;' and when it is prescribed for them to fight then a band of them fear men, as though it were the fear of God or a still stronger fear, and they say, 'O our Lord! why hast thou prescribed for us to fight, couldst thou not let us abide till our near appointed time?' Say, 'The enjoyment of this world is but slight, and the next is better for him who fears:—but they shall not be wronged a straw.
78 Wheresoe'er ye be death will overtake you, though ye were in lofty towers. And if a good thing befall them, they say, 'This is from God,' but if a bad thing, they say, 'This is from thee.' Say, 'It is all from God.' What ails these people? they can hardly understand a tale.
79 What befalls thee of good it is from God; and what befalls thee of bad it is from thyself. We have sent thee to mankind as an apostle, and God sufficeth for a witness.
80 Whoso obeys the prophet he has obeyed God; and he who turns back—we have not sent thee to watch over them.

Q 4.75

Ibn Mas'ūd read it in a different form: "Our Lord! Rescue us from this town, which was an oppressor."[90]

Q 4.77

Ibn Mas'ūd read this verse, adding the following text: "so we die naturally and not be killed lest the enemies rejoice at that."[91]

Q 4.78-79

Contradictions in the Qur'ān usually occur in verses that are apart from each other in the same sūra or in verses from different sūras. However, in this passage, the contradiction occurs in two consecutive verses. Q 4.78 teaches that the source of both good and evil is Allah, while the following verse, Q 4.79, declares that good is from Allah and evil is from man.

- Q 4.78: *"And if a good thing befall them, they say, 'This is from God,' but if a bad thing, they say, 'This is from thee.' Say, 'It is all from God....' "*
- Q 4.79: *"What befalls thee of good it is from God; and what befalls thee of bad it is from thyself...."*

Question: Is "what befalls...of bad" from God or from oneself?

Q 4.79

In the codex of Ibn Mas'ūd, this verse reads as "from thy (own) soul, however I ordained it to you," by adding *wa innamā qaḍaytuhā 'alayk* ("however I ordained it to you"). Ibn 'Abbās read it in the same manner as well.

It is also said that both Ibn 'Abbās and Ibn Mas'ūd read this text as "from thy (own) soul, but I wrote it upon you," by adding *wa anā katabtuhā 'alayk* ("but I wrote it upon you"). It is further told that Ibn Mas'ūd and Ubayy Ibn Ka'b read this verse as "from thy (own) soul and I enumerated it upon you," by adding *wa anā 'adadtuhā 'alayk* ("and I enumerated it upon you").[92]

These variant readings are trying to correct a contradiction between verses 78 and 79 in the current Arabic Qur'ān, as described in the previous comment. (See the critical analysis of Q 4.78-79, page 345.)

Q 4.80

This principle was the standard until it was abrogated by the Sword verse, Q 9.5: *"...kill the idolaters wherever ye may find them...."*[93]

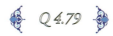

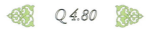

81 They say, 'Obedience!' but when they sally forth from you, a company of them brood by night over something else than that which thou hast said; but God writes down that over which they brood. Turn then from them and rely on God, for God sufficeth for a guardian.

82 Do they not meditate on the Qur'an? if it were from other than God they would find in it many a discrepancy.

83 And when there comes to them a matter of security or fear they publish it; but if they were to report it to the Apostle and to those in authority amongst them, then those of them who would elicit it from them would know it; but were it not for God's grace upon you and His mercy ye had followed Satan, save a few.

84 Fight, then, in the way of God; impose not aught on any but thyself, and urge on the believers; it may be that God will restrain the violence of those who misbelieve, for God is more violent and more severe to punish.

85 Whoso intercedes with a good intercession shall have a portion therefrom; but he who intercedes with a bad intercession shall have the like thereof, for God keeps watch over all things.

86 And when ye are saluted with a salutation, salute with a better than it, or return it;—verily, God of all things takes account.

87 God, there is no God but He! He will surely assemble you on the resurrection day, there is no doubt therein; who is truer than God in his discourse?

88 Why are ye two parties about the hypocrites, when God hath overturned them for what they earned? Do ye wish to guide those whom God hath led astray? Whoso God hath led astray ye shall not surely find for him a path.

89 They would fain that ye misbelieve as they misbelieve, that ye might be alike; take ye not patrons from among them until they too flee in God's way; but if they turn their backs, then seize them and kill them wheresoever ye find them, and take from them

Q 4.81

There is a command to Muḥammad in this verse to not busy his mind with those who outwardly appear to have faith but act contrarily to that faith.[94] It is said that the meaning here is for Muḥammad to forgive them. However, this request to forgive is abrogated by the Sword verse, Q 9.5: *"...kill the idolaters wherever ye may find them...."*[95]

Q 4.82

In an effort to prove the divine source of the Qur'ān, this verse states that if the Qur'ān had been *"from other than God they would find in it many a discrepancy."*

Thus, according to this verse, the standard of proof that the Qur'ān is *"from other than God"* would be if many discrepancies were found in its pages. In applying this standard, please refer to any number of previous entries.

Note: The original language of this verse seems to imply that the Qur'ān contains a few discrepancies. Otherwise, there would be no need to describe the contradictions as *"**many** a discrepancy."*

M. al-Rāzī answered this issue with this statement: "The emphasis on describing the contradiction as 'much' is to prove the association of a few contradictions, as if to say, 'had it been from other than Allah they would surely have found therein much discrepancy in addition to the few.'"[96]

Question: Based on our discussion thus far, it is clear that the Qur'ān contains many discrepancies, not just a few. How can Allah allow any discrepancies in his holy book, the Qur'ān?

Q 4.84

A group of scholars says this verse tells the Muslim to be responsible only for one's own self. Therefore, they say it is abrogated with the Sword verse, Q 9.5: *"...kill the idolaters wherever ye may find them...."*[97]

Q 4.88

This verse encourages Muslims to be of one mind regarding the hypocrites (idolaters) among them, lest believers be tempted to befriend them (89). The verse is abrogated with the Sword verse, Q 9.5: *"...kill the idolaters wherever ye may find them...."*[98]

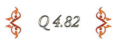

neither patron nor help,—

90 save those who reach a people betwixt whom and you is an alliance—or who come to you while their bosoms prevent them from fighting you or fighting their own people. But had God pleased He would have given you dominion over them, and they would surely have fought you. But if they retire from you and do not fight you, and offer you peace,—then God hath given you no way against them.

91 Ye will find others who seek for quarter from you, and quarter from their own people; whenever they return to sedition they shall be overturned therein: but if they retire not from you, nor offer you peace, nor restrain their hands, then seize them and kill them wheresoever ye find them;—over these we have made for you manifest power.

92 It is not for a believer to kill a believer save by mistake; and whosoever kills a believer by mistake then let him free a believing neck; and the blood-money must be paid to his people save what they shall remit as alms. But if he be from a tribe hostile to you and yet a believer, then let him free a believing neck. And if it be a tribe betwixt whom and you there is an alliance, then let the blood-money be paid to his friends, and let him free a believing neck; but he who cannot find the means, then let him fast for two consecutive months—a penance this from God, for God is knowing, wise.

93 And whoso kills a believer purposely, his reward is hell, to dwell therein for aye; and God will be wrath with him, and curse him, and prepare for him a mighty woe.

94 O ye who believe! when ye are knocking about in the way of God be discerning, and do not say to him who offers you a salutation, 'Thou art no believer,' craving after the chances of this world's life, for with God are many spoils! So were ye aforetime, but God was gracious to you, be ye then discerning; verily, God of what ye do is well aware.

Q 4.90

The verse allows Muslims to be at peace with whomever they have made pacts and treaties. Later, the Qur'ān abolishes all previous peace treaties and abrogates it with the following verses:

A. Q 9.1: *"An immunity from God and His Apostle to those idolaters with whom ye have made a league...."* [99]

B. Q 9.5: *"...kill the idolaters wherever ye may find them...."* [100]

C. Q 9.36: *"...fight the idolaters, one and all...."* [101]

Q 4.91

This verse tells Muslims that they will meet people who will agree with what they say, as well as with what their opponents say, in order to be safe from both the Muslims and the non-Muslims. The verse permits Muslims to grant this "in between" category of peace. However, that permission is abrogated with verse Q 9.5: *"...kill the idolaters wherever ye may find them."* [102]

Q 4.92

The majority of scholars agree that this verse orders the paying of compensation (blood money) for an inadvertent killing. Therefore, some scholars say the verse is conserved.[103] Other scholars believe that the verse points to those "idolaters" who had a covenant and a temporary treaty with Muḥammad, thus the verse is abrogated by the following verses:

A. Q 9.1: *"An immunity from God and His Apostle to those idolaters with whom ye have made a league...."* [104]

B. Q 9.5: *"...kill the idolaters wherever ye may find them...."* [105]

C. Q 8.58: *"...throw it back to them in like manner...."* [106]

Q 4.92

Some of the Shiite readers read this verse as "Never should a believer kill a believer; not even by mistake."[107]

Q 4.93

This verse is problematic. It deals with the case of the premeditated killing of a Muslim, which led al-Makkī to elaborate on its discussion.[108] He commented, "This verse needs lengthy explanation. I want to write a separate book in its regard. However, I will write in this book what is proper and sufficient to it, as compared to others."[109]

95 Not alike are those of the believers who sit at home without
harm, and those who are strenuous in God's way with their wealth
and their persons. God hath preferred those who are strenuous
with their wealth and their persons to those who sit still, by many
degrees, and to each hath God promised good, but God hath
preferred the strenuous for a mighty hire over those who sit still,—
96 degrees from him, and pardon and mercy, for God is forgiving
and merciful.
97 Verily, the angels when they took the souls of those who had
wronged themselves, said, 'What state were ye in?' they say, 'We
were but weak in the earth;' they said, 'Was not God's earth wide
enough for you to flee away therein?' These are those whose resort
is hell, and a bad journey shall it be!
98 Save for the weak men, and women, and children, who could
not compass any stratagem, and were not guided to a way;
99 these it may be God will pardon, for God both pardons and
forgives.
100 Whosoever flees in the way of God shall find in the earth
many a spacious refuge; and he who goes forth from his house,
fleeing unto God and His prophet, and then death catches him

The scholars were divided into two groups with respect to this verse.

One group of scholars says the verse ruled that the murderer would eternally dwell in hell, but this ruling is abrogated by verse Q 4.48: *"Verily, God pardons not associating aught with Him, but He pardons anything short of that to whomsoever He pleases...."* Other scholars say this verse is abrogated with the verses Q 25.68, 70: *"and who call not upon another god with God....save he who turns again* [repents]...."[110]

Another group says the verse is conserved, but they differ on the basis of its conservation:

A. A killer of a Muslim will be punished perpetually in hell. This is a report (*khabar*), and reports cannot be abrogated.[111]

B. "It is general, but with reservations shown by the evidence that if an infidel killed a Muslim, but later the infidel converted to Islām, then the penalty in this life and the hereafter would be dropped...."[112]

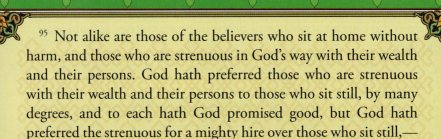

up,—his hire devolves on God, and God is forgiving and merciful.
101 And when ye knock about in the earth, it is no crime to you
that ye come short in prayer, if ye fear that those who disbelieve
will set upon you; verily, the misbelievers are your obvious foes.
102 When thou art amongst them, and standest up to pray with
them, then let a party of them stand up with thee, and let them
take their arms; and when they adore, let them go behind you, and
let another party who have not yet prayed come forward and pray
with thee; and let them take their precautions and their arms. Fain
would those who misbelieve that ye were careless of your arms
and your baggage, that they might turn upon you with a single
turning. And it is no crime to you if ye be annoyed with rain or
be sick, that ye lay down your arms; but take your precautions,—
verily, God has prepared for those who misbelieve a shameful woe.
103 But when ye have fulfilled your prayer, remember God
standing and sitting and lying on your sides; and when ye are in
safety then be steadfast in prayer; verily, prayer is for the believers
prescribed and timed!
104 And do not give way in pursuit of the people; if ye suffer they
shall surely suffer too, even as ye suffer; and ye hope from God,

Q 4.104

The reading of this verse by the majority of readers is ***wa lā tahinū*** ("**and do not give way**") from *wahina*, meaning to be weak. But, 'Ubayd Ibn 'Umayr read this as *wa lā tūhānū* from *ihāna*, which means "insult." This reading prohibits, then, that a Muslim would act in such a way that would bring insult to him.[113]

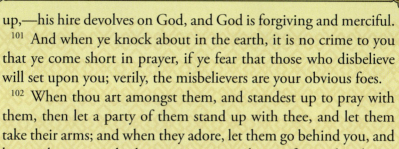

but they hope not! and God is knowing, wise.
105 Verily, we have revealed to thee the Book in truth that thou mayest judge between men of what God has shown thee; so be not with the treacherous a disputant;
106 but ask God's pardon: verily, God is forgiving, merciful.
107 And wrangle not for those who defraud themselves; for God loves not him who is a fraudulent sinner.
108 They hide themselves from men; but they cannot hide themselves from God, for He is with them while they brood at night over speeches that please Him not;—but God doth compass what they do!
109 Here are ye, wrangling for them about this world's life;—but who shall wrangle with God for them on the day of judgment, or who shall be a guardian over them?
110 Yet whoso does evil and wrongs himself, and then asks pardon of God, shall find God forgiving and merciful;
111 and whoso commits a crime, he only commits it against himself, for God is knowing, wise.
112 And whoso commits a fault or a sin and throws it on the innocent, he hath to bear a calumny and a manifest sin.
113 Were it not for God's grace upon thee, and His mercy, a party of them would have tried to lead thee astray; but they only lead themselves astray; they shall not hurt you in aught: for God hath sent down upon thee the Book and the wisdom, and taught thee what thou didst not know, for God's grace was mighty on thee.
114 There is no good in most of what they talk in private; save in his who bids almsgiving, or kindness, or reconciliation between men; and whoso does this, craving the good pleasure of God, we will give to him a mighty hire.
115 But he who severs himself from the prophet after that we have made manifest to him the guidance, and follows other than

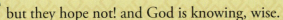

the way of the believers, we will turn our backs on him as he hath turned his back; and we will make him reach hell, and a bad journey shall it be.

116 Verily, God forgives not associating aught with Him, but He pardons anything short of that, to whomsoever He will; but whoso associates aught with God, he hath erred a wide error.

117 Verily, they call not beside Him on aught save females; and they do not call on aught save a rebellious devil.

118 God curse him! for he said, 'I will take from thy servants a portion due to me;

119 and I will lead them astray; and I will stir up vain desires within them; and I will order them and they shall surely crop the ears of cattle; and I will order them and they shall surely alter God's creation;' but he who takes the devil for his patron instead of God, he loses with a manifest loss.

120 He promises them, and stirs up vain desires within them; but the devil promises only to deceive.

121 These, their resort is hell; they shall not find an escape therefrom!

122 But those who believe, and do what is right, we will make them enter into gardens beneath which rivers flow, to dwell therein for aye,—God's promise in truth; and who is truer than God in speech?

123 Not for your vain desires, nor the vain desires of the people of the Book. He who doeth evil shall be recompensed therewith, and shall not find for him beside God a patron, or a help.

124 But he who doeth good works,—be it male or female,—and believes, they shall enter into Paradise, and they shall not be wronged a jot.

125 Who has a better religion than he who resigns his face to God, and does good, and follows the faith of Abraham, as a 'Hanif?'—for God took Abraham as a friend.

126 And God's is what is in the heavens and in the earth, and God encompasses all things!
127 They will ask thee a decision about women; say, 'God decides for you about them, and that which is rehearsed to you in the Book; about orphan women to whom ye do not give what is prescribed for them, and whom ye are averse from marrying; and about weak children; and that ye stand fairly by orphans;—and what ye do of good, verily, that God knows.'
128 And if a woman fears from her husband perverseness or aversion, it is no crime in them both that they should be reconciled to each other, for reconciliation is best. For souls are prone to avarice; but if ye act kindly and fear God, of what ye do He is aware.
129 Ye are not able, it may be, to act equitably to your wives, even though ye covet it; do not however be quite partial, and leave one as it were in suspense; but if ye be reconciled and fear, then God is forgiving and merciful;
130 but if they separate, God can make both independent out of His abundance; for God is abundant, wise.
131 God's is what is in the heavens and what is in the earth! We have ordained to those who have been given the Book before you, and to you too that ye fear God;—but if ye misbelieve, verily, God's is what is in the heavens and what is in the earth, and God is rich and to be praised!
132 God's is what is in the heavens and what is in the earth! and God sufficeth for a guardian!
133 If He will He can make ye pass away, O men! and can bring others ;—God is able to do all that.
134 He who wishes for a reward in this world,—with God is the reward of this world and of the next, and God both hears and sees.
135 O ye who believe! be ye steadfast in justice, witnessing before God though it be against yourselves, or your parents, or your

kindred, be it rich or poor, for God is nearer akin than either. Follow not, then, lusts, so as to act partially; but if ye swerve or turn aside, God of what ye do is well aware.

136 O ye who believe! believe in God and His apostles, and the Book which He hath revealed to His Apostle, and the Book which He sent down before; for whoso disbelieves in God, and His angels, and His Apostle, and the last day, has erred a wide error.

Q 4.129

Ubayy Ibn Ka'b read this verse as "as it [as if she] were a prisoner."[114] He used the phrase *kal masjūna* ("as it [as if she] were a prisoner") instead of the current Arabic Qur'ān's ***kal mu'allaqa*** ("**as it** [as if she] **were in suspense**").

Q 4.136

This verse demands of Muslims to believe in Allah and his messenger. Linguistic scholars call these forms of speech "clarifying the obvious."

How could a believer be asked to believe? This is why scholars attempted to remove the redundancy in the verse by suggesting the following possibilities:

1. The first possibility is that the verse addresses Muslims, telling them, "O you who believe; stay firm in your faith."[115] In other words, it is exhorting Muslims to have steadfast faith always.
2. The second possibility is that the verse addresses non-Muslims, which, in turn, implies either of the following two options:
   - The People of the Book: The verse requests Jews and Christians to believe in Muḥammad.
   - The hypocrites: The verse is meant to say, "O you who believe only by tongue [superficial or nominal faith], believe with the heart [deep or real faith]."[116]

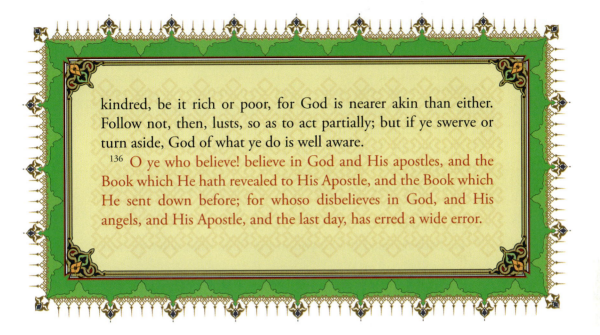

[137] Verily, those who believe and then misbelieve, and then believe and then misbelieve, and then increase in misbelief, God will never pardon them, nor will He guide them in the path.
[138] Give to the hypocrites the glad tidings that for them is grievous woe!
[139] Those who take the misbelievers for their patron rather than believers,—do they crave honour from them? Verily, honour is altogether God's!
[140] He hath revealed this to you in the Book, that when ye hear

3. The third possibility is that the verse is Muḥammad's answer to some Jews who came to him saying, "We believe in you and your book, as well as in Moses and the Torah, but we do not believe in any other books or messengers."[117]
4. The fourth possibility is that this verse was addressed to the idolaters, meaning, "O you who believe in al-Lāt, al-'Uzzā [al-Lāt and al-'Uzzā were two pagan Meccan goddesses believed to be daughters of God], and Ṭāghūt (the devil), believe in Allah, i.e., believe in Allah and his books."[118]

If we accept the first two possibilities, then what was the purpose of the verse clarifying the obvious?

As to the third possibility that this was Muḥammad's answer to some Jews who told Muḥammad that they believed in him, this response is clearly a fabrication. If someone declared that he believed in Muḥammad, he would then become a Muslim and no longer a Jew, so it would not be logical to ask him to believe.

The fourth possibility, which suggests the verse was addressed to polytheists, is naïve at best. How could the verse say, *"O you who believe,"* and address those who don't believe in Allah? If it was addressing the idolaters, a different phrase than *"O you who believe"* would have been used. Even if we accept this opinion, then we would have to add the pagans to the list of people considered People of the Book, which, in turn, means that Muslims should have collected the *jizya* (head tax) from them, rather than fighting them until they believed in Islām.

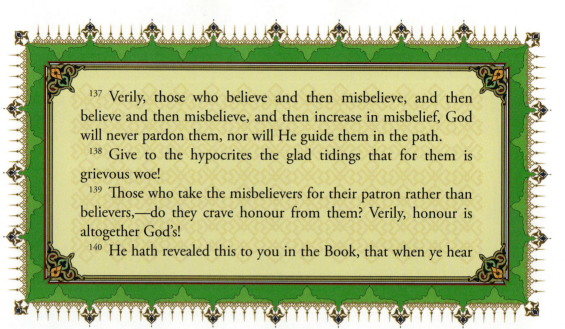

the signs of God disbelieved in and mocked at, then sit ye not
down with them until they plunge into another discourse, for
verily, then ye would be like them. Verily, God will gather the
hypocrites and misbelievers into hell together.
141 Those who lie in wait for you, and if the victory be yours
from God, say, 'Were we not with you?' and if the misbelievers
have a chance, they say, 'Did we not get the mastery over you, and
defend you from the believers?' But God shall judge between you
on the resurrection day; for God will not give the misbelievers a
way against believers.
142 Verily, the hypocrites seek to deceive God, but He deceives
them; and when they rise up to pray, they rise up lazily to be seen
of men, and do not remember God, except a few;
143 wavering between the two, neither to these nor yet to those!
but whomsoever God doth lead astray thou shall not find for him
a way.
144 O ye who believe! take not misbelievers for patrons rather
than believers; do ye wish to make for God a power against you?
145 Verily, the hypocrites are in the lowest depths of hell-fire, and
thou shalt not find for them a help.
146 Save those who turn again, and do right, and take tight hold
on God, and are sincere in religion to God; these are with the
believers, and God will give to the believers mighty hire.
147 Why should God punish you, if ye are grateful and believe?
for God is grateful and knowing.
148 God loves not publicity of evil speech, unless one has been
wronged; for God both hears and knows.
149 If ye display good or hide it, or pardon evil, verily, God is
pardoning and powerful!
150 Verily, those who disbelieve in God and His apostles desire to
make a distinction between God and His apostles, and say, 'We
believe in part and disbelieve in part, and desire to take a midway

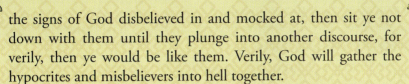

course between the two:'
151 these are the misbelievers, and we have prepared for misbelievers shameful woe!
152 But those who believe in God and His apostles, and who do not make a distinction between any one of them,—to these we will give their hire, for God is forgiving and merciful!
153 The people of the Book will ask thee to bring down for them a book from heaven; but they asked Moses a greater thing than that, for they said, 'Show us God openly;' but the thunderbolt caught them in their injustice. Then they took the calf, after what had come to them of manifest signs; but we pardoned that, and gave Moses obvious authority.
154 And we held over them the mountain at their compact, and said to them, 'Enter ye the door adoring;' and we said to them, 'Transgress not on the Sabbath day,' and we took from them a rigid compact.
155 But for that they broke their compact, and for their misbelief in God's signs, and for their killing the prophets undeservedly, and for their saying, 'Our hearts are uncircumcised,'—nay, God hath stamped on them their misbelief, so that they cannot believe except a few,—
156 and for their misbelief, and for their saying about Mary a mighty calumny,
157 and for their saying, 'Verily, we have killed the Messiah, Jesus the son of Mary, the apostle of God'....but they did not kill him, and they did not crucify him, but a similitude was made for them. And verily, those who differ about him are in doubt concerning him; they have no knowledge concerning him, but only follow an opinion. They did not kill him, for sure!
158 nay, God raised him up unto Himself; for God is mighty and wise!
159 And there shall not be one of the people of the Book but shall

Q 4.145

Scholars unanimously agree that the dwelling of hypocrites is in the lowest depths of hellfire, because of the danger the hypocrites present to Muslim society. However, some scholars consider this verse abrogated with the statement from verse Q 4.146: *"Save those who turn again...."* [119]

Ibn al-Jawzī says it is an exception, not an abrogation.[120]

Q 4.153

See the comment on Q 2.55, page 181.

Q 4.157-158

This verse recounts a discussion where the Jews said that they were responsible for the crucifixion of Jesus. But Muḥammad twisted this declaration in order to enforce his own teachings that Jesus was not crucified. Therefore, he said that the Jews did not crucify Jesus, but they instead crucified another man who resembled him, and that Allah had raised Jesus up to himself.[121]

This verse does not describe the crucifixion event. But the commentaries record the following details:

- The first commentary states that when the authorites who wanted to kill Christ surrounded the house where he was staying with his disciples, they could not see clearly into the house. So they took another person who they thought was Christ and killed him instead.[122]
- Another commentary records that when the attackers surrounded the house where Jesus was staying with his disciples, he asked his disciples if anyone would give his life in his stead. One of the disciples volunteered for the mission, so Allah made him resemble Jesus. Then the disciple was taken to be crucified and killed. "They thought they killed 'Īsā [Jesus] and likewise, the Christians thought it was Christ; but Allah had raised Christ from that day."[123]
- Another story states that there was a hypocrite who followed Jesus. When the enemies of Jesus wanted to kill him, the hypocrite volunteered to lead them into Jesus' house. So, Allah raised Jesus up to heaven and put his resemblance on that hypocrite who was killed under the assumption that he was Jesus.[124]

According to all of these accounts, Christians did not fabricate the event of the crucifixion, because they really thought that Christ was crucified, a view supported by al-Ṭabarī: "Likewise, the Christians thought that he was Christ."[125] In that case, the Muslims should have asked themselves why Allah would raise Christ while making the Christians believe that he had been crucified. One of them was actually willing to sacrifice himself for Jesus' sake, as they claim in one of the accounts.

These stories portray Allah as a deceiver because he raised Jesus while allowing another man to be conformed to Jesus' likeness and thus be crucified. If we hypothetically assume that this is a true account, regardless of whether or not this man was one of the disciples or a hypocrite, this story of Allah's deceitfulness would be an insult to Allah alone and not to Christians.

On the other hand, the fact that the Qur'ān denies the crucifixion is actually a contradiction against its claim of being the true and final word. Muslims have always claimed that the validity of the Qur'ānic text depends on the verbal recitation that transfers and communicates its stories among the people. Many Muslims participate in memorizing the Qur'ān, and, based on that recurrence, Muslims claim that the current Arabic Qur'ān is the same Qur'ān that was recited by Muḥammad. How then could the Muslims reject the crucifixion, when that event was communicated verbally as well, especially when those who witnessed the crucifixion were many more in number than those who participated in the writing of the Qur'ān?

Al-Rāzī is the only scholar who attempted to deal with this problem. He noticed that denying the crucifixion of Jesus, which was a recurrent report, would make the principle of recurrence (*tawātur*) subject to disqualification as a reliable transmission method. "This would necessitate the disqualification of all laws…and would collectively open the door for questioning the validity of recurrence, also rendering the validity of the prophecies of all prophets questionable."[126]

However, what he did not mention was that questioning the validity of the crucifixion would necessitate questioning the validity of Muḥammad's status as a prophet as well and not just the Qur'ān. For this reason, al-Rāzī suggested this solution: "When the Jews wanted to arrest Christ, Allah raised him up [to heaven], so they arrested another man and crucified him but said to the people that he was Christ. People believed this ploy because Christ 'did not mingle much with people.' Therefore, the Christians were deceived by a small, conspiring group of people."[127]

This attempt from al-Rāzī to deny Christ's crucifixion does not agree with historical facts that, to the contrary, show that Jesus preached regularly among the people and was well known by both Jews and pagans. In addition, a great number of people—those who believed in him, as well as his enemies—witnessed his crucifixion. However, since al-Rāzī was the only scholar to realize the danger that Islām could face if Christ's crucifixion was denied, he might have possibly invented this story. Nonetheless, al-Rāzī remained confused after briefly mentioning other narrations in other documentaries and, noticing several differences in them, ended his commentary by saying, "These aspects are opposing and contradicting each other, and only Allah knows the truth of the matter."[128]

Thus, the question remains: What is the origin of Muḥammad's phrase, "but a similitude was made for them?"

believe in him before his death; and on the day of judgment he shall be a witness against them.
160 And for the injustice of those who are Jews have we forbidden them good things which we had made lawful for them, and for their obstructing so much the way of God,
161 and for their taking usury when we had forbidden it, and for their devouring the wealth of people in vain,—but we have prepared for those of them who misbehave a grievous woe.

It seems that Islām has replicated the heretical views regarding Jesus that were in circulation at the time. These include the Apollinarian[D] and Docetic doctrinal view that teaches about the dual nature of Christ, "that Jesus was neither crucified nor killed, but that crucifixion and murder were inflicted on a man resembling him instead—or that Jesus (the divine part) was separated from the physical Jesus at the time of crucifixion and death."[129]

This doctrine was identical to one that was declared by Basilides and documented by Irenaeus in his book, *Against the Heresies*. Basilides taught his followers that Christ never experienced the agony of crucifixion, and that Simon of Cyrene, who carried the cross for Christ, was mistakenly crucified by ignorant soldiers. Later, when Islām was spread by the sword across the ancient world, Muslims used Basilides' doctrine as a weapon against Christianity.[130]

This doctrine is in conflict with the implied testimony to Jesus' crucifixion and resurrection by other Qur'ānic verses (Q 3.55; Q 5.117; Q 19.33). (See also the comment on Q 3.55.)

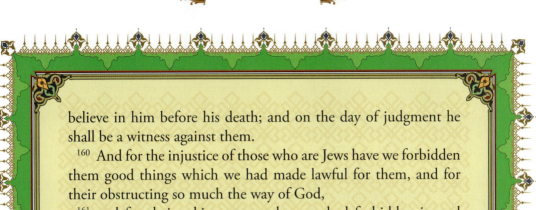

[162] But those amongst them who are firm in knowledge, and the believers who believe in what is revealed to thee, let what is revealed before thee, and the steadfast in prayer, and the givers of alms, and the believers in God and the last day,—unto these we will give a mighty hire.

[163] Verily, we have inspired thee as we inspired Noah and the prophets after him, and as we inspired Abraham, and Ishmael, and Jacob, and the tribes, and Jesus, and Job, and Jonas, and Aaron, and Solomon; and to David did we give Psalms.

[164] Of apostles we have already told thee of some before; and of apostles some we have not told thee of;—But Moses did God speak to, speaking;—

[165] apostles giving glad tidings and warning, that men should have no argument against God, after the apostles, for God is mighty, wise!

[166] But God bears witness to what He has revealed to thee: He revealed it in His knowledge, and the angels bear witness too; though God is witness enough.

[167] Verily, those who misbelieve and obstruct the way of God, have erred a wide error.

[168] Verily those who misbelieve and are unjust, God will not pardon them, nor will He guide them on the road—

[169] save the road to hell, to dwell therein for aye;—that is easy enough to God!

[170] O ye folk! the Apostle has come to you with truth from your Lord: believe then, for it is better for you. But if ye misbelieve, then God's is what is in the heavens and the earth, and God is knowing, wise.

[171] O ye people of the Book! do not exceed in your religion, nor say against God aught save the truth. The Messiah, Jesus the son of Mary, is but the apostle of God and His Word, which He cast into Mary and a spirit from Him; believe then in God and His

Q 4.162

Refer to the comment on Q 20.63 in the second volume of this book.

Q 4.162

In their codices Ibn Mas'ūd and Ubayy Ibn Ka'b wrote *wa al-muqīmūna al-ṣalāt* ("and the steadfast in prayer") according to what preceded it: ***al-rāsikhūna*** ("**who are firm in knowledge**"), which was also the reading of other readers.[131] The reading of the current Arabic Qur'ān is ***wa al-muqīmīna al-ṣalāt*** ("**and the steadfast in prayer**"), contradicting the rules of grammar.

'Ā'isha said that writing this Arabic word with the "ي: *ī* " is a mistake made by the writers of the codices.[132] The readings of Ibn Mas'ūd and Ubayy Ibn Ka'b correct that mistake.

Q 4.164

The majority read this phrase as shown above, where Allah is the speaker, or subject, and Moses is the object, or person being addressed. However, we have a Mu'tazilite reading: "And spoke to Allah Moses direct," where Allah is the object and Moses is the subject.

This reading was also the way it was read by 'Amr Ibn 'Ubayd,[133] Ibrāhīm al-Nakh'ī, and Yaḥyā Ibn Wathāb.[134]

The majority's reading shows Allah as the subject of the verb, whereas the Mu'tazilite reading shows Moses as the subject of the verb.

Question: Who is the subject—Allah or Moses?

Q 4.171

This verse accuses Christians of worshipping three gods. (See also Q 5.73). This accusation seems to be based on a distorted interpretation of the doctrine of the Trinity.

Christianity does not believe in multiple gods but in the oneness of God. The Torah and the Old Testament both declare the oneness of God. The Old Testament explicitly declares, "Hear, O Israel: The Lord our God, the Lord is one" (Deut. 6.4). In the New Testament, Christ repeats this verse when one of the scribes asks him, "'Of all the commandments, which is the most important?' 'The most important one,' answers Jesus, 'is this: 'Hear, O Israel, the Lord our God, the Lord is one'" (Mark 12.28-29). The Nicene Creed (AD 325) declares the oneness of God in Christianity with its opening statement: "We believe in one God," and the Constantinople revision of the

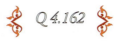

Nicene Creed (AD 381) repeats the same declaration. Even when Saint Athanasius (c. AD 293-373), who resisted various heresies, explained the doctrine of the Trinity, he exhorted Christians: "To believe in one God in trinity and trinity in unity," and added in his first creed, "The Father, the Son and the Holy Spirit are not three gods, but One God."

The Qur'ān and the Heresies

This verse defines the Person of Christ: "Christ Jesus the son of Mary was (no more than) a messenger of Allah, and His Word, which He bestowed on Mary, and a spirit proceeding from Him...." This definition of Christ, according to the Nestorian doctrine, which was widespread in the eastern part of the Arabian Peninsula from Najran to al-Hira and to Iraq and Persia, states that Christ is two persons—'Īsā, son of Mary, and Allah's word—and that these two persons became united at the time he was deposited into Mary's womb.

The phrase *"His Word"* did not mean that Jesus was created by Allah's word. Rather, it meant that he was a person deposited into Mary, "*a spirit proceeding from Him,*" which means he is from Allah and was "*bestowed on Mary.*" Allah did not create Jesus in her because Jesus existed in Allah before being deposited. According to this theory, it is not appropriate to call 'Īsā, the son of Mary, the one birthed from her, the son of Allah. Nor is it appropriate to call his mother, the mother of Allah, because the one birthed from her is different than the one deposited into her. In other words, it was a temporary and transient union.

The first Meccan portion of the Qur'ān was more inclined to the Jacobite doctrine, which was widespread in the western part of the Arabian Peninsula from Abyssinia to Yemen and the borders of Syria at Beni Ghassan. This view considers 'Īsā, the son of Mary, birthed from her, and the word of Allah, [as] one person, as suggested by the description of him found in Q 19.

(al-Ḥaddād, *Aṭwār al-Da'wa al-Qur'ānīya* 823)

apostles, and say not 'Three.' Have done! it were better for you. God is only one God, celebrated be His praise that He should beget a Son! His is what is in the heavens and what is in the earth; and God sufficeth for a guardian.

172 The Messiah doth surely not disdain to be a servant of God, nor do the angels who are nigh to Him; and whosoever disdains His service and is too proud, He will gather them altogether to Himself.

173 But as for those who believe and do what is right, He will pay their hire and will give increase to them of His grace. But as for those who disdain and are too proud, He will punish them with a grievous woe, and they shall not find for them other than God a patron or a help.

174 O ye folk! proof has come to you from your Lord, and we have sent down to you manifest light.

175 As for those who believe in God, and take tight hold of Him, He will make them enter into mercy from Him and grace; and He will guide them to Himself by a right way.

176 They will ask thee for a decision; say, 'God will give you a decision concerning remote kinship.' If a man perish and have no child, but have a sister, let her have half of what he leaves; and he shall be her heir, if she have no son. But if there be two sisters, let them both have two thirds of what he leaves; and if there be brethren, both men and women, let the male have like the portion of two females. God makes this manifest to you lest ye err; for God all things doth know.

Introduction

The name of this sūra, al-Mā'ida, literally means "a table spread with food." It is named after the story of "the table," when the disciples of Jesus asked him to bring "a table of food from heaven" down to them.[1] (See also comments on Q 5.112-115, page 399.)

This sūra will address the following subjects:

- Ritualistic matters pertaining to purification, food, and pilgrimages (Q 5.1-7, 38, 87, 91, 94-100 and others)
- Speeches against the Jews (Q 5.12-13, 18-26) and Muḥammad's opponents (Q 5.41)
- Debates about the nature of Christ and the Holy Trinity (Q 5.14, 17, 72, 110-118)

This sūra represents two opposing attitudes toward Christianity. The first encompasses the hostile mindset formed at the end of the Medinan period. The second, a friendlier mindset, describes Christians as *"nearest in love to those who believe"* (Q 5.82) and belongs to the Meccan period.

There is some disagreement among Muslims over whether Q 5 or Q 9 is chronologically the last sūra written. Despite the apparent chronological proximity between the two sūras, Q 9 displays anti-Christian speech that is in sharp contrast to the cordial expression in Q 5.82. Therefore, it is possible that the cordial verse belongs to an earlier period and was added to the body of Q 5.

It is interesting to note that negative pronouncements about the Jews and Muḥammad's opponents ("the hypocrites") are already expressed in Q 3. Al-Ḥaddād holds that these verses pertaining to the Jews and the opponents were inserted later into Q 5 because the threat of the Jews and the opponents was vanquished after the conquest of Mecca, making such inflammatory verses unnecessary. Therefore, al-Ḥaddād believes these verses have to be from Q 3.[2]

The opinion of al-Ḥaddād could be accepted if the sūras were arranged chronologically, or if the verses of each sūra were chronologically or thematically consistent. However, as we have seen in the previous sūras, the long sūras reflect extended periods of time, possibly as many as eight years. (See Q 2.)

We find in this sūra an example of the nonsequential arrangement of Qur'ānic sūras and verses. Islāmic scholars have informed us that the first revealed verses of this sūra are verses 15 and 16.[3] Therefore, according to chronological order, those verses should have been listed at the beginning of the sūra, in place of verses 1 and 2.

Furthermore, in this sūra (which covers a time period of more than two years) is a verse that we know to be one of the last verses. With this verse from Muḥammad's "Farewell Pilgrimage" speech, *"Today is perfected for you your religion"* (Q 5.3), he announced the completion of his message. We do not exclude the possibility that Muḥammad could have said it on his deathbed and that he didn't have it in mind as a Qur'ānic verse. It could be that it was simply a farewell expression.

In the name of the merciful and compassionate God!
[1] O ye who believe! fulfil your compacts.—Lawful for you are brute beasts, save what is here recited to you, not allowing you the chase while ye are on pilgrimage; verily, God ordaineth what He will.

Q5.1

This verse first commands Muslims to keep all their obligations (compacts, covenants or contracts). Then it adds this declaration: *"Lawful for you are brute beasts...."* This statement means that these animals, *al-an'ām* or "cattle" in Arabic (e.g., camels, cows, and sheep), have been made lawful to be eaten as food after slaughter. What is the connection between the fullfilment of compacts and the lawfulness of certain types of meats?

There are several different definitions to the term "compacts":[4]

- **Covenants:** General contracts.
- **Oaths:** Obligations or commitments pledged by Muslims before the Islāmic era. The following speech is attributed to Muḥammad: "Remain faithful to the oaths of *jāhilīya* (the pre-Islāmic era) and do not introduce new oaths in Islām."
- **Covenants:** Binding agreements or promises, specifically those which Allah made with his servants because of their faith in him and their obedience toward what he had made lawful or unlawful to them.
- **Contracts:** Agreements between people, or agreements that an individual makes with him or herself. Examples of contracts issued are marriage contracts, business contracts, sworn contracts, covenant contracts, and oath contracts.
- **Allah's command:** To the People of the Book to remain faithful to the covenant found in the Torah and the Injīl with regard to believing what Muḥammad has also commanded.

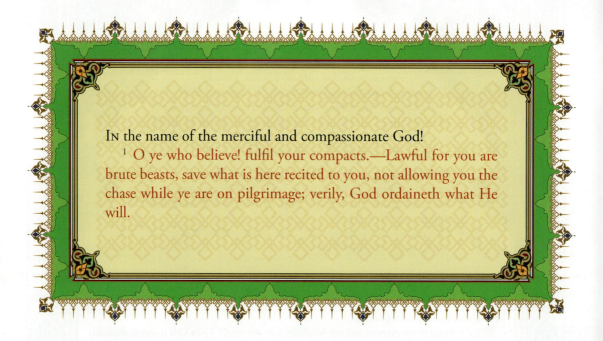

Even if we take any of these suggested interpretations regarding these types of "compacts," we continue to wonder where the link exists between the two parts of this verse.

If we are to read, *"O ye who believe! fulfill your compacts.—Lawful for you are brute beasts,"* we again see a problem we have encountered with other Qur'ānic verses. Although undetected in the English translation of the verse, there is a missing expression in the Arabic—in this case, before the word *"lawful,"* there is no break in this verse. The period found in the English translations after the word "compacts" is not in the Arabic text that unites the two phrases as one sentence. This omission indicates that the writing down of the Qur'ān was not subjected to strict standards. Of course, this laxity resulted from the lack of sufficient education and literacy among the Muslims of that era. This gap in the verse was noticed by Islāmic apologists who state that it refers to the contracts that are required by Allah of the believers, concerning what he (Allah) has permitted, forbidden, and commanded.[5]

The renowned scholar, al-Zamakhsharī, offers this summary:[6]

> It appears to be Allah's covenants with his people in his religion permitting what was permitted and forbidding what was forbidden. And that the entire topic (fulfilling of contracts) was introduced in the first part of the verse and then was followed by more details when Allah said, 'Lawful for you.'

Notice that al-Zamakhsharī uses the phrase, "It appears," denoting doubt.

In an attempt to call attention away from the weakness of eloquence in the verse, a fabricated story is told about al-Kindī, known as the philosopher of the Arabs. When he was asked by his friends to make them a book similar to the Qur'ān, he replied with this assessment:[7]

> "Yes, I can make parts like it." Then he went into seclusion for many days, and then he reappeared and said, "By God, I cannot, and no one can endure to do so! I have opened the Qur'ān and there appeared before me sūra al-Mā'ida, and so I looked and there Allah had spoken of faithfulness and forbade breaking the oath. He also gave a general injunction of what is permissible, and then made one exception after another. Then He told of his omnipotence and wisdom in two lines."

Since Q 5.1 is an example of the weakness in structure and meaning found in the Arabic, this story was invented to conceal these facts, claiming that the philosopher of the Arabs, al-Kindī, was unable to imitate them.

[2] O ye who believe! do not deem the monuments of God to be lawful, nor the sacred month, nor the offering, nor its neck garlands, nor those who sojourn at the sacred house, craving grace from their Lord and His pleasure. But when ye are in lawful state again, then chase; and let not ill-will against the people who turned you from the Sacred Mosque make you transgress; but help one another in righteousness and piety, and do not help one another to sin and enmity; but fear God,—verily, God is keen to punish.
[3] Forbidden to you is that which dies of itself, and blood, and the flesh of swine, and that which is devoted to other than God,

Q5.2

In the current Arabic Qur'ān, ***aāmmīna*** means "**those who sojourn**." Using other codices of the Qur'ān, Ibn Mas'ūd and others read *aāmmīna* as *aāmmī* by dropping the final "na", which is based on Arabic grammar rules. The scholar, Ibn Khalawayh, considers *aāmmī* a proper reading, but he has reservations about it because it is not found in the current official Qur'ān.[8]

Question: Why was the better quality reading not written in the Qur'ān?

Q5.2

This verse orders Muslims to adhere to the inherited rituals of the pilgrimage, including the use of "garlands." Accordingly, the man who wants to go on pilgrimage is to wear a necklace made from a certain kind of tree bark (from the Samor tree), to indicate that he is on pilgrimage. Wearing this special article forbids others from obstructing his pilgrimage or attacking him.[9] This verse is abrogated based on the following discussion:

A. *"...nor those who sojourn at the sacred house"*: Some scholars believe this verse is a prohibition against attacking those on pilgrimage to Mecca, even if the person is one of the idolaters. This particular part of the verse is abrogated with the following verse: *"...when the sacred months are passed away, kill the idolaters wherever ye may find them..."* (Q 9.5). It is also abrogated with another verse (Q 9.28): *"O ye who believe! it is only the idolaters who are unclean; they shall not then approach the Sacred Mosque after this year...."*[10]

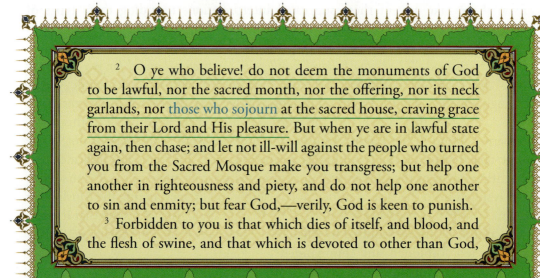

and the strangled and the knocked down, and that which falls down, and the gored, and what wild beasts have eaten—except what ye slaughter in time—and what is sacrificed to idols, and dividing carcases by arrows. To-day shall those who disbelieve in your religion despair; do ye not then fear them, but fear me—To-day is perfected for you your religion, and fulfilled upon you is my favour, and I am pleased for you to have Islam for a religion. But he who is forced by hunger, not inclined wilfully to sin, verily, God is forgiving, compassionate.

4 They will ask thee what is lawful for them? say, 'Lawful for you

B. Other scholars say the verse is abrogated by this verse (Q 9.17): *"It is not for idolaters to repair to the mosques of God, bearing witness against themselves to unbelief…."*[11]

C. A third group of scholars believe that the abrogation of this verse includes everything related to the idolaters. Fighting and slaying idolaters is no longer forbidden during the sacred months. Idolaters no longer have the right to offer sacrifices or to enjoy safety, even while wearing the garlands. Any amnesty seemingly afforded them is abrogated with verse Q 9.5: *"…kill the idolaters wherever ye may find them…."*[12]

Some scholars, however, consider part of the verse, *"do not deem the monuments of God to be lawful,"* to be conserved. Thus, it is forbidden to violate the rites and rituals of pilgrimage.[13]

Q 5.3

The current Arabic Qur'ān uses ***mutajānifin*** (**"inclined"**). However, some readers remove the Arabic *alif* (long "ā" sound) and say *mutajanifin*, a reading considered by Ibn Jinnī and other scholars to be more eloquent.[14] Does this preference imply that the Qur'ān does not contain the most eloquent forms, which is contrary to the prevalent opinion that it is the measuring scale for eloquence?

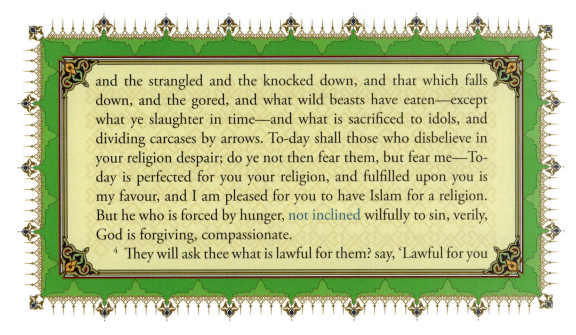

are good things and what ye have taught beasts of prey (to catch), training them like dogs;—ye teach them as God taught you;—so eat of what they catch for you, and mention the name of God over it, and fear God, for verily, God is swift in reckoning up.
5 Lawful for you to-day are good things, and the food of those to whom the Book has been given is lawful for you, and your food is lawful for them; and chaste women of those who believe, and chaste women of those to whom the Book has been given before

Q 5.5

This verse allows the Muslim to eat the food of Jews and Christians. A controversy arose as to whether or not this verse is abrogated and led to these different viewpoints:

A. The verse allows eating the sacrifices of the People of the Book without any condition. Therefore, this verse abrogates the following one: *"But eat not of what the name of God has not been pronounced over…"* (Q 6.121).[15]
B. The verse allows eating the sacrifices of the People of the Book; however, it is abrogated with this verse: *"But eat not of what the name of God has not been pronounced over..."* (Q 6.121).[16]
C. The verse allows eating what the People of the Book have slaughtered. But if it is known that the People of the Book have mentioned a name other than Allah when slaughtering the animal, then eating the slaughtered animal is forbidden. Therefore, the verse is conserved.[17]

The contradiction between the first and second viewpoints reveals the obscure history of the Qur'ānic verses, for if it is known which of the two verses is foremost in revelation, then the abrogated verse would also be known. This situation caused embarrassment for a group of Islāmic scholars, prompting them to suggest an idea unsupported by the context of these two verses. This group of scholars suggests that Q 5.5 deals with the sacrifices of the People of the Book, and Q 6.121 refers to the sacrifices of the pagans. Therefore, the two verses address two different subjects.[18]

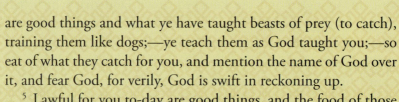

you,—when you have given them their hire, living chastely and not fornicating, and not taking paramours. But whoso disbelieves in the faith, of a truth his work is vain, and he shall be in the next life of those who lose.

6 O ye who believe! when ye rise up to prayer wash your faces, and your hands as far as the elbows, and wipe your heads, and your feet down to the ankles. And if ye are polluted, then purify

Q5.6

Various opinions have arisen as to which actions apply for each part of the body. For example, in the last part of the verse, the Arabic does not have the word "wash" in it, omitting the verb entirely. So what action should be applied to "**your feet**"? The Sunnīs believe the word "wash" is a good choice because the Arabic word for "feet" is shown in the objective (accusative) case ***wa'arjulakum***, and the Arabic words for "faces," "hands," and "elbows" in the first part of the sentence are also shown in the objective case. Thus, they believe this verb should apply to "feet" as well. Hence, the Sunnī jurisprudents rule that the feet should be washed.

However, a large group of readers use a variant reading of this verse, linking the possessive case of "**your** feet," *wa'arjulikum*, with the verb "wipe." Thus the meaning becomes "**wipe** your feet" rather than "wash your feet." They believe that because the verb "wipe" in "wipe your heads" comes just before the words "your feet," it makes more sense to associate these two elements together. Al-Ṭabarī leans toward this reading.[19]

The differences between the readings have led to differences in the rituals of *wuḍū'* (ablutions or washings). Should the feet be **washed** as the Sunnī scholars say, according to the context of "wash your faces, and your hands…and your feet"? Or should they be **wiped**, as the Shiites mandate, based on the context of "and wipe your heads and your feet to the ankles"?[20]

This issue is important because the principle of *wuḍū'* ("ablutions") for the Islāmic prayer requires fastidious attention to the minutest detail concerning these rituals. Prayers cannot be performed properly and receive acceptance without proper *wuḍū'*.

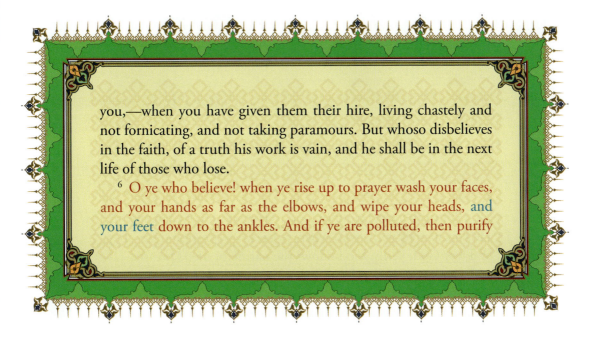

yourselves. But if ye are sick, or on a journey, or if one of you comes from the privy, or if ye have touched women and cannot find water, then take fine surface sand and wipe your faces and your hands therewith. God does not wish to make any hindrance for you; but he wishes to purify you and to fulfill his favour upon you; haply ye may give thanks.

7 Remember the favour of God to you and His covenant which He covenanted with, you, when ye said, 'We hear and we obey;' and fear God, verily, God knows the nature of men's breasts.

8 O ye who believe! stand steadfast to God as witnesses with justice; and let not ill-will towards people make you sin by not acting with equity. Act with equity, that is nearer to piety, and fear God; for God is aware of what ye do.

Q 5.6

This verse points out the causes that would break one's ablution, including, *"if one of you comes from the privy, or if ye have touched women..."* (Q 5.6).

This phrase is also found verbatim in Q 4.43: *"...or one of you come from the privy,"* which al-Rāzī explains as "meaning answering nature's call, which is explained by Muslim scholars as whatever comes out of the two orifices (meaning urination and defecation)."[21]

As to the meaning of the phrase, *"have touched women,"* there are several detailed explanations, ranging from sexual intercourse to simply touching a woman.[22]

Question: Is moving from answering nature's call to touching a woman a sign of superior rhetoric? More importantly, doesn't this verse degrade the value of women when it puts women side by side with answering nature's call? It appears to make the two equal by connecting them as agents of breaking the ablution by the use of the word "or."

9 God has promised to those who believe and work righteousness,
that for them is pardon and a mighty hire.
10 But those who disbelieve and call our signs lies, these are the
fellows of hell.
11 O ye who believe! remember God's favour towards you,
when a people intended to stretch their hands against you, but He
withheld their hands from you; and upon God let believers rely.
12 God did take a compact from the children of Israel, and
raised up of them twelve wardens; and God said, 'Verily, I am with
you, if ye be steadfast in prayer, and give alms, and believe in my
apostles, and assist them, and lend to God a goodly loan; then will
I cover your offences and make you enter gardens beneath which
rivers flow: and whoso disbelieves after that, he hath erred from
the level way.'

Q5.9

Although forgiveness is typically offered to those who commit wrongdoings, this verse states that Allah promises forgiveness and a grand reward to those who are already good: *"God has promised to those who believe and work righteousness."* This difference seems, therefore, to be a contradiction.

Q5.11

Some authoritative readers pronounce the Arabic word for "**favour**" as ***ni'mata*** with an ending "ta", according to the language of Tai'. It is written this way in the current Arabic Qur'ān. On the other hand, others use a variant reading and pronounce this word as *ni'mah* ("his favor") with an "h".[23]

Question: Why did this word get written according to the language of Tai', which is contrary to the common rules of the Arabic writing? Does that choice not indicate the absence of systematized editing of the Qur'ān?

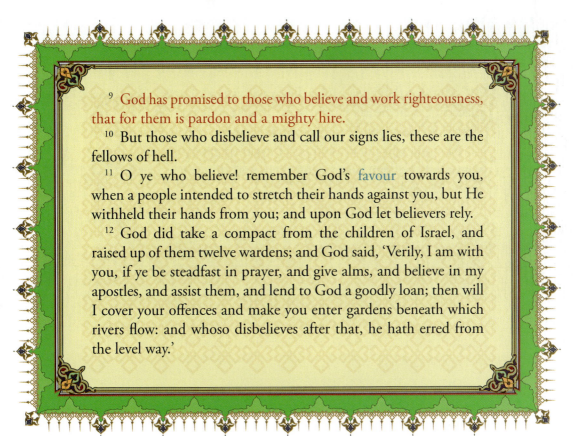

[13] And for that they broke their compact, we cursed them, and placed in their hearts hardness, so that they perverted the words from their places, and forgot a portion of what they were reminded of. But thou wilt not cease to light upon treachery amongst them, save a few of them; but pardon them and shun them; verily, God loves the kind.

[14] And of those who say, 'Verily, we are Christians,' we have taken a compact; but they have forgotten a portion of what they were reminded of; wherefore have we excited amongst them enmity and hatred till the resurrection day; but God will tell them of what they have done.

[15] O ye people of the Book! our Apostle has come to you to explain to you much of what ye had hidden of the Book, and to pardon much. There has come to you from God a light, and a perspicuous Book;

Q 5.13

According to Islāmic sources, this verse is related to a claim that a group of Jews had planned a conspiracy against Muḥammad, but he discovered their plot. These Islāmic sources say that this verse gave Muḥammad the right to pardon the Jews for their conspiracy because there was a covenant between them and him. However, the Muslim scholars differ on whether the verse is abrogated or not.[24]

The primary perspective of most Islāmic scholars says the verse is abrogated, a view that gives rise to the following opinions:

A. It is abrogated with verse Q 9.5: *"...kill the idolaters wherever ye may find them...."*[25]
B. It is abrogated with verse Q 9.29: *"Fight those who believe not in God and in the last day...."*[26]
C. It is abrogated with verse Q 8.58: *"And shouldst thou ever fear from any people treachery...."*[27]

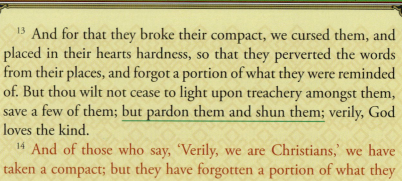

The second perspective suggests the verse is conserved because it is related to a specific event, for there was a covenant between Muḥammad and the Jews concerned. The holders of this perspective are bound to the premise that Q 9 precedes Q 5 in revelation.[28]

Q5.14

This verse tells us that Allah mandated that Christians enter into a covenant with him. Al-Rāzī clarifies that this covenant was the belief in Muḥammad; however, when Christians broke the covenant, Allah declared, *"...we excited amongst them enmity and hatred till the resurrection day* [Day of Judgment]. *"*[29]

As documented in the Islāmic commentaries, this part of this verse—*"we excited amongst them enmity and hatred"*—means "agitated them." Scholars have also said that this declaration means, "We adhered to them (enmity)"[30] or "We adhered to them animosity and hatred."[31]

The verse clearly states that Allah created animosity and hatred among Christians, but the commentators are divided as to whether the animosity is between Jews and Christians or among the Christians themselves.

Question: Is it appropriate to portray Allah as the "creator of animosity" among people?

Q5.15

This verse addresses both the Jews and Christians, stating that Muḥammad had come to them, *"to explain to you much of what ye had hidden of the Book."* However, Muḥammad did not present or explain the documents that were allegedly concealed by the Jews and Christians. Therefore, the scholars are obliged to present an opinion in this regard. They say that the concealed matters are (a) the news about the coming of Muḥammad and (b) the verse on the stoning of adulterers (*al-rajm*).[32]

But the Qur'ān does not support these opinions of the scholars, for there is nothing in the Qur'ān pointing to any concealed documents. Muḥammad himself did not outline the nature of the concealed things. As stated in this part of the verse, *"and to pardon much,"* al-Qurṭubī offers this comment: "[I]t means he overlooked many things that he did not inform you about. *"*[33]

This verse clearly states that Muḥammad did not "reveal" these hidden issues. Moreover, the scholars' ruling—that the concealed issues are the prophecy of Muḥammad (as the messenger of Allah) and the verse on stoning—is not supported by the Qur'ān or by any events recorded about the life (*sira*) of Muḥammad.

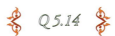

Even after the Muslim fighters and invaders had spread into the world and entered many worship centers of the Jews and Christians, discovering and examining their libraries, did they ever find any of these concealed manuscripts—especially those pointing to a prophecy announcing Muḥammad's status as prophet?

Although this verse states that Muḥammad did not specifically mention the concealed issues, nevertheless, one account portrays Muḥammad's silence as a miracle—yes, a miracle, not an inability:[34]

> A Jewish rabbi[D] came to Muḥammad and asked him about that which he had opted not to mention. However, Muḥammad did not show him but "avoided him." So the Jew went back to his people, saying, "I think he was honest in what he said." Because he (the rabbi) had found a prophecy in his book (stating) that what he asked him (Muḥammad) would not be revealed to him (Muḥammad)."

Questions: (1) How did the narrator of this account know about the dialogue that took place between the Jewish man and his people? (2) If, according to the story, the rabbi confessed that Muḥammad was honest, then why did he not become one of Muḥammad's followers?

The question posed by the Jewish scholar to Muḥammad is expected, since an accuser should provide evidence. When the rabbi came to Muḥammad, he was expecting to hear a clear explanation; however, avoidance was Muḥammad's answer.

Perhaps the following story is a more plausible version:

- Muḥammad accused the Jews of concealing certain matters.
- A Jewish scholar, representing his people, came to Muḥammad and asked him to present the proof of his accusation and to reveal what the Jews had allegedly concealed.
- When Muḥammad did not have an answer, his inability to provide the information embarrassed him in front of his followers. Therefore, he decided to ignore the Jew, which made the Jew uncomfortable and caused him to leave.
- After the Jew left, Muḥammad told his fellow Muslims that he had ignored the Jew because he did not receive a revelation from heaven.

M. al-Rāzī mentions in his book that Muḥammad possibly did not reveal the hidden matters for the following reason:[35]

> [H]e (Muḥammad) followed the heavenly commands and did not deal with any religious matters on his own but only according to inspiration. So whatever he was commanded to reveal he did reveal, and whatever he was not commanded to reveal he refrained from revealing until the time at which he was ordered to reveal it.

[16] God guides thereby those who follow His pleasure to the way
of peace, and brings them into a right way.
[17] They misbelieve who say, 'Verily, God is the Messiah the son
of Mary;' say, 'Who has any hold on God, if he wished to destroy
the Messiah the son of Mary, and his mother, and those who are
on earth altogether?' God's is the kingdom of the heavens and the
earth and what is between the two; He createth what He will, for
God is mighty over all!
[18] But the Jews and the Christians say, 'We are the sons of
God and His beloved.' Say, 'Why then does He punish you for
your sins? nay, ye are mortals of those whom He has created! He
pardons whom He pleases, and punishes whom He pleases; for
God's is the kingdom of the heavens and the earth, and what is
between the two, and unto Him the journey is.
[19] O people of the Book! our Apostle has come to you, explaining
to you the interval of apostles; lest ye say, 'There came not to us a
herald of glad tidings nor a warner.' But there has come to you now
a herald of glad tidings and a warner, and God is mighty over all!
[20] When Moses said to his people, 'O my people! remember the
favour of God towards you when He made amongst you prophets,
and made for you kings, and brought you what never was brought
to anybody in the worlds.
[21] O my people! enter the Holy Land which God has prescribed

Following M. al-Rāzī's reasoning, if Muḥammad was following commands from heaven when he would not reveal what was concealed, why then for this verse did he not reveal later those "matters" that the People of the Book had supposedly hidden?

An accusation without evidence is pure fabrication. If one accepts, for the sake of argument, the accusation that the People of the Book hid certain facts , then Muḥammad is an accomplice in this crime as he, too, did not reveal the hidden things.

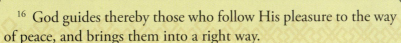

for you; and be ye not thrust back upon your hinder parts and retreat losers.

22 They said, ' O Moses! verily, therein is a people, giants; and we will surely not enter therein until they go out from thence; but if they go out then we will enter in.'

23 Then said two men of those who fear,—God had been gracious to them both,—'Enter ye upon them by the door, and when ye have entered it, verily, ye shall be victorious; and upon God do ye rely if ye be believers.'

24 They said, 'O Moses! we shall never enter it so long as they are therein; so, go thou and thy Lord and fight ye twain; verily, we will sit down here.'

25 Said he, 'My Lord, verily, I can control only myself and my brother; therefore part us from these sinful people.'

26 He said, 'Then, verily, it is forbidden them; for forty years shall they wander about in the earth; so vex not thyself for the sinful people.'

27 Recite to them the story of the two sons of Adam; truly when they offered an offering and it was accepted from one of them, and was not accepted from the other, that one said, 'I will surely kill thee;' he said, 'God only accepts from those who fear.

28 If thou dost stretch forth to me thine hand to kill me, I will not stretch forth mine hand to kill thee; verily, I fear God the Lord of the worlds;

29 verily, I wish that thou mayest draw upon thee my sin and thy sin, and be of the fellows of the Fire, for that is the reward of the unjust.'

30 But his soul allowed him to slay his brother, and he slew him, and in the morning he was of those who lose.

31 And God sent a crow to scratch in the earth and show him how he might hide his brother's shame, he said, 'Alas, for me! Am I too helpless to become like this crow and hide my brother's

shame?' and in the morning he was of those who did repent.
32 For this cause have we prescribed to the children of Israel that
whoso kills a soul, unless it be for another soul or for violence in
the land, it is as though he had killed men altogether; but whoso
saves one, it is as though he saved men altogether. Our apostles
came to them with manifest signs; then, verily, many of them did
after that commit excesses in the earth.
33 The reward of those who make war against God and His

Q 5.23

According to the codex of Ibn Mas'ūd, the reading of this verse is "Then said two men of those who fear,—God had been gracious to them both,—'Woe to you! Enter ye upon them by the door....'" This reading has the additional word in Arabic, *wailakum*, which means "woe to you."[36]

Q 5.33

A nomadic group from the 'Ukl tribe came to Muḥammad to declare that they had embraced the Islāmic faith. They were having difficulty securing the food they needed to live, so they went to Muḥammad to claim faith in his religion so that he would allow them to live in Medina. Muḥammad accepted them as believers. After a while he asked them to supervise the care of his camels. While in the pasture one day the group killed the shepherd and ran away, taking Muḥammad's camels with them.

Muḥammad responded by sending a company after them, which eventually found and arrested the group. Muḥammad punished them by cutting off their hands and feet, poking out their eyes, and leaving them to bleed to death.[37] Another account says that Muḥammad burned them.[38] Therefore, this verse came to abrogate what Muḥammad did and to create laws in a series of punishments for similar cases.[39]

What is ordered by this verse is killing, crucifixion, dismemberment, or banishment. But there is some disagreement among the scholars regarding the suggested punishments. Are the punishments listed according to the order that needs to be followed, or would any punishment from the list be as acceptable for the crime?[40] Muslim scholars have debated these punishments and under which circumstance each of them should take place.[41]

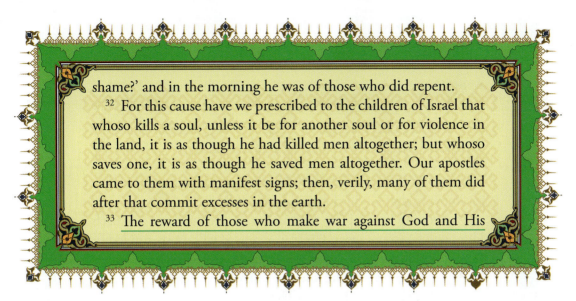

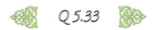

Apostle, and strive after violence in the earth, is only that they
shall be slaughtered or crucified, or their hands cut off and their
feet on alternate sides, or that they shall be banished from the
land;—that is a disgrace for them in this world, and for them in
the next is mighty woe;
34 save for those who repent before ye have them in your power,
for know ye that God is forgiving, merciful.
35 O ye who believe! fear God and crave the means to approach
Him, and be strenuous in His way, haply ye will prosper then.
36 Verily, those who disbelieve, even though they had what is
in the earth, all of it, and the like thereof with it, to offer as a
ransom from the punishment of the resurrection day, it would not
be accepted from them; but for them is grievous woe.
37 They may wish to go forth from the Fire, but they shall not
go forth therefrom, for them is lasting woe.

According to statements of Islāmic jurisprudence scholars, the ruling contained in this verse is not abrogated. Rather, some have said it is possible to exclude from this punishment *"those who repent before ye have them in your power…"* (Q 5.34).[42] It must be pointed out that Ibn al-Jawzī finds this opinion to be questionable.[43]

Q 5.38

This verse outlines the punishment of theft as the amputation of the thief's hand. Most modern Muslims do not know that this punishment was practiced before Islām. In fact, the first person to order this form of punishment was al-Walīd Ibn al-Maghīra[N].[44]

Muḥammad copied this penalty from al-Walīd Ibn al-Maghīra, the most prominent elder of the Quraysh and an enemy of Muḥammad. It was known that al-Walīd was one of Muḥammad's staunchest mockers. Nevertheless, Muḥammad borrowed the penalty from him and made it a law in the Qur'ān.

For al-Walīd to legalize this punishment would be quite understandable, since the Quraysh was a group of tribes without any state laws or prisons. History informs us that these primitive societies used extremely brutal punishments. But for Islām to present

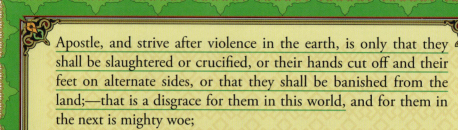

[38] The man thief and the woman thief, cut off the hands of
both as a punishment, for that they have erred;—an example from
God, for God is mighty, wise.
[39] But whoso turns again after his injustice and acts aright,
verily, God will turn to him, for, verily, God is forgiving, merciful.
[40] Do ye not know that God, His is the kingdom of the heavens
and the earth; He punishes whom He pleases, and forgives whom
He pleases, for God is mighty over all?
[41] O thou Apostle! let not those grieve thee who vie in misbelief;
or those who say with their mouths 'We believe,' but their hearts
do not believe; or of those who are Jews, listeners to a lie,—listeners
to other people, but who come not to thee. They pervert the words
from their places and say, ' If this is what ye are given, take it; but
if ye are not given it, then beware!' but he whom God wishes to
mislead, thou canst do nothing with God for him; these are those

itself as a religion and a state, while behaving like a primitive society in incorporating these forms of punishment learned from its own enemies, raises many questions about the true source of Muḥammad's inspiration.

Q 5.38

This verse in the current Arabic Qur'ān does not specify which hand is to be cut off, leaving it to the reader's speculation. However, the codex of Ibn Mas'ūd specifies that the right hand is the one that should be cut off.

Despite determining which hand is to be cut off, the codex of Ibn Mas'ūd still offers two variant readings of this verse: "The man thief and the woman thief, cut off their right hands" (*aymānahum*—in the plural form) and "their right hands of both" (*aymānahumā*—in the dual form).[45]

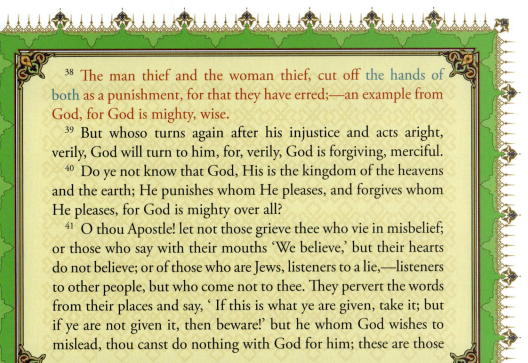

whose hearts God wishes not to purify, for them in this world is disgrace, and for them in the next is mighty woe,—

42 listeners to a lie, eaters of unlawful things! But if they come to thee, then judge between them or turn aside from them; but if thou turnest aside from them they shall not harm thee at all, but if thou judgest, then judge between them with justice, verily, God loves the just.

43 But how should they make thee their judge, when they have the law wherein is God's judgment? Yet they turn back after that, for they do not believe.

44 Verily, we have revealed the law in which is guidance and light; the prophets who were resigned did judge thereby those who were Jews, as did the masters and doctors by what they remembered of the Book of God and by what they were witnesses of. Fear not men, but fear me, and sell not my signs for a little price; for whoso will not judge by what God has revealed, these be the misbelievers.

45 We have prescribed for thee therein 'a life for a life, and an eye for an eye, and a nose for a nose, and an ear for an ear, and a tooth for a tooth, and for wounds retaliation;' but whoso remits it, it is

Q 5.42

Some Jewish people came to Muḥammad to ask him to judge someone accused of committing an offense. The defendant was allegedly a Jewish man of high rank. (It has also been narrated that it was a Jewish woman). There are other differing details: one account says the crime was adultery, while another says the crime was murder.[46] Therefore, this verse was revealed to Muḥammad to give him permission or refusal to judge.

In the references, there are two points of view about the abrogation or the conservation of this verse:

A. The first viewpoint states that the verse is abrogated with these two verses: *"...judge then between them by what God has revealed..."* (Q 5.48) and *"Wherefore judge thou between them by what God has revealed, and follow not their lusts..."* (Q 5.49).[47]

an expiation for him, but he whoso will not judge by what God
has revealed, these be the unjust.
46 And we followed up the footsteps of these (prophets) with
Jesus the son of Mary, confirming that which was before him and
the law, and we brought him the gospel, wherein is guidance and
light, verifying what was before it of the law, and a guidance and
an admonition unto those who fear.
47 Then let the people of the gospel judge by that which
is revealed therein, for whoso will not judge by what God has
revealed, these be the evildoers.
48 We have revealed to thee the Book in truth verifying what
was before it, and preserving it; judge then between them by what
God has revealed, and follow not their lusts, turning away from
what is given to thee of the truth. For each one of you have we
made a law and a pathway; and had God pleased He would have
made you one nation, but He will surely try you concerning that
which He has brought you. Be ye therefore emulous in good
deeds; to God is your return altogether, and He will let you know
concerning that wherein ye do dispute.

B. The second viewpoint is that it is conserved. Those who hold this opinion say the ruler of the Muslims has the right to choose whether to judge between parties who are under a protection pact with Muslims (e.g., the Christians and the Jews) or to decline to judge between them.[48] But if the case is between a Muslim and a person under such a protection pact, then the ruler is obligated to judge between them.[49]

Q 5.48

The word translated as "**a law**" is written in the 'Uthmānic codex, the official Qur'ān, as *sharīʿatan*. But, al-Ḥajjāj (AH 40-95/AD 660-714) changed it to the current ***shirʿatan***.[50] Both words have the same meaning. However, this explanation tells us that the Qur'ānic revision process continued to take place until half a century after the death of Muḥammad.

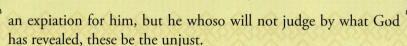

[49] Wherefore judge thou between them by what God has revealed, and follow not their lusts; but beware lest they mislead thee from part of what God has revealed to thee; yet if they turn back, then know that God wishes to fall on them for some sins of theirs,—verily, many men are evildoers.

[50] Is it the judgment of the Ignorance they crave? but who is better than God to judge for people who are sure?

[51] O ye who believe! take not the Jews and Christians for your patrons : they are patrons of each other; but whoso amongst you takes them for patrons, verily, he is of them, and, verily, God guides not an unjust people.

[52] Thou wilt see those in whose hearts is a sickness vieing with them; they say, 'We fear lest there befall us a reverse.' It may be God will give the victory, or an order from Himself, and they may awake repenting of what they thought in secret to themselves.

[53] Those who believe say, 'Are these they who swore by God with their most strenuous oath that they were surely with you?'—their works are in vain and they shall wake the losers.

[54] O ye who believe! whoso is turned away from his religion—God will bring (instead) a people whom He loves and who love Him, lowly to believers, lofty to unbelievers, strenuous in the way of God, fearing not the blame of him who blames. That is God's grace! He gives it unto whom He pleases, for God both comprehends and knows.

[55] God only is your patron, and His Apostle and those who believe, who are steadfast in prayer and give alms, bowing down.

[56] Whoso taketh as patrons God and His apostles and those who believe;—verily, God's crew, they are victorious!

[57] O ye who believe! take not for patrons those who take your religion for a jest or a sport, from amongst those who have been given the Book before and the misbelievers; but fear God if ye be believers.

over all.
[118] If Thou shouldst punish them, verily, they are Thy servants; if Thou shouldst forgive them, verily, Thou art the mighty and the wise.'
[119] God said, 'This is the day when their confession shall profit the confessors, for them are gardens beneath which rivers flow, to dwell therein for ever and for aye.' God is well pleased with them, and they well pleased with Him; that is the mighty happiness.
[120] God's is the kingdom of the heavens, and the earth, and all that is therein, and He is mighty over all.

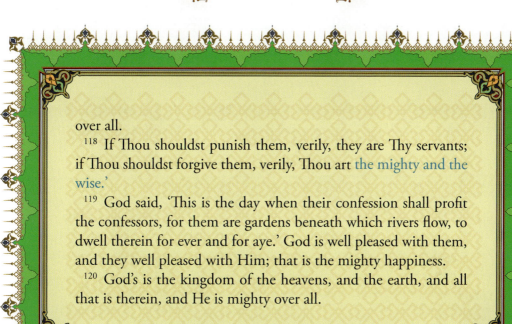

Introduction

The name of this sūra, al-An'ām, which means "the cattle," refers to the repetition of the word *an'ām* six times within the sūra.[1] It is mentioned three times in verse Q 6.138 and once in each of the following verses: Q 6.136, Q 6.139, and Q 6.142.

According to Islāmic sources, this sūra was revealed in its entirety in Mecca.[2] The sūra marks the eve of migration (*Hijra)* where, as evidenced by the verse *"and shun the idolaters"* (Q 6.106), Muḥammad seemed totally frustrated by the resistance to his message by his own tribe, the Quraysh.

However, despite the assertion that this sūra was fully revealed in Mecca, it clearly also contains Medinan elements. According to some Islāmic narratives, the verses Q 6.91-93 and 6.151-152 are from the Medinan period. Other Muslim scholars consider verse Q 6.111 to be Medinan also.[3]

The sūra contains a ruling that rejects the Quraysh's pagan sacrifices (Q 6.139, 143-144). However, we also find in it rules about permitted (*ḥalāl*) and forbidden (*ḥarām*) foods in Q 6.145-146, which belong to the later Medinan time period. It is possible that Muḥammad developed the section that deals with sacrifices in the Meccan period and reworded the verses in Medina, under the influence of Jewish thought.

In the name of the merciful and compassionate God!
1 Praise belongs to God who created the heavens and the earth,
and brought into being the darkness and the light. Yet do those
who misbelieve hold Him to have peers.
2 He it is who created you from clay; then He decreed a term,
a term,—ordained with Him. And yet ye doubt thereof.
3 He is God in the heavens and the earth. He knows your secret
conduct and your plain, and He knows what ye earn.
4 There came not to them any sign of the signs of their Lord,
but they turned away;
5 and they have called the truth a lie now that it has come to
them, but there shall come to them the message of that at which
they mocked.
6 Do not they see how many a generation we have destroyed before them, whom we had settled in the earth as we have not settled
for you, and sent the rain of heaven upon them in copious showers,
and made the waters flow beneath them? Then we destroyed them
in their sins, and raised up other generations after them.
7 Had we sent down to thee a book on paper, and they had
touched it with their hands, still those who misbelieve would have
said, 'This is naught but obvious magic.'
8 They say, 'Why has not an angel been sent down to him?' but

Q 6.15

This verse expresses Muḥammad's fear of committing transgressions against Allah. However, a group of scholars state it is abrogated with verse Q 48.2 that reads, *"that God may pardon thee thy former and later sin."* [4]

Q 6.16

Several authorities read this verse as ***yuṣraf*** ("**it is averted**") in the passive.[5] What is meant by the pronoun *it,* in *"it is averted,"* is the torment mentioned in the previous verse.

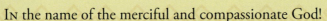

if we had sent down an angel, the affair would have been decided, and then they would have had no respite.

[9] And had we made him an angel, we should have made him as a man too; and we would have made perplexing for them that which they deem perplexing now.

[10] There have been prophets before thee mocked at, but that encompassed them which the scoffers among them mocked at.

[11] Say, 'Go about in the earth, then wilt thou see how has been the end of those who called them liars.'

[12] Say, 'Whose is what is in the heavens and the earth?' Say, 'God's, who has imposed mercy on himself.' He will surely gather you together for the resurrection day. There is no doubt in that, but those who waste their souls will not believe.

[13] His is whatsoever dwells in the night or in the day, He both hears and knows.

[14] Say, 'Other than God shall I take for a patron, the Originator of the heavens and the earth? He feedeth men, but is not fed.' Say, 'I am bidden to be the first of those resigned;' and it was said to me, 'Be not thou of the idolaters.'

[15] Say, 'I fear, if I rebel against my Lord, the torment of the mighty day.'

[16] Whomsoever it is averted from on that day, God will have had mercy on; and that is obvious happiness.

Another group read it as *yaṣrif* ("he averts"), without mentioning the subject, (i.e., Allah). Al-Ṭabarī favors this last form.[6] Ubayy Ibn Ka'b read the Qur'ān as saying, "The one whom Allah averts it from him." That is, he [Allah] is the one who removes. It is mentioned that he read it as "the one whom Allah averts from him" as well.[7]

In both forms Allah is the one who removes the torment. But the second form, where the subject is mentioned, is stronger and clearer.

Question: If the expression is stronger when the subject is mentioned, why is it written in the Qur'ān in the weaker form?

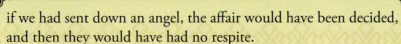

[17] And if God touch thee with harm, there is none to take it off
but He; and if He touch thee with good, He is mighty over all.
[18] He is sovereign over His servants, He is the wise, the aware!
[19] Say, 'What is the greatest witness?' Say, 'God is witness between you and me.' This Qur'an was inspired to me to warn you and those it reaches. Do ye really bear witness that with God are other gods? Say, 'I bear not witness thereto:' say, 'He is but one God, and I am clear of your associating (gods with him).'

Q 6.19

Historic sources cite that the leaders of the Quraysh tribe told Muḥammad they did not believe in his prophetic calling. They informed him of their attempts to verify his claims to prophethood with the Jews and the Christians. However, both the Jews and the Christians told the Quraysh leaders they did not have anything in their religious books that validated Muḥammad's claim to prophethood.

Having found no proof of Muḥammad's prophethood with the People of the Book, the Quraysh asked Muḥammad to provide a miracle as proof, something that would testify to his truthfulness. Muḥammad then answered them with this verse: *"Say,* [O Muḥammad!] *'What is the greatest witness?'"* and *"Say, 'God is witness'* for my prophethood because he inspired me with this Qur'ān which is miraculous."[8]

Another source reads that the phrase, *"Say, 'What is the greatest witness?'"* came down from Allah because the polytheists said to Muḥammad, "Who testifies on your behalf that you are Allah's messenger?"[9]

Muḥammad combined the following meanings in this verse:

- It is Allah who testifies to his prophethood and to the veracity of his claims.
- The Qur'ān itself is tangible evidence of his prophethood.

The following discussion focuses on whether or not the above points were enough to satisfy the leaders of the Quraysh.

The verse states that Allah testified on behalf of Muḥammad, but this cannot act as evidence because that claim could be made by anyone who wanted to be recognized as a prophet.

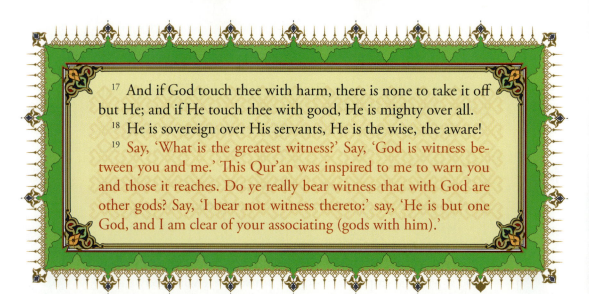

[20] Those to whom we have brought the Book know him as they know their sons;—those who lose their souls do not believe.
[21] Who is more unjust than he who forges against God a lie, or says His signs are lies? verily, the unjust shall not prosper.
[22] On the day when we shall gather them all together, then shall we say to those who have associated others with ourself, 'Where are your associates whom ye did pretend?'

Additionally, this verse presents the Qur'ān as the ultimate proof of Muḥammad's truthfulness, authenticity, and Allah's bestowed approval upon Muḥammad as a prophet. But this claim cannot be substantiated because there is no physically verifiable witness that the text came from Allah, except the prophet himself. So Muḥammad is trying to prove his own prophethood by claiming that a verse he supplied came from Allah. If this claim is valid proof of his prophethood, then once again, any self-proclaimed prophet could use this method to confirm his or her authenticity.

It has been noted also that Muḥammad had borrowed ideas and legislation from both pagans and non-pagans and added them to the Qur'ān. Therefore, the claim that the Qur'ān has a heavenly source has no practical basis, because copying other people's ideas and legislation into the Qur'ānic text testifies against its authenticity.

There are stories that were copied into the Qur'ān and presented in a distorted form. (For an example, see the comments on Q 2.125-129, page 207, and Q 2.247-251, page 249.)

There were also rituals that were adopted from other religions. The inclusion of the pagan *ḥajj* ritual in Islām is such an example. (See the comment on Q 2.158, page 213, and Q 2.196, page 227.)

Q 6.21

To lie means to make a false statement. This verse says, *"who forges against God a lie,"* or the literal translation, "who makes a fabricated statement against Allah by lying."

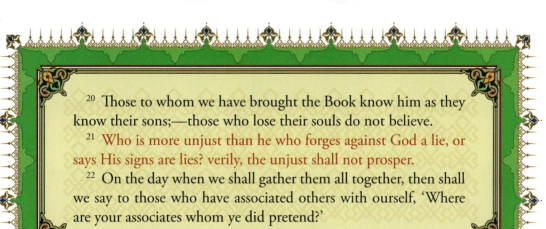

23 Then they will have no excuse but to say, 'By God our Lord, we did not associate (others with thee)!'
24 See how they lie against themselves, and how what they did forge deserts them!
25 And they are some who listen unto thee, but we have placed a veil upon their hearts lest they should understand it, and in their ears is dulness of hearing; and though they saw each sign they would not believe therein; until when they come to thee to wrangle with thee, the unbelievers say, 'These are but old folks' tales.'
26 They forbid it and they avoid it;—but they destroy none but themselves; yet they do not perceive.
27 But couldst thou see when they are set over the fire and say, 'Would that we were sent back! we would not call our Lord's signs lies, but we would be of the believers?'
28 Nay! now is shown to them what they did hide before; and could they be sent back, they would return to that they were forbidden, for they are very liars.
29 They say there is naught but this life of ours in the world and we shall not be raised.
30 But couldst thou see when they are set before their Lord; he says, 'Is not this the truth?' They say, 'Yea, by our Lord !' he says, 'Then taste the torment, for that ye did misbelieve!'
31 Losers are they who disbelieved in meeting God, until when the hour comes suddenly upon them they say, 'Woe is us for our neglect thereof!' for they shall bear their burdens on their backs, evil is what they bear.
32 The life of this world is nothing but a game and a sport, and surely the next abode were better for those who fear. What! do they not understand?
33 Full well we know that verily that which they say grieves thee; but they do not call thee only a liar for the unjust gainsay the signs of God.

In the Arabic phrasing, the use of the wording seen in the literal translation above is not for emphasis but rather to explain something that does not need further explanation. Is there such a thing as an honest fabricated statement? The use of the word *"lie"* in the verse is considered poor Arabic rhetoric, which contradicts Islāmic claims that the Qur'ān represents the most eloquent of Arabic speech.

Q 6.23

The verse states that those who worship many gods will deny their polytheism on the Day of Judgment: *"By God our Lord, we did not associate (others with thee)!"* (Q 6.23). Yet, in another part of the same sūra, it reads that they will admit their polytheism: *"and they bear witness against themselves that they were unbelievers"* (Q 6.130). In addition, their confession of a lack of faith is confirmed by another verse, *"but they cannot hide the news from God"* (Q 4.42).

Question: So will those unbelievers deny their blasphemous worship, or will they bear witness against themselves and reveal their unbelief in Allah while on the earth?

Q 6.25

It is told that 'Alī Ibn Abī Ṭālib and Ibn Mas'ūd read this verse as "but We have thrown veils on their hearts, so they understand it not, and on their eyes a covering." Compared to the current Arabic Qur'ān, their codices included the additional phrase "and on their eyes a covering."[10]

Q 6.32

In Arabic, the Qur'ān reads ***ta'qilūna*** ("**you understand**"), which addresses those who were present with Muḥammad, who denied the resurrection.[11]

Yet, several readers read it as *ya'qilūna* ("they understand") that addresses those who are righteous.[12]

Question: Does the verse address the righteous or those who deny the resurrection?

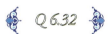

[34] Called liars too were apostles before thee; but they were patient of being called liars and of being hurt until our help came
to them; for there is none to change the words of God—now has
there come to thee the story of those He sent.
[35] And if their turning from thee be hard for thee, and if thou
canst seek for a shaft down into the earth, or a ladder up into the
sky, to bring them a sign—but if God pleased He would bring
them all to guidance, be thou not then of the ignorant.
[36] He only answers the prayer of those who listen; but the dead

Q 6.37, 50

Muḥammad's opponents had repeatedly requested a miracle from him to prove that he was a prophet. It appears that a discussion had taken place between Muḥammad and his opponents indicating that if Muḥammad was the true prophet as he claimed, Allah would have given him a miracle or a sign.[13] The people of Mecca shared this view. Their belief came from their contact with the Jewish tribes around them.

When Muḥammad heard about this opposition from the people, he said to them, *"Verily, God is able to send down a sign..."* (Q 6.37). But he was satisfied with this saying without presenting a sign. It seems that some people wanted Muhammad to live a life of prosperity as a proof of the verity of his prophecy. However, Muhammad continued defending himself by saying that he was not wealthy and did know what the future held: *"I do not say to you, mine are the treasuries of God"* (Q 6.50; see page 414).

These two verses clearly declare that Muḥammad did not perform a single miracle and they also confirm his inability to perform any miracles.

Question: Was simply saying *"Verily, God is able to send down a sign"* a sufficient proof of the prophetic reliability of any self-proclaimed prophet? Would anyone be satisfied with his saying that *"God is able"* without performing a corresponding, tangible miracle or getting any result from it?

A defender of Islām might say, "The Qur'ān is Muḥammad's miracle." Such a defender is invited to read these very pages and consider Muḥammad's "miracle" is truly a miracle.

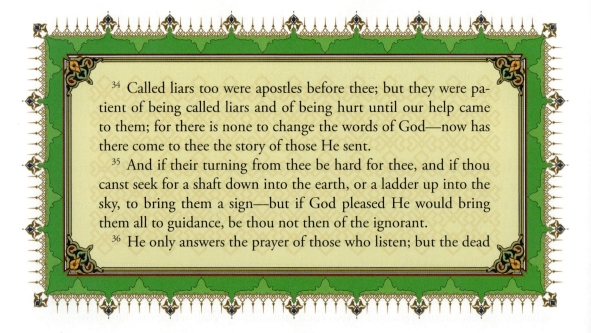

will God raise up, then unto Him shall they return.
37 They say, 'Unless there be sent down some sign from his Lord'—say, 'Verily, God is able to send down a sign, but most of them do not know.'
38 There is not a beast upon the earth nor a bird that flies with both its wings, but is a nation like to you; we have omitted nothing from the Book; then to their Lord shall they be gathered.
39 Those who say our signs are lies—deafness, dumbness, in the

Q 6.38

There are three comments regarding this verse:

A. **First comment:** There is a redundancy in the verse. It says *"a bird that flies with both its wings,"* which is what the Arabic literally says. The verse clarifies something that does not need to be clarified, because a bird clearly cannot fly unless it has two wings.

Because the redundancy in the sentence, *"a bird that flies with both its wings"* needed to be justified, al-Rāzī uses extreme measures to provide an answer, saying there are several possibilities:[14]

1. It is possible that the redundancy is for assertion.
   Our Comment: The problem with this view is that redundancy here, even if it is for assertion, disregards the linguistic taste.

2. The redundancy used in the phrase could be to clarify that the action mentioned in the verse is actual flight. In Arabic, the term used for "flying" might not be in reference to flight, like that of a bird. For instance, one can say, "fly to my need," meaning to hurry. Therefore, the phrase "with its two wings" clarifies that the meaning is literal flight.
   Our Comment: In this case, the listener should be capable of differentiating between what is literal or abstract when talking about a bird. To assume otherwise belittles the listener's ability to understand.

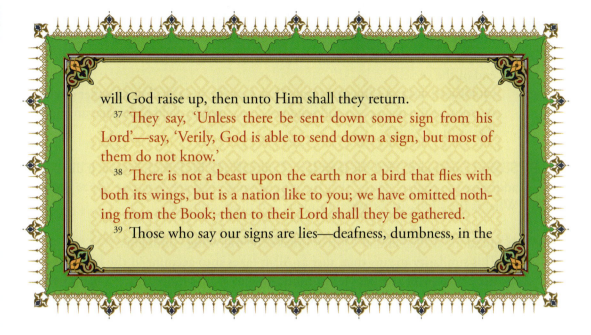

3. This redundancy is possibly used to ensure that the reader doesn't think that the phrase *"with both its wings"* is referring to angels, so it was added to the end of the verse.
   OUR COMMENT: Adding the term *"with both its wings"* will not further clarify the idea, as the reader can still hold to the commonly held belief that an angel flies with its wings.

B. **Second comment:** After the mention of animals and birds in this verse, it directly addresses the reader, stating that the animals and birds are *"a nation like to you."* What is the similarity between humans and these animals?

On this question, al-Rāzī and al-Qurṭubī make the following comments:[15]

1. This similarity means that, just as Allah takes into account in the book all of the concerns of the people's condition—life span, wealth, future, happiness, and toil—he also takes into account all these same conditions for the animals. This position was sufficient for al-Zamakhsharī.[16]
   OUR COMMENT: This view attributes logic to the verse, which is why al-Zamakhsharī, a Muʿtazilite scholar, was satisfied with it. But we do not find this logic fits the context of the verse. The scholar is assuming something that the verse never states.

2. When Allah says, *"like you,"* he is making a comparison between animals and people—that the people will look like animals when herded together for judgment on the Day of Judgment.
   OUR COMMENT: This interpretation does not seem to coincide with the overall meaning of the verse and is an arbitrary interpretation because the verse has nothing to do with the Day of Judgment.

3. All humans share at least some similar characteristics with animals; people can attack like a lion, run like a wolf, bark like a dog, or act like a pig.
   OUR COMMENT: The verse says *"a nation like you"* and not "you are like them." The verse compares animals to humans, not humans to animals.

C. **Third Comment:** The verse concludes, *"we have omitted nothing from the Book...."* This ending implies that the Qur'ān contains all subjects and all sciences. But because the scientific facts alone negate the truth of this statement, some scholars have claimed that *"the Book"* only refers to the Preserved Tablet.[17] However, because the context of the phrase clearly indicates that *"the Book"* refers to the Qur'ān, al-Qurṭubī was satisfied to make this statement: "We have left nothing of religious issues without pointing to it in the Qur'ān."[18]

dark! whom He pleases does God lead astray, and whom He pleases He places on the right way.

40 Say, 'Look you now! if there should come God's torment, or there should come to you the hour, on other than God would ye call, if ye do tell the truth?'

41 Nay, it is on Him that ye would call, and He will avert that which ye call upon Him for if He but please; and ye shall forget that which ye did associate with Him.

42 Ere this we sent unto nations before thee, and we caught them in distress and trouble that haply they might humble themselves.

43 And do they not, when our violence falls upon them, humble themselves?—but their hearts were hard, and Satan made seemly to them that which they had done.

44 And when they forgot what they were reminded of, we opened for them the gates of everything, until when they rejoiced at what they had, we caught them up suddenly, and lo! they were in despair.

45 And the uttermost part of the people who did wrong were cut off; praise be to God, Lord of the worlds!

46 Say, 'Look you now! if God should catch your hearing and your sight, and should set a seal upon your hearts—who is god but God to bring you it again?'

47 Say, 'Look you now! if God's torment should come upon you suddenly or openly, would any perish save the people who do wrong?'

Q 6.47

Some have read the verse as "suddenly and openly" with "and" instead of "**or**."[19]

Question: How did the punishment come—suddenly, openly, or both?

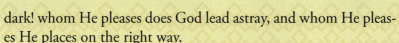

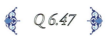

48 We do not send our messengers save as heralds of glad tidings and of warning, and whoso believes and acts aright, there is no fear for them, and they shall not be grieved,
49 but those who say our signs are lies, torment shall touch them, for that they have done so wrong.
50 Say, 'I do not say to you, mine are the treasuries of God, nor that I know the unseen; I do not say to you, I am an angel—if I follow aught but what I am inspired with—:' say, 'Is the blind equal to him who sees—?' what! do ye not reflect?
51 Admonish therewith those who fear that they shall be gathered unto their Lord; there is no patron for them but Him, and no intercessor; haply they may fear.
52 Repulse not those who call upon their Lord in the morning and in the evening, desiring His face; they have no reckoning against thee at all, and thou hast no reckoning against them at all;—repulse them and thou wilt be of the unjust.
53 So have we tried some of them by others, that they may say, 'Are these those unto whom God has been gracious amongst ourselves?' Does not God know those who give thanks?
54 And when those who believe in our signs come to thee, say, 'Peace be on you! God hath prescribed for Himself mercy; verily, he of you who does evil in ignorance, and then turns again and does right,—verily, He is forgiving and merciful.'
55 Thus do we detail our signs, that the way of the sinners may be made plain.
56 Say, 'I am forbidden to worship those ye call upon beside God;' say, 'I will not follow your lusts, for then should I err and not be of the guided.'
57 Say, 'I stand on a manifestation from my Lord, which ye call a lie. I have not with me what ye fain would hasten on, [The decision rest with Allah alone. He explains the truth and He is the Best of Judges.']
58 [Say, 'If that which you desire to be hastened were in my pow-

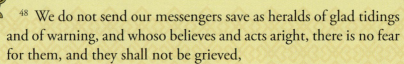

er,] that the matter might be settled between me and you; but God knows best who are the unjust.'
59 With Him are the keys of the unseen. None knows them save He; He knows what is in the land and in the sea; and there falls not a leaf save that He knows it; nor a grain in the darkness of the earth, nor aught that is moist, nor aught that is dry, save that is in His perspicuous Book.
60 He it is who takes you to Himself at night, and knows what ye have gained in the day; then He raises you up again, that your appointed time may be fulfilled; then unto Him is your return, and then will He inform you of what ye have done.
61 He triumphs over His servants; He sends to them guardian angels, until, when death comes to any one of you, our messengers take him away; they pass not over any one,
62 and then are they returned to God, their true sovereign. Is not His the rule? but He is very quick at reckoning up.
63 Say, 'Who rescues you from the darkness of the land and of the sea?' ye call upon Him in humility and in secret, 'Indeed, if He would rescue us from this, we will surely be of those who give Him thanks.'

Q 6.56

A few readers have read this verse as ***ḍalaltu*** ("**err**") with the letter *"ḍād"* instead of *ṣalaltu* ("rotted") with the letter *"ṣād."*

When one speaks of meat and uses the verb *ṣalla*, it means the meat became rotten.[20]

Q 6.57

The reading in the current Arabic Qur'ān is "The decision rest with Allah alone. He explains [***yaquṣṣu***, literally "tells"] the truth…" [Sale trans.]. However, the context is one of judgment between groups. Ibn Mas'ūd, Ubayy Ibn Ka'b, Ibn 'Abbās, and others strengthen the reading by using this form: "The command rests with none but Allah: He judges by the truth," replacing *yaquṣṣu* ("tells") with *yaqḍi* ("judges").[21]

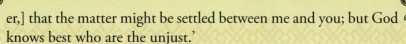

[64] Say, 'God rescues from the darkness thereof, and from every trouble, yet ye associate others with Him.'
[65] Say, 'He is able to send torment on you from above you and from beneath your feet, and to confuse you in sects, and to make some of you taste the violence of others.' See how we turn about the signs, that haply they may discriminate.
[66] Thy people called it a lie, and yet it is the truth. Say, 'I have

Q 6.66

There are two scholarly opinions about the meaning of this verse:

The first group of scholars say that Muḥammad is declaring that his sole duty is to warn and deliver the Islāmic message. However, they believe this "peaceful" announcement is abrogated with the Sword verse, Q 9.5: *"...kill the idolaters wherever ye may find them...."*[22]

A second group of scholars believes the verse is conserved. Some understand it to mean that Muḥammad was neither responsible for others, nor was he anyone's overseer. He had to deal with the deeds based on the way they appeared to be. This verse is a report (*khabar*), and a report is conserved.[23]

Q 6.68

Muḥammad was socializing with a group of individuals from the Quraysh in order to invite them to the Islāmic faith. What he got from them in return was mockery of the Qur'ān. It was then that this verse came down, commanding Muḥammad to stay away from anyone who objects to the Qur'ān.[24]

The Qur'ān does not detail the exact nature of this mockery. But what is apparent in this story is that the people of the Quraysh, who were especially famous for their linguistic abilities, had clearly mocked the Qur'ān. Based on the Islāmic argument that the Qur'ān is unrivaled in its eloquent language, they should instead have been awestruck by it.

Scholars note that this verse required Muḥammad to withdraw from the people of the Quraysh because they were mocking the Qur'ān. But the verb used in the verse is *"plunge,"* which does not indicate mockery or ridicule.

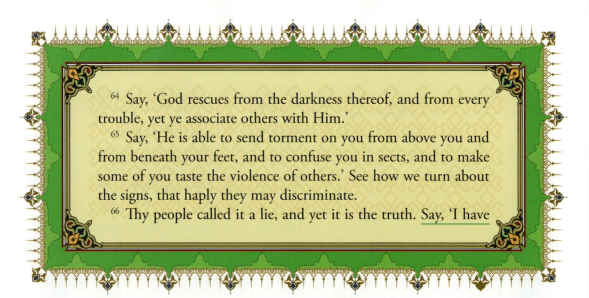

not charge over you;
67 to every prophecy is a set time, and in the end ye shall know.'
68 When thou dost see those who plunge deeply into the discussion of our signs, turn from them until they plunge deeply into
some other discourse; for it may be that Satan may make thee
forget; but sit not, after thou hast remembered, with the unjust
people.

The verb *"plunge"* is used again in the very same verse that demands of Muḥammad to withdraw from the Quraysh *"until they plunge deeply into some other discourse."*

If we are to accept the view of the scholars that the meaning of this phrase, *"those who plunge deeply into the discussion of our signs,"* is also "those who ridicule our verses," then the meaning of the verse would be "stay away from those who ridicule the Qur'ān until they ridicule other matters."

However, it is doubtful that this interpretation is the intended meaning.

It seems the real issue in this verse is that when Muḥammad was unable to argue with or persuade his critics when discussing controversial matters, he would withdraw and stay away from them. It is believed that Muḥammad used avoidance as a coping mechanism in a similar situation when a Jewish rabbi wanted to discuss the accusations that he had directed toward Muḥammad. Muḥammad chose not to engage the rabbi in the difficult matter. (See the comment regarding this incident on Q 5.15, page 377.)

So the eloquent people of the Quraysh, in whose language the Qur'ān is written, criticized the Qur'ān, and, therefore, Muḥammad decided to stay away from them. Was staying away from them evidence in favor of Muḥammad or evidence against him?

The verse then instructs Muḥammad that, if he ever sat with them and the devil made him forget what he was supposed to say, he should get up and remove himself from them until he remembered. This part of the verse admits Muḥammad's forgetfulness. (See the forgetfulness phenomenon in the comment on Q 2.106, page 198.)

Q 6.68

This verse commands Muḥammad to turn away from those who disbelieve his message. However, it is abrogated with the following verses:

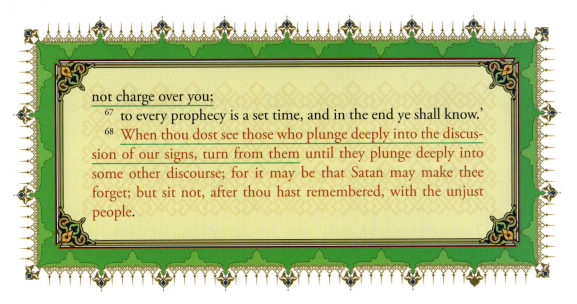

69 Those who fear are not bound to take account of them at all,
but mind!—haply they may fear.
70 Leave those who have taken their religion for a play and a
sport, whom this world's life hath deceived, and remind them
thereby that a soul shall be given up for what it has earned; nor has
it, beside God, patron or intercessor; and though it should compensate with the fullest compensation, it would not be accepted.
Those who are given up for what they have gained, for them is a
drink of boiling water, and grievous woe for that they have misbelieved.
71 Say, 'Shall we call on what neither profits us nor harms us,
and be thrown back upon our heels after God has guided us, like
him whom Satan hath led away bewildered in the earth, who has
companions who call him to guidance, "Come to us?"' Say, 'Verily, God's guidance is the guidance, and we are bidden to resign
ourselves unto the Lord of the worlds,
72 and be ye steadfast in prayer and fear Him, for He it is to
whom we shall be gathered.'
73 He it is who has created the heavens and the earth in truth;
and on the day when He says, 'BE,' then it is. His word is truth; to
Him is the kingdom on the day when the trumpets shall be blown;
the knower of the unseen and of the evident; He is wise and well
aware.
74 When Abraham said to his father Azar, 'Dost thou take idols
for gods? verily, I see thee and thy people in obvious error.'
75 Thus did we show Abraham the kingdom of heaven and of
the earth, that he should be of those who are sure.
76 And when the night overshadowed him he saw a star and
said, 'This is my Lord;' but when it set he said, 'I love not those
that set.'
77 And when he saw the moon beginning to rise he said, 'This is

A. Q 9.5: *"...kill the idolaters wherever ye may find them...."*[25]
B. Q 4.140: *"...then sit ye not down with them until they plunge into another discourse...."*[26]

Q 6.69

Originally, it was acceptable for Muslims to sit with pagans in Mecca. But the following verse abrogated this permission: *"He hath revealed this to you in the Book, that when ye hear the signs of God disbelieved in and mocked at, then sit ye not down with them until they plunge into another discourse..."* (Q 4.140). From that point, it became forbidden for a Muslim to even sit with those who would criticize Islām.[27]

Q 6.70

There are two viewpoints regarding the abrogation of this verse. In the first viewpoint, it is abrogated based on the following opinions:

A. Some scholars believe the verse lets idolaters remain within their own religion, but it is abrogated with the Sword verse, Q 9.5: *"...kill the idolaters wherever ye may find them...."*[28]
B. Another group of scholars say the verse refers to Jews and Christians and therefore is abrogated with verse Q 9.29: *"Fight those who believe not in God and in the last day...."*[29]

In the second viewpoint, some scholars say the verse is conserved because it contains a threat and not an invitation to peace.[30]

Q 6.74-79

This passage contains a part of Ibrāhīm's (Abraham's) biography. (See the comment on Q 2.258, page 252.)

Q 6.75

Most readers read ***nuriya Ibrāhīma malakūta*** ("**we show Abraham the kingdom**") with Allah as the subject of the verb.[31]

Another team of readers read *turiya Ibrāhīma malakūtu* ("You show Abraham the kingdom"). *Malakūtu* ("kingdom") is in the nominative, meaning that it is the subject of the verb.[32]

A third group or readers read it as *yara Ibrāhīmu* ("Abraham sees"), with Ibrāhīm as the subject of the verb.[33]

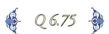

my Lord;' but when it set he said, 'If God my Lord guides me not
I shall surely be of the people who err.'
78 And when he saw the sun beginning to rise he said, 'This is
my Lord, this is greatest of all;' but when it set he said, 'O my
people! verily, I am clear of what ye associate with God;
79 verily, I have turned my face to him who originated the heav-
en and the earth, as a 'Hanif, and I am not of the idolaters.'
80 And his people disputed with him;—he said, 'Do ye dispute
with me concerning God, when He has guided me? but I fear
not what ye associate with Him unless my Lord should wish for
anything. My Lord doth comprehend all things in His knowledge,
will ye not then remember?
81 How should I fear what ye associate with Him, when ye yourselves fear not to associate with God what He has sent down to
you no power to do? Which then of the two sects is worthier of
belief, if indeed ye know?'
82 Those who believe and do not obscure their faith with wrong,
they are those who shall have security, and they are guided.
83 These are our arguments which we gave to Abraham against
his people;—we raise the rank of whom we will; verily, thy Lord is
wise and knowing.
84 And we gave to him Isaac and Jacob, each did we guide. And
Noah we guided before and all his seed,—David and Solomon
and Job and Joseph and Moses and Aaron,—for thus do we reward those who do good.
85 And Zachariah and John and Jesus and Elias, all righteous
ones;
86 and Ishmael and Elisha and Jonas and Lot, each one have we
preferred above the worlds;
87 and of their fathers and their seed and brethren; we have chosen them and guided them into a right way.
88 That is God's guidance; He guides those whom He will of

Question: Who or what is the subject of the verb—Allah, the *malakūt* (kingdom), or Ibrāhīm (Abraham)?

Q 6.84-86

These verses mention some biblical figures in the following order:
Isaac—Jacob—Noah—David—Solomon—Job—Joseph—Moses—Aaron—Zachariah—John—Jesus—Elias (Elijah)—Ishmael—Elisha—Jonas (Jonah)—Lot

Notice in these verses that the above biblical figures are mentioned in random fashion, without any chronological or alphabetical order. Although the sequence of these figures is available and consistent in both the Torah and New Testament, the absence of this order in the Qur'ān reveals Muḥammad's insufficient biblical knowledge.
Below is the biblical chronological sequence for these people:

- Job (c. twenty-first to nineteenth century BC)
- Abraham (nineteenth century BC)
- Lot (nephew of Abraham)
- Ishmael and Isaac (sons of Abraham)
- Jacob (grandson of Abraham)
- Joseph (son of Jacob; eighteenth century BC)
- Moses and brother Aaron (sixteenth century BC)
- David (eleventh century BC)
- Solomon (son of David)
- Elias (c. tenth century BC)
- Elisha (ninth century BC)
- Jonas (eighth century BC)
- Zachariah (father of John the Baptist)
- John the Baptist (b. six months before Jesus)
- Jesus (c. 5 BC)

Verse 84, which mentions that Job is a descendant of Abraham, is an apparent error. Job is from the land of Uz (some say Uz corresponds to modern-day southern Syria or western Jordan), which lies between the southern part of Judea and the northern part of the Arabian Peninsula. Conversely, the geographical area of Abraham lies outside the Arabian Peninsula. In addition, Job did not belong to the Jewish people group. (See the comment on Q 2.258, page 252.)

Verse 84 also states *"We gave him Isaac and Jacob"* in reference to Abraham, yet neglects to mention Ishmael, despite the fact that he was Abraham's eldest son. Thirteen names later, verse 86 mentions Ishmael without making the connection that he is Abraham's son.

His servants; and if they associate aught with Him,—vain is that which they have worked.

89 It is to these we give the Book and judgment and prophecy; and if these disbelieve therein we have given them in charge to a people who shall not disbelieve.

90 It is these that God hath guided, and by their guidance be thou led. Say, 'I will not ask you for it a hire: it is naught save a reminder to the worlds.'

91 They do not prize God at His true worth when they say, 'God has never revealed to mortal anything.' Say, 'Who revealed the Book wherewith Moses came, a light and a guidance unto men? Ye put it on papers which ye show, though ye hide much; and ye are taught what ye knew not, neither you nor your fathers.' Say, 'God,' then leave them in their discussion to play.

92 This is the Book which we have revealed, a blessing and a confirmation to those which were before it, and that the mother of cities may be warned, with those who are round about her. Those who believe in the last day believe therein, and they unto their prayers will keep.

93 Who is more unjust than he who devises against God a lie, or says, 'I am inspired,' when he was not inspired at all? and who says, 'I will bring down the like of what God has sent down;' but didst thou see when the unjust are in the floods of death, and the angels stretch forth their hands, 'Give ye forth your souls; to-day shall ye be recompensed with the torment of disgrace, for that ye did say against God what was not true, and were too proud to hear His signs.

94 And ye come now single-handed as we created you at first, and ye have left behind your backs that which we granted you; and we see not with you your intercessors whom ye pretended were partners amongst you; betwixt you have the ties been cut asunder;

and strayed away from you is what ye did pretend.'
95 Verily, God it is who cleaves out the grain and the date-stone;
He brings forth the living from the dead, and it is He who brings
the dead from the living. There is God! how then can ye be beguiled?
96 He it is who cleaves out the morning, and makes night a
repose, and the sun and the moon two reckonings—that is the
decree of the mighty, the wise!
97 He it is who made for you stars that ye might be guided
thereby in the darkness of the land and of the sea. Now have we
detailed the signs unto a people who do know.
98 He it is who made you spring from one soul, and gave you a
settlement and a depository. Now have we detailed the signs unto
a people who discern.
99 He it is who sends down from the heavens water; and we
bring forth therewith growths of everything; and we bring forth
therefrom green things, wherefrom we bring forth grain in full ear;
and the palm, from its spathe come clusters within reach; and gardens of grapes and olives and pomegranates, alike and unlike;—
behold its fruit when it fruits and ripens! verily, in that ye have a
sign for the people who believe.

Q 6.91

This verse encourages believers to avoid confrontation with idolaters (a practical principle), but some scholars believe it is abrogated with the Sword verse, Q 9.5: *"...kill the idolaters wherever ye may find them...."*[34]

However, in the second viewpoint, another group of scholars say the verse is conserved, believing it is not a practical principle, because it involves a threat from a "supreme authority" (Allah) and cannot be abrogated.[35]

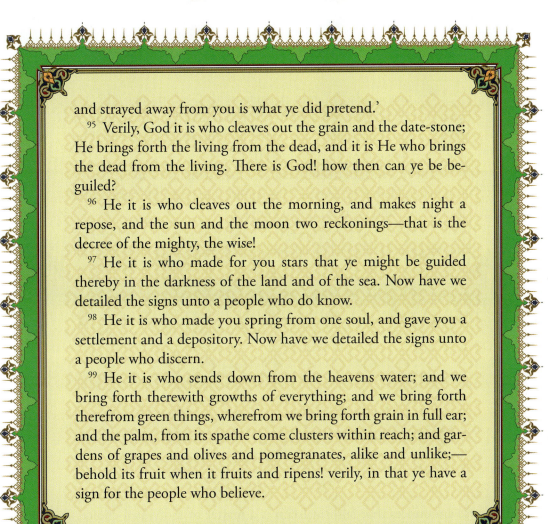

[100] Yet they made the *g*inn partners with God, though He created them! and they ascribed to Him sons and daughters, though they have no knowledge; celebrated be His praise! and exalted be He above what they attribute to Him!

[101] The inventor of the heavens and the earth! how can He have a son, when He has no female companion, and when He has created everything, and everything He knows?

[102] There is God for you,—your Lord! There is no god but He, the Creator of everything; then worship Him, for He o'er every-

Q 6.104

The verse announces that faith in Islām is a matter of individual choice. But some scholars say this right is abrogated with the Sword verse, Q 9.5: *"...kill the idolaters wherever ye may find them…."*[36]

However, a second group of scholars say the verse is conserved because the verse means that Muḥammad is not an overseer, counting the deeds of others. It is a description, and a description is not abrogated.[37]

Q 6.105

The saying in the verse is attributed to the enemies of Muḥammad who said to him, ***darasta*** ("**Thou hast studied**").

The verse means that they said to him, "O Muḥammad! You have studied 'in the ancient books what you bring to us.'" Al-Ṭabarī considers this reading to be the most accurate rendition.[38]

There are many notable readings with variations of the word *darasta* ("you studied"):

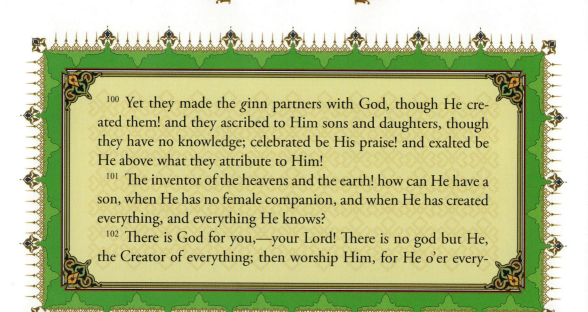

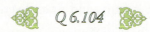

thing keeps guard!
103 Sight perceives Him not, but He perceives men's sights; for
He is the subtle, the aware.
104 Now has an insight from your Lord come unto you, and he
who looks therewith it is for himself; but he who is blind thereto,
it is against his soul; and I am not your keeper.
105 Thus do we turn about the signs, that they may say, 'Thou
hast studied,' and that we may explain to those who know.

- *dārasta* (read by Ibn 'Abbās and others): "'You *dārasta,* O Muḥammad, with someone else about these matters." They are referring to Muḥammad's studies under Salmān al-Fārisī[N] and others, including foreigners and Jews."[39]
- *dārastu* (read with the *ḍamma* "u"): This reading means they were saying that Allah taught Muḥammad, which would be an expression of ridicule and mockery toward Muḥammad.[40] Others state that the verse was a quote from a man of the People of the Book, who said, "...*dārastu* Muḥammadan," meaning "I taught him [Muḥammad]."[41]
- *darrasta* (read with a *shadda*—doubling the letter): "You, O Muḥammad, taught the ancient books."[42]
- *durrista* (read in the passive): "Someone taught you the ancient books, O Muḥammad."[43]
- *darasa* (read in the past tense): "Muḥammad studied the ancient previous books."[44]
- *darasat* (read by Ibn Mas'ūd, 'Abd Allah Ibn al-Zubayr[N], Ubayy Ibn Ka'b, and others): "The verses were repeated in their hearing so many times that they [the verses] were worn out." Al-Farrā' states, "What is meant is *taqādamat,* that is, what he [Muḥammad] was reciting to the people was something that they had heard [repeatedly in the past] and had passed by us [we heard it long before now]." [45]

Question: Does this phrase mean "you studied, O Muḥammad, with someone"; "you studied the books, O Muḥammad"; "someone taught you, O Muḥammad"; or "that the verses of the Qur'ān were repeated so many times in the hearing of non-Muslims that it became worn out?"

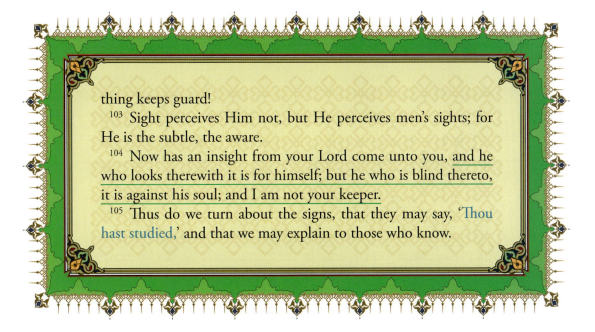

[106] Follow what is revealed to thee from thy Lord; there is no god but He, and shun the idolaters.

[107] But had God pleased, they would not have associated aught with Him; but we have not made thee a keeper over them, nor art thou for them a warder.

[108] Do not abuse those who call on other than God, for then they may abuse God openly in their ignorance. So do we make seemly to every nation their work, then unto their Lord is their return, and He will inform them of what they have done.

[109] They swore by God with their most strenuous oath, that if there come to them a sign they will indeed believe therein. Say, 'Signs are only in God's hands;—but what will make you understand that even when one has come, they will not believe?'

[110] We will overturn their hearts and their eye-sights, even as they believed not at first; and we will leave them, in their rebellion, blindly wandering on.

[111] And had we sent down unto them the angels, or the dead had spoken to them, or we had gathered everything unto them in hosts, they would not have believed unless that God pleased—but most of them are ignorant.

[112] So have we made for every prophet an enemy,—devils of men and *g*inns; some of them inspire others with specious speech to lead astray; but had thy Lord pleased they would not have done it; so leave them with what they do devise.

[113] And let the hearts of those who believe not in the hereafter listen to it; and let them be well pleased with it; and let them gain what they may gain!

Q 6.106

This verse encourages Muslims to keep their distance from idolaters, but some scholars say the verse is abrogated with the Sword verse: *"...kill the idolaters wherever ye may find them...."*[46] Whereas, others say it is abrogated with this verse, Q 9.29: *"Fight those who believe not in God and in the last day."*[47]

Q 6.107

This verse is abrogated with the Sword verse: *"...kill the idolaters wherever ye may find them...."*[48]

Q 6.108

This verse says that Allah makes the people's bad deeds attractive to them.

If Allah lures people into doing bad deeds and then justifies them in their own eyes, would he be fair (just) to judge them for those same deeds? (See the discussion of this topic in Q 3.14, page 271.)

Q 6.108

This verse is abrogated with Q 9.5: *"...kill the idolaters wherever ye may find them...."*[49]

Q 6.109

This expression in the codex of Ubayy Ibn Ka'b reads "how do you know perhaps if it came to them they would not believe?"[50]

Changes in this verse are apparent when comparing this verse from the current Arabic Qur'ān to the codex of Ubayy Ibn Ka'b:

- ***yush'irukum*** ("make you realize, sense, feel") is replaced in Ka'b's reading by *adrākum* ("make you know, comprehend").
- ***innahā*** ("it [feminine] is") is replaced in Ka'b's reading by *la'alahā* ("maybe it [feminine] is").
- ***jā'at*** ("it [feminine] came") has the third person masculine plural pronoun *hum* ("them") attached to it in Ka'b's reading.

Q 6.112

Some scholars believe that since the verse means to leave the non-Muslims in their own religion, and contains a call to not fight, it is therefore abrogated with the Sword verse: *"...kill the idolaters wherever ye may find them...."*[51]

114 Of other than God shall I crave a decree, when it is He who has sent down to you the Book in detail, and those to whom we gave the Book know that it is sent down from thy Lord, in truth? be thou not then of those who doubt.

115 The words of thy Lord are fulfilled in truth and justice; there is none to change His words, for He both hears and knows.

116 But if thou followest most of those who are in the land, they will lead thee astray from the path of God; they only follow suspicion and they only (rest on) conjecture.

However, in a second viewpoint, other scholars believe the verse contains no concrete ruling but rather includes a threat. Therefore, since a threat is treated like a report (*khabar*) and a report is not abrogated, the verse is conserved.[52]

Q 6.114

During the heat of the arguments with the polytheists of Mecca, after Muḥammad had refused or could not present miracles as proof of his prophethood, his esteemed position was greatly shaken in Mecca. As a result, Muḥammad told the tribe of the Quraysh that Allah had declared him a prophet and that Allah's testimony was enough to verify this claim.

Explaining, "and *'Of other than God shall I crave a decree,'*" al-Rāzī wrote, "'Say [Muḥammad]: Allah almighty has declared the truth of my prophecy by giving me such a detailed complete book that reached the level of inimitability.'"[53]

As pointed out earlier in the comment on Q 6.19, Muḥammad's declaration that Allah is his witness is insufficient proof of his prophethood, given that any self-proclaimed prophet could say that Allah has testified in his favor. The new point in this verse is that it introduces another witness, "to whom we gave the Book." Is Muḥammad referring to the Jews or to the Jews and Christians collectively?

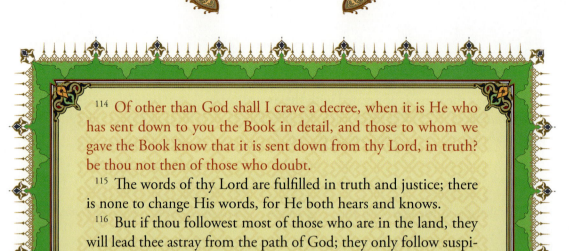

117 Thy Lord, He knows best who errs from His path, and He knows best the guided.
118 Eat then of what God's name has been pronounced over, if ye believe in His signs.
119 What ails you that ye do not eat from what God's name is pronounced over, when He has detailed to you what is unlawful for you? Save what ye are forced to; but, verily, many will lead you astray by their fancies, without knowledge. Verily, thy Lord knows best the transgressors.

The exact definition is not as important as the fact that *"to whom we gave the Book"*—whether they be Jews or Christians—they do not, have never, nor will they ever testify in his favor.

In fact, those *"to whom we gave the Book"* are witnesses against Muḥammad's prophetic claims. By remaining steadfast in their religion and holding to the truths contained in their holy books, Jews and Christians have affirmed that they do not view Muḥammad as a prophet.

Q 6.119

One group read this as ***layuḍillūna*** from the verb *aḍalla* ("to mislead another").[54] Others read it as *layaḍillūna* with a *fatḥa* (a) on the "y" from the verb *ḍalla* ("to mislead oneself [go astray]").[55]

Question: Is the final form meant to say "they mislead others" or "they mislead themselves"? There is certainly a vast difference between the two meanings.

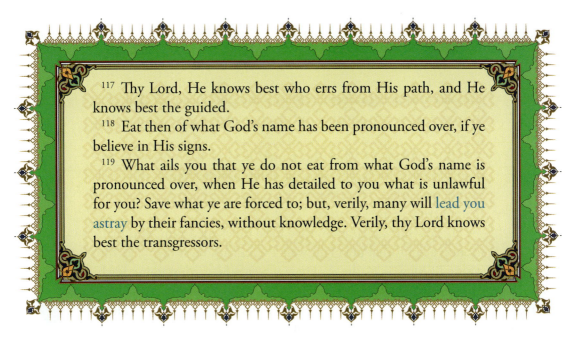

120 Leave alone the outside of sin and the inside thereof; verily, those who earn sin shall be recompensed for what they have
gained.
121 But eat not of what the name of God has not been pronounced over, for, verily, it is an abomination. Verily, the devils
inspire their friends that they may wrangle with you; but if ye obey
them, verily, ye are idolaters.
122 Is he who was dead and we have quickened him, and made
for him a light, that he might walk therein amongst men, like him
whose likeness is in the darkness whence he cannot come forth?
Thus is made seemly to the misbelievers what they have done.
123 And thus have we placed in every town the great sinners
thereof, that they may use craft therein; but they use not craft
except against themselves, although they do not understand.
124 And when there comes to them a sign, they say, 'We will not
believe until we are brought like what the apostles were brought;'
God knows best where to put His message. There shall befall those
who sin, meanness in God's eyes, and grievous torment for the
craft they used.

Q 6.121

There are two viewpoints regarding the abrogation of this verse. In the first viewpoint, the verse is considered abrogated with Q 5.5: *"...the food of those to whom the Book has been given is lawful for you...."*[56]

However, in a second viewpoint, a group of scholars say it is not permissible to eat meat over which Allah's name had not been pronounced. Therefore, the verse is conserved.

One exegetical scholar offers a further explanation: "to eat the meat of the People of the Book is loathed, if it is known that the person deliberately said a name upon it (pronounced a name over it)."[57] In other words, different religions may dictate invoking the name of their god(s) over an animal sacrifice; if the name invoked is other than "Allah," the meat is forbidden to the Muslim. For example, some Eastern Orthodox

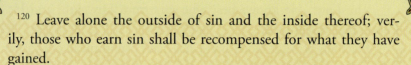

125 Whomsoever God wishes to guide, He expands his breast
to Islam; but whomsoever He wishes to lead astray, He makes
his breast tight and straight, as though he would mount up into
heaven; thus does God set His horror on those who do not believe.
126 This is the way of thy Lord—straight. We have detailed the
signs unto a mindful people;
127 for them is an abode of peace; and their Lord, He is their
patron for what they have done.
128 And on the day when He shall gather them all together, 'O
assembly of the *g*inns! ye have got much out of mankind.' And
their clients from among mankind shall say, 'O our Lord! much
advantage had we one from another;' but we reached our appointed time which thou hadst appointed for us. Says He, 'The fire is
your resort, to dwell therein for aye! save what God pleases; verily,
thy Lord is wise and knowing.'
129 Thus do we make some of the unjust patrons of the others,
for that which they have earned.

Christians may say, "In the name of the Father, Son, and Holy Spirit," or others might say, "In the name of the cross." These particular pronouncements would make such meat unacceptable to the Muslim.

Q 6.123

The one group read it as stated the current Arabic Qur'ān: ***akābir*** ("**the great**"), in the plural.

Another group read it *akbar* ("the greatest"), in the singular.

Yet, a third group read it *akthar* ("the majority").[58]

Question: Which reading is the most accurate—the elites (plural), the elite (singular), or the majority of the elites?

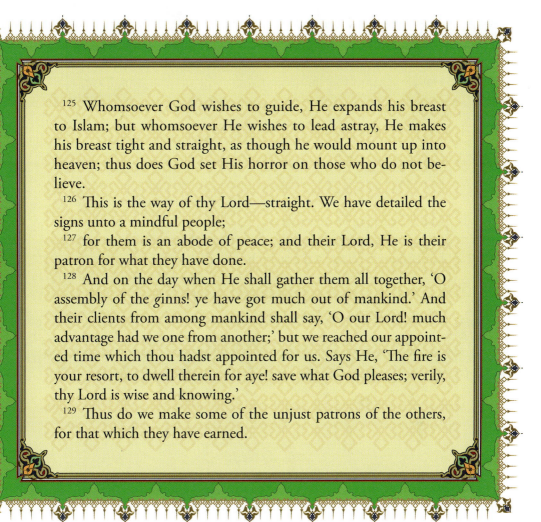

[130] O assembly of ginns and men! did there not come to you apostles from among yourselves, relating to you our signs, and warning you of the meeting of this very day of yours? They say, 'We bear witness against ourselves.' The life of this world deceived them, and they bear witness against themselves that they were unbelievers.

[131] That is because thy Lord would never destroy towns unjustly while their people are careless;

[132] but for every one are degrees of what they have done and thy Lord is not careless of that which they do.

[133] Thy Lord is rich, merciful; if He pleases He will take you off, and will cause what He pleases to succeed you; even as He raised you up from the seed of other people.

Q 6.130

The verse says that "messengers" came to mankind and also to the jinn[D] (ginn), who are believed to be invisible beings that coexist with humans. According to the way the verse reads in the Arabic text, Allah sent these messengers to the jinn from their own kind. However, Muslim scholars were divided into two opinions regarding this issue:

The first opinion states that Allah sent messengers to mankind from their own kind (men), and he sent messengers to the jinn from their own kind (jinn).

The second opinion states that messengers were sent from mankind to both the jinn and mankind.[59]

Questions:
(1) Is the existence of jinn a scientific fact? (2) If the existence of jinn is hypothetically accepted, has it ever been heard that one of the prophets was sent to the jinn? (3) According to this verse, it is assumed that the jinn world is divided into different religions. Therefore, are the jinn involved in the religious turmoil that is taking place in the world, with one group of jinn supporting the followers of one religion, while another group is supporting another religion?

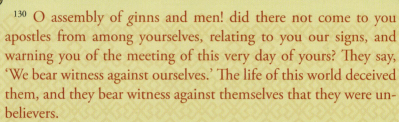

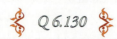

134 Verily, what ye are promised will surely come, nor can ye frus-
trate it.
135 Say, 'O my people! act according to your power, verily, I
am acting too; and soon shall ye know whose is the future of the
abode!' verily, the unjust shall not prosper.
136 They set apart for God, from what He raises of tilth and of
cattle, a portion, and they say, 'This is God's;'—as they pretend—
'and this is for our associates;' but that which is for their associates
reaches not to God, and that which was for God does reach to
their associates;—evil is it what they judge.
137 Thus too have their associates made seemly to many of the
idolaters the killing of their children, to destroy them, and to obscure for them their religion; but had God pleased they would not

Based on the first view, verse Q 6.130 conveys the idea that Allah sends jinn messengers from among the jinn. However, there are other verses with texts that emphasize that all the messengers are men of human origin: *"Nor did we ever send before thee any save men whom we inspired"* (Q 12.109). Other verses use similar words: *"Nor did we send before them any but men whom we inspired"* (Q 21.7) and *"We have not sent before thee any messengers but that they ate food and walked in the markets"* (Q 25.20).

Q 6.135

Those scholars who say this verse means "compel not into Islām" also say it is abrogated with the Sword verse: *"...kill the idolaters wherever ye may find them...."*[60]

However, other scholars who say the verse includes a threat consider the verse to be conserved.[61]

Q 6.137

The majority of the readers read ***zayyana*** ("**made seemly**") with ***shurakā'ūhum*** ("**their associates**") as the subject of the verb *zayyna.* The word ***qatla*** ("**the killing**") is the object of the verb. The word ***awlādihim*** ("**their children**") is part of the *idafa*

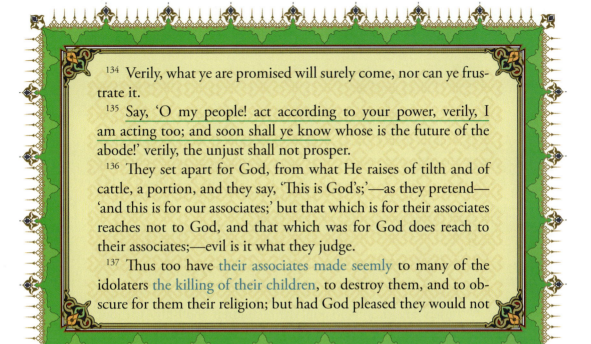

have done it, leave them alone and that which they have forged.
138 And they say, 'These cattle and tilth are inviolable; none shall
taste thereof, save such as we please'—as they pretend—'and there
are cattle whose backs are prohibited, and cattle over whom God's
name is not pronounced,—forging a lie against Him! He shall
reward them for what they have forged.
139 And they say, 'What is in the wombs of these cattle is unlawful for our wives, but if it be (born) dead, then are they partners
therein.' He will reward them for their attribution; verily, He is
wise and knowing.
140 Losers are they who kill their children foolishly, without
knowledge, and who prohibit what God has bestowed upon them,
forging a lie against God; they have erred and are not guided.
141 He it is who brought forth gardens with trailed and untrailed
vines, and the palms and corn land, with various food, and olives,

grammatical structure. The meaning is that the partners are the ones who make the killing of their children alluring in the sight of the idolaters. The same meaning is found in the reading of the codex of 'Alī Ibn Abī Ṭālib, but he read *zuyyina qatlu* ("it was made seemly the killing") in the passive. He and others thus read, "It was made seemly....the killing of their children, their associates."[62]

Another group read it as *zuyyina qatlu* ("it was made seemly the killing") of their children *shurakā'ihim* ("their associates"), where *zuyyina* is in the passive and *shurakā'ihim* is in the possessive, as a substitute for the children. This reading means that the children are the partners in life that are killed.[63]

Question: Are the partners the ones that make the killing seemly, or are they the victims of the killing?

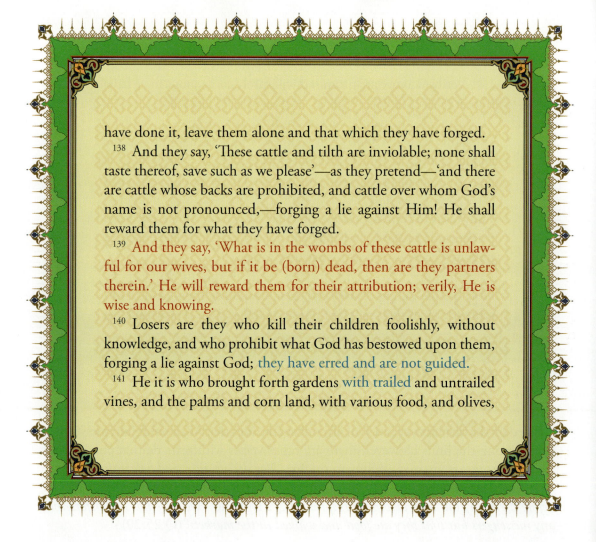

Q 6.139

In the current Arabic Qur'ān the word *khāliṣa* ("specially reserved") is used in the feminine, while the word *muḥarram* ("forbidden") is used in the masculine. The question then becomes, why did these two descriptions, "specially reserved" and "forbidden," come in two forms of the language—one in feminine and the other in masculine?

The scholars have given various linguistic reasons for writing, "specially reserved" in the feminine:

- What is in the belly of these cattle is feminine, just like the mother cow. The word *"what"* refers to the embryos.
- In Arabic, the last letter in the word *khāliṣa,* which makes it feminine, is for hyperbole.[64]

The scholars have said that the reason the word "forbidden" is written in the masculine form is because it refers to the word *"what,"* so "it was mentioned in reference to that word, but, had the meaning been considered, it should have read as feminine."[65]

It seems that Ibn Mas'ūd saw a defect in the verse, so he wrote in his version of the Qur'ān the word *khāliṣ* ("specially reserved") as masculine.[66]

It is worth noting that whenever the Muslim scholars encountered a written linguistic error, they came up with explanations and justifications for the error. This justification does not reinforce the rhetoric of the Qur'ān but shows arbitrariness in the use of the language, as well as a skewing of the text.

The Qur'ān's editing committee ('Uthmān's committee) could have saved the interpreters a tremendous effort had they followed the codex of Ibn Mas'ūd, which reads *khāliṣ* ("specially reserved") in the masculine form.

Q 6.140

The verse was read by some as "they have erred before that and are not guided." In other words, they added "before that" to the verse.[67]

Q 6.141

This verse was read by 'Alī Ibn Abī Ṭālib as "It is he who produces gardens planted and unplanted."[68]

The word used in the current Arabic Qur'ān, ***ma'rūshāt*** ("**with trailed...vines**"), comes from the verb *'arasha* ("to build a wooden structure"). When one says *i'tarasha al-'arish,* the meaning is "the vines have climbed the trellises." The gardens that are *ma'rūshāt* in the verse are the vineyards. As to the planted ones, *maghrūsāt* from the verb *gharasa,* it means to plant in the ground. This is a difference in the technical imaging of the verse.

and pomegranates, alike and unlike. Eat from the fruit thereof whene'er it fruits, and bring the dues thereof on the day of harvest, and be not extravagant; verily, He loves not the extravagant.
142 Of cattle are there some to ride on and to spread. Eat of what God has bestowed upon you, and follow not the footsteps of Satan; verily, he is to you an open foe.
143 Eight pairs,—of sheep two, and of goats two; say, 'Are the two males unlawful, or the two females, or what the wombs of the two females contain? inform me with knowledge if ye tell the truth.'
144 And of camels two, and cows two; say, 'Are the two males unlawful, or the two females, or what the wombs of the two females contain? Were ye witnesses when God ordained for you these?—

If the reading had come from one source, we would not have found this difference. One reading highlights the vines on the trellises, and another refers to the plants planted in the ground.

Q 6.141

The opinion of the scholars on whether the verse is abrogated or conserved is based on their understanding of the word "*dues*":

A. Some scholars have said that "*dues*" means the almsgiving imposed on crops. Therefore, they believe the verse is conserved.[69]
Our Comment: However, sūra al-An'ām (Q 6) is considered Meccan and the principle of almsgiving was only enacted later in Medina. If the verse refers to almsgiving, then this reference means the verse was added to the sūra later.

B. Another group has said that "*dues*" does not mean almsgiving because "alms [are] collected not during harvest [as the verse states], but after the weighing."[70] The "giving of dues" mentioned here was an obligation performed during harvest time. Therefore, those present at harvest were given a portion of whatever was available.[71] This giving of dues is thereby abrogated by the imposition of almsgiving.[72]

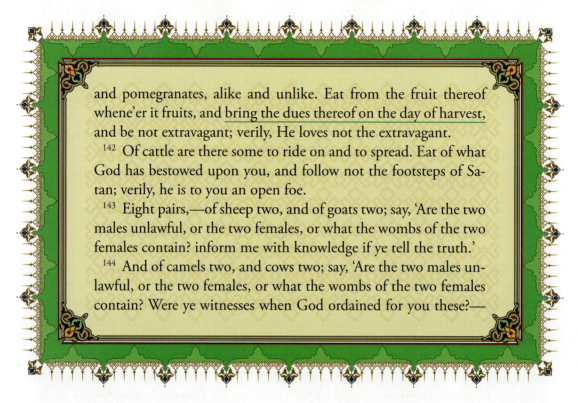

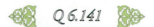

Then who is more unjust than he who devises a lie against God, to lead men astray without knowledge? verily, God guides not the unjust people.'
145 Say, 'I cannot find in what I am inspired with anything unlawful for the taster to taste; unless it be dead (of itself), or blood that has been shed, or the flesh of swine,—for that is a horror—or an abomination that is consecrated to other than God. But he who is forced, not willfully nor transgressing,—then, verily, thy Lord is forgiving and merciful.'
146 To those who were Jews did we prohibit everything that hath a solid hoof; and of oxen and sheep did we prohibit to them the fat, save what the backs of both do bear, or the inwards, or what

C. It is said that "*dues*" means feeding the workers who had contributed to the harvest, leaving behind whatever portion of the crop that had fallen to the ground, so the poor could gather it up. This practice is abrogated with almsgiving and tithing, and half the tithe mentioned in the narratives (*ḥadīths*) is attributed to Muḥammad.[73]

Q 6.145

In this verse, Muḥammad allowed the eating of the food of the Quraysh tribe with the following exceptions: "*...unless it be dead (of itself), or blood that has been shed....*" He said, "I do not find in what is revealed to me a forbidden thing of what you used to find permissible, except for this. There are things that they forbade and it now is indeed forbidden."[74] Since these exceptions are still forbidden in Islām, a group of scholars say this verse is conserved.[75]

In a second viewpoint, another group of scholars say that this verse is abrogated with the following text:

A. Q 5.3: "*...the strangled and the knocked down, and that which falls down, and the gored, and what wild beasts have eaten....*"[76]
B. A narrative (*ḥadīth*) by Muḥammad forbids "...domestic donkeys, as well as every tusked beast, and birds with claws."[77]

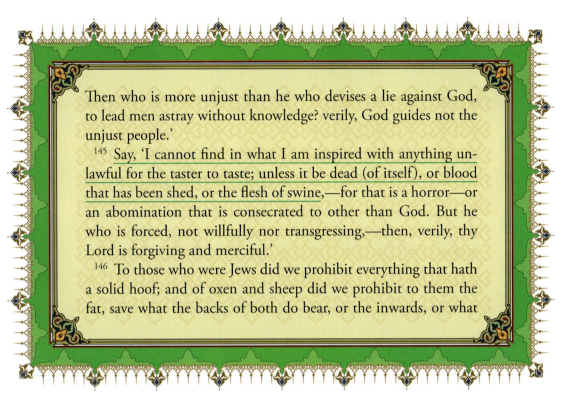

is mixed with bone; with that did we recompense them for their
rebellion, for, verily, we are true.
147 And if they give thee the lie, say, 'Your Lord is of ample mercy, nor shall His violence be turned back from the sinful people.'
148 Those who associate others with God will say, 'Had God
pleased, we had not so associated, nor our fathers; nor should we
have forbidden aught.' Thus did they give the lie to those who
came before them, until they tasted of our violence! Say, 'Have ye
any knowledge? if so, bring it forth to us: ye only follow suspicion,
and ye do but conjecture.'
149 Say, 'God's is the searching argument; and had He pleased He
would have guided you all.'
150 Say, 'Come on then with your witnesses, who bear witness
that God has prohibited these!' but if they do bear witness, bear
thou not witness with them; nor follow the lust of those who say
our signs are lies, and those who do not believe in the last day, or
those who for their Lord make peers.
151 Say, 'Come! I will recite what your Lord has forbidden you,
that ye may not associate aught with Him, and (may show) kindness to your parents, and not kill your children through poverty;—we will provide for you and them;—and draw not nigh to
flagrant sins, either apparent or concealed, and kill not the soul,
which God hath forbidden save by right; that is what God ordains
you, haply ye may understand.'
152 And draw not nigh unto the wealth of the orphan, save so as
to better it, until he reaches full age; and give weight and measure
with justice. We do not compel the soul save what it can compass;
and when ye pronounce, then be just, though it be in the case of a
relative.
153 And God's compact fulfill ye; that is what He ordained you,
haply ye may be mindful. Verily, this is my right way; follow it
then, and follow not various paths, to separate yourselves from His

way; that is what He has ordained you, haply ye may fear!
154 Then we gave Moses the Book, complete for him who acts
aright, and a decision and a guidance and a mercy; haply in the
meeting of their Lord they will believe.
155 This is the Book which we have sent down; it is a blessing;
follow it then and fear; haply ye may obtain mercy.
156 Lest ye say, 'The Book was only sent down to two sects before
us; verily, we, for what they read, care naught.'
157 Or, lest ye should say, 'Had we had a book revealed to us we
should surely have been more guided than they;' but there is come
to them a manifest sign from their Lord, and a guidance and a
mercy; who then is more unjust than he who calls God's signs lies,
and turns from them? we will reward those who turn from our
signs with an evil punishment for that they turned away.
158 What do they expect but that the angels should come for
them, or that thy Lord should come, or that some signs of thy
Lord should come? On the day when some signs do come, its
faith shall profit no soul which did not believe before, unless it has
earned some good by its faith. Say, 'Wait ye expectant, then we
wait expectant too.'

Q 6.158

One group of scholars believes the verse is about avoiding conflict with non-Muslims, but it is abrogated with the Sword verse: *"...kill the idolaters wherever ye may find them...."*[78]

However, other scholars say the verse is not about enjoining peace but contains a threat. Therefore, it is conserved.[79]

Q 6.158

The Qur'ān as read by Abū Hurayra[N] uses "nor earned *ṣāliḥān* ("a righteous deed"), instead of the current Arabic Qur'ān's reading ***khayrān*** ("**good**.")[80] This is a change made by Abū Hurayra in the formatting of the word.

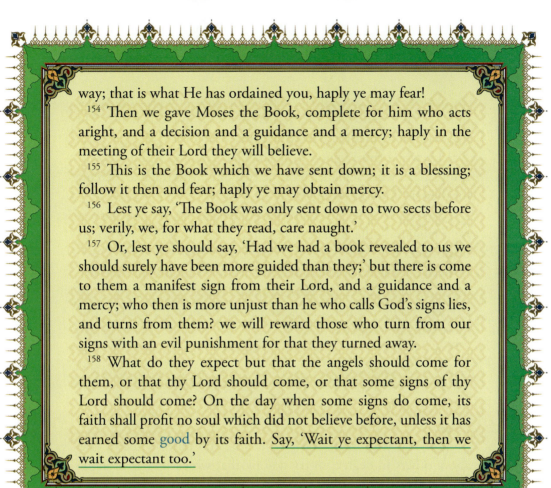

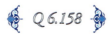

[159] Verily, those who divided their religion and became sects, thou hast not to do with them, their matter is in God's hands, He will yet inform them of that which they have done.

[160] He who brings a good work shall have ten like it; but he who brings a bad work shall be recompensed only with the like thereof, for they shall not be wronged.

[161] Say, 'As for me, my Lord has guided me to the right way, a right religion,—the faith of Abraham the 'Hanif, for he was not of the idolaters.'

[162] Say, 'Verily, my prayers and my devotion and my life and my death belong to God, the Lord of the worlds.

[163] He has no partner; that is what I am bidden; for I am first of those who are resigned.'

[164] Say, 'Other than God shall I crave for a Lord when He is Lord of all?' but no soul shall earn aught save against itself; nor shall one bearing a burden bear the burden of another; and then unto your Lord is your return, and He will inform you concerning that whereon ye do dispute.

[165] He it is who made you vicegerents, and raised some of you above others in degree, to try you by that which he has brought you;—verily, thy Lord is swift to punish, but, verily, He is forgiving and merciful.

Q 6.159

Some scholars believe that it is a call to avoid fighting, but the call is abrogated with the Sword verse: "*...kill the idolaters wherever ye may find them....*"[81] and with Q 9.29: "*Fight those who believe not in God....*"[82]

Another group of scholars believes that the verse discusses the circumstances of Muḥammad, saying, "He does not belong to the pagans and they do not belong to him." Therefore, the verse is conserved.[83]

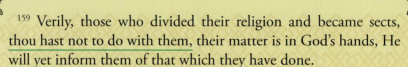

Q 6.164

This verse mentions that every human who is an evildoer will endure the consequences of his own deeds and that no person will be punished on another's behalf: "*...but no soul shall earn aught save against itself; nor shall one bearing a burden bear the burden of another...*" (Q 6.164).

However, another verse states that the transgressors will endure the consequences of their own deeds in full, as well as bearing the weight of some of the transgressions of those who followed and obeyed them: "*Let them bear the burden of their sins entirely on the resurrection day* [Day of Judgment], *and some of the burdens of those whom they led astray without knowledge...*" (Q 16.25).

Additionally, a third verse threatens that the transgressors will bear both their own burdens and the burdens of others: "*But they shall surely bear their own burdens, and burdens with their burdens...*" (Q 29.13).

Introduction

The name of this sūra, al-Aʿrāf, is an expression that is only mentioned in this sūra (Q 7.46, 48). Al-Aʿrāf, meaning "the Battlements," is the name of the barrier that separates paradise from hell.

The general objective of this sūra is to establish Muḥammad's claims to prophetic revelation. To this end, a number of prophets' stories were included. The prophets' experiences and the consequences that befell those who refused to believe in them were meant to compel the hearers from among the Quraysh people to believe in Muḥammad. It is interesting to note that the prophets' stories, including their characteristics, messages, and the opposition they faced from their people, are portrayed as exact reflections of Muḥammad and his own similar challenges.[1]

Though this sūra is distinctly Meccan, it is interspersed with Medinan verses. The following list provides evidence of these included Medinan verses:

Q 7.157-158 is a Medinan segment.[2]

- This segment uses the description, "*the ummī Prophet.*" The word *ummī* could mean "illiterate" or "gentile." This description was mentioned in Medina to distinguish Muḥammad from the prophets of the Jews and Christians.
- A second expression in this segment, *"the law and the Gospel,"* is mentioned only in those portions of the Qur'ān that were given, or "came down" in Medina.
- A third expression, *"those who believe in him and aid him and help him"* refers to the Helpers (Anṣār) in Medina.
- This segment, verses 157-158, constitutes an interruption in the context of the rest of the verses, which resumes at verse Q 7.159.

Q 7.163-172 is another Medinan segment, according to the Islāmic accounts.[3]

- Within the sūra is a remark in Q 7.94 about the economic inflation that dominated Mecca at that time.[4]
- The general style of the sūra signifies that its revelation was received on the eve of the migration (*Hijra*).[5]

This sūra is also concerned with the history of humanity and the stories of the prophets:

- Beginning of creation and the fall of Adam into temptation (Q 7.1-58)
- History of certain prophets, such as Noah, Ṣāliḥ, Shuʿayb (Q 7.59-102) and Moses (Q 7.103-174)
- Attempt to understand the end of history and the end of the world, or "the last hour" (Q 7.187-206)

In the name of the merciful and compassionate God.
1 A. L. M. S.
2 A book revealed to thee,—so let there be no straitness in thy
breast, that thou mayest warn thereby,—and a reminder to the
believers.
3 Follow what has been revealed to you from your Lord, and
follow not beside Him patrons; little is it that ye mind.
4 Yet how many a town have we destroyed, and our violence
came upon it by night, or while they slept at noon; and their cry,
when our violence came upon them,
5 was only to say, 'Verily, we were unjust!'
6 But we will of a surety question those to whom the prophets
were sent,
7 and we will narrate to them with knowledge, for we were not
absent.
8 The balance on that day is true, and whosesoever scales are
heavy, they are prosperous;
9 but whosesoever scales are light, they it is who lose themselves, for that they did act unjustly by our signs.
10 We have established you in the earth, and we have made for

Q 7.3

The common reading from the current Arabic Qur'ān that is read by the majority is ***ittabi'ū...wa lā tattabi'ū*** (**"follow...and follow not"**) from *al-ittibā'* ("following").

But another group read this verse as *ibtaghū...wa lā tabtaghū* ("seek...and seek not") from *al-ibtighā'* ("seeking").[6]

This verse from the current Arabic Qur'ān instructs Muslims to closely follow what was revealed, meaning that they should follow its teachings alone and heed no others.

On the other hand, the second way this verse is read demands an action—the pursuit of a goal, where "seeking something" means to want it and go after it. This second reading of the verse implies that what was revealed is not readily available to those addressed; they must seek it out.

Q7.4

Literally, this verse reads, "How many towns have we caused to be destroyed, then our punishment took her [it] on a sudden by night...."

How did the destruction come? Did it come first and then the punishment came after? Does not destruction logically follow punishment? In the Arabic, the verb is in the form *if'āl*, meaning "to cause to perish," rather than "destruction."

A Muslim scholar observes, "In the verse there are some actions that were listed first and other actions that were listed last, out of order. It is as if he was saying, 'how many a town did our punishment come to her [it] and so we destroyed her [it]....'"[7]

Notice that the scholar rearranged his observation so that the punishment now comes first and the destruction afterwards.

Al-Zamakhsharī said that this phrasing describes the intention to destroy, not the act of destruction itself.[8] Another similar opinion states that destruction is the plunging of the town into disobedience: "Therefore, Allah's destruction of the town is his abandoning them to their disobedience of him, hence, the coming of the *ba's* (vengeance or punishment) of Allah onto them becomes a recompense for their disobedience to their lord through his abandoning of them."[9]

The scholars made an effort to prove that there is no error in the order of the terms; however, the existence of multiple interpretations and explanations indicates that the scholars themselves were not satisfied with their own explanations.

It is also noted that if the verse is talking about the people of the town, it would require the use of the pronoun *hum* ("them") in Arabic instead of *hā* ("her"). (See literal translation of the verse: "our punishment to them.")

This conflict was resolved in English by some translations (e.g., Yusuf Ali), but it remains an issue in the original Arabic text.

In response to the issue, al-Rāzī replied, "There is something removed in the verse. It is something like: how many people of a town." However, al-Zajjāj said, "If he said, 'our punishment overtook them,' it would have been correct."[10]

The words of the early Islāmic scholar al-Zajjāj are an implicit confession of the existence of complications in the verse, if not even linguistic errors. This disclosure caused embarrassment to some scholars in explaining the verse. So they said that there is no omission in the verse, but that what is meant is the actual destruction of the town itself.[11]

Q7.6

Ibn Mas'ūd read this verse in a different form: "Then shall we question those to whom we sent our messengers before you and those by whom we sent it."[12]

you therein livelihoods; little is it that ye thank;
11 and we created you, then we fashioned you, then we said
unto the angels, 'Adore Adam,' and they adored, save Iblis, who
was not of those who did adore.
12 Said He, 'What hinders thee from adoring when I order thee?'
he said, 'I am better than he; Thou hast created me from fire, and
him Thou hast created out of clay.'
13 Said He, 'Then go down therefrom; what ails thee that thou
shouldst be big with pride therein? go forth! verily, thou art of the
little ones.'
14 He said, 'Respite me until the day when they shall be raised.'
15 He said, 'Verily, thou art of the respited;'
16 said he, 'For that Thou hast led me into error, I will lie in wait
for them in Thy straight path;
17 then I will surely come to them, from before them and from
behind them; and most of them Thou shalt not find thankful.'
18 He said, 'Go forth therefrom, despised, expelled; whoso follows thee, I will surely fill hell with you altogether.
19 But, O Adam, dwell thou and thy wife in Paradise and eat
from whence ye will, but draw not nigh unto this tree or ye will be

Q 7.13

In this verse, Allah orders Satan to leave heaven, for he is not allowed to exalt himself there, as if the passage implies that it is allowable for Satan to exalt himself on earth. Al-Ṭabarī responded to this ambiguity:[13]

> [T]he meaning of this is the opposite of what you arrived at. What is meant is "descend from [get out of] al-Janna [Islāmic paradise], for there is no dwelling in al-Janna for anyone who exalts himself above the will of Allah, but other places besides al-Janna can be dwelt by both the one who exalts oneself above Allah's will and those who are obedient to his will.

Al-Ṭabarī's explanation does not coincide with the logic of the verse, which shows us that Allah prohibited exaltation in a specific place—only al-Janna—while leaving the act as allowable in other locations.

Q 7.16

After Satan was ordered to leave al-Janna, he accused Allah of being the one who tempted him: "I will repel the sons of Adam from worshipping and obeying You; I will lure them as You lured me and mislead them as You misled me."[14]

This verse makes Allah the inciter of Satan's deviant behavior, because it neither replies to Satan's accusation, nor does it refute the charge that Allah lured him.

The passage also reiterates other verses from the Qur'ān in which Allah appears to make evil appealing to people. (See the discussion concerning this issue in Q 3.14, page 271, and compare it with Q 6.108, page 427.)

Q 7.16

One reader read this verse as "Because you have thrown me out of the way, lo! *la'ajlisanna* ("I will sit") in wait for them on your straightway…."[15] While it is true that the two words "lie" and "sit" are close in meaning, the replacement of one word with another indicates that the reader who read the verse had a role in choosing which word he would use.

If the Qur'ān was composed by just one author, we would not have so many variances. This issue of using synonyms or "close enough" words is widespread throughout Q 7:

- Q 7.47: *"But when their sight is turned towards the fellows of the Fire* [the damned]*"* was read by Ibn Mas'ūd and other readers with a word that has a similar meaning. The word ***ṣurifat*** of the current Arabic Qur'ān was replaced with the word *qulibat* for "turned."[16]
- Q 7.131: "*...and if there befell them an evil, they took the augury*." This verse was read with a similar meaning by replacing the word ***yaṭṭayyarū*** ("**they took the augury**") with the word *tashā'amū* ("they ascribed it to evil omens") in the verse.[17]
- Q 7.154: "*And when Moses' wrath calmed down*" was read by Ibn Mas'ūd and others with the word ***sakata*** ("**calmed down**") replaced with the similar word *sakana* in the verse.[18]
- Q 7.201: "*Verily, those who fear God, if a wraith from the devil touch*" appears in the codex of Ubayy Ibn Ka'b with the word *ṭāfa* instead of the similar word ***massahum*** ("**touch**") in the current Arabic Qur'ān.[19]

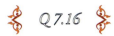

of the unjust.'
20 But Satan whispered to them to display to them what was
kept back from them of their shame, and he said, 'Your Lord has
only forbidden you this tree lest ye should be twain angels, or
should become of the immortals;'
21 and he swore to them both, 'Verily, I am unto you a sincere adviser;'
22 and he beguiled them by deceit, and when they twain tasted
of the tree, their shame was shown them, and they began to stitch
upon themselves the leaves of the garden. And their Lord called
unto them, 'Did I not forbid you from that tree there, and say to
you, Verily, Satan is to you an open foe?'
23 They said, 'O our Lord! we have wronged ourselves—and if
Thou dost not forgive us and have mercy on us, we shall surely be
of those who are lost!'
24 He said, 'Go ye down, one of you to the other a foe; but for
you in the earth there is an abode, and a provision for a season.'
25 He said, 'Therein shall ye live and therein shall ye die, from it
shall ye be brought forth.'
26 O sons of Adam! we have sent down to you garments wherewith
to cover your shame, and plumage; but the garment of piety, that is
better. That is one of the signs of God, haply ye may remember.
27 O sons of Adam! let not Satan infatuate you as he drove your
parents out of Paradise, stripping from them their garments, and
showing them their shame; verily, he sees you—he and his tribe,
from whence ye cannot see them. Verily, we have made the devils
patrons of those who do not believe,
28 and when they commit an abomination they say, 'We found
our fathers at this, and God bade us do it.' Say, 'God bids you not to
do abomination; do ye say against God that which ye do not know?'
29 Say, 'My Lord bids only justice:—set steadfastly your faces at
every mosque and pray to Him, being sincere in your religion. As
He brought you forth in the beginning, shall ye return.
30 A sect He guides, and for a sect of them was error due; verily,

Q 7.26

The verse says that Allah sent down garments to cover the nakedness of the "*sons of Adam.*" The verse continues to say that the covering is a sign or a miracle from Allah that shows his mercy and might; because of this bestowal to them, people should remember his greatness and what is due him.

Question: Could it be that the failure of Muḥammad to provide a miracle as proof of his claims led him to say that clothing is a sign, meaning a miracle?

Q 7.26

It is told that Muḥammad recited ***rīshan*** ("**plumage**") in the plural *riyāshan*. Ubayy Ibn Ka'b read his Qur'ān with a different word, replacing *rīshan* with *zīnatan* ("*adornment*".)[20]

Please note these differences:

First, that the plural, which was the way Muḥammad recited the verse, is not the form that is written down in the current Arabic Qur'ān.

Second, that there is a difference between *rīshan* and *zīnatan*. The first word *rīshan* mentioned in the verse of the current Arabic Qur'ān means "goods and money." In other renderings, it means "clothes" only.[21] Whereas, *zīnatan* means everything that is used for adornment, or it can mean jewelry.

Q 7.29-30

Ubayy Ibn Ka'b read the verse by adding the word *farīqayn* ("two sects") before the first word ***farīqan*** ("**A sect**"). His reading of this verse is based on the expression "*...shall ye return. A sect He guides,*" meaning, "shall ye return as two [opposite] groups: happy and miserable."[22]

The difference in the variant readings of these verses leads to two matters:

First, it is not permissible to pause at the word "return."[23] Instead, the two verses must be read as one continuous, related thought.

Second, the reading of these verses as given in the codex of Ubayy Ibn Ka'b is clearer and distinguishes three groups: the happy, the miserable, and those who deserve to be lead astray.

they did take the devils for their patrons instead of God, and they did count that they were guided.'

31 O sons of Adam! take your ornaments to every mosque; and eat and drink, but do not be extravagant, for He loves not the extravagant.

32 Say, 'Who has prohibited the ornaments of God which He brought forth for His servants, and the good things of His providing?' say, 'On the day of judgment they shall only be for those who believed when in the life of this world.' Thus do we detail the signs unto a people that do know.

33 Say, 'My Lord has only prohibited abominable deeds, the apparent thereof and the concealed thereof, and sin, and greed for that which is not right, and associating with God what He has sent down no power for, and saying against God that which ye do not know.'

34 Every nation has its appointed time, and when their appointed time comes they cannot keep it back an hour, nor can they bring it on.

35 O sons of Adam! verily, there will come to you apostles from amongst you, narrating unto you my signs; then whoso fears God and does what is right, there is no fear for them, nor shall they grieve.

Q 7.35

Ubayy Ibn Ka'b and others read the verse with *ta'tiyannakum* ("comes to you") in the singular feminine, grammatically applied to the apostles as a group. The current Arabic Qur'ān, on the other hand, uses the masculine ***ya'tiyannakum*** ("**come to you**"), because it is followed by the word ***rusulun*** ("**apostles**"), who are males.[24]

The difference here indicates that the readers read the verse using their own personal choice of words, because one group used a feminine verb referring to a group of apostles and another used a masculine verb referring to *rusulun* ("apostles").

36 But those who say my signs are lies, and who are too big with
pride for them, these are the fellows of the Fire, they shall dwell
therein for aye!
37 Who is more unjust than he who devises against God a lie, or
says His signs are lies? These, their portion of the Book shall reach
them, until when our messengers come to take their souls away,
and say, 'Where is what ye used to call upon instead of God?' they
say, 'They have strayed away from us;' and they shall bear witness
against themselves that they have been misbelievers.
38 He will say, 'Enter ye—amongst the nations who have
passed away before you, both of *g*inns and men—into the fire;'
whenever a nation enters therein, it curses its mate; until, when
they have all reached it, the last of them will say unto the first,
'O our Lord! these it was who led us astray, give them double
torment of the fire!' He will say, 'To each of you double! but ye
do not know.'
39 And the first of them will say unto the last, 'Ye have no preference over us, so taste ye the torment for that which ye have
earned!'
40 Verily, those who say our signs are lies and are too big with
pride for them; for these the doors of heaven shall not be opened,
and they shall not enter into Paradise until a camel shall pass into
a needle's eye.
41 It is thus that we reward the sinners; for them is a couch of
hell-fire, with an awning above them! thus do we reward the unjust!
42 But those who believe and do what is right—we will not
oblige a soul more than its capacity—they are the fellows of Paradise, they shall dwell therein for aye.
43 We will strip away what ill feeling is in their breasts—there
shall flow beneath them rivers, and they shall say, 'Praise belongs

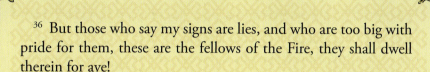

to God who guided us to this! for we should not have been guided
had not God guided us!—the apostles of our Lord did come to
us with truth!' And it shall be cried out to them, 'This is Paradise
which ye have as an inheritance for that which ye have done!'
44 And the fellows of Paradise will call out to the fellows of the
Fire, 'We have now found that what our Lord promised us is true;
have ye found that what your Lord promised you is true?' They
will say, 'Yea!' And a crier from amongst them will cry out, 'The
curse of God is on the unjust
45 who turn from the way of God and crave to make it crooked,
while in the hereafter they do disbelieve!'
46 And betwixt the two there is a veil, and on al Aaraf are men
who know each by marks; and they shall cry out to the fellows of
Paradise, 'Peace be upon you!' they cannot enter it although they
so desire.
47 But when their sight is turned towards the fellows of the Fire,
they say, 'O our Lord! place us not with the unjust people.'
48 And the fellows on al Aaraf will cry out to the men whom
they know by their marks, and say, 'Of no avail to you were your
collections, and what ye were so big with pride about;
49 are these those ye swore that God would not extend mercy to?

Q 7.44

The majority read the word as it appears in the current Arabic Qur'ān: ***na'am*** ("**yea**"). This reading was supported by al-Ṭabarī because it was the most common reading in the Muslim countries at that time.

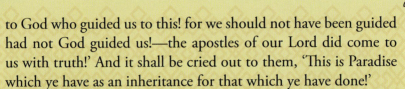

However, some read *na'im* ("yes") with a *kasra* (an "i" accent) on the middle letter *'ain*. It is said that even Muḥammad himself, 'Umar Ibn al-Khaṭṭāb, and 'Alī Ibn Abī Ṭālib used to read it with the *kasra*. They read it as such so it could be distinguished from another word, *naʿam*, which is a name for camels, cattle, and sheep.[25] Ibn Masʿūd read it as *naḥam* ("uh-huh"), replacing the letter *ʿain* (ع) with the letter *ḥa* (ح).[26]

This issue is repeated in Q 7.114: *"He said, 'Yea! and ye shall be of those who draw nigh unto me.'"*

Q 7.46

This verse in the current Arabic Qur'ān is read with the word ***yaṭmaʿūna*** ("**they so desire**"). In addition to the above rendering, some read the same above word as *yuṭāmiʿūna*.[27] There are also other renderings: *ṭāmiʿūna* and *sākhiṭūna*.[28]

The current Arabic Qur'ān shows the word *yaṭmāʿūna,* meaning "to hope for something." The rendering *yuṭāmiʿūna* means that they make one another covet. Another rendering, *sākhiṭuna*, expresses a situation different than hoping. Instead, it means "angry" or "disgruntled."

Q 7.48

Many read this verse with the word *tastakthirūna* ("to deem excessive," as in excessive time or money), which comes from the word *kathra* ("abundance, large quantity").[29]

The current Arabic Qur'ān uses ***tastakbirūna*** ("[to be] **so big with pride**") which means "to be haughty," while the variant reading means "to find it to be much or to begrudge." This difference in the rendering of the word is repeated again in Q 7.48.[30]

Comment on Verse 50 of Sūra al-Aʿrāf

I wonder, where are the ones to whom the blindness, muteness and deafness are attributed in the verse [Q 17.97]....Despite the fact that they are in the tortures of hellfire and, from the horrors of hell, they are still able to see the people of al-Janna in their bliss and ask them in a clear Arabic tongue to "Pour down to us water or anything that Allah doth provide for your sustenance." [Q 7.50 states:] *"But the fellows of the Fire shall cry out to the fellows of Paradise, 'Pour out upon us water, or something of what God has provided you with.' They will say, 'God has prohibited them both to those who misbelieve....'"*

(ʿAbd al-Nūr, *Miḥnatī maʿ al-Qur'ān wa maʿ Allah fī al-Qur'ān* 174-175)

[Q 7.50 contradicts Q 17.97, which states *"and we will gather them upon the resurrection day upon their faces, blind, and dumb, and deaf; their resort is hell."* In Q 7.50 the ones in hellfire see and speak; in Q 17.97 they are blind and dumb.]

Enter ye Paradise; there is no fear for you, nor shall ye be grieved.'
50 But the fellows of the Fire shall cry out to the fellows of Paradise, 'Pour out upon us water, or something of what God has provided you with.' They will say, 'God has prohibited them both to those who misbelieve;
51 who took their religion for a sport and a play; whom the life of the world beguiled.'—To-day do we forget them as they forgot the meeting of this day, and for that they did deny our signs!
52 Now we have brought them a book explaining it in knowledge, a guidance and a mercy to a people who believe.
53 Do they wait now for aught but its interpretation?—on the day when its interpretation shall come, those who forgot it before will say, 'There did come to us the apostles of our Lord in truth, have we intercessors to intercede for us? or, could we return, we would do otherwise than we did.' They have lost themselves, and that which they devised has strayed away from them.
54 Verily, your Lord is God who created the heavens and the earth in six days; then He made for the Throne. He covers night with the day—it pursues it incessantly—and the sun and the moon and the stars are subject to His bidding. Aye!—His is the creation and the bidding,—blessed be God the Lord of the worlds!
55 Call on your Lord humbly and secretly, verily, He loves not the transgressors.
56 And do not evil in the earth after it has been righted; and call upon Him with fear and earnestness; verily, the mercy of God is nigh unto those who do well.
57 He it is who sends forth the winds as heralds before His mercy; until when they lift the heavy cloud which we drive to a dead land, and send down thereon water, and bring forth therewith every kind of fruit;—thus do we bringforth the dead; haply ye may remember.

Q 7.54

The verse describes the attribute of Allah that he has the right to create and command. Based on this idea, the linguists said that the words of Allah are ancient (eternal), not caused (or created). They declared that Allah "distinguished between creating and commanding, and if the commanding was created, it would not be right to make a distinction between the two."

Traditional Sunnī scholars rejected this opinion. Therefore, a theological discussion arose concerning the essence and nature of Allah's word. This discussion can be found in al-Rāzī's commentary.[31]

This verse is an example that shows the lack of clear vision regarding the absolute oneness of Allah as portrayed in the Qur'ān.

Q 7.55

The current Arabic Qur'ān uses the word ***khufyatan*** ("**secretly**"). There are some readers, however, who use the word *khifyatan*.[32] But to call [Allah in prayer] *khifyatan* means to call on him in fear and reverence. Calling on God ought to be in reverence, whether one calls on him privately or publicly. However, both renderings do not require the presence of the two conditions simultaneously. One demands reverence, while the other commands it to be in private. Based on what the text appears to say, a Muslim might call on Allah in private but not necessarily in a state of reverence.

This problematic issue with word choice is repeated in Q 7.205: "*And remember thy Lord within thyself humbly and with fear,*" where the word ***khiyfatan*** ("**with fear**"), this time, is read by some as *khufyatan* ("secretly").[33]

Q 7.57

One group read this expression from the current Arabic Qur'ān as ***bushran*** ("**heralds** [of glad tidings]"). This reading has several forms: *bushuran, bashran,* and *bushra*.[34] All these forms mean "to give glad tidings."[35] In this verse, the "winds that give glad tidings" are the ones that give the good news that rain is coming.

Ibn Mas'ūd and Ibn 'Abbās also read the verse with *nushran* ("widespread") instead of *bushran*.[36] This phrase also has several forms: *nushuran*, *nushran*, and *nasharan*.[37] All these different forms mean "spreading."

Question: Does the wind spread the rain or does it herald the glad tidings that are coming?

[58] And the good land brings forth its vegetation by the permission of its Lord; and that which is vile brings forth naught but
scarcity. Thus do we turn about our signs for a people who are
grateful.
[59] We did send Noah unto his people, and he said, 'O my people! serve God, ye have no god but Him; verily, I fear for you the
torment of the mighty day.'
[60] Said the chiefs of his people, 'Verily, we do surely see you in
obvious error.'
[61] Said he, 'O my people! there is no error in me; but I am an
apostle from the Lord of the worlds.
[62] I preach to you the messages of my Lord, and I give you sincere advice; and I know from God what ye know not.
[63] What! do ye wonder that there came to you a reminder from
your Lord by a man from amongst yourselves, to warn you, and
that ye may fear? but haply ye may receive mercy.'
[64] But they called him a liar, and we rescued him and those who
were with him in the ark; and we drowned those who said our
signs were lies, verily, they were a blind people.
[65] And unto 'Ad (we sent) their brother Hud, who said, 'O my
people! serve God, ye have no god save Him; what! will ye not
then fear?'
[66] Said the chiefs of those who misbelieved amongst his people,
'Verily, we see thee in folly, and, verily, we certainly think thou art
of the liars.'
[67] He said, 'O my people! there is no folly in me; but I am an
apostle from the Lord of the worlds;
[68] I preach to you the messages of your Lord; and, verily, I am
to you a faithful adviser.
[69] What! do ye then wonder that there comes to you a reminder
from your Lord by a man from amongst yourselves, to warn you?
remember when He made you vicegerents after Noah's people and

increased you in length of stature; remember, then, the benefits of
God,—haply ye may prosper!'

70 They said, 'Hast thou come to us that we may worship God
alone, and leave what our fathers used to worship? then bring us
what thou dost threaten us with, if thou art of those who tell the
truth!'

71 He said, 'There shall fall upon you from your Lord horror and
wrath; do ye wrangle with me about names, which ye and your fathers have named yourselves, for which God sent down no power;
wait then expectant, and I with you will wait expectant too!

72 But we rescued him and those with him, by mercy from ourselves, and we cut off the hindermost parts of those who said our
signs were lies and who were not believers.'

73 Unto Thamud (we sent) their brother Zali'h, who said,
'O my people! worship God; ye have no god but Him: there has
come to you a manifest sign from your Lord. This she-camel of
God's is a sign for you; leave her then to eat in the land of God,
and touch her not with evil, or there will overtake you grievous
woe.

74 And remember how he made you vicegerents after 'Ad and
stablished you in the earth, so that ye took for yourselves castles on
its plains and hewed out mountains into houses; and remember
the benefits of God, and waste not the land, despoiling it.'

75 Said the chiefs of those who were big with pride from amongst
his people to those who were weak,—to those amongst them who
believed, 'Do ye know that Zali'h is sent from his Lord?' They
said, 'We do believe in that with which he is sent.'

76 Said those who were big with pride, 'Verily, in what ye do
believe we disbelieve.'

77 Then they did hamstring the camel, and rebelled against the
bidding of their Lord and said, 'O Zalih! bring us what thou didst
threaten us with, if thou art of those who are sent.'

[78] Then the earthquake took them, and in the morning they lay prone in their dwellings;
[79] and he turned away from them and said, 'O my people! I did preach to you the message of my Lord, and I gave you good advice! but ye love not sincere advisers.'
[80] And Lot, when he said to his people, 'Do ye approach an abomination which no one in all the world ever anticipated you in?
[81] verily, ye approach men with lust rather than women—nay, ye are a people who exceed.'
[82] But his people's answer only was to say, 'Turn them out of your village, verily, they are a people who pretend to purity.'
[83] But we saved him and his people, except his wife, who was of those who lingered;
[84] and we rained down upon them a rain;—see then how was the end of the sinners!
[85] And unto Midian did we send their brother Sho'haib, who said, 'O my people! serve God, ye have no god save Him. There has come to you a manifest sign from your Lord; then give good weight and measure, and be not niggardly of your gifts to men, and do not evil in the earth after it has been righted. That is better for you if ye are believers;
[86] and sit not down in every path, threatening and turning from the path of God those who believe in Him, and craving to make it crooked. Remember when ye were few and He multiplied you; and see what was the end of the evildoers!
[87] And if there be a party of you who believe in what I am sent with, and a party who believe not, then wait patiently until God judges between us, for He is the best of judges.'
[88] Said the crowd of those who were big with pride amongst His people, 'We will of a surety turn thee out, O Sho'haib! and those who believe with thee, from our village; or else thou shalt return unto our faith.' Said he, 'What even if we be averse there-

from?
89 We shall have devised a lie against God if we return unto your
faith, after God has saved us from it; and what should ail us that
we should return thereto, unless that God our Lord should please?
our Lord embraces everything in His knowledge;—on God do
we rely. O our Lord! open between us and between our people in
truth, for Thou art the best of those who open.'
90 And the chiefs of those who disbelieved amongst his people
said, 'If ye follow Sho'haib, verily, ye shall be the losers;'
91 then there took them the earthquake, and in the morning
they lay in their dwellings prone.
92 Those who called Sho'haib a liar, (were) as though they had
not dwelt therein!—Those who called Sho'haib a liar, they were
the losers then!
93 And he turned away from them and said, 'O my people! I
preached to you the messages of my Lord, and I gave you good
advice; how should I be vexed for a people who do misbelieve?'
94 We have not sent unto a city any prophet except we overtook
the people thereof with trouble and distress, that haply they might
humble themselves;
95 and then did we give them, in exchange for evil, good, until
they increased and said, 'Distress and joy both touched our fathers;' then we overtook them suddenly ere they could perceive.—
96 Had the people of the town but believed and feared, we
would have opened up for them blessings from the heavens and
from the earth; but they said it was a lie, so we overtook them for
that which they had earned.
97 Were the people of these cities then secure that our violence
would not come on them by night, while they slept?
98 were the people of these cities secure that our violence would
not come on them in the morning whilst they played?
99 were they secure from the craft of God? none feel secure from

the craft of God except a people that shall lose.
100 Is it not shown to those who inherit the earth after its (former) people, that, did we please, we would smite them in their
sins, and would set a stamp upon their hearts, and then they
should not hear?
101 These cities, we do relate to thee their stories. There came to
them our apostles with manifest signs; but they did not at all believe in what they called a lie before.—Thus doth God set a stamp
upon the hearts of those who misbelieve.
102 Nor did we find in most of them a covenant; but we did find
most of them workers of abomination.
103 Then we raised up after them Moses with our signs to Pharaoh and his chiefs; but they dealt unjustly therewith, and see
what was the end of the evildoers!
104 Moses said, 'O Pharaoh! verily, I am an apostle from the Lord
of the worlds;
105 it is not right for me to speak against God aught but the
truth. I have come to you with a manifest sign from my Lord; send
then the children of Israel with me.'
106 Said he, 'If thou hast come with a sign, then bring it, if thou
art of those who speak the truth.'
107 Then he threw his rod down, and lo! it was an obvious snake;
108 and he drew out his hand, and lo! it was white to the behold-
ers.
109 Said the chiefs of Pharaoh's people, 'Verily, this is surely a
knowing magician;
110 he desires to turn you out of your land;—what is it then ye
bid?'
111 They said, 'Give him and his brother some hope; and send
into the cities to collect
112 and bring you every knowing magician.'
113 And the magician came to Pharaoh and said, 'Is there indeed

a reward for us if we are conquerors?'
114 He said, 'Yea! and ye shall be of those who draw nigh unto me.'
115 They said, 'O Moses! wilt thou cast down (thy rod) or shall
we be (first) to throw?'
116 Said he, 'Throw down;' and when they threw down, they did
enchant the people's eyes, and made them dread, and brought a
mighty magic.
117 But we inspired Moses (saying), 'Throw down thy rod, and it
will gulp down that which they devise;'
118 and the truth stood fast, and vain was that which they had done;
119 and they were conquered there, and turned back feeling small!
120 and the magicians threw themselves down adoring.
121 Said they, 'We believe in the Lord of the worlds,
122 the Lord of Moses and Aaron!'
123 Said Pharaoh, 'Do ye believe in him ere I give you leave? This
is craft which ye have devised in the land, to turn its people out
therefrom, but soon shall ye know!
124 I will cut off your hands and your feet from opposite sides,
then I will crucify you altogether!'

Q 7.117-122

This story recounts a competition arranged by Pharaoh between Moses and a band of sorcerers that ends in Moses' victory. As a result, the sorcerers declare their belief in "*the Lord of Moses and Aaron*" (Q 7.117-122; Q 20.69-73; Q 26.45-48).

This competition is also mentioned in Q 10.83, but the text in this passage states a different result: "*But none believed in Moses, save a race of his own people* [meaning the people of Israel]."

Therefore, did the sorcerers believe or disbelieve after Moses won the competition?

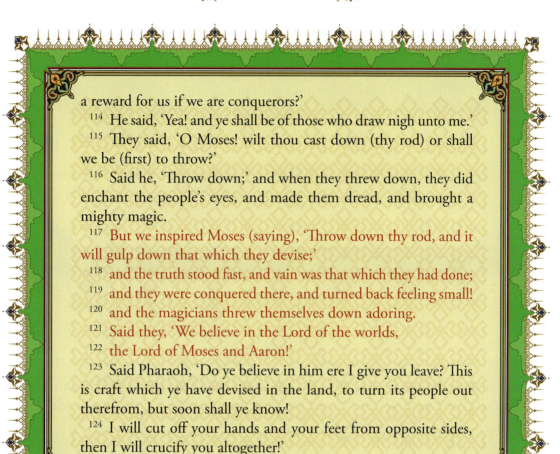

125 They said, 'Verily, we unto our Lord return!
126 nor dost thou take vengeance on us, save for that we believe
in the signs of our Lord, when they come to us. 'O our Lord! pour
out upon us patience, and take us to Thyself resigned.'
127 And the chiefs of Pharaoh's people said, 'Will ye leave Moses
and his people, to do evil in the land, and to leave thee and thy
gods?' Said he, 'We will have their sons slain and their women we
will let live, for, verily, we are triumphant over them.'

Q 7.127

The majority of the readers read this expression from the current Arabic Qur'ān as ***ālihataka*** ("**thy gods**"), which is the plural of the word *ilah* ("god"). It is a reference to the gods that Pharaoh worshipped.[38]

Ibn Mas'ūd, 'Alī Ibn Abī Ṭālib, and Ibn 'Abbās also read it as *ilhataka*, with two explanations:

- "Pharaoh, the people cease to worship [deify] you." This is the opinion of Ibn 'Abbās, who criticized the reading of the current reading using "gods," as he said that Pharaoh "was worshipped; he did not worship."
- They also said *ilhataka* is in reference to the sun that Pharaoh used to worship, as the sun was called *ilha.*[39]

Question: Is the verse here talking about Pharaoh as the one who is worshipped, or is it talking about the gods that Pharaoh worshipped?

Q 7.127

This verse says that some Egyptian leaders asked Pharaoh if he would take any action against Moses and the Israelites. The passage does not clearly state what Moses and the Israelites had done, referring only to their spreading "mischief," which apparently included their abandoning the worship of Egyptian gods. But earlier, in verse 105, it speaks of Moses coming before Pharaoh with a *"manifest sign"* and asking Pharoah to *"send then the children of Israel with"* him (Moses). The verse 127 adds that the

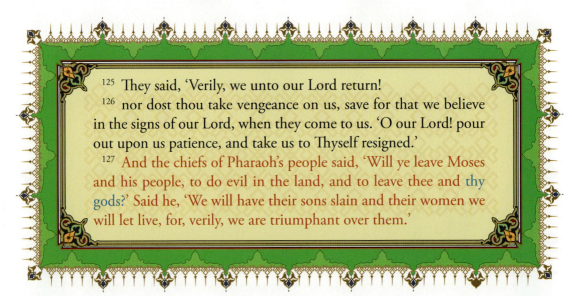

Egyptians had expressed fears that if they ignored the activities of Moses, it might have a negative impact on their religion and the political status of their country. So, Pharaoh replied, *"'We will have their sons slain and their women we will let live, for, verily, we are triumphant over them'"* (Q 7.127).

According to this verse, Pharaoh decided to kill the sons of the children of Israel and enslave their women *after* Moses began his spiritual mission. This fact is confirmed by another verse: *"'Kill the sons of those who believe with him, and let their women live!'"* (Q 40.25).

From these two verses it is apparent that the command to kill the sons of Israel occurred after Moses came to present *"the truth."*

However, in other parts of the Qur'ān it states that Pharaoh ordered the killing of the boys while Moses was still in the cradle—long before Moses' mission began as a prophet of God. The following verses recount the instructions given to Moses' mother to spare him from the slaughter ordered by Pharaoh:

> *When we inspired thy mother with what we inspired her, "Hurl him into the ark, and hurl him into the sea; and the sea shall cast him on the shore, and an enemy of mine and of his shall take him...."* (Q 20.38-39)

Again the Qur'ān repeats this version of the story: *"And we inspired the mother of Moses, 'Suckle him; and when thou art afraid for him then throw him into the river, and fear not and grieve not; verily, we are going to restore him to thee, and to make him of the apostles!'"* (Q 28.7).

Thus, in some places the Qur'ān states that the order to kill the male children of the Israelites occurred after Moses began his spiritual mission, while in other places, the Qur'ān states that Pharaoh decided to kill the male Israeli children when Moses was still an infant.

Most Islāmic commentators ignored the differences between these verses. However, al-Ṭabarī notes that there are some contradictions among them. Therefore, he attempted to resolve the issue by stating that the decision to kill the boys, which he said came after the coming of Moses with *"the truth,"* was the second decision; Pharaoh's decision to kill them was only aimed at "the sons of those who believed in Moses." But al-Ṭabarī does not specify which Qur'ānic text suggests that this killing was the second decision. Moreover, there is no reference in these verses, even implicitly, to validate al-Ṭabarī's statement that the second matter is "about the killing of the sons of those who believed in Moses."[40]

In his comment on Q 40.25, al-Zamakhsharī states that the decision to kill the boys was the second decision, without providing any specifics or support for his point of view.[41]

Their justification for this contradiction, as presented by al-Ṭabarī and al-Zamakhsharī, has no basis in the Qur'ān and, therefore, these two scholars were unable to substantiate their suggestions with a verse. Thus, the contradiction remains a mystery to be solved.

128 Said Moses unto his people, 'Ask for aid from God and be patient; verily, the earth is God's! He gives it for an inheritance to whom He pleases of His servants, and the future is for those who fear.'
129 They said, 'We have been hurt before thou didst come to us, and since thou hast come to us.' Said he, 'It may be that your Lord will destroy your foe, and will make you succeed him in the earth; and He will see how ye act.'
130 We had overtaken Pharaoh's people with the years (of dearth) and scarcity of fruits, that haply they might remember;
131 but when there came to them a good thing they said, 'This is ours;' and if there befel them an evil, they took the augury from

Q 7.128-129

This text refers to a promise made by Moses to the people of Israel, stating that they will inherit the land of Egypt. While the verse does not specifically say "Egypt," verse 129 talks about Allah destroying the enemy (in this case, Pharaoh) and giving the land of the enemy to the people of Israel, so a reference to Egypt can be assumed.

Some of the commentators defined this promise:

AL-BAYḌĀWI: "It is a promise of victory and a reminder to them of his [Allah's] pledge to destroy the Copts and bequeath to them their [the Copts'] land—to fulfill this promise. It is said that Egypt was a conquest for them in the time of David...."[42]

AL-RĀZĪ: "This is a promise made by Moses to entice his people that Allah will bequeath them the land of Pharaoh after his [Pharaoh's] destruction."[43]

AL-ṬABARĪ: "Moses says, 'Perhaps Allah will bequeath the land upon you if you show patience in the face of the misfortune incurred upon you and your children at the hand of Pharaoh...if you keep this in mind and perfect your religion, Pharaoh's land and his people are yours as a reward.'"[44]

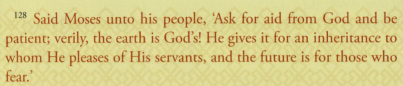

Moses and those with him;—is not their augury only in God's
hands?—but most of them know not.
132 And they said, 'Whatever thou dost bring us as a sign to enchant us therewith, yet will we not believe in thee.'
133 Then we sent upon them the flood and the locusts and the
lice and the frogs and the blood,—signs detailed; but they were
big with pride and were a people who did sin.
134 And when there fell upon them the plague, they said, 'O Moses! call upon thy Lord for us, as He has covenanted with thee;
verily, if thou dost remove the plague from us, we will believe in
thee; and we will assuredly send with thee the children of Israel.'

This promise (inheritance of Egypt) is not mentioned in the Torah or in any other source. Rather, such a promise was made about the Holy Land (the land of Canaan). The Qur'ān itself refers to this other promise in several verses: "*And we gave as an inheritance unto the people who had been weak, the eastern quarters of the earth and the western quarters thereof…*" (Q 7.137).

It is the land that the commentators declare is in al-Shām (Syria).[45]

Q 7.133

This verse mentions only five plagues that fell on the Egyptians: "*Then we sent upon them the flood and the locusts and the lice and the frogs and the blood….*"

However, according to the biblical account, ten plagues were sent against the Egyptians: blood, frogs, mosquitoes, gnats, flies, the death of livestock, boils, hail, locusts, darkness, and the death of "every firstborn son in Egypt" (Exod. 7-11).

This verse attributes the miracle of the flood to Moses. But again, according to the biblical account, this cataclysmic event happened during the time of Noah.

The limitation of the plagues to only five and the attribution of the flood to Moses are evidence of inaccurate recording of biblical and historical information.

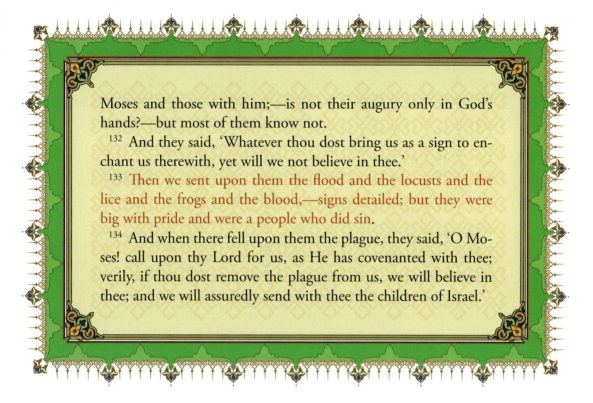

[135] But when we removed from them the plague until the appointed time which they should reach, lo! then they broke their promise.
[136] But we took vengeance on them, and we drowned them in the sea, for that they said our signs were lies and were careless thereof.
[137] And we gave as an inheritance unto the people who had been weak, the eastern quarters of the earth and the western quarters thereof, which we had blest; and the good word of thy Lord was fulfilled on the children of Israel, for that they were patient; and we destroyed that which Pharaoh and his people had made and that which they had piled.
[138] And with the children of Israel we passed across the sea; and they came unto a people devoted to their idols, and said, 'O Moses! make for us a god as they have gods.' Said he, 'Verily, ye are ignorant people.'
[139] Verily, these—destroyed shall be that which they are given to; and vain is that which they have done.
[140] He said, 'Other than God then do ye crave for a god, when He has preferred you above the worlds?'
[141] And when we saved you from Pharaoh's people who wrought you evil woe, killing your sons, and letting your women live; and in that was a mighty trial from your Lord.
[142] And we appointed for Moses thirty nights, and completed them with ten (more), so that the time appointed by his Lord was completed to forty nights. And Moses said unto his brother Aaron, 'Be thou my vicegerent amongst my people, and do what is right, and follow not the path of the evildoers.'
[143] And when Moses came to our appointment, and his Lord spake unto him, he said, 'O my Lord! show me,—that I may look on thee!' He said, Thou canst not see me; but look upon the mountain, and if it remain steady in its place, thou shalt see me;' but when his Lord appeared unto the mountain He made it dust,

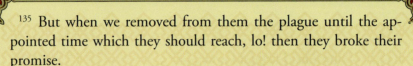

and Moses fell down in a swoon! And when he came to himself,
he said, 'Celebrated be thy praise! I turn repentant unto Thee, and
I am the first of those who are resigned.'
144 He said, 'O Moses! verily, I have chosen thee over the people
with my messages and my words, take then what I have brought
thee, and be of those who thank.'
145 And we wrote for him upon tablets an admonition concerning
everything, and a detailing of everything: 'Take them then
with firmness, and bid thy people take them for what is best thereof.
I will show you the abode of those who work abominations;
146 I will turn from my signs those who are big with pride in the
earth without right; and if they see every sign they shall not believe
therein, and if they see the path of rectitude they shall not take it
for a path; but if they see the path of error they shall take it for a
path;—that is because they have said our signs are lies and have

Q 7.141

The majority read this expression from the current Arabic Qur'ān as ***anjaynākum*** ("**we saved you**"), using the "n" of magnification (in reference to Allah). The Iraqi school followed this path. But in the codices of al-Shām (Syria) and Ḥijāz[D], it is read as *anjākum* ("he rescued you").[46] The difference is that the first reading is given in the first person with Allah as the speaker, whereas the second is given in the third person, speaking about Allah.

Q 7.145

This verse states that Allah communicated his message to Moses "*upon tablets an admonition concerning everything.*" But according to the Torah, what was communicated by God was written on only two tablets, not multiple tablets, and the Ten Commandments were written without details (Exod. 31.18, 34.1).

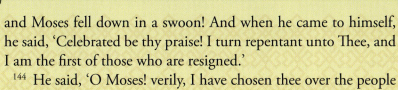

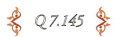

been careless of them.'

147 But those who say our signs and the meeting of the last day are lies,—vain are their works: shall they be rewarded save for that which they have done?

148 And Moses' people after him took to themselves of their ornaments a corporeal calf that lowed; did they not see that it could not speak with them, nor could it guide them in the path? They took it and they were unjust;

149 but when they bit their hands with fruitless rage and saw that they had gone astray, they said,' Verily, if our Lord have not compassion on us and forgive us we shall surely be of those who lose!'

150 And when Moses returned unto his people angry and grieved, he said, 'Evil is it that ye have done after me! Would ye hasten on the bidding of your Lord?' and he threw down the tablets and took his brother by the head to drag him towards him, but he said, 'O son of my mother! verily, the people weakened me and wellnigh killed me; make not then mine enemies glad about me, and put me not with the unjust people.'

151 He said, 'O Lord! pardon me and my brother, and let us enter into Thy mercy; for Thou art the most merciful of the merciful.

152 Verily, these have taken to themselves a calf; there shall reach them wrath from their Lord, and abasement in the life of this world; for thus do we reward those who forge a lie.

153 But those who have done bad works, and then turn again after them and believe,—verily, thy Lord, after that, is forgiving and merciful.'

154 And when Moses' wrath calmed down he took the tables, in the inscription of which was guidance and mercy for those who dread their Lord.

155 And Moses chose from his people seventy men for our appointment; and when the earthquake took them he said, 'O my Lord! hadst Thou willed, Thou hadst destroyed them before and

me. Wilt Thou destroy us for what the fools amongst us have done? This is naught but Thy trial, wherewith Thou dost lead astray whom Thou pleasest and guidest whom Thou pleasest; Thou art our patron! forgive us and have mercy on us, for Thou art the best of those who do forgive!

156 'And write down for us in this world good, and in the future too; verily, we are guided unto Thee.' He said, 'My punishment—with it I fall on whom I will; and my mercy embraceth everything; and I will write it down for those who fear, and who give alms, and those who in our signs believe,—

157 who follow the Apostle—the illiterate prophet, whom they find written down with them in the law and the gospel, bidding them what is reasonable and forbidding them what is wrong, and making lawful for them what is good, and making unlawful evil

Q 7.148

This verse recounts the story of a calf idol being made from the golden ornaments. The verse refers to the calf as a body "with a *khuwār* [mooing sound]."[47] In another reading ascribed to 'Alī Ibn Abī Ṭalib, the verse reads "he has a *ju'ār* sound [holler or bleat sound]," meaning "to shout."[48] The part dealing with the sound is not mentioned in the Torah, which is likely where this story originated. Perhaps this Qur'ānic account was adapted from the oral traditions told by the Jewish tribes who lived in the Arabian Peninsula. (Compare with Exodus 32.1-4.)

Q 7.157

The verse describes Muḥammad as the *ummī* prophet, translated by Palmer as *"the illiterate prophet."*

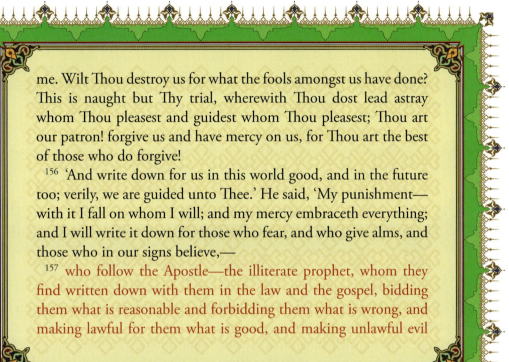

The exegetes explain that the meaning of the *ummī* prophet is one who is sent to the Arabs (who were an illiterate people).[49] The verse adds that the description of Muḥammad as an *ummī* prophet is found in the holy books, the Jewish Torah and the

things; and setting down for them their burdens and the yokes which were upon them;—to those who believe in him and aid him and help him and follow the law which has been sent down with him—they shall be the prosperous.'

158 Say, 'O ye folk! verily, I am the Apostle of God unto you all'—of Him whose is the kingdom of the heavens and the earth, there is no god but He! He quickens and He kills! believe then in God and His Apostle, the illiterate prophet,—who believes in God and

Christian gospels: *"in the law* [the Torah] *and the gospel."* However, examination of this claim presents the following inconsistencies:

- If the description of Muḥammad is not found in the *"law and the gospel,"* that omission might suggest that the Jews and Christians removed Muḥammad's description from their holy books. How then did the religious people of both religions, Judaism and Christianity, conspire to complete such a task?
- For the sake of argument, if the Christians and the Jews had conspired to make this alteration, would not some Christians and some Jews refuse to accept such alterations to their holy books and leave their religion or create a separate sect?
- Again, for the sake of argument, if both sides conspired and removed the description and, further assume, that no religious split took place as a result of such an alteration, why didn't the Christian cults use such an occasion to show that they held the "true" scriptures (containing Muḥammad's description) and use that to prove the veracity and legitimacy of their claims?
- Since Muḥammad revealed this "secret" (his claim that there is written record in the holy books of his legitimacy), he must have had these writings hidden somewhere. Where are they now?
- In defense, one might reply that there is a narrative that mentions the omitted text. 'Abd Allah Ibn 'Amr Ibn al-'Āṣ read, *"'O thou prophet! verily, we have sent thee as a witness and a herald of glad tidings and a warner'"*(Q 33.45). To this verse, commentator al-Qurṭubī adds that Muḥammad is "a refuge to the gentiles, ...[Allah's] servant and...messenger....attribute is *al-mutawakil* [("one who trusts or relies")]: neither harsh nor coarse, nor clamorous in the markets...[and] does not repay an iniquity for an iniquity but pardons and forgives."[50] Ka'b al-Aḥbār repeated this text with slight variations in expressions.

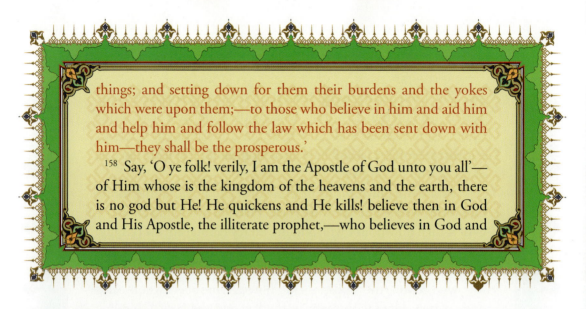

Notice the following about this text:

First, it is spoken by two witnesses, 'Abd Allah Ibn 'Amr Ibn al-'Āṣ and Ka'b al-Ahbar. However, 'Abd Allah Ibn 'Amr Ibn al-'Āṣ was not a Jew. He and his father were pagans following the religion of the Quraysh. All that is attributed to him is that he "read the Qur'ān and the previous books."[51] Which previous books did he read and in what language?

Second, the text based on this reading by 'Abd Allah Ibn 'Amr Ibn al-'Āṣ does not specify Muḥammad but can be applied to a large number of people.

Third, how much of this reading could truly be applied to Muḥammad himself? Did he truly "not repay an iniquity for an iniquity but pardoned and forgave," or does his life record (*sīra*) show otherwise? (See comment on Q 5.33, page 381)

Fourth, why don't others mention this particular text? The composition of the Bible took about fifteen hundred years. If Muḥammad or his description was mentioned in any of the Bible's books, the people through the ages would have written and discussed the person whom "they find written down." Therefore, even if the Jews and the Christians were to intentionally remove such a text from the Bible, such a mention would be recorded in the historical records and the narratives of the nations and the poems of the poets.

Fifth, when the Old Testament speaks about a prophet who would come after Moses, it speaks of him as a prophet from among the Israelites: "The LORD your God will raise up for you a prophet like me from among your fellow Israelites…" (*NLT*, Deut. 18.15). The condition "from among your fellow Israelites" means that the prophet will come from one of the twelve tribes of Israel. Does this condition apply to Muḥammad?

In the New Testament, there is no mention of a prophet to come but an announcement by Christ about the Holy Spirit: "And I will ask the Father, and he will give you another advocate to help you and be with you forever—the Spirit of truth. The world cannot accept him, because it neither sees him nor knows him. But you know him, for he lives with you and will be in you" (John 14.16-17).

Notice that the Holy Spirit, who will be forever with those addressed, cannot be a person who lives for a short while in the Arabian Peninsula. (Compare the comments on Q 3.3-4 and Q 5.15.)

in His words—then follow him that haply ye may be guided.
159 Amongst Moses' people is a nation guided in truth, and
thereby act they justly.
160 And we cut them up into twelve tribes, each a nation; and
we revealed unto Moses, when his people asked him for drink,
'Strike with thy staff the rock!' and there gushed forth from it
twelve springs, each folk knew their drinking place. And we overshadowed them with the cloud; and sent down upon them the
manna and the quails, 'Eat of the good things we have provided
you with!'—Yet they did not wrong us, but it was themselves they
wronged.
161 And when it was said unto them, 'Dwell in this city and eat
therefrom as ye will, and say 'hi*tt*atun and enter the gate adoring; so
will we pardon you your sins;—we will increase those who do well.'
162 But those amongst them who did wrong changed it for another word than which was said to them; and we sent upon them
a plague from heaven for that they were unjust.
163 Ask them too about the city which stood by the sea, when
they transgressed upon the Sabbath; when their fish came to them
on the Sabbath day sailing straight up to them; but on the days
when they kept not the Sabbath, they came not to them, thus did
we try them for the abominations that they wrought.
164 And when a nation from amongst them said, 'Why do ye warn
a people whom God would destroy, or punish with severe torment?'
they said, 'As an excuse to your Lord, that haply they may fear.'
165 But when they forgot what they had been reminded of, we
saved those who forbade evil, but we overtook those who did
wrong with punishment;—evil was the abomination that they did,
166 but when they rebelled against what they were forbidden, we
said to them, 'Become ye apes, despised and spurned!'

[167] and then thy Lord proclaimed that He would surely send against them till the resurrection day, those who should wreak them evil torment; verily, thy Lord is quick at following up, but, verily, He is forgiving, merciful.

[168] We cut them up in the earth into nations. Of them are the righteous, and of them are the reverse of that; we have tried them

Q 7.160

For more discussion about the incident of the twelve springs, see the comment on Q 2.60, page 184.

Q 7.161

This verse states *"and say 'hittatun and enter the gate adoring. . . .'"* However, the words seem to have been rearranged. Elsewhere in the Qur'ān, the order is stated this way: "*and enter the gate worshipping and say 'hittatun. . . .*" (Q 2.58). (The word *ḥiṭṭatun* is an ambiguous word. Muslim scholars suggest the following possible meanings: asking for forgiveness, humility, or prostrating, to name a few.)

Al-Zamakhsharī comments on this discrepancy: "It is all right if the two expressions are different, as long as there is no contradiction."[52]

Yes, there should be no contradiction. But which of the two terms is more correct according to the linguistic miracle of the Qur'ān? Regardless of which answer is the correct one, we are still left with a more eloquent verse and a less eloquent one.

Question: If God is the author of both of these verses, why is there a less eloquent verse still in the Qur'ān?

Q 7.166

Refer to the comments on Q 2.65, page 188.

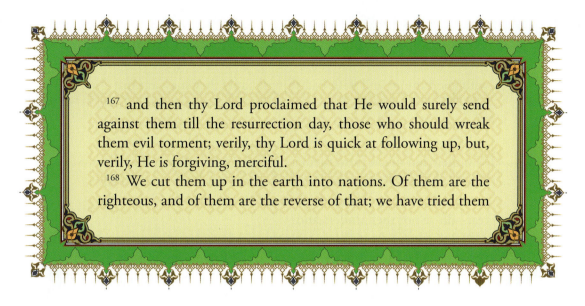

with good things and with bad things; haply they may return.
[169] But there succeeded them successors who inherited the Book!
They take the goods of this lower world and say, 'It will be forgiven
us.' But if the like goods came to them they would take them too!
Was there not taken from them a covenant by the Book, that they
should not say against God aught but the truth? Yet they study
therein! But the abode of the future life is better for those who
fear—do ye not then understand?
[170] But those who hold fast by the Book and are steadfast in
prayer—verily, we will not waste the hire of those who do right.
[171] And when we shook the mountain over them, as though it
were a shadow, and they thought it would fall upon them (saying),
'Take ye what we have given you with firmness, and remember
what is therein; haply ye may fear.'
[172] And when thy Lord took from the children of Adam out of their
loins their seed, and made them bear witness against themselves, 'Am
I not your Lord?' They said, 'Yea! we do bear witness'—lest ye should
say on the day of resurrection, 'Verily, for this we did not care;'
[173] or say, 'Verily, our fathers associated others with God before
us, and we were but their seed after them: wilt Thou then destroy
us for what vaindoers did?'—
[174] Thus do we detail the signs; haply they may return.
[175] Read to them the declaration of him to whom we brought
our signs, and who stepped away therefrom, and Satan followed
him, and he was of those who were beguiled.
[176] Had we pleased we would have exalted him thereby, but he
crouched upon the earth and followed his lust, and his likeness
was as the likeness of a dog, whom if thou shouldst attack he
hangs out his tongue, or if thou should leave him, hangs out his
tongue too. That is the likeness of the people who say our signs are
lies. Tell them then these tales—haply they may reflect.
[177] Evil is the likeness of a people who say our signs are lies;
themselves it is they wrong!

178 [He whom Allah guides, is on the right path. And they whom He leaves in error, these it is who shall be the losers.]
179 We have created for hell many of the ginn and of mankind; they have hearts and they discern not therewith; they have eyes and they see not therewith; they have ears and they hear not therewith; they are like cattle, nay, they go more astray! these it is who care not.
180 But God's are the good names; call on Him then thereby,

Q 7.169

Ibn Mas'ūd and others read the current Arabic Qur'ān's word ***darasū*** ("**they studied**") as *addakarū*.[53] The word *addakarū* means "they memorized and remembered," whereas the reading of the Qur'ān means "they read."

Question: Does this verse require one to read or to remember?

Q 7.176

This verse likens the unbeliever to a dog: *"and his likeness was as the likeness of a dog, whom if thou shouldst attack he hangs out his tongue, or if thou should leave him, hangs out his tongue too..."* (Q 7.176). The verse uses this analogy to imply the lowliness of the unbeliever. It is said that the verse uses this depiction because he "who lolls out his tongue is doing this because of tiredness or thirst. The dog is an exception. It lolls out its tongue, whether tired or rested, in sickness and in health, whether having water or thirsty. Allah used this analogy as an example concerning those who deny his signs."[54]

Question: Does this representation reflect the eloquence of Allah or the eloquence of a son of the desert?

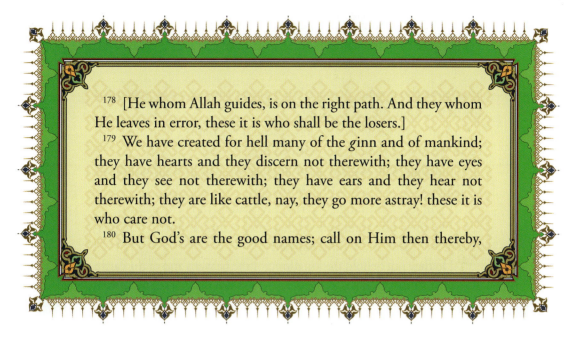

and leave those who pervert His names; they shall be rewarded
for that which they have done.
181 And of those whom we have created is a nation who are guided in truth and thereby act with equity;
182 but they who say our signs are lies, we will bring them down
by degrees from whence they know not.
183 I will let them range;—verily, my stratagem is efficacious!
184 Do they not then reflect that their companion is not possessed? he is but an obvious warner!
185 Do they not behold the kingdoms of the heavens and of the earth,
and what things God has created, and (see that), it may be, their time
is already drawing nigh? in what relation then will they believe?
186 He whom God leads astray there is no guide for him! He
leaves them in their rebellion, blindly wandering on.
187 They will ask you about the Hour, for what time it is fixed?—
say, 'The knowledge thereof is only with my Lord; none shall manifest it at its time but He; it is heavy in the heavens and the earth,
it will not come to you save on a sudden.' They will ask as though
thou wert privy to it, say, 'The knowledge thereof is only with
God,'—but most folk do not know.
188 Say, 'I cannot control profit or harm for myself, save what
God will. If I knew the unseen I should surely have much that is
good, nor would evil touch me; I am but a warner and a herald of
good tidings unto a people who believe.'
189 He it is who created you from one soul, and made therefrom
its mate to dwell therewith; and when he covered her she bore a
light burden and went about therewith; but when it grew heavy
they called on God, Lord of them both, 'Surely if thou givest us a
rightly-shaped child we shall of a surety be of those who thank.'
190 And when He gave them both a rightly-shaped child they
joined partners with Him for that which He had given them, but
exalted be God above that which they associate with Him.

Q 7.180

This verse commands Muslims to let the pagans alone. However, most scholars have said it has been abrogated with the Sword verse, Q 9.5: *"...kill the idolaters wherever ye may find them...."*[55]

Others have said the verse does not command Muslims to let the pagans alone but rather contains a threat and a warning. Therefore, there is no abrogation.[56]

Q 7.183

There are several opinions as to whether this verse is abrogated or conserved.

Within the first viewpoint, which supports abrogation, there is some disagreement about the basis of the claim to abrogation. Some scholars have said that, "*I will let them range*" means too "abandon them, O Muḥammad, and leave them to their own. I will prolong their life without neglecting their transgressions. I will repay them for their transgressions that have increased by their overstepping their boundaries." But scholars supporting this viewpoint believe the verse is abrogated with the Sword verse, *"...kill the idolaters wherever ye may find them...."*[57]

There is another lone viewpoint in favor of abrogation. This scholar believes the "meaning of the verse is an order for Muḥammad to participate [in the killing] with them [his followers]." The scholar who holds this viewpoint also maintains the verse is abrogated with the Sword verse: *"...kill the idolaters wherever ye may find them...."* However, Ibn al-Jawzī rejects this opinion and considers it based on a misunderstanding of the meaning of the verse.[58]

In the second viewpoint, which says the verse is conserved, some scholars believe that what is intended by the word *"stratagem"* was a threat to punish the people who deceive. This is a report (*khabar*), which is always conserved.[59]

Q 7.190

This verse refers to Adam and Eve. (See verse 189.) It tells us that after they were blessed with a son, they associated others with Allah (became idolaters). Again there is a problem in the Arabic text that is not apparent in the English translation. In the first part of the verse, the couple is referred to in the Arabic dual form. But at the end of the verse, it refers to them in the plural form.

What is the escape for this grammatical contradiction? Several commentators offer these explanations:

[191] Will they associate with Him those who cannot create aught,
but are themselves created,
[192] which have no power to help them, and cannot even help
themselves?
[193] But if ye call them unto guidance they will not follow you. It
is the same to them if Thou dost call them or if Thou dost hold thy
tongue.
[194] Those whom ye call on other than God are servants like yourselves. Call on them then, and let them answer you, if so be ye tell
the truth!
[195] Have they feet to walk with? or have they hands to hold with?
or have they eyes to see with? or have they ears to hear with? Call
upon your partners; then plot against me, and do not wait.
[196] Verily, my patron is God, who hath sent down the Book, and
He is the patron of the righteous.
[197] But those whom ye call on beside Him cannot help you, nor
can they even help themselves.
[198] But if ye call them unto the guidance they will not hear, thou
mayest see them looking towards thee, yet they do not see.

- "Most scholars said, *'but exalted be God above that which they associate with Him.' 'They'* means the idolaters among Arabs specifically, and he is not talking about Adam and Eve."[60]
- According to al-Ṭabarī, "The idolaters that ascribe partners with him [Allah] did not mean Adam and Eve."[61]

We find in this verse the absence of unity of thought. Even if it were possible to find justification for such literary leaps from one group to another and from one epoch to another within a single sūra, how can one justify the lack of care for the logical historical sequence within the same verse? When the verse speaks of Adam and Eve, why does it then insert the subject of the Arab pagans, particularly those "idolaters" who, without dispute, lived in a later era and with different convictions from Adam and Eve?

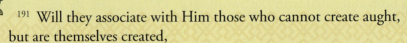

[199] Take to pardon, and order what is kind, and shun the ignorant;
[200] and if an incitement from the devil incites you, then seek
refuge in God: verily, He both hears and knows.
[201] Verily, those who fear God, if a wraith from the devil touch,
mention Him, and lo! they see.
[202] And their brethren he shall increase in error, then they shall
not desist.
[203] Shouldst Thou not bring them a sign they say, 'Hast Thou
not yet made choice of one?' Say, 'I only follow what is inspired to
me by my Lord. These are perceptions from my Lord, and a guidance and a mercy to a people who believe.'
[204] And when the Qur'ān is read, then listen thereto and keep
silence; haply ye may obtain mercy.
[205] And remember thy Lord within thyself humbly and with fear,
not openly in words, in the morning and in the evening; and be
not of those who do not care.
[206] Verily, they who are with my Lord are not too big with pride
for His service, but they do celebrate His praise, and Him they do
adore.

The Islāmic apologists unintentionally criticize the eloquence of the Qur'ān, for they affirm the existence of such discontinuity in a single verse.

Q 7.196

Ibn Mas'ūd read this as "Verily, my patron is God, who hath sent down the Book in truth," by adding *bilḥaqqi* ("in or with truth").[62]

Q 7.199

Questions regarding the abrogation of this verse revolve around two separate issues: the meaning of *"pardon"* and the meaning of *"ignorant."*

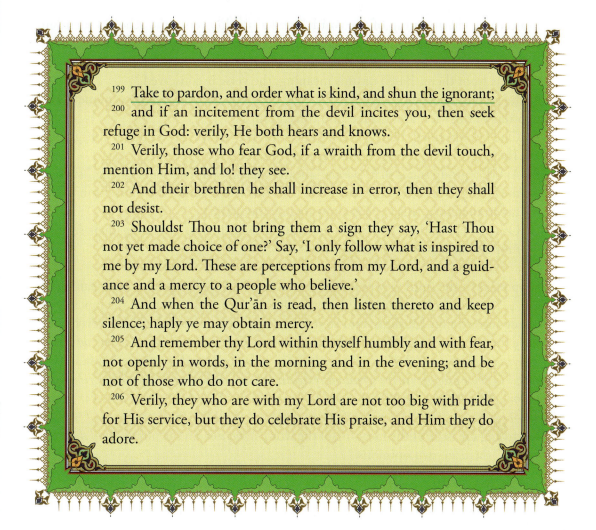

Concerning the meaning of the word *"pardon"* in this verse, the scholars mention three viewpoints. In the first, scholars say the verse is asking the reader to accept the moral standards of others without demanding extreme moral requirements and conditions from them. Based on this meaning, the verse is conserved.[63]

In the second viewpoint, scholars say that the term *"pardon"* refers to money. The supporters of this view are divided into three groups:

A. One group ruled that *"pardon"* refers to the *zakāt*, or required almsgiving. Therefore, the meaning of this verse is conserved.[64]

B. Another group states that *"pardon"* means *ṣadaqa*, or a "charitable giving," such as the giving of an offering to the poor. This was taken before the imposition of the *zakāt*; therefore, this verse is abrogated by the *zakāt*.[65]

C. Others believe that *"pardon"* is an order to Muslims to give away their surplus money, but it is abrogated by the *zakāt*.[66]

Supporters of the third viewpoint are even further divided regarding the meaning of *"pardon."* Some scholars maintain that what is intended by this verse is the practice of leniency toward non-Muslims, and so it is saying to leave them alone. However, they believe the verse is abrogated with the Sword verse, Q 9.5: *"...kill the idolaters wherever ye may find them...."*[67] Yet, other scholars say it is abrogated by virtue of these two verses: "*O thou prophet! strive strenuously against the misbelievers and the hypocrites, and be stern against them...*" (Q 9.73) and *"O ye who believe! fight those who are near to you of the misbelievers, and let them find in you sternness..."* (Q 9.123).[68]

Regarding the issue of the meaning of the word *"ignorant"* in the phrase *"and shun the ignorant,"* there are two opinions:

In the first opinion, *"ignorant"* refers to the idolaters. Therefore, the order to "turn away" from the idolaters is abrogated with Q 9.5, the Sword verse, *"...kill the idolaters wherever ye may find them...."*[69]

In the second opinion, the word *"ignorant"* means fools. Therefore, the verse is conserved.[70] In his work, al-Makkī also inclines toward this opinion.[71]

Introduction

This sūra was named al-Anfāl, meaning "spoils of war," because it begins by talking about them and contains explanations as to how spoils of war should be distributed. Other narrators call it sūra Badr because its revelation is said to have been given after that battle.[1] In fact, the largest portion of this sūra was given immediately after the Battle of Badr.[2] However, a portion of the text, verses 64-65, was revealed before the battle, which implies that the verses of the sūra were not organized in chronological order.[3]

It appears that this particular text (verses 64-65) was written in the concluding portion of this sūra. It is further probable that verse 64 is Meccan, for we are told that it refers to the conversion of ʻUmar Ibn al-Khaṭṭāb to Islām.[4]

The sūra possesses a high tone of confidence and even pride as a result of the joyous victory at Badr. As the voices of the opposition were hushed, Muḥammad made his victory a divine attestation to the truthfulness of his claims to being a prophet. This sūra is in great contrast to the third sūra (Q 3) that was revealed after the defeat in the Battle of Uḥud[D]. (See the introduction to Q 3, page 263.)

Such a dichotomous comparison is another possible indication that this revelation may not have come down from the Preserved Tablet but rather out of Muḥammad's personal circumstances and creative mind.[5]

In the name of the merciful and compassionate God.
[1] They will ask thee about the spoils. Say, 'The spoils are God's
and the Apostle's; fear God and settle it amongst yourselves; obey
God and the Apostle if ye do believe.'
[2] Verily, the believers are those who, when God's name is
mentioned, their hearts sink with fear; and when His signs are
rehearsed to them they increase them in faith; and on their Lord
do they rely;
[3] who are steadfast in prayer, and of what we have bestowed
upon them give in alms;
[4] these are in truth believers; to them are degrees with their
Lord, and forgiveness, and a generous provision.
[5] As thy Lord caused thee to go forth from thy house with the
truth, although a sect of the believers were averse therefrom.
[6] They wrangled with thee about the truth after it was made
plain, as though they were being driven on to death and looked
thereon;
[7] and when God promised you that one of the two troops
should be yours, and ye would fain have had those who had no
arms. God wished to prove the truth true by His words, and to cut
off the hindermost parts of those who misbelieve—
[8] to prove the truth true, and to make vain the vain, although
the sinners are averse.
[9] When ye asked for succour from your Lord, and He answered
you, 'I will assist you with a thousand angels, with others in reserve.'
[10] God made it only glad tidings to quiet your hearts therewith;
for victory is only from God! verily, God is mighty and wise.
[11] When drowsiness covered you as a security from Him, and
He sent down upon you from the heavens water to purify you
withal, and to take away from you the plague of Satan, and to tie
up your hearts and to make firm your footsteps.
[12] When your Lord inspired the angels—'Verily, I am with you;

Q 8.1

This verse says that *"the spoils* [of war] *are God's and the Apostle's,"* which means that Muḥammad was the judge of how they are distributed. But this passage is abrogated with a later verse: *"and know that whenever ye seize anything as a spoil, to God belongs a fifth thereof, and to His Apostle…"* (Q 8.41). Hence, the verse stipulates that a fifth of the spoils came under Muḥammad's control.[6]

Another group states that there is no abrogation in this verse, but the second verse, Q 8.41, merely provides a further clarification of Q 8.1.[7]

Note: Some Muslim scholars argue that "spoils of war" were forbidden in the laws of previous prophets." However, Ibn al-Jawzī notes that the law of prohibition was cancelled with Muḥammad.[8]

Q 8.2

Ibn Mas'ūd read *fariqat* and Ubayy Ibn Ka'b read *fazi'at*.[9] Both of the readings mean "to be frightened."

The word used in the current Arabic Qur'ān, ***wajilat*** ("**sink with fear** [out of reverence]"), differs from the above two readings because it indicates the feeling of the fear and reverence that is due to the greatness of Allah.

Question: When Allah is mentioned, does the Muslim sense the majesty of Allah or is he frightened by Him?

Q 8.6

Ibn Mas'ūd read this verse with the passive form *buyyina* ("*was made clear*").[10] The reading of the current Arabic Qur'ān ***tabayyana*** ("**was made** [lit., became] **plain**") means that the truth appeared to them in themselves or in their own heart and mind. But the reading of Ibn Mas'ūd means that someone revealed the matter to them.

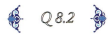

make ye firm then those who believe; I will cast dread into the hearts of those who misbelieve,—strike off their necks then, and strike off from them every finger tip.'

13 That is, because they went into opposition against God and His Apostle; for he who goes into opposition against God and His Apostle—verily, God is keen to punish.

14 There, taste it! since for the misbelievers is the torment of the Fire.

15 O ye who believe! when ye meet those who misbelieve in swarms, turn not to them your hinder parts;

16 for he who turns to them that day his hinder parts, save turning to fight or rallying to a troop, brings down upon himself wrath from God, and his resort is hell, and an ill journey shall it be!

17 Ye did not slay them, but it was God who slew them; nor didst thou shoot when thou didst shoot, but God did shoot, to try the believers from Himself with a goodly trial; verily, God both hears and knows.

18 There! verily, God weakens the stratagem of the misbelievers.

19 If ye wish the matter to be decided, a decision has now come to you; but if ye desist, it is better for you; and if ye turn back we will turn too, and your troop shall avail nothing, great in number though it be, since God is with the believers!

20 O ye who believe! obey God and His Apostle, and turn not from Him while ye hear,

21 and be not like those who say, 'We hear,' and yet they hear not.

22 Verily, the worst of beasts in God's sight are the deaf, the dumb who do not understand.

23 Had God known any good in them, He would have made them hear; but had He made them hear, they would have turned back and have swerved aside.

24 O ye who believe! answer God and His Apostle when He calls you to that which quickens you; and know that God steps in

Q 8.16

The verse refers to those taking part in the Battle of Badr.[11] It warns that those who flee from the fight will be punished by hellfire.[12] However, since the verse concerns the battle rules of Muslims, the scholars disagree on whether or not it is abrogated. They split into two groups with following viewpoints:

In the first viewpoint, some scholars state the verse is abrogated with the following verse in the same sūra: *"Now has God made it light for you; He knows that there is a weakness amongst you: but if there be amongst you but a patient hundred, they will conquer two hundred…"* (Q 8.66).

In this view, and according to this reference, it is suggested that the Muslim fighter was allowed to withdraw from a battle when the number of foes against him was more than double.[13]

In the second viewpoint, two opinions are given for the conservation of the verse. In the first opinion, the verse gives an order forbidding a soldier to flee from battle. This order is a rule of engagement in battle. Therefore, it is conserved.[14]

In the second opinion, one of the exegetes points out that since the verse talks about the people of Badr, this verse is a specific reference to that group; thus, it does not apply to everyone else and therefore it is conserved.[15]

Q 8.22, 55

The people of Mecca were critical of Muḥammad and his revelations. When a group of the tribe of Banū 'Abd al-Dār defeated him in a debate, Muḥammad responded by reciting, *"…the worst of beasts in God's sight are the deaf, the dumb who do not understand,"* as a description of them.[16] Al-Rāzī writes that the comparison "to the beasts is for their willful ignorance and the way they refrain from paying attention to what they say and what is said to them," and "calling them beasts here is because it is a name for all that walk the earth, not for way of resemblance, but merely calling them names appropriate to them in an insulting fashion."[17]

The verse adds to the insult and names them *"beasts in God's sight are the deaf, the dumb"* and ends its lampoon by describing them as beasts, *"who do not understand"*—as if some animals do speak and some do understand.

The verse's description of Muḥammad's debaters as *"the worst of beasts…the deaf, the dumb who do not understand,"* is an analogy that aims to revile them. Evidently, the author of the Qur'ān could not stand anyone rejecting him or opposing his view, displaying spite towards his opponents. This derogation is repeated after some verses where those who refused to accept the call of Muḥammad are described as *"the worst of beasts"* bar none (Q 8.55). (Compare with the comment on Q 7.176, page 475.)

between man and his heart; and that to Him ye shall be gathered.
25 And fear temptation, which will not light especially on those
of you who have done wrong; but know that God is keen to punish.
26 Remember when ye were few in number and weak in the
land, fearing lest people should snatch you away; then He shel-
tered you and aided you with victory, and provided you with good
things; haply ye may give thanks.
27 O ye who believe! be not treacherous to God and His Apostle; nor be treacherous to your engagement while ye know!
28 Know that your wealth and your children are but a temptation, and that God—with Him is mighty hire!
29 O ye who believe! if ye fear God He will make for you a discrimination, and will cover for you your offences, and will forgive
you; for God is Lord of mighty grace.
30 And when those who misbelieve were crafty with thee to detain thee a prisoner, or kill thee, or drive thee forth; they were
crafty, but God was crafty too, for God is best of crafty ones!
31 But when our verses were rehearsed to them they said, 'We

Q 8.27

Ibn Mas'ūd read it by adding another *lā* ("not") before the word ***takhūnū*** ("**be treacheous**") to the Arabic text, which is not present in the current Arabic Qur'ān.[18] The word "*nor*" was added by Palmer to the above verse before "*be treacherous.*"

Q 8.30

The majority of the readers read the verse with the word ***liyuthbitūka*** ("**to detain thee a prisoner**"), meaning to hold you captive.[19]

- Some also read *liyubayyitūka* from *bayāt*, meaning "to raid you at night."[20]
- Ibn 'Abbās read it *liyuqayyidūka* from *qayyada,* meaning "to bind you."[21]
- It is told that a group of readers read *liyuʿbidūka* from *aʿbada*, meaning a person becomes a slave or is enslaved.[22]

Question: Were the enemies of Muḥammad plotting to jail him, attack him at night, bind him, or enslave him?

Q 8.31-33

Muḥammad was reciting Qur'ānic verses to the Quraysh people and telling them tales and news of the ancients as proof of his calling as a prophet. But all of this recitation was not convincing to most of the people of the Quraysh tribe. They declared his recitations "nothing new," that he was merely telling them stories of ancient times or myths: "*this is nothing but tales of those of yore*" (Q 8.31).

The people of Quraysh did not see in the Qur'ān anything linguistically or anecdotally miraculous. Rather, they saw a creativity that could be emulated. "We could say likewise," they said, "and even surpass it." Since the Qur'ānic verses were a repetition of what they already knew of the "tales of the ancients," they called upon the god of Muḥammad to prove to them—even by torture if necessary, the truthfulness of Muḥammad: *"O God! if this be truth, and from Thee, then rain upon us stones from heaven or bring us grievous woe!"* (Q 8.32).

That taunting call was a great challenge. Since Muḥammad knew the divine proof was not forthcoming, he cleverly evaded the challenge by telling the people of Quraysh that Allah would not punish them while he, Muḥammad, dwelt among them. "*But God would not torment them while thou art amongst them*" (Q 8.33). The verse also adds, "*...nor was God going to torment them while they asked Him to forgive.*"

Yet, if the Quraysh were not Muslims and did not accept Muḥammad's calling, how could they then be expected to ask for pardon? An exegete tries to justify what cannot be justified by stating that the pagan Quraysh used to seek forgiveness during the Kaʿba circumambulation ritual (*ṭawāf*) by saying "your pardon." Another view states that asking for pardon belongs to the Muslims who are among the pagans—meaning, Allah was not going to punish the pagans while the Muslims who ask for pardon were among them.[23]

Question: If the presence of Muḥammad and the other Muslims shielded the Quraysh from the torment of Allah, why didn't Allah send down his torment upon the Quraysh after Muḥammad and his Companions emigrated? Did God not burn down Sodom and Gomorrah after he led Lot out of them?

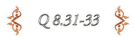

have already heard.—If we pleased we could speak like this; verily, this is nothing but tales of those of yore.'

32 When they said, 'O God! if this be truth, and from Thee, then rain upon us stones from heaven or bring us grievous woe!'

33 But God would not torment them while thou art amongst them; nor was God going to torment them while they asked Him to forgive.

34 But what ails them that God should not torment them while they turn folk away from the Holy Mosque, though they are not the guardians thereof—its guardians are only the pious?—but most of them know not.

35 Their prayer at the House was naught but whistling and clapping hands!—taste then the torment for that ye misbelieved!

36 Verily, those who misbelieve expend their wealth to turn folk from the path of God; but they shall spend it, and then it shall

Q 8.33

This verse says that suffering will not befall the Quraysh tribe because Muḥammad resides among them. Some scholars feel this verse is abrogated by the verse immediately following it (Q 8.34): *"But what ails them that God should not torment them…."*[24]

Another group of scholars say the wording of the verse means that suffering will not fall on them as long as Muḥammad is among them. Even though they are deserving of suffering as pagans, Muḥammad and the Muslims' presence among them prevents its swift coming. According to this latter group, Q 8.33 is a report (*khabar*); therefore, the verse is not abrogated.[25]

Q 8.38

It is said that this verse is abrogated with Q 8.39: *"Fight them then that there should be no sedition, and that the religion may be wholly God's…."*[26] Other scholars say this verse contains a warning and a threat from Allah. Since this threat comes from a "supreme authority," it is not subject to abrogation.[27]

be for them sighing, and then they shall be overcome! Those who
misbelieve, into hell shall they be gathered!—
37 that God may distinguish the vile from the good, and may
put the vile, some on the top of the other, and heap all up together, and put it into hell!—These are those who lose!
38 Say to those who misbelieve, if they desist they will be forgiv-
en what is past; but if they return,—the course of those of former
days has passed away.
39 Fight them then that there should be no sedition, and that
the religion may be wholly God's; but if they desist, then God on
what they do doth look.
40 But if they turn their backs, then know that God is your
Lord; a good Lord is He, and a good help;
41 and know that whenever ye seize anything as a spoil, to God
belongs a fifth thereof, and to His Apostle, and to kindred and

Q 8.41

This verse specifies the beneficiary groups of *"a fifth."* It says that *"a fifth"* goes to the *"His Apostle,"* meaning Muḥammad.

> **The fifth,** means the fifth part of the plunder and a fifth of what is discovered by men of minerals, precious metals, and buried treasures. The origin of the law of the fifth is rooted in the pre-Islāmic Arabic customs of the Arabian Peninsula. It was the percentage of plunder entitled to the head of the tribe as well as his entitlement to extend his influence over any piece of land. He would then declare it under his protection. Thereafter, no one was allowed to come near to the protected location without his permission.

We therefore note that the verse endorses one of the common *jāhilīya* (pre-Islāmic) Arab practices—a practice that originated and was implemented by groups described by the Qur'ān as blasphemers and the lost, the very ones whom Muḥammad came to guide to repentance. Thus, does a true prophet carry out wars and keep a percentage of the spoils according to the *jāhilīya* customs?

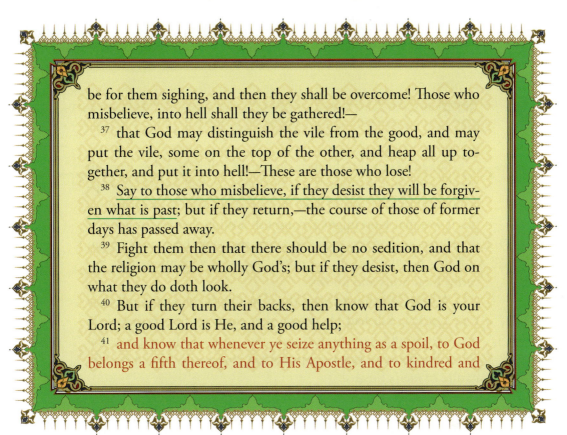

orphans, and the poor and the wayfarer; if ye believe in God
and what we have revealed unto our servants on the day of the
discrimination,—the day when the two parties met; and God is
mighty over all.
42 When ye were on the near side of the valley, and they were on
the far side, and the camels were below you; had ye made an appointment then ye would have failed to keep your appointment—
but it was that God might accomplish a thing that was as good as
done! that he who was to perish might perish with a manifest sign;
and that he who was to live might live with a manifest sign; for,
verily, God hears and knows!
43 When God showed thee them in thy dream as though they
were but few; but had He shown thee them as though they were
many, ye would have been timid, and ye would have quarrelled
about the matter;—but God preserved you; verily, He knows the
nature of men's breasts!
44 And when He showed them to you, as ye encountered them,
as few in your eyes; and made you seem few in their eyes; that God
might accomplish a thing that was as good as done; for unto God
do things return!
45 O ye who believe! when ye encounter a troop, then stand firm
and remember God; and haply ye may prosper!
46 and fear God and His Apostle, and do not quarrel or be timid, so that your turn of luck go from you; but be ye patient, verily,
God is with the patient.
47 And be not like those who went forth from their homes with
insolence, and for appearance sake before men, and to turn folks
off God's way; for all they do God comprehends.
48 And when Satan made their works appear seemly to them,
and said, 'There is none amongst mankind to conquer you to-day,
for, verily, I am your neighbour!' and when the two troops came
in sight of each other, he turned upon his heels and said, 'Verily,

I am clear of you! verily, I see what you see not! verily, I fear God, for God is keen to punish!'

49 And when the hypocrites and those in whose hearts was sickness said, 'Their religion hath beguiled these men, but he who relies upon God, verily, God is mighty and wise.'

50 Couldst thou see when the angels take away the souls of those who misbelieve; they smite them on their faces and hinder parts.—

Q 8.42

Ibn Mas'ūd read *al-suflā* ("the lowest") instead of ***al-quṣwā*** ("**the far side**") found in the current Arabic Qur'ān.[28]

Question: Were they in the farthest or the lowest area?

Q 8.48

The verse says that the devil lured the people of Quraysh into fighting the Muslims. When the battle appeared to tip in favor of the Muslims, Satan retreated and said, *"'Verily, I am clear of you! verily, I see what you see not! verily, I fear God…'"* (Q 8.48).

If we accept this verse's portrayal of Satan's ability to see behind the battle scene and his abandoning of Muḥammad's enemies, how can we believe what is said in this verse about Satan's declaration that he is *"clear of"* the Quraysh (disowns them) and that he fears Allah?

Moreover, if we accept what is in the verse, that Satan declared his fear of Allah, then he would have repented before Allah and, therefore, we should have seen a shift in the entire course of history.

M. al-Rāzī intervenes to reveal what is hidden:[29]

- When Satan saw the descending of angels in this unique way, he feared the coming of the hour of judgment and the falling of punishment on him, OR
- He feared that the angels might do him harm, but he had no fear of perishing.

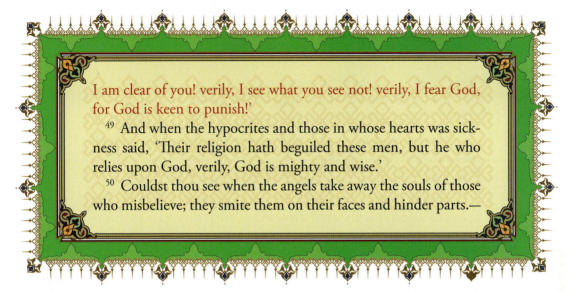

'Taste ye the torment of burning!
[51] that is for what your hands have sent on before; and for that
God is no unjust one towards his servants.'
[52] As was the wont of Pharaoh's people and those before them!
they disbelieved in the signs of God, and God overtook them in
their sins; verily, God is strong and keen to punish.
[53] That is because God is not one to change a favour He has
favoured a people with, until they change what they have in themselves, and for that God both hears and knows.
[54] As was the wont of Pharaoh's people and those before them!
they said our signs were lies, and we destroyed them in their sins,
and drowned Pharaoh's people; and all of them were evildoers.
[55] Verily, the worst of beasts in God's eyes are those who misbelieve and will not believe;
[56] with whom if thou dost make a league, they break their league
each time, for they fear not God;
[57] but shouldst thou ever catch them in war, then make those
who come after them run by their example, haply they may remember then.
[58] And shouldst thou ever fear from any people treachery, then
throw it back to them in like manner; verily, God loves not the
treacherous.
[59] Deem not that those who misbelieve can win; verily, they
cannot make (God) powerless!
[60] Prepare ye against them what force and companies of horse
ye can, to make the enemies of God, and your enemies, and others beside them, in dread thereof. Ye do not know them, but God
knows them! and whatever ye expend in God's way He will repay
you; and ye shall not be wronged.
[61] But if they incline to peace, incline thou to it too, and rely
upon God; verily, He both hears and knows.
[62] But if they wish to betray thee, then God is enough for thee!

He it is who supports thee with His help and with the believers;
63 and reconciles their hearts! Didst thou expend all that is in
the earth thou couldst not reconcile their hearts, but God recon-

Whatever the reason for Satan's fear, if the verse is true, he should have repented after this experience. So, why didn't Satan repent? On answering this question, the exegetes remain silent and the defenders mute.

8.55

See the critical analysis of Q 8.22, page 487.

Q 8.61

There are four differing viewpoints concerning the abrogation of this verse. In all four viewpoints, scholars believe the verse is abrogated. In three of the four viewpoints, the identity of the enemy is central to the basis of its abrogation.

In the first viewpoint, scholars believe the verse refers to the polytheists. Therefore, they feel it is abrogated with the Sword Verse, Q 9.5 : *"...kill the idolaters wherever ye may find them...."* Other scholars also agree that the verse refers to idolaters, but they believe it is abrogated with Q 9.29: *"Fight those who believe not in God...."*[30] In the second viewpoint, some scholars believe the verse talks about the Jews of Medina, and that it is also abrogated with Q 9.29.[31]

In the third viewpoint, yet another group states the verse is abrogated with Q 47.35: *"Then faint not, nor cry for peace while ye have the upper hand."* However, this group does not specify who should *"cry for peace."*[32]

In the fourth viewpoint, still other scholars say the verse deals with the issue of peace with the People of the Book, and that they should be treated with gentleness. However, these scholars feel that this gentleness is abrogated with the *jizya* (head tax) of Q 9.29.[33]

Note: There is an opinion that tries to reconcile the issues here. It branches off from the fourth view. It says the verse concerns the People of the Book and that it is conserved only under the condition of paying the *jizya* of Q 9.29: *"...until they pay the tribute by their hands and be as little ones."*[34]

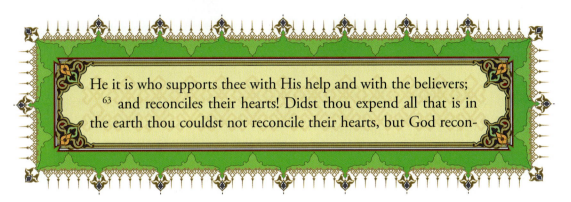

ciled them, verily, He is mighty and wise!
64 O thou prophet ! God is sufficient for thee, with those of the believers who follow thee!
65 O thou prophet! urge on the believers to fight. If there be of you twenty patient men, they shall conquer two hundred; if there be of you a hundred, they shall conquer a thousand of those who misbelieve, because they are a people who did not discern.—
66 Now has God made it light for you; He knows that there is a weakness amongst you: but if there be amongst you but a patient

Q 8.65

Some scholars have said this verse urges an attitude of perseverance in fighting, regardless of the number of the enemy, but that it is abrogated with Q 8.66: *"Now has God made it light for you; He knows that there is a weakness amongst you...."* These scholars believe that the verse "orders a man to be steadfast against two men, but if there are more, then he is allowed to flee."[35] (Compare with Q 8.16, page 487.)

Q 8.67

The verse arrives at the conclusion that it is allowable for the prophet to take prisoners of war, "but under the condition that he thoroughly subduing the land, and what is meant by thoroughly subdued the land is 'killing and extreme terrorizing.'"[36] The verse states that the prophet is the one who wields his sword against his enemies before he takes prisoners and ends by stating this condition is a sign that Allah "*wishes for the next.*"

Questions: (1) Will God, the merciful, send a prophet who is not satisfied with taking prisoners until after he has plunged the sword of death deeper? (2) Will God, the merciful, accept the glorification of his religion by shedding the blood of its detractors? (3) Is the way to execute the salvation plan of God paved with the skulls of mankind?

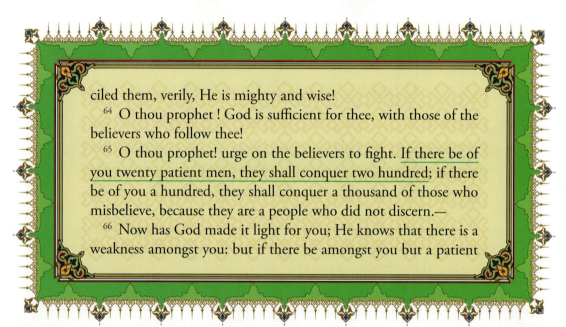

hundred, they will conquer two hundred; and if there be of you a thousand, they will conquer two thousand, by the permission of God,—for God is with the patient!

67 It has not been for any prophet to take captives until he hath slaughtered in the land! Ye wish to have the goods of this world, but God wishes for the next, for God is mighty, wise!

68 Were it not for a book from God that had gone before, there would have touched you, for that which ye took, a mighty punishment.

Q 8.67

After the great victory achieved by the Muslims over the Quraysh tribe in the Battle of Badr[D] (AH 2/AD 624), they were able to take a number of the Quraysh captive. As a result, an argument ensued within the Islāmic leadership on how to deal with the captives. This argument split the leadership into two opposing factions. The first faction, represented by Abū Bakr, said they should release the captives and take a ransom for them. The opposing faction, represented by 'Umar Ibn al-Khaṭṭāb, said the captives must be killed.

But Muḥammad, motivated by financial and tribal factors, took the side of the first faction and agreed to take a ransom.

Even though Muḥammad was aware that some Muslims would question the correctness of his conduct, he realized that the side represented by 'Umar Ibn al-Khaṭṭāb might cause him trouble. For that reason, he said, "*It has not been for any prophet to take captives until he hath slaughtered in the land!*" (Q 8.67). By this declaration, Muḥammad admitted that he should not have accepted the ransom but should have killed the captives.[37]

This verse reveals the political practicality of Muḥammad. On the one hand, he pleased the party asking for the ransom, but, on the other hand, he confirmed the morality of the opposing faction by recognizing that killing must come first. However, this debate continued and was reflected later in the differences about whether or not this verse ought to be abrogated.

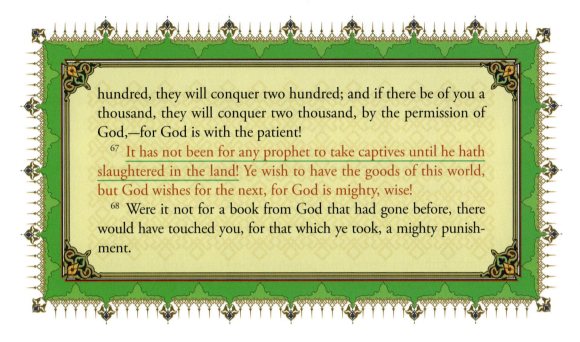

69 Eat of what spoils ye have taken, what is lawful and good; and fear God, verily, God is forgiving and merciful.
70 O thou prophet! say to such of the captives as are in your hands, 'If God knows of any good in your hearts, he will give you better than that which is taken from you, and will forgive you; for God is forgiving and merciful.'
71 But if they desire to betray thee,—they have betrayed God before! but He hath given you power over them; for God is knowing, wise!
72 Verily, those who believe and have fled and fought strenuously with their wealth and persons in God's way, and those who have given refuge and help, these shall be next of kin to each other. But those who believe, but have not fled, ye have naught to do with their claims of kindred, until they flee as well. But if they ask you for aid for religion's sake, then help is due from you, except against a people between whom and you there is an alliance; for God on what ye do doth look.
73 And those who misbelieve, some of them are next of kin to others—unless ye act the same there will be sedition in the land, and great corruption.
74 Those who believe and have fled and fought strenuously in God's cause, and those who have given a refuge and a help, those it is who believe; to them is forgiveness and generous provision due.
75 And those who have believed afterwards and have fled and fought strenuously with you; these too are of you, but blood relations are nearer in kin by the Book of God. Verily, God all things doth know.

Some scholars state the verse is abrogated by the principle of Q 47.4: *"Then either a free grant (of liberty) or a ransom...."*[38]

Most scholars refuse to abrogate the verse: "[I]t is a condition that the Muslims should kill a large number of the enemy before taking any captives."[39]

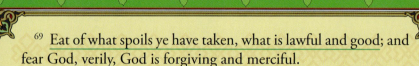

Q 8.69

This verse encourages Muslim fighters to enjoy the booty acquired in battle. This policy was permissible during Muḥammad's time, so there is no abrogation of the verse. But scholars state the verse abrogates a rule followed by prophets prior to Muḥammad. This rule forbade benefitting from the spoils of war. The scholars attributed the following saying to Muḥammad: "Spoils of war were not permitted to anyone who preceded us."[40] Thus, Muḥammad was not talking about his current times but about prior times: "anyone who preceded us."

It is noteworthy that this verse does not abrogate another verse of the Qur'ān but abrogates a rule that is thought to have been prevalent in pre-Islāmic times. Therefore, this verse has no place in the realm of abrogation and substitution but more precisely fits into the science of comparative religion. However, as it is mentioned in Islāmic references as an abrogation, we thought it is worth mentioning here.[41]

Q 8.72

This verse has two issues regarding abrogation:

1. The first issue regards the phrases, *"those who believe and have fled" and "until they flee as well."* There are several opinions expressed by scholars to validate the abrogation of these phrases.

   In the first opinion, scholars stated that the customary practice of allowing emigrant Muslims to will or bequeath only to other emigrant Muslims, excluding non-emigrant Muslims from any inheritance is abrogated with Q 8.75: *"but blood relations are nearer in kin."*[42]

   In the second opinion, scholars believed that inheritance was not allowed between the bedouin (nomads) and the Emigrants[D]. But this prohibition is cancelled with Q 8.75: *"but blood relations are nearer in kin."*[43] Thus, the verse is abrogated.

   In the third opinion, the verse refers to the brotherhood established by Muḥammad (after his arrival in Medina) between the Emigrants and the Helpers[D]. Those united with the host (literally, "those becoming brothers to each other") received an inheritance among them until Q 8.75 came down to abrogate Q 8.72: *"but blood relations are nearer in kin."* Therefore, inheritance distribution reverted to the rule of kindred of blood.[44]

2. The second issue of abrogation in this verse concerns the phrase, *"...but if they ask you for aid for religion's sake, then help is due from you."* This phrase refers to agreements of peace and aid between Muḥammad and the Arab tribes but is abrogated with Q 9.5: *"...kill the idolaters wherever ye may find them...."*[45]

Introduction

Because a decree prohibiting the practice of pagan rituals in the Arabian Peninsula was revealed in this sūra, it represents, in tangible form, Muḥammad's victory over the Meccan and Arabian tribes neighboring Mecca. This decree took place during the year AH 9 (AD 630), when Muḥammad sent 'Alī on pilgrimage to recite the first verses of this sūra. The sūra also includes the consummate position of Islām towards Jews and Christians.

Some scholars have said that Q 5 (al-Mā'ida) is the last given sūra of the Qur'ān. However, most Islāmic accounts consider al-Tawba to be the last given sūra. The majority of Qur'ānic scholars also agree that this sūra was revealed all at once.[1] Therefore, this analysis of the sūra leads to the conclusion that it was composed over several periods. That is to say, it is not the last sūra in the absolute sense, and it could not have been revealed all at once.

Despite the fact that the date of the first portion clearly refers to the year AH 9, a detailed analysis of the sūra exposes the following chronological deviations:

- Q 9.13-16 encourage the invasion of Mecca because the Quraysh did not comply with the terms of the Treaty of Ḥudaybīya, an event that occurs at least one year before year AH 9.[2]
- Q 9.25 refers to the Battle of Ḥunayn, which took place immediately after the conquest of Mecca (AH 8/AD 629).
- Q 9.40 refers to praise of Abū Bakr for joining Muḥammad in the migration (and includes the phrase, "*they two were in the cave,*" where Abū Bakr calmed the worries of Muḥammad after they were chased there during their migration to Medina by a band of Quraysh).
- Q 9.113, a Meccan verse, discusses Muḥammad's desire to seek forgiveness for his uncle, Abū Ṭalib, who died before the migration.[3]
- Q 9.128-129 also exhibit Meccan language, according to some scholars, and thus belong to the period before the Hegira.[4]

The following subjects and rulings are addressed in this sūra:

- Bans on pagan rituals describing non-Muslims as defiled (unclean): "*...it is only the idolaters who are unclean*" (Q 9.28)
- Imperative to launch crusades against Jews and Christians (Q 9.29-35)
- Command to submit to the lunar calendar only and the outlawing of al-Nasī', an extra month added every third year to the lunar calendar to make it align with the solar calendar (Q 9.36-37)
- Incitement to *jihād* in most of the verses (Q 9.111 and others)

[1] An immunity from God and His Apostle to those idolaters with whom ye have made a league.
[2] Roam ye at large in the land for four months, but know that

Q 9.1

Unlike all other sūras of the Qur'ān, Q 9 does not start with the Basmala, "*In the name of the merciful and compassionate God.*" According to the Islāmic exegetical sources, omitting the Basmala as a heading in this sūra is due to one of the following possibilities:

1. Starting with the Basmala denotes mercy and safety, conditions which are not represented in this sūra because of the Sword verse (Q 9.5) and other verses that incite to kill. Hence, omitting the Basmala as a header became imperative.[5]
   Our Comment: To say that the Basmala is a declaration of safety and thus an inappropriate header to a text where there is a command to kill the enemies with the sword is not a good reason to omit it from Q 9. There are other sūras that contain verses commanding the killing of enemies by the sword. In spite of such violent content, they still start with the Basmala as a header. (See Q 2.191, page 224; Q 4.90, page 349; Q 5.33, page 381.)

2. Another opinion states that there was a disagreement among Muḥammad's Companions whether Q 9 (sūra al-Tawba) was an independent sūra or a part of Q 8 (sūra al-Anfāl). Since both groups were firm and unyielding in their opinions, a compromise was reached to write both sūras, al-Tawba and al-Anfāl, as two independent sūras but without writing the Basmala as a heading in sūra al-Tawba.[6]
   Our Comment: The division of opinions among the Companions mentioned in the sources, regarding the independence of Q 9 and the subsequent omission of the Basmala as a compromising solution, is proof that even in the golden era of Islām, the early Muslims were not in agreement about the Qur'ān. This compromise also proves that the transcription of the Qur'ān was subjected to considerations, opinions, and the decisions of individuals.

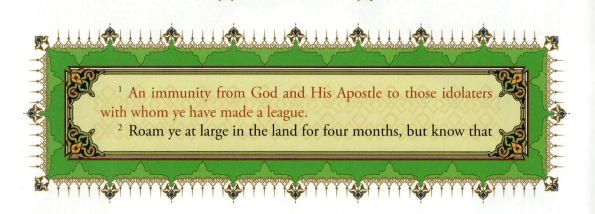

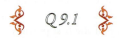

ye cannot make God helpless, and that God disgraces the misbelievers.

3 A proclamation from God and His Apostle to the people on

3. This sūra had undergone abrogation, so the Basmala was omitted with the abrogated part. Sa'īd Ibn Jubayr mentioned that "its number of verses was equal to those of sūra al-Baqara" (Q 2).[7]
   Our Comment: Lastly, the third opinion stating that Q 9 "had [an] equal number of verses to those of sūra al-Baqara (Q 2)," means that the majority of the verses for this sūra have been omitted. Such a large omission does not support the claim that the Qur'ān is divinely preserved in its text, words, and letters, as mentioned in verse Q 15.9: "*Verily, we have sent down the Reminder, and, verily, we will guard it.*"

Q 9.2

The Islāmic scholars differed regarding which group was given four months. The following are the four various perspectives:

A. Some said the verse gave safety to those who had a treaty with Muḥammad. They stated that the peace period was *"four months,"* which is neither to be increased nor decreased. As to those who had no treaty with Muḥammad, he offered them a period of fifty nights for respite.[8] (See comment on Q 9.5.)
B. It is also said by others that the verse gave safety for *"four months"* to all unbelievers, both to those who had a treaty and those who did not.[9]
C. It is said also that Muḥammad gave the "safety" mentioned in the verse to everyone who had a treaty with him. He standardized the four-month period for both the ones with whom a safety period of less than four months had been stipulated and those whose safety period was more than four months. As to those with no safety treaty with him, he declared holy war against them.[10]

   Some scholars also said the verse gave safety to the ones who had no treaty. For those who had a treaty, their treaty remained in effect until the expiration of the period stipulated in the treaty's document.[11]

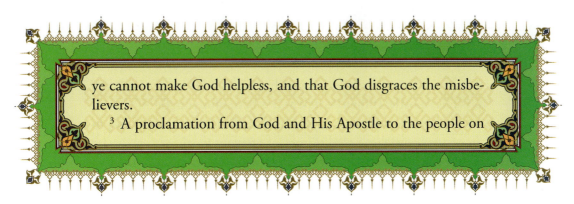

the day of the greater pilgrimage, that God is clear of the idolaters as is His Apostle! If then ye repent it is better for you; but if ye turn your backs, then know that ye cannot make God helpless. Give to those who misbelieve glad tidings of grievous woe!-

4 Except to those of the idolaters with whom ye have made a league, and who then have not failed you at all, and have not backed up any one against you. Fulfill for them then your covenant until the time agreed upon with them; verily, God loves those who fear.

Regardless of the disagreement among the scholars as to whom the verse concerns, they all agreed that the verse is abrogated with the Sword verse (Q 9.5): "*...kill the idolaters wherever ye may find them....*" Others said it is abrogated with verse Q 8.58: *"And shouldst thou ever fear from any people treachery, then throw it back to them in like manners....*"[12]

Q 9.4

The current Arabic Qur'ān reads ***yanquṣūkum*** ("**failed you**"), and those who read accordingly say that it appropriately corresponds to *ilayhim* ("to them"). Another group of readers read *yanquḍūkum* ("violated or breached [a treaty] with you"), saying that it appropriately corresponds to the mention of *al-'ahd* (*"the covenant"*) in the verse.[13]

The variations in the choice of words reflect the differences among the readers. The group that saw that the context included the act of completion as explained above, chose *yanquṣūkum* as their verb when they read it. But, the second group considered that the word had to appropriately correspond to the word *al-'ahd*, so they read *yanquḍūkum*. This dissimilarity is a result of a difference in understanding, an issue that is repeated in more than one location in this sūra:

- Q 9.28: "*it is only the idolaters who are unclean....*"
  The Arabic word ***najasun*** ("**unclean**") is used, meaning "filthy." But others read it with the Arabic word *nijsun*, meaning they are intrinsically unclean as a people group or a race. Yet, a third group read *anjāsun*, in the plural.[14]
- Q 9.81: *"Say, 'The fire of hell is hotter still, if ye could but discern!"*
  The Arabic word used in the current Arabic Qur'ān is ***yafqahūna*** ("**they discern**"). Ibn Mas'ūd read it as *ya'lamūn* ("they know") instead.[15]

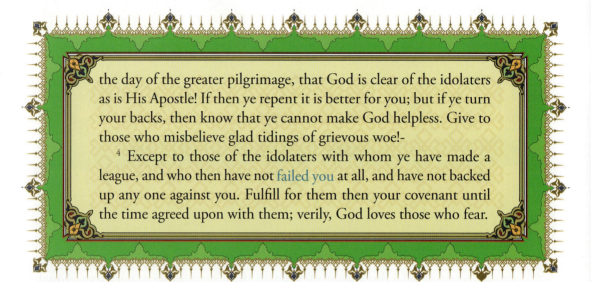

5 But when the sacred months are passed away, kill the idolaters wherever ye may find them; and take them, and besiege them,
and lie in wait for them in every place of observation; but if they
repent, and are steadfast in prayer, and give alms, then let them go
their way; verily, God is forgiving and merciful.
6 And if any one of the idolaters ask thee for aid, then aid him,
in order that he may hear the word of God; then let him reach his
place of safety,-that is, because they are a folk who do not know.

Q 9.5

There are three views concerning this verse. In the first view (in which it is abrogated) the killing of captives would be compulsory. Hence, the ruling of this verse is abrogated with the verse that stipulates *"a free grant (of liberty) or a ransom"* (Q 47.4).[16]

In the second view, it is an abrogating verse. The holders of this view state "the ruling regarding the captives did not allow killing them patiently ('patient killing' means imprisonment until death). Instead, it made permissible their release (out of generosity) or their ransom." This ruling was made according to verse Q 47.4, *"Then either a free grant (of liberty) or a ransom...,"* but was subsequently abrogated with the ruling of verse Q 9.5: *"...kill the idolaters wherever ye may find them."* Therefore, in this second view, the ruling regarding captives is to kill them and reject their ransom.[17] One Muslim scholar presented a view that stipulates that there are only two choices available for the captives: "either the sword or Islām."[18]

In the third view, some scholars declared both verses to be conserved. The verse Q 9.5 orders the killing and the taking of captives. According to verse Q 47.4, when a captive is taken, it is up to the ruler to either grant the captive freedom or accept a ransom. The ruler could also choose, according to prevailing political considerations, to kill him.[19]

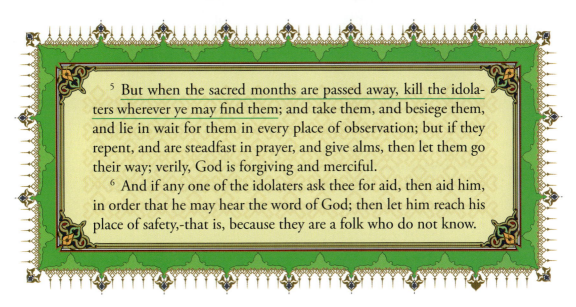

[7] How can there be for the idolaters a treaty with God and with His Apostle, save those with whom ye have made a league at the Sacred Mosque! Then while they stand by you, stand ye by them; verily, God loves those who fear.

[8] How!-if they prevail against you, they will not observe either ties of blood or ties of clientship; they please you with their mouths, but their hearts refuse; and most of them do work abomination.

Q 9.7

There are three suggestions regarding the identity of the treaty signers (*"those with whom ye have made a league"*): Banū Ḍumra, the Quraysh, and Khuzā'a.[20]

Whatever the true reference, however, the text in this verse was subsequently abrogated with the Sword verse, Q 9.5: *"...kill the idolaters wherever ye may find them...."*[21]

Q 9.7

Ibn Mas'ūd read the verse in a different form by adding *wa lā dhimmatun* ("nor a pact"). It is also said that he read it by substituting ***lilmushrikīna*** ("**for the idolaters**") with *lahum* ("for them") and adding *wa lā dhimmatun* ("nor a pact") to the verse.[22]

Q 9.17

Ibn 'Abbās and a group of readers read it *masjid* ("mosque") in the singular instead of ***masājid*** ("**mosques**").[23] The same variation is repeated in Q 9.18: "*He only shall repair to the mosques of God,*" which was read by some as *masjid* ("mosque").[24]

Those who preferred to read it in the singular interpreted the reference to mean al-Masjid al-Ḥarām[D] (the Sacred Mosque).[25]

Question: Do the verses speak of one specific mosque or a group of mosques as the current Arabic Qur'ān states?

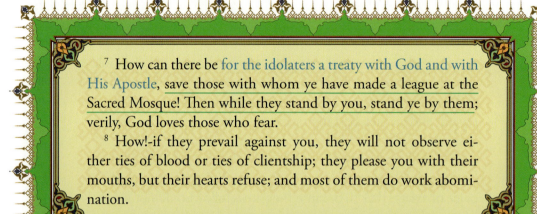

9 They barter God's signs for a little price, and they turn folk
from His way; verily, they-evil is that which they have done.
10 They will not observe in a believer ties of kindred nor ties of
clientship; but they it is are the transgressors.
11 But if they repent and are steadfast in prayer and give alms,
then they are your brethren in religion-we detail the signs unto a
people that do know.
12 But if they break faith with you after their treaty, and taunt
your religion, then fight the leaders of misbelief; verily, they have
no faith, haply they may desist.
13 Will ye not fight a people who broke their oaths, and intended to expel the Apostle? They began with you at first, are ye afraid
of them? God is more deserving that ye should fear Him! If ye be
believers,
14 kill them! God will torment them by your hands, and disgrace them, and aid you against them, and heal the breasts of a
people who believe;
15 and will remove rage from their hearts; for God turns unto
Him whomsoever He pleases, and God is knowing, wise!
16 Did ye reckon that ye would be left, when God knows not
as yet those of you who fought strenuously, and who did not take
other than God and His Apostle, and the believers for an intimate
friend? for God is well aware of what ye do.
17 It is not for idolaters to repair to the mosques of God, bearing
witness against themselves to unbelief; they it is whose works are
vain, and in the Fire shall they dwell for, aye!
18 He only shall repair to the mosques of God who believes in God
and the last day, and is steadfast in prayer, and gives the alms, and
fears only God;-it may be that these will be of those who are guided.
19 Have ye made out the giving drink to the pilgrims and the re-
pairing to the Sacred Mosque to be like being one who believes in
God and in the last day, and is strenuous in the way of God?-they
are not equal in God's sight, and God guides not an unjust people.

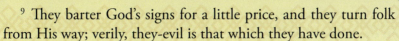

20 Those who believe and who have fled and been strenuous
in the way of God, with their wealth and with their persons, are
highest in rank with God, and these it is who are happy.
21 Their Lord gives them glad tidings of mercy from Himself, and
goodwill; and gardens shall they have therein and lasting pleasure,
22 to dwell therein for aye! Verily, God, with Him is mighty here.
23 O ye who believe! take not your fathers and your brothers
for patrons if they love misbelief rather than faith; for whosoever
amongst you takes them for patrons these are the unjust.
24 Say, 'If your fathers, and your sons, and your brethren, and
your wives, and your clansmen, and the wealth which ye have
gained, and the merchandise which ye fear may be slack, and the
dwellings which ye love are dearer to you than God and His Apostle, and than fighting strenuously in His way,-then wait awhile,
until God brings His bidding, for God guides not a people who
work abomination!'
25 God has helped you in many a place, and on the day of 'Ho-
nein when ye were so pleased with your numbers; but it did not
serve you at all, and the road grew too strait for you, where it had
been broad; and then ye turned your backs retreating;
26 then God sent down His shechina upon His Apostle and
upon the believers; and sent down armies which ye could not see,
and punished those who misbelieved;
27 for that is the reward of the misbelievers, then God turns after
that to whom He will, for God is forgiving and merciful!
28 O ye who believe! it is only the idolaters who are unclean;
they shall not then approach the Sacred Mosque after this year.
But if ye fear want then God will enrich you from His grace if He
will; verily, God is knowing, wise!
29 Fight those who believe not in God and in the last day, and
who forbid not what God and His Apostle have forbidden, and
who do not practice the religion of truth from amongst those to
whom the Book has been brought, until they pay the tribute by

I would be ashamed to even say this word

How I wish the Qur'ān had been more honorable than to describe the idolater as *najasun* ("unclean"), which is a rude word. I thought the "superiority" of the Qur'ān would forgo such mention, especially about one of its enemies.

I would be embarrassed to pronounce this word and I absolutely refuse to mention it in my writings. How could I possibly use it to describe another human being who has every right to exercise freedom of thought and expression of opinion, no matter how much this opinion differs from mine?

But for Allah to pronounce this word in a sent-from-heaven Qur'ān, which people are supposed to read—meditating over it in prayers and practices—is beyond my comprehension. Allah should be elevated above this.

This word could have been very easily replaced by another less impudent, yet more meaningful one consistent with the inimitability attributed to the Qur'ān, which is above human taste and beyond human abilities and talents [to reproduce].

Or is it through the use of this dirty word and other similar words that the Qur'ān wants us to view others and progress with our civilization? Through the use of this dirty word does the Qur'ān intend to subvert the future of our relationship with others and the way we deal with them for no reason other than that they are different in religion and beliefs?

('Abd al-Nūr, *Miḥnatī ma'a al-Qur'ān wa ma'a Allah fī al-Qur'ān* 232-233)

Q 9.28

The verse describes the *mushrikūn* (blasphemers, idolaters) as *najasun* (the unclean, defiled, impure). Some exegetes explain the description *najasun* to be an abstraction for their insult and contempt. Others say that the reason they are described as *najasun* is because they neglect the rules of hygiene. But another group of scholars say that non-Muslims are *najasun* based on their biological composition![26]

Some legal scholars produced a *fatwa* (religious ruling) that it is forbidden to shake their hands: "whoever shakes their hands, should perform ablutions *(wuḍū')*."[27]

Question: Does such a description and such an absolute ruling against non-Muslims that they are *najasun* indicate that the Qur'ān is a heavenly book?

their hands and be as little ones.
30 The Jews say Ezra is the son of God; and the Christians say
that the Messiah is the son of God; that is what they say with their
mouths, imitating the sayings of those who misbelieved before.-
God fight them! how they lie!
31 They take their doctors and their monks for lords rather than
God, and the Messiah the son of Mary; but they are bidden to
worship but one God, there is no god but He; celebrated be His
praise, from what they join with Him!
32 They desire to put out the light of God with their mouths,

Q 9.30

The verse accuses the Jews of saying that 'Uzayr (Ezra) is the son of Allah. This is a false accusation that has no basis, neither in the Pentateuch nor in the rest of the Old Testament. Historically speaking, the truth is that Ezra the priest, who is honorably titled as a scribe, was highly regarded by the Jews, like Moses, because of his knowledge of the Torah. He played an important role in the history of the Israelites in the fifth century BC. As to the stipulated charge mentioned in the Qur'ānic verse that the Jews declared Ezra to be the Son of God, it is a clear fabrication of the Qur'ān's composer.[28]

This verse also addresses Christians in a hostile manner. This is a contradictory message to the Qur'ānic verses given in Mecca, which are friendly and peaceful. But when Muḥammad moved to Medina and found support among his new helpers there, his messages against Christians became very incentive and full of hatred.

In contradiction to other verses, this verse accuses Christians of blasphemy. (See the comments on these verses: Q 2.62, 221; Q 3.42, 45, 46, 49, 55, 59; Q 4.157, 158, 171.)

Q 9.31

Concerning the accusation, "*They take their doctors and their monks for lords rather than God…,*" see the comment on Q 4.51, page 339.

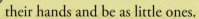

but God will not have it but that we should perfect His light,
averse although the misbelievers be!
33 He it is who sent His Apostle with guidance and the religion
of truth, to make it prevail over every other religion, averse although idolaters may be!
34 O ye who believe! verily, many of the doctors and the monks
devour the wealth of men openly, and turn folk from God's way;
but those who store up gold and silver and expend it not in God's
way,-give them glad tidings of grievous woe!

Q 9.34

Regarding this verse, which prohibits the hoarding of money, Islāmic scholars offer the following opinions:

In the first view, this prohibition applies equally to the People of the Book (Jews and Christians) and to Muslims.[29]

In the second view, the prohibition is specifically for the People of the Book.[30]

In the third view, the prohibition is specifically for all Muslims.[31] In this view, there are two divergent branches of thought:

A. The intended spending is the giving of alms, or *zakāt*. This opinion is the opinion of the majority of scholars. Therefore, the verse is conserved.[32]

B. The intended spending is the giving of the surplus. Therefore, the verse is abrogated with the enactment of *zakāt* mentioned in the verse, "*Take from their wealth alms...*" (Q 9.103).[33]

Q 9.34

The verse accuses the majority of Jewish and Christian scholars of "*openly*" devouring people's money and turning people away from "*God's way.*"

The verse directs this detestable accusation toward "the (Jewish) rabbis and the (Christian) monks" (Pickthall trans.) with the intention of tarnishing their image. The true reason is also mentioned in the text of the verse, that they "*turn folk from God's way* [Islām]." In other words, they are capable of debating Islām and refuting it.

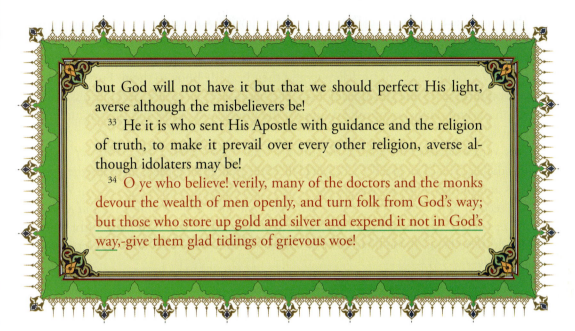

There is a lack of logic in the verse. If the Jewish scholars and the priests were falsely devouring people's money and abusing their trust, those who were robbed of their money would have rushed to embrace Islām to find support in it against their "oppressive" rabbis and priests. Islām would then be a life buoy to them. Furthermore, why would these people (if suffering from the hypocrisy, overreach, and oppression of their priests and rabbis) continue to support the priests and rabbis and their arguments against Islām?

This verse's accusation against the monks, that they "*devour the wealth of men,*" contradicts a friendly verse (Q 5.82), which states that among the Christians there are priests and monks who "*are not proud.*"

The second part of the verse reads, "*but those who store up gold and silver and expend it not in God's way.*" The pronoun in the term "*expend it*" is in the singular form when it should have been in the dual form in Arabic[D]. Otherwise, what does "it" represent: gold or silver?

M. al-Rāzī mentions several possibilities:[34]

A. The pronoun stands for *silver*, because this word is closer to the pronoun.
B. The pronoun stands for the meaning, since the hoarded things are dinars, dirhams, and other currencies.
C. When Arabs mention two things, i.e., gold and silver, with a common meaning, they only repeat the pronoun that stands for one of them.

The author concealed the linguistic error in the term "*expend it*" by making the pronoun carry multiple meanings.

We also notice the presence of two different topics in the verse:

- Accusation against the rabbis and monks (priests and anchorites)
- Prohibition against the hoarding of money

Question: What kind of eloquence addresses two different topics in one and the same verse?

Notice that the verse contains a warning against hoarding gold and silver, threatening those that do with *"glad tidings of grievous woe."* However, this verse is abrogated by another verse (Q 9.103): *"Take from their wealth alms to cleanse and purify them thereby."*

Manipulating the Verse

Forbidding the hoarding of money was abrogated or cancelled as a compromise for the rich Companions of Muḥammad. The history of Islām and Muḥammad's biography are full of similar events that reflect the [opportunistic] policy of the founders of Islām. The conflict never stopped, despite that it is seen as settled in the area of legislation. Some of the guiding indicators to that direction are the verses of *al-'afū* [forgiveness] and *al-kanz* [the treasure], which were not omitted from the Qur'ān after their abrogation. So, their status was the same as the verses that were abrogated in meaning or judgment but remained for reading purposes....

Abū Dharr [al-Ghifārī] crafted his message of prohibition of acquisition relying on the text of this verse. He continued to hold on to the verdict of the verse in spite of its confirmed abrogation, which, in turn, directed the *sharī'a* [Islāmic law] to apply the rules based on permission of acquisition. In his effort, he [Abū Dharr al-Ghifārī] relied on his social base as well as on the support of 'Alī Ibn Abī Ṭālib, with his religious and social significance, to help him take a stance...against the official explanation. In this respect, the opposing group had better justification for their position—the verse of *zakāt* and the verses of inheritance....Nonetheless, the continued presence of the verse in the Qur'ān...gave Abū-Dhar a winning card in his confrontation, causing his opponents a great embarrassment that compelled them to try and find a way out.

The context of the verse helped them to suggest an interpretation that would exclude the rich Muslims from its verdict and limit it to the rich People of the Book—the Jews and the Christians....To justify their interpretation, they tried to take advantage of the process of gathering the Qur'ān to perform a change in the configuration of the verse, bringing it closer to the desired meaning. In the book of *al-Durr al-Manthūr* by al-Suyūtī, an account by an old author called Ibn al-Dharis recalls when they [the compilers] sat down to gather the Qur'ān, they wanted to omit the word and, which is in sūra Barā'a—*"and those who hoard* [those who bury gold and silver…]." So Ubayy Ibn Ka'b stood up, saying, "Surely I will put my sword on me if you do not keep it…," so they kept it....

If the word and had been omitted, the two parts of the verse would have been connected so that the conjugate noun "who" would have been concerning the rabbis and/or the monks, making the verdict of the verse about the Jews as indicated by the rabbis, and the Christians as indicated by the monks. But by keeping the word *and,* the statement would become separated from the preceding one so that the verdict of the verse would be all-inclusive. (al-'Alawī, *Min Qāmūs al-Turāth* 82-84)

[35] On the day when it shall be heated in the fire of hell, and
their brows shall be branded therewith, and their sides and their
backs!-'This is what ye stored up for yourselves, taste then what ye
stored up!'
[36] Verily, the number of months with God is twelve months
in God's Book, on the day when He created the heavens and the
earth; of these are four that are sacred; that is the subsisting religion. Then do not wrong yourselves therein, but fight the idola-

Q 9.35

Ubayy Ibn Ka'b read the verse in a different form by substituting ***ẓuhūruhum*** ("**their backs**") with *buṭūnuhum* ("and their abdomens").[35] He made the punishment fall on the abdomens, whereas the current Arabic Qur'ān's reading makes it fall on the backs.

Q 9.36-37

The calendar in the Arabian Peninsula before Islām was based on lunar months. The total days of the Arabian lunar months number 354, which is eleven days less than that of the calendar months. For this reason, the Arabs used to add a month every three years, calling it the al-Nasī'[D] (forgotten month) so that the lunar Arabian calendar would coincide with the solar year. This practice of adding another month was done for agricultural and commercial reasons.

Most probably, Muḥammad decided to keep a sacred season for the Muslims, so he chose to abide by the lunar calendar, because he knew the difficulty in dealing with a dual lunar/solar system. Just as Muḥammad turned the pagan rituals of Ḥajj into Islāmic rituals, so he did likewise with the lunar calendar and made it sacred. Then, he abolished the Nasī' system.

The abolition of al-Nasī' system is understandable. But if the Arabs' inability to deal with a dual lunar/solar system is justification for the abolition of al-Nasī', then why didn't Muḥammad just say that it was a complicated issue? Instead, he used the term *"misbelief"* (unbelief or blasphemy), or even more, as in verse Q 9.37, *"an increase in misbelief"*?

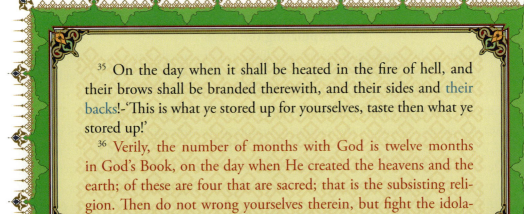

ters, one and all, as they fight you one and all, and know that God is with those who fear.

[37] Verily, putting off is but an increase in misbelief to lead astray therewith those who misbelieve. They make it lawful one year, but they make it unlawful another year, that they may come to an understanding as to the number which God has made sacred, and make lawful what God has prohibited. Seemly to them are their evil works, but God guides not a misbelieving people.

(For more discussion about the integration of other pagan rituals, such as the Ḥajj in Islām, see the comments on Q 2.158 and 196, pages 213, 227.)

Q 9.37

This verse has two issues regarding the variant readings:

1. The reading of the current Arabic Qur'ān, ***yuḍallu*** (“**to lead astray**”), means that the transposing of al-Nasī' led “*those who misbelieve*” astray. In addition to this reading, there are the following variant readings:
   - *yuḍillu* (“they mislead”) means that the unbelievers use the transposing to mislead their followers.[36]
   - *nuḍillu* (“we mislead”) means here that Allah is the one doing the misleading.[37]

   Question: Does the transposing mislead the pre-Islāmic Arabs, do the unbelievers use it to mislead the people, or does Allah use it to mislead?

2. Most readers read the phrase as it appears in the current Arabic Qur'ān ***zuyyina*** (“[was made] **seemly**”) in the passive form. It is said that Allah is the one that makes it appealing, while others said that Satan is the one. Ibn Mas'ūd and others read it *zayyana* (“he made it appealing”).”[38] According to the reading of Ibn Mas'ūd, the subject of the verb is Allah. Compare this reading with the comment on Q 3.14: “*Seemly unto men is a life of lusts.*”

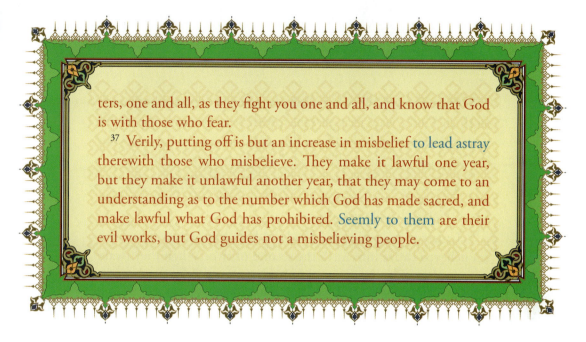

38 O ye who believe! what ailed you when ye were told to march
forth in God's way, that ye sank down heavily upon the earth?
were ye content with the life of this world instead of the next? but
the provision of this world's life is but a little to the next.
39 Unless ye march forth He will punish you with grievous woe,
and will put in your stead a people other than you! ye cannot hurt
Him at all, for God is mighty over all!
40 Unless ye help him-and God did help him, when those who
misbelieved drove him forth the second of two. When they twain
were in the cave; when he said to his comrade, 'Grieve not, verily,
God is with us;' and God sent down His shechina upon him, and

Q 9.39

Generally, it is agreed that this verse is abrogated with Q 9.122: *"The believers should not march forth altogether...."*[39] However, Ibn al-Jawzī does not agree with this opinion but instead sees that each verse deals with a particular situation. He also supports his opinion by mentioning the names of those who agree with his opinion on this matter.[40]

Q 9.40

This verse has two issues regarding the variant readings:

1. In the codex of Ḥafṣa (who was one of Muḥammad's wives), it was written "then Allah sent down His peace upon them both, and strengthened them both with forces which you did not see...."

   The reading in the current Qur'ān uses the singular *"him,"* which means the peace came upon one person. The commentators said that it was either Muḥammad or Abū Bakr. However, according to the reading in the dual ("them"), Ḥafṣa's reading, the meaning is that the peace came upon both of them together, Muḥammad and Abū Bakr.[41]

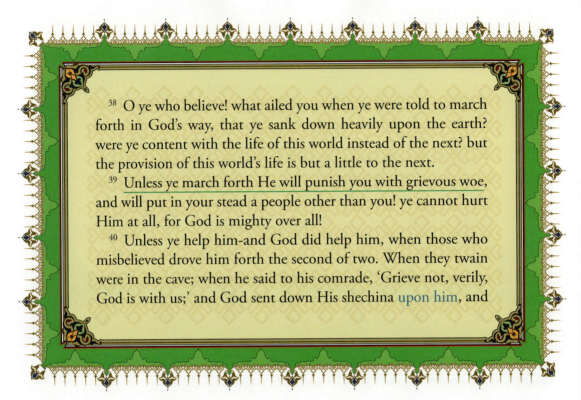

aided him with hosts ye could not see, and made the word of those
who misbelieved inferior, and the word of God superior; for God
is mighty and wise.
41 March ye then, light and heavy, and fight strenuously with
your wealth and persons in God's way; that is better for you if ye
did but know!
42 Were there goods nigh at hand, and a moderate journey, they
would have followed you; but the distance was too far for them;
they will swear by God, 'If we could, we would have gone forth
with you.' They destroy themselves, but God knows that they lie!
43 God forgive thee; why didst thou give them leave (to stay)

2. This part of the verse appears differently in the codex of Ubayy Ibn Ka'b: "and humbled to the depths the word of the Unbelievers. But made his word exalted…."[42]

Q 9.41

This verse imposed on all Muslims, whether healthy or infirm, direct participation in fighting.[43] The scholars state that the verse is abrogated with Q 9.122: "*The believers should not march forth altogether….*"[44]

It is also said this verse is abrogated with Q 9.91, which details the exceptions: "*For the weak, and the sick, and those who cannot find wherewith to expend in alms there is no hindrance….*"[45]

Ibn al-Jawzī reiterates his note referenced in the previous verse, saying, these verses do not abrogate one another, but each one is concerned with a different practical circumstance.[46]

Q 9.43

It is mentioned that this verse is abrogated with Q 24.62: *"But when they ask thy leave for any of their own concerns, then give leave to whomsoever thou wilt of them…."*[47]

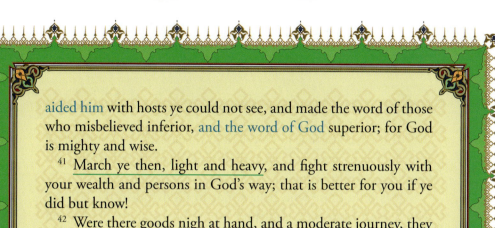

until it was made manifest to thee who spake the truth-until thou mightest know the liars?

44 Those who believe in God and in the last day will not beg off from fighting strenuously with their wealth and their persons; but God knows those who fear.

45 It is only those who believe not in God and in the last day who beg off from thee, and those whose hearts are in doubt, and in their doubt do hesitate.

46 Had they wished to go forth, they would have prepared for it a preparation; but God was averse from their starting off, and made them halt, and they were told to sit with those who sit.

47 Had they gone forth with you they would but have made you more trouble, and they would have hurried about amongst you craving a sedition; amongst you are some who would have listened to them; but God knows those who are unjust!

48 They used to crave sedition before and upset thy affairs; until the truth came, and God's bidding was made manifest, averse although they were.

49 Of them are some who say, 'Permit me, and do not try me!'

Q 9.44

The scholars state that this verse is also abrogated with Q 24.62: "*But when they ask thy leave for any of their own concerns, then give leave to whomsoever thou wilt of them....*"[48]

Q 9.55

How could wealth and children be instruments of torture in life, according to this verse, while the Qur'ān itself mentions in another verse (Q 18.46), "*Wealth and children are an adornment of the life of this world*"?

Interpreters and linguists implicitly acknowledge this conflict. For this reason, a group of them have said that the verse should be read, "Do not admire their money or their children in this life, but Allah wants to punish them with these in the afterlife."

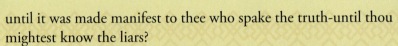

Have they not fallen into the trial already, but hell shall encompass
the misbelievers.
50 If good befall thee it seems ill to them; but if a calamity befall
thee they say, 'We had taken care for our affair before;' and they
turn their backs and they are glad.
51 Say, 'Nought shall befall us save what God has written down
for us; He is our Lord, and upon God believers do rely!'
52 Say, 'Do ye await for us aught but one of the two best things?' we
too await for you that God will inflict on you torment from Himself,
or by our hands. Wait then; and we with you are waiting too!
53 Say, 'Expend ye in alms, whether ye will or no, it shall not be
accepted from you; verily, ye are a people who do work abomination.'
54 But nought hinders their alms-giving from being accepted
save that they misbelieve in God and His Apostle, and perform
not prayer save lazily, and expend not in alms save reluctantly.
55 Let not their wealth please you nor their children, God only
wishes to torment them therewith in the life of this world, and
that their souls may pass away while still they misbelieve.
56 They swear by God that, verily, they are of you; but they are

Al-Ṭabarī writes, "Some said: Muḥammad, do not admire the wealth of those hypocrites or their children in this life, but Allah wants to use them for their torture in the afterlife."[49] This interpretation denotes advancement of one event and delay of another. Ibn 'Abbās supports this interpretation.[50]

Indeed, since the verse does not contain any delay or advancement of events and since the term *afterlife* is not present in the verse but assumed by the interpreters, the commentators have drifted from the right path. For this reason, the grammar specialists state the verse has an omitted phrase, as if to say, "But Allah wants **to dictate to them in it** to torment them [our emphasis]."[51]

So where is the eloquence, when we have to refer to interpretations to know of the omissions and the meaning of the verse?

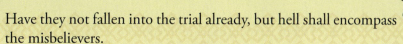

not of you, and they are a people who do stand aside in fear.
57 Could they but have found a refuge, or some caves, or a place
in which to creep, they would have turned round in haste thereto.
58 Of them are some who defame thee, with respect to alms;
though if they are given a part thereof, they are content; and if
they are not given a part thereof, then are they in a rage.
59 Would that they were content with what God and His Apostle had brought them, and would say, 'God is enough for us! God
will bring us of His grace, and so will His Apostle; verily, unto
God is our desire!'
60 Alms are only for the poor and needy, and those who work
for them, and those whose hearts are reconciled, and those in captivity, and those in debt, and those who are on God's path, and for
the wayfarer;-an ordinance this from God, for God is knowing,
wise.

Q 9.60

The verse states that part of the donations (alms) should go "to attract the hearts of those who have been inclined (towards Islâm)" (al-Hilali trans.) or "*and those whose hearts are reconciled*" or "those whose hearts are made to incline" (Shakir trans.). So who were those whose hearts have been reconciled?

After the victory of Muḥammad's army over Thaqif in the Battle of Ḥunayn, the fighters seized large amounts of plunder and took captive thousands of women and children. When the amount of seized spoils was great, Muḥammad decided to give part of it to some leaders of the Arab tribes, especially to the Quraysh leaders, in order to ensure their loyalty to him.[52]

Muḥammad gave one hundred camels each to Abū Sufyān Ibn Ḥarb, his son Mu'āwīya, and Ṣafwān Ibn Umaīya, his worst enemy in Mecca, even though he had not yet confessed faith in Islām. In addition to these three men, he also gave plunder to Ḥakīm Ibn Ḥizām, al-Ḥārith Ibn al-Ḥārith Ibn Kalada , al-Aqra' Ibn Ḥābis , 'Uyayna Ibn Ḥiṣn and al-'Abbās Ibn Mirdās. Those whose hearts became more attracted to Islām were almost forty people.[53]

61 And of them are some who are by the ears with the prophet,
and say, 'He is all ear.' Say, 'An ear of good for you!' he believes in
God, and believes in those who do believe, and is a mercy unto
such of you as believe; but those who are by the ears with the
Apostle of God, for them is grievous woe!
62 They swear by God to please you; but God and His Apostle
are more worthy for them to please if they be believers.
63 Do they not know that whoso setteth himself against God
and His Apostle, for him is the fire of hell, to dwell therein for aye?
and that is mighty shame!
64 The hypocrites are cautious lest there be revealed against them
a surah to inform them of what is in their hearts; say, 'Mock ye!
verily, God will bring forth that of which ye are so cautious!'
65 But if thou shouldst ask them, they will say, 'We did but discuss and jest;' say, 'Was it at God and His signs, and His Apostle,

Question: Is it possible for a heavenly book to legitimize the bribing of the tribal leaders?

Q 9.63

In the current Arabic Qur'ān it is written ***ya'lamū*** ("**they...know**") with a "y", where the context is about the enemies of Muḥammad. Others, however, read it with a "t", *ta'lamū* ("you...know"). Some said that the ones addressed are the enemies of Muḥammad, yet others said it was the Muslims.[54] In the codex of Ubayy Ibn Ka'b it is *ya'lam* ("he knows") with a "y", but others read it *ta'lam* ("you know"). The commentators said that Muḥammad is the one addressed in both of those readings, while some said that any hearers are the intended audience.[55]

Question: Is the address in the verse directed to non-Muslims, Muslims, Muḥammad, or to the hearer of the verse?

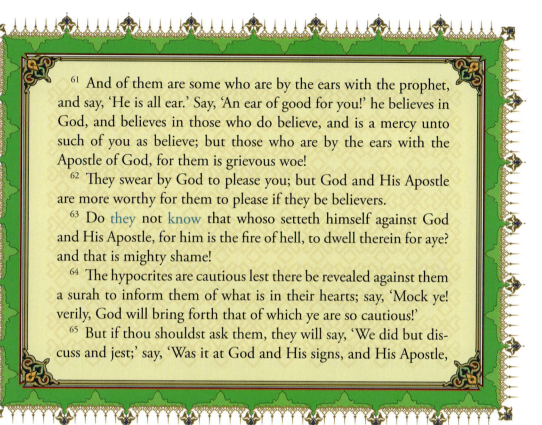

that ye mocked?'
66 Make no excuse! Ye have misbelieved after your faith; if we
forgive one sect of you, we will torment another sect, for that they
sinned!
67 The hypocrites, men and women, some of them follow others, bidding what is wrong and forbidding what is right, and they
clench their hands. They forget God and He forgets them! Verily,
the hypocrites, they are the doers of abomination!
68 God has promised unto the hypocrites, men and women, and
unto the misbelievers, hell-fire, to dwell therein for aye; it is enough
for them! God shall curse them, and theirs shall be enduring woe.
69 Ye are like those who were before you. They were stronger
than you and more abundant in wealth and children; they enjoyed
their portion then, and ye enjoy your portion, as they enjoyed
their portion before you; and ye discuss as they discussed. Their
works are vain in this world and the next, and they it is who lose.
70 Did there not come to them the declaration of those who were
before them? of the people of Noah and 'Ad and Thamud, and of
the people of Abraham, and the people of Midian? and of the overturned (cities)? Their apostles came to them with manifest signs; for
God would not wrong them, but it was themselves they wronged.
71 And the believers, men and women, are some the patrons of
others; they bid what is reasonable, and forbid what is wrong, and
are steadfast in prayer, and give alms, and obey God and His Apostle. On these will God have mercy; verily, God is mighty, wise!
72 God has promised to believers, men and women, gardens beneath which rivers flow, to dwell therein for aye; and goodly places
in the garden of Eden. But good-will from God is the greatest of
all! that is the mighty happiness!
73 O thou prophet! strive strenuously against the misbelievers
and the hypocrites, and be stern against them; for their resort is
hell, and an ill journey shall it be.

Q 9.73

The Shiites read "strive hard against the unbelievers by the hypocrites."[56]

It seems that this reading is an attempt to avoid the problem in the verse. When the scholars discussed *jihād* against the hypocrites, they said that warring against non-Muslims is a certain matter because the non-Muslims openly reject Islām. However, the hypocrites are the ones who outwardly declare Islām. How then could one fight someone who has not openly shown himself to be non-Muslim?

Hence, the commentators offer the following explanations for the reading of this verse:[57]

- The verse stipulates fighting the unbelievers and speaking harshly to the hypocrites.
- The verse demands *jihād* against the unbelievers and hypocrites, since *jihād* is not limited only to the sword and the tongue but has other tools as well.
- The punishments of Islām must be carried out against the hypocrites.

But these opinions did not settle the discussion for the following reasons:

- Since the hypocrite does not show his rejection of Islam, how is he to be rebuked or have *jihād* carried out against him?
- Applying the punishment of the *sharīʿa* is not limited to the hypocrites alone but is on all those who are under the authority of a Muslim country.

All these endeavors in exegeses fail when compared to the Shiite reading of the verse: "strive hard against the unbelievers by the hypocrites."[58]

Yet this reading, in turn, is not free of the issue of how to know the identity of the hypocrites so they can be pushed to fight the unbelievers. If they are known to the Muslims, wouldn't there be fear that they would join the enemy's camp instead of sacrificing their lives for the cause of Islām, in which they do not believe anyway?

The verse thus remains a conundrum in both the Sunnī and the Shiite readings.

[74] They swear by God they did not speak it, but they did speak
the word of misbelief; and they disbelieved after they had embraced Islām, and they designed what they could not attain; and
they only disapproved it because God and His Apostle had en-
riched them of His grace. If they turn again 'tis better for them;
but if they turn their backs, God will torment them with mighty
woe in this world and in the next, nor shall they have upon the
earth a patron or protector.
[75] And of them are some who make a treaty with God, that 'If
He bring us of His grace, we will give alms and we will surely be
among the righteous.'
[76] But when He gave them of His grace they were niggardly
thereof, and turned their backs and swerved aside.
[77] So He caused hypocrisy to pursue them in their hearts unto
the day when they shall meet Him,-for that they did fail God in

Q 9.78

The majority read ***ya'lamū*** ("**they…know**") with a "y", where the context is about the enemies of Muḥammad and the expression is in the interrogative, with the intention to rebuke. Whereas, the rest of the readers read *ta'lamū* ("you…know") with a "t", where the Muslims are the ones intended.[59]

Question: Does the verse address the Muslims or their enemies?

Q 9.79

The verse states that Allah ridicules those who ridicule Muslims. Is portraying Allah as a cynic consistent with Allah's transcendence? (Compare the comment on Q 3.54, where Allah is described as a deceiver.)

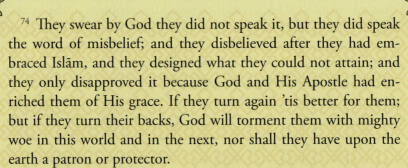

what they promised Him, and for that they were liars!
78 Do they not know that God knows their secrets and their
whisperings, and that God knows the unseen things?
79 Those who defame such of the believers as willingly give their
alms, and such as can find nothing to give but their exertions, and
who mock at them,-God will mock at them, and for them is grievous woe!
80 Ask forgiveness for them or ask not forgiveness, for them! if
they shouldst ask forgiveness for them seventy times, yet would
not God forgive them; that is because they disbelieved in God and
His Apostle, for God guides not a people who work abomination.
81 Those who were left behind rejoiced in staying behind the
Apostle of God, and were averse from fighting strenuously with
their wealth and their persons in God's way, and said, 'March not
forth in the heat.' Say, 'The fire of hell is hotter still, if ye could but
discern!'
82 Let them then laugh little, and let them weep much, as a recompense for that which they have earned!
83 But if God bring thee back to a sect of them, and they ask
thee then for leave to sally forth; say, 'Ye shall by no means ever
sally forth with me, nor shall ye ever fight a foe with me! verily,
ye were content to sit at home the first time, sit ye then now with
those who stay behind.'
84 Pray not for any one of them who dies, and stand not by his
tomb; verily, they disbelieved in God and His Apostle and died
workers of abomination!
85 Let not their wealth and their children please you, God only
wishes to torment them therewith in this world, and that their
souls may pass away the while they misbelieve.
86 Whenever a surah is sent down to them, 'Believe ye in God,
and fight strenuously together with His Apostle,' those of them
who have the means will ask thee for leave to stay at home and say,

'Let us be amongst those who stay behind.'
87 They are content to be with those who are left behind. A
stamp is set upon their hearts that they should not discern.
88 But the Apostle and those who believe with him are strenuous with their wealth and with their persons; these shall have good
things, and these it is shall prosper.
89 God has prepared for them gardens beneath which rivers
flow, to dwell therein for aye; that is the mighty happiness!
90 There came certain desert Arabs that they might be excused;
and those stayed behind who had called God and His Apostle liars.
There shall befal those of them who misbelieved, a mighty woe.
91 For the weak, and the sick, and those who cannot find wherewith to expend in alms there is no hindrance, so they be only sincere towards God and His Apostle. There is no way against those
who do well; for God is forgiving and merciful.
92 Nor against those to whom, when they came to thee that thou
shouldst mount them, thou didst say, 'I cannot find wherewith to
mount you,' turned their backs while their eyes poured forth with
tears, for grief that they could not find wherewith to expend.
93 Only is there a way against those who ask thee for leave, to
stay at home while they are rich; content to be with those who
are left behind; on whose hearts God has set a stamp, so that they

Q 9.97-98

Verse 97 reads, "*The Arabs of the desert are keener in misbelief and hypocrisy*" and verse 98 reads, "*...some* [of the desert Arabs]*...take what they expend to be a forced loan....*" Both of these accusations are abrogated with Q 9.99: *"And of the Arabs of the desert are some who believe in God and the last day...."*[60]

Yet other scholars state there is no relationship of abrogation between the verses. Instead, these verses speak of the religious positions of the desert Arabs.[61]

should not know.
[94] They make excuses to you when ye return to them: say, 'Make
no excuse, we believe you not; God has informed us concerning
you. God sees your works and His Apostle too!' Then shall ye be
brought back unto Him who knows the unseen and the seen; and
He shall inform you of that which ye have done.
[95] They will adjure you by God when ye have come back to
them, to turn aside from them; turn ye aside then from them; verily, they are a plague, and their resort is hell! a recompense for that
which they have earned!
[96] They will adjure you to be pleased with them; but if ye are
pleased with them, God will not be pleased with a people who
work abomination.
[97] The Arabs of the desert are keener in misbelief and hypocrisy,
and are more likely not to know the bounds which God has sent
down to His Apostle; but God is knowing and wise.
[98] And of the Arabs of the desert are some who take what they
expend to be a forced loan, and they wait a turn of fortune against
you; against them shall a turn of evil fortune be; for God both
hears and knows.
[99] And of the Arabs of the desert are some who believe in God
and the last day, and who take what they expend in alms to be a

Q 9.97, 99, 101

The sūra accuses the Arabs of being "*keener in misbelief and hypocrisy*" (verse 97). Then after only two verses it contradicts itself, excluding "some" of the Arabs: "*And of the Arabs of the desert are some who believe in God and the last day…*" (verse 99).

To resolve what appears to be an obvious contradiction, the scholars of Islām said that there is no contradiction, but that it is a case of abrogating and being abrogated.

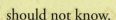

means of approach to God and to the Apostle's prayers,-is it not a
means of approach for them? God will make them enter into His
mercy; verily, God is forgiving and merciful.
100 As for the foremost in the race, the first of those who fled, and
the helpers, and those who followed them in their kindness, God
is well pleased with them, and they are well pleased with Him; He
has prepared for them gardens beneath which rivers flow, to dwell
therein for aye; that is the mighty happiness.
101 And of those who are round about you of the Arabs of the
desert, some are hypocrites, and of the people of Medinah, some
are stubborn in hypocrisy; thou dost not know them-we know
them; we will torment them twice over; then shall they be sent off

This situation is a very strange form of abrogation. Not only does verse 99 abrogate verse 97 (*"The Arabs of the desert are keener in misbelief and hypocrisy…"*) but it also abrogates verse 101 (*"And of those who are round about you of the Arabs of the desert, some are hypocrites…"*).

Questions: How could the abrogating and abrogated verses occur side by side like this, so that a verse abrogates both the verse before it and after it? How can these three verses be revealed at the same time with one abrogating the other two? How could we find abrogating and abrogated verses in sūra al-Tawba (Q 9) when it is said to be the last given sūra of the Qur'ān?

The juxtaposition of abrogating and abrogated verses in this way, and the presence of abrogation in the last given sūra, proves the arbitrary transcription of the Qur'ān. Where is the intended meaning and the final opinion among these contradictory rulings?

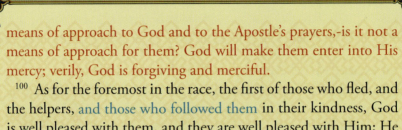

into mighty woe.
102 And others have confessed their sins,-that they have mixed with a righteous action another evil action;-haply it may be God will turn again to them; verily, God is forgiving and merciful.
103 Take from their wealth alms to cleanse and purify them thereby; and pray for them; verily, thy prayer is a repose for them; for God both hears and knows.
104 Do they not know that God accepts repentance from His servants, and takes alms; and that God is He who is easily turned and merciful.
105 And say, 'Act ye;' and God and His Apostle and the believers shall see your acts, and ye shall be brought back to Him who

Q 9.100

'Umar Ibn al-Khaṭṭāb read this text "the first of those…the helpers who followed them" without the *waw* ("and"). So the phrase "who followed them" becomes a description of the Anṣār.[62]

According to most of the readers, the verse mentions three groups: *al-Muhājirūn*[D] ("the Emigrants"), *al-Anṣār* (*"the Helpers"*), and those who followed Muḥammad. However, 'Umar Ibn al-Khaṭṭāb comments that the verse deals with two groups only: *al-Muhājirūn* and *al-Anṣār*.

Q 9.101

The majority reading is ***sanu'adhibuhum*** ("**we will torment them**") with an "n", where the speaker is Allah. It was written in the codex of Anas Ibn Mālik as *sayu'adhibuhum* ("he will torment them") with a "y", the report being about Allah. Ubayy Ibn Ka'b read *satu'adhibuhum* ("they [lit. *she*: feminine singular used grammatically for nonhuman plural] will torment them") with a "t", with the interpretation that the angels, or the keepers of hellfire, will torment them.[63]

Therefore, there are three possibilities for the explanation of the verse: Allah is the one speaking, Allah is the one spoken about, or the angels are the ones spoken about.

knows the seen and the unseen, and He shall inform you of that
which ye have done.
106 And others are in hopes of God's bidding; whether He will
torment them, or whether He turn again towards them; for God
is knowing, wise.
107 And there are those who have taken to a mosque for mischief,
and for misbelief, and to make a breach amongst the believers,
and for an ambush for him who made war against God and His
Apostle before; they surely swear, 'We only wished for what was
good;' but God bears witness that they are liars.
108 Never stand up therein!-there is a mosque founded on piety from the first day: it is more right that thou shouldst stand
therein;-therein are men who love to be clean; for God doth love
the clean.
109 Is he who has laid his foundation upon the fear of God and
of His good-will better, or he who has laid his foundation upon a
crumbling wall of sand, which crumbles away with him into the
fire of hell?-but God guides not a people who do wrong.
110 The building which they have built will not cease to be a
source of doubt in their hearts until their hearts are cut asunder;
but God is knowing, wise.
111 Verily, God hath bought of the believers their persons and

Q 9.106

Ibn Mas'ūd read it differently: "and Allah is forgiving merciful."[64]

Q 9.109

The verse was read in a different form. Ubayy Ibn Ka'b read it with the addition of *qawā'iduhu* ("his bases") and the feminine singular of the verb *fa-inhārat* ("they crumbled"), which is grammatically used for nonhuman plural, instead of the current

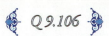

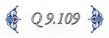

their wealth, for the paradise they are to have; they shall fight in the way of God, and they shall slay and be slain: promised in truth, in the law and the gospel and the Qur'ān;-and who is more faithful to His covenant than God ? Be ye glad then in the covenant which ye have made with Him, for that is the mighty happiness!
112 Those who repent, those who worship, those who praise, those who fast, those who bow down, those who adore, those who bid what is right and forbid what is wrong, and those who keep the bounds of God,-glad tidings to those who believe!
113 It is not for the prophet and those who believe to ask forgiveness for the idolaters, even though they be their kindred, after it has been made manifest to them, that they are the fellows of hell.
114 Nor was Abraham's asking pardon for his father aught else but through a promise he had promised him; but when it was made manifest to him that he was an enemy to God, he cleansed himself of him; verily, Abraham was pitiful and clement.
115 Nor will God lead astray a people after He has guided them until that is made manifest to them which they have to fear; verily, God all things doth know.
116 Verily, God's is the kingdom of the heavens and the earth! He quickens and He kills! Nor have ye beside God a patron or protector.

Arabic Qur'ān's masculine singular ***fa-inhāra*** ("[it] **crumbles**"), in reference to the wall of sand. Ubayy Ibn Ka'b read "and doth his bases crumbled [fem.] to pieces with him, into the fire of hell." Ibn Mas'ūd read the verb in the singular, like the current Arabic Qur'ān, but added *qawā'iduhu* ("his bases") like Ubayy Ibn Ka'b.[65]

Q 9.111

'Umar Ibn al-Khaṭṭāb and others read it differently, replacing ***bi-anna lahumu al-jannata*** ("**for the paradise they are to have**") with *bi-l-jannati* ("by the garden").[66]

[117] God has now turned towards the prophet and those who fled with him, and towards the helpers who followed him in the hour of difficulty, after that the hearts of a part of them had well-nigh gone amiss. Then He turned unto them; verily to them He is kind and merciful:-

[118] unto the three who were left behind, so that the earth with all its ample space was too strait for them, and their souls were straitened for them, and they thought that there was no refuge for them from God save unto Him. Then He turned again towards them that they might also turn; verily, God, He is easily turned and merciful!

Q9.117

Ibn Mas'ūd read it by removing *kāda* ("had well-nigh") and replacing the word ***fariqin*** ("a part of them") with *ṭā'ifa* ("a sect").[67]

The term *kāda* means to almost do the act without actually doing it. The meaning of it in the verse is that their hearts were close to having gone amiss but had not. However, according to the reading of Ibn Mas'ūd, their hearts did go amiss from the truth. There is a clear difference between the one who almost went amiss and those who actually did go amiss. What a difference of condition and implications the two recitations present.

Q9.119

Most read ***al-ṣādiqīna*** ("**those who speak the truth**") in the plural, as it is in the current Arabic Qur'ān. We have a reading for some of the readers that reads *al-ṣādiqayni* ("the two who speak the truth") in the dual form. It is said that the two are Allah and Muḥammad, yet others say the two are Abū Bakr and 'Umar Ibn al-Khaṭṭāb.[68]

In addition to that, there is a reading attributed to Ibn 'Abbās and to Ibn Mas'ūd that reads *al-ṣādifīna* with an *"f"*. This reading means those who turned away from both falsehood and those who ascribe to falsehood.[69]

Thus, the readings disagree about the command given to Muslims:

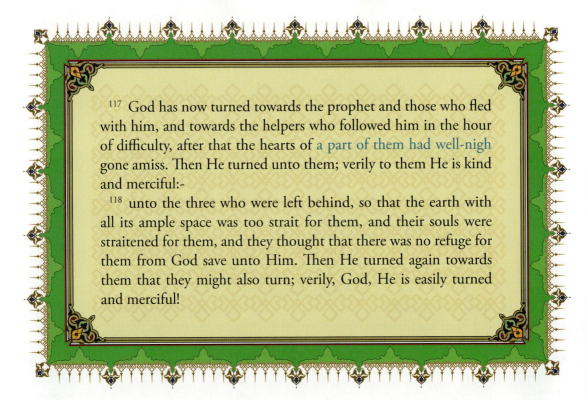

119 O ye who believe! fear God and be with those who speak the truth.
120 It was not for the people of Medinah, and those around about them of the Arabs of the desert, to stay behind the Apostle of God and not to prefer their souls to his: that is because neither thirst, nor toil, nor heat, nor hunger befel them on God's way. Nor do they stop to anger the misbelievers, nor do they get any (harm) from the enemy without a good work being written down to them; verily, God wastes not the hire of those who do well.
121 Nor do they expend in alms a small or great expense, nor do they cross a wady without it being written down to them; that God

- Muslims should be with those who speak the truth, in general.
- Muslims should be with Allah and Muḥammad or with Abū Bakr and ʻUmar Ibn al-Khaṭṭāb.
- Muslims should be with those who turn away from falsehood.

However, there are those who reject all these readings because Ibn Masʻūd and Ibn ʻAbbās read it from Muḥammad as *min al-ṣādiqīna* ("from those who speak the truth") instead of the Arabic Qur'ān's ***maʻa al-ṣādiqīna*** ("**with those who speak the truth**").[70]

They consider that a person can be *maʻa al-ṣādiqīna* ("with those who speak the truth") without being true himself. But the reading *min al-ṣādiqīna* ("from those who speak the truth") means that one is to be with them and one of them.[71]

Q 9.120

A group of scholars state that the verse means "it was not permitted for any of the settlers of Medina and the surrounding area to decide to stay behind and not join Muḥammad in battle." The verse is abrogated with Q 9.122: *"The believers should not march forth altogether."*[72] Another group of scholars states that it is conserved because it contained a command to the Muslims of that time to meet the call of Muḥammad to go to war, "if he needed them and mobilized them, no one could stay behind."[73]

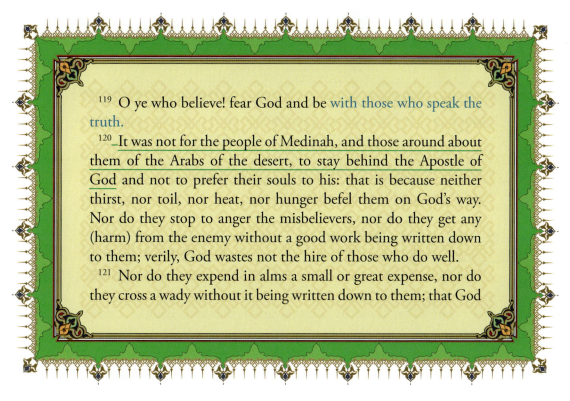

may reward them with better than that which they have done.
[122] The believers should not march forth altogether; and if a troop of every division of them march not forth, it is only that they may study their religion and warn their people when they return to them, that haply they may beware.
[123] O ye who believe! fight those who are near to you of the misbelievers, and let them find in you sternness; and know that God is with those who fear.
[124] And whenever a surah is sent down, there are some of them who say, 'Which of you has this increased in faith?' But as for those who believe, it does increase them in faith, and they shall rejoice:
[125] but as for those in whose hearts is sickness, it only adds a

Q 9.126

The current Arabic Qur'ān reads ***awa lā yarūna*** ("**Do they not see**"), which goes back to Q 9.125: "*...but as for those in whose hearts is sickness....*"[74]

On the other hand, Ibn Mas'ūd and others read *awa lā tarā* ("Do you not see"), where Muḥammad is the one addressed. It is also said that Ibn Mas'ūd wrote in his codex *awa lam tara* ("have you not seen"), where Muḥammad is also addressed.[75]

Question: Who is addressed here—Muḥammad or those *"in whose hearts is a sickness"*?

Q 9.128

The majority of the readers read ***min anfusikum*** ("**from amongst yourselves**") as it is in the current Arabic Qur'ān. Ibn 'Abbās and a group of readers read *min anfasikum*, meaning "the most esteemed or the noblest." They said that Muḥammad, his daughter Fāṭima, and his wife, 'Ā'isha, read by this reading.[76]

Is it reasonable that what is written in the Qur'ān is different than what Muḥammad himself read, as well as his daughter and his wife? For after Muḥammad used to read *min anfasikum*, meaning that he is of a higher status, the editors of the Qur'ān wrote, *min anfusikum*, "from amongst yourselves," meaning from "you."

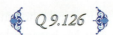

plague to their plague, and they die misbelievers.
126 Do they not see that they are tried in every year once or twice?
Yet they do not turn again, nor do they mind!
127 And whenever a surah is sent down, some of them look at
the others-'Does any one see you?'-Then they turn away! God has
turned their hearts, for that they are a people who do not discern.
128 There has come to you an apostle from amongst yourselves;
hard for him to bear is it that ye commit iniquity; he is anxious
over you after the believers, pitiful, compassionate.
129 But if they turn their backs, then say, 'God is enough for me!
there is no god but He! upon Him do I rely, for He is Lord of the
mighty throne!'

In the Qur'ān, it appears *min anfusikum* ("from amongst yourselves") goes back to the comprehension of the editing committee of the Qur'ān that Muḥammad was not from the social or financial elite of the Quraysh. So they corrected the Muḥammadan claim by making him one of them, instead of one of their nobles. If that had not been done, the claim would had been confirmed and established by making the reading of the word according to the way Muḥammad and his house read it.

Q 9.129

The majority of readers read ***al-'aẓīmi*** ("**the mighty**") with a *kasra* ("i"), making the word an adjective of the word *al-'arshi* ("the throne"), according to Arabic grammar.

Other readers read it *al-'aẓīmu* ("the mighty") with a *ḍamma* ("o" or "u"), making the word an adjective of the word *rabbu* ("Lord").[77]

Does the adjective *al-'aẓīm* ("the mighty") describe the lord or the throne?

Question: Is it permissible to mention the lord without the adjective of exaltation, when the throne is exalted? If not, why do Muslims, even today, read this verse which gives exaltation to the throne yet neglect the reading that gives exaltation to the lord?

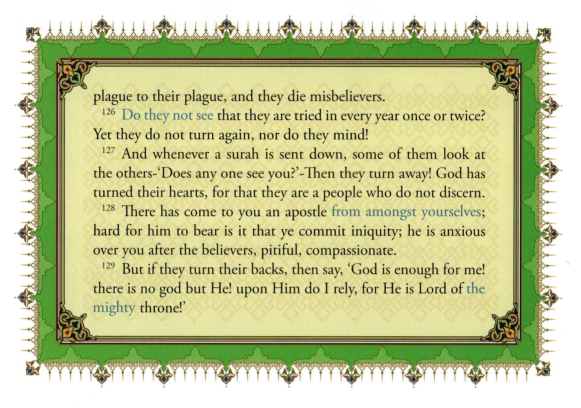

Part III
Resources and References

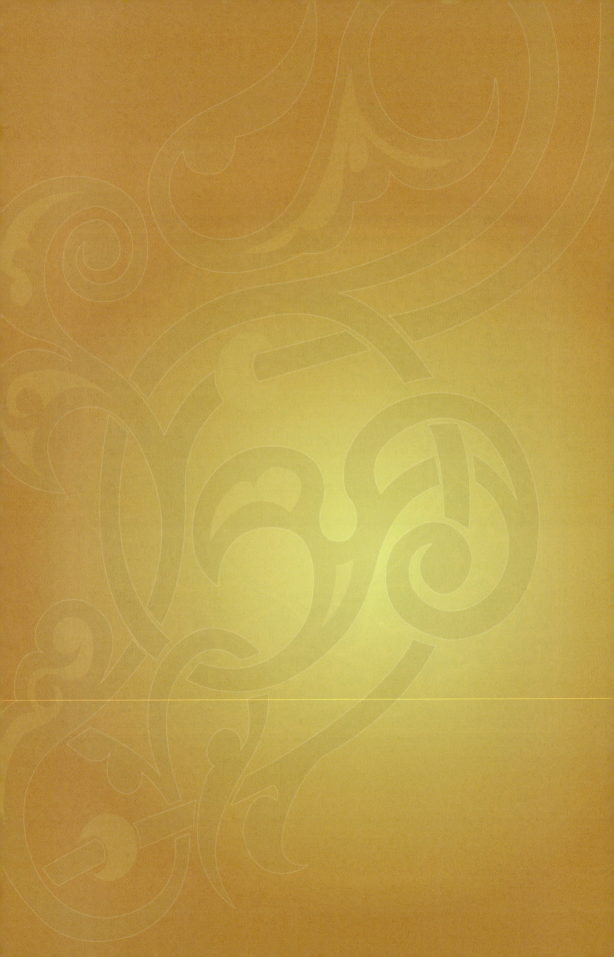

Summary of Resources and References

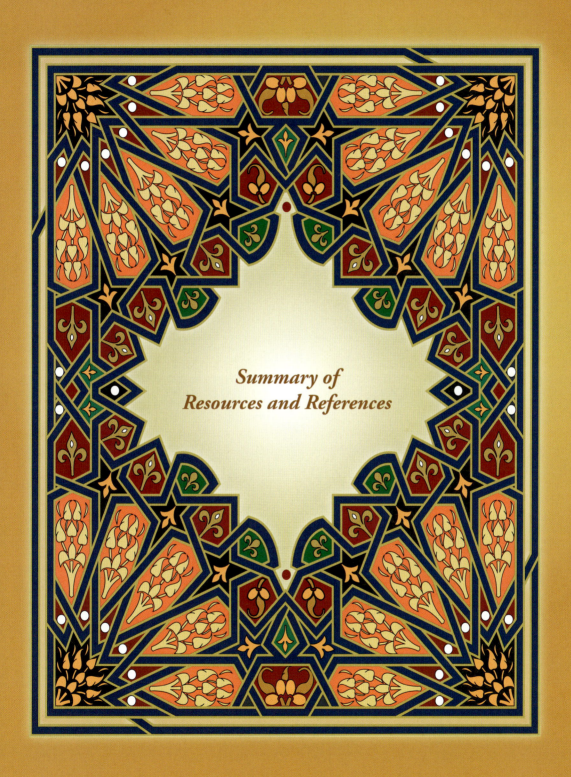

Summary of Resources and References

The third part of this book contains traditional references as well as other resources to assist the reader in understanding various aspects of the book. All the resources will better familiarize the reader with important concepts particular to the Qur'ān, help the reader in topic searches and related information, and enhance the reader's contextual understanding and knowledge concerning the beginnings and spread of Islām.

Suggested Readings
This section contains annotated lists of both print and online readings to extend the discussion on selected topics mentioned in this book.

Selected Proper Names
This section contains additional information about individuals mentioned in this book who impacted—or were affected by—Islām or the Qur'ān, particularly during the early centuries.

Selected Definitions
Brief definitions for important Islāmic subjects and other related terms are presented in this section.

Controversial Qur'ānic Texts
Three suras—al-Khal', al-Ḥafd, and al-Nūrayn—that are not included in the current Arabic Qur'ān are presented in this section in Arabic and paired with an adjacent English translation.

Timeline
The vertical graphic with accompanying captions notes important leaders and identifies major dates in the early history of Islām and the Qur'ān from 54 BH/AD 570 to AH 1342/AD 1925.

Maps
Four maps are included to provide a visual geographical and political representation of the Arabian Peninsula during the early history of Islām. The first two maps show major cities and tribes in the area and the last two illustrate major raids and the expansion of Islām into the Mediterranean region (sixth to seventh century AD):

- Cities and Tribes of Arabia
- Yathrib (Medina) Tribes
- Major Raids of Arabia
- The Spread of Islām

Endnotes
Because of the extensive research contained in this book, endnotes (rather than parenthetical documentation) were used to cite the textual references. Each set of endnotes is organized sequentially by chapter—articles first, followed by the suras.

Works Cited

All references cited in this book are contained in this section and are divided into three sections: Arabic Commentaries, Arabic Sources, and Non-Arabic Sources.

Subject Index

Major topics discussed in this book are alphabetically arranged and linked with corresponding page numbers to enhance and expedite reader access to the content.

Suggested Readings

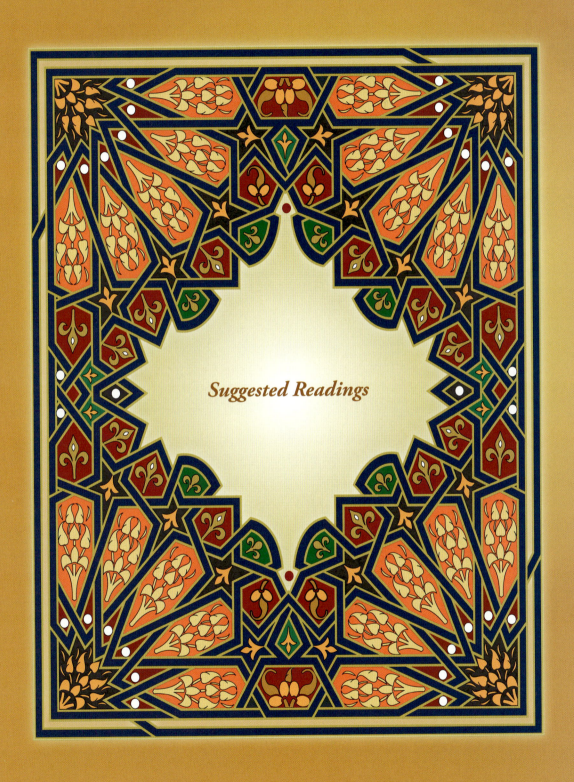

Suggested Readings

The following list of print and online resources provides additional information about selected topics addressed in this book. Though not comprehensive, this list does offer readers—especially those with little previous knowledge of the Qur'ān and its exegetes—another opportunity to clarify or deepen their understanding of a particular concept, issue, or event mentioned in this book that they find interesting yet still puzzling.

These suggested readings are organized by where the particular topic is highlighted in a given article or chapter.

Articles

Compilation of the Qur'ān

These sources discuss the compilation and revisions of the Qur'ān.

Gilliot, Claude. "Reconsidering the Authorship of the Qur'an: Is the Qur'an Partly the Fruit of a Progressive and Collective Work." *The Qur'an in Its Historical-Context.* Ed. Gabriel Said Reynolds. London: Routledge, 2008. 88-108. Print.

Jeffery, Arthur, ed. *Materials for the History of the Text of the Qur'ān: The Old Codices.* New York: AMS Press, 1975. Print. The only in-depth study of variations in the Qur'ānic text in early Islāmic history. Originally published in 1937; requires knowledge of Arabic.

Sell, Edward. *The Recensions of the Qur'an.* Madras: Christian Literature Society, 1909. Print.

This article details Shiite additions to the Qur'ān, especially sūra al-Wilāya:

St.-Clair Tisdall, William. "Shi'ah Additions to the Koran." *Moslem World* 3.3 (1913): 227-241. Print.

These sources discuss the restoration, research, and controversy concerning the Ṣan'ā'(Sana) manuscripts, discovered in 1972.

Lester, Toby. "What Is the Koran?" *Atlantic Monthly*. Jan. 1999. *Atlantic Monthly Group*. Web. 31 Aug. 2010. <http://www.theatlantic.com/doc/199901/koran>.

Taher, Abul. "Querying the Koran." *Guardian.* 8 Aug. 2000. *Guardian News and Media Limited.* Web. 7 Aug. 2010. <http://www.guardian.co.uk/Archive/Article/0,4273,4048586,00.htm>.

Muḥammad's Jibrīl

This reference manual about hallucinations and other sensory deceptions provides information regarding possible physical reasons for the symptoms Muhammad experienced during his revelations.

Blom, Jan Dirk. *A Dictionary of Hallucinations.* New York: Springer, AD 2010. Print. See Akoasm, Auditory Aura, Auditory Hallucination, and Visual Hallucination.

Sūras

Q 1.1-7

German Semitic scholar, Theodor Nöldeke, has written a well-regarded analysis of the Jewish and Christian origin of sura al-Fatiha (Q 1), now available in an Arabic translation.

Nöldeke, Theodor. *History of the Qur'an* [*Tārīkh al-Qur'ān*]. Trans. Georges Tamer. Beirut: Konrad-Adenauer-Stiftung, AD 2004. 98-104. Print.

Q 2.1

Many Western scholars have tried to decipher the *muqaṭṭa'āt*. Although their attempts have not provided any convincing conclusions, it is still worthwhile to read some of them. The article, "The Mystic Letters of the Koran," by well-respected Orientalist Arthur Jeffery, summarizes these attempts.

Jeffery, Arthur. "The Mystic Letters of the Koran." *The Muslim World.* 13 (1924): 247-260. Print.

Jeffery, Arthur. "The Mystic Letters of the Koran." *Answering Islam.* N.p. 2009-2010. Web. 10 Aug. 2010. <http://www.answering-Islām.org/Books/Jeffery/mystic_letters.htm>.

Q 2.125-129

A review of Abraham's life story can be found in the biblical narrative—the book of Genesis (11.26-25.18).

The New International Study (NIV) Study Bible. Eds. Kenneth Barker, Donald Burdick, John Stek, et al. Grand Rapids: Zondervan, 1985. Print.

Rich information about the Ka'ba can be found in a multivolume encyclopedic work by Dr. Jawād Ali, a prominent Iraqi historian (d. AD 1987).

Ali, Jawād. *al-Mufaṣṣal fī Tārīkh al-'Arab Qabl al-Islām.* Vol. 6. Beirut: Dār al-'Ilm, AH 1413/AD 1993. Print.

Q 2.194

For further information about the Ḥajj (major pilgrimage) and the 'Umra (minor pilgrimage) in pagan and Islāmic contexts, see the comment on Q. 2.158 and the following resources.

'Alī, Jawād. "Al-Ḥajj and Al-'Umra." *al-Mufaṣṣal fī Tārīkh al-'Arab Qabl al-Islām.* section: 347-397. Beirut: Dār al-'Ilm, AH 1413/AD 1993. Print.

Q 2.258

Narrative accounts of the Abraham and Nimrod story can be found in the *Midrash Rabbah* and other sources.

Freedman, H., trans. and ed. *Midrash Rabbah.* Vol 1. London: Soncino, AD 1939. 310-311. Print.

St. Clair-Tisdall, W[illiam]. *The Original Sources of Qur'an.* London: Society for Promoting Christian Knowledge, AD 1911. 66-80. Print.

St. Clair-Tisdall, W[illiam]. *The Sources of Islam: A Persian Treatise.* abr. Trans. William Muir. Edinburgh: T. & T. Clark, AD 1901. 16-24. Print.

"Nimrod."*JewishEncyclopedia.com.* The Kopelman Foundation. 2002. Web. 22 Aug. 2010. <http://www.jewishencyclopedia.com/>.

Q 3.46, 49

The story of creation, "out of clay, as it were, the figure of a bird," can be found in Chapter 4 of the apocryphal text, *The Infancy Gospel of Thomas*, in the English translation from Latin, and in Chapter 2 in the English translation from Greek.

The Infancy Gospel of Thomas. Trans. M.R. James. Oxford: Clarendon, 1924. *PseudepigraphaWeb.* Ed. Joshua Williams. 2002. Web. 2 October 2009. <http://www.pseudepigrapha. com/LostBooks/TheInfancyGospelOfThomas.html>.

Q 3.183

The following sources discuss the biblical significance of fire and the prophet Isaiah.

Dufour, Xavier Leon, et al. [Arabic translation]. *Mu'jam al-Lāhūt al-Kitābī* [A Theological Lexicon of the Bible]. 5th ed. Beirut: Dār al-Mashriq, 2004. Print. See "Fire" in the index.

"Fire." *JewishEncyclopedia.com.* The Kopelman Foundation. 2002. Web. 22 Aug. 2010. <http://www.jewishencyclopedia.com/view.jsp?artid=158&letter=F&search=fire>.

"Isaiah." *JewishEncyclopedia.com.* The Kopelman Foundation. 2002. Web. 22 Aug. 2010. <http://www.jewishencyclopedia.com/view.jsp?artid=261&letter=I&search=ISAIAH>.

Kitāb Murshid al-ṭālibīn ilā al-Kitāb al-muqadas al-thamīn. Open Library. *Internet Archive.* 2010. Web. 22 Aug. 2010. <http://openlibrary.org/books/OL14027192M/Kitab_Murshid_al-talibin_ila_al-Kitab_al-muqaddas_al-thamin>.

Souvay, Charles. "Isaias." *The Catholic Encyclopedia.* Vol. 8. New York: Robert Appleton Company, 1910. *New Advent.* Web. 27 Aug. 2010. <http://www.newadvent.org/cathen/08179b.htm>.

Q 4.2-3

For those who can read the Arabic القرآن واغتيال الفصاحة العقل والبيان, an article that deals critically with Q 4.3 is available online.

Elia, N. "Qur'ān and the Murder of Eloquence, Logic, and Clarity." *Annaqed: The Critic.* 2 Feb. 2008. Web. 31 Aug 2010. <http://www.annaqed.com/ar/content/show.aspx?aid=16053>.

Q 4.15, 16

Additional sources are available for further study of the verse on stoning (*al-rajm*): "As to the old man and old woman, if they committed adultery, stone them with no hesitation, a punishment from Allah, for Allah is All-Knowing and Wise."

Gairdner, W[illiam] H[enry] T[emple], Iskander 'Abdu'l-Masih al-Bajouri and Boulos Fawzi al-Remawi. *al-Rajm Verse in the Torah and the Qur'an.* Bulaq, Egypt: English American, 1909. Print.

Gairdner, W[illiam] H[enry] T[emple], Iskandar 'Abdu'l-Masih and Sali 'Abdu'l-Ahad. *The Verse of Stoning in the Bible and the Qur'ān.* London: Christian Lit. Soc., 1910. Print.

Q 4.157-158

Additional reading on Irenaeus' documentary on the teachings of Basilides is available online.

Irenaeus, "Against Heresies (Book I, Chapter 24): Doctrines of Saturninus and Basilides." *New Advent*. Kevin Knight. 2010. Web. 25 Aug 2010. <http://www.newadvent.org/fathers/0103124.htm>.

Q 4.171

These sources discuss the Christian Trinity for the Arabic reader.

Jadid, Iskandar. *Wiḥdānīyat al-Thālūth fī al-Masīḥīya wa al-Islām*. Rikon: The Good Way, n.d. <http://www.alkalema.net/pdf/wehdanietalsalos.pdf>.

Boulad, Henri. *Manṭiq al-Thālūth*. Beirut: Dār al-Mashriq, n.d. Print.

al-Tikritī, Abū Ra'iṭa [ninth century AD]. *fī al-Thālūth al-Muqaddas*. Thesis. Study and text by Father Salīm Dakkāsh the Jesuit. N.p.: Dār al-Mashriq, 1996. Print. (It is a thesis from the Arabic Christian heritage.)

Q 7.127

This article discusses the differences and similarities between the Qur'ān and the Bible on the topic of Moses' confrontations with Pharoah and the slaying(s) of the Israelites' infant sons.

Katz, Jochen. "Qur'ān Contradiction: Was There a Second Period of Slaying the Sons of the Israelites? *Answering Islam*. 2010. Web. 2 Sept. 2010. <http://answering-Islām.org/Quran/Contra/pharaoh_slaying_sons.html>.

Q 8.41

The following source contains more information regarding "the fifth".

'Alī, Jawād. *al-Mufaṣṣal fī Tārīkh al-'Arab Qabl al-Islām*. 2nd ed. Vol 5. Beirut: n.p., AH 1413/AD 1993. Print. See sections "al-ḥurūb" and "fī al-Fiqh al Jāhilī."

Selected Proper Names

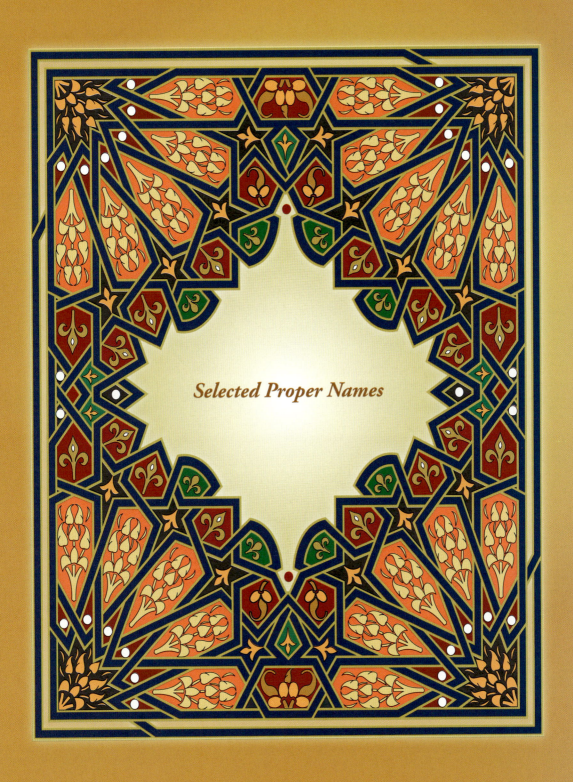

Selected Proper Names

'Abd Allah Ibn 'Abbās

('Abd Allah Ibn 'Abbās Ibn 'Abd al-Muṭṭalib)

3 BH-AH 68/AD 619-687

In the Islāmic sources, he is commonly referred to as Ibn 'Abbās. He was born in Mecca and was one of Muḥammad's Companions at a young age. Revered by Muslims for his knowledge of the Qur'ān and his authority and narration of the *ḥadīths*, he is often given the title, "the Interpreter of the Qur'ān."

'Abd Allah Ibn Jaḥsh

('Abd Allah Ibn Jaḥsh Ibn Ri'āb)

d. AH 3/AD 625

He was a well-known Companion of Muḥammad and the brother of Zaynab, a daughter-in-law (and later, wife) of Muḥammad. He was from the tribe of Assad, a branch of the Quraysh, and commanded the first successful expedition (at Nakhla) on behalf of Muḥammad. He was killed in the Battle of Uhud.

'Abd Allah Ibn Mas'ūd

d. c. AH 32/AD 653

An early convert, 'Abd Allah Ibn Mas'ūd was one of the most prominent Companions of Muḥammad. Courageous in his faith, he was the first one to read the Qur'ān openly in Mecca. Ibn Mas'ūd participated in all of Muḥammad's battles and devotedly served Muḥammad, earning Muḥammad's complete trust and respect. Despite his high standing and reputation, he was not asked to participate in the compilation of the Qur'ān after Muḥammad's death. Ibn Mas'ūd has his own codex of the Qur'ān.

'Abd Allah Ibn al-Zubayr

AH 1-73/AD 622-692

'Abd Allah Ibn al-Zubayr was from the Assad family of the Quraysh tribe and the first one to be born in Medina from among the *Muhājirūn* (those who emigrated from Mecca to Medina with Muḥammad). He supported 'Ā'isha in the war against 'Alī Ibn Abī Ṭālib. After the death of Mu'āwīya, the founder of the Umayyad Empire, 'Abd Allah Ibn al-Zubayr refused to give allegiance to Mu'āwīya's son, Yazīd Ibn Mu'āwīya. When Yazīd Ibn Mu'āwīya died in AD 683, the majority of the Islāmic provinces declared their allegiance to 'Abd Allah Ibn al-Zubayr, except for al-Shām (Syria), which remained a firm stronghold for the Umayyad. The wars continued for ten years until al-Ḥajjāj Ibn Yūsuf al-Thaqafī (during the governance of 'Abd al-Malik Ibn Marwān) killed 'Abd Allah Ibn al-Zubayr on the battlefield. His corpse was beheaded and crucified.

Abū Bakr

c. 51 BH-AH 13/AD 573-634

Abū Bakr was one of the earliest followers of Muḥammad. He was a rich merchant from the Quraysh tribe. His daughter 'Ā'isha became Muḥammad's third wife. Abū Bakr accompanied Muḥammad on many of the early missions and became the first caliph (successor) to rule the emerging Muslim empire (AH 11).

Abū Dharr al-Ghifārī

(Jundub Ibn Junāda)

d. c. AH 32/AD 652

A tribesman of the Banū Ghifār, he was among the earliest of those who embraced Islām as a faith. When he criticized the pomp of the authorities during the reign of 'Uthmān Ibn 'Affān, al-Ghifārī was consequently banished to al-Ribdha outside of Medina, where he later died.

Abū Ḥanīfa

(al-Nu'mān Ibn Thābit)

AH 80-150/AD 699-769

Though born in Kufa, Iraq, Abū Ḥanīfa was of Persian ancestry. An esteemed scholar, he founded the Hanafī branch of Islāmic faith, which is one of the four main Sunnī branches. During his lifetime, he enjoyed a position of great respect and admiration among his Muslim colleagues. When he refused to work for the government, he was jailed and tortured. He died in prison.

Abū Hurayra

('Abd al-Raḥman Ibn Ṣakhr al-Dūsī)

d. AH 59/AD 679

It is told that his original name was 'Abd Shams before converting to Islām in Medina. When he became a Muslim, Muḥammad named him 'Abd al-Raḥmān. He accompanied Muḥammad and spent long periods of time with him, achieving renown for his memorization of the many *ḥadīths* (sayings) of Muḥammad.

A debate, however, exists over the authenticity of his *ḥadīth* narrations. The Sunnīs view his narrations as trustworthy, whereas the Shiites reject them. During the reign of 'Umar Ibn al-Khaṭṭāb, the historical records allude to Abū Hurayra's conviction as a liar (adding his own ideas to the *ḥadīths*, etc.) and his support of enemies of Muḥammad's family and descendants.

Abū Isḥāq al-Zajjāj

(Ibrāhīm Ibn al-Sarīy Ibn Sahl)

AH 241-311/AD 855-923

This great linguistic scholar lived in Baghdad and contributed several categorical works in the fields of the Arabic language and the sciences of the Qur'ān. Most notable among his works: *Ma'ānī al-Qur'ān wa I'rābahu* [*The Qur'ān's Interpretation and Parsing*].

'Ā'isha Bint Abī Bakr

9 BH-AH 58/AD 613-678

'Ā'isha was the daughter of Abū Bakr, a close friend of Muḥammad and one of his Companions throughout Muḥammad's claim to prophethood. When Muḥammad was over fifty years old, he married 'Ā'isha, who was barely nine years old. Of all his wives, it is said she was the only virgin before her marriage to Muḥammad, and she was his favorite. She is quoted as a source for many *ḥadīths* about Muḥammad's personal life and is considered a learned scholar of Islām's early age. She is highly regarded by Sunnīs, esteemed as a role model for Muslim women, but the Shiites discredit her because she was vehemently opposed to 'Alī Ibn Abī Ṭālib.

'Alī Ibn Abī Ṭālib

('Alī Ibn Abī Ṭālib Ibn 'Abd al-Muṭṭalib)

c. 23 BH-AH 40/AD 600-661

Married to Fāṭima, the daughter of Muḥammad, 'Alī was Muḥammad's son-in-law as well as his first cousin. He accepted Islām when he was young. He later participated in most of Muḥammad's battles as a young man.

The Shiites consider him and his descendants the rightful successors to Muḥammad and believe the first three caliphs (Abū Bakr, 'Umar Ibn al-Khaṭṭāb, and 'Uthmān Ibn 'Affān) illegally usurped 'Alī's power and position as Islām's first legitimate successor after Muḥammad. This position eventually divided Islām into Sunni and Shiites branches.

'Alī became the fourth caliph in AH 35/AD 656, but his reign was full of conflicts and disputes among the Muslims that led to his assassination five years later in Kufa.

'Amr Ibn 'Ubayd

(Abī 'Uthmān al-Baṣrī)

AH 80-144/AD 699-761

'Amr Ibn 'Ubayd was of Persian origin. He was a prominent Mu'tazila who was known for his asceticism. Among his writings are *al-Tafsīr* and *al-Rad 'alā al-Qaddarīya.* He died while traveling from Basra to Mecca.

al-Ḥajjāj Ibn Yūsuf al-Thaqafī

AH 40-95/AD 660-714

He was born in Ta'if and worked with the police of the Umayyad Empire, rising in rank until he became the *wālī* (governor) of Iraq. He ruled with an iron fist and is credited with establishing the authority of the Umayyad in the region. He was also known for his eloquence and introduced changes to the Qur'ān in fourteen different places, according to the Islāmic sources.

al-Ḥārith Ibn Suwayd al-Ṣāmit, al-Ḥārith Ibn Suwayd al-Taymī

Two men named al-Ḥārith Ibn al-Suwayd are mentioned in Islamic sources. The first is al-Ḥārith Ibn Suwayd Ibn al-Ṣāmit from the Anṣar tribe of Aws. This al-Ḥārith Ibn Suwayd al-Ṣāmit, a Muslim, became an enemy of al-Mujadhar (another Muslim) for killing al-Ṣāmit's father in pre-Islāmic times. During the Battle of Uḥud, Ibn al-Ṣāmit killed al-Mujadhar and recanted his Islam, taking refuge with the Quraysh. Later, Ibn al-Ṣāmit returned to Islam but was killed by Muḥammad, despite Ibn al-Ṣāmit's reconversion to Islām, because Muḥammad did not forgive him for killing al-Mujadhar.

The second is al-Ḥārith Ibn Suwayd al-Taymī from Kufa. He left Islām, rejoining his people for a time, only to return to Islām. His return to Islam was accepted. He later became one of the narrators of the *hadīths*.

al-Ḥassan al-Baṣrī

(al-Ḥassan Ibn Yassār; Abī Sa'īd)

AH 21-110/AD 642-728

Though born in Medina, al-Baṣrī later moved to Basra where he received his education and became one of the most famous jurisprudents of his time. During his lifetime, divisions among Muslims had spread in Iraq, but he supported the peaceful resolution of policies among the populace.

Jawād 'Alī

AD 1907-1987

Jawād 'Alī was a prominent Iraqi historian who received his doctorate from the University of Hamburg in 1939 for his dissertation, *al-Mahdi and His Four Emissaries*. After returning to Iraq, he became the secretary of the Authorship and Translation Committee. Jawād 'Alī worked as a professor in the history department at the College of Education in Baghdad and was also a visiting professor at Harvard (1957-1958). Among his most famous works is his eight-volume encyclopedia, *Tārīkh al-'Arab Qabl al-Islām*, published from 1956 until 1960.

Ka'b Ibn al-Ashraf

Ka'b Ibn al-Ashraf was a poet and a prominent figure from the Jewish tribe of Banū al-Nuḍayr. He was among those who leveled criticisms against Muḥammad. When the Quraysh tribe was defeated in the Battle of Badr and some of its leaders were killed, Ka'b Ibn al-Ashraf expressed sorrow over the defeat by satirizing the Muslims. Later, he went to Mecca to incite the Quraysh to avenge the defeat at Badr. Muḥammad then ordered that Ka'b be killed, and the company that executed the order brought his head to Muḥammad.

Khadīja Bint al-Khūwaylid

c. 68-3 BH/AD 556-620

Khadīja was Muḥammad's first wife and his only wife until her death after twenty-four years of marriage. Before their marriage, Khadīja was a wealthy, influential businesswoman with important social connections. She became acquainted with Muḥammad when she employed him to be her trade representative and lead her caravans.

Muḥammad married Khadīja when she was forty and he was in his early twenties. She bore Muḥammad two sons (both died when very young) and four daughters. Over the course of their marriage, Muḥammad relied heavily on her support, counsel, and business acumen. Her love, loyalty, and devotion to him proved crucial for his call and success. She was the first person to declare Muḥammad a prophet and became his first convert.

Muḥammad Ibn al-Ḥassan al-'Askarī

(al-Mahdī)

b. c. AH 255/AD 869

According to the Shiite Twelvers, this man did not die but was "hidden" by God. He is also known as Muḥammad al-Muntaẓar, the Hidden Imām, and the Twelfth Imām.

Musaylima Ibn Ḥabīb

(Musaylima Ibn Thamāma Ibn Ḥabīb)

d. AH 12/AD 633

A member of the tribe of Banū Hanyfa of Yamāma, he was known as the Raḥman of Yamāma because he used to call people to faith in the god, al-Raḥmān ("the Merciful"). Although it is not clearly known when he started his religious activities, historical records mention that he and Muḥammad corresponded, and in those letters, he is said to have asked Muḥammad to split strategic areas between themselves. These records also mention some of Musaylima's own revelations, which he would deliver to the public. However, the sources treat him disparagingly, always denouncing him as Musaylima al-Kadhāb ("Musaylima the Liar"). Because of this negative treatment, it is difficult to obtain unbiased information about him.

Abū Bakr sent a massive army under the leadership of Khālid Ibn al-Walīd to vanquish Musaylima's movement. Hundreds died on both sides, including Musaylima. Thus, this rival of Islām died leaving Islām to have the final word in the region.

Naṣr Ḥāmid Abū Zayd

AD 1943-2010

Zayd was an Egyptian researcher of linguistics and a teacher at Cairo University in the college of literature. In the mid-1990s, the Islāmists filed a suit against him, accusing him of apostasy. The lawsuit called for a judicial injunction to separate him from his wife, Ibtihāl Yūnis, a professor of French literature. Faced with a growing hate campaign against him and a legal system influenced by extremists, Naṣr left Egypt with his wife and moved to Netherlands.

He completed several works regarding the Qur'ān, most notably *Mafhūm al-Naṣṣ: Dirāsa fī 'Ulūm al-Qur'ān* [*The Concept of the Text: A Study of the Qur'anic Sciences*].

Qatāda Ibn al-Nu'mān

d. AH 23/AD 644

Qatāda was from the Anṣār tribe of Aws and participated in all of Muḥammad's battles. During the conquest of Mecca he carried the banner of the family of Banū Ẓafr, a branch of the Aws tribe. He saved Muḥammad's life at the Battle of Uhud.

Sa'd Ibn Abī Waqqāṣ

(Sa'd Ibn Mālik)

d. AH 55/AD 675

He was among the first ten to follow Muḥammad. He participated in all of Muḥammad's battles and was a military leader during the reign of 'Umar Ibn al-Khaṭṭāb, leading the invasion of Iraq and the Persian cities. He became the head of Kufa during the reign of 'Umar.

Sa'īd Ibn Jubayr

AH 45-95/AD 665-714

Of Abyssinian descent, Sa'īd Ibn Jubayr was among the second generation of Muslims. He lived in Kufa and taught the Islāmic religious sciences. When a revolt against the Umayyad started under the leadership of 'Abd al-Raḥmān Ibn al-Ash'ath, he joined in the revolt. When the revolt failed, he disappeared, but later he was arrested and executed by orders of al-Ḥajjāj Ibn Yūsuf al-Thaqafī.

Salmān al-Fārisī

(Salmān the Persian)

d. c. AH 36/AD 656

It is said that he was a Magi of Persian origin who traveled from one country to another. When he was in the Arabian Peninsula, he was kidnapped and sold as a slave in Medina, where he later became a Muslim. Known for living simply during his lifetime, he holds a position of great respect among all Sunnīs and Shiites. There are many legends woven around his person and travels.

ʻUbayd Ibn ʻUmayr

(ʻUbayd Ibn ʻUmayr Ibn Qatāda al-Makkī)

d. AH 68/AD 687

He was born during the life of Muḥammad and became a prominent exegete and preacher among *al-Tābiʻīn* ("the Followers"), the second generation of Muslims.

Ubayy Ibn Kaʻb

d. c. AH 32/AD 652

Born in Medina into the Khazraj tribe, Ubayy Ibn Ka'b became one of Muḥammad's early followers among *al-Anṣār* ("Helpers"). After converting to Islām, he started writing some of the revealed verses for Muḥammad, who considered him to be one of four trustworthy keepers of the Qur'ān.

ʻUmar Ibn al-Khaṭṭāb

40 BH-AH 23/AD 584-644

He was one of Muḥammad's fathers-in-law and influential in strengthening Islām in Mecca. His daughter Ḥafṣa was entrusted with an early codex, which contained parts of the Qur'ān. He also participated in most of the battles of Islām. ʻUmar played a major role in installing Abū Bakr as the first caliph. ʻUmar then succeeded Abū Bakr as the second caliph and ruled for about a decade before his assassination. During his caliphate, Islām expanded geographically into Asia and Africa.

ʻUthmān Ibn ʻAffān

47 BH-AH 35/AD 577-656

ʻUthmān was a wealthy merchant who converted to Islām during its early stages and became a Companion of Muḥammad and his son-in-law. He became the third caliph, following ʻUmar's assassination (AH 23) and was himself later assassinated by Muslims who objected to his policies. His most notable achievement was his effort to collect manuscripts from Muḥammad's followers to compile a written Qur'ān and make it the official codex. He formed a committee headed by Zayd Ibn Thābit to accomplish that task. One of the unfortunate results of this act was the burning of other early codices of the Qur'ān. In his zeal to have a unified codex for the entire Muslim empire, ʻUthmān deprived future generations of manuscripts that might have shed light on some of the earlier contents of the Qur'ān.

al-Walīd Ibn al-Maghīra

(Ibn 'Abd Allah Ibn 'Amr)

d. AH 1/AD 622

He was famous for his sharp mind, which prompted people to seek his counsel to resolve their disputes. He prohibited the drinking of wine, even before Islām. When Muḥammad announced himself as a prophet, al-Walīd refused to follow him and became one of Muḥammad's staunchest enemies. He died after Muḥammad's migration to Medina.

Zayd Ibn Thābit

d. c. AH 45/AD 655

He was from the tribe of Khazraj, among the Anṣār ("Helpers"). He was one of the scribes who wrote down what was revealed to Muḥammad. It is told that Muḥammad asked him to learn the Hebrew and Syriac languages, which he supposedly did in only a few weeks. However, there is no record that shows his proficiency in either of these two languages. Zayd Ibn Thābit participated in both of the Qur'ān's compilation committees from the caliphate of Abū Bakr until the caliphate of 'Uthmān. There are several reports critical of his leadership of the last compilation committee by Ibn Mas'ūd.

Selected Definitions

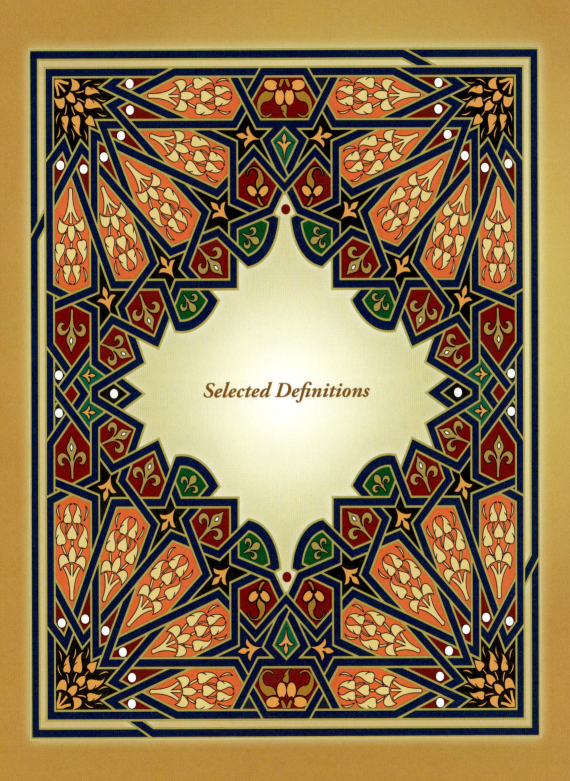

Selected Definitions

abrogated verses

Abrogated verses are verses that have been annulled or overridden by another verse or verses. An abrogated verse can be classified into one of three kinds:

- Verse whose wording remains in the Qur'ān but its ruling is abrogated by another verse.
- Verse whose ruling remains in the *sharī'a* (Islāmic law) but whose words are no longer in the Qur'ān.
- Verse whose wording and ruling are no longer applicable. The words are no longer in the Qur'ān and its ruling is not in the *sharī'a*.

Verses that are untouched by abrogation are considered *muḥkamāt* (conserved). See **khabar**. (See the article "Abrogation and the Abrogated" on page 81.)

AH

This term stands for the Latin *anno Hegirae* ("in the year of the *Hijra*"). According to the Islāmic calendar, the prophet Muḥammad embarked on his emigration from Mecca to Medina in AH 1/AD 622. This event eventually became the reference marker for numbering years when Islām adopted the Arabic lunar calendar. Most Muslim countries today use both the Islāmic and Gregorian calendars.

To convert from an Islāmic (H) or Gregorian (G) calendar year to the other, use one of the following equations:

$$G = 0.97023 \times H + 621.57$$

$$H = (G - 621.57)/0.9702$$

Allah

Allah is the name of the divine being in Islām. He is transcendent, unreachable, and unknowable—beyond comprehension. He is also known by his different attributes (a total of ninety-nine names).

al-Anṣār

Muḥammad and his followers, who were known as *al-Muhājirūn* ("the Emigrants"), migrated from Mecca to Medina in AH 1/AD 622. The Anṣār are those tribesmen from the Aws and Khazraj who supported Muḥammad among the people of Medina. The Anṣār became Muslim and joined Muḥammad in his raids against the Quraysh.

Apocrypha

This Greek word ἀπόκρυφα means "hidden, concealed" or "spurious." The term refers to those writings not included in the Hebrew or Protestant Christian church canon (holy books). In the fourth century AD, they were declared inferior and inauthentic by Church Fathers, who restricted their use in public worship.

During the first few centuries of the Christian era, a large quantity of other noncanonical writings emerged, intended primarily to provide more information about Jesus and the apostles. In content, these works ranged from the orthodox to the bizarre. None of these writings has been accepted as canonical by the Church. See **Infancy Gospel of Thomas**.

Since the eighteenth century, however, Western scholars have collected and classified apocryphal texts of both the Old and New Testaments, so that researchers and theologians can subject them to scientific and historical study.

Apollinarianism

Apollinarianism is a Christian heresy named after its author, Apollinaris, Bishop of Laodicea (AD 310-390). The followers of Apollinarianism state that Jesus had a human body and a soul with senses. However, they believed he had a divine Logos instead of a spirit, meaning that his spirit as a human was replaced with the second person of the Trinity. Like Docetism, another heretical doctrine, Apollinarianism rejected that Jesus was fully human. Denounced and condemned by different Christian councils, this once popular sect soon became extinct.

Arabic dual form (*al-muthannā*)

Unlike the English language, which uses a singular form for one and a plural form for more than one, the Arabic language uses an additional dual form for two subjects or entities.

al-Basmala

This term refers to the saying, *"In the name of the merciful and compassionate God"* (Palmer translation). The Basmala is found at the beginning of every sūra in the Qur'ān except Q 9. On the other hand, the Basmala is mentioned twice in sura al-Naml (Q 27): once at the beginning and in verse 30.

Battle of Badr

This decisive battle (AH 2/AD 624) was a turning point for the early Muslims in their goal to establish themselves and subdue their opponents. Unlike previous skirmishes, this battle was the first large-scale engagement between Muḥammad's military forces and their main adversaries, the Quraysh. After killing several important leaders, including including a high-ranking tribal chief, Abū al-Ḥakam ʿAmr Ibn Hishām al-Makhzūmī, the Muslims were able to claim their victory. The Battle of Badr is one of the few battles specifically mentioned in the Qur'ān.

Battle of the Trench

In the fifth year after *Hijra* (AD 627) the Quraysh and their supporters, the tribes of Ghaṭafān and Kināna, lay siege to Medina. Its defenders, the Muslims (led by Muḥammad) dug a trench around parts of the city on the advice of Salmān al-Fārisī (the Persian). This strategy prevented the enemies' ability to advance with their camels and horses. The resulting stalemate, along with decreasing morale and poor weather conditions, eventually forced the retreat of the Quraysh and their allies.

Battle of Uḥud

Occurring after the Battle of Badr, this battle was the second major military engagement between the Quraysh and the Muslims in AD 625. Fighting on the slopes and plains of Mount Uḥud, the Muslims initially had the advantage only to lose it when some Muslim archers left their posts to loot the Meccan camp. The Meccan army successfully routed the unprotected Muslim troops with a surprise attack. Many Muslims were killed and Muḥammad was badly injured. This Muslim defeat was a serious but ultimately temporary setback. See **Battle of the Trench**.

c. ("circa")

This abbreviation means "approximately."

codex/codices

A codex is a manuscript volume, especially of a classic work or scriptures. For the purposes of this book, the word codex (plural: codices) is used interchangeably with the Arabic word *muṣḥāf* (plural: *maṣāḥif*) and refers to any literary collection of the Qur'ānic sūras and verses by Muslim scribes (including the work completed by 'Uthmān's committee, AD 653-654.) These collections, or codices, may differ from one scribe to another in terms of the number of sūras or verses included or excluded. Some of the better known of these other Qur'ānic versions include Ibn Mas'ūd's codex and Ibn Ka'b's codex.

Companions (*al-Ṣaḥāba*)

Refers to a group of Muslims who accompanied Muḥammad for a long period of time.

d.

This abbreviation means "died." The date shown after this abbreviation indicates the date of death.

Day of Judgment

This term refers to the Day of Reckoning when God will judge each person according to his or her deeds. Islām makes a distinction between the Day of Judgment, Yawm al-Hisab, and the final day, Yawm al-Qiyama, the cataclysmic day.

d. c.

This abbreviation means "died circa" or "died approximately."

al-Dhikr

The word means "that which is mentioned verbally" from the verb *dhakara*. It also can mean "remembrance" from the verb *tadhakara*. This word appears in the Qur'ān with several meanings. One of these meanings is the Bible; Q 16 and Q 21 state that *al-Dhikr* had been revealed to prophets before Islām. At the end of Q 21, *al-Dhikr* clearly refers to the Torah. In Q 38, the *al-Dhikr* is described as the main origin from which the Qur'ān branches. Since the Qur'ān states that *al-Dhikr* is not changeable, despite the many clear verses that *al-Dhikr* was given before Muḥammad, Muslims believe that the term applies to the Qur'ān.

diacritical marks

An important feature of the Arabic language is the markings applied to Arabic characters (or a combination of characters) indicating a phonetic value different from that given the unmarked character. Because several letters in the Arabic alphabet share the same shapes and vowels are not clearly indicated, some kind of diacritical marking was necessary to avoid confusion.

According to Islāmic sources, al-Du'ali devised the earliest form of distinguishing the letters of the Qur'ān at the end of the seventh century AD. This primitive form was improved in the eighth century AD by al-Khalīl Ibn Aḥmad al-Farāhidī, who devised a diacritical system of dots and accents that helped to better distinguish the Arabic letters.

His system became universal by the early eleventh century and includes six diacritical marks: *fatḥa* (a), *ḍamma* (u), *kasra* (i), *sukūn* (vowel-less), *shadda* (double consonant), and *madda* (vowel prolongation; applied to the *alif*). He also added the *hamza* to the long vowels. The lack of these markings on any letter or word can change the pronunciation of the letter or the word and the subsequent meaning of that word.

Emigrants

See **al-Muhājirūn**.

Farewell Pilgrimage

In AH 10/AD 632, Muḥammad made his last pilgrimage (Farewell Pilgrimage). At that time, Muḥammad made a pilgrimage to Mecca to define the rites of the pilgrimage. He also gave an address, later called the Farewell Address. He died of an illness shortly afterward.

Fast of ʿĀshūra'

The term applies to fasting the tenth day of the lunar month Muharram. The Quraysh and the Jews both used to observe this fast. When Muḥammad migrated to Medina, he inquired of the Jews there about their reasons for observing this fast. They responded that they commemorated the day God delivered Moses and his people from Pharaoh by this fast. Muḥammad replied that Moses more rightfully belongs to Muslims and commanded that Muslims also honor this fast. When Ramadan was imposed later, Muḥammad left the decision to Muslims' personal preferences whether or not to observe the Fast of ʿĀshūra'.

al-Furqān

See the article "Introduction" on page 21.

Gabriel

See **Jibrīl**.

ginn

See **jinn**.

ḥadīth

The word *ḥadīth* can be translated as a speech, a saying, or even small talk. In Islāmic theology, the term refers to a narrative concerning a deed or utterance of Muḥammad reported by his Companions.

al-Ḥanifiya

This term refers to a group of Arabs who chose monotheism over idol worship. (For a complete treatment of this definition, see Q 3.67, page 290.)

Helpers

See **al-Anṣār**.

Ḥijāz
This geographical region is located on the west coast of modern day Saudi Arabia along the Red Sea. It extends from the northern tip of the Red Sea by the Gulf of Aqaba and all the way southward. It includes such major cities as Jeddah and Medina, with Mecca as its chief city.

al-'idda
This term is applied to the period a divorced woman or widow has to wait before remarriage in Islām. This prescribed waiting period was enacted to ensure the woman is not pregnant before she remarries. (See the article "Women in the Qur'ān" on page117.)

ifṭār
Each day during Ramadan, Muslims abstain from food, drink, and sexual relations from sunrise to sunset. The evening meal that breaks the day's fast is called *ifṭār.*

imām
The title "imām" represents someone who is imitated and followed as a leader. The definition of an imām varies from one Islāmic sect to another. According to the Sunnī sect, an imām is someone who is more knowledgeable in religious matters, *sharī'a* law, and has memorized more of the Qur'ān. He can lead others in prayers, but a woman is not allowed to be an imām (a prayer leader) in the presence of a man. However, according to the Shiite sect, an imām carries additional attributes; he represents the prophet of Islām (except for receiving a revelation) in his functional role as a spiritual guide to all people and is a source of their earthly and eternal happiness.

Infancy Gospel of Thomas
The *Infancy Gospel of Thomas* is an apocryphal writing dating from the second or third centuries AD. It is a collection of tales purportedly about Jesus from the ages of five to twelve. This work was eventually considered inauthentic and unacceptable by Church Fathers for inclusion in the official canon of Christian scripture.

Its content portrays Jesus as a god-child, with supernatural powers (not unlike a young god in a Greek myth). At times, this young Jesus displays a revengeful, arrogant nature by cursing or even killing those who upset him. (See Q 3.46, 49 on page 282.)

Injīl (Gospel)
The term Injīl, or Gospel, has its roots from the Greek word "evangelion," meaning "to evangelize" or "to share the good news." Even though this is a foreign word, it is included in the Qur'ān. This word is referenced twelve times in the Qur'ān, predominantly during the Medinan period. According to Islām, the Injīl is a book that Allah has revealed directly to Jesus. Muslims believe that the Injīl contains a prophecy

concerning Muḥammad's birth and coming (Q 7.157; Q 61.6). While the Qur'ān does not make any distinction between the Injīl and the New Testament Gospels, the use of the singular Injīl in the Qur'ān has led Muslim theologians to make accusations against Christians by asserting that they have corrupted the original Gospel (Injīl) to accommodate later Christian doctrines, such as the Trinity. According to these Muslim critics, the existence of four Gospels in lieu of one is evidence of such corruption.

Jibrīl (Gabriel)

According to Islāmic belief, Jibrīl is the deliverer of inspiration to Muḥammad. The name "Jibrīl" was known before Islām and is mentioned in the Bible in Daniel 8.16 and 9.21. It is believed that the name "Jibrīl" reached Muḥammad through a Syriac source. The first Islāmic appearance for the name "Jibrīl" is in Medina. (See the article "Muḥammad's Jibrīl" on page 39.)

jihād

According to Islāmic theologians, the term *jihād* represents the physical and spiritual struggle in the cause of Allah. The concept of *jihād* as armed struggle appears to be the predominant understanding of most Muslims since the last days of Muḥammad. Muslim scholars agree that the command for *jihād* is mandatory for all Muslims, but they present two views specifying how Muslims should obey it: (1) In the case of an Islāmic war launched against non-Muslims, only able-bodied Muslims are expected to fight, or (2) *jihād* mandates the participation of all Muslims, including elders, women, and children.

jinn

Muslims believe the jinn are invisible beings who coexist with humans on earth. According to Muslim tradition, the jinn are considered to be like men, subject to future salvation and damnation. Even though they are separate from humanity, they share certain qualities with humans, such as intellect, discrimination, and the capacity for freedom. They have the power to choose between true and false; hence, they can accept or reject the messages revealed by Allah. According to the Qur'ān, a group of jinn converted to Islām after hearing the Qur'ān. (See Q 72.1-7 and Q 15.27, in the second volume of this book.)

jizya

It is the head tax imposed by Islām on any People of the Book who do not embrace Islām as a religion. The purpose of the tax is to subdue and humiliate the payee. In return, payees can live and practice their own faith among Muslims in their community. The amount of the tax is not fixed and, based on the ruling of the local governor, can change from region to region in compliance with Q 9.29: *"Fight those who believe not in God and in the last day, and who forbid not what God and His Apostle have forbidden, and who do not practice the religion of truth from amongst those to whom the Book has been brought, until they pay the tribute by their hands and be as little ones".* (See more discussion about the *jizya* in the article "The Qur'ān and People of Other Faiths" on pages 137.)

al-Ka'ba
Since Islām, this term refers to the cubical structure in Mecca, considered the most sacred site in Islām. According to Islāmic tradition, the structure was erected in the time of Abraham, who built it with the help of his son Ishmael. This granite structure, draped in a black silk and cotton covering with embroidered Qur'ānic verses, stands about 43 feet high. Located at its eastern corner is the Black Stone, a sacred relic that Islāmic tradition dates back to the time of Adam and Eve.

Five times a day Muslims everywhere face the Ka'ba when they kneel to pray. At least once during their lifetime, Muslims (if they are able) are required to complete the Ḥajj (pilgrimage) to Mecca, where they circumambulate the Ka'ba seven times as one of the Five Pillars of Islām. (See also Q 2.158. For more discussion about other ka'bas, see the comment Q 2.125-129, page 207.)

kāfir/kuffār
From an Islāmic standpoint, anyone who does not believe in Muḥammad as a prophet nor embrace Islām as a religion is considered an infidel, or *kāfir* (plural: *kuffār*).

khabar
A narration about an event that has happened is called a report, or khabar. In the Qur'ān such a report cannot be abrogated because it would mean the event did not happen and imply that it is a lie. See **abrogated verses**.

Last Day
See **Day of Judgment**.

liturgy
This word originated from a Greek composite word, *leitourgos* ("a man who performs a public duty"). Over time, this word has taken on a religious sense when Christians used the word to mean the public official service of the Church. Today, the word generally means all the rites, ceremonies, prayers, and sacraments of the Church, as opposed to private devotions.

Magians

Members of this ancient Persian religious cult (c. sixth century BC) incorporated fire altars and sacrifices to perform their many rituals. In time they assimilated and formalized some ideas and beliefs from Zoroasterism: monotheism, the belief in one supreme deity and dualism, the constant struggle between light (good) and darkness (evil). At their height, the reach of the Magians spread into Bahrain, Oman, and Yamāma (a region in Saudi Arabia currently called Najd).

al-Mahdī (Muḥammad Ibn al-Ḥassan al-'Askarī)

In Arabic, al-Mahdī means "the Guided One." According to the Islāmic belief, al-Mahdī, a descendent of Muḥammad, will come at the end of time accompanied by 'Īsā (Jesus) to establish an utopian Islāmic kingdom.

The Shiites differ from the Sunnis in believing that al-Mahdī (the twelfth imām) disappeared. The Shiite Twelvers believe this man did not die but was "hidden" by God.

Mecca (Makka)

This city is the birthplace of Muḥammad and, during his time, it was an important financial center. Over the centuries, Mecca has been called many other names, including *Umm al-Qurā,* "Mother of Towns," and Bakka. (See Q 3.96).

Meccan Qur'ānic text

It is the portion of the Qur'ān that was revealed in Mecca, according to Islāmic teachings. There are sixty-eight chapters (sūras) in this section. See **Medinan Qur'ānic text**.

Medina (Yathrib)

In AD 622, Muḥammad migrated to this flourishing agricultural settlement to spread his message about Islām. At the time of Muḥammad's *Hijra* (Hegira), this oasis city was known as Yathrib. In time, Muḥammad prohibited this name, calling it instead the "City of Light" or al-Madīna al-Munawara. Today it is considered Islām's second holiest city. Muḥammad is buried there in the al-Masjid al-Nabawī (Mosque of the Prophet).

Medinan Qur'ānic text

It is the portion of the Qur'ān that was revealed in Medina, according to Islāmic teachings. There are twenty-eight chapters (sūras) in this section. See **Meccan Qur'ānic text**.

messenger

According to the Islāmic teaching, a messenger is someone whom Allah chooses to deliver a divine message. Islām counts Moses, David, and Jesus among these unique messengers; however, Muḥammad is considered the last and greatest messenger. (It is worthy to note that there are no female messengers according to Islāmic teachings.)

Midrash Rabbah

The word *midrash* means commentary, explanation, research, and study. The Midrash Rabbah refers to a group of commentaries and myths regarding the first five books of the Old Testament known as the Pentateuch, or the Torah. These commentaries eventually moved from oral recitation to the written form and were compiled into a massive work by the end of the third century AD.

Mishnah

It is the first record of the oral religious legislations in Judaism and considered second only to the Tanakh (entire Old Testament) regarding its authority on religious matters. The penning down of these oral traditions started after the destruction of the temple in Jerusalem in AD 70.

The Mishnah contains six divisions known as sedarim. Each sedarim consists of seven to twelve articles. A section called the Gemara was added during the three centuries after AD 70. The Gemara and Mishnah together constitute the Talmud.

The religious teachers in the Mishnah are known as tannaim. The Mishnah includes their opinions regarding different religious matters and some of their dialogues with one another.

***al-Muhājirūn* ("the Emigrants")**

This title applies to the early followers of Muḥammad, who emigrated with him from Mecca to Medina during the *Hijra* (AD 1/AD 622).

muḥkamāt* and *mutashābihāt

The Qur'ān states that it contains two kinds of verses; both are fundamental parts of the book and both must be accepted even if readers do not always understand. (See Q 3.7). Verses that are clear and unambiguous with only one interpretation are called *muḥkamāt* ("decisive and clear revelations"). Verses with unclear or multiple interpretations are called *mutashābihāt* ("similar, ambiguous, allegorical").

al-mushrikūn

In Arabic, the word *mushrikūn* literally means "those who take a partner [to God]." In the Qur'ān this term refers to idolaters and polytheists.

al-mut‘a (temporary marriage)
Al-mut‘a is a special type of marriage, where the man and woman mutually agree to a marital arrangement of a specified period of time (one hour, one day, one week, etc.). Like a regular marriage, a certificate is issued, a dowry (payment for the time together) is paid, and *al-‘idda* is observed. However, the marriage ends as stipulated in the marital contract. In case of death, no inheritance is awarded to the surviving party.

In early Islām, the Sunnī initially viewed this kind of marriage as permissible until Muḥammad abrogated this practice with *a ḥadīth* forbidding it. However, Shiites still hold to the legitimacy of *al-mut‘a*. (See the article "Women in the Qur'ān" on page 117.)

al-Mutakallimūn
This term was first given to a group of people who studied and practiced *kalām*, an Islāmic philosophical discipline that began in the second century AH. Now this term is a common name for all seeking philosophical demonstration in confirmation of religious principles. Al-Mutakallimūn seek theological knowledge through debate and argument, using reason to establish and support Islām's tenets. The purpose behind this movement was to transition the Muslims from traditional beliefs to verifiable doctrine and present a reasoned response to cultic movements within Islām, or *al-firaq al-ḍālla*.

Mu‘tazila, Mu‘tazilite
One of the significant theological schools in the study of the Qur'ān is the Mu‘tazila. Established in the second century AH (eighth century AD), this movement flourished during the Abbasid era. Its name derives from the expression "those who withdraw (separate) themselves" because the founder of this group did not support the predominant opinions of two other schools, Ahl al-Sunna and al-Khawārij, during a theological dispute.

al-Nasī'
The term applies to one of the lunar months in the Arab calendar; originally it was the first month of the year. Because the Arab calendar consists of twelve lunar months in a year of 354 or 355 days, this month was extended additional days (an extra month) every three years by early Arabs to make up for the difference between the solar and lunar years (about eleven days per year). This practice of periodically adding another month was done for agricultural and commercial reasons. However, after AH 10/AD 632 the extension of al-Nasī' was prohibited and the Muslim year was restricted to only twelve lunar months.

Orientalists, Orientalism
Orientalism is the study of Near and Far Eastern societies and cultures by Westerners. In terms of Islāmic research, Orientalists ("al-Mustashriqūn") of the past have tried

to restore Qur'ānic text and related sacred writing and reconstruct the chronology of such texts. Many have examined the history of exegesis by reading and reviewing the writings of Islāmic scholars and commentators.

Palmyrian inscriptions
Discovered near Palmyra and adjacent regions, these ancient inscriptions (attributed to Palmyrene merchants and soldiers) helped scholars in their studies of Semitic epigraphy. The earliest inscription dates to 44 BC and the latest dates to AD 274.

People of the Book
The jurisprudents of Islām agree that the People of the Book are the Jews and the Christians. Some also include the Sabaeans and the Magians. When Islām grew in strength, Muḥammad proclaimed that the People of the Book must pay *al-jizya* (head tax) if they did not convert to Islām (Q 46).

Preserved Tablet
According to the teaching of Islām this is a celestial book in which Allah wrote his Qur'ān and preserved it from any additions or deletions. Allah sent it down to Muḥammad on various occasions over a period of thirteen years.

prophet
According to Muslim scholars the distinction between a prophet and a messenger is that a prophet receives a message through an angel, hears it in his heart, or receives a vision. The messenger receives a higher revelation through Jibril (Gabriel).

Quraysh
They were the tribes of Mecca and its surrounding areas during the early history of Islām. It was said that the first person to unite them was Quṣay Ibn Kilāb. These tribes were in the trade business and not in farming or shepherding.

rabbi/rabbis
Though sometimes a spiritual leader, a rabbi is an officially ordained teacher and master of Jewish law. He has the necessary education to teach the Halacha (see **rabbinical literature**) and issue instructions regarding social traditions. The fifth sūra of the Qur'ān is also named the Rabbis Chapter.

rabbinical literature
This term refers to the Halacha, which is the body of traditions that rely on the oral Jewish law. The commentaries and explanations contained in the Halacha are used by devout Jews as a guide to living a religious, ethical and moral life. In the historical studies, as well as in this book, the term is used in reference to the early rabbis' commentaries

on the holy books, e.g., Torah, prior to the seventh century AD. The rabbis verbally taught and explained the holy books to their disciples, who when rabbis themselves, would transmit these explanations and add their own as well. These oral commentaries and explanations were eventually written down in the second century AD.

Ramadan

Ramadan is one of the lunar months in the Muslim calendar. Every year during this month, Muslims have fasted since the second year of the Hijra (AH 2). During Ramadan, Muslims abstain from eating, drinking, and sexual relations from sunrise till sunset. Exemption from fasting is only granted to sick people, menstruating or pregnant women, travelers, young children, and mentally-challenged persons. All others are commanded to fast during this month. The punishment for intentionally breaking the fast during Ramadan is to feed sixty poor people or to fast two consecutive months.

al-Sab ʿal-Mathānī

This title refers to the entire Qur'ān or several portions of it. It also refers to the first sūra of the Qur'ān, which contains seven (sabʿ) verses. The word *mathānī* has several meanings and applications:

- Means to repeat (or second) and applies to the first sūra because it is repeated during every prayer.
- Applies to verses that speak of praising (*thanā'*), such as the verses of Q 1.
- Applies to a group of several sūras, starting with Q 2 and ending with Q 9 (considered the last sūra). It is similarly applied to a list of twenty-five sūras, excluding Q 1.
- Refers to sūras with more than ten but less than a hundred verses.
- Refers to the Mithnā, a written "Record of Deeds," which will be read on the Day of Judgment. In such an interpretation, the Qur'ān has primary authority.
- Refers to the Mishnah (Mithnā in Arabic), a Jewish literary work that was written as a source of religious instruction in addition to the Old Testament.
- Refers to a term mentioned in Q 15.87: "*We have already brought thee Seven of the Repetition, and the mighty Qur'ān.*"

Note that the above verse (Q 15.87) separates the work, Sabʿ al-Mathānī, from the Qur'ān by the use of "and."

Sabaeans

There are several groups that carry this name in the Middle East. (One of those groups, followers of Mandaeism, live along the banks of the rivers Tigris and Euphrates today.) The early Sabaeans mentioned in the Qur'ān could be in reference to those who lived before Islām in Egypt and the southern Arabian Peninsula. At the peak of their political empire, they were known for their wealth and commercial activity, especially in the lucrative spice trade. Today, this early group no longer exists.

sacred months

During these months Arabs must cease from fighting each other and allow trade caravans to travel freely without fear of attack. These sacred months include Rajab, Dhū-l-Qi'da, Dhū-l-Ḥijja, and Muḥarram.

Sacred Mosque (Masjid al-Ḥarām)

This religious site, located in Mecca, is considered the most sacred public worship center in Islām. It is the largest mosque in the world. At the center of its inner courtyard stands the Ka'ba, the holiest shrine in Islām.

ṣadaqa* and *zakāt

Ṣadaqa (charity) is freely giving to another without religious obligation. A person may perform *ṣadaqa* to draw closer to Allah and to foster a friendly relationship with the receiver of the gift. Thus, *ṣadaqa* is similar in meaning to a gift.

Zakāt, on the other hand, is the third pillar of Islām. It is a religious obligation to give a "fourth of the tenth," meaning 2.5% of one's wealth to specified recipients (see Q 9.60):

1. Poor
2. Needy
3. *Zakāt* collectors (literally, "those who work for it")
4. Infidels who would convert to Islām if they received the *zakāt* offering "those whose hearts are reconciled"
5. Slave-owners (to free a Muslim slave)
6. Debtors who cannot repay their debts (to individuals, i.e., not corporations, etc.)
7. Allah (to fund conquests and *jihād* campaigns)
8. Muslim "wayfarers" (travelers who are stranded)

al-Ṣaḥāba

See **Companions**.

al-Sayf

See **Sword verse**.

schools of reading

After 'Uthmān's committee had finished its work and its codex was dispersed to the Muslim-controlled regions, five schools arose that specialized in the reading of the codex of 'Uthmān, training and educating their followers according to the readings of certain respected scholars:

- school of Basra (reading of Abū 'Umar Ibn al-'Alā')
- school of Kufa (readings of 'Āṣim Ibn Abī al-Nujūd, 'Alī Ibn Ḥamza, and Ḥamza Ibn Ḥabīb)
- school of Damascus (reading of 'Abd Allah Ibn 'Āmir)
- school of Mecca (readings of 'Abd Allah Ibn Kathīr and Muḥammad Ibn 'Abd al-Raḥman Ibn Muḥayṣin)
- school of Medina (reading of Nāfi' Ibn Abī Na'īm)

Shiite Twelvers

This Shiite group is the largest branch of Shī'a Islām. The name Twelvers comes from their belief in twelve divinely ordained leaders, known as the Twelve Imāms.

The Shiite Twelvers are also the largest denomination that adopts the Ja'fari doctrine (the teachings of the sixth Imām Abū Ja'far al-Ṣādiq (AH 83-148). Because this group follows the teachings of this imām, the Twelvers are also called Imāmīya. This denomination believes that the Twelve Imāms, as well as Fāṭima and her father Muḥammad, were sinless.

Another belief holds that the twelfth imām, Muḥammad Ibn al-Ḥassan al-'Askarī (AH 255), who disappeared from sight when he went down into a tunnel to escape the Abbasid, is still alive. But no one can meet him except those who are sincere among his companions. See **al-Mahdī**.

stoning verse (*āyat al-rajm*)

In the *sharī'a* (Islāmic law), the ruling for a married adulterer is death by stoning. According to Ibn Kathīr, in his *Tafsīr* (commentary), this ruling appears to have come from a *hadith* (traditional saying of Muḥammad), which states, "The old man and the old woman, if they commit adultery, stone them outright. A model of punishment from Allah. And Allah is Mighty, Wise." This verse was once part of Q 33, but it was eventually removed from the Qur'ān. Despite its removal, its ruling is still valid according to the Islāmic belief.

sunna/sunan

According to Islāmic beliefs, *sunna* is the prescribed way of life based on the narrative records of Muḥammad's sayings (*ḥadīths*) or actions. See **ḥadīths**.

Sword verse (*al-Sayf*)

This verse is found in verse 5 in sūra al-Tawba (Q 9.5) in the Qur'ān. (The context for this verse is contained in Q 9.1-29.) The Sword verse is considered by many scholars to be one of the very last commands revealed by Muḥammad to his followers. It commands the Muslims to fight by the sword against idolaters, including Christians and Jews. It is also believed that this verse has abrogated 114 verses that promote peace ("peace" verses) in the Qur'ān and nullified them.

Ṭāghūt

This word appears six times in the Qur'ān with several different meanings: "the idols," "Satan," and "the diviner." It is said that the word might be of foreign origin, similar to other words in the Qur'ān, such as Ṭālūt and Jālūt. It is also said that the word has a Syriac root that means "error, or to lead into error." In the old Hebrew, it means "idol."

al-taqīya

Hiding or disguising personal thoughts and beliefs under false appearances for the sake of safety is called *al-taqīya* (dissimulation). Examples of this type of behavior might include the pretense of pledging allegiance to a particular ruler or country or observing local religious practices to protect or further one's interests. The Qur'ān allows Muslims the use of *al-taqīya* to protect themselves from harm (Q 16.106). Shiites have used this doctrine during the times when they were persecuted by the Sunnīs and continue to use it even today.

Some of the Sunnī groups also made use of this doctrine during the Abbasid era when the issue of the creation of the Qur'ān was raised. Every Muslim who publicly took the position that the Qur'ān was eternal and not created was executed during that era.

Targum

The word *targum* is a Hebrew-Aramaic word that means the interpretation and explanation of the Torah for the synagogues. The ancient Targum was transmitted orally for centuries. This oral transmission was continually modified to adapt to its audience and prevailing conditions. Because of these changes over time, there are now several copies of the written Targum concerning the first five books of Moses. The commentary found in the Targum, called the Midrash, reflects the scriptural interpretations of the ancient Jews.

Treaty of Ḥudaybīya

In AH 6/AD 628, Muḥammad and 1400 of his followers set out to Mecca to perform a small pilgrimage. The Quraysh, Muḥammad's enemies, intercepted the Muslims at Ḥudaybīya, located outside of Mecca. To resolve the crisis without bloodshed, the two parties signed a treaty with the purpose of establishing a ten-year truce. The Muslims hoped the truce would enable them to freely expand their influence, territory, and military power over the next decade. Two years after the treaty was signed (AH 8/AD 629), Muḥammad returned to Mecca with 10,000 Muslims and conquered the city.

'Uthmān's committee

In approximately AH 30/AD 650, this committee (which included Zayd Ibn Thābit, Sa'īd Ibn al-'Āṣ, 'Abd al-Raḥman Ibn al-Ḥārith Ibn Hishām, 'Abd Allah Ibn al-Zubayr, and others) was commissioned by 'Uthmān, the third caliph, to compile and write the

Qur'ān in the language of the Quraysh. (See the article "Compilation of the Qur'ān" on page 49).

al-Ẓāhirīya

Al-Ẓāhirīya, a school of law founded in the ninth century AD, follows an ideological and legislative method that calls for holding fast to the Qur'ān and the *sunna* of Muḥammad. It rejects all other opinions outside these sources and considers them to be speculative.

zakāt

See **ṣadaqa** and **zakāt**.

Controversial Qur'ānic Texts

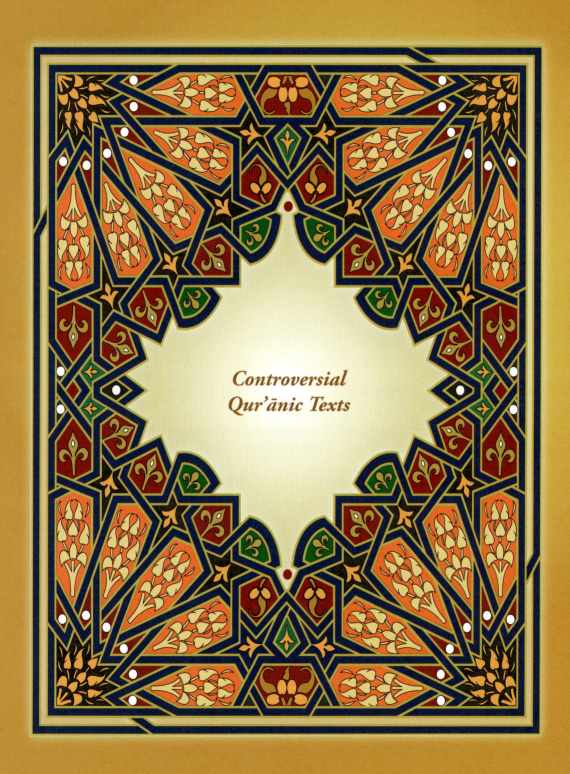

Controversial Qur'ānic Texts

Sūra al-Khal‘ سُورة الخلع

In the Name of God, the Merciful, the Compassionate. بسم الله الرحمَن الرَّحيْم

1 O God we pray Thee for help and forgiveness[;]

(١) اللَّهُمَّ إِنَّا نَسْتَعِينُكَ، وَنَسْتَغْفِرُكَ،

2 we praise Thee and are not unthankful towards Thee,

(٢) وَنُثْنِي عَلَيْكَ، وَلَا نَكْفُرُكَ

3 and we let go and forsake every one who trespasses against Thee.

(٣) وَنَخْلَعُ وَنَتْرُكُ مَنْ يَفْجُرُكَ

Sūra al-Ḥafd سُورة الحفد

In the Name of God, the Merciful, the Compassionate. بسم الله الرحمَن الرَّحيْم

1 O God we serve Thee,

اللَّهُمَّ إِيَّاكَ نَعْبُدُ، (١)

2 and to Thee do we pray, and Thee do we worship;

وَلَكَ نُصَلِّي، وَنَسْجُدُ، (٢)

3 we hasten to Thee; we strive after Thee;

وَإِلَيْكَ نَسْعى وَنَحْفِدُ، (٣)

4 we hope for Thy pity, and we fear Thy punishment.

نَرْجُو رَحْمَتَكَ، وَنَخْشى عَذابَكَ، (٤)

5 Truly, Thy punishment overcomes the unbelievers."

إِنَّ عَذابَكَ بِالكُفَّارِ مُلْحَقٌ (٥)

The current Arabic Qur'ān does not include al-Khal‘ and al-Ḥafd, two sūras that were included in the codex of Ubayy Ibn Ka‘b. Additionally, one version of the Shiite Qur'ān once included sūras al-Nūrayn and al-Wilāya.

The authenticity of sūra al-Khal‘ and al-Ḥafd has generated debate and disputes among Muslim scribes during the early history of Islām. However, all Sunnī scholars refute sūra al-Nūrayn (though Orientalists hold various views about its validity). The opinion regarding sūra al-Wilaya is more consensual, with the majority of Orientalists and Sunnī (including some Shiite) scholars declaring this sūra to be a fabrication.

Three of these controversial sūras—al-Khal‘, al-Ḥafd, and al-Nūrayn—are presented above and on the following pages in Arabic and the corresponding English translation (Sell 14, 19-22). (See the article "Compilation of the Qur'ān" on page 49.)

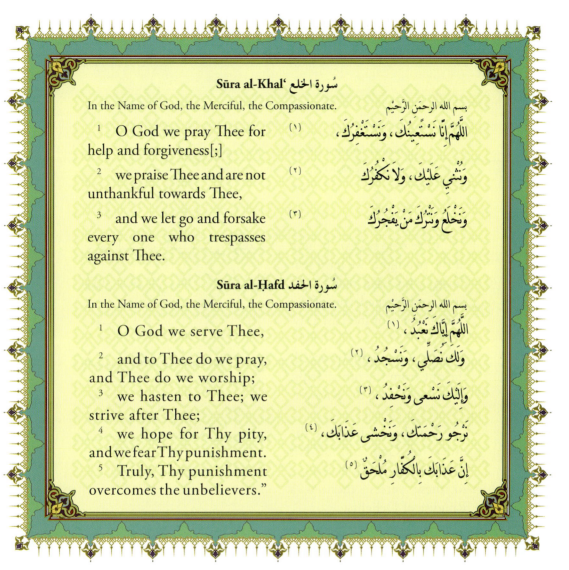

Sūra al-Nūrayn (Nūrain): Two Lights سُورة النُّورَيْن

In the Name of God, the Merciful, the Compassionate. بسم الله الرحمَنِ الرَّحيْم

1 O ye who believe, believe in the two lights we have sent down, who have recited our signs and warned you of the punishments of the Last Day.

يا أيُّها الَّذينَ آمَنُوا آمِنوا بالنُّورَيْن أنْزَلْنَاهُمَا
يَتْلوان عَلَيْكُمْ آياتي وَيُحَذِّرَانِكم عَذْابَ يَوْمٍ
عَظِيْمٍ (١)

2 These two lights (proceed) the one from the other. Truly, I am the Hearer, the Knower.

نُوران بَعْضُهُمَا مِنْ بَعْضٍ. وَإِنا لَسميع
عَليم (٢)

3 For those who obey the orders of God and of His Prophet, for them, according to these verses, there is a Paradise of Delights;

إِنَّ الَّذِينَ يُوفُونَ بَعَهْدِ الله وَرَسُوْلِه في
آيَاتٍ لَهُمْ جَنَّاتُ نَعِيْم (٣)

4 but those who disbelieve after they have believed, and who break their promise and that which the Prophet had stipulated for them, shall be cast into Hell.

وَالَّذِينَ كَفَرُوا مِنْ بَعْدِ مَا آمنوا بنَقْضِهِمْ
مِيثَاقهُمْ وَمَا عَاهَدَهُمُ الرَّسُولُ عَلِيْهِ
يُقْذَفُونَ في الجَحِيْمِ (٤)

5 They who have injured their own souls and have been disobedient to the executor of the Prophet (i.e., Ali), they shall drink of the scalding water.

ظلمُوْا أَنْفُسَهُمْ وَعَصَوْا لِوَصِيّ الرَّسُوْل،
أُولَئِكَ يُسقَونَ مِنْ حَمِيْم (٥)

6 Truly, God is He who gives light to the heavens and to the earth, and who chooses the angels, the prophets, and who makes believers;

إِنَّ الله الَّذِي نَوَّرَ السَّمَوَاتِ وَالأَرْض
بِمَا شَاءَ وَاصْطَفَى مِن الْمَلائِكَةِ
وَالرَّسلِ وَجَعَلَ مِنَ الْمُؤْمِنِيْن (٦)

7 they are His creation, He creates what He wills: there is no God but He, the merciful and gracious.

أُولَئِكَ مِنْ خَلْقِهِ يَفْعَلُ الله ما يَشَاءُ لا
إِلَهَ إِلاَّ هُوَ الرَّحْمَنُ الرَّحِيم (٧)

8 Truly, those who were before them have deceived their prophets. I have punished them for their deceit, and my punishment is severe and strong.

قَدْ مَكَرَ الَّذِينَ مِنْ قَبْلِهِمْ بِرُسُلِهِمْ فَأَخَذْتُهُمْ
بِمَكْرِهِمْ إِنَّ أَخذي شَدِيْدٌ أَلِيْمُ (٨)

9 Truly, God has destroyed 'Ad and Samud on account of what they did and has made them as a memorial to you, but ye did not believe.

إن اللهَ قَدْ أَهْلَكَ عَاداً وَثَمُودَ بِمَا كَسَبُوا
وَجَعَلَهُمْ لكُمْ تَذْكِرَةً فلا تَتَّقُونَ (٩)

10 And He did the same with regard to Pharaoh for his opposition to Moses and his brother Aaron. He drowned him and all who followed him

وَفِرْعَونَ بمَا طغى عَلى مُوسىَ وأخيْهِ
هَرُونَ أغْرقتُه وَمَنْ تَّبعَهُ أجْمَعيْنَ (١٠)

11 as a sign to you, yet most of you are perverse.

لِيَكُونَ لكُمْ آيَةً وَإنَّ أكْثَرَكُمْ فاسِقون (١١)

12 Truly, God will gather them together in the day of resurrection, and they will not be able to answer when questioned:

إنَّ الله يَجْمَعُهُمْ يَوْمَ الحَشَر فَلا يسْتَطيْعُونَ
الجَوابَ حِيْنَ يُسألوْنَ (١٢)

13 for them is the Hell, for God is knowing and wise.

إنَّ الْجَحَيْمَ مأواهُمْ وَإِنَّ الله عَليْمُ
حَكِيْمُ (١٣)

14 O Prophet! publish my warnings, perhaps they will follow them.

يَا أيُّهَا الرَّسُولُ بَلِّغْ إنذاري فسَوفَ
يَعْمَلونَ (١٤)

15 In truth, they who turned from my signs and my orders have perished.

قدْ خَسِرَ الَّذِينَ كَانُوا عَنْ آيَاتي
وحُكْمي مُعْرِضُونَ (١٥)

16 As to those who keep thy covenant, I reward them with the Paradise of Delights.	مَثَّلُ الَّذِينَ يُوْفُونَ بِعَهْدِكَ إِنِّي جَزَيْتُهُم جَنَّاتِ النَّعيم (١٦)
17 Truly, God is the Pardoner and the great rewarder.	إِنَّ اللهَ لَذوْ مَغْفِرةٍ وأَجْرٍ عَظيم (١٧)
18 Truly, Ali is one of the pious men,	وَإِنَّ عَلَيّاً لَمِنَ الْمُتَّقِين (١٨)
19 and we will restore his rights to him at the Day of Judgment.	وَإِنَّا لَنُوَفيهِ حَقَّهُ يَوْمَ الدَّين (١٩)
20 We are not ignorant of the injustice done to Him.	وَما نَحْنُ عَنْ ظُلْمِهِ بَغَافِلي (٢٠)
21 We have exalted him above all thy family,	وَكَرَّمنَاهُ عَلىَ أَهْلِكَ أَجْمَعْينَ (٢١)
22 and he and his posterity are patient	وَإِنَّه وَذُرِّيَتَهُ لصَابُرون (٢٢)
23 and his enemies are the chief of sinners.	وَإِنَّ عَدُوَّهُمْ إِمَامُ الْمُجْرِمين (٢٣)

24 Say to those who have disbelieved after they had believed, "You have sought the glory of worldly life and have hastened to gain it, and have forgotten what God and His prophet promised you" and you broke the promises after a strict order about them." We have given you examples, perhaps, you may be guided.

قُلْ لِلَّذِينَ كَفَرُوا بَعْدَمَا آمَنُوا طَلَبْتُمْ زِينَةَ الْحَيَوةِ
الدُّنْيَا وَاسْتَعْجَلْتُمْ بِهَا وَنَسِيتُمْ مَا وَعَدَكُمُ اللهُ
وَرَسُولُهُ وَنَقَضْتُمُ الْعُهُودَ مِنْ بَعْدِ تَوْكِيدِهَا
وَقَدْ ضَرَبْنَا لَكُمُ الأَمْثَالَ لَعَلَّكُمْ تَهْتَدُونَ (٢٤)

25 O Prophet! We have sent the manifest signs; in them are shown who will believe on him ('Ali) and who after thee will turn away from him ('Ali).

يَا أَيُّهَا الرَّسُولُ قَدْ أَنْزَلْنَا إِلَيْكَ آيَاتٍ
بَيِّنَاتٍ فِيهَا مَنْ يَتَوَفَّهُ مُؤْمِناً وَمَنْ يَتَوَلَّهُ
مِنْ بَعْدِكَ يُظْهَرُونْ (٢٥)

26 Turn from them; certainly they turn aside

فَاعْرِضْ عَنْهُمْ إِنَّهُمْ مُعْرِضُونَ (٢٦)

27 and certainly We will summon them on the Day (of Judgment), when nothing shall avail them and no one shall pity them.

إِنَّا لَهُمْ مُحْضِرُونَ فِي يَوْمٍ لا يُغْنِي عَنْهُم
شَيْءٌ وَلا هُمْ يُرْحَمُونَ (٢٧)

28 Truly, there is a place for them in Hell and they shall not return.

إنَّ لَهُم في جَهَنَّم مَقَاماً عَنْهُ لا
يَعْدِلُونَ (٢٨)

29 Praise the name of thy Lord and be of those who worship Him.

فَسَبِّحْ باسْم رَبَكَ وَكُنْ مِن
السَّاجدِيْنَ (٢٩)

30 Truly, we sent Moses and Aaron with what was needed and they rebelled against Aaron. Patience is good, so we changed them to monkeys and pigs, and have cursed them till the day of resurrection.

وَلَقَدْ أرْسَلْنَا مُوسى وَهَرُون بما
اسْتُخْلفَ فَبَغَوْا هَرونَ فصَبْرٌ جَمِيْلٌ
فجَعَلْنَا مِنْهُمُ الْقِرَدَةَ والخَنَازِيْر ولَعَنَّاهُمْ
إلى يَوْمَ يُبْعَثُونَ (٣٠)

31 Be patient, they will be punished.

فاصْبرْ فسَوفَ يبْلونَ (٣١)

32 We have sent thee an order, as we did to preceding prophets.

وَلَقَدْ أتَيْنَا بكَ الْحُكْمَ كَالَّذِينَ مِنْ قبْلِكَ
مِنَ الْمُرْسَلِيْنَ (٣٢)

33 We have appointed to thee a successor from among them: perhaps they will return.

وَجَعَلْنَا لكَ مِنْهُمْ وَصيّاً لَعَلَّهُمْ
يَرْجِعُونَ (٣٣)

[34] He who turns from my order, from him I will turn, they get but little benefit from their unbelief. Do not ask about those who break the law.

وَمَنْ يَتَّوَلَّ عَنْ أَمْرِي فَإِنِّي مُرْجِعُهُ
فَلْيَتَمَتَّعُوا بِكُفْرِهِمْ قَلِيْلًا فَلا تَسْأَلْ
عَنِ النَّاكِثِين (٣٤)

[35] O Prophet! We have made for thee a compact on the neck of those who believe; possess it and be of the number of those who are thankful.

يَا أَيُّهَا الرَّسُولُ قَدْ جَعَلْنَا لَكَ في
أَعْنَاقِ الَّذِينَ آمَنُوا عَهْداً فَخُذهُ وَكُنْ مِنْ
الشَّاكِرِيْنَ (٣٥)

[36] Truly, Ali is constant in prayer at night making the prescribed prostrations (sajidan), and he fears the Last Day and hopes for mercy from his God. Say, how can those be compared who make tyranny, and those who know my troubles.

إِنَّ عَلِيّاً قَانِتاً بِاللَّيْلِ سَاجِداً يَحْذر الآخِرةً
وَيَرْجُو ثُوابَ رَبِّهِ قل هَلْ يَسْتَوي الَّذِين
ظَلَمُوا وَهْمْ بَعَذابي يُعْلَمُونَ (٣٦)

[37] They will place charms on their necks and they will repent of their works.

سَيُجَعَلُ الأغلالُ في أَعْنَاقِهِمْ وَهْمْ عَلى
أَعْمَالِهِمْ يَنْدِمُون (٣٧)

38 We gave good news to thee of pious descendants,

إِنَّا بَشَرْنَاكَ بذُرِّيَةِ الصَّالِحِيْنَ (٣٨)

39 and they will not be disobedient;

وإِنَّهُمُ لأَمْرِنَا لا يَخْلُفُون (٣٩)

40 my peace and my mercy is on them, living or dead, and on the day when they shall rise again.

فَعَلَيْهِمْ مِنَّي صَلوة وَرَحْمَةً أَحْيَاءً وَأَمْواتاً
وَيَوْمَ يُبْعَثُّون (٤٠)

41 My anger is on those who after thee transgress amongst them. Truly, they are a bad people and will wander from the right way;

عَلَى الَّذِينَ يَبْغَونَ عَلَيْهُم مِنْ بَعْدِكَ
غَضَبِي إِنَّهُمْ قومُ سُوءٍ خَاسِرِينْ (٤١)

42 but those who go on in the way, on them is my mercy and they will be safe in the lofty rooms (of Paradise).

عَلى الَّذِينَ سَلَكُوا مَسْلَكَهُمْ مِنِّي رَحْمَةً
وَهُمْ في الغُرُفاتِ آمِنُون (٤٢)

43 Praise be to the Lord of both worlds.

وَالْحَمدُ للهِ رَبِّ الْعَالِمِيْنْ (٤٣)

Amen.

آمين.

Timeline

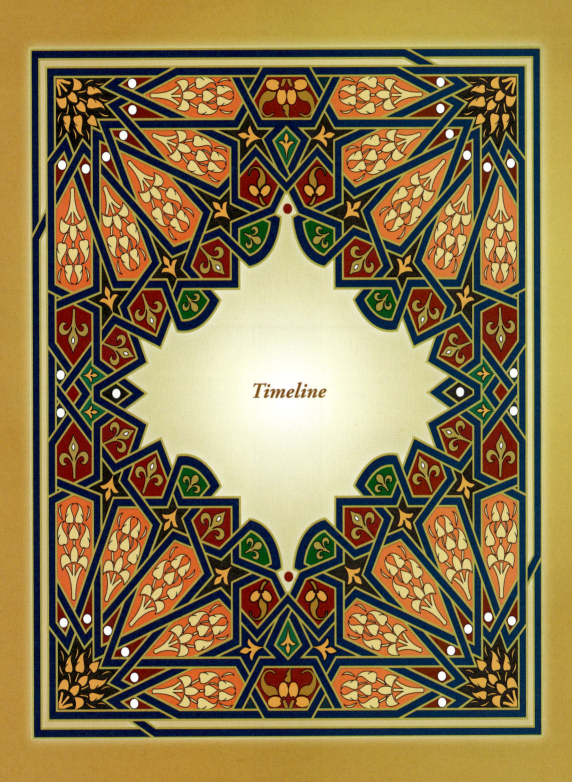

BH | AD

54 • 570 **Birth of Muḥammad**

29 • 594 **First Marriage**
Muḥammad marries Khadīja Bint Khūwaylid.

13 • 610 **First Revelation**
Muḥammad tells his wife, Khadīja, that he received the revelation of the first sūra of the Qur'ān (Q 96).

3 • 619 **Death of Khadīja Bint Khūwaylid**
Muḥammad's first wife and financial supporter dies. Until her death, Muḥammad takes no other wives.

3 • 619 **Death of Abī Ṭālib**
Muḥammad's uncle dies, leaving Muḥammad without protection and provision.

3 • 619 **Engagement to 'Ā'isha**
Muḥammad becomes engaged to 'Ā'isha, the six-year-old daughter of Abū Bakr.

AH | AD

1 • 622 **Hijra (Hegira)**
The Muslims migrate to Yathrib (Medina). The date of this migration, known as the *Hijra*, eventually marks the beginning of the Islāmic calendar, established in the time of 'Umar Ibn al-Khaṭṭāb.

1 • 622 **Marriage to 'Ā'isha**
Muḥammad marries 'Ā'isha, daughter of Abū Bakr, when she is nine years old.

2 • 623 **First Muslim Expedition**
'Abd Allah Ibn Jaḥsh leads a company that raids a commercial caravan of the Quraysh during an Arab holy month. Such action was prohibited by the Arabs.

2 • 624 **Battle of Badr**
The Muslims attack a Quraysh commercial caravan, an incident that leads to the Battle of Badr, during the month of Ramadan.

2 • 624 **Raid of Banū Qaynuqā'**
The Muslims force out the Jewish tribe Banū Qaynuqā' and seize their lands.

3 • 625 **Battle of Uhud**
The Quraysh army avenges the Battle of Badr by soundly defeating the Muslims in the Battle of Uhud.

4 • 626 **Raid of Banū al-Naḍīr**
The Muslims force out the Jewish tribe of Banū al-Naḍīr and seize their lands.

5 • 627 **Raid of Banū al-Muṣṭaliq**
The Muslims seize exorbitant spoils from Banū al-Muṣṭaliq (or the Raid of al-Muraysī').

5 • 627 **Battle of the Trench**
The Quraysh army besieges Medina and withdraws after several skirmishes. Muslims also call this incident the Raid of Khandaq.

5 • 627 **Raid of Banū Qurayẓa**
The Muslims attack the Jewish tribe of Banū Qurayẓa. After the tribe surrenders, the Muslims behead 900 men and enslave the women and children.

5 • 627 **Marriage to Zaynab**
Muḥammad reveals a Qur'ānic verse condoning his marriage to Zaynab, after she was divorced by Muḥammad's adopted son. At that time, this ruling was contrary to the Arabs' ethics, which prohibited such actions.

6 • 628 **Treaty of Ḥudaybīya**
Muḥammad signs this treaty with the Quraysh. This peace treaty is intended to last for ten years, but Muḥammad breaks it within two years.

7 • 629 **Raid of Khaybar**
The Muslims attack the Jewish tribe of Khaybar, beheading 93 men and deporting its people.

8 • 630 **Surrender of Mecca**
The people of Mecca surrender to the Muslims without a fight.

11 • 632 **Death of Muḥammad**

Note: Dates are approximate due to disagreements among Islāmic sources.

Copyright© 2011 by TheQuran.com®. All rights reserved.

AH | AD

11 | 632 — First Caliph
Abū Bakr, Muḥammad's close friend and father of 'Ā'isha, becomes the first caliph, marking the beginning of the "four caliphs" reign.

11 | 632 — Battle of Yamāma
Khālid Ibn al-Walīd leads the Muslim armies against Banū Ḥanīfa and kills the self-proclaimed prophet, Musaylima Ibn Ḥabīb.

12 | 633 — First Compilation
First compilation of the Qur'ān is completed around this date, during the caliphate of Abū Bakr.

13 | 634 — Second Caliph
'Umar Ibn al-Khaṭṭāb, father of Ḥafṣa (a wife of Muḥammad), becomes the second caliph after Abu Bakr's death.

13 | 634 — Battle of Yarmūk
The Muslims defeat the Byzantine forces in Syria.

14 | 635 — Battle of Qādisīya
The Muslims defeat the Persians forces in Iraq.

23 | 644 — Third Caliph
'Uthmān Ibn 'Affān, the son-in-law of Muḥammad, becomes the third caliph after the assassination of 'Umar Ibn al-Khaṭṭāb by a Persian slave.

30 | 650 — Burning of Codices (Maṣāḥif)
As disagreement grows over the content of the Qur'ān, 'Uthmān forms a committee to unify it. Once the committee completes its work (second compilation), 'Uthmān commands that all other *maṣāḥif* be burned around this date.

35 | 656 — Fourth Caliph
'Alī Ibn Abī Ṭālib, Muḥammad's cousin and husband of his daughter Fāṭima, becomes the fourth caliph after the assassination of 'Uthmān during escalating social tension among Muslims.

40 | 661 — Schism of Sunnīs and Shiites
'Alī is assassinated and political power transfers from Medina to Damascus, marking the beginning of division within the ranks of Muslims. This led to the later schism of Muslims to Sunnis and Shiites. Sunnīs hold 'Alī as the Seal of the (four) Caliphs, whereas Shiites believe 'Alī is the only rightful caliph.

90 | 709 — Predominant Reader
Ḥafṣ Ibn Sulaymān al-Asadī (d. AH 180/AD 796) becomes one of the seven sanctioned readers whose reading of the 'Uthmānic codex becomes the most predominant.

110 | 728 — Prominent Reader
Born 'Uthmān Ibn Sa'īd Ibn 'Abdullah Ibn 'Amr Ibn Sulaymān but better known as Warsh, this esteemed Egyptian Qur'ānic reader (d. AH 197/AD 812) eventually immigrates to Medina to develop and transmit the reading of his teacher Nāfi'.

224 | 839 — Early Important Commentator
Born nearly 200 years after Muḥammad's death, Muḥammad Ibn Jarīr al-Ṭabarī (d. AD 923) becomes the earliest, most prominent exegete and commentator of the Qur'ān.

245 | 859 — Seven Readings
Ibn Mujāhid limits the readings of the Qur'ān to only seven and leads a campaign to abolish all other readings.

604 | 1208 — Preeminent Commentator
Born nearly 600 years after Muḥammad's death, Abū 'Abd Allah Muḥammad Ibn Aḥmad Al-Qurṭubī (d. AD 1272), distinguished Islāmic scholar and writer, produces *Tafsīr al-Qurṭubī*, a 20-volume work that introduces a new investigative approach to Qur'ānic commentary.

1250 | 1834 — Numbering of Verses (First)
German Orientalist, Gustav Leberecht Flügel, adds the first verse-numbering system to the Qur'ān.

1323 | 1905 — Warsh Reading Publication
Al-Tha'labīya Press publishes the reading of Nāfi' as told by Warsh, a reading used primarily by Muslims living in western North Africa.

1342 | 1925 — Numbering of Verses (Current)
Al-Azhar Islāmic University in Cairo modifies the verse-numbering system and publishes a printed copy of the Qur'ān based on the reading of Ḥafṣ.

1342 | 1925 — Ḥafṣ Reading Publication
Al-Azhar Islāmic University in Cairo publishes the reading of 'Āṣim as told by Ḥafṣ, the reading used today by the majority of Muslims worldwide.

Copyright© 2011 by TheQuran.com®. All rights reserved.

Maps

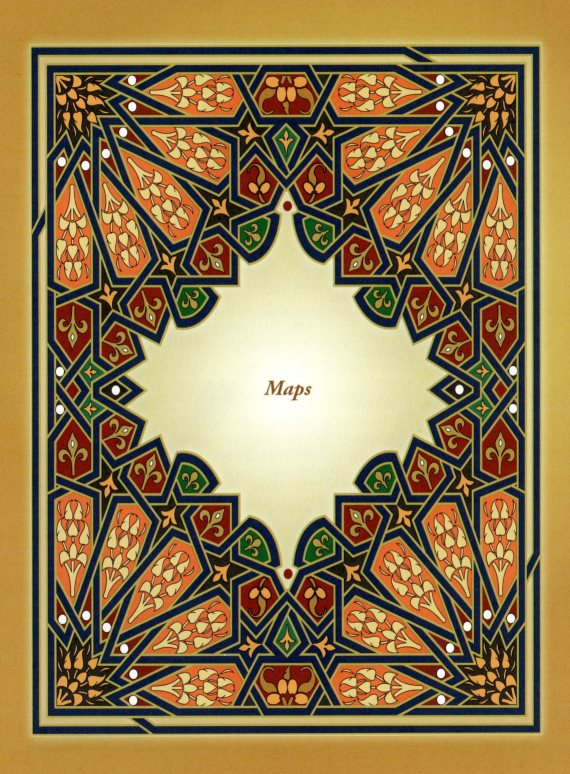

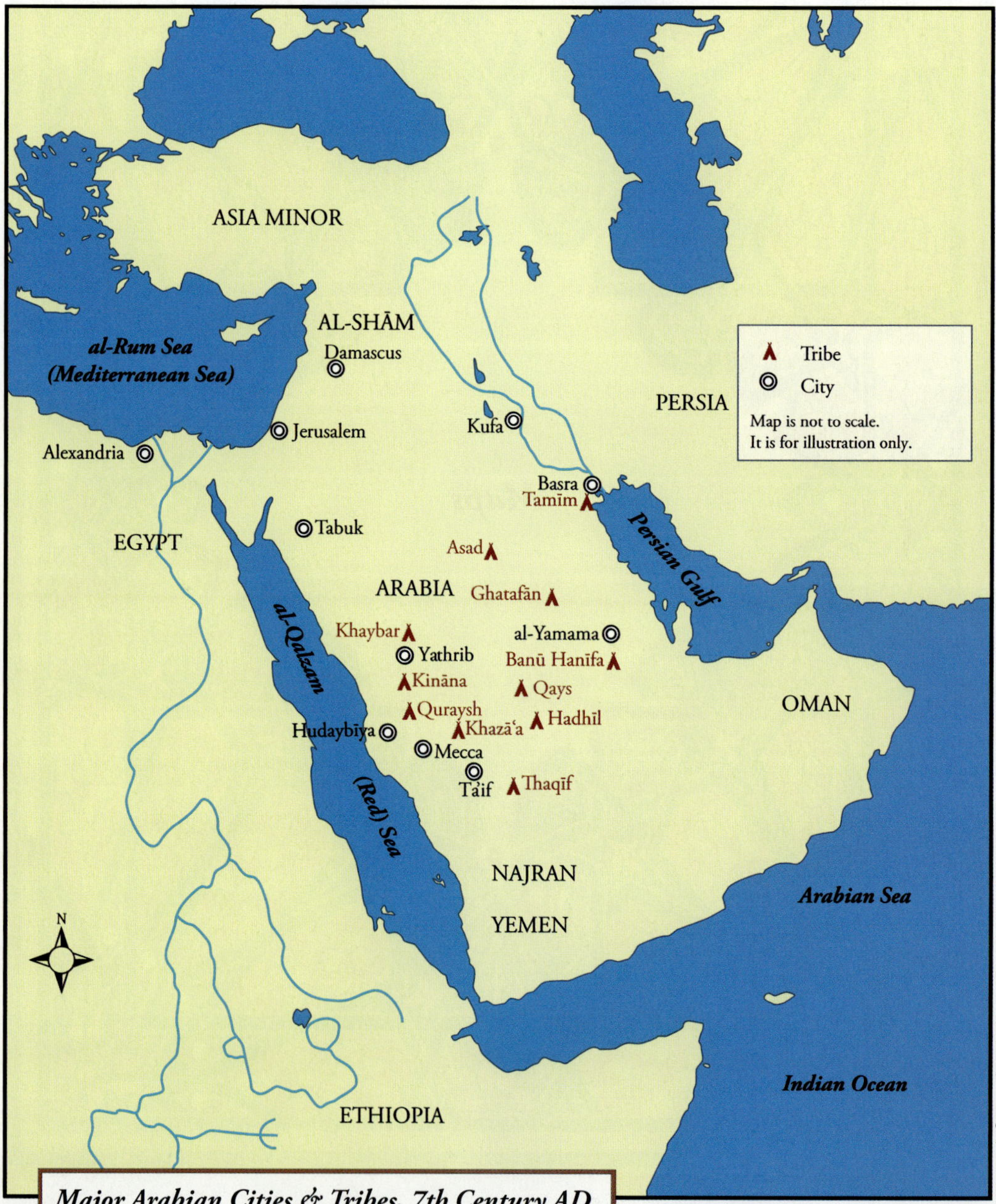

Major Arabian Cities & Tribes, 7th Century AD

Copyright© 2011 by TheQuran.com®. All rights reserved.

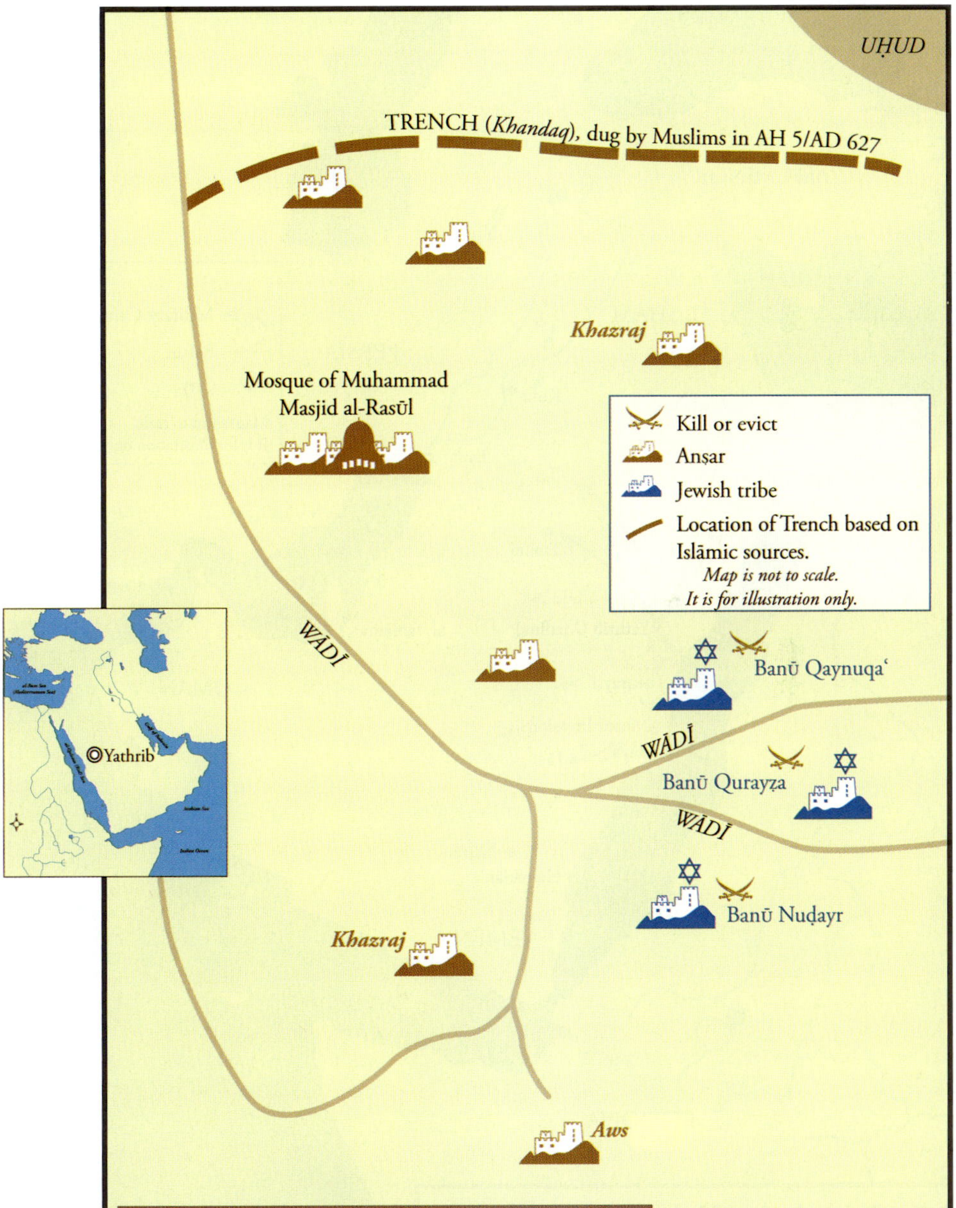

Selected Tribes of Yathrib (Medina)

Copyright© 2011 by TheQuran.com®. All rights reserved.

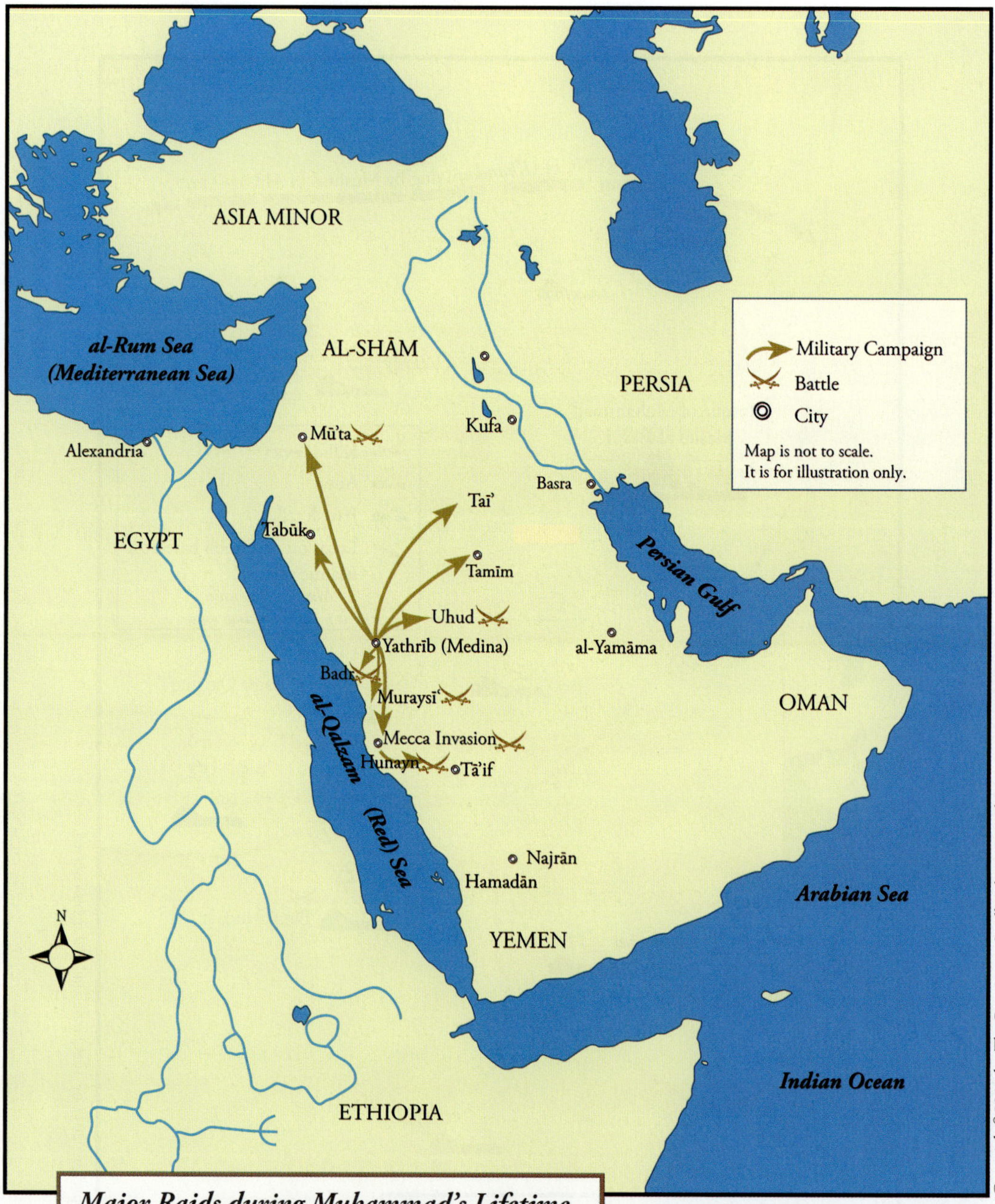

Major Raids during Muhammad's Lifetime

Copyright© 2011 by TheQuran.com®. All rights reserved.

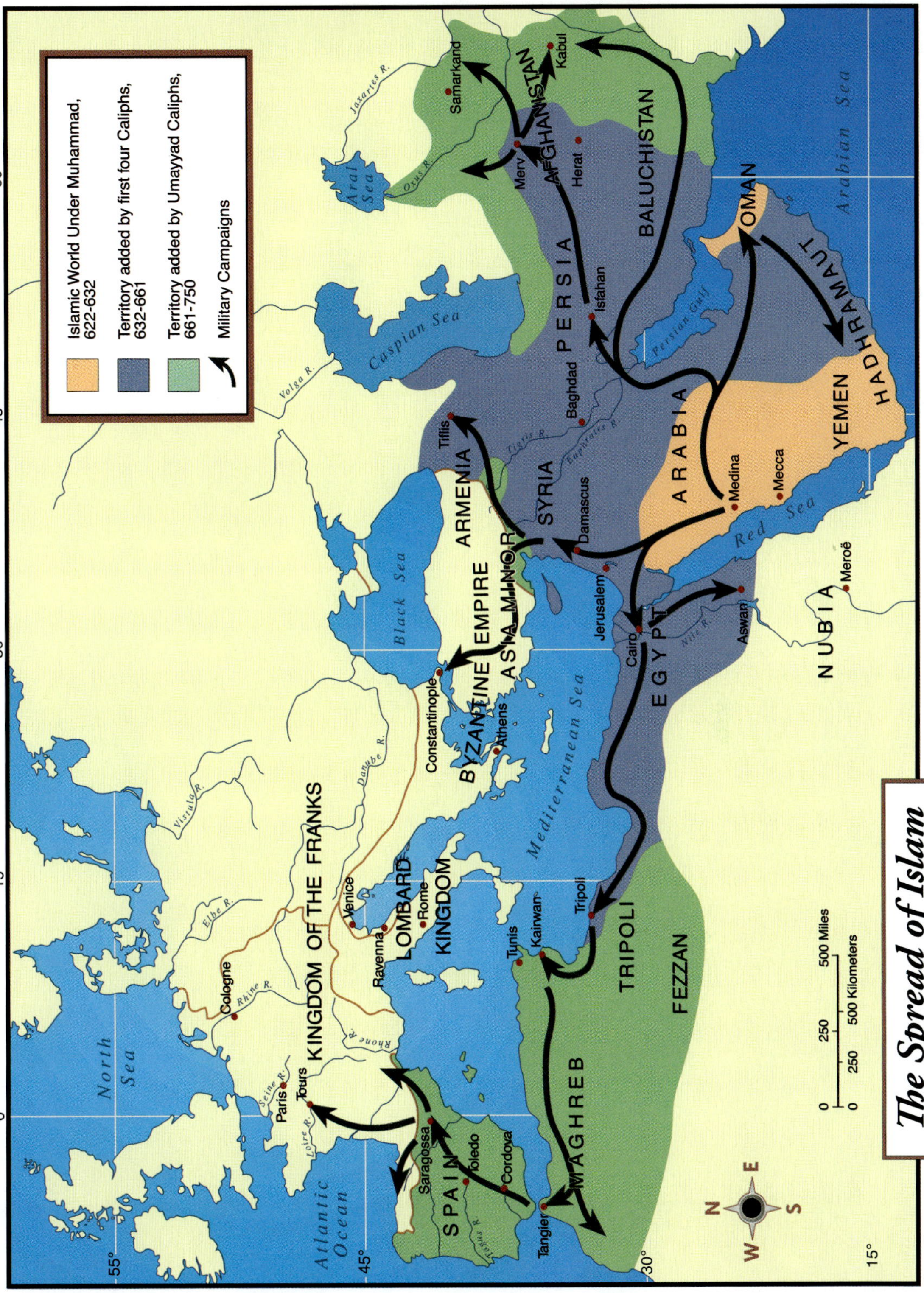
Islamic World Under Muhammad, 622-632
Territory added by first four Caliphs, 632-661
Territory added by Umayyad Caliphs, 661-750
Military Campaigns
The Spread of Islam
0 250 500 Miles
0 250 500 Kilometers
N
E
S
W
KINGDOM OF THE FRANKS
LOMBARD KINGDOM
BYZANTINE EMPIRE
ASIA MINOR
ARMENIA
SYRIA
PERSIA
AFGHANISTAN
BALUCHISTAN
ARABIA
OMAN
YEMEN
HADHRAMAUT
EGYPT
NUBIA
TRIPOLI
FEZZAN
MAGHREB
SPAIN
North Sea
Atlantic Ocean
Black Sea
Caspian Sea
Aral Sea
Mediterranean Sea
Red Sea
Persian Gulf
Arabian Sea
Paris
Tours
Cologne
Venice
Ravenna
Rome
Constantinople
Athens
Saragossa
Toledo
Cordova
Tangier
Tunis
Kairwan
Tripoli
Cairo
Jerusalem
Damascus
Aswan
Meroë
Medina
Mecca
Baghdad
Tiflis
Isfahan
Herat
Merv
Samarkand
Kabul
Seine R.
Loire R.
Rhine R.
Rhone R.
Elbe R.
Vistula R.
Danube R.
Volga R.
Tigris R.
Euphrates R.
Nile R.
Oxus R.
Jaxartes R.
Tagus R.
0°
15°
30°
45°
60°
55°

Endnotes

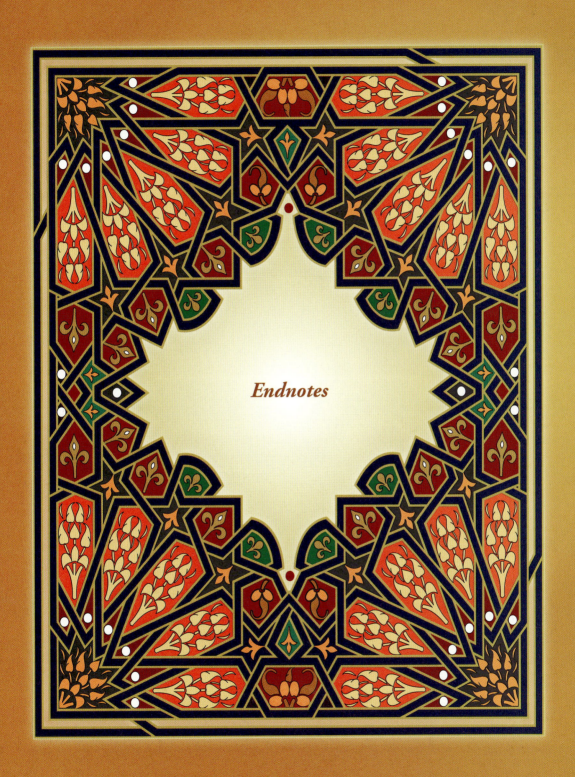

Endnotes

Introduction

1. Abū Shuhba 17.
2. al-Suyūṭī, *al-Itqān* 341; Abū Shuhba 17.
3. al-Suyūṭī, *al-Itqān* 340.
4. Ibid.
5. Ibid. 339; Abū Shuhba 18.
6. Jeffery, *Foreign Vocabulary of the Qur'ān* 233.
7. Ibid. 234; Nöldeke, *Tārīkh al-Qur'ān* 29-32.
8. Jeffery, *Foreign Vocabulary of the Qur'ān* 233.
9. al-Zarkashī 1: 281-282.
10. Jeffery, *Foreign Vocabulary of the Qur'ān* 226.
11. Geiger 41-42.
12. Jeffery, *Foreign Vocabulary of the Qur'ān* 228-229.
13. al-Suyūṭī, *al-Itqān* 336-338; al-Zarkashī 1: 273-276.
14. al-Suyūṭī, *al-Itqān* 336.
15. Jeffery, *Foreign Vocabulary of the Qur'ān* 181-182.
16. al-Suyūṭī, *al-Itqān* 422.
17. Ibid. 423.
18. Ibid. 427.
19. Ibid. 362.
20. Jeffery, *Foreign Vocabulary of the Qur'ān* 73.
21. Ibid. 72.
22. Ibid. 72-73.
23. al-Dānī, *al-Bayān* Ḥa'-Ṭa'.
24. Ibid. 296.
25. al-Raṣāfī 561-562.
26. Ibid. 561-570; compare with the analysis of *fāṣila* in Nöldeke, *Tārīkh al-Qur'ān* 34-38 and *Sketches* 33-34.
27. Nöldeke, *Sketches* 36.
28. al-Raṣāfī 604-605.
29. Lane cv-cvi.
30. al-Raṣāfī 554.
31. Ibid. 608.
32. al-Zarkashī 1: 255.

Critical Analysis

1. al-Zarkashī 1: 229-330; compare with Abū Zayd 42, 45 and al-Ḥaddād *I'jāz al-Qur'ān* 14-15.
2. Badawī 80.
3. Ibid. 90-93.
4. Muir, *Apology of al-Kindy* 78-80.
5. Badawī 250.
6. Ibid. 250-251.
7. Ibn al-Nadīm 39.

Muḥammad's Jibrīl

1. al-Bukhārī 1: 542.
2. Ibn Sa'd 1: 165.
3. al-Bukhārī 1: 13-14; this tale is also repeated in 2: 425.
4. 'Alī 6: 761.
5. Muslim 3: 415.
6. al-Bukhārī 4: 43-46.
7. Ibn Sa'd 1: 165.
8. 'Alī 6: 755.
9. Ibid. 6: 757.
10. al-Bukhārī 2: 425.
11. 'Alī 6: 759.
12. Ibid. 6: 758.
13. Muslim 4: 311.
14. Ibid. 4: 312.
15. al-Suhailī 1: 408-409.
16. Ibn Sa'd 1: 165.
17. 'Alī 6: 760.
18. Jeffery, *Foreign Vocabulary of the Qur'ān* 100-101.
19. Houtsma et al. 1: 2652.
20. al-Ṭabarī 23: 251, 24: 547.

Compilation of the Qur'ān

1. al-Suyūṭī, *al-Itqān* 378.
2. Ibid. 377.
3. Jabal 162-163.
4. al-Zamakhsharī 2: 372; al-Ṭabarī 9: 405-406.
5. Ibn Sa'd 2: 306-307.
6. Nöldeke, *Tārīkh al-Qur'ān* 39.
7. al-Sijistānī 11-12; al-Dānī 13.

8. al-Sijistānī 13; al-Dānī 15.
9. al-Sijistānī 12.
10. al-Suyūṭī, *al-Itqān* 378.
11. Stipčević 1: 219-220; compare with Déroche 173.
12. al-Dānī 16; al-Zarkashī 1: 233; al-Suyūṭī, *al-Itqān* 379.
13. al-Zarkashī 1: 233; al-Sijistānī 14, 15, 28; compare with al-Dānī 13-14.
14. Jar Allah 26.
15. Ibid. 27.
16. al-Suyūṭī, *al-Itqān* 383.
17. Ibid. 385.
18. Jabal 187.
19. al-Sijistānī 15.
20. Ibn Sa'd 2: 307.
21. al-Suyūṭī, *al-Itqān* 389.
22. al-Sijistānī 20.
23. Ibid. 26-28.
24. Nöldeke, *Tārīkh al-Qur'ān* 297.
25. al-Sijistānī 18.
26. Ibid. 29; al-Dānī 17.
27. al-Sijistānī 32.
28. al-Ḥarīrī 169.
29. Jar Allah 28.
30. al-Dānī 14.
31. al-Sijistānī 33-34.
32. Ibid. 17-18.
33. al-Sijistānī 26; al-Dānī 16.
34. al-Dānī 19.
35. al-Sijistānī 16.
36. Ibid. 32.
37. Ibid. 28.
38. al-Dānī 18.
39. al-Sijistānī 30; compare with al-Suyūṭī, *al-Itqān* 391.
40. al-Dānī 18; compare with al-Suyūṭī, *al-Itqān* 393.
41. al-Sijistānī 24-25.
42. Ibid. 21-22.
43. Nöldeke, *Tārīkh al-Qur'ān* 280, 339.
44. *Encyclopedia of the Qur'ān* 1: 348.
45. Nöldeke, *Tārīkh al-Qur'ān* 253.
46. al-Suyūṭī, *al-Itqān* 391.

47. Ibid. 392.
48. al-Sijistānī 41.
49. Ibid. 42.
50. al-Qurṭubī 14: 90.
51. Jeffery, Introduction 7-8.
52. al-Sijistānī 59-130.
53. al-Ḥarīrī 164-166; compare with Nöldeke, *Tārīkh al-Qur'ān* 259-261, which has a list with less numbers; also compare with al-Sijistānī 92-98.
54. al-Sijistānī 98-102.
55. Jabal 176.
56. Nöldeke, *Tārīkh al-Qur'ān* 266-267.
57. al-Sijistānī 16.
58. al-Bāqilānī 71.
59. Nöldeke, *Tārīkh al-Qur'ān* 322-323.
60. Ibid. 324.
61. Ibid. 323.
62. Leaman 31.
63. Nöldeke, *Tārīkh al-Qur'ān* 229-231; compare with Sell 22-24.
64. al-Sijistānī 16.
65. Ibid. 17.
66. al-Suyūṭī, *al-Itqān* 378.
67. *Encyclopedia of the Qur'ān* 1: 331-332.
68. Ibid. 1: 334; compare with Jeffery, Introduction 8-9.
69. Leaman 31.
70. Lester.
71. *Encyclopedia of the Qur'ān* 1: 334; Böwering 74.
72. Donner 33.

Chronological Sequence of the Qur'ān

1. *Encyclopedia of the Qur'ān* 1: 321-322.
2. al-Suyūṭī, *al-Itqān* 45; al-Zarkashī 1: 187.
3. Ibn al-Nadīm 28.
4. al-Suyūṭī, *al-Itqān* 428.
5. *Encyclopedia of the Qur'ān* 1: 322.
6. al-Suyūṭī, *Asrār Tartīb* 68-72.
7. al-Zarkashī 1: 244-245.
8. Ibn al-Nadīm 29-30.
9. al-Suyūṭī, *al-Itqān* 423; compare with al-Zarkashī 1: 251; Ibn al-Jawzī, *Funūn al-Afnān* 235-236.
10. al-Suyūṭī, *al-Itqān* 427.

11. al-Ya'qūbī 2: 135.
12. Ibn al-Nadīm 30.
13. Nöldeke, *Tārīkh al-Qur'ān* 245.
14. al-Zamakhsharī 2: 372.
15. al-Ṭabarī 9: 406.
16. Ibid. 9: 405.
17. Ibn al-Jawzī, *Funūn al-Afnān* 197-198.
18. al-Ḥarīrī 140.
19. Nöldeke, *Tārīkh al-Qur'ān* 297-298.
20. Ibid. 298.
21. Ibn 'Āshūr 6: 71.
22. al-Zarkashī 1: 199-203.
23. al-Suyūṭī, *al-Itqān* 177; Ibn al-Ḍurays 36.
24. al-Suyūṭī, *al-Itqān* 176; Ibn al-Ḍurays 35.
25. Goldziher 310.
26. Ibid. 311-312.
27. Ibid.
28. Ibid.
29. Ibid.
30. Ibid.
31. Ibid.
32. Ibid.
33. Sell 19.
34. al-Rāzī, *Tafsīr* 3: 222.
35. al-Suyūṭī, *al-Itqān* 44.
36. *Encyclopedia of the Qur'ān* 1: 322.
37. al-Ḥaddād, *Aṭwār al-Da'wa* 291-298.

Abrogation and the Abrogated

1. Ibn Kathīr 10: 84-85.
2. al-Ṭabarī 16: 603-604.
3. al-Suyūṭī, *al-Itqān* 1435-1436; al-Zarkashī 2: 29.
4. al-Suyūṭī, *al-Itqān* 1435; al-Zarkashī 2: 29.
5. Ibn al-Jawzī, *Nawāsikh* 104-110.
6. al-Ṭabarī 2: 388.
7. al-Zarkashī 2: 40.
8. Ibid. 2: 35.
9. al-Zarkashī 2: 35; compare with al-Baghdādī 52-53 and Ibn al-Jawzī, *Nawāsikh* 114-116.
10. Abū Zayd 130.

11. al-Suyūṭī, *al-Itqān* 1441.
12. al-Zarkashī 2: 37.
13. Ibn al-Jawzī, *Nawāsikh*137.
14. al-Suyūṭī, *al-Itqān* 1440; al-Zarkashī 2: 39.
15. al-Suyūṭī, *al-Itqān* 1440-1441; al-Zarkashī 2: 39; compare with Ibn al-Jawzī, *Nawāsikh* 110-113.
16. al-Ṭabarī 2: 391.
17. Ibid. 2: 392.
18. al-Suyūṭī, *al-Itqān* 1436-1437; al-Zarkashī 2: 31; compare with Shu'la 44.
19. al-Makkī 79.
20. Ibid. 78-79.
21. al-Suyūṭī, *al-Itqān* 1436.
22. al-Zarkashī 2: 38.
23. al-'Alawī, *Min Qāmūs al-Turāth* 195.
24. al-Rāzī, *Tafsīr* 3: 244.
25. *Encyclopedia of the Qur'ān* 1: 13.
26. Shu'la 46.
27. Abū Zayd 131.
28. Ibid.
29. al-Ṭabarī 11: 522.
30. al-'Alawī, *Min Qāmūs al-Turāth* 200.

Variant Readings of the Qur'ān

1. Ibn Qutayba, *Ta'wīl* 35; Ibn al-Khaṭīb 125.
2. Nöldeke, *Tārīkh al-Qur'ān* 559.
3. al-Rāfi'ī 40; compare with Brockelmann 4: 2.
4. al-Dumyāṭī 1: 33.
5. Ibid. 34.
6. al-Ashwaḥ 61-63.
7. Ibid. 65.
8. al-Dhahabī 343-347; compare with Brockelmann 4: 3-4; Ḍayf 18.
9. al-Dhahabī 384.
10. Ibid. 384-385.
11. Nöldeke, *Tārīkh al-Qur'ān* 560-561; al-Dhahabī 384; compare with Brockelmann 4: 3-4 and Ḍayf 19.
12. Ḍayf 16-17.
13. Ibid. 18.
14. Nöldeke, *Tārīkh al-Qur'ān* 566; al-Ashwaḥ 45, 65; al-Rāfi'ī 41-42.
15. al-Ashwaḥ 69.
16. Ibid. 65.
17. 'Azzūz 21.

18. Nöldeke, *Tārīkh al-Qur'ān* 556.
19. al-Ashwaḥ 84.
20. Ibid. 42.
21. Ibid. 100.
22. Nöldeke, *Tārīkh al-Qur'ān* 589.
23. Ibn Jinnī 1: 32.
24. al-Khaṭīb 3: 496-497.
25. 'Azzūz 50-51.
26. Ibid. 65.
27. Ibid. 69.
28. Ibn al-Khaṭīb 126.
29. Ibid.
30. 'Azzūz 16-18.
31. Ibn Khalawayh 1: 20; compare with Ibn Qutayba, *Ta'wīl* 39-40.
32. Compare with al-Khaṭīb 2: 69-70.
33. Ibn Manẓūr 2686.
34. Compare with al-Khaṭīb 9: 299.
35. al-Khaṭīb 1: 83.
36. Compare with al-Khaṭīb 9: 105-106.
37. Ibn Qutayba, *Ta'wīl* 36-38; compare with al-Zarkashī 1: 214-215.
38. al-Suyūṭī, *al-Itqān* 423.
39. Nöldeke, *Tārīkh al-Qur'ān* 266-267.
40. al-Sijistānī 22.
41. Ibn Sa'd 2: 306-307.
42. Brockelmann 4: 2.
43. al-Ṭabarī 18: 446; al-Zamakhsharī 4: 564.
44. Goldziher 30-31.
45. al-Rāzī, *Tafsīr* 25: 96.
46. al-Khaṭīb 7: 137.
47. al-Qurṭubī 16: 396.
48. Goldziher 31.
49. Wherry 3: 282.
50. Nöldeke, *Tārīkh al-Qur'ān* 617-619; Ibn al-Jazrī 8-12.
51. Nöldeke, *Tārīkh al-Qur'ān* 619; Ibn al-Jazrī 12-14.
52. al-Ashwaḥ 152-153; Nöldeke, *Tārīkh al-Qur'ān* 619-620.

Muqaṭṭa'āt (The Stand-alone Letters)

1. al-Qurṭubī, 1: 239.
2. al-Rāzī, *Tafsīr* 2: 7.
3. al-Andalusī 1: 82.

4. al-Burhān 1: 176.
5. al-Qurṭubī 1: 237.
6. al-Rāzī, *Tafsīr* 2: 6. (Al-Rāzī does not discuss the letter Y.)
7. Ibid. 2: 7.
8. Ibid. 2: 6.
9. al-Qurṭubī 1: 238.
10. al-Rāzī, *Tafsīr* 2: 7.
11. al-Andalusī 1: 82.
12. al-Rāzī, *Tafsīr* 2: 6.
13. al-Ṭabarī 1: 220.
14. Ibn Kathīr 1: 257.
15. al-Rāzī, *Tafsīr* 2: 9.
16. al-Zarkashī, *al-Burhān* 1: 170-171.
17. Ibn Kathīr 1: 255.

Women in the Qur'ān

1. al-ʻAqqād 4: 407.
2. al-Zamakhsharī 5: 433; compare with al-Qurṭubī 19: 20.
3. al-Rāzī, *Tafsīr* 27: 203.
4. Ibn Kathīr 12: 306.
5. al-ʻAqqād 4: 399.
6. Ibid. 4: 400.
7. Ibid. 4: 401.
8. al-Qurṭubī 15: 215.
9. Ibn Kathīr 10: 217.
10. al-Qurṭubī 17: 230.
11. al-Zamakhsharī 5: 98.
12. Ibn Kathīr 11: 243.
13. al-Ṭabarī 19:181, 183; Ibn Kathīr 11: 243.
14. al-Qurṭubī 17: 233.
15. al-ʻAqqād 4: 398.
16. Ibid.
17. Abū Khalīl 234.
18. al-Qurṭubī 6: 286.
19. al-Ghazālī 69.
20. al-Suyūṭī, *al-Durr al-Manthūr* 4: 391.
21. al-Ghazālī 70.
22. al-Suyūṭī, *al-Durr al-Manthūr* 4: 399; compare with Kishk 96, 97.
23. al-Suyūṭī, *al-Durr al-Manthūr* 4: 388, 392, and 397-398.

24. al-Ghazālī 69; compare with al-Suyūṭī, *al-Durr al-Manthūr* 4: 390 and Ibn Kathīr 4: 23.
25. al-Suyūṭī, *al-Durr al-Manthūr* 4: 393, 398; Kishk 100.
26. al-Rāzī, *Tafsīr* 3: 238; compare with al-Ṭabarī 6: 696-697.
27. al-Rāzī, *Tafsīr* 10: 93.
28. al-Ṭabarī 6: 698; al-Suyūṭī, *al-Durr al-Manthūr* 4: 397.
29. al-Ṭabarī 6: 701; Ibn Kathīr 4: 25.
30. Ibn al-ʿArabī 1: 533.
31. al-Ṭabarī 6: 704; compare with al-Qurṭubī 6: 284 and al-Suyūṭī, *al-Durr al-Manthūr* 4: 403.
32. al-Ṭabarī 6: 705
33. Ibid. 6: 707; al-Qurṭubī 6: 285.
34. al-Zamakhsharī 2: 70.
35. al-Ghazālī 71.
36. Kishk 100.
37. Ibn Kathīr 4: 25.
38. al-Ṭabarī 6: 709-710.
39. Ibid. 6: 708.
40. Ibid. 6: 711.
41. al-Ṭabarī 6: 711-712; al-Thaʿālibī 2: 230; al-Qurṭubī 6: 285.
42. al-Qurṭubī 6: 286.
43. al-Shaʿrāwī 98.
44. al-Ṭabarī 3: 748.
45. al-Qurṭubī 4: 8.
46. Ibid.; Ibn Kathīr 2: 312.
47. al-Ṭabarī 3: 745.
48. Ibid. 7: 569.
49. al-Qurṭubī 6: 37.
50. ʿAlī 5: 547.
51. al-Qurṭubī 6: 33.
52. Abd al-Raḥmān (Bint al-Shāṭi') 605.
53. Ibid. 606.
54. Ibid. 609.
55. Abū Khalīl 229.
56. al-Suyūṭī, *Asbāb al-Nuzūl* 44.
57. ʿAlī 5: 557.
58. Ibid. 5: 556.
59. Ibid. 5: 536.
60. Ibid. 5: 537.
61. Ibn al-Jawzī, *Nawāsikh* 271; al-Makkī 230.
62. Ibn al-Jawzī, *Nawāsikh* 270; al-Suyūṭī, *Tārīkh al-Khulafā'* 165.

63. al-Baghdādī 289.
64. Calder 57-58.
65. al-'Alawī, *Fuṣūl 'An al-Mar'a* 54.
66. Ibid. 54.
67. Ibn Manẓūr 3479.
68. al-Sha'rāwī 57-58.
69. Ibid. 59.
70. 'Alī 5: 562.
71. Ibid. 5: 563, 565.
72. Abū Khalīl 241.

The Qur'ān and People of Other Faiths

1. 'Abdu 10: 175.
2. al-Maḥallī and al-Suyūṭī, *Tafsīr al-Jalālayn* 187.
3. al-Shanqīṭī 2: 501.
4. al-Bayḍāwi 4: 426.
5. 'Abdu 10: 181.
6. Ibid. 10: 199.
7. Ibid. 10: 322.
8. al-Zamakhsharī 3: 30.
9. al-Zamakhsharī 3: 30; compare with *Encyclopedia of the Qur'ān* 1: 410.
10. al-Bayḍāwi 4: 448.
11. *Encyclopedia of the Qur'ān* 1: 343.
12. al-Qurṭubī 10: 170.
13. Ibid.
14. Ibid.
15. al-Ṭabarī 11: 407.
16. Ibid. 11: 408.
17. al-Zamakhsharī 3: 32.
18. al-Baghawī 4: 33-34.
19. al-Ṭabarī 11: 408.
20. Ibn Kathīr 7: 176.
21. Ibid 7: 178.
22. Ibn Manẓūr 2249.
23. al-Bayḍāwi 4: 449.
24. Ibn Kathīr 7: 174; al-Zamakhsharī 3: 30-31.
25. 'Abdu 10: 324.
26. al-Zuḥailī 192.
27. 'Abdu 10: 174.
28. Ibid. 11: 57.

29. al-Zuḥailī 190.
30. al-Ṭabarī 11: 369.
31. Ibn Kathīr 7: 237.
32. Ibid. 7: 155.
33. ʿAbdu 10: 229.
34. Ibid. 10: 230.
35. Ibid.

Key to Reading Part II

1. al-Rāzī, *Tafsīr* 8: 47; Ibn Kathīr 3: 69.
2. al-Baghawī 2: 207; al-Ṭabarī 6: 688.
3. al-Zamakhsharī 2: 67.
4. al-Baghawī 2: 44.

Sūra 1 (al-Fātiḥa)

1. Ibn ʿĀshūr 1: 131.
2. Ibid. 1: 136.
3. al-Khaṭīb 1: 9.
4. Ibid. 1: 10.
5. al-ʿAkbarī 1: 92.
6. al-Khaṭīb 1: 17.
7. Ibid.
8. al-Sijistānī *Kitāb al-Maṣāḥif* 21-22.
9. al-Qurṭubī 1: 174.
10. Ibid. 1: 177.
11. Nöldeke, *Tārīkh al-Qur'ān* 100, marginal note.
12. Jeffery, *Foreign Vocabulary of the Qur'ān* 140-141.
13. Nöldeke, *Tarikh al-Qur'ān* 98-100.
14. M. al-Rāzī, *Min Gharā'ib* 2.
15. al-Ṭabarī 1: 178.
16. al-Rāzī, *Tafsīr* 1: 260.

Sūra 2 (al-Baqara)

1. Nöldeke, *Tārīkh al-Qur'ān* 166.
2. al-Ḥaddād, *Aṭwār al-Daʿwa* 764.
3. Muir, *Life of Mahomet* 3: 311.
4. Ibn al-Jawzī, *Nawāsikh* 127-128.
5. Ibid. 128-129; Ibn Salāma 11.
6. Ibn al-Jawzī, *Nawāsikh* 128.
7. al-Khaṭīb 1: 39.

8. Ibid.
9. Ibid.
10. Ibid. 1: 55.
11. Ibid. 1: 82.
12. Ibid. 1: 59.
13. Ibid. 1: 63.
14. Ibid. 1: 64.
15. Ibid. 1: 66.
16. al-Ṭabarī 1: 510.
17. Ibid. 1: 491.
18. Ibn Kathīr 1: 338.
19. al-Zamakhsharī 1: 252.
20. al-Maḥallī and al-Suyūṭī, *Tafsīr al-Jalālayn* 6.
21. al-Ṭabarī 1: 516.
22. al-Ḥaddād, *Aṭwār al-Da'wa* 351.
23. Ibn Kathīr 1: 365.
24. al-Khaṭīb 1: 83-84.
25. Ibid. 1: 83.
26. Ibid. 1: 93.
27. Ibid. 1: 94; al-Zamakhsharī 1: 264.
28. Goldziher 27.
29. al-Ṭabarī 1: 687.
30. al-Rāzī, *Tafsīr* 3: 89.
31. Ibid. 3:88.
32. al-Maḥallī and al-Suyūṭī, *Tafsīr al-Jalālayn* 9-10.
33. al-Andalusī 1: 156.
34. Ibn Qutayba, *Tafsīr Gharīb al-Qur'ān* 5.
35. al-Ṭabarī 2: 18; al-Qurṭubī 2: 146.
36. Ibn al-Jawzī, *Nawāsikh* 129-130.
37. Ibid. 130; al-Makkī 124; Ibn Ḥazm 19.
38. al-Makkī 124.
39. Ibn al-Jawzī, *Nawāsikh* 131.
40. al-Ṭabarī 2: 61.
41. al-Qurṭubī 2: 171.
42. al-Rāzī, *Tafsīr* 3: 119-120.
43. Ibid. 3: 118.
44. al-Khaṭīb 1: 123
45. Ibid. 1: 127.
46. Ibid. 1: 162.

47. Ibid. 1: 132.
48. Ibid. 1: 133.
49. Ibid. 1: 203-204.
50. Ibid. 1: 210.
51. Ibid. 1: 214.
52. Ibn al-Jawzī, *Nawāsikh* 131-132.
53. Ibid. 131.
54. Ibid. 133; al-Makkī 124; Ibn Ḥazm 21.
55. Ibn al-Jawzī, *Nawāsikh* 133; Ibn Salāma 12.
56. al-Naḥās 23-24.
57. al-Makkī 124.
58. al-Rāzī, *Tafsīr* 3: 190; compare with al-Ṭabarī 2: 221-225.
59. al-Qurṭubī 12: 427.
60. al-Khaṭīb 1: 163-164.
61. Ibn al-Jawzī, *Nawāsikh* 134-135; al-Makkī 125; al-Naḥās 24.
62. al-Makkī 125.
63. Ibn al-Jawzī, *Nawāsikh* 135.
64. al-Khaṭīb 1: 173.
65. al-Ṭabarī 2: 390-391.
66. Ibid 2: 391-392.
67. al-Rāzī, *Tafsīr* 3: 244.
68. al-Ṭabarī 2: 388.
69. al-Qurṭubī 2: 301.
70. al-Maḥallī and al-Suyūṭī, *Tafsīr al-Jalālayn* 17.
71. al-Ṭabarī 2: 391.
72. Ibid. 2: 392.
73. al-Maḥallī and al-Suyūṭī, *Tafsīr al-Jalālayn* 17.
74. Ibn al-Jawzī, *Nawāsikh* 136-137; al-Makkī 125-126; Ibn Salāma 12; al-Naḥās 25; al-Ṭabarī 2: 423- 424.
75. Ibn al-Jawzī, *Nawāsikh* 137.
76. Ibid.; compare with al-Makkī 126 and Ibn al-Jawzī, *Zad al-Masir* 1: 132.
77. al-Khaṭīb 1: 179.
78. Ibid.
79. Ibn al-Jawzī, *Nawāsikh* 139-140.
80. Ibid. 142.
81. al-Makkī 131.
82. Ibn al-Jawzī, *Nawāsikh* 142-145; Ibn Salāma 13; al-Suyūṭī, *al-Durr al-Manthūr* 2: 7.
83. al-Naḥās 14-15.
84. al-Makkī 127.

85. al-Naḥās 15; Ibn al-Jawzī, *Nawāsikh* 149; al-Ṭabarī 2: 456- 458.
86. al-Khaṭīb 1: 183.
87. Ibid.
88. Ibid. 1: 184.
89. al-Ṭabarī 2: 516.
90. Ibid.
91. al-Rāzī, *Tafsīr* 4: 45.
92. al-Khaṭīb 1: 189.
93. Ibid. 1: 190.
94. 'Alī 6: 398.
95. Ibid.
96. al-Ṭabarī 2: 600; compare with Goldziher 39.
97. al-Khaṭīb 1: 201.
98. Ibn al-Jawzī, *Nawāsikh* 150.
99. Ibid. 150-151.
100. al-Ṭabarī 3: 722-723; al-Rāzī, *Tafsīr* 4: 177.
101. al-Andalusī 1: 229.
102. Ibn al-Jawzī, *Nawāsikh* 151-153.
103. 'Alī 6: 380.
104. Ibid.
105. al-Rāzī, *Tafsīr* 4: 177.
106. 'Alī 6: 380-381.
107. al-Ṭabarī 2: 715.
108. Ibid.
109. Abū Ḥaīyān 1: 631.
110. al-Ṭabarī 2: 716.
111. Ibid.
112. al-Ṭabarī 2: 722-723; al-Rāzī, *Tafsīr* 4: 177.
113. al-Andalusī 1: 229.
114. Ibn Ḥazm 22; Ibn Salāma 14.
115. Ibn al-Jawzī, *Nawāsikh* 154; al-Makkī 133.
116. Ibn al-Jawzī, *Nawāsikh* 155; Ibn Ḥazm 23; Ibn Salāma 15.
117. Ibn al-Jawzī, *Nawāsikh* 155.
118. al-Makkī 134; al-Naḥās 17.
119. Ibn al-Jawzī, *Nawāsikh* 156; Ibn Salāma 15.
120. Ibn Salāma 15.
121. Ibid. 16.
122. al-Makkī 135.
123. Ibid. 135-136.

124. Ibid.
125. Ibid. 137.
126. Ibn al-Jawzī, *Nawāsikh* 158.
127. Ibid. 160-161; al-Naḥās 18.
128. al-Makkī 141.
129. Ibn al-Jawzī, *Nawāsikh* 163.
130. Ibid. 164-165; al-Makkī 141, 143.
131. Ibn al-Jawzī, *Nawāsikh* 166-168; al-Makkī 145; Ibn Ḥazm 26; Ibn Salāma 17-18; al-Naḥās 19-20.
132. al-Makkī 146.
133. Ibid. 147.
134. Ibid. 146.
135. al-Ṭabarī 3: 152-160.
136. Ibn al-Jawzī, *Nawāsikh* 172-175; al-Makkī 149; al-Naḥās 21-23; al-Ṭabarī 3: 159; al-Suyūṭī, *al-Durr al-Manthūr* 2: 178.
137. Ibn al-Jawzī, *Nawāsikh* 175-177; al-Makkī 150.
138. al-Khaṭīb 1: 250.
139. Ibid. 1: 270.
140. Ibid. 1: 252.
141. Ibn al-Jawzī, *Nawāsikh* 179.
142. Ibid. 180.
143. Ibn Salāma 18-19; al-Makkī 155-156; al-Naḥās 25.
144. al-Naḥās 26.
145. Ibn al-Jawzī, *Nawāsikh* 181-182; al-Makkī 157; al-Naḥās 26.
146. Ibn al-Jawzī, *Nawāsikh* 182; al-Makkī 157; al-Naḥās 27.
147. Ibn al-Jawzī, *Nawāsikh* 182; al-Makkī 157.
148. Ibn Ḥazm 27.
149. al-Naḥās 27.
150. Ibn al-Jawzī, *Nawāsikh* 182-183.
151. al-Khaṭīb 1: 265.
152. Ibn al-Jawzī, *Nawāsikh* 184; al-Ṭabarī 3: 298.
153. Ibn al-Jawzī, *Nawāsikh* 185; Ibn Kathīr 2: 217.
154. Ibn al-Jawzī, *Nawāsikh* 185; Ibn Ḥazm 27.
155. Ibid.
156. Ibn al-Jawzī, *Nawāsikh* 186; al-Suyūṭī, *al-Durr al-Manthūr* 2: 320.
157. Ibn al-Jawzī, *Nawāsikh* 186.
158. Ibid. 187-188; compare with al-Makkī 159 and al-Naḥās 28.
159. al-Naḥās 32.
160. Ibn al-Jawzī, *Nawāsikh* 189-190.
161. ʿAlī 6: 348.

162. 'Alī 6: 375.
163. Ibid. (Other forms are also mentioned).
164. al-Khaṭīb 1: 273.
165. al-Ṭabarī 3: 510; compare with Goldziher 24.
166. al-Khaṭīb 1: 290
167. Ibid. 1: 291.
168. Ibid. 1: 294.
169. Ibn al-Jawzī, *Nawāsikh* 191-192; Ibn Salāma 20; al-Ṭabarī 3: 642-643.
170. Ibn al-Jawzī, *Nawāsikh* 192; Ibn al-Jawzī, *Zad al-Masir* 1: 234.
171. Ibn al-Jawzī, *Nawāsikh* 193; al-Naḥās 29.
172. Ibn al-Jawzī, *Nawāsikh* 194.
173. Ibid.
174. al-Naḥās 29.
175. Ibn al-Jawzī, *Nawāsikh* 196.
176. al-Ṭabarī 3: 664.
177. Ibn al-Jawzī, *Nawāsikh 197;* al-Makkī 160; Ibn-Ḥazm 28; al-Naḥās 30.
178. Ibn al-Jawzī, *Nawāsikh* 197; al-Makkī 160.
179. al-Naḥās 31.
180. al-Makkī 166; al-Naḥās 39.
181. Ibn al-Jawzī, *Nawāsikh* 199; al-Makkī 167; Ibn Salāma 22; al-Naḥās 39-40.
182. Ibn al-Jawzī, *Nawāsikh* 200-202; Ibn-Ḥazm 28-29.
183. al-Makkī 168.
184. al-Khaṭīb 1: 301.
185. Ibn al-Jawzī, *Nawāsikh* 202-203.
186. Ibid. 203-204; al-Naḥās 56.
187. Ibn al-Jawzī, *Nawāsikh* 204.
188. al-Makkī 171.
189. Ibid. 169-170.
190. al-Ṭabarī 3: 745.
191. Ibid. 3: 748.
192. Ibid. 3: 751; Ibn Kathīr 2: 310.
193. Ibid.
194. al-Ṭabarī 3: 753; Ibn Kathīr 2: 311.
195. al-Ṭabarī 3: 754.
196. Ibn Kathīr 2: 312.
197. al-Qurṭubī 4: 8.
198. Ibn al-'Arabī 1: 238.
199. al-Qurṭubī 4: 10.
200. al-Ṭabarī 4: 45, 47.

201. al-Makkī 175.
202. al-Ṭabarī 4: 87.
203. Ibn al-Jawzī, *Nawāsikh* 205.
204. Ibid. 206.
205. Ibid.
206. Ibid. 207.
207. Ibid.
208. al-Khaṭīb 1: 315.
209. al-Suyūṭī, *Asbāb al-Nuzūl* 44.
210. al-Ṭabarī 4: 169-177; al-Suyūṭī, *al-Durr al-Manthūr* 2: 691-692.
211. al-Suyūṭī, *al-Durr al-Manthūr* 2: 696.
212. Abū Ḥaīyān 2: 211.
213. Ibid. 2: 689.
214. Ibn al-Jawzī, *Nawāsikh* 211; al-Makkī 179; Ibn Salāma 26.
215. Ibn al-Jawzī, *Nawāsikh* 211; al-Ṭabarī 4: 245; Ibn Kathīr 2: 373-377.
216. al-Makkī 179.
217. al-Ṭabarī 4: 367.
218. Ibid. 4: 359-363.
219. Ibid. 4: 342-359.
220. Ibid. 4: 366-367.
221. al-Khaṭīb 1: 336; compare with Goldziher 24-25.
222. al-Ṭabarī 4: 363.
223. Ibid. 4: 364-366.
224. Ibid. 4: 400-404.
225. Ibn al-Jawzī, *Nawāsikh* 214-216; Ibn Salāma 26; al-Naḥās 72; al-Suyūṭī, *al-Durr al-Manthūr* 3: 110-111.
226. al-Khaṭīb 1: 357.
227. Ibn al-Jawzī, *Nawāsikh* 219.
228. Ibid. 220; al-Makkī 193; al-Naḥās 79.
229. Ibn al-Jawzī, *Nawāsikh* 217; al-Makkī 193; al-Ṭabarī 4: 551.
230. Ibn al-Jawzī, *Nawāsikh* 218 and *Zad al-Masir* 1: 306.
231. *Midrash Rabbah* 17: explanation of Gen. 15.7.
232. Freedman and Simon 310-311.
233. St. Clair-Tisdall, *Original Sources* 79-80.
234. al-Khaṭīb 1: 402.
235. Ibn al-Jawzī, *Nawāsikh* 222-223; al-Makkī 196; Ibn Ḥazm 30; al-Naḥās 83.
236. al-Makkī 196.
237. Ibn al-Jawzī, *Nawāsikh* 221; al-Makkī 196; Ibn al-Jawzī, *Zad al-Masir* 1: 340.
238. Ibn al-Jawzī, *Nawāsikh* 225-231; Ibn Ḥazm 30; al-Naḥās 85.

239. Ibn al-Jawzī, *Nawāsikh* 231.
240. Ibid. 232; Ibn Salāma 27-28; al-Makkī 200.
241. Ibn al-Jawzī, *Nawāsikh* 233; al-Naḥās 85.
242. Ibn al-Jawzī, *Nawāsikh* 233-234; al-Makkī 200; al-Naḥās 85.
243. al-Khaṭīb 1: 433-434.
244. Ibid. 1: 431.
245. Ibid. 1: 432-433.
246. Ibn al-Jawzī, *Nawāsikh* 236; Ibn Ḥazm 30.
247. Ibn al-Jawzī, *Nawāsikh* 235-236.

Sūra 3 (Āl-i 'Imrān)

1. Wherry 2: 1.
2. al-Ḥaddād, *Aṭwār al-Da'wa* 798; compare with Wherry 2: 1.
3. al-Ḥaddād, *Aṭwār al-Da'wa* 804; compare with Wherry 2: 1.
4. al-Ṭabarī 5: 180.
5. al-Rāzī, *Tafsīr* 7: 170.
6. al-Zamakhsharī 1: 527.
7. Ibn Kathīr 3: 6.
8. al-Ṭabarī 16: 431-434; see comment on Q 21.105.
9. al-Rāzī, *Tafsīr* 7: 174.
10. Ibid 7: 174.
11. al-Qurṭubī 5: 10; M. al-Rāzī, *Min Gharā'ib* 38.
12. al-Khaṭīb 1: 444; al-'Akbarī 1: 302.
13. al-Khatīb 1: 445.
14. Ibid. 1: 452-453.
15. Ibid. 455.
16. Ibid.
17. al-Rāzī, *Tafsīr* 7: 209.
18. al-Zamakhsharī 1: 533.
19. al-Ṭabarī 5: 254; al-Qurṭubī 5: 42.
20. al-Rāzī, *Tafsīr* 7: 209-210.
21. Ibid. 209.
22. al-Qurṭubī 5: 43-44.
23. al-Khaṭīb 1: 460.
24. Ibid.; compare Goldziher 32-33.
25. al-Khaṭīb 1: 464.
26. Ibid.
27. al-Makkī 201.
28. Ibid. 202.

29. Ibn al-Jawzī, *Nawāsikh* 237; Ibn Ḥazm 30-31; Ibn Salāma 29.
30. Ibn al-Jawzī, *Nawāsikh* 237.
31. al-Khaṭīb 1: 467.
32. Ibn al-Jawzī, *Nawāsikh* 238; compare with Ibn Salāma 29.
33. Shu'la 120.
34. Ibn al-Jawzī, *Nawāsikh* 238; Shu'la 120.
35. Ibn al-Jawzī, *Nawāsikh* 238.
36. al-Khaṭīb 1: 478.
37. al-Zamakhsharī 1: 548.
38. St. Clair-Tisdall, *Original Sources* 159.
39. al-Khaṭīb 1: 486.
40. al-Maḥallī and al-Suyūṭī, *Tafsīr al-Jalālayn* 55.
41. al-Rāzī, *Tafsīr* 8: 46.
42. al-Khaṭīb 1: 493.
43. Ibid. 1: 498; compare with Goldziher 21.
44. *Infancy Gospel* ch. 1.
45. *Infancy Gospel* chs. 1, 36; repeated variations, ch. 46.
46. al-Ṭabarī 5: 450.
47. al-Rāzī, *Tafsīr* 8: 74.
48. al-Ṭabarī 5: 447-448.
49. al-Rāzī, *Tafsīr* 8: 75.
50. Ibid. 8: 74.
51. Ibn Kathīr 3: 69.
52. al-Hamadānī 67.
53. al-Qurṭubī 5: 156.
54. M. al-Rāzī, *Min Gharā'ib* 48.
55. al-Qurṭubī 5: 157.
56. al-Rāzī, *Tafsīr* 8: 84.
57. Ibid.
58. al-Qirdāḥī 428.
59. Bell 120-125.
60. Murūwa 1: 309.
61. Shīkhū 118-119, 451; compare with 'Alī 6: 456 (Orientalist opinion).
62. al-Ḥaddād, *Aṭwār al-Da'wa* 45, 49, 89, 90, 230, 298, 675.
63. al-Khaṭīb 1: 533.
64. Ibid.
65. Ibid. 641.
66. Ibn al-Jawzī, *Nawāsikh* 239.
67. Ibn Ḥazm 31.

68. Ibn al-Jawzī, *Nawāsikh 239*; al-Ṭabarī 5: 560.
69. Ibn al-Jawzī, *Nawāsikh* 240.
70. Ibid. 240-241; Ibn Ḥazm 31.
71. Ibn al-Jawzī, *Nawāsikh* 241; Ibn Salāma 29.
72. Ibn al-Jawzī, *Nawāsikh* 241.
73. Ibn Ḥazm 31.
74. Ibn al-Jawzī, *Nawāsikh* 242-243; compare with al-Makkī 203, Ibn Salāma 30, and al-Naḥās 88.
75. Ibn al-Jawzī, *Nawāsikh* 244-245.
76. al-Makkī 203.
77. al-Khaṭīb 1: 553; compare with Goldziher 48-50.
78. Ibn al-Jawzī, *Nawāsikh* 245; compare with Ibn Salāma 30.
79. al-Zamakhsharī 1: 626-627; al-Ṭabarī 6: 53.
80. al-Qurṭubī 5: 313.
81. Ibid. 315; al-Ṭabarī 6: 54.
82. al-Qurṭubī 5: 316.
83. Ibid. 342-343.
84. Ibid.
85. Ibn al-Jawzī, *Nawāsikh* 246.
86. Ibid.
87. al-Khaṭīb 1: 607.
88. Ibid. 610.
89. al-Ṭabarī 6: 194-195.
90. Ibn Manẓūr 3285-3286.
91. al-Ṭabarī 6: 195-197; compare with al-Khaṭīb 1: 612 and Goldziher 40.
92. al-Makkī 205.
93. al-Khaṭīb 1: 624.
94. Ibid.
95. Ibid.
96. al-Qurṭubī 5: 444-445.
97. al-Zamakhsharī 1: 668.
98. al-Ṭabarī 6: 284.
99. al-Qurṭubī 5: 445.
100. Ibn al-Jawzī, *Nawāsikh* 246.
101. Ibn Salāma 31.
102. Ibn al-Jawzī, *Nawāsikh* 246.
103. al-Khaṭīb 1: 645.

Sūra 4 (al-Nisā')

1. Ibn 'Āshūr 4: 211.
2. Wherry 2: 64.
3. Nöldeke, *Tārīkh al-Qur'ān* 176; al-Ḥaddād, *Aṭwār al-Da'wa* 809.
4. Ibn 'Āshūr 4: 212.
5. Ibid.
6. al-Rāzī, *Tafsīr* 9: 177; al-Qurṭubī 6: 23-24; al-Andalusī 2: 6-7.
7. al-Rāzī, *Tafsīr* 9: 178.
8. al-Andalusī 2: 7.
9. al-Rāzī, *Tafsīr* 9: 178.
10. al-Andalusī 2: 7.
11. al-Rāzī, *Tafsīr* 9: 178.
12. al-Qurṭubī 6: 23-24.
13. Ibn al-Jawzī, *Nawāsikh* 247; al-Makkī 208.
14. Ibn al-Jawzī, *Nawāsikh* 249-250; compare with al-Makkī 209.
15. Ibid.
16. Ibn al-Jawzī, *Nawāsikh* 250.
17. Ibid.
18. Ibn al-Jawzī, *Nawāsikh* 251-252; al-Makkī 208; al-Naḥās 92.
19. al-Makkī 208; al-Naḥās 92; Shu'la 122.
20. Ibn Salāma 31.
21. Ibn al-Jawzī, *Nawāsikh* 253.
22. Ibid. 254.
23. Ibn al-Jawzī, *Nawāsikh* 255-257; Ibn Ḥazm 31; Ibn Salāma 31-32.
24. Ibn al-Jawzī, *Nawāsikh* 253-254.
25. al-Makkī 210-211; Shu'la 123; compare with al-Ṭabarī 6: 432-434.
26. Ibn al-Jawzī, *Nawāsikh* 258-259.
27. Ibid. 259.
28. Ibid.
29. Ibid. 260; compare with Ibn Salāma 32.
30. Ibn al-Jawzī, *Nawāsikh* 260-261.
31. Ibid. 262; Ibn Ḥazm 32.
32. al-Khaṭīb 2: 24.
33. Ibid. 2: 31.
34. Ibid. 2: 32.
35. al-Rāzī, *Tafsīr* 9: 242; al-Zamakhsharī 2: 41.
36. Ibn al-Jawzī, *Nawāsikh* 262-263; al-Naḥās 96; al-Ṭabarī 6: 494.
37. al-Ṭabarī 6: 499, 503; compare with Ibn Ḥazm 32; Ibn Salāma 33.
38. al-Ṭabarī 6: 494, 496; al-Naḥās 97.

39. Ibn al-Jawzī, *Nawāsikh* 263; al-Makkī 215; al-Ṭabarī 6: 496, 504-405.
40. Ibn al-Jawzī, *Nawāsikh* 264-265; compare with Ibn Salāma 33.
41. Ibid. 265.
42. Ibid. 267.
43. al-Makkī 215.
44. Ibid. 217.
45. Ibid.; compare with Ibn Ḥazm 33.
46. al-Khaṭīb 2: 41.
47. Ibid.
48. Ibid. 2: 44.
49. M. al-Rāzī, *Min Gharā'ib* 64.
50. al-Rāzī, *Tafsīr* 10: 15.
51. al-Ṭabarī 6: 549.
52. Ibn al-Jawzī, *Nawāsikh* 267; Ibn Ḥazm 33.
53. Ibn al-Jawzī, *Nawāsikh* 267-268.
54. Ibid. 268; Ibn Ḥazm 33.
55. al-Khaṭīb 2: 50; compare with Goldziher 23.
56. al-Makkī 218.
57. Ibn al-Jawzī, *Nawāsikh* 269; al-Ṭabarī 6: 585-586.
58. Ibn al-Jawzī, *Nawāsikh* 269.
59. Ibid. 270; compare with al-Makkī 221-222.
60. al-Makkī 222-223; Shu'la 125.
61. Ibn Ḥazm 33; Ibn Salāma 36; al-Naḥās 100; Shu'la 125.
62. Ibn al-Jawzī, *Nawāsikh* 271; compare with al-Makkī 223, Ibn Ḥazm 33, and al-Naḥās 100.
63. Ibn al-Jawzī, *Nawāsikh* 270.
64. al-Makkī 220.
65. al-Ṭabarī 6: 627.
66. Ibid. 6: 627-628.
67. Ibn al-Jawzī, *Nawāsikh* 273; compare with al-Makkī 225, Ibn Ḥazm 33-34, and Ibn Salāma 36.
68. Ibn al-Jawzī, *Nawāsikh* 272.
69. al-Khaṭīb 2: 58.
70. Ibn al-Jawzī, *Nawāsikh* 273-274.
71. Ibid. 275.
72. Ibid.; al-Makkī 226-227; al-Naḥās 105.
73. al-Makkī 228.
74. al-Khaṭīb 2: 63.
75. Ibid. 2: 72.
76. Ibn al-Jawzī, *Nawāsikh* 279-280; al-Makkī 228-229; Ibn Salāma 37.
77. Ibn Salāma 37.

78. al-Khaṭīb 2: 81.
79. Ibid. 2: 81.
80. al-Qurṭubī 6: 408.
81. al-Rāzī, *Tafsīr* 10: 130.
82. al-Qurṭubī 6: 411-412.
83. al-Zamakhsharī 2: 91; al-Rāzī, *Tafsīr* 10: 132.
84. al-Ṭabarī 7: 143.
85. al-Khaṭīb 2: 92.
86. Ibn al-Jawzī, *Nawāsikh* 281; al-Makkī 252; Ibn Ḥazm 34; Ibn Salāma 37; Shu'la 127.
87. Ibn al-Jawzī, *Nawāsikh* 281-282; Ibn Ḥazm 34; Ibn Salāma 37-38.
88. Ibn al-Jawzī, *Nawāsikh* 282-283; al-Makkī 252; Ibn Ḥazm 34; Ibn Salāma 38.
89. Ibn al-Jawzī, *Nawāsikh* 283.
90. al-Khaṭīb 2: 109.
91. Ibid. 2: 110.
92. Ibid. 2: 115.
93. Ibn al-Jawzī, *Nawāsikh* 284; Ibn Ḥazm 34; Ibn Salāma 38.
94. al-Ṭabarī 7: 250.
95. Ibn Ḥazm 34.
96. M. al-Rāzī, *Min Gharā'ib* 76.
97. Ibn al-Jawzī, *Nawāsikh* 284; Ibn Ḥazm 35; Ibn Salāma 38.
98. Ibn Ḥazm 35; Ibn Salāma 40.
99. Ibn al-Jawzī, *Nawāsikh* 285-287.
100. Ibid. 287; al-Makkī 230; Ibn Ḥazm 34; Ibn Salāma 38; al-Naḥās 109.
101. al-Makkī 230.
102. Ibn al-Jawzī, *Nawāsikh* 287; Ibn Ḥazm 34-35; Ibn Salāma 38.
103. Ibn al-Jawzī. *Nawāsikh* 288; al-Ṭabarī 7: 327-328.
104. Ibn al-Jawzī, *Nawāsikh* 288; Ibn Ḥazm 35; Ibn Salāma 39.
105. al-Makkī 231-232.
106. Ibn al-Jawzī, *Nawāsikh* 288.
107. Goldziher 309.
108. al-Makkī 232-248.
109. Ibid. 232.
110. Ibn al-Jawzī, *Nawāsikh* 289; Ibn Ḥazm 35; Ibn Salāma 39-40; compare with Shu'la 127-128.
111. Ibn al-Jawzī, *Nawāsikh* 289-293; al-Ṭabarī 7: 343.
112. Ibn al-Jawzī, *Nawāsikh* 293.
113. al-Khaṭīb 2: 146-147.
114. Ibid. 2: 170.
115. al-Rāzī, *Tafsīr* 11: 76.
116. Ibid. 11: 76-77.

117. Ibid. 11: 76; al-Zamakhsharī 2: 163.
118. al-Qurṭubī 7:181.
119. Ibn Ḥazm 35; Ibn Salāma 40.
120. Ibn al-Jawzī, *Nawāsikh* 296.
121. al-Ṭabarī 7: 650.
122. Ibid.
123. Ibid. 7: 651.
124. al-Zamakhsharī 2: 175.
125. al-Ṭabarī 7: 651.
126. al-Rāzī, *Tafsīr* 11: 101.
127. Ibid. 11: 102.
128. Ibid.
129. Qazzī 154.
130. Irenaeus.
131. al-Khaṭīb 2: 199.
132. Ibid.; compare with Goldziher 46-47.
133. al-ʿAkbarī 1: 421.
134. al-Khaṭīb 2: 203; compare with Goldziher 195-196.

Sūra 5 (al-Mā'ida)

1. Ibn ʿĀshūr 6: 69.
2. al-Ḥaddād, *Aṭwār al-Daʿwa* 937.
3. Ibn ʿĀshūr 6: 71.
4. al-Ṭabarī 8: 6-12.
5. al-Hamadānī 109.
6. al-Zamakhsharī 2: 191.
7. al-Qurṭubī 7: 245-246.
8. al-Khaṭīb 2: 217.
9. al-Ṭabarī 8:28.
10. al-Makkī 256; Ibn al-Jawzī, *Nawāsikh* 298-299; al-Naḥās 115; compare with al-Ṭabarī 8: 35-37.
11. Ibn al-Jawzī, *Nawāsikh* 299.
12. Ibid. 299-301; al-Naḥās 115-116; al-Ṭabarī 8: 40.
13. al-Makkī 257; Ibn al-Jawzī, *Nawāsikh* 298.
14. al-Khaṭīb 2: 228.
15. Ibn al-Jawzī, *Nawāsikh* 302-303.
16. Ibid. 303.
17. Ibid. 305.
18. al-Makkī 261.
19. al-Khaṭīb 2: 232.

20. Ibid.; compare with Goldziher 14-15 and Ibn Khalawayh 1: 143.
21. al-Rāzī, *Tafsīr* 11: 172.
22. al-Ṭabarī 7: 62-75.
23. al-Khaṭīb 2: 237.
24. al-Ṭabarī 8: 255.
25. al-Makkī 269; Ibn al-Jawzī, *Nawāsikh* 307-308.
26. Ibn al-Jawzī, *Nawāsikh* 308; Ibn Salāma 41; Ibn Ḥazm 35-36; al-Naḥās 123.
27. al-Makkī 269; Ibn al-Jawzī, *Nawāsikh* 309.
28. al-Makkī 270.
29. al-Rāzī, *Tafsīr* 11: 194.
30. al-Qurṭubī 7: 384.
31. al-Zamakhsharī 2: 217; al-Rāzī, *Tafsīr* 11:193.
32. al-Zamakhsharī 2: 218; al-Qurṭubī 7: 385.
33. al-Qurṭubī 7: 385.
34. Ibid. 385-386.
35. M. al-Rāzī, *Min Gharā'ib* 97.
36. al-Khaṭīb 2: 252.
37. al-Ṭabarī 8: 361-366; compare with al-Naḥās 123-124.
38. al-Ṭabarī 8: 363.
39. Ibid. 368.
40. al-Makkī 270-271.
41. Ibn al-Jawzī, *Nawāsikh* 310; al-Naḥās 124-125.
42. Ibn Salāma 41; al-Naḥās 127; al-Makkī 270; Ibn Ḥazm 36.
43. Ibn al-Jawzī, *Nawāsikh* 310; al-Ṭabarī 8: 396.
44. al-Qurṭubī 7: 449-450.
45. al-Khaṭīb 2: 270.
46. al-Ṭabarī 8: 436-438.
47. al-Naḥās 129; al-Makkī 271-272; Ibn al-Jawzī, *Nawāsikh* 311-312; al-Ṭabarī 8: 442-444.
48. Ibn al-Jawzī, *Nawāsikh* 313-314; al-Ṭabarī 8: 440-441.
49. al-Makkī 272.
50. al-Khaṭīb 2: 286; al-Sijistānī 59, 130.
51. al-Khaṭīb 2: 301.
52. al-Ṭabarī 8: 553-554.
53. al-Qurṭubī 8: 81.
54. Ibid. 82.
55. al-Khaṭīb 2: 330; compare with al-'Akbarī 1: 454-455.
56. al-Khaṭīb 2: 332.
57. al-Makkī 273.
58. al-Khaṭīb 2: 337

59. Ibn al-Jawzī, *Nawāsikh* 315; Ibn Salāma 42; Ibn Ḥazm 36.
60. Ibn al-Jawzī, *Nawāsikh* 315; Ibn al-Jawzī, *Zad al-Masir* 2: 432.
61. al-Makkī 274; Ibn al-Jawzī, 315.
62. Ibn al-Jawzī, *Nawāsikh* 315.
63. Ibn Salāma 42; Ibn al-Jawzī, *Nawāsikh* 316; Ibn Ḥazm 36; Ibn al-'Arabī 2: 229.
64. Ibn Salāma 42.
65. Ibn al-Jawzī, *Nawāsikh* 316; compare with al-Makkī 274; Ibn al-Jawzī, *Zad al-Masir* 2: 443.
66. Ibn al-Jawzī, *Nawāsikh* 317-318.
67. al-Ṭabarī 9: 55-58; Ibn al-Jawzī, *Nawāsikh* 319.
68. Ibn al-'Arabī 2: 240; al-Makkī 275; Ibn al-Jawzī, *Nawāsikh* 320.
69. Ibn al-Jawzī, *Nawāsikh* 320.
70. al-Makkī 277.
71. Ibid. 275; Ibn al-Jawzī, *Nawāsikh* 321.
72. al-Khaṭīb 2: 369.
73. Ibid.
74. St. Clair-Tisdall, *Original Sources* 176-179.
75. al-Khaṭīb 2: 378.
76. Ibid.

Sūra 6 (al-An'ām)

1. Ibn 'Āshūr 7: 121.
2. Ibid.
3. Ibid.; compare with Nöldeke, *Tārīkh al-Qur'ān* 146.
4. Ibn al-Jawzī, *Nawāsikh* 323; Ibn Ḥazm 37; Ibn Salāma 44; Shu'la 136.
5. al-Khaṭīb 2: 397.
6. Ibid. 2: 397-398.
7. Ibid. 2: 398.
8. al-Rāzī, *Tafsīr* 12:185; compare with al-Ṭabarī 9:181.
9. al-Qurṭubī 8: 336.
10. al-Khaṭīb 2: 407- 408.
11. Ibid. 2: 415- 416.
12. Ibid. 2: 416.
13. al-Rāzī, *Tafsīr* 12: 220.
14. Ibid. 12: 223.
15. Ibid. 12: 224-225; al-Qurṭubī 8: 370-371.
16. al-Zamakhsharī 2: 343.
17. Ibid. 2: 342.
18. al-Qurṭubī 8: 371.
19. al-Khaṭīb 2: 430.

20. Ibid. 2: 440.
21. al-Khaṭīb 2: 441; note that the Yusuf ʿAlī (not the Palmer) translation uses the word *truth*.
22. Ibn al-Jawzī, *Nawāsikh* 324; al-Makkī 281; Ibn-Salāma 44; al-Naḥās 136.
23. Ibn al-Jawzī, *Nawāsikh* 324; al-Makkī 281; al-Naḥās 137.
24. al-Qurṭubī 8: 418.
25. Ibn al-Jawzī, *Nawāsikh* 324; Shuʿla, 137.
26. Ibn-Ḥazm 37; Ibn Salāma 44-45.
27. Ibn al-Jawzī, *Nawāsikh* 325; al-Makkī 282; Shuʿla 137; al-Naḥās 137.
28. Ibn al-Jawzī, *Nawāsikh* 326; al-Makkī 282; al-Naḥās 137.
29. Ibn Ḥazm 37; Ibn Salāma 45.
30. Ibn al-Jawzī, *Nawāsikh* 326-327; al-Makkī 283; Shuʿla 138; al-Naḥās 137.
31. al-Khaṭīb 2: 464.
32. Ibid.
33. Ibid.
34. Ibn al-Jawzī, *Nawāsikh* 327; Ibn Ḥazm 37; Ibn Salāma 45.
35. Ibn al-Jawzī, *Nawāsikh* 327.
36. Ibn al-Jawzī, *Nawāsikh* 327; Ibn Ḥazm 37; Ibn Salāma 45.
37. Ibn al-Jawzī, *Nawāsikh* 328.
38. al-Khaṭīb 2: 510-511.
39. Ibid. 2: 511; compare with al-ʿAkbarī 1: 504.
40. al-Khaṭīb 2: 512; compare with al-ʿAkbarī 1: 506.
41. al-ʿAkbarī 1: 507.
42. al-Khaṭīb 2: 512.
43. Ibid.; al-ʿAkbarī 1: 506.
44. al-ʿAkbarī 1: 506.
45. al-Khaṭīb 2: 512; compare with al-ʿAkbarī 1: 505 and Ibn Khalawayh 1: 166.
46. Ibn al-Jawzī, *Nawāsikh* 328; *al-Iḍāḥ* 286; Ibn Ḥazm 37.
47. al-Naḥās 148.
48. Ibn al-Jawzī, *Nawāsikh* 328; Ibn Ḥazm 38; Ibn Salāma 45.
49. Ibn al-Jawzī, *Nawāsikh* 329; Ibn Ḥazm 38; Ibn Salāma 46.
50. al-Khaṭīb 2: 521.
51. Ibn al-Jawzī, *Nawāsikh* 329; Ibn Ḥazm 38; Ibn Salāma 46.
52. Ibn al-Jawzī, *Nawāsikh* 329.
53. al-Rāzī, *Tafsīr* 13: 167.
54. al-Khaṭīb 2: 534.
55. Ibid. 2: 535.
56. Ibn al-Jawzī, *Nawāsikh* 329-330; Ibn Salāma 46.
57. al-Makkī 287.
58. al-Khaṭīb 2: 537.

59. al-Ṭabarī 9: 560.
60. Ibn al-Jawzī, *Nawāsikh* 330; Ibn Ḥazm 38; Ibn Salāma 46.
61. Ibn al-Jawzī, *Nawāsikh* 331.
62. al-Khaṭīb 2: 552-553.
63. Ibid. 2: 553-554.
64. al-Rāzī, *Tafsīr* 13: 219, al-Qurṭubī 9: 46.
65. al-Qurṭubī 9: 4.7
66. al-Ṭabarī 9: 586, al-Zamakhsharī 2: 403.
67. al-Khaṭīb 2: 568.
68. Ibid.
69. Ibn al-Jawzī, *Nawāsikh* 331-333; Shu'la 138; al-Naḥās 138-141; al-Ṭabarī 9: 595.
70. al-Makkī 284.
71. al-Ṭabarī 9: 600-601, 607, 611; compare with al-Rāzī, *Tafsīr* 13: 225.
72. al-Naḥās 138.
73. Ibn al-Jawzī, *Nawāsikh* 333-334; al-Makkī 283; al-Naḥās 140; al-Ṭabarī 9: 609-611.
74. al-Ṭabarī 9: 632.
75. Ibn al-Jawzī, *Nawāsikh* 335; al-Makkī 288.
76. Ibn al-Jawzī, *Nawāsikh* 336.
77. Shu'la 140; al-Naḥās 144.
78. Ibn al-Jawzī, *Nawāsikh* 337; Ibn Salāma 46.
79. Ibn al-Jawzī, *Nawāsikh* 337.
80. al-Khaṭīb 2: 595.
81. Ibn al-Jawzī, *Nawāsikh* 337; Ibn Ḥazm 38; Shu'la 140.
82. al-Naḥās 146.
83. Ibn al-Jawzī, *Nawāsikh* 337-338; compare with Shu'la 140.

Sūra 7 (al-A'rāf)

1. Wherry 2: 201.
2. Ibid.; compare with Nöldeke, *Tārīkh al-Qur'ān* 144.
3. Ibn 'Āshūr 9: 146-166.
4. Nöldeke, *Tārīkh al-Qur'ān* 143.
5. Wherry 2: 201.
6. al-Khaṭīb 3: 4; al-'Akbarī 1: 529.
7. al-Hamadānī 143.
8. al-Zamakhsharī 2: 424.
9. al-Ṭabarī 10: 59.
10. al-Rāzī, *Tafsīr* 14: 23.
11. al-Ṭabarī 10: 61.
12. al-Khaṭīb 3: 7.

13. al-Ṭabarī 10: 88-89.
14. Ibid. 10: 93.
15. al-Khaṭīb 3: 14.
16. Ibid 3: 60.
17. Ibid 3: 140.
18. al-Khaṭīb 3: 174; al-'Akbarī 1:565.
19. al-Khaṭīb 3: 248.
20. al-Khaṭīb 3: 26; compare with al-'Akbarī 1: 533- 534.
21. Ibn Jinnī 1: 246.
22. al-Qurṭubī 9: 190-191; compare with al-Andalusī 2: 392.
23. al-Khaṭīb 3: 31.
24. Ibid. 3: 37; compare with Ibn Jinnī 1: 247.
25. al-Khaṭīb 3: 57; compare with al-'Akbarī 1: 541-542.
26. al-Khaṭīb 3: 57.
27. al-'Akbarī 1: 543.
28. al-Khaṭīb 3: 60.
29. Ibid. 3: 61.
30. Ibid.
31. al-Rāzī, *Tafsīr* 14: 128-132.
32. al-Khaṭīb 3: 74.
33. Ibid. 3: 253.
34. Ibid. 3: 76-77; compare with Ibn Jinnī 1: 255.
35. al-'Akbarī 1: 548.
36. al-Khaṭīb 3: 78.
37. Ibn Jinnī 1: 255; al-'Akbarī 1: 546-547.
38. al-Khaṭīb 3: 136.
39. Ibid.
40. al-Ṭabarī 20: 308.
41. al-Zamakhsharī 5: 340.
42. al-Bayḍāwi 4: 278.
43. al-Rāzī, *Tafsīr* 14: 221.
44. al-Ṭabarī 10: 371.
45. Ibid 10: 404.
46. al-Khaṭīb 3: 148.
47. al-Ṭabarī, 10: 447.
48. al-Rāzī, *Tafsīr* 15: 8.
49. al-Qurṭubī 9: 353.
50. Ibid. 9: 354; compare with al-Ṭabarī 10: 491-492 and al-Baghawī 3: 289.
51. Usud al-Ghāba 3: 346.

52. al-Zamakhsharī 2: 523.
53. al-Khaṭīb 3: 211; compare with Ibn Jinnī 1: 267-268.
54. al-Qurṭubī 9: 387.
55. Ibn al-Jawzī, *Nawāsikh* 339; al-Makkī 291; Ibn Ḥazm 38.
56. Ibn al-Jawzī, *Nawāsikh* 339; al-Makkī 291.
57. Ibn Salāma 47.
58. Ibn al-Jawzī, *Nawāsikh* 339-340.
59. Ibid. 339.
60. M. al-Rāzī, *Min Gharā'ib* 152.
61. al-Ṭabarī 10: 630.
62. al-Khaṭīb 3: 246.
63. Ibn al-Jawzī, *Nawāsikh* 340; al-Makkī 292; al-Naḥās 147.
64. Ibn al-Jawzī, *Nawāsikh* 341; al-Makkī 292; al-Naḥās 147.
65. Ibn al-Jawzī, *Nawāsikh* 341.
66. Ibn Ḥazm 38; Ibn Salma 47; al-Naḥās 147; Shu'la 141.
67. Ibn al-Jawzī, *Nawāsikh* 341; al-Makkī 292; Shu'la 141.
68. al-Naḥās 147.
69. Ibn al-Jawzī, *Nawāsikh* 341; al-Makkī 293; Ibn Ḥazm 38; Ibn Salāma 47.
70. Ibn al-Jawzī, *Nawāsikh* 341-342.
71. al-Makkī 293.

Sūra 8 (al-Anfāl)

1. Ibn 'Āshūr 9: 245.
2. Wherry 2: 249.
3. Ibn 'Āshūr 9: 246.
4. al-Bayḍāwi 4: 414.
5. Wherry 2: 249.
6. Ibn al-Jawzī, *Nawāsikh* 343; al-Makkī 295; Ibn Salāma 49; al-Naḥās 149.
7. Ibn al-Jawzī, *Nawāsikh* 344; al-Makkī 295.
8. Ibn al-Jawzī, *Nawāsikh* 343.
9. al-Khaṭīb 3: 258.
10. Ibid 3: 260.
11. Ibn al-Jawzī, *Nawāsikh* 344-345.
12. al-Makkī 296.
13. Ibn al-Jawzī, *Nawāsikh* 345; al-Makkī 297; al-Naḥās 152.
14. Ibn al-Jawzī, *Nawāsikh* 346; al-Makkī 297; al-Naḥās 152.
15. al-Makkī 297; al-Naḥās 152.
16. al-Ṭabarī 11: 100; al-Qurṭubī 9: 482.
17. al-Rāzī, *Tafsīr* 15: 149.

18. al-Khaṭīb 3: 283.
19. Ibid 3: 284.
20. Ibid.
21. Ibid.
22. Ibid 3: 285.
23. al-Qurṭubī 9: 497.
24. Ibn al-Jawzī, *Nawāsikh* 346; al-Makkī 297; Ibn Ḥazm 39; al-Naḥās 154; Shu'la 142; Ibn Salāma 49.
25. Ibn al-Jawzī, *Nawāsikh* 346-347; compare with al-Makkī 298; al-Naḥās 153; Shu'la 142.
26. Ibn Ḥazm 39; Ibn Salāma 50.
27. Ibn Salāma 50.
28. al-Khaṭīb 3: 298.
29. M. al-Rāzī, *Min Gharā'ib* 160-161.
30. Ibn al-Jawzī, *Nawāsikh* 347-348; compare with al-Makkī 300.
31. Ibn Ḥazm 39; Ibn Salāma 49.
32. al-Makkī 300; al-Naḥās 156; Shu'la 142.
33. Ibn al-Jawzī, *Nawāsikh* 348-349; compare with al-Makkī 300.
34. Ibn al-Jawzī, *Nawāsikh* 348.
35. Ibn al-Jawzī, *Nawāsikh* 349-351; compare with al-Makkī 300-301; Ibn Ḥazm 39; Ibn Salāma 49; al-Naḥās 157; Shu'la 143.
36. al-Rāzī, *Tafsīr* 15: 205.
37. al-Ṭabarī 11: 271-274.
38. Ibn al-Jawzī, *Nawāsikh* 352; al-Makkī 301; al-Ṭabarī 11: 272.
39. Ibn al-Jawzī, *Nawāsikh* 352-353; al-Makkī 302.
40. al-Makkī 303; al-Naḥās 158.
41. Compare with Ibn al-Jawzī, *Nawāsikh* 343-344.
42. Ibn al-Jawzī, *Nawāsikh* 353-354; al-Makkī 304; compare with Ibn Ḥazm 39; Ibn Salāma 50; al-Naḥās 158; Shu'la 143.
43. Ibn al-Jawzī, *Nawāsikh* 355; al-Makkī 305; al-Naḥās 159-160.
44. al-Makkī 305.
45. Ibn Salāma 50.

Sūra 9 (al-Tawba)

1. Ibn 'Āshūr, 10: 97.
2. Nöldeke 200; al-Ḥaddād, *Aṭwār al-Da'wa* 966-967.
3. Ibn 'Āshūr 10: 97.
4. Ibid.
5. al-Shanqīṭī 2: 501.
6. Ibn Kathīr 7: 135-136, al-Shanqīṭī 2: 501.
7. al-Shanqīṭī 2: 501-502.

8. Ibn al-Jawzī, *Nawāsikh* 357; al-Makkī 307; Ibn Salāma 51; al-Naḥās 161-162.
9. Ibn al-Jawzī, *Nawāsikh* 358.
10. Ibid.; al-Makkī 307-308; al-Naḥās 162.
11. Ibn al-Jawzī, *Nawāsikh* 358; compare with al-Makkī 308.
12. Ibn al-Jawzī, *Nawāsikh* 357.
13. al-Khaṭīb 3: 346; compare with al-ʿAkbarī 1: 607-608.
14. al-Khaṭīb 3: 366.
15. Ibid. 3: 432.
16. Ibn al-Jawzī, *Nawāsikh* 359; al-Makkī 309; al-Naḥās 165.
17. Ibn al-Jawzī, *Nawāsikh* 360; al-Makkī 309; compare with Ibn Salāma 51; al-Naḥās 164.
18. al-Makkī 309.
19. Ibn al-Jawzī, *Nawāsikh* 360; al-Makkī 309.
20. Ibn al-Jawzī, *Nawāsikh* 361-362.
21. Ibid. 362; Ibn Salāma 51.
22. al-Khaṭīb 3: 348.
23. Ibid. 3: 356.
24. Ibid. 3: 357.
25. al-Ṭabarī 11: 375.
26. al-Bayḍāwi 4: 448.
27. al-Zamakhsharī 3: 30-31; Ibn-Kathīr 7: 174.
28. *Encyclopaedia Judaica* 6: 652. See entry on "Ezra."
29. Ibn al-Jawzī, *Nawāsikh* 362.
30. Ibid. 363.
31. Ibid.
32. Ibid.
33. Ibn al-Jawzī, *Nawāsikh* 363-364; al-Makkī 314; compare with Ibn Ḥazm 40; Ibn Salāma 51.
34. M. al-Rāzī, *Min Gharā'ib* 166.
35. al-Khaṭīb 3: 377.
36. Ibid. 3: 382.
37. Ibid. 3: 383.
38. Ibid. 3: 384-385.
39. Ibn al-Jawzī, *Nawāsikh* 364-365; al-Makkī 314; compare with Ibn Ḥazm 40; Ibn Salāma 52; al-Naḥās 167.
40. Ibn al-Jawzī, *Nawāsikh* 365-366.
41. al-Khaṭīb 3: 388.
42. Ibid. 3: 390.
43. Shuʿla 145.
44. Ibn al-Jawzī, *Nawāsikh* 366; al-Makkī 315; Shuʿla, 145.
45. Ibn al-Jawzī, *Nawāsikh* 366.

46. Ibid. 366-367; compare with Shu'la 145.
47. Ibn Ḥazm 40.
48. Ibn al-Jawzī, *Nawāsikh* 367-368; al-Makkī 316; Ibn Salāma, 52; al-Naḥās 168.
49. al-Ṭabarī 11: 500.
50. al-Qurṭubī 10: 240.
51. al-Rāzī, *Tafsīr* 16: 95.
52. Ibn Sa'd 2: 139-142.
53. al-Ṭabarī 11: 519-520; al-Qurṭubī 10: 262-265.
54. al-Khaṭīb 3: 416.
55. Ibid.
56. Ibid. 3: 425.
57. al-Rāzī, *Tafsīr* 16: 137-138; compare with al-Ṭabarī 11: 566-567.
58. al-Khaṭīb 3: 425.
59. Ibid. 3: 428.
60. al-Makkī 318; Ibn Ḥazm 40; Ibn Salāma 52.
61. al-Makkī 318.
62. al-Khaṭīb 3: 445-446.
63. Ibid. 3: 447.
64. Ibid. 3: 452.
65. Ibid. 3: 461.
66. Ibid. 3: 465.
67. Ibid. 3: 472.
68. Ibid. 3: 475.
69. Ibid.
70. Ibid.
71. Goldziher 45-46.
72. Ibn al-Jawzī, *Nawāsikh* 370; al-Makkī 321-322; Shu'la 145; al-Naḥās 176.
73. al-Makkī 322; compare with Shu'la 145; al-Naḥās 176.
74. al-Khaṭīb 3: 481-482.
75. Ibid. 3: 482.
76. Ibid. 3: 484.
77. Ibid. 3: 484-485.

Works Cited

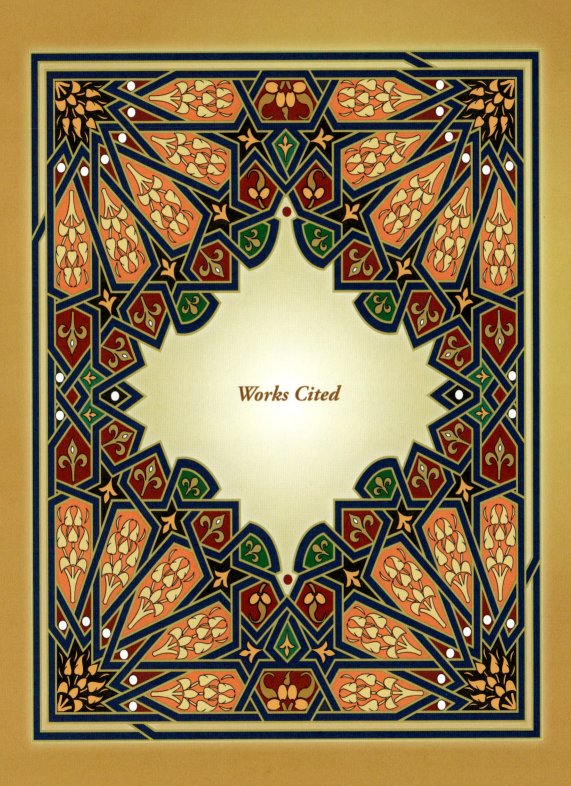

Works Cited

Arabic Commentaries

'Abdu, Imām Muḥammad. *Tafsīr al-Qur'ān al-Karīm* [a.k.a. *Tafsīr al-Manār*]. Comp. Muḥammad Rashīd Riḍā. 12 vols. Cairo: n.p., AH 1366/AD 1947. Print.

Abū Ḥaīyān, Muḥammad Ibn Yūsif al-Andalusī. *Tafsīr al-Baḥr al-Muḥīṭ.* Ed. 'Abd al-Mawjūd 'Ādil Aḥmad, et al. 8 vols. Beirut: Dār al-Kutub al-'Ilmīya, AH 1413/AD 1993. Print.

al-Andalusī, Abū Muḥammad 'Abd al-Ḥaq Ibn Ghālib Ibn 'Aṭṭīya. *al-Muḥarir al-Wajīz fī Tafsīr al-Kitāb al-'Azīz.* 6 vols. Beirut: Dār al-Kutub al-'Ilmīya, AH 1422/AD 2001. Print.

al-Baghawī, Abū Muḥammad al-Ḥussayn Ibn Mas'ūd. *Tafsīr al-Baghawī* [a.k.a. *Ma'ālim al-Tanzīl*]. 8 vols. Riyadh: Dār Ṭība, AH 1409/AD 1989. Print.

al-Bayḍāwī, Abū Sa'īd 'Abdullah Ibn 'Umar. *Tafsīr al-Qāḍī al-Bayḍāwī.* [Rare edition containing marginal note by Sheikh Muḥyī al-Dīn Zāda.] Ed. Muḥammad 'Abd al-Qādir Shāhīn. 8 vols. Beirut: Dār al-Kutub al-'Ilmīya, AH 1419/AD 1999. Print.

Ibn 'Āshūr, Muḥammad al-Ṭāhir. *Tafsīr al-Taḥrīr wa al-Tanwīr.* 30 vols. Tunis: al-Dār al-Tunisīya, AD 1984. Print.

Ibn Kathīr, al-Ḥāfiẓ 'Imād al-Dīn Abū al-Fidā'. *Tafsīr al-Qur'ān al-'Aẓīm.* Ed. Muṣṭafā al-Saīyd Muḥammad, et al. 15 vols. Giza: Qurṭuba Est., AH 1420/AD 2000. Print.

Ibn Qutayba, Abū Muḥammad 'Abd Allah Ibn Muslim. *Tafsīr Gharīb al-Qur'ān.* Ed. al-Saīyd Aḥmad Ṣaqr. Beirut: Dār al-Kutub al-'Ilmīya, AH 1398/AD 1978. Print.

al-Maḥallī, Jalāl al-Dīn Muḥammad and Jalāl al-Dīn 'Abd al-Raḥman al-Suyūṭī. *Tafsīr al-Jalālayn.* Damascus: Dār Ibn Kathīr, AH 1407/AD 1986. Print.

al-Qurṭubī, Abū 'Abd Allah Muḥammad Ibn Aḥmad. *al-Jāmi' li-Aḥkām al-Qur'ān wa al-Mubayīn li-mā Taḍammanahu min al-Sunna wa Āay al-Furqān.* Ed. 'Abd Allah Ibn 'Abd al-Muḥsin al-Turkī. 24 vols. Beirut: al-Risāla Est., AH 1427/AD 2006. Print.

al-Rāzī, Muḥammad. *Tafsīr al-Fakhr al-Rāzī* [a.k.a. *al-Tafsīr al-Kabīr wa Mafātīḥ al-Ghayb*]. 32 vols. Beirut: Dār al-Fikr, AH 1401/AD 1981. Print.

al-Shanqīṭī, Muḥammad al-Amīn. *Aḍwā' al-Bayān fī Iḍāḥ al-Qur'ān bi-l-Qur'ān.* 9 vols. Jeddah: Majma' al-Fiqh al-Islāmī, n.d. Print.

al-Suyūṭī, Jalāl al-Dīn 'Abd al-Raḥman. *al-Durr al-Manthūr fī al-Tafsīr bi-l-Ma'thūr*. Ed. 'Abd Allah Ibn 'Abd al-Muḥsin al-Turkī. 17 vols. Cairo: Hajr Center, AH 1424/AD 2003. Print.

al-Ṭabarī, Abū Ja'far Muḥammad Ibn Jarīr. *Jāmi' al-Bayān 'an Ta'wīl Āay al-Qur'ān* [a.k.a. *Tafsīr al-Ṭabarī*]. Ed. 'Abd Allah Ibn 'Abd al-Muḥsin al-Turkī. 26 vols. Cairo: Hajr Center, AH 1422/AD 2001. Print.

al-Tha'ālibī, Abū Zayd 'Abd al-Raḥman Ibn Muḥammad. *Tafsīr al-Tha'ālibī al-Musammā bi-l-Jawāhir al-Ḥisān fī Tafsīr al-Qur'ān*. 5 vols. Beirut: Dār Iḥyā' al-Turāth al-'Arabī; Mu'assasat al-Tārīkh al-'Arabī, AH 1418/AD 1997. Print.

al-Zamakhsharī, Jar Allah Abū al-Qāsim Maḥmūd Ibn 'Umar. *al-Kashāf 'an Ḥaqā'iq Ghumūḍ al-Tanzīl wa 'Uyūn al-Aqāwīl fī Wujūh al-Ta'wīl*. Ed. 'Ādil Aḥmad 'Abd al-Mawjūd and 'Alī Muḥammad Mu'awaḍ. 5 vols. Riyadh: al-'Ubaykān, AH 1418/AD 1998. Print.

al-Zuḥailī, Wahba. *al-Tafsīr al-Wajīz 'ala Hāmish al-Qur'ān al-'Aẓīm*. 2nd ed. Vol. 1. Damascus: Dār al-Fikr, AH 1415/AD 1994. Print.

Arabic Sources

'Abd al-Karīm, Khalīl. *al-Judhūr al-Tārīkhīya li-l-Sharī'a al-Islāmīya*. Cairo: Sinai Production, AD 1990. Print.

'Abd al-Nūr, 'Abbās. *Miḥnatī ma'a al-Qur'ān wa ma'a Allah fī al-Qur'ān*. Egypt: Damanhur, AD 2004. Print. A trial edition.

Abū Khalīl, Shawqī. *al-Islām fī Qafaṣ al-Itihām*. Damascus: Dār al-Fikr, AH 1407/AD 1986. Print.

Abū Shuhba, Muḥammad Muḥammad. *al-Madkhal li-dirāsat al-Qur'ān al-Karīm*. 3rd ed. Riyadh: Dār al-Liwā', AH 1407/AD 1987. Print.

Abū Zayd, Naṣr Ḥāmid. *Mafhūm al-Naṣṣ: Dirāsa fī 'Ulūm al-Qur'ān*. 2nd ed. Beirut: al-Markaz al-Thaqāfī al-'Arabī, AD 1994. Print.

al-'Akbarī, Abū al-Baqā'. *I'rāb al-Qira'āt al-Shawādh*. Ed. 'Azzūz, Muḥammad al-Sayīd Aḥmad. Vol. 1. Beirut: 'Ālam al-Kitāb, AH 1417/AD 1996. Print.

al-'Alawī, Hādī. *Fuṣūl 'an al-Mar'a*. Beirut: Dār al-Kunūz al-Adabīya, AD 1996. Print.

—. *Min Qāmūs al-Turāth*. Damascus: Dār al-Ahālī, AD 1988. Print.

'Alī, Jawād. *al-Mufaṣṣal fī Tārīkh al-'Arab Qabl al-Islām*. 2nd ed. 10 vols. Beirut: Dār al-'Ilm, AH 1413/AD 1993. Print.

al-'Aqqād, 'Abbās Maḥmūd. *al-Mar'a fī al-Qur'ān (Mawsu'at 'Abbās Maḥmūd al-'Aqqād al-Islāmīya)*. 5 vols. Beirut: Dār al-Kitāb al-'Arabī, AH 1390/AD 1971. Print.

al-Ash'arī, Abū al-Ḥassan 'Alī Ibn Ismā'īl. *Maqalāt al-Islāmīyīn wa Ikhtilāf al-Muṣallīn.* Ed. Muḥammad Muḥyī al-Dīn 'Abd al-Ḥamīd. Cairo: al-Nahḍa al-Misrīya, AH 1369/ AD 1950. Print.

al-Ashwaḥ, Ṣabrī. *I'jāz al-Qira'āt al-Qur'ānīya: Dirāsa fī Tārīkh al-Qira'āt wa Itijahāt al-Qurrā'.* Cairo: Wahba, AH 1419/AD 1998. Print.

'Azzūz, Muḥammad al-Saīyd Aḥmad. *Mawqif al-Lughawīyīn min al-Qira'āt al-Qur'ānīya al-Shādha.* Beirut: 'Ālam al-Kutub, AH 1422/AD 2001 AD. Print.

Badawī, 'Abd al-Raḥman. *Min Tārīkh al-Ilḥād fī al-Islām.* 2nd ed. Cairo: Sina, AD 1993. Print.

al-Baghdādī, Abū Manṣūr 'Abd al-Qāhir Ibn Ṭāhir Ibn Muḥammad. *al-Nāsikh wa al-Mansūkh.* Ed. Ḥilmī Kāmil As'ad 'Abd al-Hādī. Amman: Dār al-'Adawī, n.d. Print.

al-Bāqilānī, Abū Bakr Ibn al-Ṭayīb. *al-Intiṣār li-l-Qur'ān.* Ed. Muḥammad 'Iṣām al-Quḍāt. Beirut: Dār Ibn Ḥazm, AH 1422/AD 2001. Print.

Bint al-Shāṭi'. 'A'isha 'Abd al-Raḥman. *Tarājim Sayīdāt Bayt al-Nubūwa.* Cairo: Dār al-Ḥadīth, AH 1422/AD 2002. Print.

Brockelmann, Carl. *History of Arabic Literature.* Trans. 'Abd al-Ḥalīm al-Najjār. 5th ed. 5 vols. Cairo: Dār al-Ma'ārif, n.d. Print.

al-Bukhārī, Abū 'Abd Allah Muḥammad Ibn Ismā'īl. *al-Jāmi' al-Ṣaḥīḥ* [a.k.a. *Ṣaḥīḥ al-Bukhārī*]. Ed. Muhīb al-Dīn al-Khaṭīb, Muḥammad Fū'ād 'Abd al-Bāqī, and Quṣay Muhīb al-Dīn al-Khaṭīb. 9 vols. Cairo: al-Salafīya, AH 1400/AD 1979. Print.

al-Dānī, Abū 'Amr. *al-Bayān fī 'Addi Āay al-Qur'ān.* Ed. Ghānim Qaddūrī al-Ḥamd. Kuwait: Markaz al-Makhṭūṭāt wa al-Turāth wa al-Wathā'iq, AH 1414/AD 1994. Print.

Ḍayf, Shawqī. Introduction. Ibn Mujāhid. *Kitāb al-Sab'a fī al-Qira'āt.* By Ibn Mujāhid. Ed. Shawqī Ḍayf. 3rd ed. Cairo: Dār al-Ma'ārif, AD 1988. Print.

al-Dhahabī, Shams al-Dīn Abū 'Abd Allah. *Ṭabaqāt al-Qurrā'.* Ed. Aḥmad Khān. Riyadh: Markaz al-Malik Fayṣal li-l-Buḥūth wa al-Dirasāt al-Islāmīya, AH 1418/AD 1997. Print.

al-Dumyāṭī, Aḥmad Ibn Muḥammad al-Bannā. *Itḥāf fuḍalā' al-Bashar bi-l-Qira'āt al-Arba'at 'Ashar.* Ed. Sha'bān Muḥammad Ismā'īl. Cairo: al-Kullīyāt al-Azharīya, AH 1407/AD 1987. Print.

al-Ghazālī, Abū Ḥāmid. *Adāb al-Nikāḥ wa kasr al-Shahwatayn.* Tunis: Dār al-Ma'ārif li-l-Ṭiba'a wa al-Nashr, AD 1990. Print.

Goldziher, Ignaz. *Madhāhib al-Tafsīr al-Islāmī.* Trans. 'Abd al-Ḥalīm al-Najjār. Cairo: al-Khānjī, AH 1375/AD 1955. Print.

al-Ḥaddād, Yūsuf Durra. *Aṭwār al-Da'wa al-Qur'ānīya*. 2nd ed. Jounieh: al-Būlisīya, AD 1986. Print. al-Qur'ān wa al-Kitāb 2.

—. *I'jāz al-Qur'ān*. 2nd ed. Jounieh: al-Būlisīya, AD 1982. Print.

al-Ḥamadānī, 'Abd al-Jabbār Ibn Aḥmad. *Tanzīh al-Qur'ān 'an al-Maṭā'in*. Beirut: Dār al-Nahḍa al-Ḥadītha, AD 1980. Print.

al-Ḥarīrī, Abū Mūsā (Father Joseph Qazzī). *'Ālam al-Mu'jizāt*. Beirut: Dār li-Ajl al-Ma'rifa, AH 1403/AD 1982. Print. Silsilat al-Ḥaqīqa al-Ṣa'ba 3.

Houtsma, M.T., et al., eds. *Da'irat al-Ma'ārif al-Islāmīya*. 1st ed. Sharja: Markaz al-Shāriqa li-l-Ibdā' al-Fikrī, AH 1418/AD 1998. Print.

Ibn al-'Arabī, Abū Bakr Muḥammad Ibn 'Abd Allah. *Aḥkām al-Qur'ān*. Ed. T. Muḥammad 'Abd al-Qādir 'Aṭa. 4 vols. Beirut: Dār al-Kutub al-'Ilmīya, AH 1424/AD 2003. Print.

Ibn al-Athīr, 'Alī Ibn Muḥammad al-Jazrī. *Usud al-Ghāba fī Ma'rifat al-Ṣaḥāba*. Ed. 'Alī Muḥammad Mu'awaḍ and 'Ādil Aḥmad 'Abd al-Mawjūd. Beirut: Dar al-Kutub al-'Ilmīya, AH 1417/AD 1996.

Ibn al-Ḍurays, Abū 'Abd Allah Muḥammad Ibn Ayūb al-Bajalī. *Faḍā'il al-Qur'ān wa mā Unzila min al-Qur'ān bi Makka wa mā Unzila bi-l-Madina*. Ed. 'Urwa Bidayr. Beirut: Dār al-Fikr, AH 1408/AD 1987. Print.

Ibn Ḥabīb, Abū Ja'far Muḥammad. *Kitāb al-Muḥabbar: Riwāyat Abū Sa'īd Ibn al-Ḥussayn al-Sukkarī*. Ed. Lise Lichtenstadter. Vol. 6. Hyderabad, India: Matba'at Jam'īyat Dā'irat al-Ma'ārif al-'Uthmānīya, AH 1361/AD 1942. Print.

Ibn Ḥazm al-Andalusī, Abū 'Abd Allah Muḥammad. *al-Nāsikh wa al-Mansūkh fī al-Qur'ān al-Karīm*. Ed. 'Abdul-Ghaffār Sulayiman al-Bendari. Beirut: Dār al-Kutub al-'Ilmīya, AH 1406/1986 AD. Print.

Ibn al-Jawzī, Abū al-Faraj 'Abd al-Raḥman. *Funūn al-Afnān fī 'Uyūn 'Ulūm al-Qur'ān*. Beirut: Dār al-Bashā'ir al-Islāmīya, AH 1408/AD 1987. Print.

—. *Nawāsikh al-Qur'ān*. Ed. Muḥammad Ashraf 'Alī al-Milbārī. Medina: al-Majlis al-'Ilmī, AH 1404/AD 1984. Print.

—. *Zād al-Masīr fī 'Ilm al-Tafsīr*. 4 vols. Beirut: al-Maktab al-Islāmī, AH 1404/AD 1984. Print.

Ibn al-Jazrī, al-Imām Shihāb al-Dīn Abū Bakr al-Dimashqī. *Sharḥ Ṭayībāt al-Nashr fī al-Qira'āt al-'Ashr*. Comments by Anas Mahrah. 2nd ed. Beirut: Dār al-Kutub al-'Ilmīya, AH 1420/AD 2000. Print.

Ibn Jinnī, Abū al-Fatḥ 'Uthmān. *al-Muḥtasib fī Tabyīn Wujūh Shawādh al-Qira'āt wa al-Iḍāḥ 'anhā*. Ed. 'Alī al-Najdī Nāsif, 'Abd al-Ḥalīm al-Najjār, 'Abd al-Fattāh Ismā'īl Shalabī. Vol. 1. Cairo: Wizārat al-Awqāf, lajnat Ihyā' Kutub al-Sunna, AH 1415/AD 1994. Print.

Ibn Khalawayh, Abū 'Abd Allah al-Ḥussayn Ibn Aḥmad. *I'rāb al-Qira'āt al-Sab' wa 'Ilalihā.* Vol. 1. Cairo: Maktabat al-Khānjī, AH 1413/AD 1992. Print.

Ibn al-Khaṭīb. *al-Furqān.* Beirut: Dār al-Kutub al-'Ilmīya, n.d. Print.

Ibn Manẓūr. *Lisān al-'arab.* Ed. Dār al-Ma'ārif. Cairo: Dār al-Ma'ārif, n.d. Print.

Ibn Mujāhid. Abū Bakr Aḥmad Ibn Mūsā Ibn al-'Abbās. *Kitāb al-Sab'a fī al-Qira'āt.* Ed. Shawqī Ḍayf. 3rd ed. Cairo: Dār al-Ma'ārif, AD 1988. Print.

Ibn al-Nadīm, Muḥammad Ibn Abī Isḥāq. *al-Fihrist.* Ed. Riḍā Tajaddad al-Māzindarānī. Tehran: Dar al-Masira, AD 1971. Print.

Ibn Qutayba, Abu Muḥammad 'Abd Allah Ibn Muslim. *Ta'wīl Mushkil al-Qur'ān.* Ed. Aḥmad Ṣaqr. Cairo: Dār al-Turāth, AD 1972. Print.

Ibn Sa'd. *Kitāb al-Ṭabaqāt al-Kubrā.* Ed. 'Alī Muḥammad 'Umayr. 8 vols. Cairo: al-Khānjī, AH 1421/AD 2001. Print.

Ibn Salāma, Abū al-Qāsim Hibat Allah. *al-Nāsikh wa al-Mansūkh.* Ed. Sheikh Māhir 'Abd al-'Aẓīm al-Ṭanṭāwī. Beirut: Dār al-Yusef, n.d. Print.

Jabal, Muḥammad Ḥassan Ḥassan. *Wathāqat Naql al-Naṣṣ al-Qur'ānī.* Tanta: Dār al-Ṣaḥāba li-l-Turāth, AD 2001. Print.

Jar Allah, Mūsā. *Tārīkh al-Qur'ān wa al-Maṣāḥif.* Petersburg: al-Matba'a al-Islāmīya, AD 1905. Print. [Author also known as Bigiev (Western sources) and Rostovdoni (Arabic sources)].

Jeffery, Arthur. Introduction. *al-Maṣāḥif.* By Abū Bakr 'Abd Allah Ibn Abī Dāwūd Ibn al-Ash'ath al-Sijistānī. Damascus: Dār al-Takwīn, AD 2004. Print.

al-Khaṭīb, 'Abd al-Laṭīf. *Mu'jam al-Qira'āt.* 11 vols. Damascus: Dār Sa'd al-Dīn, AH 1422/AD 2002. Print.

Kishk, 'Abd al-Ḥamīd. *Min Waṣāyā al-Rasūl al-Mūwajaha li-l-Nisā'.* Cairo: Al-Tawfiqīya, n.d. Print.

Kitāb Murshid al-Ṭālibīn ilā al-Kitāb al-Muqaddas al-Thamīn. Beirut, AD 1869. Print.

al-Makkī, Abū Muḥammad Ibn Abī Ṭālib. *al-Iḍāḥ li-Nāsikh al-Qur'ān wa Mansūkhuhu wa Ma'rifat Uṣūluhu wa Ikhtilāf al-Nāṣṣ Fīhi.* Ed. Aḥmad Ḥassan Faraḥāt. Jeddah: Dār al-Manāra, AH 1406/AD 1986. Print.

Murūwa, Ḥussayn. *al-Naza'āt al-Māddīya fī al-Falsafa al-'Arabīya al-Islāmīya.* 6th ed. Vol. 1. Beirut: Dār al-Fārābī, AD 1988. Print.

Muslim, Abū al-Ḥussayn Muslim Ibn al-Ḥajjāj. *Minnat al-Mun'im fī Sharḥi Ṣaḥīḥ Muslim.* Sharḥ al-Mubārakafūrī [Annotated by al-Mubārakafūrī]. Riyadh: Dār al-Salām, AH 1420/AD 1999. Print.

al-Naḥās, Abū Ja'far Muḥammad Ibn Aḥmad. *al-Nāsikh wa al-Mansūkh fī Kitāb Allah 'Azza wa Jalla wa Ikhtilāf al-'Ulamā' fī Dhalik*. Ed. Sulaymān Ibrāhīm Ibn 'Abd Allah al-Lāḥim. 1st ed. Egypt: al-Risāla, AH 1412/AD 1991. Print.

Nöldeke, Theodor. *Tārīkh al-Qur'ān*. Trans. Georges Tāmir. Beirut: Konrad-Adenauer-Stiftung, AD 2004. Print.

Qazzī, Joseph. *Bayn al-Masīḥīya wa al-Islām*. Beirut: Dār li-Ajl al-Ma'rifa, AD 2006. Print. Silsilat al-Ḥaqīqa al-Ṣa'ba 18.

—. *Masīḥ al-Qur'ān wa Masīḥ al-Muslimīn*. Beirut: Dār li-Ajl al-Ma'rifa, AD 2006. Print. Silsilat al-Ḥaqīqa al-Ṣa'ba 17.

al-Qirdāḥī, Jibrā'īl. *al-Lubāb: A Syriac-Arabic Dictionary*. Ed. Yūḥannān Ibrāhīm. 2nd ed. Ḥalab: Dār Mārdīn, AD 1994. Print.

al-Rāfi'ī, Muṣṭafā Ṣādiq. *I'jāz al-Qur'ān wa al-Balāgha al-Nabawīya*. Beirut: Dār al-Kitāb, AH 1425/AD 2005. Print.

al-Raṣāfī, Ma'rūf. *Kitāb al-Shakhṣīya al-Muḥammadīya aw Ḥal al-Lughz al-Muqqaddas*. Koln: Manshūrat al-Jamal, AD 2002. Print.

al-Rāzī, Muḥammad Ibn Abī Bakr Ibn 'Abd al-Qādir. *Min Gharā'ib Āay al-Tanzīl*. Beirut: al-'Aṣṣrīya, AH 1423/AD 2002. Print.

al-Sha'rāwī, Muḥammad Mitwallī. *al-Mar'a fī al-Qur'ān al-Karīm*. Cairo: Akhbār al-Yawm, AD 1998. Print.

Shīkhū, Father Lewis. *al-Nuṣrānīya wa Adābihā bayna 'Arab al-Jāhilīya*. 2nd ed. Beirut: Dār al-Mashriq, AD 1989. Print.

Shu'la, Abū 'Abd Allah. *Ṣafwat al-Rāsikh fī 'Ilm al-Mansūkh wa al-Nāsikh*. Ed. Muḥammad Ibrāhīm 'Abd al-Raḥman Fāris. Cairo: al-Thaqāfa al-Dīnīya, AH 1415/AD 1995. Print.

al-Sijistānī, Abū Bakr 'Abd Allah Ibn Abī Dāwūd Sulaymān Ibn al-Ash'ath. *Kitāb al-Maṣāḥif*. Beirut: Dār al-Kutub al-'Ilmīya, AH 1405/AD 1985. Print.

Stipčević, Aleksandar. *Tārīkh al-Kitāb*. Trans. Muḥammad al-Arnā'ūṭ. Kuwait: al-Majlis al-Waṭanī li-l-Thaqāfa wa al-funūn wa al-Adāb, AD 1993. Print. Silsilat 'Ālam al-Ma'rifa 169-170.

al-Suhailī, 'Abd al-Raḥman Ibn 'Abd Allah. *al-Rawḍ al-Unuf fī Tafsīr al-Sīra al-Nabawīya l-Ibn Hishām*. Beirut: Dār al-Kitāb al-'Arabī, n.d. Print.

al-Suyūṭī, Jalāl al-Dīn 'Abd al-Raḥman. *Asrār Tartīb al-Qur'ān*. Egypt: Dār al-I'tiṣām, AH 1398/ AD 1978. Print.

—. *al-'Itqān fī 'Ulūm al-Qur'ān*. Ed. Markaz al-Dirāsāt al-Islāmīya. Kingdom of Saudi Arabia: Wizārat al-Shu'ūn al-Islāmīya wa al-Awqāf wa al-Da'wa, AH 1397/AD 1977. Print.

—. *Lubāb al 'Uqūl fī Asbāb al-Nuzūl*. Beirut: Dār al-Kitāb al-'Arabī, AH 1426/AD 2006. Print.

—. *Tārīkh al-Khulafā'*. Ed. Ibrāhīm Ṣāliḥ. Damascus: Dār al-Bashā'ir, AH 1417/AD 1997. Print.

al-Ya'qūbi, Aḥmad Ibn Abī Ya'qūb. *Tārīkh al-Ya'qūbī*. Beirut: Dār Ṣādir, AH 1415/AD 1995. Print.

al-Zaraklī, Khayr al-Dīn. *al-A'lām*. 15th ed. Beirut: Dār al-'Ilm li-l-Malāyīn, AD 2002. Print.

al-Zarkashī, Abū 'Abd Allah Badr al-Dīn. *al-Burhān fī 'Ulūm al-Qur'ān*. 3rd ed. Ed. Muḥammad Abū al-Faḍl Ibrāhīm. 4 vols. Cairo: Dār al-Turāth, AH 1404/AD 1984.

Non-Arabic Sources

Ali, 'Abdullah Yusuf, trans. *The Holy Qur'an: Text Translation and Commentary*, 3rd ed. Lahore: Sh. Muhammad Ashraf, AH 1356/AD 1938. Print.

Bell, Richard. "Who Were the Hanifs?" *Muslim World* 29 (1949): 120-125. *Answering Islām*. Web. 3 Sept. 2010.<http://www.answering-Islām.org/Books/Bell/ hanifs.htm>.

Blom, Jan Dirk. *A Dictionary of Hallucinations*. New York: Springer, AD 2010. Print.

Böwering, Gerhard. "Recent Research on the Construction of the Qur'an." *The Qur'an in Its Historical Context*. Ed. Gabriel Said Reynolds. Abingdon: Routledge, AD 2008. Print.

Calder, Norman, Jawid Mojaddedi and Andrew Rippin, eds. *Classical Islām: A Sourcebook of Religious Literature*. London: Routledge, AD 2003. Print.

Déroche, François. "Written Transmission." *The Blackwell Companion to the Qur'an*. Ed. Andrew Rippin. Carlton, Australia: Blackwell, AD 2006. Print.

Donner, Fred M. "The Historical Context." *The Cambridge Companion to the Qur'an*. Ed. Jane Dammen McAuliffe. Cambridge: Cambridge UP, AD 2006. Print.

Encyclopedia Judaica. Eds. Fred Skolnik and Michael Berenbaum. 2nd ed. 22 vols. Detroit: Macmillan, AD 2006. Print.

Encyclopedia of the Qur'an. Gen. ed. Jane Dammen McAuliffe. 5 vols. plus index. Boston: Brill, AD 2001. Print.

Freedman, H., trans. and ed. and Maurice Simon. *Midrash Rabbah.* Vol. 1. London: Soncino, AD 1939. 310-311. Print.

Geiger, Abraham. *What has Mohammad Taken from Judaism?* [Prize Essay]1833. *Judaism and Islām.* Trans. F. M. Young. Madras, AD 1896. Print.

al-Hilali, Muhammad Taqi al-Din and Muhammad Muhsin Khan, trans. *The Noble Qur'an in the English Language.* Riyadh: Darussalam, AD 1996. Print.

Hirschfeld, Hartwig. *New Researches into the Composition and Exegesis of the Qoran.* London: Roy Asiatic Society, 1902. *Internet Archive.* Web. Dec. 2010. <http://www.archive.org/details/newresearchesint00hirs>.

Holy Bible: New Living Translation [*NLT*]. 2nd ed. Wheaton, IL: Tyndale House, 2004.

The Infancy Gospel of Thomas. Trans. M[ontague] R[hodes] James. Oxford: Clarendon, 1924. *Pseudepigrapha Web.* Ed. Joshua Williams. 2002. Web. 2 October 2009. <http://www.pseudepigrapha.com/LostBooks/TheInfancyGospelOfThomas.html>.

Irenaeus. "Doctrines of Saturninus and Basilides." *Against Heresies* 1.24. Rpt. in *Ante-Nicene Fathers.* Vol. 1. Trans. Alexander Roberts and William Rambaut. Ed. James Donaldson and A. Cleveland Coxe. Buffalo, 1885. *New Advent.* Ed. Kevin Knight. 2009. Web. 10 Dec. 2009. <http://www.newadvent.org/fathers/ 0103124.htm>.

Jeffery, Arthur. *The Foreign Vocabulary of the Qur'an.* Baroda: Oriental Institute, AD 1938. Print.

—. "The Mystic Letters of the Koran." *The Muslim World* 13 (1924): 247-260. Print.

Lane, Edward William. *Selections from the Kur'an.* London, AD 1878. Print.

Leaman, Oliver, ed. *The Qur'an: An Encyclopedia.* London: Routledge, 2006. Print.

Lester, Toby. "What Is the Koran?" *Atlantic Monthly* Jan. 1999: n. pag. *The Atlantic.* Web. 31 Aug. 2010.

Lundquist, John M. *The Temple of Jerusalem: Past, Present and Future.* London and Westport: Praeger, AD 2008. Print.

Muir, William, trans. and ed. *The Apology of Al Kindy. Risalat al-Kindi.* By al-Kindi. London, AD 1887. Print.

—. *Life of Mahomet.* 4 vols. London, AD 1861. Print.

The NIV Study Bible: New International Version Eds. Kenneth Barker, et al. Grand Rapids: Zondervan, AD 1985. Print.

Nöldeke, Theodor. *Sketches from Eastern History.* Trans. John Sutherland Black. London and Edinburgh, AD 1892. Print.

Palmer, E[dward] H[enry], trans. "The Qur'ân." *Sacred Books of the East.* Ed. F. Max Müller. Vol. 6. Oxford: Clarendon, 1880. *Internet Archive.* Web. Nov. 2010. <http://www.archive.org/details/qurn00palmgoog >.Pickthall, Muhammad Marmaduke, trans. *The Meaning of the Glorious Koran.* Hyderabad: Hyderabad Govt P, AD 1930. Print.

St. Clair-Tisdall, W[illiam]. *The Original Sources of the Qur'an.* London: Society for Promoting Christian Knowledge, AD 1911. Print.

—. *The Sources of Islām: A Persian Treatise.* abr. Trans. William Muir. Edinburgh: T. & T. Clark, AD 1901. Print.

Sale, George. trans. *The Koran: commonly called the the Alcoran of Mohammed.* 5th ed. Philadelphia: J. W. Moore, 1856. *Google books.* Web. Nov. 2010. <http://books.google.com/books?id=6osxHeW6XDsC&output=pdf>.

Sell, Edward. *The Recensions of the Qur'an.* Madras: Christian Lit. Soc., AD 1909. Print.

Shakir, M. H., trans. *The Qur'an.* Elmhurst: Tahrike Tarsile Qur'an, AD 1985. Print.

Sher 'Ali, Maulawi, trans. *The Holy Qur'an: Arabic Text and English Translation.* Tilford: Islām International, 2004.

The Spread of Islam Map, 622-750 CE. Map. *Maps.com.* Magellan Geographix. n.d. Web. Nov. 2010. <http://www.maps.com/ref_map.aspx?cid=694,725,739,1027&pid=11393&nav=MS>.

Wherry, E[lwood] M[orris]. *A Comprehensive Commentary on The Qur'an: Comprising Sale's Translation and Preliminary Discourse with Additional Notes and Emendation.* 4 vols. London, AD 1898. Print.

Subject Index

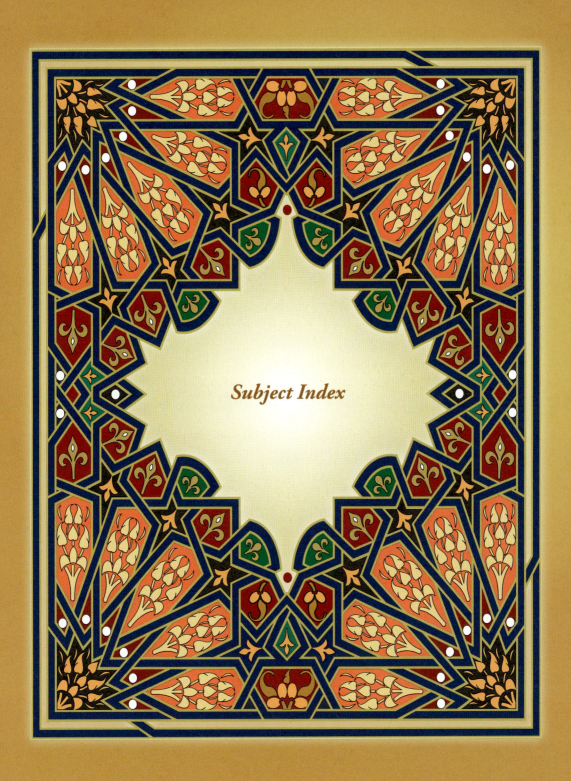

Subject Index